University of South Wales

2062352

KT-452-068

SIXTH EDITION

BUSINESS IN CONTEXT
AN INTRODUCTION TO BUSINESS AND ITS ENVIRONMENT

DAVID NEEDLE

CENGAGE
Learning

Australia • Brazil • Japan • Korea • Mexico • Singapore • Spain • United Kingdom • United States

CENGAGE Learning®

Business in Context
6th Edition

David Needle

Publisher: Andrew Ashwin

Development Editor: Abbie Jones

Content Project Manager: Sue Povey

Manufacturing Buyer: Elaine Willis

Marketing Manager: Amanda Cheung

Typesetter: Cenveo Publisher Services

Cover design: Adam Renvoize Creative

Text design: Design Deluxe Ltd

© 2015, Cengage Learning EMEA

ALL RIGHTS RESERVED. No part of this work covered by the copyright herein may be reproduced, transmitted, stored or used in any form or by any means graphic, electronic, or mechanical, including but not limited to photocopying, recording, scanning, digitizing, taping, Web distribution, information networks, or information storage and retrieval systems, except as permitted under Section 107 or 108 of the 1976 United States Copyright Act, or applicable copyright law of another jurisdiction, without the prior written permission of the publisher.

While the publisher has taken all reasonable care in the preparation of this book, the publisher makes no representation, express or implied, with regard to the accuracy of the information contained in this book and cannot accept any legal responsibility or liability for any errors or omissions from the book or the consequences thereof.

Products and services that are referred to in this book may be either trademarks and/or registered trademarks of their respective owners. The publishers and author/s make no claim to these trademarks. The publisher does not endorse, and accepts no responsibility or liability for, incorrect or defamatory content contained in hyperlinked material.

All the URLs in this book are correct at the time of going to press; however the Publisher accepts no responsibility for the content and continued availability of third party websites.

For product information and technology assistance, contact **emea.info@cengage.com**.

For permission to use material from this text or product, and for permission queries, email **emea.permissions@cengage.com**.

British Library Cataloguing-in-Publication Data
A catalogue record for this book is available from the British Library.

ISBN: 978-1-4080-9521-8

Cengage Learning EMEA
Cheriton House, North Way, Andover, Hampshire, SP10 5BE
United Kingdom

Cengage Learning products are represented in Canada by Nelson Education Ltd.

For your lifelong learning solutions, visit
www.cengage.co.uk

Purchase your next print book, e-book or e-chapter at
www.cengagebrain.com

Printed in Singapore by Seng Lee Press
Print Number: 02   Print Year: 2016

To Jacquie

To Jacquie

BRIEF CONTENTS

BRIEF CONTENTS

CONTENTS

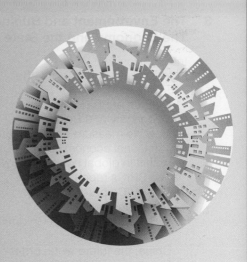

PART TWO ORGANIZATIONAL AND STRATEGIC CONTEXTS

PART THREE THE ACTIVITIES CONTEXT

LIST OF CASES

PREFACE

The origins for this book lie in courses I have developed and taught at the University of East London, at Queen Mary, University of London and, for the last several years at King's College, London. An important theme of all those courses has been the inter-related nature both of business activities themselves and their relationships with the strategic, organizational and environmental contexts in which they operated. A second important theme was the identification of what were considered at the time to be key issues in business. These two themes remain the basis of Business in Context in the sixth edition.

The book was aimed originally at first and second-year undergraduates studying business and management, to give them a multidisciplinary approach to their studies and an insight into the real world of business and management. The book has been found to be useful wherever there is a need for an overview of business or a treatment of business and the environment. As a result, the book has been adopted on MBA and specialist masters programmes and on some professional courses.

A number of key themes appear throughout the book:

- Businesses are perceived as operating through a complex network of interrelationships and our model is a simplification of this complexity.

- While business activities are undoubtedly influenced by their strategic, organizational and environmental contexts, those same business activities help shape those very same contexts.

- In all aspects of business life we need to remind ourselves that decisions are made by people. An understanding of behavioural and political issues is therefore important, as is the need to view issues from a number of different perspectives to gain a more complete understanding.

- Very rarely can we view business activities in isolation, as decisions made in one area inevitably have significant consequences, not only for other parts of the same business but for other businesses and even the wider community.

- Many of the new ideas, issues and techniques that have emerged over the years are undoubtedly products of influences that were operating at the time. While some have stood the test of time, others have become passing fashions and fads.

In this edition all the chapters have been updated and changed in some way. There are significant additions to the section on leadership in Chapter 7 and significant changes in marketing involving digital marketing and the use of social media are reflected in Chapter 12. Some cases have disappeared and new ones have been added, including Abercrombie & Fitch and Southwest Airlines. The case of the Spanish company Zara has been specially written for this edition by colleagues at the Universities of Valencia and Vigo. Almost all the other cases have been updated and in the Chapter 13 case study on British Airways a new dimension has been added.

The first chapter offers an explanation of the Business in Context model. The other chapters are split into three parts. Part One contains Chapters 2–5 and examines the environment of business, starting with globalization and ending with culture. In between we examine economic, political, technological and labour market influences. Part Two deals with organization and management. Chapter 6 examines the organizational context and reviews issues relating to goals, ownership, size, structure and organizational culture. Chapters 7–9 focus on management issues. Chapter 7 examines the nature of management and leadership, followed in Chapter 8 by a review of strategy. Chapter 9 deals with business ethics and corporate social responsibility. Part Three deals with specific functions and business activities and Chapters 10–14 cover innovation, operations, marketing, human resource management, and finance and accounting. Aspects of all these activities are clearly defined and, in addition, they are placed within their environmental, organizational and strategic contexts. The book therefore offers both general and specific views of business.

The core elements of previous editions are retained:

- Each chapter starts with a set of learning objectives.

- Each chapter highlights key concepts and provides a separate explanation of these.

- Throughout each chapter students are invited to reflect on key ideas and concepts and link them to their own experiences.

- Each chapter illustrates key issues by using cases, all written by the author, to support the information in the chapter.

- Each chapter is supported by a summary, a list of discussion questions and suggestions for further reading.

- There is a glossary at the back containing useful short definitions of all the major concepts in the book.

This book, like its predecessors, takes a broad sweep of business and its environment. A great deal of selectivity is inevitable and the main criteria for the inclusion of material has always been that it interested me. Many of the ideas are attributed to their rightful source, but many are the product of years discussing business issues with students, friends and colleagues. I thank all of them for their contribution, with the rider that the misinterpretations and mistakes are all my own.

David Needle

ACKNOWLEDGEMENTS

There are several who deserve my thanks for their help in producing this book. My students at King's College, London have been using previous editions of this text for the last seven years and their feedback has helped shape some of the changes in the new edition. An ex-student, Grace Merkin, has been an invaluable help. She has not only compiled many of the updated tables and provided current information on many of the cases but is responsible for much of the research and writing for the new Abercrombie and Fitch case. I am grateful to colleagues in Spain, Paco Puig from the University of Valencia and Miguel González-Loureiro from the University of Vigo, for writing the new Zara case. At King's I am particularly grateful to colleagues in the Department of Management, especially Doug West and Ali Budjanovcanin, for suggesting new approaches and providing materials for the chapters on Marketing and Management and Leadership respectively. Finally, I thank Abbie Jones, my patient and supportive editor from Cengage.

The publisher would like to thank the following academics for their helpful advice when reviewing draft chapter material:

Peter Cook
Henley Business School

Allan Smith
University of Aberdeen

Olga Kuznetsova
Manchester Metropolitan University

David Sunderland
University of Greenwich

Eliot Lloyd
University of Bedfordshire

Denise Kendry
University of Gloucestershire

Ludo Gelders
Katholieke Universiteit Leuven

Michael Marck
University of Strathclyde

Digital Support Resources

All of our Higher Education textbooks are accompanied by a range of digital support resources. Each title's resources are carefully tailored to the specific needs of the particular book's readers. Examples of the kind of resources provided include:

- A password protected area for instructors with, for example, a testbank, PowerPoint slides, and an instructor's manual
- An open-access area for students including, for example, useful weblinks and glossary terms

Lecturers: to discover the dedicated lecturer digital support resources accompanying this textbook please register here for access: **http://login.cengage.com**.

Students: to discover the dedicated student digital support resources accompanying this textbook, please search for BUSINESS IN CONTEXT on: **www.cengagebrain.co.uk**

THE CONCEPT OF BUSINESS IN CONTEXT

1

LEARNING OBJECTIVES   At the end of this chapter you should be able to:

- Define and illustrate business as a broadly-based and varied activity.
- Identify and illustrate the key activities of business and the relationships between them.
- Identify the strategic, organizational and environmental contexts within which business operates.
- Articulate the complex interactions that operate within and between business activities and their contexts.
- Use the Business in Context model to analyse a variety of business situations and cases.
- Define systems and contingency theories as they apply to business and assess their contribution to an understanding of business.

INTRODUCTION

The theme of this book is that businesses are complex. They cannot be understood by reference to their activities alone. These activities – which include innovation, operations, marketing, human resource management, finance and accounting – take place in a set of contexts. It is our contention that they can only be understood fully when those contexts within which they operate are also understood. In this first chapter we will explain what we mean by business and identify the relevant contexts. It is also our contention that the relationship between

FIGURE 1.1   Business in Context Model

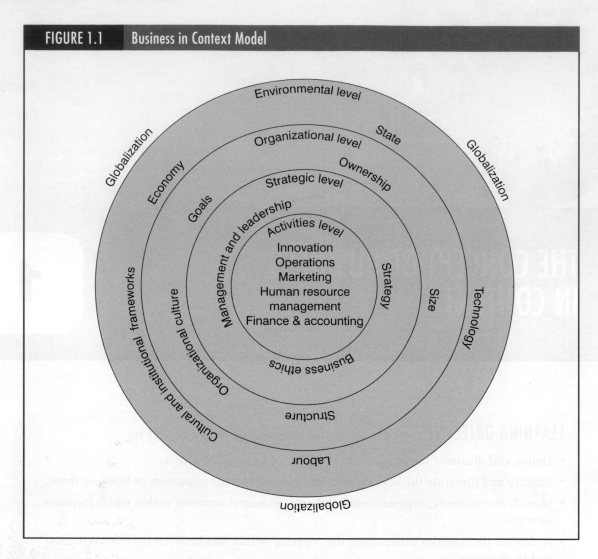

business activities and these contexts is dynamic. The Preface introduced a model of business. We present the model in Figure 1.1 and use it to illustrate the elements of this dynamic relationship. This model can be used to analyse industrial and service sectors as well as the events at a single firm.

We introduce briefly two theoretical approaches to the analysis of business organizations: the systems and contingency approaches. These are often used as the starting point for our analysis throughout this book and reference will be made to them in other chapters. We will conclude this first chapter by outlining the layout of this book.

BUSINESSES AND THEIR CONTEXTS

In this text we present a broad view of business. Businesses operate in all kinds of areas, including manufacturing industry, retailing, banking and other financial services, transport, media and entertainment. The publishers of this book are engaged in a business activity, involving the production, marketing and selling of books to generate income both to make profits and to finance future operations. Businesses also vary considerably in terms of size. The corner newspaper and grocery store is a business as is the Japanese car giant, Toyota.

We challenge the view that businesses are exclusively profit-oriented. Business systems and methods operate in all kinds of organizations. In 2013, 12 UK universities operated with income in excess of £500 million and Oxford and Cambridge each had income of over £1 billion. The figures are much higher in the USA and most universities are fairly complex organizations in which all the activities normally associated with business may be identified. For example, there are few colleges that do not market their courses, or have to operate in dynamic and competitive markets both at home and overseas. Hospitals, too, are large complex organizations experiencing the type of management problems found in businesses anywhere. In any case, the distinction between profit and non-profit organizations has become blurred. All universities and colleges must rely increasingly on generating their own income owing to changes that have taken place in public funding. In the UK, the growth of medical provision outside the National Health Service (NHS) has seen the growth of profit-oriented private hospitals which compete in the marketplace for customers and advertise their services internationally as well as nationally. In countries such as the USA this has always been the case.

KEY CONCEPT 1.1   BUSINESS

A business is the organized effort of individuals to produce and provide goods and services to meet the needs of society. We view business as a broad concept, incorporating profit-making concerns such as manufacturing firms and banks, and non-profit-making or not-for-profit concerns such as schools, hospitals and charities.

Business activities

As can be seen from Figure 1.1, a number of business activities have been identified. In this book we deal with them as five groups:

- innovation
- operations
- marketing
- human resource management
- finance and accounting.

Each of these groups is sufficiently broad to cover a number of related functions. When examining business activities there are two points to consider. First, the activities interact with one another. For example, operations decisions influencing the quantity and quality of the goods produced and the services provided will have implications for the other functional areas. Can products and services be designed to differentiate them from competitors' offerings? Is there a market and where does it exist? Can staff be recruited in sufficient numbers and with sufficient skills? Can the planned operation be financed? Second, as we have already indicated, these activities do not exist in a vacuum, but are shaped by, and in turn shape, the contexts within which they operate. In the Business in Context model we have identified three types of context: strategic, organizational and environmental. In addition we view these within the context of globalization.

Business contexts

At the **strategic level** we are concerned with those management decisions, and the influences on those decisions, that determine the direction of business activities. Strategic decisions will influence such factors as the range of products and services, the amount spent on advertising, the numbers and type of people employed as well as the shape and nature of the organization. Strategies are often a question of reconciling opportunities and constraints which exist within both the organization and the environment in which it operates. The managing director of a small firm with a potentially profitable innovation often faces a strategic dilemma. Its organizational size means that expanding production capacity is impossible and its credit standing is such that it may be unable to raise sufficient development capital. The availability of finance is, in any case, a function of the economic and political climate. The options may be to sell the idea for development by a larger firm or simply sell out to a larger organization, both of which may be personally unacceptable to the owner of the small business. In this way, strategic issues are inseparable from the organization and environment in which they operate and can, in fact, alter those two other contexts. It is widely accepted that the structure of a firm is often a product of its strategy (Chandler, 1962, offers a forceful argument for this). Economic, cultural and political globalization have changed the nature of business and created globally complex business structures. The overseas investment strategies of large multinational corporations have been seen to have considerable influence on the economic and political affairs of other nations, especially those in the developing world.

Strategies are invariably the product of managers and we explore the concept of management and leadership in Chapter 7, which sets the immediate context for strategic decisions. A theme in business strategy and a currently popular rhetoric of business leaders and annual reports is that of corporate social responsibility (CSR). We explore both the rhetoric and reality of business ethics and CSR in Chapter 9

KEY CONCEPT 1.2   STRATEGY

A strategy comprises a set of objectives and methods of achieving those objectives. A strategy is usually formulated by top management and is based on a mixture of careful analysis of the environment and the organization, the personal preferences of the managers involved, and a process of negotiation with various other stakeholders.

At the **organizational level** we are concerned with issues grouped under the following headings:

- goals
- structure
- ownership
- size
- organizational or corporate culture.

Many such issues are interrelated. The public ownership of business firms may well mean the pursuit of social as well as business goals, and publicly-owned firms invariably have bureaucratic structures. This is partly a function of organizational culture, and partly a function of the large size of most public sector operations. All firms as they increase in size tend to adopt more formalized structures. Such organizational factors can place limitations on the nature of business activities. Formalized structures can inhibit certain types of product and process development and size, when the business is small, can be a restriction on expansion, as we saw in our illustration of strategic issues. In more general terms these organizational factors combine with management strategy to create distinctive organizational cultures.

KEY CONCEPT 1.3   ORGANIZATION

An organization refers to the way in which people are grouped and the way in which they operate to carry out the activities of the business. We define the key elements of the organization as the goals of the business and the way they are formulated, ownership and control, size, structure and organizational culture.

We have identified five factors that operate at the **environmental level**:

- the economy
- the state
- technology
- labour
- cultural and institutional differences.

The influence of all these elements and their interaction with individual organizations takes place within the context of **globalization**. The increasing need to view all businesses in a global context is dealt with in Chapter 2.

Some of these factors are deliberately broad. We examine the workings of the economy and its interaction with business activity as well as the nature of competition. Coverage of the state includes discussion of government, legal and political issues. The examination of labour focuses on the workings of the labour market. The review of cultural and institutional differences examines those issues that differentiate businesses in different countries and covers historical, cultural, political and economic differences.

As with the other factors in the model, there is considerable interaction between these environmental factors. The behaviour of labour markets is a function of the level of economic activity as well as legal provisions dealing with issues such as trade union membership and discrimination, which in turn reflect the policy of governments. The composition of the labour market reflects changes in technology, economic and social changes and government policy. The mobility of labour within and between countries varies with the social and cultural traditions of those countries as well as with the laws on immigration and work permits. Technological innovations are often motivated both by declining economic fortunes and by direct state intervention. Similarly, we can cite illustrations of the interaction between the environment and our other contexts. The technological complexity of the product market in which the firm operates will largely determine the extent of its research and development (R&D) activity, and hence its strategies and structure. In the 21st century, human resources policies and practices are determined by cost considerations in an increasingly competitive global business environment.

The interplay that typifies the relationship between business activities and the contexts in which they operate will be a constant theme in this book. We will attempt to show that many of the relationships are two-way. The economic environment referred to above not only shapes businesses but is, in turn, a product of business activity. Changes in technology are products of innovation activity at the level of the firm. We are thus able to build up a model of business as a constant interplay of interactions and influences.

INTERACTION–INFLUENCE, SYSTEMS AND CONTINGENCY APPROACHES

It has been stressed elsewhere in this introductory chapter that the various elements of the Business in Context model interact with one another and influences go backwards and forwards across the various levels (see Figure 1.1). We are presenting an **interaction–influence model**. The idea of such a model for businesses is not new but forms the basis of the systems and contingency approaches that have been developed as part of organization theory. It is not our intention to present either a comprehensive review or a critique of these two approaches. Instead, we present a brief summary of their main ideas. Their importance as far as we are concerned is that they offer the student of business an important framework for analysis.

The systems approach

The systems approach assumes that all organizations are made up of interdependent parts which can only be understood by reference to the whole. As such, organizations may be analysed in terms of inputs, processes and outputs, as illustrated in Figure 1.2. It may be seen from this that there are many similarities with the Business in Context model.

The development of systems thinking from an organizational perspective starts with the analogy of the firm as a living organism. To be effective, the firm, like the organism, must adapt to its environment to survive. The inputs, processes and outputs must be balanced so the firm can obtain equilibrium, especially with its environment. The application of the systems approach in organizational analysis first gained prominence through the use of a socio-technical systems perspective. This is based on the assumption that the social system of the firm and its technical system interact in a complex way.

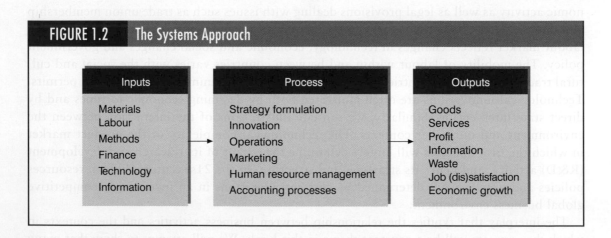

FIGURE 1.2   The Systems Approach

Inputs	Process	Outputs
Materials	Strategy formulation	Goods
Labour	Innovation	Services
Methods	Operations	Profit
Finance	Marketing	Information
Technology	Human resource management	Waste
Information	Accounting processes	Job (dis)satisfaction
		Economic growth

KEY CONCEPT 1.4   THE SYSTEMS APPROACH

The systems approach is a view of business involving two related concepts. First, businesses are made up of a series of interactions, involving business activities, the various aspects of the organization, and aspects of the environment. What we identify as a business is the sum total of all these influences and interactions. Second, the systems approach views business as a series of inputs from the environment, internal processes and eventual outputs.

The contingency approach

The contingency approach starts with an analysis of the key environmental variables, which shape the organization. It then proceeds with the assumption that the successful firms are those that adapt to the key influences and achieve some kind of best fit with their environment. This approach has been very influential in the area of corporate strategy. The strategist attempts to match the environmental opportunities and threats with the organization's own strengths and weaknesses to develop an optimum strategy for the firm in question.

Both the systems and contingency approaches are based on the concept of an organization interacting with elements in its environment and adapting to them. Both systems and contingency approaches have been criticized for focusing on a limited range of environmental variables, for being deterministic, and for ignoring both the influence of the organization on its environment and the values and behaviour of management and the workforce. It is our view that such criticisms place unnecessary limits on the use and value of both approaches. In developing our model of business we wish to use systems and contingency thinking to present a broad analytical framework, enabling us to gain a greater insight into the way businesses operate. We are concerned to show, however, that businesses, while influenced by their environments, are not wholly determined by them. Business strategies can and do influence environmental contingencies.

KEY CONCEPT 1.5   THE CONTINGENCY APPROACH

The contingency approach focuses on the relationship between the organization and its environment. It embraces the notion that business activities and the way they are organized are products of the environment in which they operate. The most successful businesses are therefore those that are organized to take advantage of the prevailing environmental influences. The contingency approach can be traced through the work of Woodward (1965) and Burns and Stalker (1966), although the term itself was popularized in the work of Lawrence and Lorsch who wrote:

Organizational variables are in a complex interrelationship with one another and with conditions in the environment. If an organization's internal states and processes are consistent with external demands ... it will be effective in dealing with the environment.

(Lawrence and Lorsch, 1967, p. 157)

THE STRUCTURE OF THIS BOOK

The chapters that follow will analyse each of the elements of the Business in Context model. The chapters have been grouped into three parts. The first part will examine the environmental context and begins with a review of globalization. The second part focuses on the organizational and strategic aspects and includes coverage of both management and leadership and business ethics, both linked to strategy.

Part 1: The environmental context

Chapter 2	Globalization
Chapter 3	Economy and the state
Chapter 4	Technology and labour
Chapter 5	Cultural and institutional frameworks

Part 2: The organizational and strategic contexts

Chapter 6	Business and organization
Chapter 7	Management and leadership
Chapter 8	Strategy
Chapter 9	Business ethics and corporate social responsibility

Part 3: The functional context

Chapter 10	Innovation
Chapter 11	Operations
Chapter 12	Marketing
Chapter 13	Human resource management
Chapter 14	Finance and accounting

SUMMARY

- In this introductory chapter the workings of the Business in Context model have been outlined and in so doing mapped out the rest of this book.

- In the model, variables are identified that interact with business. These variables have been arranged in levels, which have been termed environmental, organizational and strategic. It is believed that understanding the way businesses and their activities operate is enhanced by placing them in this contextual framework.

- The theoretical underpinnings of the model are discussed with reference to the systems and contingency approaches to organizational analysis.

DISCUSSION QUESTIONS

1   The five environmental, five organizational variables, and five business activities have been identified in the model. By necessity these represent broad categories. What elements might be considered under the various headings used in the model of business?

2   Take in turn an industry, a firm and a specific issue, and analyse each using the Business in Context model.

3   What is the value of the systems and contingency approaches to an understanding of business?

PART ONE
THE ENVIRONMENTAL CONTEXT

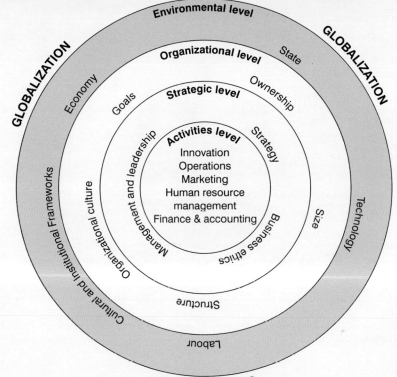

GLOBALIZATION

2

LEARNING OBJECTIVES At the end of this chapter you should be able to:

- Define globalization and the key issues and debates associated with it.
- Describe and assess the different perspectives on globalization.
- Assess the main causes and drivers of globalization as a concept.
- Assess the impact of globalization on the economy and on the production of goods and services.
- Assess the relationship between globalization and political change and between globalization and culture change.
- Identify the limitations of globalization.
- Articulate the links between globalization and the development of the multinational and transnational corporations.
- Articulate the links between globalization and offshore outsourcing and between globalization and strategic alliances and joint ventures.

INTRODUCTION

Globalization is seen by many to be the dominant force in business today. The term is frequently used by academics, journalists and politicians. It is clear that something has happened that has changed whole economies and changed the markets, strategies and the behaviour of people in most organizations. However, a problem with all these usages is the imprecise and variable nature of the definition of globalization itself. Dicken (2011, p. 2) argues:

> *(Globalization) has become not only one of the most used, but also one of the most misused and one of the most confused words around today.*

In this chapter we will examine the key developments, leading to some definitions of globalization. We will analyse the driving forces and pose the question, 'when did it start?' We will then turn to examine three specific aspects, reviewing globalization economically, politically and culturally. Given the view of Dicken, expressed above, and of other sceptics we will review a number of perspectives on globalization. The chapter will then focus on the role played by multinational companies and, within that, the growth of strategic alliances, joint ventures and outsourcing. We start, however by reviewing aspects of globalization within the framework of our Business in Context model.

KEY CONCEPT 2.1	GLOBALIZATION

Globalization is a process in which the world appears to be converging economically, politically and culturally. Globalization is seen by many as a fundamental change where national borders become irrelevant, a process accelerated by developments in information communication technology. It is considered by many to be the dominant force in modern business. In economic terms, many firms are producing goods and services for global markets, using labour in various locations in the world and using global sources for raw materials and components. In the past 20 years there has been an acceleration of cultural exchange across the globe, helped, in part, by advances in travel and communications. Business and cultural globalization have been accompanied by political globalization through the activities of supranational bodies such as the United Nations, World Trade Organization and the European Union. There are strong links between globalization and the multinational corporation (Key Concept 2.3).

GLOBALIZATION AND THE BUSINESS IN CONTEXT MODEL

Globalization is pervasive and has an impact on all areas of business activity and the context within which those activities operate.

In terms of the **environmental context,** we shall see in this chapter how globalization has affected all aspects of our model.

- The world economy is now more closely interlinked through global markets and the global organization of the production of goods and services.
- Linked to the above, trade has increased dramatically in the past 50 years, largely through the activities of multinational companies.
- Nation states have been brought together to form alliances for trade and defence.
- Key features of a global economy are the speed and coverage of both technology transfer and information transfer, the latter facilitated by the Internet.
- As well as the increase in the trade of manufactured goods, there is strong evidence of increased flows of services, money, ideas and people.
- There is also evidence to suggest that cultures around the world are moving more closely together both in terms of lifestyle and certain core values.

In terms of the **organizational context** the following aspects can be observed:

- Ownership patterns of organizations around the world have become more complex as a result of cross-border acquisitions and joint ventures and the creation of transnational corporations.

- We shall see that the impact of globalization is not confined to large organizations and that many changes have occurred in the **small business** sector.

- In many organizations new structures and cultures have emerged to respond to global changes.

In terms of **strategy,** there has been a shift in emphasis from a national competitive focus to a global focus. Global strategies have emerged in product development, the production of goods and services, distribution and the management of labour. These in turn have affected **business activities.** For example:

- The ease of technology transfer and the increase in collaborative ventures have changed the nature of innovation and R&D and the production processes in many firms.

- Operations now involve the coordinated efforts of a number of organizations across the globe.

- For most organizations marketing is by definition a global activity, with the complexities that that entails.

- Firms must devise policies for attracting, retaining and relocating staff operating globally.

- Finance has become a global resource with the acquisition of funds, the movement of money and taxation becoming global issues. This has led to a corresponding adaptation of accounting procedures.

However, as we shall see as this chapter unfolds, not everyone is convinced of the all-embracing impact of globalization and some are critical of its impact. Students should be aware that many issues related to globalization are contentious.

WHAT IS GLOBALIZATION?

A standard definition of globalization is offered by the World Bank:

The global circulation of goods, services and capital, but also of information, ideas and people. It has shaped all of the 20th century, albeit with large cyclical variations and has become an increasingly visible force in recent decades.

(World Bank, 2000, p. 1)

Scholte (2005) acknowledges the main elements of this definition as part of a framework he uses to define globalization. He identifies five elements: internationalization; liberalization; universalization; westernization; and deterritorialization. He argues that while globalization is dependent upon all five strands, it is only the last that provides a true understanding of globalization and marks it as a distinctive change in the conduct of human affairs. We examine each of the elements briefly.

- **Internationalization** involves the rapid growth in international trade of goods, services, money and information and the development of global networks for both production and finance activities.

- **Liberalization** involves the creation of free markets around the world, incorporating changes that have taken place in such countries as China and the former Soviet Union. It also involves the liberalization of information, by making much more information available to many more people through the Internet.

- **Universalization** is a process of convergence due to regulatory frameworks. The World Trade Organization has established rules of free trade for member nations, which currently include the majority of active trading nations in the world. The EU has a legal framework, within which member states must operate. Such universalization has extended to product requirements such as the regulation of fuel emissions on motor vehicles.

- **Westernization** involves the dominance of western values with particular influence from the USA. This has resulted in the convergence of some cultural values such as a move to individualism over collectivism and a preference for rules over relationships in the conduct of business. We return to these cultural themes later in this chapter and again in Chapter 5.

Scholte argues that all the above have been present for some time and have emerged and re-emerged as powerful forces at certain times in history. This is acknowledged also by the World Bank definition. However, Scholte sees the distinctiveness of globalization as:

- **Deterritorialization.** This is a relatively recent phenomenon and is a process that places less emphasis on national boundaries and geographical barriers. Goods, money, people, knowledge and ideas now flow between countries as never before. Scholte argues that each of the other four developments can take place in a world that is made up of distinct territories and can be defined in terms of national boundaries. Globalization makes national boundaries less relevant.

As a consequence, Scholte prefers to see globalization as a 'reconfiguration of social geography by the transplanetary and supraterritorial connections between people'. (Scholte, 2005, p. 8).

This theme is also taken up by Waters, who defines globalization as:

A social process in which the constraints of geography on social and cultural arrangements recede and in which people become increasingly aware that they are receding.

(Waters, 1995, p. 3)

Both Scholte and Waters see globalization as a fundamental change in social relations at all levels. The key issue is one of geography or territory. Oceans, mountain ranges and deserts no longer pose insurmountable barriers; we can fly over them. Through telephone calls, the Internet and the electronic transfer of finance we can undertake instant transactions across many countries. Satellite television is now commonplace and is taken for granted, so that, in almost all parts of the world, there was access to live broadcasts of every game in the 2014 soccer World Cup in Brazil and of most events in the 2012 Olympic and Paralympic Games in London.

When General Motors expanded its operations into Europe through the acquisition of Opel in Germany in 1929 there were no passenger flights linking the two countries and travel was a tedious and lengthy journey involving train and boat. There was no fax, no email and the ability to place a direct dial telephone call was some 40 years away. The main form of communication was by letter or telegraph.

What is happening now is that, through developments in electronic communications and travel, the world of many people has expanded beyond their national territory. We interact with others and gain access to information across borders with relatively few barriers and state controls. Unfortunately, this widening of our horizons also means that the lack of environmental care in one country can affect the lives of people in a different country.

The next two definitions focus on the changes that have taken place in the economy and in markets, stressing the role played by developments in electronic communications and travel. Castells considers that significant changes have taken place and are attributed to information and communications technology. This has enabled people and organizations to interact and work together as never before. For example, in both manufacturing and finance, activities in different firms across the globe are linked. Dealers in the stock exchanges and finance houses of Tokyo, Hong Kong, Frankfurt, London and New York are in continuous 24-hour communication. Changes in one country have an immediate impact on others. Nowadays, it is not necessary for designers of a new car at General Motors to travel between the USA and Germany. Americans and Germans can work together as a team at the same time on the same project using the same computer software, although one team is working in Germany and the other in the USA.

> *A global economy is something different: it is an economy with the capacity to work as a unit in real time on a planetary scale.*

(Castells, 1996, p. 92)

> *The globalization of markets has only been made possible in the late twentieth century by dramatic changes in transportation and communications technologies, for information, people, goods and services.*

(Castells, 1996, p. 96)

We return to these themes later in our discussion of the global factory and global supply chains.

REFLECTION POINT

What are the main similarities and differences between the definitions of globalization offered in the last section? Which definition do you prefer and why?

WHEN DID GLOBALIZATION START?

Michael Porter traces globalization back to the 19th century (Porter, 1990) with developments in industrialization and the expansion of trade. Geoffrey Jones charts the rise of what he terms 'the first global economy' from 1880 to its peak in 1914 (Jones, 2005). Others go back much further, citing the Roman Empire and the spread of Islam as examples of globalization before the 14th century.

A key factor in the move to a global economy has been those developments that have led to growth in capitalist economies. Marx identified that capitalism was concerned with **accumulation.** In a competitive capitalist system firms must increase the scale of production to continue to accumulate profit. This leads inevitably to them seeking new markets as national markets become too small to fulfil their needs. Capitalism is also concerned with **commodification;** this involves broadening the scale of consumption. New products and services must be developed to contribute to the process of accumulation. According to Marx this resulted in the opportunity to make money in ways previously not considered by putting a price on something that was previously thought to have no economic value. We can see this today, as in the selling of information via mobile phones or from telephone chat lines or even from the sale of mobile phone ring tones.

As a result of these processes, firms have sought to develop products and services and to increase sales volume by seeking global markets. Through global production and global markets, firms are able to achieve economies of scale and move costs to where they are cheapest, e.g. manufacture products or establish call centres in low-wage countries.

Many assume that globalization has been essentially a linear development with periods of acceleration. However, as we noted in the previous section, the World Bank definition speaks of 'cyclical variations'. Jones (2005) goes much further, charting the disintegration of the global economy between 1914 and 1950. The factors involved in this disintegration were as follows:

- Two world wars, 1914–18, 1939–45.
- The Great Depression of the late 1920s and early 1930s causing a fall in the economies of most countries, the rise of mass unemployment and the collapse of the international financial system.
- The Cold War of the post-1945 era.
- The rise of Eastern European and Chinese communism.
- Economic problems after the Second World War in Germany and Japan.
- Protectionism by governments through the introduction of import tariffs to discourage trade and by companies creating cartels (agreements with other companies on price and on which markets to enter).

The result of these impediments was a reduction in trade and in foreign investment and the closure of large areas of the world to free trade.

The period after 1950 saw a growth in trade and foreign direct investment. Commentators such as Scholte and Castells identify the greatest changes, if not the most significant trends, as occurring since the 1960s, the era of the post-industrial revolution. For example, the first international direct dialling systems did not appear, and then only between London and Paris, until 1963. While we can watch live sporting events from around the world almost every night, the first satellite television broadcast did not occur until 1967 (Scholte, 2005).

Straw and Glennie (2012) now speak of the 'third wave of globalization' that features much greater interconnectivity especially between businesses and a changing balance of economic power (see Chapter 3), not just involving China and the rest of the BRIC economies (Brazil, Russia, India and China) but also Korea, Mexico, Indonesia and Turkey.

Globalization has been made possible by a number of developments.

THE CAUSES AND DRIVERS OF GLOBALIZATION

Linked to the historical development of globalization, we can identify a number of causal factors and driving forces:

- **The importance of rational knowledge.** In the 19th century the primacy of rational knowledge emerged and influenced most cultures. Rational knowledge emphasizes knowledge derived from scientific, objective methods and sees the importance of knowledge to solving problems and controlling our lives and environment. Knowledge related to science and technology became especially important.

- **The growth of trade.** From 1950 to 2000 there was a 20-fold increase in the international trade of merchandise. This compares with an increase in production of only 6-fold for the same period (Dicken, 2011). From 1995 to 2006 the value of international trade rose from $5 trillion to $12 trillion (Straw and Glennie, 2012). Individual national economies have become interconnected through trade. This relatively recent trend adds support to the view of globalization as a modern phenomenon.

- **The growth of foreign direct investment (FDI).** FDI is the investment and management of overseas operations by companies, leading to the growth of multinational companies (see below and discussed later in this chapter). The most dramatic increases in investment occurred in the 1990s. Between 1990 and 2000 outflows of FDI rose from US$200 billion to US$1200 billion (United Nations, 2004).

- **Multinational corporations.** Multinational companies are, like regional and global organizations, both products and drivers of globalization. Multinational corporations (MNCs) or multinational enterprises (MNEs) are the product of global expansion. They have also contributed towards the diffusion of technology and ideas and the convergence of processes and management practices. A feature of MNCs in the past 20 years has been the increase in the number of joint ventures and strategic alliances, which have resulted in yet greater integration. We examine the role of multinationals and alliances in more detail later in this chapter. In particular we will focus on the changing role of the multinational enterprise and the emergence of the concept of the transnational corporation.

- **Costs.** In the need to accumulate and to remain in business in an increasingly competitive world economy, attention to costs has become paramount. Global sales mean that economies of scale in production can be achieved. Global sourcing means that raw materials, components, labour and finance can be accessed from anywhere in the world and, often, price is the key driver. The ever-present need to develop new products increases the cost. Particularly in scientifically and technologically complex industries such as cars, mobile phones and pharmaceuticals, the cost of R&D (research and development) has risen disproportionately to other costs. Competition has driven firms to bring out products at more frequent intervals as product life cycles are shortened. The net result of these developments is that most national markets are too small to achieve a return on investment and global markets and operations become a necessity. Yip (2003) refers to all these developments as cost globalization.

- **Technological innovations.** A world economy that is networked electronically is only possible through developments in transport, particularly air travel, communications and data processing. The developments in computer technology and the falling costs of information storage, transmission and processing are particularly significant here. The key developments have taken place in information and communications technology (ICT), involving computers, microelectronics and fibre optics and the creation of the Internet. (We deal with ICT in more detail in Chapter 4). Such innovations in transport and communications have facilitated the easier movement and increased flows of people, goods, money, information and ideas.

- **Changing world politics.** In Europe, the fall of the Berlin Wall symbolized a changing political map with the liberalization of former state controlled economies and the creation of emerging markets in such countries as Russia, Poland, Hungary and the Czech Republic. In some of those countries the political transformation to free market economies has facilitated their membership of the European Union. Changes towards liberalization have also taken place in the large economies of China and India. Not only have such changes led to increased trade, they have led to the expansion of multinational firms and foreign investment in new areas. Bartlett and Ghoshal (1995) believe that changing government policies linked to changing political economies have influenced trade and investment more than anything else.

- **Changing markets.** Yip (2003) refers to this as market globalization, a process that involves two elements: the emergence of groups of customers around the world with similar needs that are satisfied by global products; and the emergence of new market economies such as the Asian tigers (Hong Kong, Singapore, South Korea and Taiwan), China and Russia.

- **Regulations.** A networked world economy has been made that much easier to achieve by the agreement on global standards. Standardization can be seen in such fields as computer systems, civil aviation and intellectual property rights. The role of governments has been crucial in the promotion of standardization and integration. Global and regional organizations such as the UN, WTO, EU, North American Free Trade Association (NAFTA) and the Association of South East Asian Nations (ASEAN) have contributed to the standardization process as well as being products of globalization and integration.

Two general points can be made from our discussion of the causes of globalization:

- All the above have at some time contributed to the phenomenon we refer to as globalization. However, some authors stress the importance of some factors over others. Scholte and Castells give prominence to information and communications technology while Bartlett and Ghoshal emphasize the role of changing government regulations.

- Some of the drivers of globalization could be viewed as consequences. So, globalization is clearly a product of increased trade. However, increased trade is also a product of a globally linked economy.

We now turn our attention to examine the features of globalization by looking at economic and production aspects, political aspects and cultural aspects.

REFLECTION POINT

Which of the causes and drivers identified above do you consider the most influential and why?

ECONOMIC AND PRODUCTION ASPECTS OF GLOBALIZATION

The emergence of global competition, markets and globally organized production systems have had a radical effect upon management strategies and business behaviour.

Global markets

Global markets have been created in a wide variety of consumer goods. The globalization of markets was referred to in a seminal article by Levitt (1983). He identified that a qualitative change had occurred in markets with the appearance of standardized global products. He argued that cultural difference was an overstated barrier and that many products had gone global. He cited jeans, pizzas and Chinese food among others as examples of national products that had gone global. However, the expansion of the global market was seen more in terms of electrical goods and automobiles. He argued that as products had become more technical and competition had increased, then the rising cost of product development could only be met by economies of scale, standardized global products and larger markets. He further argued that the global media and the reduced costs of communication and travel had created the demand for such products.

While Levitt's argument is logical there are limits to the growth of standardized global products. There are political barriers in the form of import quotas and taxes and economic barriers in that some products may not be affordable in some countries. We know also that so-called global products are customized to satisfy local tastes, McDonalds being a prime example. While it can be argued that there are even greater pressures for cost reduction now than in 1983, organizations have developed a greater capacity for flexible manufacturing and product variation.

The idea of the global product has been supported by global branding and global advertising campaigns and the growth in global retailers such as Zara. In addition to consumer goods, financial goods are also traded globally, including foreign exchange, shares and insurance. To meet the expansion of global trade in the financial sector, stock exchanges have emerged around the world. Flows of capital now account for the majority of cross-border transactions. Financial markets are linked and work together in real time. The availability of information across the world is instantaneous. Such networked financial markets have been held responsible for the crash that affected many Asian economies in 1997. The rapid economic growth of many Asian economies attracted considerable overseas investment. At the first hint of trouble, many of those investors withdrew. This was apparent to all in a networked information system and others followed. Most recently, we have seen global markets emerge for communication and information products such as mobile phones alongside new forms of product, where profit is derived from telephone calls and obtaining information from the Internet.

Globally organized production

Globally organized production systems have been established to integrate production across many countries. Dicken (2011), while casting doubt on the truly global nature of globalization, acknowledges the extent of integration of production networks involving many firms in many different types of activity in different countries.

Cars and computers are now assembled using components from several countries. A company such as Nike sources trainers and other goods from low-wage economies. In one example, Nike used South Korean firms located in Indonesia with components shipped from China, and the operation was financed by the Japanese.

Understanding of the processes involved in globally organized production depends upon our understanding of a number of related concepts. We examine in turn outsourcing and offshoring, the global factory and the global supply chain.

Outsourcing and off-shoring

In the literature these terms are often confused.

Outsourcing involves getting another company to carry out part of the process. It is a contractual and therefore a 'market' relationship. In manufacturing, another company is often contracted to provide components or even large parts of the finished product. This happens in industries such as the automotive and computer industry where many of the parts are outsourced. Many firms outsource the provision and maintenance of their IT needs or get another firm to handle their payroll. In many universities the catering and cleaning functions are outsourced to private firms. Much of the outsourcing is done by firms within the same country.

Off-shoring involves moving a process to another country. In many multinationals, the process is performed by a unit in the same firm that is located overseas and therefore is not a form of outsourcing. This involves equity in another country and is a relationship based on 'hierarchy'. However, where a firm not only locates an activity in another country but contracts this activity to another firm, it is referred to as offshore outsourcing.

Initially, such activities involved relatively low-skilled operations in manufacturing industry. Two developments have occurred. The range of activities has expanded to include the service sector and high-skilled work. For example, Hill (2007) cites the Bank of America moving IT work to India, the Massachusetts General Hospital in the USA outsourcing the interpretation of CT scans to radiographers, also in India, and the consulting firm Accenture moving thousands of IT jobs to the Philippines and India.

Off-shoring and offshore outsourcing have created a variety of organization forms, including: offshore centres; mergers and acquisitions forming wholly-owned subsidiaries; joint ventures and strategic alliances; and sub-contracted operations. In all cases these organizations become part of a global network. The rationale for these developments is similar to the drivers of globalization identified in this chapter, and includes increased competition, the need for cost reduction, lower shipping costs and cheaper and faster telecommunications. Both off-shoring and offshore outsourcing have attracted a great deal of interest and generated considerable debate. We will examine this debate in terms of the assumed benefits and problems. Such benefits and problems apply both to firms and the countries in which they are located. The home firm and country refers to the original location of the multinational. The host firm and country refers to the firm and country to which the activity has been transferred.

Assumed benefits of off-shoring and offshore outsourcing The benefits for the home firm and country are listed below. Not all these benefits are accepted by everyone and they should be viewed alongside the section on problems and issues which offers an alternative perspective:

- Inevitably operations are moved to countries where labour costs are substantially lower. This applies to higher skilled jobs as well. Such cost savings can be reinvested at home. A US company relocating its call centre to India can reduce its labour cost by 90 per cent (Batt, Doellgast and Kwon, 2006).
- The displaced workforce can move to jobs of higher value. This is good for both the employee, through higher wages and the economy, through improved gross domestic product (GDP). Farrell (2005), while supporting this claim, identifies greater difficulty in less flexible labour markets such as Germany.
- Consumers gain through cheaper goods and services.
- The market for home country products is increased. For example, IT firms in India working for US companies will buy US computers and related equipment.
- Firms overseas in lower-cost economies can offer round the clock working at much cheaper shift rates.

- Firms can make use of time zone differences. This has enabled many USA firms to use Indian-based software engineers to service their computer systems when they are not being used.

The benefits for the host country include:

- The creation of new jobs with higher wages.
- Increased GDP through export sales.
- The development of local economies through the establishment of local supply chains and increased purchasing power of local workers.

Farrell (2005) citing her earlier research involving US and Indian firms, argues that for every US$1 spent by US companies shifting work to India, US$1.46 new wealth is created. This is made up of US$0.33 to India in the form of wages, company profits and increased taxes and US$1.13 to the USA in terms of cost savings and the export of equipment. Moreover, she argues that the value added by reemploying US workers in better jobs gives an additional benefit of US$0.47 for every dollar spent.

However, many of these benefits have been questioned and off-shoring and offshore outsourcing raises a number of problems and issues. As before, we can identify these for both the home and the host countries.

Assumed problems associated with off-shoring and offshore outsourcing The problems and issues focusing on the home country include:

- Moving operations offshore can create unemployment at home. Not all displaced workers find jobs (estimates range from 30–40 per cent of those displaced).
- Evidence suggests that those who find work do not move to jobs with enhanced skills and pay but rather move to lower paid work. Levy (2005) estimates as many as 80 per cent move to jobs with lower pay.
- Levy (2005) also argues that the home beneficiaries are limited to the shareholders of the lead company.
- Offshore outsourcing carries the additional risk of lower quality products and lower standards because of lack of training and effective controls by the home firm.
- There may be the risk that by transferring technology and know-how, this can be copied and the firm in the host country emerges as a competitor, with some advantages in its own market.
- The argument that off-shoring creates income for the home country in the form of goods purchased is also challenged. Many branded goods from home country firms are themselves produced by offshore outsourcing and not all the revenues flow back to the home country.

The problems and issues focusing on the **host country** include:

- Smaller local firms in the host country can be forced out of business by the financial and market power of large multinationals operating in that host country. An advantage of multinationals lies in their ability to manage complex offshore networks.
- While employees at some host country firms benefit through higher wages, those working for second- and third-tier suppliers may be worse off as leading firms drive harder bargains to gain greater rewards.
- The major gains are made by the owners of lead firms in the supply chain in the host countries rather than the employees. Wages may be kept at low levels to maintain profits.

Many of the problems are summed up by Levy (2005). He argues that many brands, especially in the footwear and clothing industries, are built upon relatively unsophisticated products. The power of the brand enables such firms to charge premium prices yet hold down costs by paying relatively low wages for relatively unskilled work.

REFLECTION POINT

What conclusions do you draw from the advantages and disadvantages of off-shoring and offshore outsourcing identified above?

Global factory

The global factory encompasses the activities of a global firm, or a global network of firms, that organizes servicing production, distribution, marketing, design, branding and innovation of a set of products and services. As will be seen, these products and services and their subcomponents, inputs and intellectual property may not be owned by a single firm at any one time but their component activities are controlled by a system described here as the global factory.

(Bartels, Buckley and Mariano, 2009, p. 1)

A typical example of how the global factory operates is where components are made by a number of different firms in different locations around the world and then brought together at the stage of final assembly. This is sometimes referred to as the fine slicing of the production process and as a modular supply chain.

The process is illustrated by Friedman (2006). He bought a Dell Inspiron notebook computer and set about tracking down the origin of its parts. His findings are summarized in Table 2.1 and in Figure 2.1 and illustrate the concept of globally organized production.

TABLE 2.1	Friedman's Dell Notebook
Activity	**Place**
Design	Texas, USA and Taiwan
Assembly	Malaysia
Component	**Place of origin**
Hard drive	US firm in Singapore or Japanese firm in Thailand
Microprocessor	US firm in Costa Rica, Philippines, Malaysia or China
Power cord	UK firm in India, Malaysia or China
Power adaptor	Thailand
Battery	US firm in Mexico or Malaysia
Graphics card	China
CD/DVD drive	Philippines
Memory	Germany, S. Korea, Japan or Taiwan
Motherboard	Taiwan
Keyboard	Japanese firm in China
Wireless card	US firm in China or Malaysia
Modem	China

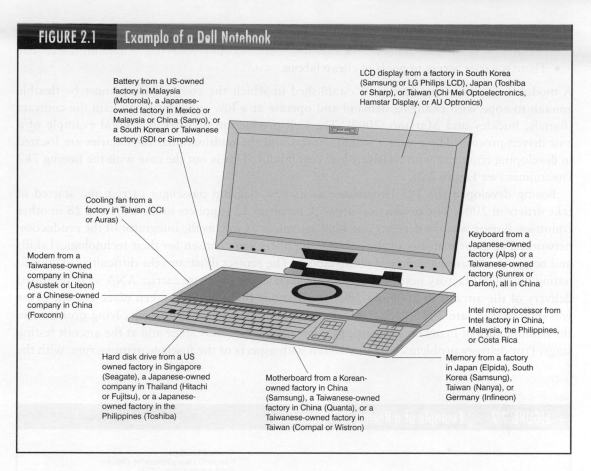

FIGURE 2.1   Example of a Dell Notebook

Battery from a US-owned factory in Malaysia (Motorola), a Japanese-owned factory in Mexico or Malaysia or China (Sanyo), or a South Korean or Taiwanese factory (SDI or Simplo)

LCD display from a factory in South Korea (Samsung or LG Philips LCD), Japan (Toshiba or Sharp), or Taiwan (Chi Mei Optoelectronics, Hamstar Display, or AU Optronics)

Cooling fan from a factory in Taiwan (CCI or Auras)

Modem from a Taiwanese-owned company in China (Asustek or Liteon) or a Chinese-owned company in China (Foxconn)

Keyboard from a Japanese-owned factory (Alps) or a Taiwanese-owned factory (Sunrex or Darfon), all in China

Intel microprocessor from Intel factory in China, Malaysia, the Philippines, or Costa Rica

Hard disk drive from a US owned factory in Singapore (Seagate), a Japanese-owned company in Thailand (Hitachi or Fujitsu), or a Japanese-owned factory in the Philippines (Toshiba)

Motherboard from a Korean-owned factory in China (Samsung), a Taiwanese-owned factory in China (Quanta), or a Taiwanese-owned factory in Taiwan (Compal or Wistron)

Memory from a factory in Japan (Elpida), South Korea (Samsung), Taiwan (Nanya), or Germany (Infineon)

The illustration of the Dell notebook demonstrates some key features of the global factory:

- A product assembled in one country using parts made in many other countries.
- Some of the parts are made by multinational firms from advanced industrial economies, operating in developing economies either as wholly-owned subsidiaries or joint ventures.
- The same part can be made by several firms in different locations.

KEY CONCEPT 2.2   THE GLOBAL FACTORY

A global factory relates to the disaggregation of the production process across a number of different firms in different countries. This form of manufacture and even the production of services has become increasingly common and is generally driven by the need to reduce costs and enabled by changes in both production technology and communications.

The factors which have made the global factory possible are similar to those that have brought about globalization that we discussed earlier. With the global factory, the key components are:

- Technology change has enabled the mass production of standardized products to the same quality in any number of different locations. In this way the production process has been codified to make the manufacture of components possible in contractor firms that were not involved in the design and development of the original product.

- Technology change in information and communications technology has made possible low cost global communications aiding both information flows and effective control.
- There is easier access to pools of cheap labour.

A modular system of production is established in which the contract firms must be flexible enough to cope with changing demand and operate at a low enough cost to gain the contract (Bartels, Buckley and Mariano, 2009). The Dell production network is a good example of a cost driven process. The contract manufacturers and the multinational subsidiaries are located in developing countries with relatively low cost labour. This is not the case with the Boeing 787 Dreamliner (see Figure 2.2).

Boeing developed the 787 Dreamliner as its new flagship passenger carrier and started to take orders in 2004. The production network involved 22 suppliers in the USA and 28 in other countries. Boeing was the designer and final assembler as well as the integrator of the production network. The great majority of the overseas suppliers were chosen for their technological skills and not on the basis of a supply of cheap labour. The project illustrates the difficulties of coordinating the global factory network. Customers such as the Japanese carrier ANA were promised delivery of the aircraft in 2008. By 2009 the first test flight had not taken place and the plane was delivered in late 2011. Delay was due to a combination of factors involving problems in the manufacture of many components, problems at the assembly stage and at the aircraft testing stage. Post delivery problems were discovered with aspects of the fuselage manufacture, with the

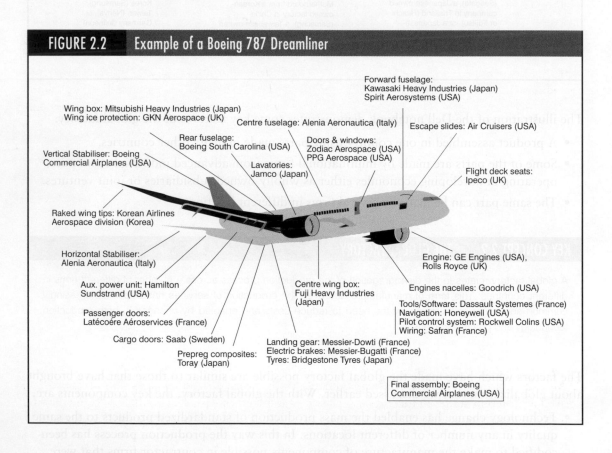

FIGURE 2.2   Example of a Boeing 787 Dreamliner

Forward fuselage:
Kawasaki Heavy Industries (Japan)
Spirit Aerosystems (USA)

Wing box: Mitsubishi Heavy Industries (Japan)
Wing ice protection: GKN Aerospace (UK)   Centre fuselage: Alenia Aeronautica (Italy)   Escape slides: Air Cruisers (USA)

Rear fuselage:
Boeing South Carolina (USA)   Doors & windows:
Zodiac Aerospace (USA)
PPG Aerospace (USA)

Vertical Stabiliser: Boeing
Commercial Airplanes (USA)   Lavatories:
Jamco (Japan)   Flight deck seats:
Ipeco (UK)

Raked wing tips: Korean Airlines
Aerospace division (Korea)

Horizontal Stabiliser:
Alenia Aeronautica (Italy)   Engine: GE Engines (USA),
Rolls Royce (UK)

Aux. power unit: Hamilton
Sundstrand (USA)   Centre wing box:
Fuji Heavy Industries
(Japan)   Engines nacelles: Goodrich (USA)

Passenger doors:
Latécoére Aéroservices (France)   Tools/Software: Dassault Systemes (France)
Navigation: Honeywell (USA)
Pilot control system: Rockwell Colins (USA)
Wiring: Safran (France)

Cargo doors: Saab (Sweden)   Landing gear: Messier-Dowti (France)
Electric brakes: Messier-Bugatti (France)
Prepreg composites: Tyres: Bridgestone Tyres (Japan)
Toray (Japan)

Final assembly: Boeing
Commercial Airplanes (USA)

engine and with the hydraulic system. These problems continued throughout 2013 and on more than one occasion the aircraft was grounded.

The global factory concept extends to the service industry. Globally interlinked service provision operates in such areas as accounting (e.g. PricewaterhouseCoopers), and consulting (e.g. McKinsey). Some of the administration for British Airways and Lufthansa is done in India. Some firms use accounting staff in offshore locations to chase bad debts when paying head office accounting staff to do this would not be cost-effective. Some hospitals in the USA and the UK use radiographers in India to analyse scans.

Some of these examples see the global outsourcing of service work moving into skilled, high value-added work. Yet many regard operating services in this way to be more difficult than manufacturing. The main reason is that most services require human interaction and are often customized to the needs of individual clients. This can make service work more expensive to operate and more difficult to outsource. As a result, service work in many organizations tends to be kept in-house.

Even with these difficulties there is plenty of evidence of the outsourcing of call centre work. Taylor et al. (2013) note an increase in call centre employment in India of 700 per cent between 2002–2009 and estimate revenues derived from international call centre work in India at over $26 billion. There are a number of reasons for this increase in outsourced call-centre activity. Indian call centres operate at 10 per cent of the cost of those in the USA (Batt, Doellgast and Kwon, 2006); the transactions have been standardized in such a way that those interacting with customers have little discretion and follow tightly controlled scripts. This type of service work has therefore been codified as is the case in manufacturing; and developments in communications technology enable interaction with customers over great distances, which in the case of India is supported by a reliable telecommunications network. There does however remain a potential conflict between customer focus and cost efficiency (Taylor, 2010). This is partly resolved in that the majority of call centres in India deal with high volume, low discretion, simple transactions, while more complex customer focused work as in business to business transactions is retained in-house (Taylor et al., 2013).

REFLECTION POINT

What do you consider to be the main problems and issues involved in managing a global production network? Consider something you have bought. Do you think it was the product of a global production chain? If so can you identify the origins of its component parts?

Global value chains

The global value chain is closely associated with the concept of the global factory and represents the build-up of value along a supply chain made up of a number of international partners. This has resulted in the vast increase in the international trade of components rather than of finished products. We examine the value chain again in relation to strategy in Chapter 8.

An examination of most global value chains reveals that different values and revenues are derived at different stages in the chain. A classic example of this process is offered by the iPhone (see Figure 2.3)

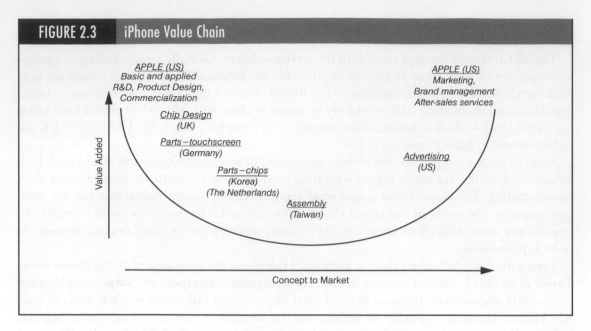

FIGURE 2.3   iPhone Value Chain

APPLE (US)
Basic and applied
R&D, Product Design,
Commercialization

APPLE (US)
Marketing,
Brand management
After-sales services

Chip Design
(UK)

Parts – touchscreen
(Germany)

Advertising
(US)

Parts – chips
(Korea)
(The Netherlands)

Assembly
(Taiwan)

Value Added

Concept to Market

We can see from the value chain of the iPhone that the key value-added activities are either kept in-house by Apple and include R&D, design, branding and marketing, or sub-contracted to companies in the UK or Germany as with chip design and the touchscreen. The least value-added component is manufacture which is outsourced either to Taiwan or China and represents about 1 per cent of the cost of the iPhone. In this way the greatest potential for profit accumulation is retained by Apple. This is typical of many global supply chains and there is little wonder that its shape is sometimes referred to as the 'smiley curve'.

Gereffi (1999) identifies two main types of global value chain. **Producer driven chains** coordinate production across several companies as in the manufacture of computers and mobile phones illustrated in Table 2.1 and Figs 2.1 and 2.3. The original designer usually develops and controls key technologies and organizes the production and assembly of components across a number of sub-contractor firms. **Buyer-driven chains** are typically found in large retail operations and large clothing and footwear manufacturers. These companies establish chains, often in low wage economies, to provide low-cost goods that are branded to represent the retailer or the clothing or footwear manufacturer. Nike is a good example of a buyer-driven approach and buys relatively unsophisticated products from a range of low-cost producers, which Nike then sells at a relatively high price on the strength of a global brand.

Later work by Gereffi, Humphrey and Sturgeon (2005) offer a further classification of global supply chains based on how they are governed. A broad distinction can be made between those governed by markets and those governed by hierarchies. Within this they identify:

- **Modular chains** involving a range of suppliers making components to the lead firm's design typical of the electronics, automobile and computer industries.

- **Captive chains** exist where small supplies are dependent on powerful large buyers as often found in the fresh food industry or with such firms as Nike as it operated prior to 2000.

- **Relational chains** in which the lead firm and the suppliers build up a close relationship based on trust and the experience of working together. This is often seen as a desired model in many sectors whereby close coordination can create synergies and flexible operating systems that are mutually beneficial. Nike moved in this direction following criticisms of their captive approach.

However, with all chains the key issues are issues of coordination and control as we saw with the case of the Boeing 787 Dreamliner.

POLITICAL ASPECTS OF GLOBALIZATION

Since the end of the Second World War a large number of supranational and regional organizations have been formed. Some, like the North Atlantic Treaty Organization (NATO), have defence as their primary concern. The EU was formed with the objective of uniting European countries in free-market trade, thus avoiding the divisions that occurred as a result of the war. Other trading blocs were formed, such as NAFTA. At global level, the greatest activity is attributed to the UN and its many specialist arms and to the WTO (see the case study in Chapter 3) and the World Bank. Outside these structures, there are forums like the G8 (one of several groups) for politicians of the major economies of the world to come together and set agendas to control world economic as well as social policy.

Such organizations had their origins in the furtherance of trade or as an alliance for defence purposes. However, more recent trends have seen a focus on social, environmental and political objectives rather than on trade and defence. In recent years the EU has focused on social issues and the G8 on poverty and debt in developing countries and the effects of global warming.

The key debate is whether such supranational organizations are able to overrule democratically elected governments in individual countries. Some claim that nation states have lost their sovereignty and are subsumed within regional and supranational structures. People in the UK are subject to laws passed in Brussels by the EU and in many countries in Europe national currencies have been abolished in favour of the euro. The sceptics rebuff such views, maintaining that nation states still hold considerable power, and that some, such as the USA, extend that power outside their territorial borders. Whichever side of the debate is taken there have been observable changes in the way countries are governed. While the majority of decisions are still made by national governments, the influence of supranational bodies is present.

A relatively recent phenomenon in many parts of the world has been a move towards decentralization of decision-making with regionalism becoming more of a force. The former Yugoslavia has broken up into a number of smaller states. In the UK, regional assemblies have been created for Scotland and Wales, and through the creation of the office of mayor, London has moved towards becoming a city state. In the UK also there is much evidence of the influence of local politics on industry location as with Japanese transplants of Nissan and Toyota in the UK.

CULTURAL ASPECTS OF GLOBALIZATION

There is the view that globalization has brought about cultural convergence. We can illustrate this in a number of ways:

- English has maintained its position as a global language and is the working language in many global organizations. British and US universities now teach MBA programmes in English to Chinese students in China. Many of the leading French business schools now offer modules taught in both French and English.

- Through increased travel, television and identification with global causes such as HIV/Aids and our response to disasters, a global consciousness has emerged uniting people across the world.

- The mass media is highly oligopolistic and controls what we read in newspapers and see on television across the world. By the mid-1990s Rupert Murdoch's News Corporation was a global network of companies. The network embraces national and regional newspapers and magazines and book publishers. It controls cable and satellite companies in the UK, USA, Latin America, Australia and Asia, including the Sky and Star networks. It owns 20th Century Fox Films and the TV company Fox Broadcasting as well as television stations in the USA and Australia. Both CNN and BBC World consider themselves to be global channels. Around the world, people are subjected to the same news and television programmes.

- We may also observe a change in some values. Individualism is replacing collectivism in many countries, as more traditional societies modernize. Societies built more around relationships than rules are changing to embrace universal rules. In some societies, such as those in the Middle East or in Latin America, it is common to find that doing business is a slow process involving getting to know the people you are dealing with and establishing a relationship based on trust. However, where business involves the coordination of complex global activities as we saw with the example of the Dell Notebook, then doing business solely on the basis of relationships between individuals is either impossible or very inefficient. More formalized, universal systems have to be developed. (A fuller account of such changes in values is found in our discussion of culture in Chapter 5).

PERSPECTIVES ON GLOBALIZATION

A number of perspectives have emerged on globalization. In this section we identify three: the globalist perspective, the anti-globalization perspective and the sceptical perspective. This classification is similar to the one used by Kirkbride *et al.* (2001).

The globalist perspective

This perspective recognizes that convergence has taken place through the creation of global products, services and markets. It recognizes cultural convergence in that many people around the world share the same tastes. Global products, services and markets are served by a global integration of production, distribution and marketing. Great economies of scale are achievable and the system favours large organizations in oligopolistic markets (a few big firms dominating an industry as in automobiles, pharmaceuticals, banking and the media). The globalist perspective believes we are living in an increasingly borderless world with ever-increasing flows of goods, services, money, people and ideas. As a result, firms become global and links with their country of origin are weakened. These ideas are to be found in seminal works by globalists such as Yip (1995). Variations within the globalist thesis exist as to the extent and rate of change and about its impact.

All globalists believe that a significant change has taken place, that such changes have resulted in economic growth, for many if not for all, and that the process is irreversible. One of the more fervent globalists is Martin Wolf (2004). He rejects most of the claims of the anti-globalists and argues that trade and FDI are not the instruments of exploitation used by rich countries on the developing world, but are in fact wealth creators. He cites evidence of western multinational companies investing in developing countries and paying better wages than local firms. He also rejects the view that globalization is a cause of environmental problems, seeing them instead as the product of national government intransigence.

Like Wolf, the supporters of globalization cite a number of advantages. These are:

- Increased prosperity for most with considerable gains made by the newly industrialized countries (NICs) such as the Asian tigers. Straw and Glennie (2012, p. 1) go further. They state that 'the progressive integration of the global economy has helped drive economic growth that has contributed to lifting millions of people out of poverty around the world'.

- Improvements in rates of literacy and numeracy.

- Improvements in health, especially a reduction in infant mortality.

- Increased security resulting in an absence of global wars. Some attribute this to the growth of international alliances and others, such as Friedman (2006), to the interconnected nature of the global economy.

- A greater number of products and services available to a greater number of people. This is due in part to productivity increases resulting from greater efficiencies. This has reduced the costs and the price of many consumer goods.

- Access to greater information and knowledge.

- Global action on poverty, health and environmental problems.

The anti-globalization perspective

This perspective accepts that changes have occurred but that the net result is exploitative and has resulted in a widening of the gap between rich and poor nations. Large multinationals are singled out as exploiters. International agencies such as the World Bank, World Trade Organization (WTO) and International Monetary Fund (IMF) are accused of being influenced too much by the rich and powerful nations and, in making loans to Third World countries, simply saddle those countries with debts they can never repay.

The opponents of globalization claim a number of disadvantages:

- The beneficiaries are in a minority and include those living in prosperous countries. The rest of the world has been marginalized, none more so than Africa. In terms of trade, the so-called TRIAD (countries of North America, Western Europe and Japan) dominates. Only China features alongside the TRIAD countries in terms of the export and import of manufactured goods and services. A similar pattern occurs in terms of outward flows of FDI (Dicken, 2011).

- The gap between rich and poor nations and between rich and poor people in those nations has widened.

- Globalization is accused of causing economic crashes of the sort experienced by Mexico, South-East Asia and Russia. In some cases, economic crashes of the sort found in South East Asia and the banking crisis of 2008 are seen as the product of the rapid transfer of economic problems from one country to another, facilitated by globalization.

- There are still fierce local and regional wars. Indeed the number of civil wars has increased as the power of the state is weakened (Straw and Glennie, 2012). The challenges to authority in parts of the Arab world since 2012 are in part a product of the increased access to global media, changing social values and the increased ease of communication via communications technologies such as mobile phones and websites such as Facebook. Paradoxically, many anti-globalists would see such social changes calling for greater democracy, undoubtedly products of globalization, as highly desirable.

- Globalization has brought with it new kinds of conflict related to the lack of control over the increased movement of goods and capital. In particular, global production occurs in criminal activities in such areas as money-laundering and international drugs cartels (illegal drugs are thought by many to be one of the world's largest industries).

- Globalization is associated with ecological disasters such as the erosion of the ozone layer, the extinction of animal and plant species, global warming, and the rapid spread of diseases such as HIV/Aids and avian influenza (bird flu).

As a result of the above, some anti-globalists believe that globalization must be stopped or at least controlled. This has led to protests, some of them violent, at summits in Seattle and Genoa.

The pro- and anti-globalization perspectives are not as clear cut as they are portrayed here. The World Bank (2000) speaks of 'compelling' evidence that globalization has created economic growth and reduced poverty in the developing world, yet acknowledges that it has created inequalities, especially in poor countries. Friedman (2006) sees globalization bringing the world together (in his book he refers to this as a 'flat' world). He acknowledges also that half the world's population, including rural India, rural China and most of Africa, live in a distinctively 'unflat' world, where poverty is the norm. This uneven impact of globalization takes us into the third perspective inhabited by the sceptics. Scholte (2005) argues that globalization has had a positive effect on security, equality and democracy but is, at the same time, associated with increased insecurities and widening inequalities.

The sceptical perspective

A number of writers, typified by Hirst and Thompson (1999), have argued that globalization represents nothing new and is part of a trend in world economics that can be traced back several centuries. Sceptics argue that the globalists have failed to come up with a convincing model of the global economy. The sceptics question whether the changes that can be seen are really global, citing the concentration of production and investment within the advanced economies of Europe, America and Japan. They also question the concept of the borderless world, seeing large multinationals such as Mitsubishi retaining strong links with its home country (Japan). In fact, they argue that most multinationals are still identified by their country of origin and that the concept of the truly global, stateless company is rare if not non-existent.

Dicken (2011) rejects the major claims of both the globalists and the anti-globalists lobby, at least in their extreme form. He labels the extreme globalists as the 'hyper-globalists of the right' and the extreme anti-globalists as the 'hyper-globalists of the left'. He states that their respective claims for increased prosperity and increased inequalities are both myths based on inadequate evidence. He rejects the notion of the global economy seeing an international economy based on nation states with significant differences between them.

In many ways the sceptics have much in common with the anti-globalists and they suggest limitations to globalization as follows:

- Many countries still limit the flow of goods and services in an attempt to protect their own markets.

- Most countries have currency and banking regulations, which limit the flow of capital.

- Labour mobility does not occur on a great scale, restricted, in the main, by immigration laws. It is the movement of production to use labour as a global resource that is the key feature of globalization. While there has been a rise in absolute numbers of migrants, the percentage of the population has remained constant at 3 per cent. What has changed is the number of internal migrants moving for work in such countries as China, where it is estimated at 150 million (Straw and Glennie, 2012).

- Nation states still wield considerable power and most aim to preserve their own sovereignty.

- While multinationals have expanded both in number and location they tend to retain strong ties with their country of origin in terms of the distribution of population, R&D, and the nationality of both owners and senior management groups.

- We can still see considerable cultural diversity among peoples of the world.

- The impact of globalization is highly uneven. Most advantages fall to Western Europe, the USA and Japan. Even in the UK those advantages tend to be felt more by the young and the middle classes living in cities. While emerging economies show high growth rates, living standards have been slow to catch up (Straw and Glennie, 2012).

The three perspectives are summarized in Table 2.2. However, a fourth perspective may be emerging, that of acknowledging the problems that globalization brings but at the same time having confidence that such problems can be solved or are at least manageable. Scholte (2005) argues that the problems are not inevitable but are the outcomes of policies (or lack of them) that politicians have the power to change. Straw and Glennie (2012) offer similar sentiments and call for improved and new forms of global collaboration particularly in areas such as the regulation of financial markets.

TABLE 2.2 Perspectives on globalization		
Globalists	**Anti-globalists**	**Sceptics**
• Growth of global products, services and markets	• Agree with globalists that changes have occurred but disagree on the impact	• Globalization not new but a continuation of existing trend
• Convergence of cultures	• Widening gap between rich and poor nations and people	• No plausible model exists of the global economy
• Global integration of production, marketing and distribution with increased efficiencies and reduced costs	• International agencies serve needs of rich nations	• Changes are not global but focus on industrial nations
• Dominance of oligopolies	• Exploitation by big business	• In all nations the effect is uneven
• Borderless world	• Benefits rich nations	• Firms still identify with country of origin
• Firms no longer represent nation states	• Creates economic problems	• Flows of goods, services, money and labour are restricted by nation states
• Increased flows of goods, services, money and ideas	• Conflict has not been eliminated	
• All results in economic growth		

(Continued)

TABLE 2.2   (Continued)

Globalists	Anti-globalists	Sceptics
• Increased wages and prosperity and reduced poverty • Reduced international military conflict • Greater access to information and knowledge • Global action on poverty, disease and environmental problems	• Globalization has occurred in criminal activity • Creation of ecological problems and hastening of spread of disease	• Nation states still wield considerable power • Cultural diversity is a distinguishing feature

REFLECTION POINT

Which of the above perspectives do you agree with and why?

THE MULTINATIONAL AND TRANSNATIONAL CORPORATION

We have already noted that an important aspect of globalization has been the market dominance of the multinational corporation. In this section we will explore the characteristics and activities of MNCs. We also examine what some commentators see as the transformation of the traditional MNC into the transnational corporation (TNC), a key organizational form in the development of globalization. However, we use the generic term MNC, despite the fact that this term has different meanings to different writers. We shall attempt to clarify those differences within this section. Trade and finance have always been international and there are many interesting examples of early multinationals, e.g. the Hudson Bay Company and the Dutch East India Company. Kikkoman, the Japanese company manufacturing soy sauce, established a factory in Denver, USA in the 1890s to supply the Chinese who were working on the expanding rail network. The British American Tobacco Corporation had established itself in China by 1914 and employed 25 000 Chinese workers by 1920. The company invested in cinemas and the film industry in China in the 1920s, not only to sell cigarettes and tobacco at cinemas but also to feature cigarette smoking in its films to promote sales (Jones, 1996). It was not until the post-war period that the large US conglomerate with its divisional structure was attracted to expanding European markets. While Europe initially provided an open door to such investment, later protectionist policies, set up by the then European Economic Community (EEC), accelerated the growth of US subsidiaries in Europe. Japanese firms have also invested in both Europe and the USA for the same reasons.

KEY CONCEPT 2.3   THE MULTINATIONAL CORPORATION

A multinational firm is one that operates and is managed from bases in a number of countries. Ownership of assets in a foreign country was considered a defining feature of the multinational. However, changes in the global economy involving the rapid expansion of global networks of supply and production have focused the defining feature of the MNC in terms of the range of global activities over which the firm has influence. While small firms can and do operate multinationally, most multinationals are large corporations with diverse interests coordinated by a centrally planned global strategy. Multinational growth was originally associated with firms from the USA and Europe, although there has been a significant growth in multinational activity from firms in Asia, notably from Japan and more recently from China. Over 80 per cent of the world's largest 500 MNCs originate from the USA, the EU or Japan.

Characteristics of the multinational corporation

There seems to be no agreed definition for a multinational corporation. The United Nations Conference on Trade and Development (UNCTAD) publishes its transnationality index comprising the unweighted average of 3 measures:

per cent foreign to total assets;

per cent foreign to total sales;

per cent foreign to total employment.

Whilst the data produced by UNCTAD identifies the world's largest multinational corporations it offers no guidance as to what level should be reached on each of the three measures before a company can be considered a multinational. We maintain that the characteristics of a multinational company must include more than a simple engagement in a foreign country and involves:

- A headquarters and operations in one country and operations in one or more other countries.
- Foreign direct investment (FDI), implying both ownership and overseas operations.
- Control of a globally networked supply chain and systems of production.
- A substantial management presence overseas.
- Some form of centrally planned global strategy.
- The diffusion of management ideas and practices.

The significant expansion of coordinated activities as part of the global factory and the global supply chain, discussed earlier, has led to a revised definition of the multinational as:

A coordinated system or network of cross-border value generating activities, some of which are carried out within the hierarchy of the firm, and some of which are carried out through informal social ties or contractual relationships. Thus an MNE is not defined by the extent of the foreign production facilities it owns but by the sum total of its value creating activities over which it has significant influence.

(Cantwell, Dunning and Lundan, 2010, p. 569)

MNCs and the global economy

The multinational has influenced national economies in a variety of ways. Many multinational companies are very large indeed, controlling much of global production, global resources and global money flows. The past 25 years have seen a significant growth in the number and scope of multinationals. In 1990, around 35 000 multinationals could be identified. By 2001 that number had increased to 65 000 with around 850 000 affiliate companies between them (UNCTAD cited in Chandler and Mazlish, 2005). Between 1983 and 2001 the world GDP rose 173 per cent but the capital assets of the world's biggest 50 firms rose 686 per cent (UNCTAD cited in Chandler and Mazlish, 2005). This growth in capital assets is a measure of the expansion of these firms. While some of that expansion is accounted for by growth in their country of origin, a greater part is due to the growth of foreign direct investment (FDI). We have already referred to this in our earlier section on the causes of globalization. It should be noted that although the largest growth in FDI has been experienced by multinationals in the developing countries (with much investment currently flowing into China), by far the greatest amount of capital flow in terms of FDI is between countries in the developed economies as between the USA and Western Europe. The developed economies also possess the greatest amount of FDI stock, the total overseas capital assets of multinationals.

Table 2.3 shows that if we equate GDP with sales, then 7 of the largest 50 economic entities are companies. Such data raise issues about the relative power of corporations and nation states and the impact that the former can have on the latter. Whilst, in most cases, governments are accountable to their electorate, multinationals are accountable, if at all, to only their most powerful global shareholders.

TABLE 2.3	The world's top 50 economic entities in 2012 by GDP or Revenues in $US million
USA	15 684 750
China	8 227 037
Japan	5 963 969
Germany	3 400 579
France	2 608 699
UK	2 440 505
Brazil	2 395 968
Russia	2 021 960
Italy	2 014 079
India	1 824 832
Canada	1 819 081
Australia	1 541 797
Spain	1 352 057
Mexico	1 177 116
South Korea	1 155 872
Indonesia	878 198
Turkey	794 468
The Netherlands	773 116
Saudi Arabia	727 307

TABLE 2.3	(Continued)
Switzerland	632 400
Iran	548 895
Sweden	526 192
Norway	501 101
Poland	487 674
Belgium	484 692
Royal Dutch Shell (Neth/UK)	484 489
Argentina	474 954
Taiwan	473 971
Exxon Mobil (USA)	452 926
Wal-Mart (USA)	446 950
Austria	398 594
BP (UK)	386 463
South Africa	384 315
Venezuela	382 424
Sinopec Group (China)	375 214
Colombia	366 020
Thailand	365 564
United Arab Emirates	358 940
China National Petroleum (China)	352 338
Denmark	313 637
Malaysia	303 527
Singapore	276 520
Nigeria	268 708
Chile	268 177
Hong Kong (China)	263 021
State Grid (China)	259 142
Egypt	256 729
Philippines	250 126
Finland	250 126
Greece	249 201

The number of companies in the top 50 has fallen from 11 in 2005 to 7 in 2012. However, the significant change in this table is the inclusion of 3 Chinese companies reflecting the emergence of China as a major economic force. The table also confirms the relative decline of Japanese companies. A similar table published in 1998 reveals 6 Japanese companies in the top 40, but by 2005 only Toyota remained No Japanese company features in the current listings.

Legrain (2002) believes that such tables are highly misleading. He believes that a comparison of GDP and sales revenue is not comparing like with like and argues that a better representation of a firm's worth is its value added: the difference between the value of its sales and the cost of its inputs. Under this measure he calculates that few would appear in the top 50. Furthermore, he argues that nation states have far more power than individual companies, in that they can impose taxes, go to war, and make laws which affect the lives of every citizen. (We examine the role of the state in more detail in the next chapter.) Chandler and Mazlish (2005) agree that equating sales revenue with economic output exaggerates the economic power of the multinational and that value added is a better indicator. Nonetheless they conclude that the economic size of some of these companies gives them considerable political power.

REFLECTION POINT

Do you believe that firms can be as powerful as nation states? What arguments and evidence can you bring to support your position?

Rationale for the development of MNCs

Many reasons have been put forward to explain why multinationals have emerged. Many of these factors operate together. For example, the growth of multinational activity in China, through joint ventures, is both a product of access to a potentially large market and to cheap labour. The following points identify the main reasons:

- Expansion overseas enables firms to protect themselves against the cyclical problems of national economies. The early expansion of US firms, such as Esso and General Motors, overseas was a product of a home market that was both in recession and saturated.

- The traditional motivation for multinational growth was associated with accessing raw materials. Through vertical integration and the acquisition of firms further down the supply chain, key supplies could be secured for both domestic and overseas operations.

- The need for new markets was an imperative due to the growing investments in process and product technologies. The size of such investments meant that home markets were too small and overseas expansion was imperative to exploit economies of scale. Large markets are particularly attractive, hence the amount of FDI in the USA, the EU and more recently China.

- MNC expansion particularly through mergers, acquisitions and joint ventures was also seen as protection against competition. Such collaborations gave access to both expanded markets and economies of scale. Indeed, any expansion offers the potential for the exploitation of economies of scale.

- A major motivation was the need to reduce costs. Locations were favoured that gave access not only to low-cost materials, but also low-cost labour, rents and low rates of corporate taxation. The expansion of multinational manufacturers in China, Vietnam and Indonesia has been to transfer labour-intensive activities to low-cost labour markets. Part of the attractiveness of Singapore to overseas firms was the availability of government-built factory shells, government rent subsidies and favourable tax rates.

- Overseas location is often motivated by the need to overcome import controls and tariff barriers. Under EU law, firms operating within an EU country, irrespective of their origin, are classed as an EU producer and therefore not subject to import restrictions. This resulted in large numbers of US and Japanese firms locating operations within the EU.

- The expansion of multinationals has been facilitated by changes in organizational structure to assist control. These have included such structural developments as the creation of divisions and profit centres and by developments in transport and electronic communications.

An analysis of the above rationale reveals a combination of reactive and proactive explanations. In part MNEs are reacting to such factors as downturns and market saturation at home and being proactive by moving into growth markets and reducing costs by accessing low cost labour markets.

A theory of multinationals?

Many of the above reasons have been incorporated in attempts to develop a theory of multinationals. Most of these theories have emerged since 1960, although some, notably economies of scale and scope and transaction cost theory, have their origins in much earlier work. However, in all cases the predictive capability of such 'theories' leaves much to be desired.

A simple explanation is based on economies of scale and economies of scope. The concept of economies of scale suggests that increased size of operation brings with it a reduction in unit costs. In other words, the larger a firm becomes, the cheaper it is to produce goods and services. This is due to a range of factors including benefits from increased specialization, the experience of staff and the ability of larger firms to borrow more money at favourable rates. A related concept, economies of scope, refers to reduced costs associated with a range of products. Such benefits may include the centralization and sharing of functions such as marketing, distribution and accounts, the opportunity to create a family of brands and the ability to cross-subsidize by transferring revenues across the firm. The size and scope of multinationals enables them to benefit from such advantages.

The Uppsala School (see for example Johanson and Vahlne, 1977) based a theory largely on the basis of the development of Swedish firms such as Sandvik, Volvo and Atlas-Copco. They concluded that going multinational is generally an incremental process that begins with exporting and moves to establishing operations in another country. The choice of country is important and the most favourable locations are those with the greatest similarity to the country of origin in terms of culture, language and business practices. They refer to this as 'psychic distance'. Firms move first to countries where they feel most comfortable and the greater the psychic distance the greater the barriers to expansion in that country. IKEA took several years to establish itself in Sweden before moving first into Norway and then to Denmark. Its rapid global expansion beyond Scandinavia only began a few years later.

Not all multinationals appear to follow this incremental sequence. Attention has been given in recent years to a group of companies that have been labelled as **'born globals'**. Such companies move rapidly into a wide range of foreign markets, Google being a prime example. Many, however, are relatively small high-tech companies such as Logitech that have developed leading edge products and/or operate in niche markets. The product is designed for the global market and the founders usually have international backgrounds with existing global networks in place.

The Eclectic Paradigm, probably the most comprehensive approach to theory to date was conceived by John Dunning (1993). He argues that three factors are necessary to explain a company 'going multinational'. He took the approaches of three different attempts at theoretical explanation and placed them together. The three factors he identifies are:

- **Ownership factors**. Dunning argues that to be successful in an overseas market, a multinational must possess certain advantages over local firms. Such advantages could include superior technology, superior brands, greater access to finance, superior forms of distribution and superior organization and management.
- **Location factors**. The reason to operate overseas may be due to any number of reasons that operate in the host country. These might include operating in that country to avoid import tariffs or to take advantage of cheap labour or low rates of taxation or specific resources.

- **Internalization factors.** This is based on the notion of transaction costs. These are the costs involved in doing business. For example, a firm wishing to do business in a foreign market may seek a partner in that country either as a manufacturer or distributor or both. There are potential problems in such a relationship. The partner in the host country will require some form of payment and their activities will need to be monitored and controlled. Additional costs are incurred in drawing up contracts and other such legal fees. Furthermore, the firm wishing to expand in another country is often basing decisions on host country firms with limited information. How does it know it has selected the best partner possible? Risks may be involved in that the host country partner may acquire the intellectual property of the expanding firm and emerge as a competitor. For some or all of these reasons firms that wish to expand in foreign markets may wish to apply greater controls and reduce risk by keeping all activities in-house. This explains why many multinationals expand by entering new markets by establishing their own operations on a greenfield site or by purchasing a firm and creating a wholly owned subsidiary. Williamson (1975) referred to this as a choice between markets and hierarchies. Dealing with the marketplace is much less predictable than controlling operations within the same firm through an arrangement of subsidiary organizations (hierarchies).

The above approach is also referred to as the OLI theory, after the first letter of each of the three approaches, i.e. ownership, location and internalization.

REFLECTION POINT

Which of the three factors – ownership, location and internalization – is the most persuasive in explaining the growth of the multinational firm?

From multinational to transnational

In the past 10 years or so, writers have used the term transnational corporation (TNC) rather than MNC to reflect the changes brought about by globalization. Bartlett and Ghoshal (1995) and Bartlett and Beamish (2011) see the transnational as the latest culmination of changing strategic approaches focusing on the twin elements of cost and responsiveness.

The changing strategies are presented as a series of stages which Bartlett and Beamish identify as international, multidomestic, global and transnational mentalities.

The international mentality focuses on the export of products manufactured at home. Some of the marketing is local, as in the use of agents, but the product is hardly modified. Many companies operated in this way in the early stages of their development. Microsoft still operates in this way.

The multidomestic mentality sets up operations in one, but usually more, overseas countries and both produces and markets local products for local markets. There is usually considerable product variation. The car industry operated in this way for many years and many food and cosmetic companies still do. However, such a focus on local responsiveness can be costly, with duplication of R&D, marketing and other functions. In addition, several decentralized companies operating independently can create problems of coordination and control.

The global mentality is typified by increased competition and the expansion of operations. There is a focus on cost reduction, achieved through switching operations to low-cost countries. Cost reduction is also achieved by product rationalization leading to economies of scale.

Car firms switched from multidomestic to global operations as in the case of the European car industry. An integrative global strategy emerges that results in global products for global markets made at low cost in different locations, as in the case of firms producing microchips. Companies such as Coca-Cola and Sony are typical global companies.

The **transnational mentality** attempts to address the pressures of operating in a global economy. These were defined by Bartlett and Ghoshal (1995) as the need to be locally responsive; the need to be cost efficient and the demand for constant innovation to respond to changing markets and increased competition. The transnational therefore achieves both the local responsiveness of the multidomestic operation with the economies of scale and cost reduction of the global operation. The transnational company displays a number of features:

- Firms are neither centralized nor decentralized but gain competitive advantage from both the integration of global resources to achieve economies of scale and from flexibility and the capability to respond to local market needs, i.e. operating both globally and locally.

- Cross-border operation becomes a necessity for survival as high-volume sales become essential to recover investment costs, particularly those associated with shorter product life cycles.

- The strategies move away from the focus on a single issue of market, supply or cost to embrace a mixture of motives. Low-cost operation in cheap labour economies may be pursued for mass-market goods, whereas accessing skill and know-how may be more significant with more complex, high value-added products. LG, the Korean electronics firm, uses South-East Asian locations for its mass-market products, such as televisions and video recorders. The same firm uses its US operations, and the experience of its US subsidiaries to develop more advanced products. In another vein, high-cost start-up operations in such countries as China can be offset by more profitable ventures elsewhere.

- Technology transfer and the diffusion of R&D across partner companies becomes important. There is a broader exchange of ideas and core competencies and the focus becomes global learning and worldwide innovation.

- Transnational companies are associated with a corresponding growth in joint ventures and alliances. These enable the transnational corporation to share costs, access new markets, pool expertise and knowledge, and create synergies (more detail is provided in the section on joint ventures later in this chapter). In this way, transnational companies create highly interdependent networks of resources.

- The strategic and structural issues are flexibility, responsiveness, innovation, speed and integration. Different types of organization are created. Barriers are broken down vertically through the reduction in the layers of management and a reduction in the importance of hierarchies. Barriers are also broken down horizontally through the integration of suppliers and distributors.

- A transnational mentality emerges based around a corporate rather than a national culture.

- As a result of the complexity of most transnational operations, transnational companies can be expensive to coordinate and control.

There are some who question whether the transnational has emerged as defined in this way. In a study by Hu (1996), few examples were found of truly transnational companies. He argued that most so-called transnationals operate from a central base in their country of origin and they are, in most cases, owned, controlled and managed by home-country nationals. He further argues that only bi-national firms, such as Shell and Unilever, can be considered truly global. This represents a cautious view, which may be challenged by the changes that have taken place in the automotive industry. Some European car companies, such as Renault and Ford have stakes in Japanese firms and, in the case of Renault, have placed a chief executive in charge of Nissan. Fiat have expanded their network into the USA through their acquisition of Chrysler. As we will see in Case 2.1, Daimler Benz have significantly expanded their presence in China through a series of joint ventures.

KEY CONCEPT 2.4	THE TRANSNATIONAL CORPORATION

The growth of the global economy has resulted in many multinationals becoming truly international businesses with weakening ties with their original country of origin. Some writers have referred to such firms as transnational corporations. A transnational integrates global resources to achieve economies of scale which have the capability of responding to local markets. Flexibility, responsiveness and innovation replace control and cost as primary strategic objectives.

As if in support of Hu's point, many texts on international business, whilst referring to the concept of transnationality, offer few and, in some cases, no examples whatsoever. Bartlett and Beamish add to the confusion by claiming that the transnational firm is as much about a 'mentality' as it is about strategies and structures, a phenomenon that is difficult to observe. The US fast food chain McDonald's offers some of the features of the transnational company. It has an operating style that is extremely standardized, in terms of process, brand and franchise arrangements. However, it has product and marketing variations in response to local needs and preferences. A good example of this is found in the McDonald's operation in Singapore, more detail of which may be found in the case study in Chapter 12.

Figure 2.4 summarizes the differences between the four types and identifies the differences as a function of efficiency, competition and responsiveness.

FIGURE 2.4	Differences between types of multinational operation as classified by Bartlett and Ghoshal (1995)

Increasing emphasis on responding to local needs

Multi-domestic company
- Production in a number of overseas operations
- Products geared towards local markets

Transnational company
- Mix of centralization and decentralization
- Mixed motives and strategies
- Diffusion of ideas via joint ventures and R&D
- Cross-border mentality built around corporate identity

International company
- Manufacture at a home base
- Growth of exports

Global company
- Cost reduction a priority
- Global strategy to achieve lower costs – use of low-cost locations
- Global products for global markets

Increasing emphasis on creating efficiencies on a global scale/increasing competition

Another difference lies in their modes of entry into overseas markets. The international mentality favours exporting, the multidomestic mentality favours local operations and the global mentality favours centrally controlled and coordinated activities involving a mix of wholly owned subsidiaries and joint ventures. In the next section we examine briefly the routes that can be taken by international firms and we close the chapter by examining in more detail specific issues relating to joint ventures.

REFLECTION POINT

Can McDonald's be called a transnational company? What other companies do you believe meet the requirements to be called transnational and why?

MODES OF ENTRY

International firms can enter overseas markets in a number of ways, each with variations in cost, commitment, risk and ease of entry.

Exporting This is the simplest form of entry and is relatively low cost and low risk. There may be problems in the form of tariffs and barriers and transport costs may increase the price of the product. This is usually the first stage in international growth.

Licensing This allows another firm in an overseas market to offer a service or manufacture a product for a fee paid to the originators. Little investment is involved and it is relatively low risk. It usually means fast entry and can also avoid import tariffs. Pilkington, the UK glass manufacturer, found this a good way of capitalizing on the development of the float glass process for the manufacture of plate glass, particularly because exporting glass carried a high risk of damage. While licensing can be profitable it does carry the risk that the licensee learns from the process, becomes opportunistic and enters the market independently as a competitor.

Franchising This is similar to licensing but differs in that licensing usually involves a single product whereas franchising involves the whole business including a range of products, the brand and the method of operation. It allows an overseas firm to produce and market a branded product or service for an initial fee and (usually) a supply contract. Again it is relatively low cost and low risk, allows rapid entry to the market and avoids tariff barriers. The model is particularly suited to small businesses and is used by fast food companies such as McDonald's and Kentucky Fried Chicken. There may be issues of quality control and in many cases, revenues can be low.

Offshore outsourcing As we have identified earlier in this chapter many firms outsource part of their business to firms in other countries. This can be a form of market entry, although it is mainly employed to achieve cost efficiencies in the production of goods or services.

Joint ventures The classic form of joint venture in international business involves firms from one or more countries establishing a new firm. This concept is explored in detail in the next section.

Wholly-owned subsidiary This form of FDI occurs either through the acquisition of a firm in another country or by establishing a Greenfield site operation. This form of entry gives the multinational greater control of the operation and enables them to realize all revenues. It can be expensive and carries more risk than with other modes, including political risks.

In general, market entry has become a more complex business due to the increased complexity of global networks and the number of countries involved. This has resulted in a wide variety of practices and multinationals can enter different countries in different ways. This will depend on the conditions that operate in those countries and variation can be a product of market conditions, economic and political factors, legal factors and labour market skills, as well as decisions that are based on cost, risk and how much control is exerted by the multinational.

REFLECTION POINT

With each of the modes of entry identified above assess the costs, commitment and risk involved in terms of high, medium or low.

Strategic alliances and joint ventures

In all types of business, in most parts of the world, there is a long history of firms working together to achieve mutual advantages; however, the increase in alliances and joint ventures has been a phenomenon of the business world in the past 25 years. The phenomenon is a product of globalization, increased competition, the attractiveness of emerging markets in developing nations and, for advanced economies, declining growth rates and the increasing cost of home operations, particularly in terms of labour and R&D.

Strategic alliances and joint ventures are essentially strategic options, where there is some advantage in working in collaboration with another partner rather than going it alone or subcontracting to an export agency or contract provider. Alliances and joint ventures may be a faster and more effective way for new market entry, a more cost-effective means of product development or distribution, or simply a means of survival. Alliances and joint ventures represent less radical forms of collaboration than are found in mergers or acquisitions. A merger or an acquisition may not be wanted by any of the parties or they would be too costly. In some cases the kind of ownership patterns involved in a merger or acquisition would be politically difficult, as was the situation, until recently, in India and as currently operates in China in certain sectors such as the automotive industry. In general, joint ventures must add more value than either wholly-owned subsidiaries or contract outsourcing.

The difference between a strategic alliance and a joint venture is usually the depth of the contractual relationship. **Joint ventures** generally involve an element of shared ownership or involve fairly restrictive contractual obligations as with licensing and franchise agreements. In terms of ownership patterns a number of variations are possible:

- joint ownership with control by one party
- joint ownership with shared control
- majority/minority ownership with variations in control
- a third company owned and/or controlled by two or more other companies.

The final category is perhaps the most common form of joint venture, particularly between firms of different countries. When this happens it is called an **international joint venture** (**IJV**).

A **strategic alliance** occurs when two companies agree to cooperate on a specific venture or have an arrangement to share facilities. Contractual arrangements can and do exist but,

TABLE 2.4 Example of alliances in the airline industry	
Star Alliance (2013): 28 members	**One World Alliance (2013): 12 members**
Adria Airways	airberlin
Aegean Airlines	American Airlines
Air Canada	British Airways
Air China	Cathay Pacific
Air New Zealand	Finnair
ANA	Iberia
Asiana Airlines	Japan Airlines
Austrian	LAN Airlines
Avianca	Malaysia Airlines
Brussels Airlines	Qantas
Copa Airlines	Royal Jordanian
Croatia Airlines	S7 Airlines
EGYPTAIR	
Ethiopian Airlines	
EVA Air	
LOT Polish Airlines	
Lufthansa	
Scandinavian Airlines	
Shenzhen Airlines	
Singapore Airlines	
South African Airways	
SWISS	
TAM Airlines	
TAP Portugal	
Thai Airways International (THAI)	
Turkish Airlines	
United	
US Airways	

generally, they are less restrictive than those found under licensing or franchise agreements. In the manufacturing industry, a pattern is emerging where companies such as Daimler Benz establish alliances with suppliers. At the main Mercedes factory, near Stuttgart, the supplier of tyres (Continental) has established operations next to the main assembly plant, and their production plans are tied in with those of Mercedes. In the airline industry a number of national carriers have joined together to form alliances. Two of the largest, the Star Alliance and the One World Alliance, are identified in Table 2.4.

Alliances in the airline industry offer customers advantages in the form of single booking, ticketing and baggage handling across routes and airlines within the same alliance. For alliance partners, there are potential cost savings via shared ticketing, check-in facilities, baggage handling and customer interaction, with further savings possible in such areas as maintenance.

KEY CONCEPT 2.5   JOINT VENTURES

Joint ventures are forms of collaboration between firms to achieve specific strategic objectives such as technology transfer, new market entry or new product development. Joint ventures usually involve some element of shared ownership as in the case of two firms collaborating to establish a new company. Many joint ventures involve firms from different countries and these are sometimes referred to as international joint ventures or IJVs.

The remainder of this section will focus on **joint ventures,** although many of the issues raised are also applicable to strategic alliances.

Reasons for the growth of joint ventures

These can be identified as follows:

- **Survival and growth in the face of increased global competition.** In the automobile industry the need for survival and growth has also caused competitors to work together on joint projects, as with Ford and Volkswagen creating a new people carrier, built through a joint venture in Portugal. Across all types of industry, a joint venture may be the only effective way for some small firms to compete and survive.

- **Market growth and new market entry.** A joint venture can extend product distribution networks into new areas. All partners may gain access to a bigger market. This is especially true with IJVs. In some cases, a joint venture is a political necessity to gain entry into certain markets, such as China. Despite this restriction being lifted following China's membership of the WTO, it is still a requirement in some types of industry, such as automobiles and is still a preferred mode of entry for many foreign firms. In India, until relatively recently, foreign firms could only operate in a joint venture in the country where the Indian partner held the majority share. That restriction has now been lifted, reflecting the growing influence of globalization on joint venture activity and the need for more flexible arrangements. As a consequence there has been a corresponding growth in FDI in India.

- **Technology transfer** is a motivator behind many joint ventures, particularly for firms in transitional and emerging economies. In China, the key exchange in many IJVs between Chinese firms and those from the West or Japan is the **transfer of technology** to the Chinese firm in return for market entry. This happened in the case of the joint venture between Chrysler and the Beijing Auto Works to manufacture the Jeep.

- **Access to specific core competencies.** An important strand in the development of the theory of strategic management is the belief that specific knowledge, skills and technology can be harnessed to differentiate a firm from its competitors and give it competitive advantage. This is referred to as a core competence and will be discussed further in Chapter 7 in our discussion of strategic issues. A core competence could reside in a specific area of knowledge and expertise, a specific technology or operating system or even an effective system of customer care. Through joint ventures, a firm may acquire core competencies or exchange complementary core competencies to benefit both parties. In this way a specialist credit insurer may work together on a project with a specialist surety firm, each contributing their knowledge and skills.

- **Synergy** is where an outcome is achieved by an activity that is greater than the sum of its constituent parts. In a joint venture the pooling of knowledge, skills and technology may achieve such synergy. This is particularly important as many projects and even industries (such as biotechnology) are interdisciplinary by nature. Techniques can also be created, for example to reduce the time taken to develop new products, vital in an increasingly competitive market. Two different firms working together and pooling knowledge and resources can often create solutions that would not be possible in a wholly-owned subsidiary. A MNE working with a local firm can gain market and local operating knowledge that would be difficult if they were working alone.

- **Cost reduction** is the aim of many joint ventures. Through the pooling of both market demand and resource supply, two or more firms can achieve economies of scale across global operations. In the case of some IJVs, high-volume, low-tech work can be concentrated in low-labour cost regions. Better deals can be struck through bulk purchasing from suppliers. Duplicated activities can be consolidated with a saving on labour, buildings costs and overheads.

- **Reduced risk** is achieved by sharing the risk between two or more partners. The development of the Airbus is the result of a joint venture between the aerospace industries of the UK, France, Germany and Spain. The development of the project comprised high front-end expenditure and difficult market entry so that the industry of no single country was prepared to accept the risk. International joint ventures can be a better way of dealing with uncertainty through the use of local knowledge, local networks and local political knowledge. This is especially true in countries that are less well developed economically.

- **Increased control of the supply chain** may be achieved by joint ventures between manufacturers of goods and services and their suppliers and distributors. In this way News Corporation around the world operates together with a part-owned partner, TNT, to distribute its newspapers.

- **Create tailored local situations** A firm operating internationally may gain distinctive competence through partnership with a local firm to offer specific goods and services to meet the needs of local markets, to work more effectively with local labour or to increase market share through knowledge of the market.

In most joint ventures it is not one factor that predominates but a combination of the above. In the case of Airbus Industry, the collaboration between the UK, France and Germany which started in 1970, a number of factors were at work. A joint venture reduced entry costs for the companies involved in a notoriously expensive business. The partners were supported by their respective governments, initially in a move to compete on a global scale with US firms, Boeing and McDonnell Douglas. In addition, there was a clear demand from European airlines for a new type of medium-range carrier (Lyons, 1991).

However, many commentators believe that the rationale for joint ventures has changed. In the 1970s and 1980s the main motivation was one of control – of markets, resources, the supply chain and even forming alliances with competitors to discover and head off their initiatives. The model that developed in transitional and emerging markets was for a multinational from an advanced economy to form a joint venture with a local firm and gain market entry in return for limited technology transfer. In this way, Chrysler formed a partnership with the Beijing Auto Works to create the Beijing Jeep Corporation. Through the joint venture, Chrysler gained entry to the Chinese market but carefully controlled the extent of the technology transfer. The type of Jeep built in China was an older model no longer made in the USA.

While this type of relationship continues to exist, there emerged in the 1990s a new rationale. Control and competition were replaced by collaboration. This was sought with customers, suppliers, governments and even competitors as part of the development of global strategics.

Problems and issues with joint ventures

Case 2.1 illustrates many of the issues involved in a joint venture between an established western firm and a firm from a less developed but changing economy. Such economies are often referred to as transitional, a concept we deal with in Chapter 3. In their study of international joint ventures in Eastern Europe, usually involving firms from an advanced industrial country, Rondinelli and Black (2000) found there to be both convergent and divergent interests at work. The incoming multinationals enjoyed the following advantages:

- increased profits
- low risks
- market access
- cheap labour costs
- extension of the product life cycle.

The former state-owned enterprise in Eastern Europe also enjoyed a number of advantages, including:

- increased profits
- raised productivity
- access to new technology and know-how
- new products
- access to export markets.

They also noted substantial gains for East European governments in the form of reduced subsidies, tax income and assistance in the restructuring of the economy. However, they also noted problems, many of which can be seen in Case 2.1.

The problems were:

- job cuts
- conflicting goals, especially over technology transfer
- problems over power and control
- limitations resulting from a less well-developed infrastructure.

A more generic approach to evaluating joint ventures has been developed by Medcof (1997). He uses the model of the '4 Cs' based on the concepts of capability, compatibility, commitment and control. These and other issues are dealt with below.

CASE 2.1   FROM JEEP TO MERCEDES: THE STORY OF A CHINESE JOINT VENTURE

This case examines an international joint venture (IJV) in China between a western multinational and a local Chinese partner. Part One charts the development of the joint venture, in particular the early days with a US partner (AMC and then Chrysler) and focuses on the motives, problems and issues encountered, many of which are typical of many IJVs. Part Two examines the changes that occurred when Chrysler merged with Daimler Benz and was then demerged a few years later. The original IJV was set up to produce the US-designed Jeep. Production was stopped on the Jeep in 2006 as Daimler Benz assumed total control and the IJV then focused entirely on the production of Mercedes vehicles.

Part One: 1983–2006

The Beijing Jeep Corporation was established in 1983 as a joint venture between American Motors Corporation (AMC), manufacturers of the Jeep and the Beijing Auto Works, with AMC owning 31 per cent and Beijing owning 69 per cent. The intention was that AMC would be allowed to purchase more equity with profit from the operation. Production of the Jeep began in 1984 and joined the existing production of the Russian designed four-wheel drive BJ2020, the first of its kind in China, but a vehicle far less sophisticated and less reliable than the Jeep. The focus in the early years was on the production of military and government vehicles. The original joint venture between BAIC and AMC established a third, independent company, the Beijing Jeep Corporation (BJC). The original agreement was for 20 years with the option to renew if both parties and the Chinese government were agreeable.

AMC was one of the smaller motor manufacturers in the USA and the company was bought by Chrysler, the third largest US producer, in 1987. By 1998, Beijing Auto Works had become Beijing Automotive Industry Holding Company Ltd (BAIC). In the same year Chrysler merged with Daimler Benz to form Daimler-Chrysler. Responsibility for the joint venture in the West therefore passed from AMC to Chrysler to Daimler-Chrysler within a 15-year period. During that period the Chinese government had taken steps to liberalize its economy and give more freedom for decision-making to individual managers. By 1998, the stake of Daimler-Chrysler in Beijing Jeep had risen to 42.4 per cent, the Chinese holding 57.2 per cent. In 2005, the name of Beijing Jeep was changed to Beijing-Benz Daimler-Chrysler Automotive Company Ltd, and ownership was split 50-50 between Daimler-Chrysler and the Chinese.

BAIC reported directly to the Beijing municipal government and was a typical state-owned Chinese company, whose production output was a function of targets set by a centrally planned economy. BAIC was originally established in the 1950s with backing from the former USSR.

The original benefits to AMC passed on to Chrysler were many. The financial risk involved was minimal. The initial investment was low and, in any case, the Beijing municipal government contracted to pay this back as share dividend. Moreover, the Americans would be allowed to increase their stake if the company was profitable. A further financial gain for AMC/Chrysler came through the sale of kit versions of the Jeep and parts. AMC/Chrysler sold these to the Chinese joint venture at a profit. AMC/Chrysler therefore benefited both from the sale of the Jeep made by BJC and through the sale of the parts to BJC. Since a joint venture was the only route into the Chinese market (and still is in the automotive industry), AMC/Chrysler gained entry to an emerging market with considerable potential, particularly for the sales of four-wheel-drive vehicles. AMC and Chrysler were keen to control the extent of technology transfer to the new company. The model to be produced in China was an older version of that being produced in the USA. AMC/Chrysler were therefore doing what many had done before them, notably Fiat in the USSR. They were extending the product life cycle of an older product and its parts through its manufacture in an emerging economy. BJC would therefore offer no competition in export markets and AMC/Chrysler were not 'handing over' state-of-the-art technology to the Chinese. An additional benefit to AMC/Chrysler was learning more about the Chinese market and about joint ventures generally.

There were a number of benefits for BAIC and for the Chinese economy in general. They were gaining access to western technology not just in terms of product but in terms of manufacturing processes as well. They were gaining a vehicle with a global brand and reputation. AMC/Chrysler was contracted to assist BAIC set up a local R&D centre. The knowledge gained from the West and from R&D could be disseminated to other industries. As well as technology transfer, the Chinese were also gaining knowledge of management practices and techniques. The Jeep as a global brand would have export potential, with an initial focus on other emerging economies, and the promise of hard currency earnings for the Chinese. Although initially reliant on kits and parts from the USA, the intention was to shift the emphasis to local suppliers. The joint venture was therefore important in the development of the local supply chain, involving both suppliers and distributors, to the benefit of Chinese industry generally. In general, the joint venture was part of the wider process in China of learning more about the

(Continued)

CASE 2.1   (Continued)

West and its business methods. It also offered the promise of expansion and job creation.

From the early days of the joint venture in the 1980s there were several problems.

State bureaucracy. Although BJC was set up as an autonomous company it was soon clear to AMC/Chrysler that the hand of central planning by the Chinese was evident in everything the company did. In the early days, BJC was seen by the Chinese government more as a means of controlling the flow of foreign exchange than as the potential for a manufacturing company. AMC/Chrysler managers were frustrated by the politics and bureaucracy of doing business in China.

Accounting systems. BJC operated with Soviet-style accounting systems that provided vital information to a centrally planned economy. However, these were inadequate for the management of a joint venture with accountability needed in the USA. There were no cashflow statements, budget forecasts or cost accounting information, all essential parts of a USA accounting system.

Localization. The initial plan was that 80 per cent of the Jeep would be manufactured locally by the end of 1990. Only half of that target was achieved, the main problems being delivery times and quality. For example, there was a high initial investment in press shop machinery, which stamped out the body shapes. However, this was dependent on using high-quality steel, which none of the local suppliers was able to deliver. The machinery lay idle until imported steel from Japan was used.

After-sales. Income derived from servicing vehicles and parts sales make a greater contribution to the profit margins of most major vehicle manufacturers than the sales of new vehicles. This was not the case at that time in China. Chinese companies were preoccupied with meeting production targets and after-sales customer care was not a consideration. Moreover, as a manufacturer of four-wheel drive vehicles, the majority of early sales were to the state. State employees traditionally had little interest in maintenance. If something needed to be fixed it was just as easy to order a replacement vehicle.

Human resource issues. The initial joint venture employed more than 4000 Chinese and six expatriate workers from the USA. There were problems of labour discipline. Productivity at BJC was only 65 per cent of that at the Chrysler Jeep plant in Ohio. As China had a full-employment policy, there was a reluctance to dismiss poor performers. Also, there were problems involving the expatriate workers. They were paid much more than their Chinese counterparts, which caused some resentment. Of the first 25 expatriates sent by AMC/Chrysler, only one spoke Mandarin Chinese and only three completed their full tour of duty. Many expats complained about living conditions in China and all considered it a hard posting. There were differences of cultural perception based on the concept of age. The first USA workers were fairly young and China was seen as an important part of their management development. The fact that they were young disappointed the Chinese, who equate youth with inexperience. As a result, Chrysler changed its policy and sent older managers close to retirement age. The Chinese preferred this, assuming that as they were older they had more experience and status. The policy also served to revitalize the careers of some Chrysler managers.

Sales and profits. Between 1984 and 1996 over half a million vehicles were built by BJC. During that period sales increased annually by an average 29 per cent and profit by an average 7 per cent. In 1996, BJC was ranked third among the top 500 foreign-invested companies in China, and the company received several honours both locally and nationally. However, from a record production of 80 000 Jeeps in 1995, only 30 000 were made in 1998. Between 1998 and 2002 the company suffered heavy losses.

When Daimler came on the scene in 1998 it inherited a company with an ageing plant that produced two outdated models. These were the Jeep Super Cherokee and the BJ2020, which was still essentially based around 40-year-old Soviet technology. BJC had problems competing with new entrants to the four-wheel-drive market in China, notably Volkswagen and General Motors, with the Japanese not far behind. All offered newer models than the Jeep, with state-of-the-art technology, greater comfort and added features at competitive prices. Profits at BJC had disappeared and the company was inefficient even by Chinese standards. For example, while BJC was building 5 vehicles per employee per year, the VW plant at Shanghai was building 24. The labour force at BJC, which had risen to 8000 when production was soaring, had been cut back to 4000 and by 2003 was only 3200. Daimler still considered BJC to be over-staffed. Daimler-Chrysler was therefore faced with a dilemma. The contract was available for renewal in 2003. The company could be used as a platform for the introduction of the Mercedes range but massive investment would be required, and some commentators predicted that BJC would be sold off.

Daimler-Chrysler itself was facing financial problems relating to the merger and to the sluggish performance of Chrysler cars in the USA. In 2001 the company had announced 20 per cent job losses and the closure of 6 plants. Beijing, however, was relatively unscathed, benefiting in part from the switch in the locus of control from the USA to Beijing, now officially the North-East Asia headquarters of Daimler-Chrysler.

Daimler-Chrysler chose to invest, with a large capital injection in plant, the introduction of advanced technology and establishing a new management team. The investment amounted to some US$226 million. In 2001, cooperation between Daimler-Chrysler and BAIC was extended for 30 years until 2033 and it announced that the flagship model of the range, the Grand Cherokee, was to be built in Beijing. By 2003, the company was making three types of Jeep, the Grand Cherokee, the Super Cherokee and the Jeep 250. In addition, the BJ2020 was re-branded as the City Cruiser. Daimler-Chrysler pledged to introduce a new model every year and planned to assist BJC extend its sales and service network from eleven provinces in 2001 to cover all 23 provinces in China. By 2003 the company was back to profit of about US$24 million.

By 2005, the company had built two new plants, one to make the Jeep and other sport utility vehicles (SUVs), and the second to concentrate on Mercedes and Chrysler saloon cars. It had dropped the City Cruiser but produced a version as a military vehicle. The company made the Grand and Super Cherokee but the Jeep 250 became a version of the Cherokee made entirely from local parts. The company had also branched out into the manufacture of other SUVs, producing Mitsubishi Pajero Sport and Mitsubishi Outlander. At the time, Mitsubishi was 37 per cent owned by Daimler-Chrysler (although Daimler-Chrysler was soon to sell its shares). A step forward was the production of Mercedes Benz E class cars and the Chrysler 300C, a large saloon using Mercedes technology. Plans were made to build the Mercedes C class and the Chrysler Sebring. The manufacture of Mercedes cars especially offered the company much greater profit potential than the Jeep alone. The company also licensed the manufacture of small vans to Fuzhou in China and to Taiwan. A significant development was that Daimler-Chrysler became the first company in China to offer financing for both passenger and commercial vehicles.

Part Two: 2006–2013

Jeep production was halted in 2006 just before the demerger of Chrysler and Daimler Benz. In May 2007, Daimler-Chrysler announced the sale of 80.1 per cent of Chrysler US to the private equity investment company Cerberus (the remaining 19.9 per cent was sold by Daimler in 2009). The value of Chrysler at the time of the 1998 merger was US$36 billion. The sale in 2007 was worth US$7.4 billion. This was accompanied by the withdrawal from Mitsubishi. The Jeep was still available in China but only as a US import. With an increase in price to incorporate import tariffs, by 2012 sales had fallen to 46 000.

Daimler Benz kept the plant and became the sole foreign partner with 50 per cent equity in the newly named IJV, Beijing Benz Automotive Ltd (BBAC). The company was originally registered in 2005. BBAC produced Mercedes C Class, E Class cars and GLK Class SUVs. Plans were drawn up to expand facilities to build Mercedes compact cars, establish a new engine plant in 2013 and set up a new R&D centre both for vehicle testing and for joint development of components with suppliers. At the beginning of 2013 BBAC employed over 9000 people. The 2012 performance gave Daimler some concern as sales had fallen by 11 per cent and revenues by 2.8 per cent from the previous year. This was at a time when the Chinese market in car sales had been growing at around 10 per cent per year. The company appointed a new Chief Executive to oversee its China operations.

In 2013 sales had improved and not including Hong Kong, 228 000 vehicles were sold in China. The Chinese market became the third largest for Daimler Benz behind Germany and the USA

(Continued)

CASE 2.1   (Continued)

and currently one in six of all Mercedes cars sold worldwide are sold in China. Sales forecasts for 2015 are for 300000 vehicles. Seventy-five new dealer outlets were added in 2013 making 300 in all covering 150 cities. The company sees China as crucial in establishing itself as the leading brand in the luxury car market.

Daimler Benz involvement in China is coordinated by Daimler Greater China Ltd (DGRC), established in 2001 in Beijing and responsible for all activities in China, Hong Kong, Macau and Taiwan. The activities now include the manufacture of cars, vans, trucks and buses; a finance company; R&D; and a spare parts company. DRGC is involved in a number of joint ventures (most 50–50 equity with a Chinese partner).

> Beijing Benz Automotive Ltd (Established in 2005 for Mercedes cars and SUVs)
>
> Fujian Benz Automotive Limited (Established in 2007 for Mercedes vans)
>
> Beijing Foton Daimler Automotive Co Ltd (Established in 2011 for medium and heavy duty trucks and to locate a new engine plant)
>
> Shenzen BYD New Technology Co Ltd (Established in 2011 to develop electric vehicles under the Denza brand)

Chrysler and the Jeep

Chrysler was declared bankrupt in 2009 and like the other US car giant General Motors the company was effectively owned by the US and Canadian Governments and by the Union of Auto Workers (to protect the healthcare provision of current and past employees). The company has since been acquired by FIAT, the Italian car manufacturer, as the majority shareholder with plans to buy the remaining shares in 2014. Plans are in place to re-establish Jeep production in China in Changsa, the capital of Hunan Province in a new IJV with FIAT's current Chinese partner the Guanzhou Automobile Group.

Questions

1 What were the main reasons for the joint venture between AMC/Chrysler and BAIC, formerly the Beijing Auto Works? What benefits were to be gained by both parties?

2 What were the early problems and issues encountered by this joint venture?

3 Assess the dilemma facing Daimler-Chrysler in 1998. Was the company justified in its decision to invest?

4 Assess the motives of Daimler Benz since 2001?

- Many joint ventures create **organizational complexities,** which can increase costs. Project teams and coordinating committees have to be set up. Staff have to be seconded from their regular roles and much time can be taken up in meetings and travelling. The chief executives of Renault and Volvo believed that a merger would be cheaper than a joint venture in the long term as it would cut out most of the joint committees and cut down on the number of meetings.

The success of any joint venture is dependent upon a **strategic fit** between the parties concerned. Joint ventures are likely to be more successful where the partner firms offer complementary core competencies. For many years Renault and Volvo were engaged in a joint venture built on joint technical development and shared distribution. The joint venture was a success, largely because the strengths of each company were complementary. Volvo was strong in large cars, Renault in small ones; Volvo was strong in North America, while Renault had a larger market share in South America. In many joint ventures, especially between an MNE and a local partner, the relationship between partners changes over time. As the MNE gains more local knowledge they may wish to change the relationship from a joint venture to a wholly owned subsidiary.

- **Capability** is concerned with what each of the parties brings to the joint venture and is about the expectations each has of the other. In the case of General Motors and Daewoo in South Korea, GM managers felt that the alliance was weakened by the Koreans' lack of quality capability. In the Beijing Jeep Corporation, there were numerous delays due to the inability of local suppliers to produce on time and to the required quality. The service and spare parts industry was relatively undeveloped in China. Chrysler officials accused the Chinese of poor labour discipline and low productivity, while Chrysler managers, with one exception, were unable to speak Mandarin Chinese.

- Problems of **compatibility** arise in working together and often do not emerge until the implementation phase. Such problems can arise as a result of differences in culture, management style and personality and in administrative and accounting procedures. Datta (1988) found that social and cultural issues are the ones most often overlooked by managers when establishing joint ventures. A major difficulty in establishing joint ventures between universities, involving the exchange of students, occurs around differences in teaching style, differences in the academic calendar and different requirements for assessment. With Beijing Jeep there were problems arising from differences between the US and Chinese accounting systems, and the high pay of the Americans compared with the local managers became a source of resentment for the locals. The biggest problem for Chrysler, however, lay in its frustrations arising from the highly political nature of doing business in China, such as dealing with a cumbersome bureaucracy and having to accept local suppliers recommended by local government.

- **Commitment** is the extent to which the partners are willing to continue to invest resources and effort, more especially when problems arise either in fulfilling expected objectives or between the partners themselves. Many alliances fail through a lack of staying power.

- A number of problems can arise out of issues of **control.** Where one partner is dominant, then the weaker partner may have its core competencies actually weakened. In a study of Japanese joint ventures with US companies, Lei (1989) found that almost invariably the Japanese company was the dominant partner and there was a widespread fear (sometimes well-founded but sometimes not) that Japanese firms would take over the critical skills of the US partner and give little in return. One of the reasons for failure in the Renault-Volvo case was the belief among the Swedes that French management and strategies would predominate in the new company. Control becomes even more of an issue when joint ventures involve more than two partners. The collapse in 2009 of the joint venture between the French company, Danone and the Chinese soft drinks producer, Wahaha was a classic failure of both control and commitment. Wahaha brought to the joint venture a well-known Chinese brand, but then used the brand in several of its other companies when Danone believed the brand would only be used in the joint venture. Wahaha had initially entered the joint venture with a 49 per cent share. Danone had 25.5 per cent and a partner company in Hong Kong, Baifu, owned 25.5 per cent. Where Wahaha supplied the brand, Danone and Baifu supplied the investment. However, when Danone bought out Baifu, it had a majority share to the consternation of Wahaha. There was clear mistrust and a lack of commitment on both sides (Zhang and Van Deusen, 2010).

There is also the problem of **measuring performance outcomes.** Brouthers et al. (1997) argue that this is far from simple, since it depends on the rationale behind the joint venture. For example, financial criteria alone would be inappropriate if the reason for the joint venture were either technology transfer or expanding market share. They cite the case of the alliance between the airlines KLM (Holland) and Northwest (USA). The alliance would appear to be successful on financial grounds, yet, initially, the senior managers encountered difficulties in working together. Datta (1988) argues that too many joint ventures are assessed only from the perspective of the dominant partner. This is especially apparent in the entry of established firms into emerging markets. In most cases there will be trade-offs. Otis Elevators (USA) established a joint venture in Tianjin, China, to access a large potential market. The Chinese, however, were more concerned with gaining access to elevator technologies and foreign currency. Although it is a broad generalization, several studies have commented that the primary motivation of western companies in joint ventures is cost reduction, while that of eastern companies lies in knowledge acquisition. The **evidence on performance** is very mixed. Successful alliances have been shown to outperform single businesses (Medcof, 1997), but against this there are many failed joint ventures and alliances. From the above points it can also be seen that attention to such issues as strategic fit, compatibility, capability, commitment and control will do much to ensure the success of a joint venture. It is for this reason that many writers focus on the importance of careful analysis in partner selection.

REFLECTION POINT

What are the specific advantages and disadvantages for the different parties in a joint venture in a transitional economy between a local company and an established multinational from a developed economy?

CASE 2.2   SLEEK INTERNATIONAL LTD

Sleek International is a small company with its headquarters in Leyton, east London. The company was formed in 1989, selling beauty cosmetic products to the Afro-Caribbean community in the UK, but with an emphasis on the London market. There was a gap in the cosmetics market because Afro-Caribbean women had difficulty in finding affordable products to match their variety of skin shades.

The original company was joined by another, selling hair extension products, again with a focus on Afro-Caribbean women. The two companies came together as one in 1998 and, although the product markets were related, the two arms of the business continued to be run separately. Stocks and packaging, although in the same building, were kept apart as were the sales function. However, the company benefited from a shared management information and financial system.

The 1998 company was owned by two directors, each the original owner of the cosmetics and hair products company respectively. The directors

shared the same aims for the business, which were stated as:

- good quality products at a reasonable price
- a wide product range
- a focus on the Afro-Caribbean female market.

Sleek employed around 40 people in London, which served as the headquarters for a growing international operation. The company soon expanded through offices and sales teams in France (Paris), Ghana (Accra) and South Africa (Johannesburg).

Sleek has never manufactured any of the products and has always operated as an intermediary in the distribution chain. It still obtains its products from suppliers and packages and brands them as its own. It offers a full range of cosmetic products, including lipsticks, eyeliners and creams. In terms of hair products, Sleek focuses on hair extension pieces. These are made either from human or synthetic hair. Human hair is currently the preferred product, but this may change in the future. Much of the human hair comes from China. However, with a rapidly changing Chinese economy, many people have become more fashion conscious and opt for regular hairdressing rather than growing their hair for sale. In addition, there are improvements in synthetic hair technology, making it more like the real thing. The hair extension pieces are attached to the purchaser's own hair by means of glue, weaving to braided hair or weaving to a cap. In the last case the hair is worn over the customer's own hair and can be removed like a wig.

Sleek sold its products through high-street pharmacies and hairdressers as well as some supermarkets.

The focus is on those locations where there is a large Afro-Caribbean population. For the hair business, Sleek's main supplier of both human and synthetic hair has been for many years a large Chinese manufacturer in Henan province in south-central China. People in Henan have a history of selling their own hair. The company, Henan Rebecca Hair Products, not only manufactures hair extensions and wigs but operates as a distributor itself and has sales operations in Nigeria.

The global market leader and major competitor for Sleek's product range is Hair Zone, selling its products under the brand name 'Sensationnel'. This is a US company founded by South Koreans. It dominates the US market as well as the Caribbean and has made inroads into the European and African markets as well. Traditionally, the perceived advantages of the 'Sensationnel' brand are its keen pricing strategy, availability of product on demand and top-of-the-range packaging. In general, the market, especially for hair products, is highly price-sensitive as a large proportion of the market comes from lower income families. Sleek is a registered and established brand and its share of the European market in 2004 stood at around 10 per cent. The expansion of operations to France was to reach a large Afro-Caribbean population and act as a stepping point to widen coverage of the continental European market. It was also seen as a vehicle for entry into the markets of French Africa and the French Caribbean. The Ghana operation is a means of reaching a large West African population. Much is expected of the establishment of the South Africa operation. South Africa, with its emerging economy among the post-apartheid black population, offers an excellent potential for market growth. Although there is an expanding market of people concerned with their appearance, the market is still highly price sensitive. Sleek is firmly entrenched in products for the Afro-Caribbean market and, as yet, has not developed any inroads into the large Asian market, a community that dominates as an ethnic group in the east London region.

Sleek's sales value doubled between 2000 and 2003 from £1.8 to £3.6 million. Sales for 2001 represented a 73 per cent increase on the previous year and a massive 288 per cent rise in profits. A fall in profits for 2002 resulted from a large financial investment in a computer-based management information system. This is part of the owners' determination to reinvest profit, which is seen as a major factor in the dynamic growth of the company.

In 2004, the owners recognized two priorities for the future. A large drain on the cash flow of the business was the large investment in stock, which they wished to reduce. Sleek's stock position was a function of its lack of control over the supply of products from suppliers. Yet despite its large stockholding at any time, there were still occasions when Sleek was unable to meet demand because of deficiencies in supply. The second priority was the improvement in packaging and presentation.

A change in the supply position of the hair side of the business occurred in 2004. The company formed a joint venture with Henan Rebecca Hair Products, creating a new company, Noble Sleek Ltd. At the same time, the two companies that had come together in 1998 decided to split creating separate cosmetic and hair businesses, but both continued to use the 'Sleek' brand. The cosmetics side of the business was registered as SleekMakeUP and the hair products as Noble Sleek (although it was also known as Hair by Sleek). The creation of Noble Sleek had two immediate advantages. The UK operations of Sleek had strengthened its supply chain and, through Henan's presence in Nigeria, had gained access to another large African market.

The company also went for a higher profile through involvement in the London carnival scene, notably the Notting Hill carnival and introducing the search for 'Miss Sleek', the new face to appear on their promotional material. The company was also

(Continued)

CASE 2.2   (Continued)

one of the sponsors of the 2006 Oasis Music Awards for gospel music.

However both companies had begun to diversify beyond their original market. Sleek MakeUP offers 30 shades of foundation, which it claims is more than any other high-street brand and is now aimed at Caucasian, Asian and Latin as well as Afro-Caribbean customers. Noble Sleek also developed products for the Caucasian markets.

In 2010 the Chinese partner, Henan Rebecca Hair Products took complete control of Noble Sleek and strengthened its presence in South Africa and France. The distribution chain now covers over 1000 retailers worldwide.

Questions

1   What aspects of globalization are illustrated by this case?

2   What does this case tell us about the role of the small firm in globalization?

3   Do you consider Sleek to be a multinational company? What are the opportunities and threats, strengths and weaknesses of Sleek?

SUMMARY

- Globalization is a key issue in modern business and involves the interlinking of the world's nations and their economies.

- It is a product of the tremendous growth in international trade and foreign direct investment assisted more recently by developments in information and communications technology.

- The development of trade, FDI and an interlinked global economy has not been linear. There was a marked slowdown in such developments between 1914 and 1950.

- Not everyone shares the same view of globalization. The globalists argue that the process is inevitable and has made a great contribution to the lives of most people in both the developed and the developing world. The anti-globalist lobby focuses on the disadvantages, especially the uneven distribution of advantages, favouring rich nations, the undemocratic power of big business and damage to the environment. A more sceptical view challenges the global effects of globalization, reinforcing the anti-globalist view of its uneven impact.

- Whichever perspective is taken we can see its influence economically, politically and culturally. Global markets have developed in both manufacturing and service industries and in both, operations are organized and networked globally. Nation states have formed alliances and world organizations for trade, defence and to tackle social and environmental issues. There is some evidence of cultural convergence.

- The forces behind globalization are many and varied and include developments in capitalism, the need to reduce costs and technological innovations, especially those concerned with information and communications technology.

- A feature of the modern global economy is the multinational enterprise and in its modern form, the transnational corporation. There would appear to be a shift in emphasis away from cost reduction and market exploitation towards more complex strategies combining global efficiencies with local responsiveness.

- Globalization has brought with it new forms of organization and organization structure. Many of these are linked to methods of entry into international markets. There has been a growth in both off-shoring and joint ventures each presenting advantages and disadvantages to the nation states and to the firms involved.

DISCUSSION QUESTIONS

1 In what ways does globalization have an impact on either (a) your firm or a firm with which you are familiar; or (b) your college?

2 Outline the main arguments put forward by the globalists, the anti-globalization lobby and the sceptics. Which view do you support and why?

3 Examine the main drivers of globalization. Which are the most influential?

4 Assess the contribution of developments in information and communications technology to the growth of globalization.

5 To what extent can you argue the case that large corporations have become as powerful as nation states?

6 With reference to offshore outsourcing, what are the benefits and problems for home and host nations in terms of the economy, individual firms and employees?

7 Contrast the main features of a transnational corporation with those of a multinational.

8 Why have joint ventures emerged as an organizational form in a global economy? What are the main criteria for the success of a joint venture?

9 What are the features and strategic rationale for a global production system? Identify such a system in both manufacturing and the service industries.

10 Assess the advantages and disadvantages of globalization from the perspective of (a) a consumer and (b) a small firm.

FURTHER READING

Fairly broad general accounts can be found in:

Dicken, P. (2011) *Global Shift: Mapping the changing contours of the world economy,* 6th edn, Sage: London.
Scholte, J.A. (2005), *Globalization: A critical introduction,* 2nd edn, Macmillan: Basingstoke.

More critical perspectives are available in:

Held, D., McGrew, A., Goldblatt, D. and Perraton, J. (1999) *Global Transformations: Politics, economics and culture,* Polity Press: Cambridge.
Hirst, P. and Thompson, G. (1999), *Globalization in Question,* 2nd edn, Polity Press: Cambridge.

Strategic and organizational implications can be found in:

Bartlett, C.A. and Beamish, P.W. (2011) *Transnational Management: Text, cases and readings in cross-border management,* 6th edn, Irwin: Chicago.

Dunning, J.H. (1993) *Multinational Enterprise and the Global Economy*, Addison-Wesley: Harrow.
Medcof, J.W. (1997) 'Why too many alliances end in divorce', *Long Range Planning*, 30, 5: 718–32.

Interesting perspectives can be found in:

CNN Money (2007) http//:money.cnn.com/magazines/fortune/global500/index.html
Friedman, T.L. (2006) *The World is Flat: A brief history of the world in the 21st century*, Penguin: Harmondsworth.
Wolf, M. (2004) *Why Globalization Works*, Yale University Press.

THE ENVIRONMENT AND BUSINESS: THE ECONOMY AND THE STATE

3

the firm and its environment. Each of the areas selected also interacts with the others, as the matrix in Figure 3.1 shows. For the business manager, the environment comprises a number of variables, which interact with the business either alone or jointly. The complexity does not end

LEARNING OBJECTIVES At the end of this chapter you should be able to:

- Identify those aspects of the environment that most influence and are influenced by business and assess the relative importance of those influences over time.

- Illustrate and explain how aspects of the environment interact with each other and with business.

- Explain the changing nature of the global economy and assess the key changes, including the growth of the Chinese economy.

- Identify the types of state intervention and the problems associated with them.

- Assess the roles of the WTO and the EU.

- Assess the role of the business community as a pressure group.

- Critically assess the significance of, and issues related to, economic and political integration in a modern global economy.

INTRODUCTION

Chapter 1 introduced the model that forms the basis of our analysis of business. In this chapter and the next we focus on a major element of that model, namely the environment. We define the environment as comprising all factors that exist outside the business enterprise but that interact with it. As pointed out in Chapter 1, all firms are, to a greater or lesser extent, constrained by the environment within which they operate but the activities of businesses themselves also change that same environment. This two-way process is an important theme throughout the book. In Chapter 2 the concept of globalization was examined and a number of perspectives identified. Whichever perspective is taken, it is clear that changes, especially those in politics, markets, and information and communications technology (ICT), have transformed business, and that all businesses, both large and small, operate in a global environment. The concept of globalization and its processes set the scene for our discussion of the environment.

Apart from our discussion of globalization we have devoted three chapters to the business environment. Even so, the field is broad and the material is necessarily highly selective. Five areas of the environment have been identified:

- the economy
- the role of the state
- technology
- labour
- culture and institutions.

This chapter examines issues relating to the economy and the state. In Chapter 4 we look at the interaction of business, technology and labour, and in Chapter 5 we explore cultural and institutional issues. In all these chapters we identify issues that illustrate the interaction between the firm and its environment. Each of the areas selected also interacts with the others, as the matrix in Figure 3.1 shows. For the business manager, the environment comprises a number of variables, which interact with the business either alone or jointly. The complexity does not end there. These interactions may occur at a number of levels, as shown in Figure 3.2.

- At the immediate level a firm interacts with a local environment, in which plans to expand its buildings will need approval from the local council, and where its marketing and human resource strategies will be influenced by firms operating in the same local market. A shift in the economy of a local region, such as a reduction in the level of the coal-mining industry as has happened in the UK and Poland, will have implications far beyond that industry. It will affect those firms supplying the industry as well as local retail businesses.

- A second type of interaction occurs in a national environment, influenced by such matters as law, bank interest rates, the rate of inflation, and national employment and education policies. In Chapter 5 we examine two influences, those of national culture and institutional frameworks. We will demonstrate that businesses are influenced by the prevailing culture and may need to adapt practices accordingly. However, there are also examples of multinationals operating the same practices and style irrespective of location. Institutional arrangements such as the education system and the regulation of the stock market also have a significant influence on business.

- Third, we have the international environment in which the firm may be affected by international money exchange rates, competition from cheap labour economies, and the regulations of supranational bodies such as the WTO and the EU. In recent years the international environment has become increasingly significant for businesses through the process of globalization as discussed in Chapter 2. Businesses in all sectors have to adapt to increased global competition.

FIGURE 3.1	The interaction of environmental factors: some illustrations

				Economy	
				The extent and direction of state intervention in the economy The power of the multinationals in influencing policy	State
			State	State support of innovation and technical change and the specific impact on certain industries e.g. defence	The influence of innovation on economic growth	Technology
		Technology	The effect of technical change on skills and trade union policy towards such changes	Government policies to direct the supply of labour Legislation to regulate trade union activities	The influence of the economy on the type and levels of employment	Labour
	Labour	Cultural influences on human resource strategies	The impact of changes in technology on society Cultural attitudes towards technology	Cultural explanations for the differences between nations regarding state intervention	The nature of the economy shaping family life e.g. agricultural vs industrial societies The influence of cultural values on the directions of economic development and specialization	Culture

As a general rule, the ability of managers to influence their environment diminishes as they move further away from the local environment. As with all such rules, there are exceptions since the ability to influence the environment tends to increase with the size of the firm and large global companies can have much political influence and so affect local economies and labour markets.

We will deal with each of our environmental variables in turn. Before that we will examine some generic models that are commonly used to assess environmental influences.

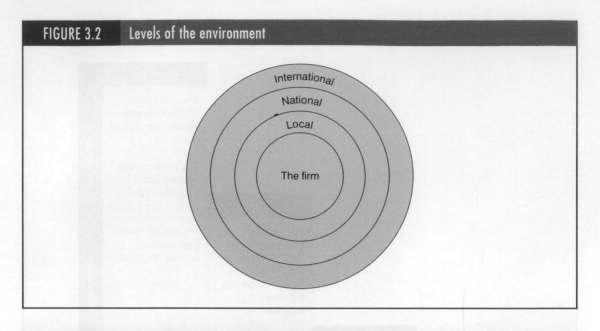

FIGURE 3.2   Levels of the environment

REFLECTION POINT

Identify a specific firm and give examples of its interaction with the local, national and international environments.

MODELS USED IN ASSESSING THE ENVIRONMENT

The Business in Context model and Figures 3.1 and 3.2 are models we have constructed to make sense of the environment in which businesses operate. They do what other models do; they simplify a very complex set of relationships. A commonly used model is that of PEST. References to this can be found in most business texts but its origins are unclear. It is used as a framework analysis in some texts and journals and tends to be popular with students.

PEST analysis comprises a review of four types of environmental influence. These are identified as follows.

Political environment This covers the nature of the political system and how that influences business. For example, the governance of business in China differs from that in the USA and that of a transitional economy and new EU member like Romania differs from that of a more established member such as Germany. Another issue here would be the laws and regulations imposed not just by national governments but by supranational bodies such as the EU and the WTO. The political environment would also encompass the influence of stakeholder groups, such as local political groups, shareholders and trade unions.

Economic environment This includes issues of economic structure, such as the relative proportion of the economy devoted to each of agriculture, mining, manufacturing and services. It also examines issues relating to economic health, including the size of the economy and indicators such as growth rates, interest rates and levels of unemployment. The role of financial institutions such as banks would also come under this heading.

Socio-cultural environment We shall see in Chapter 5 that the cultural values of a particular society have an influence on business strategy and practices. Also considered under this heading are influences resulting from the changing composition of the population such as an increase in the proportion of older people or changing attitudes in employment to gender issues. The analysis may consider also the skills composition of the labour force and linked to this the relationship between skills and the educational system.

Technological environment The issue here is the influence of new or changing technology on strategies, work practices and on jobs. A major change in this respect has been the impact of information and communications technology.

Variations of the above are used by some authors. One such is **PESTEL** or **PESTLE**. This approach extends the PEST model by considering legal and ethical issues.

Legal environment Legal regulations affect businesses in a number of ways, through stock market regulation of mergers and takeovers, through corporate law covering such issues as taxation, through contract law dealing with the relationship with customers and suppliers and through employment law dealing with how employees are treated.

Ethical environment This examines the implications of ethical and environmental issues such as rates of pay, the employment of child labour, the disposal of waste, the use of energy and how employees, suppliers and customers are treated generally. Another variation is referred to as LoNGPEST. This takes the PEST framework as its starting point and examines PEST factors in each of three contexts: local (Lo), national (N) and global (G). There is some similarity here with the model presented in Figure 3.2.

Critique of PEST

- PEST is widely used and offers a framework to assess a large number of influences.

- However, it does tend to place those influences in compartments. Many influences operate together such as the political and economic environments and cannot be understood fully on their own.

- The PESTEL approach offers even more overlap. We might argue that the legal environment can be considered as part of the political environment and the ethical environment deals with issues contained within all categories of the PEST model.

- The model is fairly deterministic in that it focuses upon factors operating on the firm. There is little or no acknowledgement that organizations, their managers and owners can influence the environment in which they operate.

- The above three elements are covered by the Business in Context model, which, while treating elements separately, emphasizes the interactive nature of all aspects of the model at all levels and further acknowledges the influence on the environment by organizations and their stakeholders.

- The model is static in that it focuses on present factors only. Consideration of those influences in the future is probably a more useful form of analysis.

- There are a number of other models for an analysis of the environment such as SWOT (or TOWS as it is sometimes called), which examines the external opportunities and threats facing an organization and assesses its ability to respond in terms of strengths and weaknesses. Michael Porter (1980, 1990) also offers models such as the 'five forces' and the 'diamond'. These models will be dealt with in Chapter 8, when we discuss strategy.

REFLECTION POINT

How useful is PEST (and its variations) to managers in offering an understanding of the business environment to enable them to develop effective strategies?

THE ECONOMY AND BUSINESS

With many aspects of our environment we are faced with the immediate problem of deciding where the environment ends and business begins and vice versa. In looking at the relationship between business and the economy this becomes particularly acute, since much of what we label as the economy is the product of business activity. By the same token, business enterprises have to react to economic developments. Figure 3.3 is an attempt to illustrate this relationship in the form of a simple model.

The economy interacts with businesses at all three levels depicted in Figure 3.2. For example, at the local level, immediate competitive issues related to firms operating in the same product market are the most significant. If Selfridges, the department store in London's Oxford Street reduces the price of popular brands of laptop and tablet by up to 15 per cent, then the managers of shops in the same area selling similar goods must determine their most appropriate strategic response. This may involve adopting the same price strategy or it may involve a more selective strategy offering larger discounts for specific brands. Competition can be fierce and many firms prefer to cooperate rather than compete on issues such as price and wage rates. In this way some businesses form themselves into cartels, which may be an effective way of controlling the immediate competitive environment and, perhaps, the wider environment too, as in influencing government policy. There are several examples of food shops getting together to buy in bulk

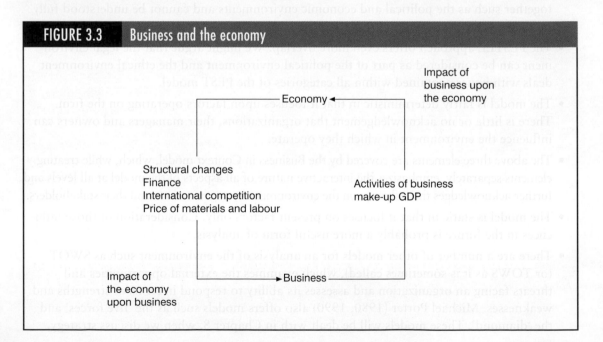

FIGURE 3.3   Business and the economy

Economy

Impact of business upon the economy

Structural changes
Finance
International competition
Price of materials and labour

Activities of business make-up GDP

Impact of the economy upon business

Business

from suppliers in an attempt to keep prices down and combat the threat posed by large super-markets. The supermarkets themselves, while not behaving as a cartel, employ staff to keep a watch on the prices displayed by their competitors and respond accordingly. We deal with the competitive environment in more detail in Chapter 8.

In this section we will examine the model by looking at the relationship between business and the economy. Starting with the fact that the USA is the world's largest economy, we will examine shifts in economic and political power and discuss the significance of fast-growing economies, notably China. We will also examine the threats to the continued dominance of the USA. We will then look at how the political economy of the world has changed through the processes of liberalization and privatization and by the growing influence of the economic system and practices associated with the USA and UK, known as the Anglo-Saxon system. However, before we do this, we need to understand how we measure and compare national economies.

How we measure and compare national economies

Economies are measured in a number of ways and we use several of these measures in the proceeding sections and throughout this book. It is important to understand how each of the measures is derived. Here, we define GDP, GNP, GNI and PPP. The measurements are complex in that they are derived from a large number of factors and there are subtle variations between them, which can be confusing. It is usual to express all measures in US dollars.

Gross domestic product (GDP) is the total value of all goods and services produced in a country in a given year. It includes the value of exports minus the value of imports. GDP is a popular measure and is often used as the basis of comparison for economies of different countries. GDP is often expressed as GDP per capita, which divides the total GDP by the population of the country. Per capita data is often used for all the measures listed below.

Gross national product (GNP) is the total value of goods and services produced in a given country in a given year plus income earned by residents from their overseas activities minus the income earned by non-residents in that country. The GNP of France will therefore include income derived from French firms operating in other countries but will not include the income gained by, for example, Japanese or US firms in France.

Gross national income (GNI) is GDP plus income received from other countries (usually in the form of interest payments or dividends) less income paid to other countries. GNI will therefore include income from a UK firm operating in other countries but would deduct income sent home by, for example, a Korean firm operating in the UK.

Purchasing power parity (PPP) is a measure of the purchasing power in different countries and is a good measure of the relative cost of living in those different countries. Indeed it is used by the World Bank as one of its indicators of poverty. PPP compares the purchasing power of the currency of one country for a basket of goods with the purchasing power of another currency in another country for the same basket of goods.

REFLECTION POINT

What uses can be made of the above ways of measuring the economy?

A shift in global economic power?

The global economy has been dominated by the USA, whose economic output in 2008 was more than three times that of its nearest rival, Japan. The 20th century has been referred to as the American century. Nonetheless, writers are keen to champion the latest economic growth phenomenon with the assumption that the world order is being or is about to be challenged. Cases have been made at various times for the growth of the Japanese economy, the rise of the Asian tiger economies, the challenges offered by the so-called BRIC economies of Brazil, Russia and especially India and China. Most recently growth predictions have been made for the emerging MINT economies of Mexico, Indonesia, Nigeria and Turkey. In this section we look at the rise of Japan and the more recent growth of the BRIC economies. We focus on the factors behind the rapid economic growth in China and end with a re-examination of the USA in the global economy.

The growing influence of Japan

Japan emerged in the post-war period as the world's second-largest economy behind the USA, although it has since been overtaken by China. There is a widely-held view that this is some kind of miracle in which a modern Japanese economy arose from the ashes of a devastated country at the end of the second world war, but the foundations of a strong economy were laid much earlier. Nevertheless, postwar growth has been significant and in Japan's case, particular advances were made from the 1950s as is shown in Table 3.1.

This growth was built upon by a rapid increase in overseas investments as shown by Table 3.2.

TABLE 3.1	The Japanese economy 1950–87				
	1987 GDP $US bn	1987 GDP per capita $US	1950–87 compound annual GDP growth %	1950–87 compound annual industrial production growth %	1950–87 average unemployment
Japan	1371	11225	7.2	9.7	1.7
USA	3679	13541	3.2	3.8	5.7
UK	629	11049	2.5	2.2	4.7
Germany	899	14691	4.6	4.6	3.5
S. Korea	63	1528	7.9	14.1	5.0
Singapore	15	5885	8.3	9.7	4.1

TABLE 3.2	Growth of Japanese overseas direct investments 1962–90 in $US billion
1962	<1
1970	1.0
1975	3.5
1980	4.9
1985	11.0
1989	66.0
1990	57.0

In addition, the focus on certain types of manufacture, exports and FDI meant that by the 1990s Japan had emerged as the world leader in product markets such as home audio, robotics, fax machines, cameras and video games (Porter et al., 2000). The net result was to lift Japan from the world's fifth largest economy in 1960 to the second largest by 1980 (Dicken, 2011).

The explanation for the growth of the Japanese economy in the 1950s and 1960s has been attributed to a number of factors:

- Japanese manufacturing firms had cost advantages that were derived initially from a labour force that worked long hours for low wages. This enabled Japanese manufacturers to make inroads into the markets of its rivals.

- The Japanese control of imports enabled the same firms to dominate the home market.

- Firms became cash-rich, which enabled them to invest in new methods and new technologies to reduce the build time of their products. As wages rose and hours of work reduced, competitive advantage was maintained by further investments in process technology and product development.

Other explanations that have been put forward include a supportive state, a supportive banking system, human resource management policies and practices, the core cultural values of the Japanese and the close relationship between suppliers and manufacturers. We will return to some of these issues in Chapter 5, when we discuss culture and in Chapter 11, when we discuss operations management.

The success of Japan has had significant influence on western management practices and led to a substantial increase in Japanese FDI in Europe and the USA as indicated by Table 3.2. However, while Japan is currently the third most powerful economy in the world (it was the second largest until superseded by China in 2010), it endured economic problems during the decade from 1992, when the average growth was only 1 per cent and both wages and prices fell (Stewart, 2004). Massive trade surpluses during the boom years had forced up the value of the yen. This in turn led to the easy credit of the late 1980s, which created in Japan a 'bubble economy', typified by land and property speculation and wasteful investment by manufacturers. In terms of the labour market, Japan had moved from a low- to a high-wage economy. In manufacturing industry, efficiency gains had kept pace with wage rises, but to some, many of the leading firms had reached the limits of cost reduction. Moreover, Japanese firms were faced with increasing competition both from lower wage economies in the region and from firms in advanced economies, whose efficiencies had improved, largely through the adoption of Japanese techniques such as just-in-time. As a result:

- There was a crisis of confidence in the financial sector and the state was blamed for a lack of regulation.

- Profits fell in most companies accompanied by redundancies and closures.

- There was a rise in unemployment.

- Domestic spending fell dramatically. This stimulated price-cutting by the department stores and the influx of cheaper imports, many from China.

- There was increased competition globally, particularly with the re-emergence of a strong US economy. Low-wage economies also posed a threat to high-wage Japan. There is a particular concern about the growth of the Chinese economy.

TABLE 3.3	The original predicted growth of the BRIC economies against the G6				
	Predicted GDP in $US billions				
	2010	2020	2030	2040	2050
Brazil	668	1333	2189	3740	6074
Russia	847	1741	2980	4467	5870
India	929	2104	4935	12367	27803
China	2998	7070	14312	26439	44453
France	1622	1930	2267	2668	3148
Germany	2212	2524	2697	3147	3603
Italy	1337	1563	1671	1788	2061
Japan	4601	5221	5810	6039	6673
UK	1876	2285	2649	3201	3782
USA	13271	16451	20833	27229	35165

The BRIC report

In an influential report in 2003, researchers at Goldman Sachs identified four countries, Brazil, Russia, India and China, where they predicted that the combined economic growth would outstrip the combined value of the G6 (France, Germany, Italy, Japan, UK and USA). Moreover, they claimed that the growth rate of the BRICs would be even greater than forecast by investors and others (Wilson and Purushothaman, 2003). Some of their predictions are presented in Table 3.3.

The researchers predicted that China would overtake Japan by 2015 and the USA by 2039. India was predicted to overtake all the G6, bar Japan and USA, by 2025 and Japan by 2035. Indeed, India was shown to have the fastest growth rate of all, largely because the decline in numbers of working age population would affect India much later than either China or Russia. China and India were predicted to be the dominant economies for manufactured goods and services, while Russia and Brazil would dominate in terms of energy and raw materials.

However dramatic the predicted growth rates appear, the Goldman Sachs report argued that people in the emerging nations will still be poorer on average than those in the G6, with the exception of Russia. For example, Table 3.4 lists the GDP per capita for the same group of countries for 2050. This shows that the current largest economies will not still be the richest by 2050.

Several economic commentators believe that Goldman Sachs had underestimated the growth rates for China. The researchers themselves recognize that the predictions are dependent on a large number of variables, not least the policy decisions of the BRIC governments themselves on matters such as inflation, trade and education.

The BRIC predictions in perspective

We are now in a position to evaluate the original Goldman Sachs prediction against actual GDP data. In Table 3.5 we compare the Goldman Sachs prediction for 2010 against the actual GDP for the four BRIC nations and the G6.

TABLE 3.4	The predicted GDP per capita of the BRIC economies against the G6 in 2050

Predicted GDP per capita in $US

	2050
Brazil	26 592
Russia	49 646
India	17 366
China	31 357
France	51 594
Germany	48 952
Italy	40 901
Japan	68 805
UK	59 122
USA	83 710

TABLE 3.5	Goldman Sachs prediction versus actual GDP for BRIC and G6 economies for 2010

Predicted GDP in $US billions

	GS prediction	Actual	Actual
	2010	2010	2011
Brazil	668	2 143	2 477
Russia	847	1 488	1 858
India	929	1 684	1 848
China	2 998	5 931	7 318
France	1 622	2 549	2 773
Germany	2 212	3 259	3 571
Italy	1 337	2 044	2 195
Japan	4 601	5 488	5 867
UK	1 876	2 252	2 432
USA	13 271	14 447	15 094

Table 3.5 shows that Goldman Sachs underestimated the economic growth not only of the G6 but also of the BRIC economies. However, the level of underestimation was far greater for the BRIC countries. For example, the actual GDP for Brazil in 2010 was 220 per cent more than predicted by Goldman Sachs in 2003. For China the 2010 GDP was 98 per cent higher than the predicted figure. The table also shows that the growth of the BRIC economies continued at a similar rate into 2011. By contrast, among the G6, the actual GDP rates, although higher, were much nearer the original prediction. The actual figures for the UK and USA were only 17 per cent and 8 per cent higher than those predicted and even the highest variance, in the case of France, was 36 per cent.

TABLE 3.6	Predicted economic rankings in 2050 according to economic forecasts			
Rank	Today	PwC	Citigroup	Goldman Sachs
		(2011)	(2011)	(2009)
1	US	China	India	China
2	China	India	China	US
3	Japan	US	US	India
4	Germany	Brazil	Indonesia	Brazil
5	France	Japan	Brazil	Russia
6	UK	Russia	Nigeria	UK
7	Brazil	Mexico	Russia	Japan
8	Italy	Indonesia	Mexico	France
9	India	Germany	Japan	Germany
10	Canada	UK	Egypt	Italy

Since the initial Goldman Sachs predictions there have been three follow-up reports. Goldman Sachs followed up with their own (O'Neill and Stupnytska, 2009) and this was joined in 2011 by reports from PricewaterhouseCoopers (PwC, 2011) and Citigroup (Buiter and Rahbari, 2011). The new Goldman Sachs report emphasized that the BRIC economies had withstood the banking crisis of 2008 in much better shape than the G6 economies and predicted an even faster acceleration for the Chinese economy than they originally predicted with a new estimate of parity with the USA by 2027. The PwC report offers broad support to the Goldman Sachs predictions and emphasizes the importance of the growing number of middle classes in the emerging economies and the increasing power of multinationals from the emerging economies. The Citigroup report highlights predicted growth in an even wider range of emerging markets. They see the growth of China and India continuing but feel there will be more opportunity for rapid growth for nine other countries including Indonesia, Nigeria, Egypt, Mongolia and Iraq. All three reports predict that only the USA, UK and Japan will remain in the top 7 of the top 10 ranked economies by 2050. This is shown in Table 3.6

Is BRICS more than a Goldman Sachs construct?

Although the BRIC countries were identified by the Goldman Sachs report in 2003, official links at government level between the four countries did not take place until 2006. In 2010 the group was expanded to include South Africa, a country that was not remotely comparable in physical or economic size or rate of economic growth with the existing four members. Its inclusion was however seen as important politically. Post-apartheid South Africa was gaining significant influence within the African continent, thus offering the existing BRIC economies trade and FDI expansion opportunities. As a consequence the BRICs (small 's') are now referred to as BRICS (large 'S') The five BRICS countries are also now members of the G20, a grouping that includes Indonesia, Mexico, Argentina, Saudi Arabia and the European Union.

The BRICS would appear to have much in common politically and economically. Since 2006 there has been increased trade between the original members. There is significant energy trade between China and Russia and China is Brazil's main market. There is a clear wish to have a greater voice in world affairs based perhaps on a shared dissatisfaction with the old global order. The BRICS share an interest in the Middle East, in Africa and in developing countries in general.

However there is little sign at present that the BRICS countries are developing as a collective political force. There are significant variations politically, economically and socially and there appears to be a lack of collective vision on such issues as climate change and the current conflict (2014) in Syria. Of the BRICS only China clearly seems to have the potential to emerge as a major global political power.

REFLECTION POINT

Is BRICS more than an invention of Goldman Sachs?

More recently attention has turned away from the BRICS and a new acronym has emerged: MINT. The acronym is attributed to Jim O'Neill who was a member of the original Goldman Sachs team that coined the term BRICs. MINT refers to Mexico, Indonesia, Nigeria and Turkey. These are predicted as the next engines of economic growth on the basis that they are large geographically and are located near to established and/or expanding markets. Each of these countries has a growing population with large numbers of young workers. This contrasts sharply with many other countries, including China, whose economies are predicted to slow as the proportion of older people increases (Elliot, 2014). The growth of the MINT economies is reflected in the Citigroup predictions presented in Table 3.6.

Whether predictions for the MINT economies turn out to be accurate Elliot (2014) points out that such speculation is indicative of a shift in the balance of power in global economy in the last 20 years, which is the central theme of this section of the chapter.

China: the future world order?

China has been the world's fastest growing economy since 1980. In 1985, its annual GDP was US$305 billion. That was more than doubled by 1995 and then trebled by 2005 (http://devdata. worldbank.org). In 2009 China contributed 18 per cent of the world's growth compared to the USA at 14 per cent. China is the world's largest exporter of manufactured goods and the second largest importer (Straw and Glennie, 2012). The average annual growth rate of just under 10 per cent in 1980–2000 has led many commentators to predict a leading economic role for China in the new global economy. This is clearly supported by the BRIC data presented in the previous section. In this section we will examine the nature and extent of economic change in China, explore some key factors behind that change and examine a number of significant issues that have arisen as a result.

Economic change and economic growth

In the late 1970s China began a process of economic liberalization to move from a centrally planned state controlled economy under a communist political regime to a free market economy still under a communist regime. Although the process of liberalization was extensive, China remains a mixed economy reflected by the different types of business organization. These can be classified as follows.

State owned enterprises (SOEs) Here the entire assets are owned by the state which also appoints the managers. Variations of state ownership exist as collective enterprises (COEs) under the control of local authorities and township/village enterprises (TVEs).

TABLE 3.7	Classification and economic contribution of firms in China by ownership 2007	
Type of firm	**% of total**	**Approximate % contribution to GDP**
SOE	3.5	35
Collective enterprises	5.78	N/A
Private enterprises	70.68	50
Foreign enterprises	20.05	15

Private companies These are shareholder owned, limited liability companies and comprise larger companies at a more mature stage of their development and private individual enterprises (PIEs), which are usually small businesses and start-ups. The PIEs could be individually funded, funded by cooperatives or funded by shareholders.

Foreign owned enterprises (FIEs) This classification includes all businesses where 25 per cent of assets are owned by a foreign investor. The Chinese government differentiates Hong Kong, Macau and Taiwan FIEs from the investment coming from other countries.

Data on the actual number of firms in each category is difficult to obtain but Table 3.7 shows how these different types of firm are distributed across the Chinese economy.

A number of points need to be made here. First, the data reveals the extent of liberalization and privatization that has taken place in China. Most firms are now privately owned and contribute 50 per cent towards Chinese GDP. Second, the data shows that although the SOE sector is relatively small (3.5 per cent), its contribution to the Chinese economy is significant at 35 per cent. The size and assets of individual SOEs is much larger than those of firms in the private sector. This is due to the presence of strategically significant companies such as those in the power industry or in banking that are still under state control. By the end of 2008 SOEs formed 3.1 per cent of the total number and their contribution had fallen from 37 per cent in 1999 to 30 per cent in 2008 (Gao, 2010). Third, the large number of private enterprises include many small business start-ups that are a direct result of liberalization policies. Fourth, it needs to be remembered that FIEs need only comprise 25 per cent foreign ownership and many are joint ventures with a Chinese partner. This partner may be either state owned or, increasingly, privately owned. Hence the picture may be more complex than indicated by this table.

The significance of economic growth in China has been the speed at which it took place and, in comparative terms, the consistency of its growth over a large number of years to become the world's second largest economy behind the USA. Tables 3.8 and 3.9 show the extent of that growth.

Table 3.9 shows clearly the consistent level of growth of the Chinese economy compared to that of other nations. It reveals also how China has coped better than most with the global economic crisis of 2008–9. There are significant differences here between China and Hong Kong, which also features in the table. Hong Kong is part of China but is treated differently as a special economic region. Part of that different treatment is the presence of many overseas firms in Hong Kong, many of them in banking and other financial services. The isolation of China from the global economic crisis is undoubtedly a function of the significant involvement of the Chinese government in the running of the economy.

By 2005 China had become the world's largest producer of computers, steel, TV sets, fish and meat (Chen and Yao, 2006) and by 2009 cars could be added to that list (see Table 3.15).

TABLE 3.8	The growth of GDP in China in US$ billion 1980–2012
1980	189.4
1985	306.7
1990	356.9
1995	728.0
2000	1 198.5
2005	2 256.9
2010	5 949.8
2012	8 358.3

TABLE 3.9	Percentage annual GDP growth 2008–2012 in selected countries				
	2008	**2009**	**2010**	**2011**	**2012**
China	9.6	9.2	10.4	9.3	7.8
USA	(–0.4)	(–3.1)	2.4	1.8	2.2
UK	(–1.0)	(–4.0	1.8	1.0	0.3
Germany	1.1	(–5.1)	4.2	3.0	0.7
Japan	(–1.0)	(–5.5)	4.7	(–0.6)	1.9
Brazil	5.2	(–0.3)	7.5	2.7	0.9
India	3.9	8.5	10	6.3	3.2
Russian Federation	5.2	(–7.8)	4.5	4.3	3.4
Hong Kong	2.1	(–2.5)	6.8	4.9	1.5

Some sectors are still heavily protected by the state, especially financial services and agriculture and, in the case of cars, foreign investment is not allowed to exceed 50 per cent of the total ownership. In this section we will look at further measures of growth, the reasons behind the growth and the issues the economic growth has raised.

Tables 3.8 and 3.9 indicate the speed and volume of China's economic growth. We have seen earlier in this chapter that such data led Goldman Sachs researchers to predict that China would overtake the USA by 2040. In 2011 the IMF forecast, based on purchasing power parity (PPP), that China would overtake the USA by 2016 (Rasiah, Zhang and Kong, 2013), although the authors acknowledge the difficulties of basing forecasts on PPP, as we have done earlier in this chapter.

Rasiah, Zhang and Kong identify general indicators of growth including: GDP growth; productivity increases, especially those between 2000–2009; increases in savings and investment; stability of the exchange rate; a strong balance of payments and the holding of international reserves; the shift to higher value-added work, especially in technology industries.

More specific measures of growth can be found in terms of exports and of Chinese acquisitions of foreign companies. In terms of exports Table 3.10 shows China's rising share of global exports in selected industries.

TABLE 3.10	China's percentage share of global exports 1980–2009	
	1980	*2009*
Clothing	4.0	34
Textiles	4.6	28
Office and telecoms	0.1	26

TABLE 3.11	Structural change in the Chinese economy 1963–2008	
	1963	*2008*
Agriculture	40	10
Industry	33	46
Services	27	44

Three major acquisitions are a further indication of China's status as a major economic power. In 2005 Lenovo acquired IBM's personal computer business for US$1.25 billion as well as taking over a $0.5 billion debt. In doing so they acquired the Think Pad brand as well as manufacturing technology and IBM's global sales network. Although the IBM brand was initially important the brand name switched to Lenovo after 3 years. This acquisition demonstrates the importance of acquiring high technology businesses. In 2014 Lenovo followed this up by buying Motorola from Google for US$2.9 billion to extend its growth in the smartphone sector and to access Motorola's position in the US market. However, the largest Chinese acquisition to date has been in the food industry. In 2013 Shuanghui International acquired Smithfield Foods (USA) for $4.7 billion. Smithfield was the world's largest producer and China is the world's largest consumer of pork products offering a sound strategic rationale for the acquisition.

The acquisitions are part of a 'Going Global' government initiative which began in 2000. However, a majority of acquisitions, like IBM, have involved foreign companies in some financial difficulty. Furthermore, inward foreign investment in China still exceeds outward investment by some margin.

The economic growth has changed the nature of the Chinese economy as shown by Table 3.11.

While Table 3.11 shows a dramatic shift away from agriculture, this sector was still, in 2008, the major source of employment in China with 300 million employed, compared to 260 million in industry and 210 million in services (Rasiah, Zhang and Kong, 2013).

The reasons for growth

There are a number of reasons for growth, most of which are interrelated. The main ones are the factors involved in globalization such as trade, FDI and the activities of multinational firms; and the policies of the Chinese government to encourage economic growth, support privatization and investment in human capital.

Globalization Many of the main reasons for the rapid growth of the Chinese economy are inter-linked under the heading of globalization. In 1973 China was ranked 23rd in terms of world trade. By 2004 it was in 3rd place behind the USA and Germany. Trade was in turn stimulated by FDI as foreign owned enterprises contributed 50 per cent of Chinese exports. FDI was in turn stimulated by the need of MNCs to access cheap Chinese labour to manufacture their products and who saw great potential in China's domestic market. The growth in FDI took off after 1992 and by 2004 China had not only become the largest recipient of foreign investment of all developing economies but was second only to the USA globally (Chen and Yao, 2006).

WTO membership While China's growth as a trading nation was boosted by it operating as a low cost manufacturer of goods that were then exported, its acceptance as a WTO member in 2001 gave a further boost. Before entry the contribution of trade to Chinese GDP was 43 per cent, but by 2007 it had reached 68 per cent (Panitch and Gindin, 2013). Case 3.2 will explore China's membership of the WTO in more detail.

Privatization A key element in the liberalization of the Chinese economy has been the creation of a private sector. This began with joint ventures between foreign MNCs and Chinese SOEs as with the creation of the Beijing Jeep (Case 2.1). However, since then the number of private firms, involving local as well as international investment has grown significantly, which in turn has led to the growth in both the size and activity of the stock market in China. In Table 3.7 we can see the extent of the private sector and its contribution to the Chinese economy. Privatization has followed a different route in China to that found in other countries. Whereas in Russia privatization was largely a central government initiative, in China it is the local governments that have been more involved as it is these who controlled the majority of small- to medium-sized SOEs (Gao, 2010). There has been some research into the process of privatization in China. Not surprisingly smaller, younger SOEs are more attractive to investors than larger, older SOEs which also tend to be less productive (Driffield and Du, 2007). The same study points to evidence of notable productivity growth accompanying privatization. The continued growth of the Chinese economy has been accompanied by what some commentators have called 'stock market fever', where large numbers of Chinese have invested savings in the stock market. This is a prime example of the liberalization of the Chinese economy.

Chinese government strategies Clearly central government policy has played a central role in the liberalization of the Chinese economy. Early reforms in the late 1970s and early 1980s focused on agriculture and the rural areas. Rural households were able to own land and collectively-owned town and village enterprises were set up (TVEs). SOEs were encouraged to be more market oriented and form joint ventures with foreign multinationals, and special economic zones were created to focus on export manufacture and encourage inward FDI. In this respect the early focus was on low value-added assembly in electronics manufacturing and in the clothing industry. As a result, Chinese firms became an important link in the global value chains of foreign multinationals. Following this the Chinese government stressed the importance of technological catch-up and the need to move into higher value-added activities. Knowledge-based firms were encouraged to cluster in the Shanghai and Beijing regions to stimulate further technological growth. We have already seen the encouragement given to Chinese companies in the purchase of key foreign companies as with the Lenovo acquisition of IBM.

Human capital development Human capital development goes hand in hand with a range of other government policies. By 2009 there was universal access to primary education, 78 per cent access to secondary and 25 per cent access to tertiary education (Rasiah, Zhang and Kong, 2013). Between 1987 and 2007 there were 50 000 Chinese enrolled on US university PhD programmes in science and engineering (Panitch and Gindin, 2013). There was general support for Chinese to benefit from overseas university education as well as significant investment at home. Several Chinese universities are now considered some of the best in the world and Peking University and Tsinghua University feature in the world's top 50 universities (Times Higher Education, 2013). Those Chinese educated overseas return to work in local firms or in FIEs in China. In addition there has been significant investment research and development both at the level of individual firms and in terms of the numbers employed.

Issues and potential problems

Despite the rapid growth of the Chinese economy a number of issues have been raised by various commentators.

Dominance of foreign firms Panitch and Gindin (2013) believe that 'China is still catching up technologically with Korea and Taiwan let alone the United States' (Panitch and Gindin 2013, p. 152). They argue that too much of the high value-added activities are dominated by foreign firms, which were responsible for a high proportion of exports in industrial machinery, computers and computer equipment (before the Lenovo acquisition of IBM) and electronics and telecommunications equipment. Nonetheless, Chinese law is still protective of some sectors, notably mining, steel, banking, transport, telecommunications systems, the Internet, and, as we have noted already, limits the amount of foreign investment in the automobile industry to 50 per cent of any company. Some, like the European Chamber of Commerce believe this to be a violation of WTO membership in that the Chinese government is refusing to grant licences to foreign companies, especially in areas where the market is expanding but the share of foreign investment is not (Anderlini, 2010). However there is a growing concern that some foreign investors are getting around restrictions through the 'creation of variable interest entities'. These are essentially a means of shifting the returns of a Chinese-owned company in China to a foreign-owned company offshore. Such arrangements have been the subject of investigation by the Chinese government and have resulted in disputes between Chinese and foreign parties as was the case between Alibaba (a Chinese Internet company) and Yahoo (The Economist, 2011).

Need to increase domestic consumption Some believe that while there is an over-dependence on foreign firms there is too great a dependence on foreign export markets as well, especially those of the USA. Domestic consumption in China has fallen as a proportion of GDP to 35 per cent, one of the lowest percentages in Asia (Bowles, 2012). Domestic consumption was identified as a priority of the 12th Five Year Plan. Policy measures included continued urbanization, increased employment, tax reforms to offer improved distribution of income, and social security measures to boost savings. Such measures may also tackle issues of inequality (see below). Bowles (2012) identifies an increase in individual savings from 15 per cent to 27 per cent of income in the period 1990–2008. However, much of this is specifically targeted towards spending on education and health care. It is suggested that increased government spending in these two areas alone would release savings to increase domestic consumption.

Increasing inequalities Without doubt, the economic growth of China has done much to raise income levels and reduce poverty. Panitch and Gindin (2013) suggest that China has now greater inequalities in income and wealth than those found in the USA. The economic transformation has widened the gap between rich and poor both in terms of individuals and regions. Eastern provinces, especially the area around Shanghai and in the north-east around Beijing and Tianjin, have benefitted more than western provinces and, in general, urban areas are much better off than rural areas. There are signs of social unrest. Younger workers have complained about long hours, relative low pay and the corruption of local officials, while there have been well-publicized strikes in foreign invested companies such as the Japanese Mitsumi Electric and Honda plants. Critics point to a lack of social spending to tackle the rising inequalities.

Purchasing power parity The purchasing power parity is a measure devised to show the real differences in the standard of living between inhabitants in different countries and is regarded by the World Bank as a good indicator of the state of a national economy. Table 3.12 shows the low base of both China and India and lends support to the Goldman Sachs predictions for GDP per capita in Table 3.4.

TABLE 3.12	Purchasing power parity per capita in $US for selected countries	
Country	**2011 GNI per capita* (current USD)**	
Norway	88 870	ranked 1
Qatar	80 440	
Luxembourg	77 390	
Switzerland	76 530	
USA	48 620	
Canada	45 550	
Japan	44 900	
Germany	44 230	
Singapore	42 930	
France	42 420	
UK	37 780	
Italy	35 320	
Korea, Rep	20 870	
Poland	20 870	
Brazil	10 720	
Romania	8 140	
South Africa	6 960	
Peru	5 150	
China	4 940	ranked 76
Namibia	4 700	
Morocco	2 970	
Indonesia	2 940	
Philippines	2 210	
India	1 420	ranked 120
Ghana	1 410	
Uganda	510	
Zambia	510	
Malawi	360	
Congo, Dem. Rep.	190	ranked 167

*GNI per capita = PPP per capita

Low levels of productivity This problem is mainly confined to SOEs and is typical of transitional economies in general. Historical policies of full employment have created overstaffing in many SOEs to achieve broader social goals. The absence of a profit motive and the lack of employee incentives often results in low levels of motivation which produces low productivity. Even in SOE joint ventures with foreign partners, productivity tends to be lower than in the foreign partner's home country. Technology lag and supply chain issues may also be contributory factors. The privatization of some SOEs and the growth of the private sector in general will have a positive impact on productivity levels.

Limited banking system The banking system in China is dominated by five large state-owned banks. Although there was an agreement made with the WTO to allow foreign banks to operate in China, this has not happened. The lack of participation in the global financial system is not just a concern of the WTO but limits China's integration in the global economy.

Rising inflation The first half of 2007 saw the Chinese economy grow by 11.9 per cent, the fastest growth in 12 years but this was accompanied by rising inflation. There was fear that the economy was overheating, resulting in the Central Bank imposing no less than five rises in the interest rate in just over a year (Singapore Straits Times, 20 July 2007). Inflation and the availability of credit remain a concern particularly in the property market and the increased borrowing by local governments.

Other problems Despite the extensive liberalization policies of the government and the growth of foreign investment, China is still seen by many investors as a potentially difficult market related to the workings of a complex state bureaucracy. There are growing concerns about levels of pollution both locally and globally and corruption is still seen as a problem in some sectors of the economy.

China versus India

The only growth rate to approach China in recent years is that of India with an average 6 per cent GDP growth in 1980–2000. There is some justification for placing China and India together. Their origins as modern nation states date from roughly the same time, both countries have very large populations with a large supply of cheap labour. The economies of both countries have until recently been subject to considerable state-control. They are facing similar problems of inequalities, rural poverty, relatively poorly developed banking systems and both are perceived by investors as being politically difficult, which does not prevent China being a popular destination for FDI. Perhaps the most significant factor is the low base of the respective economies (see Table 3.12). However, China has attracted a much greater level of FDI, US$53 billion in 2003 compared with India's US$4 billion in the same year (Roach, 2004). At the moment, India lags behind China in so many indicators, including growth rate, manufacturing base, exports, FDI and savings, that some question whether they should be treated as the same in terms of economic power. With reference to India, Dicken advises us to 'beware the hype' (Dicken, 2011, p. 34) and he feels that while China may well become an economic super power, the evidence for India is weak. Indeed, although the GDP of India continues to grow, between 2005 and 2007 it fell in the world rankings behind Brazil and the Russian Federation and 2013 was a particularly disappointing year in terms of high inflation, a rising balance of payments deficit and a weakened currency.

REFLECTION POINT

What arguments can you give both for and against the dominance of China in a future global economy?

Back in the USA

It is clear by most measures that the USA has dominated the global economy for almost a century and continues to contribute over a third of the global economic output. As we can see from Table 3.13, the USA is the largest economy in the world and is twice the size of the next largest economy, China, and three times the size of the third largest economy, Japan.

TABLE 3.13	Top 30 countries by GDP in 2011	
Ranking	**Economy**	**2011 GDP (US bn)**
1	United States	14 991
2	China	7 319
3	Japan	5 867
4	Germany	3 601
5	France	2 773
6	Brazil	2 477
7	United Kingdom	2 445
8	Italy	2 194
9	India	1 873
10	Russian Federation	1 858
11	Canada	1 736
12	Spain	1 477
13	Australia	1 379
14	Mexico	1 153
15	Korea Rep.	1 116
16	Indonesia	847
17	Netherlands	836
18	Turkey	775
19	Switzerland	659
20	Saudi Arabia	577
21	Sweden	549
22	Poland	514
23	Belgium	514
24	Norway	486
25	Argentina	446
26	Austria	418
27	South Africa	408
28	United Arab Emirates	360
29	Thailand	346
30	Denmark	334

In addition, the USA is the world leader in terms of manufacturing with 25 per cent of world total, the world leader in terms of service provision with 34 per cent of the world total, and the world leader in terms of agriculture with 15 per cent of the world total (Dicken, 2011). It is true that the USA has a very large trade deficit, but the value of the production of US companies overseas outstrips the value of exports by two and a half times. The USA has had a significant effect on world business through the operation of US multinationals in terms of both their output and influence on management practices.

However, there are signs of decline. We can argue that decline is taking place economically, politically and culturally.

- We can see from the data in Table 3.3 that Goldman Sachs predicted that China will overtake the USA economy by 2040 although subsequent predictions suggest that parity between China and the USA will come much sooner. Nonetheless, the wealth of the USA in terms of GDP per capita (see Table 3.3) and purchasing power parity (see Table 3.12) will remain strong. Currently, however, we can see a relative decline in terms of multinational operation. In 1960 the USA contributed 50 per cent of global FDI. By 2005 this figure had dropped to 21 per cent (Dicken, 2011).

- The continued strength of the USA economy combined with its military might has meant that US foreign policy has tended to dominate world affairs. The USA spends as much on defence and military capabilities as the rest of the world put together. However, its foreign policy has come under severe criticism by European powers (with the UK a notable exception) mostly in relation to its involvement in Iraq and Afghanistan. The US inability to effect 'solutions' in those countries and the threat by 'terrorist' groups against US interests have challenged its dominant political position.

- Culturally, the US has had great influence through films, television and through its products and brands. While its films and television remain influential in many product areas, such as cars, electronics and pharmaceuticals, US brands have been overtaken by those from other countries, as with Japanese cars and electrical goods. Tables 3.14 and 3.15 examine the declining fortunes of the USA in the car industry. In Table 3.14 we see that whereas in 1986 over 70 per cent of cars sold in the USA were American brands, within 20 years US brands had been overtaken by Japanese, whose brands now take around 50 per cent of the American market. Table 3.15 shows that while the USA was the second largest producer of cars in 1999 behind the Japanese, by 2009 the US had dropped to 6th place with China taking the lead as the top producer.

In this section we have looked at the evidence for a shift in global economic power. We may conclude that the USA retains its dominant position, although it is less dominant in terms of overseas investment, multinational presence and perhaps global influence than in former years.

TABLE 3.14	Market share of cars in the USA		
Origin of brand	*1986 (%)*	*2006 (%)*	*2009 (%)*
USA	71.1	39.9	31.0
Japan	21.0	42.6	47.8
Germany	4.3	9.8	10.9
S. Korea			

TABLE 3.15	Top car producers by country 1999–2009		
	1999		**2009**
1 Japan	8 100 169	1 China	10 383 831
2 USA	5 637 949	2 Japan	6 862 161
3 Germany	5 309 524	3 Germany	4 964 523
4 France	2 784 469	4 South Korea	3 158 417
5 South Korea	2 361 735	5 Brazil	2 576 628
6 Spain	2 281 617	6 USA	2 246 470
7 UK	1 786 624	7 India	2 166 238
8 Canada	1 626 316	8 Spain	1 812 688
9 Italy	1 410 459	9 France	1 819 462
10 Brazil	1 107 751	10 Iran	1 359 520
11 Mexico	993 772	11 UK	999 460
12 Russia	943 732	12 Czech Rep.	967 760
13 Belgium	917 513	13 Mexico	942 876
14 China	565 366	14 Canada	822 267

Includes all production in a country by domestic and foreign producers

The economy of China has displayed a consistent and exceptional growth rate over a considerable period. If this trend continues then its economic output will outstrip that of the USA.

We now turn our attention to other changes influencing national economies, involving liberalization, privatization and the growing influence of Anglo-Saxon capitalism. We refer to these changes as changes in the operation of national economies. They are in fact changes in political economy since they represent shifts in political ideology which have led to the reform of the economic system.

Changes in the operation of national economies

We examine two major changes, liberalization and privatization, and focus on transitional economies; those economies that have moved from state control to a free market. In Chapter 5 we examine the view that there has been a global shift towards an economic system characteristic of the USA and UK.

Liberalization and privatization

Liberalization is the process of shifting from some form of state control of the economy towards a free market. The most obvious examples are China and the former USSR and its allied states.

Political reforms in China in 1979 led to liberal measures in the Chinese economy. We have already seen the outcome of these changes. In Chapter 2 we noted the growth of joint ventures between Chinese state-owned companies and firms from other countries and we illustrated this by examining the involvement of Chrysler and then Daimler Benz in China. In this chapter we have commented on the growth of the Chinese economy fuelled by foreign investment and increases in foreign trade. However, the overall control of the economy of China remains in the hands of the state, albeit with a significant growth in the private sector (see Table 3.7).

This has not been the case with the political reforms of the USSR and its allies. The Soviet state was broken up into a number of countries, although some, like the Russian Federation, remain very large. Most countries have pursued the economics of the free market, and compared with China, the changes have been rapid (some would argue destabilizing) and wide-ranging. In addition, changes have taken place in former Soviet bloc countries such as Poland, Hungary and the Czech Republic. In such countries the liberalization process has been so far reaching that it has enabled such states to become members of the EU.

Privatization is the sale of state assets to private interests. It is an important aspect of liberalization as former state-owned enterprises become private companies. However, privatization has become a feature of many liberal economies too, as in such countries as the UK, France, Germany, Canada and Australia. In the UK, the state-owned British Telecom was privatized, as was Deutsche Telekom in Germany. The banking crisis of 2008 has led to a change in this policy, with governments around the world, including the USA and UK, taking big shareholdings in major banks and major companies such as General Motors in the US. We will discuss this change later in this chapter and examine the ownership issues of privatization in more detail in Chapter 6.

Variations in liberal economies

Variations in the extent and timing of privatization in free market economies suggests that there are variations between economies in the extent of state ownership and control. In fact those variations extend to other issues as well, including the rights of the individual, the extent of collective provision and the role played by stakeholders. We can identify three broad models: Anglo-Saxon; social market; and Asian. We identify also a fourth model representing those economies in transition from state control to private ownership. We examine the workings of these models in more detail in Chapter 5, when we explore variations in institutions and relations between stakeholders.

- The Anglo-Saxon capitalism model is sometimes called laissez-faire or competitive managerial capitalism. While all forms of capitalism see the market to be the ultimate arbiter and control of a well-regulated economy and certainly preferable to state control, this form of capitalism above all others emphasizes the workings of the free market. Such a system can be seen best in the USA and the UK but is a feature also of Australia, New Zealand and Canada.

- The social market model is also known as the German model and the Rhine-land model and is typified by the system found in Germany. Variations of the model can be found in France, the Benelux countries, the Netherlands, in the Scandinavian countries as well as in Italy and Spain. The model favours a free market, but one regulated by the state with an emphasis on job protection and social welfare. However, as we see in Chapter 5, there is considerable variation in the way the model operates in these countries.

- The Asian model is also known as the Japanese model, alliance capitalism or community capitalism. It is found throughout Asia but its core characteristics are best illustrated in Japan and the Asian tiger economies, especially South Korea. However, there are variations in the model. The underlying theme of Asian capitalism is that of the free market but with a strong state giving direction where necessary. Further insights into the model can be seen in Case 3.1 about Singapore.

REFLECTION POINT

What do you see as the key differences between the Anglo-Saxon, social market and Asian market economies?

A challenge to Anglo-Saxon capitalism?

In recent times the supremacy of Anglo-Saxon capitalism as an economic system has been called into question. Towards the end of 2008 the global economy was heading for a recession and the value of major companies such as Ford and General Motors was decimated as stock market values fell dramatically around the world.

The problem began a few years earlier in the USA as banks were lending large sums of money to large numbers of people, many of whom traditionally would have been rated as high risk (known as the sub-prime market). A similar pattern was occurring in the UK as people spent much more money than they earned. The Anglo-Saxon economies had enjoyed a long period of economic growth. As a consequence, financial institutions took bigger risks to reap even greater rewards. As with the growth of the sub-prime mortgage market, a key problem was the availability of cheap money and financial institutions, especially banks had turned their attention to the derivatives market for investment, carrying much higher risk than the traditional equities and bond markets. Three additional factors added to the problems. First, as was discovered later, the banks had poor systems of corporate governance. Second, investment bankers had significant status and power and several were appointed to government advisory roles. Third, both managers and some employees were encouraged to take risks on the back of huge bonus incentives. Certainly, many place the blame on an economic system that encouraged greed by those making economic decisions in corporations in the financial sector. (We examine this issue in our discussion of management pay in Chapter 7). The result was that banks and other financial institutions became under-capitalized; they had insufficient funds to cover the outstanding loans.

This created a banking crisis and a stock market collapse in the wake of a severe threat to the economic system. Some banks such as Lehmann Brothers were forced to close. The UK and the USA governments along with many other around the world put together rescue packages to prevent economic collapse. The UK government propped up the financial system with various measures totalling over £400 billion in return for preference shares and interest to be paid on loans. The UK government became majority shareholders in the Royal Bank of Scotland, taking initially 60 per cent. It also bought shares in HBOS (43.5 per cent) and Lloyds TSB (43.5 per cent). The US government put £143 billion into the banking system, taking minority stakes in Bank of America, Citigroup and Goldman Sachs. As the banking crisis led to an economic crisis, many major companies became at risk. The US government bailed out General Motors by taking 61 per cent of shares in the company as well as the Canadian and Ontario governments taking 12 per cent. The crisis was felt in many other countries. The Russian stock market was closed down and in Sweden, a plan to privatize six government companies was halted.

However, the response varied even in Anglo-Saxon economies. Whereas the UK bailed out the banks to the extent of 19.8 per cent of GDP and the USA to the extent of 6.8 per cent of GDP, in Australia it was only 0.1 per cent and in Canada, nothing at all. (Konzelmann, Fovargue-Davies and Schnyder, 2012) The key differences lay in the variations in the way the banking sectors were controlled (corporate governance is covered in more detail in Chapter 6). There has also been a different approach by governments in the disposal of shares. In the UK, the government still retains shares in the major banks. In the case of RBS the government increased its share to 65 per cent, although it reduced its share in Lloyds TSB (which had acquired HBOS), to 32.7 per cent. In the US, while the government has maintained its shareholding of Bank of America, by the end of 2013 it had sold all its shares in General Motors. During its period of ownership sales had fallen and the company was dubbed 'Government Motors' by the media.

Undoubtedly, the rapid escalation of the financial crisis in the banks and its rapid spread to all countries in the world highlights one of the problems of a highly integrated global economy, as we have discussed in Chapter 2.

REFLECTION POINT

Will the events of 2008 and the resulting banking and stock market crisis reverse the trend of liberalization, privatization and the move towards the Anglo-Saxon system?

State-controlled and transitional economies

In a centrally planned (state-controlled) economy, such as ones that existed in the former Soviet Union and the former communist countries of Eastern Europe, the state has total ownership and control of the means of production. The activities of all firms in all sectors of the economy are under state ownership and control. The economy is centrally planned and the state controls supply and demand, wages and prices and levels of employment. However, under most such economic regimes the reality never matched the expectations and problems have been well documented. These include the failure to match targets and allocated resources, the failure to meet targets irrespective of resources, over-production, inflexibility and inefficiencies in all sectors of the economy.

Many state-controlled economies underwent periodic reforms, but the key feature of the transitional economy is the radical nature of change, that is more far-reaching than any internal reform. Such economies present international firms, especially those from the advanced industrial nations, with opportunities for market expansion, business growth, foreign direct investment, and enable them to reap the benefits from many of the advantages associated with joint ventures. These issues were discussed in Chapter 2 and formed the basis of Case 2.1.

Features of the transitional process are liberalization and privatization together with some form of internationalization, usually through the encouragement of inward foreign investment. The extent of the transition and the experience of most transitional economies have been mixed. In Eastern Europe, countries such as Poland, Hungary and the Czech Republic have made economic advances, while the experience of many of the countries of the former USSR was an initial rapid decline into economic chaos (with the notable exceptions of the Baltic states, Latvia, Lithuania and Estonia). Such variations in performance may be attributed to both the extent and length of time of state control of the economy. In the former USSR, central planning had been a feature for 70 years whereas, for most Eastern European countries (including the Baltic states), state control was a feature from 1948 only. In the former USSR, central planning was an embedded feature of business processes and behaviour and many people had known no other system. The change, when it did arrive, was rapid and destabilizing. In countries such as Hungary and the Czech Republic, not only was the experience of state control for a shorter period, but a greater number of liberal reforms had taken place before the collapse of centralized communist control in the early 1990s.

In China, liberal reforms began at the end of the 1970s, introduced by the regime of Deng Xioaping. Such reforms accelerated rapidly during the 1990s with foreign direct investment pouring in and the establishment of joint ventures between former Chinese state-owned enterprises and western and Japanese firms such as IBM, Daimler Benz, Siemens, Hewlett Packard, VW and Mitsubishi. Such reforms culminated in 2001 with the acceptance of China as a member of the World Trade Association (see Case 3.2). The economy of China is still defined as centrally planned, although that planning incorporates liberal reforms. The transformation of major cities, especially those in the east and along the coast, has been dramatic. However, the GDP per capita for China, despite predictions of growth, still stands at a fraction of its western and Japanese counterparts and variations exist within China itself, particularly between the prosperous coastal area and the relatively undeveloped western provinces. Moreover, as we saw in the section on joint ventures in the previous chapter, tensions exist when centrally planned economies meet the free market.

The importance of joint ventures to the transition of the Chinese economy has led to a tendency for China to follow western models of capitalism rather than the Asian model, with which it is much more closely related, both culturally and structurally, in terms of a strong state apparatus (Dore, 2000). While models of capitalism are necessarily idealized, they do present emerging and transitional economies with a choice of routes.

In many ways the liberal economic reforms under a state-controlled political system in China have had a greater impact on global economics than changes in other transitional economies. As Dicken (2011) points out, the combined economies of the Russian Federation, Poland, Hungary and the Czech Republic contributed only 2 per cent of global GDP in 2005. In some countries there is also evidence of de-liberalization. In the early 1990s in Russia under the Yeltsin government, oil, gas and metals industries were sold to private firms, at what many believed to be very cheap prices. The Putin government, however, saw the strategic value of Russia's large oil and gas reserves, both in terms of international trade and as a lever to gain new global alliances (Walsh, 2005). As a result, Gazprom with the Kremlin as the major shareholder has become Russia's biggest company.

In the next two sections we examine in general terms the effect of business on the economy and of the economy on business.

REFLECTION POINT

What factors result in transitional economies taking different paths towards liberalization?

The impact of business on the economy

All businesses produce goods and services and provide employment. In doing so they contribute to a nation's income, capital assets, and economic growth. In the previous section we have seen how these contributions are measured in terms of GDP, GNP and GNI.

Furthermore, contributions can be made to a nation's economy through the investment and outputs of foreign firms. This is referred to as foreign direct investment (FDI).

In the previous chapter we explored the importance of the multinational and transnational company to the growth of the global economy. Both these types of company are also examples of FDI. Foreign direct investment is the full or partial ownership of a firm located in one country by investors in another country. The rationale behind FDI is similar to that for the existence of the multinational, although as a mode of entry it needs to have significant advantages over exporting and licensing to make the investment worthwhile. It goes without saying that FDI can have considerable influence upon a nation's economy. It was also noted in the previous chapter that FDI had replaced export volume and value as a measure of a nation's economic success.

Key issues for business managers are also key economic issues. These may be identified as products, productivity, markets, profits and the supply of labour. These themes re-emerge when we discuss the role of the economy in the chapters on the various business activities.

For example, in Chapter 10 we examine the view that economic growth is dependent upon product and process innovation.

The impact of the economy on business

There are many ways in which economic changes can affect businesses in all countries. These changes include structural changes, the supply and price of raw materials, increased international competition, and the emergence of globalization as a dominant influence. Central to the development of globalization is the impact of multinational firms. These illustrate the difficulty of isolating business and environmental influences. Many businesses in the UK have undoubtedly been influenced by a world economy increasingly dominated by multinational corporations. These same multinationals are themselves businesses with the ability to influence national and international economies.

In most countries in the world, changes in the nature of the global economy have led to structural changes. The case of coal-mining is a good example. In the UK, coal-mining was once a major industry and a major employer. Table 3.16 charts the decline of the coal-mining industry in the UK.

The changes are a product of many factors, including the discovery of North Sea oil and gas, the availability of cheaper coal from countries such as Poland, Russia and South Africa, and political choices about mine closures. By 2005, the UK was producing only about 40 per cent of the coal it was using, relying on imports. Such structural changes are not peculiar to the UK. Coal mine closures in Poland resulted in a reduction in employment in that industry of some 70 per cent from 450 000 in 1985 to 136 000 in 2003 (EU Commission statistics, 2004).

In most developed economies there has been a decline in the manufacturing sector (de-industrialization) and growth of services, especially the financial sector. In turn, these changes have caused high levels of unemployment in those areas formerly dominated by traditional manufacturing industry, while creating many jobs in financial services. The case of the UK coal-mining industry illustrates how economic changes can affect whole communities. The closure of a major employer reduces retail sales, and large scale unemployment, especially among young people faced with few prospects, creates its own social problems.

The availability of resources influences the fortunes of individual firms and can lead to structural changes. In 1973, OPEC, representing the oil-producing countries, decided to restrict the supply of oil, with a subsequent sharp increase in price. Similar price rises occurred in 1979.

TABLE 3.16	Changes in coal-mining in the UK 1947–2005			
Year	Mines	Employees	Output (million tonnes)	% of UK energy from coal
1947	1000+	1.1 million	187	90
1957	650	700 000	213	85
1977	238	242 000	108	35
1997	22	8 000	39	18
2012	5	5 600	17	N/A

TABLE 3.17	Changes in Detroit 1950–2013	
	1950	**2013**
Population	1.8 million	700 000
Manufacturing jobs	297 000	28 000
Homicides per 100 000 people	6.1	43.1

The impact on businesses in the UK were several. Increased costs were passed on in the form of higher prices or resulted in reduced profits, with some firms unable to compete. Some industries sought substitute products with corresponding increases in demand for products of the coal and gas industries. Rising petrol prices meant increased costs of transport and led to product changes in the car industry. These changes were even more significant in the USA, with a reduction in car size and the imposition of a national speed limit on all roads, the legacy of which remains today. When Britain became an oil producer, changes in the price of oil had an effect upon the exchange value of sterling. An exchange rate strengthened by an oil economy meant British exports became more expensive and was damaging for those businesses that depended for a large proportion of their revenue on exported goods.

There has been a marked increase in the international dimension of most types of business. This has taken the form of growth in international competition, initially from Japan but, more recently also from other South-East Asian economies, especially China. The decline in competitiveness of many of Britain's manufacturing industries, such as shipbuilding, motorcycles, domestic electrical products and cars, has been attributed to the rise of cheap labour economies, especially those in the Far East, or the product superiority of manufacturers in countries such as Japan and Germany.

However, our perspective of international competition must be revised constantly, so dynamic are the forces at work. While de-industrialization in many 'advanced economies' was linked to a switch of manufacturing to those aforementioned cheap labour economies, such economies are becoming less cheap and, far from lagging behind, they are beginning to take the lead in certain areas of manufacturing technology and product development.

Such economic changes can have far-reaching effects beyond businesses to affect entire communities. Overseas competition and the decline of car production in the USA (see Table 3.17) has had a major impact on the home of the US motor industry, Detroit. Table 3.16 charts the changes that have taken place since 1950.

In addition to the changes listed above 78 000 buildings have been abandoned in the city and the city authorities filed for bankruptcy as the only way to maintain essential services.

THE STATE AND BUSINESS

Taking his lead from Max Weber, John Scott (1979) defines the state as that body which has a monopoly over taxation, money supply and the legitimate use of violence. The state is normally thought of as comprising the executive, parliament, civil service, judiciary, and armed forces and police. It would be wrong to perceive the state as a united body. Tensions can and do occur, as between parliament and the civil service or between parliament and the judiciary. Variations in policy often result from differences in political ideology.

KEY CONCEPT 3.1   THE STATE

The state comprises parliament, the judiciary, the civil service, police, armed forces and so on. Traditionally, there have been tensions between the state's need to direct the economy and regulate business and the wishes of the business community to pursue their interests with a minimum of state intervention. Nevertheless, state intervention is a feature of business life and is inevitable in many countries, where the state is a major employer. Intervention occurs through the legal regulation of market transactions, inventions and employment contracts and through the state's attempt to influence demand both as a consumer and via government economic policy. The business community in turn attempts to influence the state by adopting the various tactics associated with pressure groups. Increasingly, business comes under the influence of the policies of supranational bodies, such as the EU and WTO.

The World Bank (1997) has identified five core responsibilities of the state in a modern society:

- establishing a legal framework;
- developing economic policies;
- building basic services and infrastructure;
- protecting the vulnerable;
- protecting the environment.

All these responsibilities affect business in some way. We have already noted that the state interacts with business through its management of the economy. In this section we will deal with aspects of the state's activity at both national and local levels in terms of the state's attempt to intervene in business and the efforts made by business managers to influence the workings of the state. It will also link back to the models of economic systems outlined in the previous section. This section examines also the issue of international political and economic integration and focuses on two supranational bodies, the EU and the WTO. The interaction of the state and business is illustrated by examining the relationship in our discussion of business activities in Chapters 10 to 14.

REFLECTION POINT

To what extent do you agree with the five core responsibilities of the modern state as identified by the World Bank?

Before the relationship between the state and business is examined more closely it is important to consider the ideological underpinnings that inform state involvement in business in the 20th century. For many years, two broad contending political philosophies have dominated: centralized state control typified by the former USSR and China, and liberal pluralism typified by the USA and Western Europe. As noted in the last section when we discussed political systems and business, both these philosophies have had a profound effect on business. We also noted a shift towards liberalism if not liberal pluralism.

For liberals, the state is concerned with the maintenance of order and with providing conditions so that business can prosper. The state is seen as a neutral umpire in a pluralist society dominated by voluntary cooperation and exchange, where differences are never fundamental. Under a liberal view of the state, intervention is necessary for the following reasons:

- To protect the workings of the free market against forces that might otherwise disrupt it, such as excessive monopoly power of either business or trade unions.

- To provide and/or control goods and services to individuals such as defence and education, where provision by other means would be impossible or inappropriate.

- To take a longer-term view of economic, social and environmental change than individual businesses are capable of doing.

The liberal perspective allows wide variation, as we saw in our different models of capitalism, from a highly directive economy to one in which the free market is encouraged to operate unfettered by government controls.

Those criticizing this perspective argue that the state tends to operate to preserve the status quo, that groups in society rarely have equal power to support voluntary cooperation and exchange, and that ultimately the state is not neutral. Marxists take this view a stage further and argue that the state is the instrument of the ruling class in an essentially exploitative society, where massive inequalities exist. Under a Marxist view of the state, intervention is necessary to maintain the status quo in favour of the dominant class and to protect their interests.

State intervention under different economic systems

You are referred here to the discussion of economic systems discussed earlier in this chapter and in more detail in Chapter 5. Under each system the state's relationship with business is different.

- Under systems of state control and central planning the state has total ownership of business and controls production via targets, and controls both supply and demand and wages and prices. Such a system typified the old regimes of the former Soviet Union and China. Such total intervention is now rare, existing only in a handful of countries such as North Korea and Cuba. Nearly all former state-controlled economies are in transition towards a free market system. This means that private ownership of business has been introduced and managers will have more freedom to act. The extent of state involvement in such a transitional economy varies. For example, although China allows private companies and joint ventures with foreign firms, business activities are still tightly managed by the state operating at both national and regional levels.

- The Anglo-Saxon systems of the UK and USA are based around the notion of a free market and non-intervention of the state. Yet here the state is still active in business through laws and regulations that have a significant impact on the way business is done and on internal business practices. There is much debate within the business communities of both countries that despite the rhetoric of the free market, the state is often seen as too interventionist in the affairs of private businesses. For example, in the UK the owners of small businesses have complained that employment laws relating to part-time work and maternity leave are disadvantageous to their competitive position. A complication here for the UK is that many laws governing business are not the product of the UK government but emerge from the EU, where several member nations operate under a social market system.

- The social market system has a number of variations. The state plays a key role in protecting the social welfare of its inhabitants. There is considerable investment in such areas as health and education supported by high rates of taxation. Laws are enforced to limit mergers and takeovers, which might affect jobs, and to facilitate employee involvement in business decisions. For example, the Anglo-Dutch steel firm Corus (formed from British Steel and Hoogovens and since taken over by Indian group Tata) announced large losses in 2002–03 with the inevitable threat to jobs. Far more job cuts were expected in the UK, because Dutch workers are better protected through their system of employee involvement. Such state direction in business has been labelled as corporatism. This is essentially an attempt by the government to achieve stability by integration, involving representatives of business and trade unions in the economic decision-making process. However, as we noted in the previous section, some social market countries, including Germany, have become more Anglo-Saxon in their approach to business.

- Under the Asian model the state is directive but not in terms of social welfare, which is the responsibility of individuals. The state tends to be pro-business and assists in business growth. In Japan, some sectors have been given government support and R&D has been facilitated by the establishment of government-backed centres involving representatives from several firms working in the same sector. In Singapore, the government encouraged the inward investment of foreign firms (see Case 3.1).

Difficulties with state intervention

There are a number of reasons why state intervention in business is difficult:

- The impact of government policy upon business activity is often difficult to measure and direct relationships can be difficult to prove owing to the large number of other variables which can, and do, affect the situation.

- Governments change and, with them, policies. Differences both between and within political parties can result in different approaches to intervention.

- The business community may oppose attempts by governments to control it. The majority of owners and managers of business have an ideological attachment to laissez-faire.

- As we saw in Chapter 2, many multinationals tend to have a greater allegiance to their own corporate goals than those of any single nation state.

Despite such problems the state does intervene in business in a variety of ways.

Types of state intervention

Collective provision The most obvious form of state intervention is through the provision of those goods and services that would otherwise be too expensive, too dangerous, or just ineffective if left to private control. Such aspects would include defence, the police, health, welfare and housing. The extent and nature of such collective provision is a matter of political and ideological debate. The British government, since 1979, has pursued a policy of reducing its collective provision, as we will discuss under privatization in Chapter 6.

The state as employer In the UK, the proportion of the working population employed by the state rose from 2.4 per cent in 1851 to 24.3 per cent in 1975. Policies of privatization since 1983 have led to reductions in those directly employed by the state, but it remains a major employer with a profound effect on the labour market. In many countries governments attempt to hold down wages in the public sector as part of the policy of reducing public expenditure. In the UK, this has from time to time resulted in confrontations with such groups as miners, nurses, teachers and the fire brigade.

The state as consumer The state is a consumer of many products and services. As a major employer, the state is a purchaser of office equipment and many businesses rely on government contracts as a source of revenue. The state, through its involvement in defence, health and education, influences the direction of innovation (Chapter 10 has a more comprehensive review of this aspect).

Legal regulation The legal regulation of business is extensive and complex. The law of contract is used to regulate the market place. Company law deals with such issues as the protection of consumers through the regulation of monopoly power, rules governing the provision of company information and so on. Labour law deals with both the protection of the individual worker and the regulation of collective bargaining. Patent law exists to encourage innovation by granting monopoly rights to patent holders. Illustrations of such legal provisions may be found in the chapters dealing with specific business activities. Some laws operate as constraints while others exist specifically to aid industrial development.

Demand management All governments attempt to influence and control economic growth, the balance of payments, wage and price stability and the level of unemployment. Measures used include fiscal measures, such as taxation, monetary measures, such as the control of credit, and direct measures, such as import controls and assistance to specific firms. In the 1980s both the US and UK governments attempted to stimulate economic growth through monetarist and supply-side policies.

Through taxation and monetary policies governments are able to raise revenue to finance activities and also to achieve specific objectives, as through the lower rates of taxation levied on food as opposed to tobacco. In many countries governments have given aid either for specific purposes, such as innovation (Chapter 10 contains a full discussion of this), or to assist a particular firm or industry. The UK government in the 1960s gave the nuclear, motor vehicle, and electrical industries special assistance, and in the 1970s, the machine tool and woollen textiles industries. Similar policies are pursued by other countries, notably France and Japan. Historically, UK governments have assisted specific firms such as British Leyland and Rolls Royce. However, such support for individual firms is ideologically incompatible with free market economic policies and is constrained by policies of the EU. Whether it wishes to or not, the UK government is forbidden under EU competition law to favour UK firms over those in the rest of Europe. However, funds are available within the EU, through its Social and Regional Development Funds, to stimulate the growth of firms in designated deprived regions and to retrain the workforce.

Training Governments attempt to influence the skills composition of the work force through education and training policies. Arguably, some countries have been more successful at this than others. Training features more prominently in the USA and Germany than it does, for example, in the UK.

Protection Governments have, to varying degrees, attempted to protect their industries against what is viewed as unfair competition from overseas firms and, indeed, other governments. One direct measure is the use of import tariffs and controls such as quota restrictions. Japan did this for a number of years with significant influence of the growth of home industries and firms. Government representatives will also attempt to influence the policies of supranational institutions, such as the EU or WTO, to ensure a level playing field for the conduct of international trade.

Marketing   Most governments support their own businesses in exporting goods and services. Diplomatic services will inevitably involve a trade function and embassies will act as host to trade delegations as well as influencing foreign governments and businesses through diplomatic connections.

Advisory services   In addition to its policies of regulation and assistance, the state offers advice to business people. Such advice ranges from overseas trade, as identified above, to dealing with industrial relations problems at home.

The business community as a pressure group

So far this section has concentrated on the way the state attempts to influence business. We now turn our attention to the ways in which the state can be influenced by the business community acting as a pressure group or, more correctly, as a series of pressure groups.

We have already noted that businesses are traditionally resistant to state control and are generally committed to a laissez-faire economy. However, as a pressure group, businesses tend to be fragmented with no powerful central body to coordinate policy. This of course varies from country to country. The chamber of commerce system in Germany has considerable influence on policies at a local level.

With all pressure group activity there is a difficulty both in observing it and in measuring its effect. We can only make deductions based upon open, formally reported attempts to influence. The business community tends to be secretive and many attempts to influence government policy are undoubtedly covert and informal. Nonetheless, the business community represents an important source of revenue via taxation and borrowing to enable the state to fund its activities and, this alone, constitutes an important political lobby.

We have suggested that, for the most part, managers tend to be reactive rather than proactive as far as the state is concerned and seem more concerned to predict changes in the political environment than to initiate those changes for themselves. In this way, the tobacco manufacturers predicted increased government regulation of their industry and took measures both to diversify and to transfer attention to growing Third World markets. The same companies reacted to restrictions on tobacco advertising by expanding their interests in sport sponsorship to maintain a high public profile. Some companies, of course, are better than others in resisting state intervention. Multinationals can use their protected status as members of another sovereign state to limit the extent of intervention in those countries in which they operate, and by transferring funds from country to country can minimize tax liabilities.

Political risk assessment is a technique used by some firms operating in an international environment particularly where there is considerable investment planned, as in the establishment of a manufacturing plant. Risk assessments would be built into the strategic plan and assess the stability of the country as well as the chances and likely impact of a change in regime. At a more detailed level, risk assessment will attempt to predict policy changes and their effect upon operations. There have been a number of well-documented cases where a change of government has resulted in the expropriation or nationalization of assets, as has occurred in such countries as Chile, Egypt, Iran, Iraq and Nigeria. Other risks can incorporate such diverse events as civil war, the kidnapping of managers and associated ransom demands, restrictions on borrowing, trades union activities, and policy changes concerning the hiring of local staff. Such assessment is far from easy. Governments can change without any fundamental shift in economic policy and the nationalistic rhetoric of some politicians may threaten foreign investment in the run-up to an election, but turn out to be supportive once power has been achieved.

Once genuine risks are forecast, management will wish to take some measures to prevent them. Real pressure group activity exists where the business deliberately attempts to control the political environment in which it operates. Ways in which business attempts to influence government policy include:

- Professional groups such as doctors, lawyers and accountants and employers' associations representing whole industries all attempt to influence policy.

- Industry groups lobby government bodies to secure some kind of advantage or to protect themselves from what they see as unfair competition. Thus, the fishing industry in both the UK and the rest of Europe is persistently lobbying for increased protection through the extension of territorial waters.

- Some firms seek political influence through donations to political parties. This is the source of considerable funding to political parties in the USA and a growing source in the UK as well as in other European countries. We note in the Enron case in Chapter 9, how the company gave financial support to both main parties in the USA and to the governing Labour Party in the UK. Such donations came under scrutiny in the UK in 2006 when the government was accused of offering honours to individuals who donated large amounts.

- Multinationals and large firms in any country will make some attempt at influencing government policy and may even be consulted.

- Individuals, too, represent an important channel of influence. Many references are made to the 'old boy network' that operates in government and business circles and several firms take more direct action by enlisting the services of a member of parliament on its board of directors. British Airways, before privatization, set up a powerful lobby to protect its own position. The Civil Aviation Authority had published a report recommending that BA should give up some of its routes to its competitors, particularly local routes to provincial airlines and international routes to its main competitor, British Caledonian. The report also recommended that BA should move some of its services from Heathrow to Gatwick Airport and allow its competitors to move into Heathrow. The lobby was successful and a government White Paper on airline competition policy favoured BA. Some sources indicated the role played by the then BA chairman, Lord King, who was a personal friend of the then prime minister, Margaret Thatcher. The government decision effectively prevented British Caledonian from expanding and did much to prepare for its eventual takeover by BA following privatization.

Lobbying has become an occupation. The EU for example has around 10 000 accredited lobbyists whose role is to influence policy. In recent years a number of firms that operate as professional lobbying consultants have emerged. Clients include not just private sector organizations but also local authorities who wish to influence government policy on such issues as the dumping of nuclear waste and who are resisting proposals to create nuclear waste sites in their area.

We can see that businesses attempt to influence the state in a variety of ways: through personal influence, by gaining media coverage for their views, by taking out expensive advertisements, by hiring consultants, and by submitting letters to the press often enlisting the support of other interested parties.

REFLECTION POINT

In what ways does the state intervene in the operations of individual firms? In what ways can the business community and the stakeholders of business influence government policies and decisions?

So far in this section, focus has been on the way the state exerts its influence over the business community and vice versa. Chapter 2 noted the growing trend of political globalization through trading blocs and supranational political organizations. Such organizations and their activities increase the complexity of the interaction between the state and business. In the next section the general issue of international economic and political integration is dealt with and focuses on two such organizations, the WTO and the EU.

International economic and political integration

International economic and political integration can take a number of forms. There are essentially two types: global integration as with the UN or WTO, and regional integration as with the EU. There are at least 30 regional groupings and they operate across all continents. The main types, listed in ascending order of integration, are:

- Free trade areas. Nations within these areas agree to remove barriers to trade such as tariffs and quotas, e.g. NAFTA.

- Customs unions. These are extensions of free trade areas in that members operate together to set a common tariff for all non-member states, e.g. the EU operates as a bloc in negotiations over trade with non-member states.

- Common market. This is like a free trade area and customs union, with the added freedom that people and capital can move freely between member countries as well as traded goods and services. The EU is a classic example.

- Economic union. This involves the integration and harmonization of economic policies. It is a goal of the EU but has proved to be difficult to achieve with the unwillingness of some members to surrender sovereignty on issues such as rates of taxation or a common currency.

- Political union. This involves not just economic integration but the integration of political systems. The former Yugoslavia achieved such a union after the Second World War. The difficulties of both creating and maintaining such systems in the face of different demands was in evidence with the break-up of Yugoslavia in the 1990s.

Such types of regional association and integration play a big role in management decisions and business behaviour. The operation of such a region can influence the location of production, the targeting of markets, and lead to increased FDI and joint venture activity.

The World Trade Organization

The World Trade Organization (WTO) began its life as GATT (General Agreement on Tariffs and Trade). It was founded as a supranational body shortly after the Second World War. Alongside the World Bank and the IMF, it was set up as part of the Bretton Woods system for the management of the post-war economy. Although the initial concern was for trade in goods, this was extended to include services. GATT was always seen as a temporary stage in the creation of the WTO, but it was not until the conclusion of the Uruguay Round of GATT talks in 1993 that this became a reality. The WTO, with its headquarters in Geneva, opened for business on the first day of 1995.

KEY CONCEPT 3.2	WORLD TRADE ORGANIZATION

Emerging from the General Agreement on Tariffs and Trade (GATT), the World Trade Organization (WTO) is a global organization of some 160 nations (160 members in June 2014 with a number of nations with observer status, before full membership). It is concerned with the establishment of rules of trade between member states. This it does within the framework of liberalizing world trade and offering assistance to the developing world. The full achievement of its objectives has been thwarted by trade restrictions by many nations and by the activities of some multinationals in moving operations to avoid WTO regulations.

GATT was founded on the twin assumptions that trade is associated with wealth and that an increase in trade between nations means a reduction in the risk of war. These assumptions were born out of the experience of the 1930s when many nations sought to protect their own economies during depression through the imposition of high import tariffs and through the experiences of global war in the 1940s. In 2001, when China joined, the WTO comprised 143 member countries. The issues surrounding the membership of China are explored in more detail in Case 3.2.

Agreements between members are reached through 'rounds', of which there have been eight since 1945. Each round seeks to further the liberalization of trade. In general, the WTO operates by:

- establishing rules that govern trading behaviour between nation states;
- attempting to liberalize trade through tariff and quota reduction;
- offering a facility and a legal framework, including a court, for the settlement of disputes;
- monitoring trade agreements and government policies, especially those that may contravene the WTO objective of liberalization;
- providing technical assistance and training for developing countries.

The WTO offers a more formal structure for the furtherance of trade agreements than existed under GATT. Senior ministers of member states and regions meet once a year and business is dealt with by the Council of Representatives, which meets around nine times a year. The council's work is supported by standing committees. Members should adhere to rules governing the trading of goods and services and they have a duty to apply these rules and the same tariffs to all other members. Furthermore, members must not discriminate between domestic and imported goods and services. The WTO members embrace well over 90 per cent of world trade. Its supporters point to the dramatic reduction in tariffs and the equally dramatic increase in world trade since the war.

Others are more sceptical, highlighting the continued presence of trading blocs as proof of the continued existence of protectionism, the success of countries, such as Japan, in resisting foreign imports, and the growth of informal agreements outside the jurisdiction of the WTO. Such an agreement would include the 'gentleman's agreement' between Britain and Japan and between the USA and Japan to limit the import of Japanese cars. Such agreements are contrary to the spirit of the WTO. Others have criticized the WTO for taking a weak stance on social and environmental issues, including child labour and global warming. The USA government banned the import of tuna from certain countries, on the grounds that the fishing methods used killed large numbers of dolphins and were a threat to the species. The WTO declared the ban illegal in 1991. Many USA firms manufacture in Mexico, thus avoiding more stringent USA laws on pollution, and there are many cases of multinationals exploiting cheap labour economies and sanctioning the use of child labour. The WTO draws a distinction between the traded goods and services and the methods of production, which critics regard as a flaw in its rules. The only exception is the imposition of trade restrictions on scientifically established health grounds. The perceived ambivalence of the WTO towards social and environmental issues has seen recent summits of WTO members attacked by anti-globalization protest groups, who forced the premature closure of the Seattle summit in 1999.

The Uruguay 'round' of talks began in 1986 and took 7 years to reach its conclusion at the end of 1993. This round concerned itself with the tariff issues, but also tackled foreign investment, patents and copyright, trade issues concerning service industries, and agriculture. It is this last issue, among others, that resulted in the Uruguay talks taking so long to reach a conclusion. Throughout the world, agriculture is the most highly subsidized of all industries and any proposal to reduce subsidies and hence liberalize trade have met with stern opposition and ultimately deadlock, resulting in the talks exceeding their deadline date. Even though the Uruguay round was completed at the very end of 1993, it was done amid much last-minute compromise. After talks, agreements must then be ratified by the respective governments, a process that can take years. This lengthy process and the difficulties in reaching an agreement has led many to question the ability of the WTO to regulate international business and trade effectively.

The Doha round of talks began in Qatar in 2001 picking up on unfinished business from the last round as well as raising new issues. The Doha round of talks remained unfinished at the end of 2013. It has focused on the differences between the advanced economies and the developing nations with agricultural subsidies of particular concern (see the following section on the EU). Other issues include the access of poorer countries to patented drugs, with HIV/AIDS as a big factor, concern for the environment and a call for the WTO to review the standards and conditions under which labour is employed around the world.

REFLECTION POINT

How effective is the WTO in achieving its stated objectives of unlimited free trade between member states and assisting the developing world ? What are the obstacles to achieving these goals?

The European Union

At the beginning of 2014 the European Union (EU) embraced 28 nation states. In Table 3.18 the stages in the growth of the EU since the 1950s are identified. The EU was formed out of post-war idealism as a means of putting an end to war between European nations and to assist in the post-war political, social and economic reconstruction of Europe. Politically, the EU originally saw itself as a power bloc alongside the USA and the USSR. With the break-up of the Soviet Union, its political position has almost certainly been enhanced. Economically, there was a desire to capitalize on the largest market in the advanced industrial world. Protectionism was sought both against a buoyant Japanese export trade and in response to increasing protectionism on the part of the USA. The EU, with over 400 million people, is a bigger market than either the USA (around 300 million) or Japan (around 130 million).

TABLE 3.18	Stages in the development of the European Union
1952	The European Coal and Steel Community formed by Belgium, France, West Germany, Italy, Luxembourg and the Netherlands
1957	The above six countries sign the Treaty of Rome and establish the European Economic Community. The UK is invited to join but withdraws from talks at an early stage
1958	The European Economic Community comes into being
1973	The initial six members are joined by Denmark, Ireland and the United Kingdom
1981	Greece joins
1986	Spain and Portugal join
1987	The Single European Act is passed to create a single market by 1992
1992	The Treaty on European Unity, also known as the Maastricht Treaty
1995	Austria, Finland and Sweden join
1997	Treaty of Amsterdam
2002	Euro banknotes and coins become the official currency of the EU and are adopted by 12 states
2004	10 new members join: Czech Republic, Cyprus, Estonia, Hungary, Latvia, Lithuania, Malta, Poland, Slovakia and Slovenia
2007	Bulgaria and Romania join
2013	Croatia joins

The EU is currently an independent member of the G20 in addition to those member states who are also members.

KEY CONCEPT 3.3   THE EUROPEAN UNION

The European Union (EU), which began life in 1952 as the European Coal and Steel Community, embraces 28 member states in 2014. The objective of the EU is the maximization of advantages associated with the free movement of goods, finance and people and to capitalize on a large internal European market. In achieving these objectives it is intended to bring the peoples of Europe closer together and operate a single market using a single currency. Landmarks have been the Treaty of Rome (1957), the Single European Act (1987), the Treaty on European Unity (1992), the Treaty of Amsterdam (1997) and the introduction of the euro in 1999. There are still concerns by some member states, notably the UK, about the timing of the introduction of a single currency and its impact on sovereignty and there remain differences in wage rates and standards of living between member states.

While the impetus for the creation of the EU was economic (it was originally known as the European Economic Community), the EU has formally embraced social and legal issues. Social issues pertaining to the workplace have been grouped together under the collective banner of the Social Charter, to which the UK was unable to subscribe in full at the time, the only EU member so to do.

Political changes that took place at the end of the 1980s and into the early 1990s changed the face of European business and, with the reunification of Germany, a former communist state was brought into the EU for the first time. Since then many other former communist states have become members.

In this section on the EU we will examine its objectives, the mechanisms through which those objectives are achieved and focus on specific key issues including competition, agriculture, energy, monetary union and employment.

REFLECTION POINT

What are the key issues arising from the expansion of the EU?

EU objectives and instruments

Objectives of the EU include:

- maximization of the advantages accruing from the free movement of goods, finance and people;
- increase of competition and demand;
- maintenance of stable prices and high levels of employment;
- coordination of the policies of individual governments and their central banks.

Such objectives rest on two sets of related assumptions.

- First, it is assumed that the reduction in trade barriers will lead to increased competition, which will drive more efficient methods of production and result in better quality products at cheaper prices. This in turn will lead to an increase in demand.
- Second, it is assumed that a united Europe will offer considerable economies of scale and eliminate the waste associated with nation states operating independently.

The main instruments through which these objectives are to be achieved are contained within the Treaty of Rome 1957, the Single European Act 1987, the Social Charter and the Treaty of Maastricht 1992, the Treaty on European Unity 1992 and the Treaty of Amsterdam 1997. In general terms, the instruments comprise directives, which are binding but give member states flexibility in operation, and regulations, which are binding and directly applicable.

The EU comprises a number of institutions:

- European Commission based in Brussels is the administrative heart of the EU and carries out most of the work.
- Council of Ministers is made up of the heads of state of member countries, who take it in turns to lead the EU for a specified period.
- European Parliament is made up of elected representatives from the member countries. A nation's representation is proportional to its population.
- European Court of Justice is the supreme European court to which people can appeal if they feel they have been served badly by the justice system in their own country.

A primary objective of the EU is the removal of obstacles to free trade, and hence there are proposals to eliminate frontier controls and work permits and to harmonize both taxation policies and technical standards. The creation of a single European technical standard for car manufacture would, for example, eliminate the need to produce different types of headlamps for the same model of car to meet the various legal requirements in different European countries. The elimination of such differentiation would reduce costs and be likely to lead to increase demand.

The degree to which such instruments have been introduced has varied according to the nature of the proposed change and between member nations. Not all countries have embraced the proposals as readily as others. The UK has failed to agree to the provisions of the Social Charter and opted out of the Social Chapter of the Maastricht agreement (although subsequently agreed to opt in). Particularly contentious issues include agriculture and monetary union. It is to these and other issues we now turn.

EU issues

Businesses have been influenced by a certain harmonization that has taken place in company law, employment law, accounting practice, taxation, and the role of financial institutions. There has been cooperation over policies concerning industrial development, regional aid and environmental protection. In the same way that business interests lobby national governments, attempts are made to influence EU policy. Nonetheless, there would appear to be problems for businesses in dealing with the EU:

- Concerns are expressed about the bureaucracy and protracted decision-making mechanisms of EU institutions.
- As the number of members increases, decision-making becomes more cumbersome. The increase in members from 15 to 27 in 2007 and then to 28 in 2013 is unlikely to improve things.
- There is a conflict of interests between constituent nation states. At the root of this conflict is the issue of sovereignty. The EU will assume powers that formerly belonged only to democratically elected governments of individual nation states.
- Differences exist within the EU between member states. These include differences in geographical size, population, resources, living standards and a range of economic variables that present difficulties in the move to a level playing field. Nonetheless, such convergence is a prerequisite of monetary union. Such issues are likely to be more apparent following the addition of 12 countries, 10 from East Europe in 2007. The additional 12 states have increased the EU population by a fifth but add only around 6 per cent to the GDP. There are fears that many businesses in those countries will be unable to withstand the competitive pressures that membership will bring or that the richer members will have to subsidize these countries to unacceptable levels.

We will illustrate some of the difficulties by focusing on competition policy, agricultural policy, energy policy, monetary union, the eurozone crisis, and workplace issues as part of social and labour policy.

Competition policy The competition policy of the EU has the avowed aims of preventing cartels, of controlling monopolies, especially state-controlled monopolies, and of restricting state aid to certain industries thereby creating unfair competition. Despite such aims there are many cases of protectionism and unfair competition within the EU. One reason for the decline of the British industry lay in the availability of cheaper coal elsewhere and the subsidies offered to producers in Germany.

The complexities of competition policy were illustrated by the case of Ryanair, a cut price airline and Charleroi airport in Belgium. Ryanair used Charleroi because it offered a good deal. The problem was that Charleroi was publicly owned. The EU Commission argued that Ryanair was effectively getting a state subsidy to fund its cheap deals, which was illegal under EU regulations. As a consequence, Ryanair threatened to leave Charleroi with an estimated loss of 200 jobs, apart from the loss of the service to passengers (Osborn, 2003).

Agricultural policy The common agricultural policy (CAP) subsidizes European farmers. This allows EU farmers to over-produce and sell produce below cost price. The subsidy is not unique: US farmers also receive subsidies from Washington. However, it is a contentious issue in terms of cost, its effect on the free market and on the developing world, especially Africa.

- It can be argued that CAP is contrary to the concept of free trade that underpins the EU. Farmers are protected in a way that other industries and occupations are not, for example, in the coal mining industry, where there have been closures and job losses. CAP has also been challenged by the WTO.

- CAP takes about 40 per cent of the EU budget and comprises a considerable tax burden to all in the EU (Stewart, 2005).

- As a result of the subsidies, producers from the developing world cannot compete. Many countries in Africa depend on agricultural exports and lose out to unfair competition. In some cases European produce is exported to Africa and sells at a lower price than local produce.

Any attempt to reform the system is usually met with strong opposition, especially from French farmers, who benefit more than most from CAP.

Energy policy Unlike the agricultural policy, the EU energy policy embodies most of the principles of the EU. There has been a rapid movement to a single European market at least for the 15 member states before 2004. The policy has focused on gas and electricity and aims for an open market in both industrial and domestic supply by the end of 2007. In many countries this has required the reform of their industry involving privatization and the legal separation of transmission (pipelines, cables) and distribution to customers. The EU wants to achieve a market where any purchaser of gas or electricity can buy from the cheapest supplier in any member country and aims to influence transfer prices between member states and influence each country to regulate its own prices. The goal is price reduction across the board.

Monetary union Monetary union had as its initial instrument the European Exchange Rate Mechanism (ERM). This was an attempt to keep the exchange rates of currency between member countries within fixed limits. While the ERM had its detractors, the major objections are usually reserved for the proposals associated with European Monetary Union (EMU) and the creation of a single European currency. Those in favour of EMU see advantages in terms of increased competition and trade, the reduction of transaction costs, increased certainty in planning, the reduction of inflation and the necessity for greater political cooperation. Detractors have pointed to the problems of maintaining comparable interest rates, as seen within the ERM in 1992 and 1993, and say that there would be unequal costs and benefits. For the British government EMU is seen as a loss of sovereignty and hence political control and democratic accountability. For this reason Britain has acted as the chief opponent to full-scale monetary union.

In 1999, the new single currency, the 'euro', was introduced by 11 participants. Denmark, Greece, Sweden and the UK opted out for various reasons, although all initially saw themselves as potential future members and Greece did opt in soon afterwards. By 2014, 18 countries in the EU were members of the single currency group and Denmark, Sweden and the UK remain opted out. At first, the euro was confined to paper transactions, with coins and notes used for the first time in 2002.

The development of the EU has been a reason why trade between member countries has grown much faster than trade with other nations. Its supporters see the euro as a key instrument in strengthening unity between member states and a means to enhance the role of the EU on a world stage.

The claimed advantages of the euro are seen in terms of the following:

- For the consumer it will be easier to shop, because differences in the prices of goods between EU members will become transparent. There is a view that prices will eventually converge. This may be good news for the UK car buyer, given that prices have always been more expensive than in the rest of the EU, but this could result in the loss of UK jobs.

- Currency exchange, with its expensive transaction costs and the uncertainty owing to fluctuations in the exchange rate, will become a thing of the past. This will benefit trade between firms within the EU as well as obviating the need for travellers to change money. Ford's chief executive has argued that the failure of the UK to opt in adds a quarter to the cost of operating in the UK.

- The inevitable strength of the euro and the conditions of membership within the single currency will create greater economic stability and end volatile inflation and interest rates. This will enable the EU to withstand severe fluctuations in the global economy.

- The introduction of the euro is seen as part of a package of measures, which include the reduction in the social security element of wages. This has the intention of bringing down labour costs and enhancing labour flexibility.

The claimed disadvantages of the euro are seen in terms of the following:

- Opponents of a single currency view it not so much as an economic measure, but as a political one; a step on the route to a federal Europe. This appears to be less of a problem for some members than others, the UK being the main speaker for the opposition.

- A single currency is incompatible with the management of a large economy. It reduces the freedom of individual governments to respond to economic changes that may threaten their economy more than that of other EU states. For instance, governments will be unable to use devaluation to increase competitiveness.

The arguments given by the UK government for initial non-participation are based around the notion that the currency will only work given the necessary convergence of economies across Europe in terms of economic structures, business cycles and interest rates. The UK government claimed that, by 1999, the economy had not met the necessary tests of convergence. Supporters of the euro have argued that, at the time of introduction, the UK economy was closer than ever before to the other major economies of Europe, but in the long run, the single currency will be impossible to avoid. It is interesting to note that whereas the EU's own conditions of entry to the EMU were clearly set out in terms of performance measures, the UK objections based on its own tests of entry were highly subjective.

Eurozone crisis This particular problem came to light with announcements from the incoming Greek government that Greek national debts were much larger than had been reported by previous governments. The EU stepped in and working with private sector banks assisted Greece by agreeing to cuts in interest rates and extending the loan periods. Around the same time similar help was given to Ireland and Portugal. By 2011 the problem had widened with Italy and Spain requiring assistance with their debt problems. The involvement of the private sector banks was itself problematic resulting from their poor financial health following the 2007–2008 crisis. The causes of the eurozone crisis were many and varied:

- Banks across Europe were in a weak position as many were undercapitalized following their own difficulties in 2007–2008.

- Private debt was mounting, especially in countries such as Italy and Spain as a result of easy credit in the form of business loans and mortgages.

- Public debt was a particular feature of Greece as a consequence of generous public sector pay and retirement and pension policies.

- In southern Europe especially wages had risen out of proportion to the economic health of those countries. This is in stark contrast to Germany where wage rises had been held at modest levels following agreement between employers and trade unions.

The impact resulted in splits within the EU. Germany took a strong line seeing the growing crisis as leading to the potential failure and break-up of the EU itself. Germany's tough stance was resented by many in Greece, leading to social unrest and opposition to austerity measures involving higher taxes, reductions in both public sector and private sector wages, a worsening of employment conditions and a reduction in social welfare benefits. There was opposition to austerity measures in other countries as well. A further impact was a rise in unemployment. The highest rates were seen in Greece and Spain, when by mid-2013 general unemployment was around 25 per cent in both countries and unemployment among the under 25s was 56 per cent in Spain and 63 per cent in Greece.

Germany led the call for new rules to prevent debt accumulation and further problems. They insisted that borrowing was limited to 0.5 per cent of GDP in each year and should not exceed 3 per cent of GDP overall. Although these were badged as new tough measures they were not far removed from the guideline agreed in the 1992 Maastricht Treaty.

REFLECTION POINT

How did the euro affect the banking crisis of 2008? What might have happened without the euro?

Social and labour policy Social and labour issues were central to the Social Chapter of the Treaty on European Unity, which built on the 1989 Social Charter and dealt with issues relating to wages and workplace conditions. There was an attempt to harmonize practices, not only on wages and conditions, but also on equal opportunities and mechanisms for consultation between management and labour.

The problems of unequal wages and conditions were highlighted by the decision of Hoover in 1993 to move 450 jobs from its factory in Dijon, France, to Cambuslang, Scotland. This was done on the basis that wages and, in particular, associated benefits were up to 30 per cent cheaper in the UK than in parts of the EU. Around the same period, Philips moved 150 jobs from Holland to the UK at Blackburn. Such transfer of labour for cost advantages has been dubbed 'social dumping' and threatens to undermine European harmony.

Elements in social and labour policy are:

- The right to freedom of movement for employment and training.

- The right to equal treatment and a fair wage.

- An improvement in living and working conditions for full and part-time workers.
- The right to social protection for the sick, unemployed and retired.
- The right to join and leave a trade union.
- The right to vocational training.
- A limit on working hours in any week (Working Time Directive).
- A right to be represented at the workplace (Works Council Directive).

REFLECTION POINT

What has been the effect of EU policies on individual firms in member states? Has that result been the same in each country?

CASE 3.1   BUSINESS AND MANAGEMENT IN SINGAPORE

For many years Singapore stood out from the other Asian tigers in terms of the strength of its economy, particularly its GDP per capita, and the economy was relatively resilient in the face of the 1997 East Asian collapse. Table 3.19 shows the Singapore economy at the peak of its success in 1996 in terms of GDP per capita. In 2000, it was the best performing Asian economy with a 9.9 per cent annual growth. The growth of the economy has been associated with a number of interrelated factors, which include geography, culture, the role of the state and the role played by multinational corporations of several countries. This case study will examine these factors as well as the relative decline that has affected Singapore since 2001.

Singapore is a relatively small island of some four and a half million people linked to the Malaysian peninsula by road and rail. Its geographical position made it an important staging post for world shipping. Singapore was established as a trading post by the British in 1819 and expanded rapidly in the 1860s, as a result of increasing trade with China and Japan and the opening of the Suez Canal. The growth was consolidated by the exploitation of rubber and tin in the surrounding regions, with Singapore operating as a vital export channel. This economic expansion led to considerable immigration for a virtually uninhabited island. The majority of immigrants were Chinese. This is reflected in the current ethnic mix of 76 per cent Chinese, 15 per cent

TABLE 3.19	How the Singaporean economy compared in 1996		
	GDP per capita 1996 $US	1996 ranking	1990 ranking
Switzerland	42 350	1	1
Japan	38 120	2	2
Norway	35 710	3	5
Denmark	34 620	4	6
Singapore	32 878	5	17
Germany	30 300	6	7
USA	29 600	7	9
Hong Kong	27 130	11	8
UK	20 900	17	16
South Korea	11 910	24	25

(Continued)

CASE 3.1   (*Continued*)

Malay and 7 per cent Indian. A white, largely expatriate population makes up the remainder. In 1959, Singapore achieved self-government from the British and in 1963 joined the Malaysian Federation. The political alliance with the Malay States was short-lived and Singapore became a fully independent nation state in 1965.

Throughout the 1950s and early 1960s there were a number of problems to be faced. Britain withdrew its bases and hence a source of revenue for the local economy. Relations with Malaysia became problematic. The country had no natural resources and there were insufficient jobs in trade alone to support the population. Its domestic market was small by international standards and the nation faced increasing competition from the growing economies of the region. Politically, at that time, Singapore was far from stable and its businesses were dogged by labour relations problems.

In the mid-1960s a strong government emerged under Lee Kuan Yew and outside help was enlisted. Following the recommendations of a UN task force, Singapore embarked on a policy of labour-intensive manufacturing to establish jobs and to substitute imports. Israel, a relatively new state, surrounded by potentially hostile forces and with few natural resources, was seen as a role model, and several visits were made by leading Singapore politicians. The Singapore government tackled the then regional problem of communism through creating jobs and the establishment of a vigorous public housing scheme. Trade unions were brought into the system of state capitalism by giving them the island's taxi service to manage and by enabling them to run a pension and insurance company. A senior government official became head of the trade union movement. Labour problems disappeared. Considerable investment was made in education, to create a unified system and end the division along racial grounds. Most significantly, the government established the Economic Development Board (EDB) to plan and oversee the nation's economic development.

Following the phase of job creation and import substitution, the EDB launched a campaign to attract overseas investment in the form of export-oriented multinationals. At the same time there was considerable investment in the port, which became one of the largest and most modern in the world and certainly one of the busiest. The policies were so successful in terms of job creation that the problem shifted to one of labour shortages and rising wages. The EDB sought investment that was high-tech, knowledge-based and high in added value. The country soon became a world leader in the computer disk drive industry. More recent policies have focused on establishing Singapore as a regional centre with outward investment in neighbouring countries, particularly Vietnam.

By any economic measure the policies were successful. From 1985 to 1997 the country enjoyed uninterrupted GDP growth averaging at over 8 per cent each year. Unemployment fell to below 2 per cent in 1991 and became steady at less than 3 per cent until 2001. Inflation was kept low at around 3 per cent, falling to less than 2 per cent in 1995. Over the same period, wages rose by around 9 per cent a year. A balance of payments deficit in 1980 of $3.3 million was turned into a surplus of $21.3 million by 1995. Output in manufacturing increased over 10 per cent year-on-year during the 1990s. However, the problems facing the region in 1997 meant that manufacturing output fell by 0.8 per cent and labour cuts were announced by companies such as HP, Philips and Motorola. Nonetheless, the strength of the Singapore economy meant that its problems were less severe than those of its near neighbours.

Three reasons have been given for this remarkable economic growth: cultural explanations, the role of the state and the part played by multinational corporations. FDI has played a role in the economic development of the island, but its attraction has also been government policy.

Singapore shares core cultural values with other Asian tigers. These values include the importance of the family and education; the commitment to hard work; the importance attached to personal savings; perseverance, adaptability and a long-term orientation. The core values originated from Confucianism, which also emphasizes duty and hierarchy, rule by humanity and moral persuasion, meritocracy and the supremacy of ethical standards. In business and economic life, such values are seen in loyalty to the nation's rulers and the support of officialdom, loyalty to the firm by a hard-working and responsible workforce, the importance of family firms, thrift, adaptable entrepreneurs, and a concern for education and self-improvement.

Undoubtedly, in Singapore there is a commitment to the goals of the government that is rare in other countries, although high levels of labour turnover as a result of labour shortages and subsequent spiralling wages suggests that loyalty to the firm can be compromised. The concern for education is evident in a population eager to accumulate qualifications and by a massive state support of schools, polytechnics and universities, as well as training for industry. The people clearly work hard. Singaporeans save a higher proportion of their income than anyone else, assisted largely by the state-run Central Provident Fund (CPF), which, through a combination of deduction from wages and employer contributions, produces savings of up to 38 per cent of wages. The CPF then offers interest on savings, provides finance for home ownership and acts as a retirement pension fund. Withdrawals are also possible to buy blue-chip stock.

Family firms play an important part in the economy and there are many large and powerful Chinese businesses. Some of these businesses are linked to Chinese clans, to which people belong on the basis of their family origins, traced back to a particular village in China. Among the Chinese there is also evidence that people who speak the same Chinese dialect are attracted to specific sectors. For example, Hokkien-speaking people tend to dominate in banking, finance and trade. However, there is also evidence to suggest a weakening of such traditional networks and value systems. Many of the new generation have acquired university education, often overseas, and experiences have been broadened beyond traditional values. In several local firms, family control is being replaced by professional management.

Undoubtedly, the state has helped establish the conditions for long-term economic growth and for controlling the direction and pace of that growth. Its agency, the EDB, has been particularly influential. The state is viewed as being pro-business, establishing pragmatic policies when needed to support business growth. This has been complemented by a substantial investment in education and training, particularly technical training, and in housing and welfare.

Since independence, Singapore has been effectively a one-party state, with control in the hands of the People's Action Party (PAP). The government is noted for its strong social control. Opposition parties do exist but their parliamentary representation is negligible. The November elections of 2001 saw the PAP take 82 of the 84 seats in parliament. State leadership has been highly directive and proactive, particularly in defence, education and training, and the economy. Many Singaporeans work directly for the state and government employment tends to attract the most talented from the population. Its government ministers are the most highly paid in the world, reinforcing a strong desire for stability and incorruptibility. The economic policies embrace the attraction of foreign direct investment and the establishment of government-linked companies. Some of these, like Singapore Airlines, are highly successful and pursue policies that are both aggressive and progressive. As well as the government-linked companies, the state plays a part in local investment through the Development Bank of Singapore. In more recent years economic policy has involved a closer relationship with Malaysia and Indonesia, to broaden both the product and labour market. Much of Singapore industry's unskilled labour travels daily across the causeway linking Singapore to Malaysia and the government has backed offshore manufacturing in both Malaysia and the nearby islands of Indonesia.

For many years Singapore has been an attractive location for multinational investment and many leading firms from the USA, Japan, Germany and the UK have manufacturing operations on the island. More than 3000 foreign firms operate in Singapore, attracted by a number of features. Singapore is viewed as a very safe and relatively attractive posting for expatriate employees. The EDB has led initiatives to improve the social amenities of the city in ways favoured by expatriates. The redevelopment of areas around the river to provide restaurants, bars and entertainment is one such initiative. There are tax incentives and state provision of factory shells and related infrastructure. The Singaporean government has been selective in its dealings with multinationals, favouring high-tech, capital-intensive firms. Such companies have also been attracted by the political stability of the country and the absence of effective opposition either from political parties or from hostile trade unions. The local labour

(Continued)

CASE 3.1 (Continued)

force is generally well educated and well trained, although there are labour shortages and competition for highly-skilled managerial and technical talent is fierce.

The very success of Singapore and the increasing prosperity of its population have been recognized as a problem. There are fears that the country, like Japan, will become too expensive, with a widening gap between rich and poor. The signs are there in the form of escalating salaries and rents for office and factory space. These have pushed up the cost of operating in Singapore. Increasing affluence has brought with it increasing individualism, which poses a threat to traditional values, and, perhaps, social and political stability. Labour shortages, labour mobility and continuous annual wage rises have both increased workloads and resulted in a workforce with high expectations. For some, Singapore is still too dependent upon foreign investment and foreign managerial talent. Moreover, its success has acted as a role model for others in the region with the consequence of increased competition, especially from lower-wage economies, notably China and India.

Such problems were highlighted in 2001. Unemployment rose to 4.5 per cent, the currency weakened against the US dollar and there was a substantial decline in orders in those firms manufacturing microchips and disk drives. In general,

the economy was seen to be too dependent on an increasingly volatile electronics sector. GDP fell and a recession was declared. Fears were expressed that an ageing population would become a strain on public finances as many people had invested their savings in a property market that had fallen substantially. In 2003 estimates for the GDP placed Singapore fourth in the region behind Japan, Australia and Hong Kong and with a global rating that was back at the level of 1990.

For many, the strength of the state and the strength of the national systems will overcome such potential problems. For others the 1997 slowdown and the recession of 2001–02 will act as a catalyst for change.

Questions

1 Identify and assess the role of the state in the economic growth of Singapore.

2 What other factors have influenced economic growth?

3 To what extent are the strategies followed by Singapore a key to the economic growth of other nations?

4 What threats does Singapore face in the early days of the 21st century and what are the possible remedies?

CASE 3.2 CHINA AND THE WTO

China was admitted to the WTO on 11 December 2001. China was one of the original 23 members of GATT in 1948, but withdrew in 1950 after two revolutions, a civil war and the creation of the People's Republic in 1949. China applied for re-admittance in 1986 during the Uruguay round of talks and was given observer status in 1995.

Although not a member of WTO, many foreign goods had been readily available in China for many years, and China emerged during the 1990s as the world's 7th largest exporter. Its status as an exporter and that of having the largest trade surplus with the USA, ahead of Japan, is in part due to the USA opening its doors to Chinese imports while demanding

no reciprocal arrangement. Membership of the WTO will mean that China must open its doors to foreign goods and foreign competition.

China's membership has been especially welcomed by the poorer and developing country members of WTO, accounting for 70 per cent of the total membership. They see a large power, such as China, as a counter to the traditional domination of WTO by the USA, EU, Japan and Canada. Particular issues for the developing countries are:

- The agricultural subsidies given to farmers in the USA and Europe, which work against agricultural exports from poorer countries.

- The expense of patented drugs, in particular those to combat AIDS and other epidemics. Drug companies, invariably from the West, have, through their governments, blocked the sale of cut-price goods to the developing world.

Membership of WTO will bring China a number of potential benefits, but with those benefits will be a number of threats. The benefits and threats are not just economic, but political and social as well.

- While, initially, membership is seen as largely symbolic, it is believed that market reforms, already continuing at a pace, will be locked in. As a consequence, China has moved more quickly towards a free market economy than many had predicted. As can be seen in Tables 3.7 and 3.11 in the text, the structure of the Chinese economy has changed.

- As a consequence of membership, China will have to make a number of legal reforms and many believe that the rule of law will be strengthened in the country.

- There will be an increased flow of goods, information, people and ideas. This will weaken the power of the state over individuals and, together with other economic reforms, will have the inevitable consequence of a move towards a more democratic political structure.

- There will be more privatization and deregulation with the consequence of greater freedom for individual firms.

- WTO membership will lead to still greater inflows of FDI and technology transfer.

- The bureaucracy and government machinery will need to be streamlined with faster and more transparent decision-making. Such streamlining will inevitably mean job losses among officials.

- As well as government workers, those in all sectors of the economy will be threatened as greater efficiency is sought to improve competitiveness. Many jobs in many areas of the economy are currently protected and full employment policies have resulted in chronic overstaffing.

- Currently 800 million people in China depend on agriculture. Western agriculture is more efficient and a reduction in tariffs on imported agricultural produce will threaten the agriculture sector.

- The four largest commercial banks in China have debt problems and will not be able to compete with foreign banks, which gained equal status in 2006.

- The WTO and China have not had a harmonious relationship. Despite the 12 years of membership, the WTO is still dissatisfied with the quality and detail of data that China is providing, most prominently data on the structure of subsidies and tariffs, which are at the heart of the WTO's enforcement activities.

- Chinese compliance with WTO requirements and Chinese pledges have not been prompt. For example, in 2001 China undertook to open up the credit card services market by 2006 but only in 2012 was the first foreign credit card company (Citigroup) allowed to issue its own cards in China without co-branding. As of mid-June 2013, China was involved in 11 disputes before the WTO as a complainant but found itself on the receiving end of 31 complaints. Fourteen of the complaints against China were by the United States and six were made by the European Union. Although China has claimed to be the spokesperson for the developing countries it has also received complaints from Brazil, Mexico and Guatemala.

- Labour disputes, strikes and other domestic conflicts (primarily over pay and labour conditions) threaten to undermine the price advantages of Chinese exports 'from within'.

Questions

1 What are the advantages to China of WTO membership and to what extent has membership contributed to economic change in China? Are other factors more significant?

2 What are the potential threats to China of WTO membership?

3 In an increasingly global economy, what effective role can the WTO play and does membership really mean anything?

SUMMARY

- A number of models can be used to examine and analyse the business environment, including PEST and SWOT. An alternative to these is the Business in Context model.

- A number of measures can be used to measure the economy including GDP, GNP and breakdowns of these by head of population (per capita).

- Analysis of the current global economy reveals the continued dominance of the USA. The fast growth experienced by Japan and then the Asian tigers has receded, but predictions indicate that China will be the largest economy in the world by 2040 and the biggest growth will be experienced by India. These predictions may need to be reassessed in light of economic problems in 2008–09, affecting all nations.

- It is clear that the global economy has changed towards a more liberal model. Former state controlled economies such as China and Russia have introduced liberal measures and in all nations there has been an increase in privatization.

- There are significant differences between market economies. Three major groups can be identified as Anglo-Saxon, social market and Asian. There is some evidence of a shift towards the Anglo-Saxon system, although its benefits have been questioned in light of a global banking and stock market crisis in late 2008.

- Evidence exists both for the impact of business on the economy and vice versa, especially in the areas of overseas investment and economic change.

- The state is defined as the government, civil service, judiciary, armed forces and the police.

- The state operates differently in different economic systems and is often the defining feature of variations between market economies.

- The state intervenes in the operations of individual firms in a variety of ways presenting those firms with both opportunities and difficulties. The business community acting as a pressure group can exert some influence on state policy and businesses have increased their involvement by giving financial backing to candidates in national elections.

- With globalization comes the growing trend of economic and political integration as seen in the development, polices and issues of the WTO and EU.

DISCUSSION QUESTIONS

1 In what ways can a business influence its immediate economic environment through its R&D, operations, marketing and human resource strategies?

2 Using the illustrations of (a) a mass producer of cars, (b) a university and (c) a small accountancy practice, examine how a firm interacts with its economic environment at the local, national and international level.

3 What are the uses and limitations of a model such as PEST?

4 What conclusions do you draw from Tables 3.3 and 3.4, which draw comparisons between some emerging economies and the established economies of the G6? What are the limitations of such data?

5   Using Table 3.13 as a starting point, obtain up-to-date GDP figures from UNCTAD or the World Bank websites. What changes have occurred and what conclusions do you draw?

6   What do you understand by the term 'liberalization'? Why do you think the global economy has moved in a liberal direction in the past 30 years?

7   Identify the main differences between Anglo-Saxon, social market and Asian models of capitalism. Which would be the most appropriate model for a country such as China to follow?

8   What are the problems and issues facing transitional economies from the perspective of the nation state and individual firms and their employees?

9   In what ways does the state assist and constrain business?

10 Using the illustrations of (a) a mass producer of cars, (b) a university and (c) a small accountancy practice, examine how the management of each of them can attempt to influence state policy and the directions this influence might take.

11 Does the WTO play a useful role in controlling the workings of the global economy?

12 Assess the influence of the EU on businesses in a single nation state. Is the expansion of the EU likely to strengthen or weaken its influence?

FURTHER READING

The changing nature of the interaction of business and its environment means that the best sources of current material are inevitably websites, good newspapers and the more reflective magazines. Useful websites that provide overviews of trends and a wealth of statistics are:

www.unctad.org: the United Nations Conference on Trade and Development.
www.wto.org: the World Trade Organization.
www.worldbank.org: the World Bank

Good introductions and overviews of economic issues with good coverage of issues not covered in this chapter are:

Dasgupta, P. (2007) *Economics: A Very Short Introduction*, Oxford University Press: Oxford.
McAleese, D. (2004) *Economics for Business: Competition, Macro-stability and Globalisation*, 3rd edn, FT Prentice Hall: Harlow.

Reviews of global economic changes can be found in:

Dicken, P. (2011) *Global Shift: Mapping the Changing Contours of the World Economy*, 6th edn, Sage: London.
Wilson, D and Purushothaman, R. (2003) 'Dreaming with BRICs', *Global Economics Paper*, 99, Goldman Sachs: New York.

Coverage of different economic systems and the underlying causes of that diversity are available in:

Dore, R. (2000) *Stock Market Capitalism: Welfare Capitalism: Japan and Germany versus the Anglo-Saxons*, Oxford University Press: Oxford.

Hall, P.A. and Soskice, D. (eds) (2001) *Varieties of Capitalism: The Institutional Foundations of Comparative Advantage*, Oxford University Press: Oxford.

A good overview of the role of the state can be found in:

World Bank (1997) *The State in a Changing World*, World Development Report, Oxford University Press: Oxford.

THE ENVIRONMENT AND BUSINESS: TECHNOLOGY AND LABOUR

4

LEARNING OBJECTIVES At the end of this chapter you should be able to:

- Define technology and its associated concepts and explain its role in organizations.
- Assess the extent to which managers have a choice in the selection and use of technology.
- Assess the significance of technology to strategy and the extent to which technology can contribute to competitive advantage.
- Define and assess the effect of information and communications technology and e-commerce on business.
- Assess the impact of technical change on jobs and people.
- Identify employment trends globally and assess the influence of globalization on labour mobility.
- Define the changing role of trade unions and identify the changing patterns of trade union membership.

INTRODUCTION

In the previous chapter we examined the roles of the economy and the state and how they related to business. In this chapter we continue our examination of the environmental factors in the Business in Context model. We examine the extent to which technology is a given or part of the management decision-making process and explore its contribution to strategy and competitive advantage. We examine the effect of technology in general, but more specifically technology change on organizations, jobs and people. We deal also with changes brought about by developments in information and communications technology, and e-commerce. The labour issues reviewed include an analysis of employment trends, the impact of globalization on labour mobility, and the changing nature of trade unions. Although we examine technology and labour separately, there is an obvious interaction between them. For example, technological change has an impact on the number, type and content of jobs. In this chapter we will examine those points of interaction, as well as looking at other influences on the labour market, including economic and social change.

TECHNOLOGY

Technology is probably one of the most widely used and least precisely defined terms in business. It is, however, something that affects business in all its forms and activities.

The concept has been popularly used to imply some form of process, invariably machinery-based, so we think of assembly lines, computers and cash dispensers. In this way technology represents the application of science and engineering for use in business. However, technology not only refers to the artefacts themselves but also to the way they are used and the theories governing their application. Human knowledge is therefore an essential ingredient of technology.

Technology not only impacts upon business, in many ways it has changed the vocabulary of business. We have already examined in Chapter 2 the relationship of information and communications technology to the development of globalization. We also refer to materials technology, manufacturing technology, packaging technology, transport technology and so on. Technological developments and change have led to the growth of entirely new industries such as biotechnology, which in turn has created new product and process applications in such areas as health care, agriculture, in manufacturing with biodegradable products, and in waste management.

We often distinguish between organizations according to the level of sophistication of the technology they use as in the case of high-tech versus low-tech firms. On a much broader scale we distinguish between societies according to their sum total of knowledge and skills and the application of these for the benefit of that society. This, too, is known as technology. From a business perspective we can therefore speak of technology as the application of available knowledge and skills to create and use materials, processes and products.

KEY CONCEPT 4.1   TECHNOLOGY

Technology is a broad concept referring to the application of available knowledge and skills to create and use materials, processes and products. Technology is often accorded a dominant role in business and is often viewed as determining products, processes, organization structure and the individual's attitude to work. While there are situations where the prevailing technology is undoubtedly influential, it is the product of human endeavour and many managers do have a choice.

We will examine the role of technology in business activities in Chapters 10–14. This section will examine the links between technology and strategy and examine technological change, particularly changes in information and communications technology (ICT), and the way it affects business and people at work. We select ICT because of its far-reaching impact on all types of organization, activities and jobs. However, in examining the relationships between technology and organizations we need to consider the extent to which technology determines strategies, structures and business behaviour or whether other factors are at work.

Technology: determinant or choice?

A classic view of technology is that it exists as an environmental constraint, which becomes the dominant feature of all businesses. Firms operate within certain technological imperatives, which shape not only the products and the processes they use, but the structure of the organization, relations between people, and individual job satisfaction. Galbraith (1972) painted a picture of markets being dominated by technological considerations rather than consumer choice.

Woodward (1965) argued that technology not only determined organization structure, but the relationship between individual departments and the focus of each business. For example:

- In small batch firms (those producing limited production runs of a variety of products, e.g. designer shoes), product development and specialist sales were key issues.

- In mass production organizations (long production runs of standardized products, e.g. car manufacture), fragmentation led to tensions between departments, a source of potential conflict.

- In process organizations (continuous operation performed by a series of technological tasks, e.g. oil refining), once the system had been created, high volume sales became the issue.

Woodward viewed technology as a determinant of both organization structure and of possible strategy options. She has been labelled a contingency theorist. The contingency approach puts forward a view of business whereby activities at the level of the firm result from the interrelationship of variables such as technology, the behaviour of competitors, the role of the state and so on. The end result is supposedly strategic choice for the individual manager following from an analysis of relevant variables. Woodward's view of technology would appear to give the manager no choice at all. Technology is dominant and managers fail to adapt to it at their peril.

We offer two challenges to this view of technology. First, we look briefly at its relationship with organizational size, and second, we view technology as an element of strategic choice.

- The first challenge to the notion of an all-pervasive technology is offered by those who champion size as a more influential variable than technology (e.g. Hickson et al., 1969). Studies such as these conclude that technology may well be an important determinant of the structure and work patterns in smaller plants, but as firms increase in size, it is size itself that becomes the more dominant influence. We examine the variable of size more fully in Chapter 6.

- Technology is believed by some to determine the structure and processes of business, just as the climate and weather determine agriculture. The knowledge, skills, artefacts and processes that make up technology are, unlike the weather, products of the kind of people who operate technological systems. The assembly line is not a technological imperative, but a device created to satisfy the pressures of mass markets and a product of the foresight of entrepreneurs, such as Henry Ford, and the skill of designers who made the process work. Viewed in this way, technology is not a determinant of business but rather a product of the way managers respond to other environmental influences. Furthermore, the kind of technology employed by businesses may be a matter of strategic choice. The application of socio-technical systems analysis offers managers the possibility of changing the prevailing technology to suit the needs of their own particular workforce and the prevailing social situation in which they operate. Increasingly, technology and, more especially, information technology (IT) are used as strategies for competitive advantage.

We may conclude that the relationship between technology and business is very complex. It involves the interrelationship of other variables such as size, management choice, economic and social change, available finance, industrial relations, the intervention of the state and culture. It cannot be reduced to a simple notion of determinism. This is seen in the discussion of News International in Case 4.2. Management wished to introduce computerized photo-composition into its newspaper operations in the UK, USA and Australia. The technology was available and the strategy was clear, yet the speed of the introduction varied in the three countries as a function of government attitude, industrial relations, finance and culture (Marjoribanks, 2000).

REFLECTION POINT

Do managers really have a choice or must they adopt prevailing technologies to remain competitive?

Technology and strategy

Many organizations have a technology strategy. This strategy will be based on decisions such as:

- The selection of the technology to be used and, for example, in the case of IT, the hardware and software systems to be used.
- The extent to which technology is to be standardized throughout the organization.
- Budgets and the extent of centralization versus decentralization of purchasing.
- Authorization of use, including access to equipment and information.
- Strategies for maintenance and replacement.
- Considerations for staff training.
- The extent to which staff members are allowed to use, for example, the Internet, for personal use and the limits management may wish to place upon this.

The kind of strategy identified above tends to focus on internal control mechanisms. However, the key contribution of technology to strategy is that it can be a **source of competitive advantage.** This can operate in a number of ways:

- Technologies have changed the nature of some industries. In banking, the use of ATMs, the possibility of electronic transfers of funds and the availability of online banking have all changed the nature of the industry in many countries. Online booking services have changed the nature of the travel business. Those organizations that are unable to offer the range of services provided by the new technology are less able to compete.
- For many organizations new technologies have reduced costs and made it possible to offer more diverse services with fewer staff.

- Technological developments have led to the creation of new products and processes. In some industries this has enabled some firms to dominate the market, as with Microsoft in computer software and Tetra Pak in food and drinks packaging. Process developments in terms of assembly line manufacture at Ford, just-in-time at Toyota and glass manufacture at Pilkington, provided those companies with considerable advantages over their competitors and, in the case of Pilkington considerable revenues through licence fees. The value of technology in this respect depends upon the intellectual property strategy of the firm and the extent to which such new developments are protected by copyright and patents and the ability of the firm to sustain its competitive advantage over time; Toyota, Microsoft and Tetra Pak have managed this, Pilkington have not.

- The emergence of entirely new technological applications has created new business opportunities, as has been the case in agriculture with the genetically modified breeding of animals and the genetic modification of crops to enhance food production.

- Technology can be a source of core competence, the ability to do something or offer something that competitors cannot, such as the development of the electric car or 24-hour online sales or services. The duration of that advantage will depend on the extent the process can be protected (e.g. by patents) and the ease by which it can be copied.

- In manufacturing, technology, through computerized design and control systems, can offer increased flexibility and speed of response to market demand.

- In service industries technology has provided the opportunity for improved customer service in the form of fast information retrieval or round-the-clock response to customer problems. For many, however, the reality is the depersonalized and less-than-effective call centre.

- E-commerce can lead to wider markets and cheaper products as many have experienced through Amazon.

- The rapid growth of digital and social media technologies has not only transformed communication in organizations and with consumers, it has transformed the marketing function. A fuller account of these technologies is presented in Chapter 12.

Whilst all the above can act as sources of competitive advantage, the complexity of the technology required in some industries such as oil refining, aircraft manufacture and pharmaceuticals can act as a barrier to entry. Costs can also be high acting as a barrier to entry for small firms. In some firms, such as the UK newspaper industry (see Case 4.2) there is considerable resistance to changing to new technology, which acts as an obstacle to competitive advantage.

In addition to technology as a source of competitive advantage, it is also a **source of coordination and control.**

- Through technology the work of departments and of individuals can be linked. In our discussion of globalization in Chapter 2 we referred to globally linked production systems (the global factory and the global supply chain) and technology creating the possibilities for people in different countries to work together in real time.

- A technology strategy can lead to standardization of operation.

- An internal computer network or intranet offers management greater control of the workforce. It allows remote surveillance of computer screens and hence managers can see what an employee is working on (or indeed downloading from the Internet) at any one time.

REFLECTION POINT

Examine an organization with which you are familiar, e.g. university, bank, supermarket, transport company. In what ways does that organization use technology to gain competitive advantage and how does it use it to achieve greater control?

Such use of technology as identified above can result in **changed structures.** The information storage and retrieval capabilities of computers mean that such information is potentially accessible to more people. In some organizations this has removed the need for large numbers of middle managers. In some types of work it has changed the organizational politics by changing the power balance. In manufacturing, the capability of computer-controlled machines has removed the reliance on toolmakers. In general there are fewer restrictions on location, even in service industries, where call centres have removed the need for face-to-face communication with customers.

We will return to many of these issues throughout the book, when we discuss structure in Chapter 6 and in each of the individual chapters on business activities (Chapters 10–14).

Information and communications technology

Information and communications technology (ICT) is the application through computers of miniaturized electronic circuitry to process information.

KEY CONCEPT 4.2   INFORMATION AND COMMUNICATIONS TECHNOLOGY

Information and communications technology (ICT) refers to the convergence of technological development in microelectronics, computing, telecommunications, fibre optics and lasers. This has enhanced quantity, quality and speed of transmission, enabled the development of a globally linked economy and given managers and some workers greater potential flexibility in and control over work operations. Developments in ICT have driven the rapid growth of globalization since 1980.

ICT has changed the way in which, not only business, but social relations are conducted, as the following list shows:

- We now email, text or communicate through social media such as Facebook and Twitter rather than send letters or even make a telephone call.

- Instead of visiting the library, we access information electronically from our desk at work or at home.

- In banking and finance, it has enabled money markets all over the world to be linked with instant access to information and especially market changes. The speed of information flow, the accessibility of that information around the world and the subsequent speed of response were factors in money and stock market falls during the latter part of 1987 and again in 2008 and in the fall of the Asian Tiger economies in 1997.

- In retailing, electronic point-of-sale systems (EPOS) provide instant information on sales trends, cash flows and stock levels. Through the creation of Internet sites such as eBay (see Case 4.1) traditional retailing is being challenged as customers trade with each other.

- In Chapter 12 we see how marketing has been transformed as customers use the Internet to post feedback on products and services.

CASE 4.1   EBAY

eBay is an online trading company that was founded as Auctionweb in 1995 in the USA by a computer programmer and consultant, Pierre Omidyar. The company changed its name to eBay in 1997 and became a public company a year later.

As many Internet companies have struggled to survive, eBay stands out as an overwhelming success in a highly volatile and sensitive market. Despite occasional troughs, its share price rose 500 per cent between 1998 and 2003. A UK survey of the most popular and fastest growing brands in 2004 ranked eBay first, ahead of Google, Nokia and Amazon. By the company's 10th anniversary in 2005 the sales value of goods traded reached US$40 billion, earning the company US$1 billion.

In many companies, a sales to profit ratio of 40 to 1 would be considered a poor return, but eBay is unlike many other companies. The company owns no stock, yet offers a wider range of products than most, if not all, companies. It trades in more than 30 countries yet has no warehouses and has no distribution or delivery costs. eBay operates with low staffing levels and occupies relatively few buildings. It is the ultimate low-cost operation. Until relatively recently, the company has engaged in little promotional activity, yet has become a global brand.

The company has made use of Internet technology, the growth of computer ownership and access and an increased willingness by customers to engage in ecommerce transactions. eBay is essentially a mechanism for bringing together sellers and buyers and in practice the company is operated by its customers. They produce the goods for sale, they make the decisions on price and they are responsible for promotion and distribution. Customers also form the R&D department, for it is they who have been responsible for product development through finding new types of product to sell. Customers may take a leading role, but many analysts believe a key ingredient in the success of the company has been its recruitment of experienced senior managers. In 1998, the chief executive was Meg Whitman, who later became the CEO of Hewlett-Packard. She arrived with a background that included Disney, Proctor & Gamble and Hasbro. In 2004, she was voted the most powerful woman in corporate America by *Fortune* magazine. She was succeeded in 2008 by John Donahoe, who had been running the auctions side of the business and was effectively her deputy. He was still in post in 2014.

The operating mechanisms are simple. A seller places an item for sale on the eBay website. Items are presented to would-be buyers in different categories. Search engines are available to enable potential customers to hunt down items. The item is placed at a fixed price or for a specified period on auction, in which the seller can nominate a reserve price. In an auction, buyers bid against one another up to an appointed deadline. If the reserve price is reached the item is sold to the highest bidder. Buyers also agree to pay postage in addition to the cost of each item. eBay derives its income from this exchange process. A fee is paid by the seller for listing the item. This fee varies with the cost of the item and varies between the countries in which eBay operates. Additional fees are paid for using more than one photograph to display the item and for listing an item under more than one category. Once items are sold, eBay takes a percentage of the fee received. The company is concerned that transactions proceed as smoothly as possible and encourages both buyers and sellers to rate each other at the end of each transaction.

In its early days, eBay's growth was based on a reputation for the selling of collectors' items, particularly niche products. Today, the company still trades in collectibles, but also offers clothes, computers, cars and property. Currently, the top four earners are cars, consumer electronics, clothes and books/CDs/DVDs. Press coverage of eBay however, tends to focus on the illegal or bizarre such as tickets to oversubscribed sporting events and rock concerts, a Volkswagen Golf once owned by the Pope, and the original 'Hollywood' sign.

Whilst the base of eBay's customers has remained the individual seller, there has been considerable expansion in the use of eBay by businesses. The company recognized this and in 2006 launched eBay Express in the USA and Germany. This is a conventional shopping website that allows customers to browse products from a variety of providers. It is estimated that well over 100 000 small firms worldwide trade exclusively on eBay and in the UK, 68 000 small firms obtain at least a quarter of their revenue from eBay.

By 2004, eBay was operating in 30 countries and had acquired leading online trading companies such as Alan-do.de in Germany (now renamed eBay Germany), iBazar in France, Mercado Libre in Latin America and Baazee in India. EBay also had interests

(Continued)

CASE 4.1   (Continued)

in China, Korea, Japan and Australasia as well as most European countries. Like many companies, eBay had fixed its sights on the potential growth of the consumer markets in India and China. The USA was still the biggest market but by 2004, 42 per cent of its revenue came from other countries, with the UK and Germany taking the lead.

In the past few years, eBay has expanded its operations into a range of related products. In 2002, eBay acquired PayPal, a company offering a secure online payment facility to anyone with an email account. PayPal had become the preferred channel for many eBay customers and earned 60 per cent of its revenue from eBay transactions. In addition to revenues received when items are bought, a further commission is paid on any PayPal transaction. In 2005, eBay acquired Gumtree, a jobs and accommodation website, launched initially in London but rapidly expanded to 31 other cities. Classified advertisement sites were also purchased in Spain and Germany as well as Shopping.com, which offers comparative data on products. eBay Express was launched as a fixed-price shopping site, largely to attract a different kind of buyer to eBay. In 2006, the company bought Skype for US$2.6 billion. Through this phone site, Skype software users can obtain free calls. Such ventures into related areas are seen as an important counter to a slowdown in the growth of the core business. In 2006, eBay entered into a joint venture deal with Yahoo and the eBay toolbar was redesigned to feature the Yahoo search engine, which became the exclusive search engine for advertising on eBay. PayPal was also extended across Yahoo.

The company had expanded both internationally and into related areas of activity. Throughout 2007 and early 2008, profit growth was maintained. Yet the new chief executive inherited a number of problems. The core auction business had been slowing down for some years. Skype was an expensive acquisition and had failed to produce the yields expected. The company sold 70 per cent of its share in 2009 for little more than it had paid for the company. Less than two years later Skype was bought by Microsoft for $8.5 billion. The company was facing competition from Amazon and a feeling was emerging that customers preferred fixed price goods rather than auctions. In addition, Louis Vuitton sued eBay for selling fake handbags and perfumes, at a cost to eBay of $US61 million.

The company's response was to change its strategic focus to attract more fixed price sellers.

This sector had grown 60 per cent from 2003–2008 and included a major US online seller, Buy.com. The sector was targeted with the introduction of a new fee structure with discounts for major sellers. eBay was apparently aligning itself with large sellers and not small businesses and individual buyers. A second focus was on the buyers themselves. While buyers were still asked to rate sellers, sellers were no longer allowed to rate buyers. It was felt that this system was seen as threatening and off-putting by buyers and was not used in other forms of seller–buyer exchange.

As a consequence, many individual sellers felt they were being squeezed out of eBay by large organizations and their power over 'unsuitable' buyers had been eroded. A UK Sunday newspaper saw it as:

The end for the online auction – leaving eBay looking less like a car boot sale and more like a shopping mall.

(*Observer,* 10 August, 2008)

Although eBay Express had seemed the way forward for the company, a decision was made to close it down less than two years after its launch. It was much less successful than the company had expected and failed to dent the market leadership of Amazon. The launch of a wide variety of fixed price goods alongside its traditional auction site gave the company a branding problem. eBay also lacked the expertise to source, supply and distribute products as it had no experience as a retailer. The expansion of eBay Express simultaneously in the USA, UK and Germany turned out to be a move too far and too fast.

As a consequence the company retreated to its core auction business. Between 2008 and 2012 revenues increased 65 per cent to US$ 14.1 billion.

Questions

1 What technological and social changes can be identified in this case?

2 What is the basis of eBay's success and continued growth?

3 What problems and issues may pose a threat to eBay?

4 Is the quote at the end of the case a fair assessment of the changes at eBay with a change in chief executive in 2008?

- In manufacturing, computer-controlled machines, robotics, and entire computerized flexible manufacturing systems have greatly enhanced a firm's response to changing market demands and improved product quality. More significantly, it has created the global factory and enabled manufacturing operations to be linked around the world.

- In the service industry we are confronted by automated reply systems and call centres.

- In the office the introduction of word-processing systems originally revolutionized typing and, in many organizations, has led to the elimination of the role of typist altogether, as people type their own letters and reports. Email systems can reduce the amount of paperwork in circulation and organizations have now turned to using social media.

- As we see later, electronic commerce has the potential to change the way we all do business.

REFLECTION POINT

In what ways has your life changed or been made easier by developments in ICT? What changes have you observed in the last few years?

Without doubt, developments in ICT have transformed social relations and business and driven the process of globalization. Castells (1996) sees developments in ICT as a convergence of related technologies and include:

- **Developments in microelectronics.** In particular, microchip technology paved the way for smaller and more powerful personal computers sold at a price that made them accessible to an increasing proportion of the world's population. Developments in chip technology and especially their capacity reduced the need for large mainframe computers.

- **Developments in computing.** In particular there was a convergence of developments in the 1970s and 1980s. In the 1970s Apple launched its first microcomputer based on the development of the microprocessor. In 1981, IBM introduced the term personal computer (PC) with its new product. This was not based on IBM's own technology and was soon cloned by manufacturers around the world leading to an explosion in PC ownership and use. This was facilitated through software developments and the creation of effective operating systems, the most influential of which was written by Microsoft.

- **Developments in broadcasting and telecommunications.** These include the proliferation of satellite television and use of emails, the possibility of videoconferencing and the development of the Internet and social media. Not only has this resulted in dramatic increases in the volume of information and its availability to increasing numbers, but has changed the nature of communication. We can now have 'virtual meetings' with any number of participants around the globe. As we saw in Chapter 2, such developments have made possible the creation of the global factory and global value chain and have led Castells (1996) to refer to the post-1980 era as 'informational capitalism'. For him, the developments in ICT are as significant as those in the industrial revolution of the 18th century.

- **Developments in optoelectronics.** Such developments include fibre optics and laser transmission. Developments in fibre optics have led to the increased carrying capacity of wire-based systems. The creation of broadband systems has enhanced not just capacity but also speed and quality of information delivery. Laser technology has facilitated the use of CDs and DVDs as sources of information and some predict that laser transmission of information will replace cables at some point in the future.

- **Developments in mobile communications technologies.** The more recent key developments in ICT include the widespread use of mobile telephones, the emergence of wireless computer networks and new products such as tablets and the new generation of mobile phone which have crossed the divide between telephone and computer technologies.

At the outset we said that the key development was the convergence of the above technologies. A student from India at a UK university, using her own laptop computer, can pick up emails from the university system when visiting home. She can send an essay to her tutor as an email attachment: an essay that has been researched by remote access to the university's library collection, stored electronically and accessed via the Internet. The software in her computer was installed using CDs and, as a reward for all her hard work, she can use the same laptop to download and play her favourite music or watch her favourite film on DVD. When back at university she communicates regularly with her family in India using an Internet phone system such as Skype or social media such as Facebook.

In business such developments have been made possible as a result of:

- The availability of cheaper and more powerful computers, which have improved productivity, performance and quality.
- Increased global competition, which has necessitated increased efficiency through reduced operating costs and reduced staffing levels and resulted in increased cooperation across borders.
- The creation of new forms of more flexible organization and management structures.

The changes brought about in business offer advantages to different stakeholders:

- For management, there is the possibility of cost reduction and increased competitiveness and profitability and instant response to changes in the operating environment.
- For the workforce, there are opportunities for increased job satisfaction and career development.

  For the customer, there are better-quality goods and services at competitive prices.
- For suppliers there is the opportunity of forging closer longer-term relationships with manufacturers and service providers.

We now focus on two areas; electronic commerce or e-commerce and the relationship between changing technology and jobs. We deal with each in turn.

Electronic commerce

Today's business interests sit on a fault line of the greatest seismic shift since the invention of the printing press ... e-business. We are embarking on a journey of such magnitude that it has the capacity to change the course of our entire social order.

(PricewaterhouseCoopers, 1999, p. 5)

KEY CONCEPT 4.3   E-COMMERCE AND E-BUSINESS

Such approaches connect suppliers and buyers directly through computer-based systems. E-commerce generally relates to trading activity involving information, goods and services. The initial point of contact is electronic although, in the case of goods and services, delivery is often made using more conventional systems. E-business generally refers to a much broader range of activities, incorporating all business activities. It enables the various elements of global firms to work more closely together and can form the basis of much business to business activity. The growth of e-commerce and e-business is directly associated with the development of the Internet and company-wide intranet systems. Doing business electronically reduces the supply chain and hence increases convenience, reduces costs and improves speed of delivery. It is predicted that it will revolutionize business although at present take-up rates are quite low, costs of entry are high and there are unresolved issues related to privacy and security.

Such statements as the PwC's above reflect the hype that surrounded developments in electronic commerce, also known as e-commerce and e-business. While there is no internationally agreed definition of e-commerce, it is generally held to incorporate any exchange of information at any stage in the supply chain. It thus involves suppliers and manufacturers and service providers and firms and their customers.

Commentators such as those at PwC believed that the way we do business will be revolutionized and that it will level the playing field between large and small firms. In this section we will explore the concept of electronic commerce, how it is changing business practices and the issues it raises.

For some companies, electronic commerce is little more than the creation of a website to provide information to customers, while to others it is a means of selling goods and services on an international scale. Essentially, electronic commerce is a transaction involving goods, services and information in which the parties to the transaction do not meet, but interact electronically. Much of that interaction is carried out online. This has led to the growth of Internet companies, such as Amazon, one of the pioneers of electronic retailing. Amazon began selling books, often at much cheaper rates than in shops. Its product range expanded to include DVDs, CDs, cameras and computer equipment, and then to include the Kindle range and downloaded books, clothing, sports goods, health and beauty products and car parts and accessories. In addition to retailing, information can be accessed on websites. Much of the information is free to anyone with the means of access, as with versions of many local, national and international newspapers. Some databases, such as collections of academic journal articles, require a subscription fee, and can be accessed by means of a password.

In the above cases, both the supplier and buyer gain through reduced transaction costs. Retailers are able to shorten the supply chain to the customer, thereby reducing costs, as well as gaining access to a global market. Consumers benefit through reduced prices and access to a range of products globally and those seeking information have access to a much wider range than hitherto, all of which can be accessed from the home or the office.

A large range of goods, from CDs to cars, can be bought in this way, although there are some restrictions and some reluctance to making major purchases such as a car online. E-commerce has enabled home access to personal bank accounts and a full range of banking services. The Internet has made possible ticketless air travel, a system used by most airlines.

TABLE 4.1	Top ten countries for Internet users, 2011		
Ranking	**Country**	**Internet users**	**% of population**
1	China	511 963 000	38.3
2	USA	242 614 880	77.86
3	India	119 749 712	10.07
4	Japan	101 376 528	79.53
5	Brazil	88 917 974	45.0
6	Russian Federation	69 837 538	49.0
7	Germany	67 621 622	83.0
8	France	51 962 632	79.58
9	UK	51 412 657	82.0
10	Nigeria	47 143 356	28.43

An airline seat can be purchased electronically and the customers may now select their own seat online and print off their boarding card. Applications for some university courses can be made over the Internet. Supermarket shopping orders can be placed via a website with guaranteed delivery times.

It is not only shoppers who benefit from enhanced services. Some supermarkets, such as Tesco, use e-commerce as the basis of their sales ordering system with suppliers. As with most supermarkets, items scanned at the check-out provide vital information for stock reordering levels. In the case of Tesco, the information is transferred automatically to a central computer system, which automatically raises orders to suppliers, which are then despatched to the appropriate store. This version of retailing just-in-time (see Chapter 11) eliminates the necessity for Tesco to hold large stock in central warehouses, thereby reducing costs.

While the media focus is on the impact for the general public, the size and value of business-to-business transactions far exceeds the use of e-commerce by the ordinary consumer. Businesses have shown themselves much more willing to use the Internet for transactions than the general public, even in the USA, which has one of the highest proportions of Internet users per head of population in the world. Firms use e-business to deal with both suppliers and customers. The rate of take-up of such methods by businesses would appear to be linked to the level of competition and whether Internet trading is done by competitors. It is a system that has enabled some companies to come from nowhere to be leading players in their field, as in the case of Dabs.com, founded in 1990 and sold to BT by its owner in 2006 when its turnover was approaching £200 million. It is now the UK's largest Internet trader in IT products,

There are, however, barriers to overcome before the 'seismic shift' of PwC's claim can occur.

- A major constraint is one of access to the Internet. As we can see in Tables 4.1 and 4.2 there is considerable variability in the number of Internet users in different countries and those in the population that have access to computers. There may be over 500 million Internet users in China, more than twice the number in the USA, but it is 38 per cent of the Chinese population. Internet use may have grown significantly in Nigeria but it represents only 28 per cent of the population. In India it is around 10 per cent and as Table 4.2 shows the availability of PCs in many African countries is at a very low level.

TABLE 4.2	Personal computers per 100 people in selected countries	
Country	**PCs/100 people**	**Most recent year of available data**
Canada	94.4	2006
Netherlands	90.91	2006
UK	80.23	2006
USA	78.67	2006
Israel	73.0	2004
Hong Kong	69.25	2008
Australia	69.0	2004
France	65.17	2006
South Korea	58.14	2007
Japan	54.0	2004
Romania	19.32	2007
Russian Federation	13.33	2006
Bulgaria	11.01	2008
Sudan	10.71	2006
Greece	9.43	2006
South Africa	8.25	2005
China	5.61	2006
Tanzania	0.91	2005
Mali	0.81	2007
Congo	0.56	2005
Niger Republic	0.08	2005

- Even with access, some consumers are still reluctant to make purchases online using a credit card. Evidence suggests that fraud and fear of potential fraud are problems operating against both the seller and the buyer.

- Many customers prefer more personalized shopping and the opportunity to talk to shop assistants about issues not directly related to the product. A survey by Eisingerich and Kretschmer (2008), while arguing the advantages of e-commerce, found that websites missed opportunities by focusing too heavily on the technical details of products. They feel that successful sites place products in a wider context making associations with a range of potential customer interests and lifestyle information, in an attempt to make them more personalized.

- The costs of setting up an effective e-commerce system are considerable, which poses particular problems for smaller firms.

- Surveys of smaller firms reveal there is often customer pressure behind the decision to use e-commerce. The advantages are identified as improved competitiveness and enhanced service. However most SMEs (small- and medium-size enterprises) when surveyed see it as making a greater contribution to internal communications via the introduction of email systems than they do to attracting new customers (Quayle, 2002; Daniel and Wilson, 2002).

Undoubtedly, privacy and security are important and banking services are at the forefront of developing secure firewall and filtering systems. As well as developments in security systems, e-commerce has led to the creation of laws to protect electronic transactions. Such legal rulings become particularly important where the transactions occur across national borders and hence, across different legal systems. Electronic transactions pose particular problems where there are differences in contract law, consumer protection, sales tax and customs duty. In 1999, the EU began to develop laws to clarify such issues and which country's law would apply in the case of cross-border purchase. Some countries, such as China, Singapore and Saudi Arabia, have used their legal powers as well as firewall and filtering technology to limit access to overseas web-sites. Such censorship is attacked by those who see the Internet as the main instrument for the creation of both a borderless world and the spread of democracy. As with many well-publicized developments in business, the reality is neither as extensive nor as simple as the image. We may stand on the threshold of a revolution, but that revolution is for the most part confined to the developed world. Many African nations lag behind in the computer revolution. We now examine the impact of technology on jobs.

Technology change, jobs and people

Earlier in this chapter we discussed the relationship between technology and strategy. We identi-fied the way technology could improve productivity, quality and cost efficiency across all types of business. In our discussion of information and communications technology we saw that many of these improvements had been brought about through the greater availability of cheaper and more powerful computers and through developments in online communications. In this section we focus on the impact of technology on jobs and on people doing those jobs. There would appear to be three perspectives:

- First, we have the kind of view associated with such writers as Braverman (1974). Technology change, particularly ICT, is seen as a deskilling agent reducing the amount of discretion an individual has over his or her job, at the same time increasing management control over both work process and worker. The thesis associates technology change with job cuts and rising unemployment, and the greatest impact of both deskilling and job losses is felt by skilled manual workers.
- The second perspective offers an optimistic scenario. Technology change is seen as creating opportunities for the workforce in the form of new and different types of jobs with opportunities for existing workers to learn new skills.
- The third perspective is also optimistic, viewing technology as a liberating device, eliminating the need for human labour in repetitive, dangerous or unpleasant tasks and, in some cases, freeing people to engage in socially beneficial work.

The evidence supporting these three perspectives is mixed. We will view the effect on the numbers employed, on the types of jobs involved, and on the content of those jobs.

Technology and job numbers

More pessimistic views on the influence of technology on employment levels emerged in the mid-1990s. Some estimates in the USA suggested that 2 million jobs were lost annually, and, replaced only by part-time or temporary work (Rifkin, 1995). The same author saw job losses in manufacturing and service sectors alike. In the latter, banking experienced branch closures and staff reductions in the face of automatic teller machines, telephone and online banking.

It is clear that there have been job losses in manufacturing resulting from the replacement of jobs by forms of automation. Table 4.3 identifies changes in job numbers over a 20-year

TABLE 4.3	Changing job numbers in the UK 1979–1999		
	Job numbers 1979	**Job numbers 1999**	**% change**
All Jobs	24.3 million	27.3 million	12
Top 10 areas of growth			
Care assistant	103 837	539 407	419
Software engineer	34 009	171 769	405
Management consultant	18 811	81 803	335
Computer management	43 239	178 701	313
Computer analyst	76 038	302 617	298
Education assistant	45 040	173 763	286
Hospital ward assistant	7 460	29 986	262
Entertainment	22 549	73 030	224
Corporate finance managers	37 794	119 812	217
Financial institution management	107 138	322 608	201
Top 10 areas of decline			
Drilling machinists	29 276	1 731	(−94)
Coalminers unskilled	29 782	1 818	(−94)
Coalminers skilled	73 301	5 095	(−93)
Grinding machinists	56 426	8 164	(−86)
Foundry labourers	14 801	2 505	(−83)
Engineering labourers	58 243	12 758	(−78)
Electricity plant workers	36 352	8 009	(−78)
Spinners	16 941	4 173	(−75)
Print workers	48 878	12 162	(−75)
Rail signal workers	13 761	3 571	(−74)

period in the UK based on a study carried out by the Centre for Economic Performance. The table clearly shows changes linked to technology change with the growth of jobs in computing and the loss of jobs in electricity plants, among print workers and rail signal workers. However, reviewing this table, it is difficult to isolate the impact of technology from other factors. Some of the largest rises in job numbers are the result of demographic changes, particularly the ageing population and the need for more care workers. The growth of assistants in education and hospitals reflects a change in organizational policy with less skilled tasks in both those areas being moved from professional teachers and nurses to lower paid workers. The reduction in job numbers in textiles and engineering is both a function of the switch from manufacturing to services and the impact of overseas competition including the movement of jobs overseas. Job losses in the coalmining industry are the result of changes in government policy as we discussed in Chapter 3. We examine further changes in the labour market when we discuss labour issues in the next section.

There are some positive findings regarding technological change in manufacturing Although the initial investment is generally high, many automated systems can reduce overall costs, leading to lower prices and an increase in demand. In this way, some employment levels can be maintained.

In an extensive study across the (then) 12 member states of the EU involving firms in mechanical engineering, electronics, banking, insurance and retail (Gill et al., 1992), they found that new technologies had created jobs. However, they acknowledged that job losses could well be felt in those firms not employing such technology and thus losing competitive edge and market share.

Developments in ICT place fewer restrictions on location. With the capacity to re-route telephone calls, the same job can be done equally well in Mumbai as in Frankfurt or Manchester. In this respect, both BA and Lufthansa have centralized their ticket accounting function in India, taking advantage of cheap labour. RCI, the world's largest company dealing in time-share holiday exchanges, has established its European operations centre in Cork, closing down smaller offices in other countries. Where the job involves telephone sales or telephone information, it matters little where the jobs are located. The same applies to 'call centres', used extensively in service industries. We examined this phenomenon more closely in our discussion of globalization in Chapter 2.

Variation by the type of job

In general, the demand for unskilled labour has fallen while that for skilled labour has risen. Routine, repetitive jobs have been eliminated in both manufacturing and service work and some workers have been empowered through having direct control over processes. Far from causing mass unemployment, this has led to job shortages in some areas, notably in highly skilled and specialized work. While jobs have disappeared, new jobs, particularly in IT and financial services, have emerged. This uneven impact has in some cases led to a transfer of skills from one group of workers to another. In many organizations the numbers of middle and supervisory level managers has been greatly reduced. Goos and Manning (2007) support the view that technology change has resulted in the removal of middle-ranking jobs as computers eliminate both white collar and some skilled manual jobs. They also argue that technology change cannot replace jobs requiring high skill levels, problem analysis and decision-making, nor can it replace poorly paid and low status jobs in restaurants and bar work, where personal contact with customers is essential.

Technology and job content

A popular view is that new technology is replacing 'mass labour' with 'elite labour', emphasizing more creative, knowledge-based work. In manufacturing, automation has enhanced the work environment of jobs such as paint spraying. In the office, the use of computers has reduced the drudgery of typing numerous addresses. Nevertheless, the benefits derived through the introduction of such advanced systems can be offset by the cost in manufacturing, and by the time taken to encode information in the office before such benefits can accrue. There are conflicting findings and views:

- A key debate in terms of job content is that of 'deskilling versus upskilling'. Braverman (1974) argued that technological change was reducing the discretion that individual workers had within their jobs. He called this **technological deskilling**. He also claimed that the change had increased the level of control that management had over employees. He called this **organizational deskilling**.

- The **upskilling** hypothesis argues that the skill level of many jobs has been enhanced by two factors. First, there has been a decline in the need for unskilled and semi-skilled manual work and an increase in the demand for so-called 'knowledge' work. Second, upskilling is seen in the increased demand for training and retraining.

- However, evidence of upskilling is mixed. Contrary to popular belief, there is evidence of greater upskilling of jobs in manual work as opposed to service industry work (Gallie, 1991). Some service industry work, notably in fast food and call centres, comprises highly prescribed operations and/or responses that are reminiscent of semi-skilled work on manufacturing assembly lines.

The main point to be taken from studies is that the introduction of technology should not be viewed deterministically. Its impact is based on many factors, including the nature of the product and service, the type of organization involved, the competitive environment in which it operates, the management strategy employed, and the position taken by trade unions, employees and governments. We may conclude that the direct job losses arising are fewer than originally envisaged and must be viewed in the context of job losses resulting from other causes, such as global competition and government economic policy. However, several points need to be made:

- The introduction of ICT, if not directly causing job losses, changes the nature of employment for most people. Some groups gain while others lose.

- In general, there has been a **polarization** of the workforce. For an educated group in skilled work, their jobs have often been enhanced. For many workers their jobs have been downgraded. We return to the theme of polarization in the next section dealing with labour issues.

- As well as an occupational polarization in most industrial societies, the global organization of production has brought about a **geographical polarization.** Low-skilled, labour-intensive work is located in low-wage economies such as India, China and Indonesia, while higher-skilled work predominates in the advanced industrial nations.

- As a consequence, in terms of job losses, the hardest hit group is the low-skilled male workers in advanced industrial nations.

- While there was an initial transfer of jobs from the manufacturing to the service sector, some areas of the service sector, notably banks, suffered big job losses in the 1990s.

CASE 4.2	NEWS INTERNATIONAL AND WAPPING

For almost a year, every Saturday evening the residents of a fashionable warehouse conversion on the edges of London's docklands were denied free access to their property. The residents' access was blocked by mass picketing resulting from an industrial dispute between News International and its former Fleet Street employees over the printing of newspapers at the company's newly commissioned Wapping plant.

Although what has become known as the Wapping dispute focuses on the events of the 1980s, the seeds of that dispute were laid much earlier and the implications had a significant impact on the size and structure of the newspaper industry. This case focuses on the technology and labour issues of that dispute and looks briefly at what has happened since.

News International is a company controlled by Rupert Murdoch, Australian by birth but with American citizenship. The company was founded by his father in Australia in 1923 and is still essentially family owned and controlled. News International now forms part of a large global business empire controlled by the parent company, News Corporation. The empire has considerable business interests in the UK, USA, Canada, Australia, most of Asia, the Middle East,

(Continued)

CASE 4.2   (Continued)

Central and South America and parts of the former Soviet Union. The News Corporation Annual Report 2011 identified the following revenue streams:

Total revenue	33.4 (US$ billion)
Publishing	8.8
Cable TV	8.0
Filmed entertainment	6.9
Television	4.8
Satellite TV	3.8
Other	1.1

Publishing involves mainly newspapers but also books. During 2010 there were increased revenues from Australia (where there are 150 newspaper titles) and the *Wall Street Journal*, produced in the USA, Europe and Asia. News Corporation has 30 magazine titles and the major book publisher, HarperCollins. In addition it has a controlling interest in major cable and satellite companies in the UK, USA, Germany, Latin America, Australia and Asia, including BSkyB and Star Television. It owns 20th Century Fox Films and the TV company, Fox Broadcasting, as well as control of 12 US TV stations and Network 7 in Australia. An analysis by the BBC news team based on 2009 revenues concluded that the then four titles produced by News International (*Times, Sunday Times, Sun* and *News of the World*) contributed just under 5 per cent of the total revenue stream for 2009.

News International controls two daily newspapers, *The Times* and the *Sun*, and two Sunday newspapers, the *Sunday Times* and the *Sun on Sunday*. The *Sun* and the *Sunday Times* are the best-selling newspapers of their type in Britain and *The Times* is arguably the nation's most famous daily paper. News International also published the *News of the World*, the best selling popular Sunday paper in the UK. Despite its sales the paper was closed in July 2011, following the involvement of its journalists and editors in a phone hacking scandal. The mobile phones of certain celebrities and, in one case, a murdered schoolgirl were accessed illegally by newspaper employees in pursuit of stories.

A little background on the newspaper industry

The technological breakthrough in the newspaper industry was direct input and photocomposition. This enabled the typesetting operation to be carried out by journalists or typists, eliminating the need for traditional print workers. This new method of 'cold-type' printing uses desk-top computers or PCs to input material to be stored on a central computer which also contains programs for page composition. The computer prints off its stories and advertisements on photographic paper, which are then pasted up to form the eventual pages of the newspaper. These are photographed and a negative is produced. The negative is converted into a flexible polymer plate to be clipped to the presses for the printing to commence.

Under this method around 3000 lines a minute could be typeset compared with seven lines per minute using the old technique. The traditional method uses linotype, a method involving the creation of the type from molten lead, sometimes known as the 'hot metal' process. The method is labour intensive and uses old equipment. 'Cold type' has the added advantage that stories and whole pages could be changed and mistakes corrected quickly and cheaply. The system also uses printing presses that are much cheaper and can therefore be replaced when further technical improvements are made. Cold type methods had been used by American newspapers since the early 1960s. In Britain, however, the introduction of new technology had been slow. Even where photocomposition had been introduced the process was not used to its full potential as, under management–union agreements, inputting was still performed by print workers and not journalists or typists.

Murdoch saw the new technology as central to reducing costs and enabling greater productivity across his newspaper empire in Australia and the USA as well as the UK. The only major dispute was in the UK. In Australia, the introduction proceeded at a slower rate but was achieved with some involvement by the unions, with the backing of a pro-union Australian government. In the USA the existing contracts of print workers were bought out at considerable cost. In the UK the situation was different; traditional practices of the print unions were more entrenched, there was a need to expand away from the cramped conditions of Fleet Street in Central London, Murdoch wanted complete management control and the Conservative Government of the day assisted through legal changes to weaken the powers of trades unions.

The printing industry in the UK was one of the most traditional of the craft industries with a long history. The print unions were vigilant in maintaining control over the apprenticeship system, entry to the profession, and over the way the job is done. These traditional craft controls were aided by the rigid enforcement of a union closed shop, where union membership was a necessary condition of employment. Such controls were greatest in Fleet Street where job entry was reserved only for existing members of a recognized trade union (a pre-entry closed shop). The two major unions were the National Graphical Association (NGA), covering the printers themselves, and the Society of Graphical and Allied Trades (SOGAT 1982), covering dispatch, distribution and clerical workers.

In this way the union controlled work allocation and above all, staffing levels for each job. Frequent management complaints concerned over-staffing and the inability to implement changes that would invariably be accompanied by uneconomic staffing requirements. There was considerable resistance to the introduction of new technology, as this would effectively reduce the craft control of the job and make it accessible to those not trained as printers.

The issues of new technology and trade union control over work practices lay at the heart of most major national newspaper disputes around that time. No national paper was immune and in 1985 alone 95.6 million copies were lost to industrial disputes of one type or another.

Despite management's frequent complaints, the situation was largely of their own making. Concessions to trade union control of staffing levels had been made owing to the highly competitive nature of the national newspaper industry, the highly perishable nature of the product, and the need for maximum flexibility, especially when dealing with late changes in news items. Competition was not just for readers, but for more lucrative advertising revenues. Lost production could never be regained and lost distribution could not be sold at a later date. These factors also gave the trade unions considerable strength in wage negotiation and Fleet Street workers were able to achieve higher rates than those earned by other print workers.

It was partly competition that led to Fleet Street management adopting a new approach to the introduction of new technology. The relative cheapness of cold type over hot metal reduced one of the major barriers to entry to newspaper production. The initial challenges came in the provinces with the growth of the 'free newspaper' industry. These are essentially cheaply produced local papers where advertising takes precedence over news items. The income from advertising is such that the newspapers can be distributed free to all householders in a given area. This sharpened competition in the local paper market. The response among some existing local papers was to force through the introduction of new technology. The *Nottingham Evening Post* in the face of union opposition from the NGA simply replaced the print workers.

The real focus was in 1983 with the case of the Messenger group of free local newspapers in south Lancashire and its proprietor Eddie Shah. In expanding his distribution and introducing direct input printing he overcame bitter opposition from the NGA. He was backed in his quest by new laws redefining industrial disputes and imposing greater restrictions on picketing, drawn up by a government intent on curbing the power of the unions. The NGA were fined by the courts and Shah achieved all his objectives.

Competition also came from the expansion of the television news services. The advent of breakfast television posed an even greater threat to an already declining total newspaper readership. The newspaper industry needed new technology to provide a better quality product with clearer newsprint and sharper pictures and an ability to respond quickly to changing news stories.

Events at Wapping

In 1978 land was purchased in Wapping with a view to building a large printing works using the latest technology in newspaper production, and construction began within two years. At that time News International owned just the *Sun* and the *News of the World* and the plant was part of a plan to increase both the output and the size of both newspapers. In 1981, the company purchased both *The Times* and the *Sunday Times*, despite accusations that News International would be

(Continued)

CASE 4.2   (*Continued*)

operating a monopoly against the public interest. Once again there was a desire to increase both the production runs and the size of both newly acquired newspapers. In all cases the size of the newspapers and the quantity of production were restricted by the size of the existing plants around the Fleet Street area of central London and what management saw as uneconomic staffing levels imposed by the trade unions.

Before Murdoch's acquisition *The Times* had attempted to force the new technology issue, but after an 11-month shutdown in 1978 the NGA retained exclusive control over typesetting operations. The completion of the plant at Wapping and the expense involved in interest payments alone gave new urgency to some form of agreement with the print unions. Bill O'Neill, an ex-senior trade unionist in Australia and now part of Murdoch's management team was brought in from the USA to lead negotiations.

News International wanted:

- Legally binding contracts with the unions.
- No strike agreement during the period of the contract.
- No union closed shop.
- Acceptance of management's right to manage.

The unions refused to consider the demands of News International and negotiations to move production of the *Sun* and *News of the World* to Wapping broke down in early 1984. The unions had refused to give way on the issue of staffing levels and demarcation. Murdoch was clearly frustrated by the failure to reach agreement and ensured that the design of the new Wapping print works incorporated protection against the action of pickets. Once built the print works became known as 'Fortress Wapping'.

Murdoch was determined to introduce total management control over staffing levels and achieve total labour flexibility. News International terminated all its existing collective agreements with the unions with the aim of replacing them with a legally binding contract and a no-strike clause, the elimination of the closed shop, and binding arbitration in the case of a dispute. The penalty for breaking the agreement would be instant dismissal for individuals and the right to sue the union for unlimited amounts. Such a strategy was calculated to confront the unions on the issue of job control and, not surprisingly, was rejected

by NGA and SOGAT '82. The two unions insisted that any move to Wapping should be accompanied by no redundancies and the maintenance of existing work practices. As a result Murdoch declared that negotiations were over and gave his print workers six months' notice and no option of jobs at Wapping.

One union, the Electrical, Electronic, Telecommunication and Plumbing Union (EETPU), was prepared to negotiate on the basis of the new proposals, much against the advice of the trade union movement's central body, the TUC. For some time the electricians' union had been keen to expand its membership in new areas and viewed its members as key workers in all workplaces increasingly operating under the demands of new technology. One of those areas was printing, and the union had even gone so far as to provide training for its members in newspaper production.

Electricians were recruited by News International initially to commission the new presses. However, by the end of January 1986 the Wapping plant was producing the four newspaper titles amid much secrecy, using electricians recruited from outside London and transported daily by an organized bus network. This led to considerable recriminations within the trade union movement and calls to expel the EETPU from the TUC. They were eventually expelled at the 1988 TUC Conference, not for activities at News International, but for 'poaching' members from other unions in South Wales. Many journalists on all the titles moved to Wapping for increased salaries but several refused to work under the new arrangements. For their part, the print unions held a secret ballot, and the majority was in favour of strike action. Picket lines were set up outside Wapping and SOGAT attempted to prevent the distribution of the newspapers with the help of the transport workers union (TGWU). Both unions were countered by the law. In the case of the TGWU the threat was sufficient, but SOGAT was fined £25 000 and had its assets frozen by the High Court for persistent attempts to prevent newspaper distribution.

By the following month News International agreed to the involvement of ACAS (the Government's arbitration and conciliation service). The main issue that emerged was that of redundancy payments for those on strike. The company had always maintained that those choosing this course of action forfeited their right to severance pay and had effectively dismissed

CASE 4.2 (Continued)

themselves. The company did offer the unions the old *Sunday Times* printing plant so that they could set up their own newspaper staffed by the displaced workforce. The offer was rejected by the unions, who insisted on the maximum number of workers being taken on at Wapping and generous redundancy payments for the rest. Increasingly, however, the union position was being undermined by events elsewhere. New technology agreements were being reached with unions at the Express and Mirror newspapers and several national newspapers announced their own plans to move to Docklands. In all cases the owners saw the move as an opportunity both to expand and negotiate fresh deals with the trade unions.

By May 1986 the company made what they claimed was a final offer in a bid to end the picketing at Wapping. This comprised a redundancy payment deal totalling £50 million, an opportunity for all workers to apply for vacancies at Wapping as and when they arose, a withdrawal of all legal actions against the unions, and a promise to review the issue of union recognition after a year. The offer was rejected. Picketing was intensified, accompanied by a significant involvement of the police and further legal proceedings to prevent the picketing taking place. As a result of these proceedings SOGAT estimated its losses at £1.5 million. The estimated costs of policing the dispute up to June 1986 were £1 million.

In September, News International made a revised offer of redundancy payments to the dismissed workers, again rejected by the NGA and SOGAT '82. The mounting costs of the dispute forced SOGAT to appeal for funds among its membership nationwide. The appeal was rejected.

The first anniversary of the strike in January 1987 was accompanied by the largest mass picket to date and extremely violent clashes between the police and the pickets. Part of the violence was undoubtedly attributed to a growing frustration among the workers and a realization that the unions could no longer afford to continue. The cost of legal proceedings, the general cost of running the dispute and an impending contempt of court action was too much for the NGA and SOGAT to bear and would have resulted in the elimination of all their assets. By February 1987 both unions, along with the journalists' union, accepted a redundancy package for the dismissed employees and the dispute ended. In all some 4000 staff lost their jobs.

Postscript

- At the time of the Wapping dispute, the UK newspaper industry employed over 30 000 people. By 1990, that number had fallen to less than 15 000. At the same time, newspapers had increased considerably the size of each edition and had introduced colour printing as a standard feature in almost all newspapers. Colour printing had a significant impact on advertising. In 1990 the Wapping plant benefited from a £500 million investment in state-of-the-art printing presses.

- By 2000 newspapers were seen by News Corporation as strategically less significant than developments in film and television. Nonetheless, newspapers still held considerable symbolic importance in the UK, where they have been viewed by successive governments as being able to influence the electorate through their editorial position.

- The EETPU soon lost its favoured status and was de-recognized by News International. The union merged with the Amalgamated Engineering Union (AEU) in 1992 to become the AEEU and is now part of UNITE.

- In early 2008, News International moved its printing from Wapping to a new site in Hertfordshire, just outside the M25 and away from the congestion of London. News International headquarters remained in Wapping. In 2014 the site of the printing works at Wapping was sold to a property developer and work began on demolishing 'Fortress Wapping' to replace it with houses, apartments and a school.

- The phone hacking scandal which led to the closure of the *News of the World* was subject to two UK government investigations. The Leveson Inquiry covered phone hacking within the broader remit of 'culture, practices and ethics of the press'. The second inquiry was conducted by the Culture, Media and Sport Select Committee of the House of Commons and focused specifically on phone hacking and on News International. The report of the Commons Select Committee was particularly critical of News International, highlighting 'serious wrong-doing' at the *News of the World* and criticizing the 'slow and too defensive

(Continued)

CASE 4.2 **(Continued)**

response' of News International. The Committee stated further that Rupert Murdoch was 'not a fit person to exercise stewardship of a major international company'. News International's response was to label the Committee's conclusions as 'unjustified and highly partisan'. Following publication of the report the share price of News Corporation was boosted on the New York Stock Exchange, probably based on the view that the company would be selling off its UK newspapers.

- In 2012, News Corporation was split into two groups, Media and Entertainment as one and Publishing as the other. Rupert Murdoch became Chairman of both but was CEO of only the Media and Entertainment Group.

Questions

1 Identify and assess the relative importance of the factors that led News International to move to Wapping.

2 What does the case tell us about the introduction of new technology in a traditional industry? To what extent is this case typical?

3 Many who lost their jobs at Wapping remain resentful of their treatment at the hands of News International. Have they a case? Do you believe that the management of News International behaved ethically?

4 What conclusions do you draw from the case about industrial relations in the UK in the 1980s and beyond?

LABOUR

Labour interacts with business through the workings of the labour market and through the activities of trade unions. Aspects to consider are the changes in both the level and nature of employment, the impact of globalization and the role played by trade unions in the operation of business. We have noted in Chapters 2 and 3 and earlier in this chapter how the forces of globalization, technological change and changes in both the ideologies and actions of the state have affected labour markets and trade unions. In Chapter 5 we will see how both types of employment and employee relations can be influenced by cultural factors and by regulatory and institutional frameworks in different countries. Managers influence the workings of the labour market through various strategies of recruitment, training and payment. Variations in management strategy also account for the way companies handle issues of employee relations. In this section we will look at employment trends, the impact of globalization on the labour market and the power of trade unions in influencing management decisions. A more detailed discussion of human resource and employee relations strategies may be found in Chapter 13.

Employment trends

In the previous section we focused on job changes related to technological change. We argued that it was difficult to isolate the impact of technological change on jobs from other factors. In this section we explore those factors, starting with changes that have taken place in the economic structures of many countries and the reasons behind them. We then select five related issues: unemployment, flexibility, working hours, labour market polarization and the link between globalization and job mobility.

Changes in the economic structure Jobs in the labour market can be put into one of five groups:

- The primary sector, which includes agriculture and mining.
- The manufacturing sector.

- The construction sector.
- The retailing and distribution sector, which includes wholesalers, shops and garages.
- The service sector, which includes a wide range of activities such as catering, banking, education, health and social care, computing and the professions.

Manufacturing and construction are often grouped together, as are retailing, distribution and services. The latter grouping is referred to as the tertiary sector. The following points will identify the changing trends involving these sectors. Tables 4.4, 4.5 and 4.6 reveal the extent of changes on the nature of employment for six economies. In these tables manufacturing and construction have been placed together as 'industry' and retailing is included as part of 'services'.

The data reveal a number of trends.

TABLE 4.4	Percentage of the workforce engaged in agriculture, 1960–2006		
	1960	*1980*	*2006*
France	22.5	8.7	3.4
Germany	13.8	5.2	2.3
Italy	32.5	14.2	4.3
Japan	29.5	10.1	4.1
UK	4.7	2.6	1.4
USA	8.4	3.6	1.5

TABLE 4.5	Percentage of the workforce engaged in industry, 1960–2006		
	1960	*1980*	*2006*
France	36.9	35.0	22.0
Germany	46.0	42.9	29.0
Italy	33.6	37.0	29.8
Japan	28.5	35.1	27.1
UK	46.1	36.2	21.5
USA	33.4	29.3	19.9

TABLE 4.6	Percentage of the workforce engaged in services, 1960–2006		
	1960	*1980*	*2006*
France	40.7	56.3	74.6
Germany	40.2	51.9	68.8
Italy	34.0	48.8	65.9
Japan	41.9	54.8	68.8
UK	49.2	61.2	77.1
USA	58.1	67.1	78.5

TABLE 4.7	Sector of employment as a percentage of the global workforce 2006
Services	42
Agriculture	36
Industry	22

Shift out of the primary sector Table 4.4 shows a marked decline in the numbers employed in agriculture. This trend is common to all developed countries, although the trend was marked much earlier in the UK and USA. Agriculture still had an important presence in Japan and Italy into the 1980s. However, agriculture is still a major employer in the less developed world. This is reflected in Table 4.7, when all countries are considered, agriculture has only recently been surpassed by the services sector as the main source of employment. The primary sector also includes the mining and extractive industries. In Chapter 3 we noted a marked decline in employment in these industries in the UK, where employment in coalmining fell from over 1 million in 1947 to 6000 in 2005. Similar changes have taken place in the USA and in other parts of Europe.

Shift out of manufacturing Table 4.5 reveals a shift out of manufacturing industry. The process of de-industrialization has led to considerable job losses in the manufacturing sector in most developed countries. The trend has been worldwide with a 10 per cent fall in manufacturing employment across all developed countries between 1970 and 1992. However, over the same period, manufacturing employment in the UK fell from 8.5 million to 4.9 million, over 57 per cent (ILO, 2003). This was partly as a result of government policy, but mainly the effects of global competition and the movement of jobs to cheaper labour economies. Some countries have maintained higher levels of manufacturing employment, notably Japan, but also Germany and Italy. However, in all these countries there has been a major increase in employment in the service sector.

Gains in the service sector As seen in Table 4.6, job gains have been experienced in the tertiary sector of the economy, particularly in the financial sector, catering, the professions and professional services, and health and social care. Among the 10 most developed economies, service employment rose from 127.4 million in 1970 to 216 million in 1994 (ILO, 2003). There is variation within the services sector itself, with job losses in areas such as telecommunications linked to privatization and in the public sector resulting from spending cuts.

We reiterate the point made in our discussion of technology that changes in the levels of employment are the product of a number of factors and are rarely attributed to a single cause.

Unemployment issues The changes in employment patterns by sector as identified above affect rates of unemployment. The main impact has been a rise in long-term unemployment among males, mainly those displaced by job losses in primary industries and in manufacturing. In some cases this may be temporary as displaced workers change jobs or move to other sectors. However, in some cases, as in the coalmining industry, unemployment in specific regions can rise sharply with the creation of social problems.

In most developed economies, unemployment rates have risen with the largest increase in Europe. In 1996, the OECD average was 7.5 per cent, while that of Europe was 10.5 per cent. Within most regions there are variations. In Europe, unemployment rates have fallen in the UK but risen in France, Germany and Spain. Unemployment has also declined in the USA and

TABLE 4.8	Unemployment rates (as a % of working population) in selected countries 1960–2012					
	1960	*1970*	*1980*	*1990*	*2000*	*2012*
France	1.5	2.5	6.5	8.6	9.1	10.3
Germany	1.1	0.5	2.8	5	7.8	6.5
Italy	3.7	3.2	4.4	7	10.2	10.9
Japan	1.7	1.2	2	2.1	4.8	4.4
UK	2.2	3.1	6.9	7.1	5.5	7.8
USA	5.5	4.9	7.1	5.6	4.0	8.2

Canada since 1995, and it remains low for much of the developing world. Rates for most Asian countries in 1996 were less than 3 per cent (ILO, 2003). Table 4.8 shows changing rates of unemployment in six developed economies.

A number of other trends can be identified.

- The International Labour Organization (ILO) concludes unsurprisingly that unemployment is highest in developing countries and particularly in those with little more than primary levels of education. Unemployment is also linked to education in developed countries in that those with the lowest educational qualifications are over-represented amongst the unemployed (ILO, 2007). A later report identifies that since 2008 spells of unemployment have become longer and some dramatic increases have been noted as in the Baltic States, Ireland and Spain (ILO, 2013)

- There has been a rise in female unemployment. This is a consequence of more women entering the labour force and hence registering for employment. It is also a consequence of the introduction of technology in the service industries and the displacement of lower skilled work, which was done mainly by women.

- Noon and Blyton (2007) note that in developed economies there has been an increase in numbers experiencing unemployment at some stage of their lives and a rise in job insecurity, especially with the increase in temporary and part-time work, as noted in the next section.

- The same authors also note that whereas redundancies were traditionally caused by sector changes and recession, the majority of redundancies are the result of cost-cutting exercises by companies (Noon and Blyton, 2007)

- There has been a rise in youth unemployment. In some countries this is severe. In most countries it is three times higher than adult unemployment. In North Africa and the Middle East it is six times higher (ILO, 2013). In 2013 the problem was especially severe in Greece with 63 per cent of under-25s out of work and 56 per cent in Spain. Table 4.9 illustrates this problem in six developed economies.

Flexibility Across all developed countries labour markets have become more flexible both in terms of the nature of the employment contract and the hours worked. There has been an increase in part-time work, fixed-term contracts and self-employment. Figures for the EU show much variation. Part-time working is highest in the Netherlands at 36.5 per cent of all jobs and lowest in Italy with 6.6 per cent (ILO, 2003). Part-time working dominates in the service industry and employs a high proportion of

TABLE 4.9	Unemployment rates (as a % of working population) by age in selected countries 2011		
	*Persons aged 15–19**	*Persons aged 20–24*	*25 and over*
France	29.6	20.6	7.9
Germany	9.9	8.1	5.6
Italy	47.4	26.5	7.0
Japan	9.7	7.7	3.9
UK	31.2	16.5	5.8
USA	24.4	14.6	7.6

*16–19 in US and UK

females. In the UK, 86 per cent of all part-time jobs are occupied by women and similar statistics prevail for Belgium, Germany and Switzerland. In the USA, Canada and Japan, while females still predominate in part-time work, the proportion is not nearly so marked as in Europe (ILO, 2003). The majority of part-time jobs are low paid, low status and offer limited career opportunities. As a consequence, part-time employment is used by employers to achieve their goals of cost reduction. In retailing and in some service work there has been an increase in extended opening and operating hours. Instead of paying premium rates to full-time employees, part-time workers on much lower rates of pay are used to staff the additional hours needed. Some department stores and supermarkets are staffed at weekends by a majority of part-time employees.

As well as part-time work there has been an increase in temporary employment, where spells of work are of a limited duration. This is found more often in Europe than the USA (De Cuyper et al., 2008). Invariably the main reason is the need for flexibility, the need to reduce costs and to meet specific peaks in demand as in retailing at Christmas.

Both part-time and temporary work may be the only forms of employment available for those seeking work. However, some employees prefer the flexibility it gives them to achieve a desired work-life balance or cope with the demands placed on them by parental or carer duties.

Flexibility is also increasing in the patterns of attendance. There might have been a decline in traditional manufacturing shift work, but many service industries have moved to round-the-clock, every day operations. This is particularly the case in some forms of retailing and catering. We also examine flexibility in Chapter 6 and we examine it further in our discussion of working hours.

Hours worked The total amount of working time varies between countries. In excess of 2200 hours a year were worked in Bangladesh, China, the Republic of Korea, Malaysia and Thailand, while fewer than 1600 hours were worked in Belgium, Denmark, France, Germany, the Netherlands and Sweden (ILO, 2007). Even in the EU, which stipulates a maximum of 48 hours per week that employees can be asked to work, there is variation. In France the maximum is 35 hours and many in the UK regularly work longer than 48 hours. The UK has been dubbed a 'long hours culture'. In some occupations, as with many in the finance sector, the EU maximum is willingly ignored as part of the organization culture and as a precursor to career progression. Much of the variation is the product of the move towards greater flexibility. In the UK, Noon and Blyton (2007) note a polarization, with many working in excess of 48 hours and equally many working fewer than 8 hours per week.

Within the total hours we can see variation in patterns of working time, including the amount of overtime and weekend working and the number of holidays. Four trends can be identified:

- In most countries working hours have reduced.
- Men work longer hours than women, almost certainly due to the over-representation of women in part-time work.
- There has been an increase in the numbers of employees working unsocial hours due to the need for greater flexibility, the growth of part-time and temporary work and the extension of shift work into the service sector, as in the case of 24-hour operations in telephone banking, supermarkets and call centres.
- In many countries there has been a shift from a system of working hours covering all to more individualized systems. A number of new patterns have emerged. These include: various forms of flexi-time, often where employers can choose times of attendance at work within certain parameters; compressed hours working, where employees work an increased number of hours over fewer days to create larger blocks of leisure time; and annualized hours where employees gain a guaranteed annual income in return for flexible and variable arrangements, often to allow the organization to deal with variations in demand for products and services.

Despite the wide variation in hours worked, in most countries there has been a marked reduction in working hours in the last 50 years. This is a function of:

- Legal restrictions introduced initially for reasons of health and safety.
- Collective agreements with trade unions to reduce the working week.
- A widespread and growing concern for an improved work–life balance.
- To preserve jobs, as was the case at the Volkswagen plant in Germany in the 1990s.

While some of the changes in working hours offer employees more choice and more freedom, others involve the distribution of working time to fit the needs of the organization. In some cases this has led to a worsening of terms and conditions for employees. This is certainly the case in some organizations where there has been an increase in night and weekend work paid at standard rates rather than higher rates associated with shift work or work during unsocial hours. Such changes have occurred within the context of the decline of trade unions and a reduction in the bargaining power of employees.

Polarization of the labour market We introduced this topic in our discussion of technology earlier in this chapter. Both Castells (1996) and Dore (1997) have noted changes in job allocation associated with the growth of 'graduate calibre' jobs and the raising of the educational entry requirements for jobs across the board. The prediction is that this will lead to a polarization within society. There will be those with good education and scarce skills who will obtain challenging jobs, although global competition and technological change will end the concept of a job for life. However, an increasing proportion of the population will be faced with either poor jobs or unemployment, with little chance of acquiring the skills to move into more challenging work.

Globalization and labour market mobility

While capital flows freely in the electronic circuits of global financial networks, labour is still highly constrained and will be for the foreseeable future, by institutions, culture, borders, police and xenophobia.

(Castells, 1996, p. 232)

The view that globalization has resulted in an increase in the flows of goods, services, capital, ideas and people is challenged if we examine global movements in the workforce. Overall migration figures across the world have been increasing at an annual average rate of just under 2 per cent, although the biggest growth has been within countries in the developing world (ILO, 2003). However, the proportion of the world's workforce operating outside its own country is relatively small. In 1996, it was 1.5 per cent of the total working population, with half of those working in Africa and the Middle East (Castells, 1996).

An explanation of this is that globalization actually leads to a decrease in labour migration as increased flows of FDI and trade create jobs in most developing countries. With globalization it is jobs that move and not people. However, those that do migrate are often well-educated. There is a fear that multinationals have shifted the manufacture of goods and services and hence labour to lower-cost countries, thereby creating increases in unemployment in many countries of the developed world. We presented this argument in more detail in Chapter 2 in our discussion of off-shoring. The IMF argues, however, that globalization contributes to employment growth everywhere, whereas unemployment is a function of government macro-economic and labour market policy (IMF, 2003). Direct links between globalization and labour migration on the one hand and employment levels on the other, are difficult to prove, because of the interaction of so many variables.

The EU represents an interesting case. The free movement of labour is seen to be as important as the free movement of goods and money, yet mobility remains low. In an attempt to encourage greater mobility the European Commission designated 2006 as 'the year of workers' mobility'. While surveys reveal that the freedom to move is ranked highly as a desirable factor amongst Europeans, only around 4 per cent of the EU population work in a different EU country (European Commission, 2006). Data on individual countries is revealing. Table 4.10 shows the proportion of the workforce in Europe's five largest labour markets in 2007 who are citizens of another EU country.

Within the data of Table 4.10, certain nationalities predominate in any one country. The Romanians form the largest group in Spain and Italy, the Portuguese in France, the Polish in the UK and the Italians in Germany, although the largest immigrant workforce in Germany comes from outside the EU, from Turkey.

The European Commission (2006) identified a number of obstacles to mobility. Citizens of 17 new member states since 2004 still required work permits; many citizens have dual career families, which can inhibit mobility; and Europeans traditionally have low mobility. In Europe, the average duration in one job is 10.6 years, whereas for Americans it is 6.7 years. To these reasons there are also the barriers imposed by language.

Despite the relatively low levels of labour mobility across the world, World Bank figures for 2002 revealed that money sent home by migrant workers from developing countries with jobs

TABLE 4.10	Percentage of workers in five EU countries that are citizens of another country in 2007
France	2.2
Germany	4.1
Italy	1.5
Spain	4.3
UK	3.4

in developed countries, was greater than the combined total of government aid, bank loans, IMF and World Bank aid (quoted in *The Observer*, 20 April, 2003). The figures are even more remarkable given that the majority of those workers are among the poorest paid in those countries. India and Mexico received the largest contribution from migrant workers at around US$10 billion each and the Philippines received US$6.5 billion. Such money transfers also accounted for 37 per cent of the GDP of Tonga.

REFLECTION POINT

Did you expect such low levels of mobility in the global labour force? What explanations can you offer?

Attempts have been made to set minimum standards for employment across the world. The International Labour Organization was founded in 1919 as part of the peace treaty that ended the First World War and became an agency of the United Nations in 1946. Its aims are stated as:

The International Labour Organization (ILO) is devoted to advancing opportunities for women and men to obtain decent and productive work in conditions of freedom, equity, security and human dignity.

(www.ilo.org)

The ILO is an advisory body dealing with human rights, working conditions, equality, social security and migrant worker issues. The ILO has been criticized for its inability to enforce such standards, although there is greater evidence of its impact in the development of employment systems and standards in developing countries.

The close links between the growth of international trade, of multinationals and of the networked global economy has meant that labour issues are now a major item on the agenda of the WTO.

Trade unions

Trade unions are formally organized groups of employees with the aims of protecting jobs, the improvement of pay and conditions, and the widening of industrial democracy, among others. Such aims can bring unions into conflict with their employers, a conflict normally resolved by a process known as collective bargaining. We will examine first the changing nature of trade union membership before assessing the power unions can use to influence business decisions.

KEY CONCEPT 4.4   TRADE UNIONS

A trade union is a group of employees who formally come together to achieve mutual goals. Such goals normally include job protection, improving pay and conditions and attempting to influence management decisions.

The membership, power and role of trade unions vary considerably across the world. In the USA, overall membership is low. By 2011 only 6.9 per cent of all US private sector workers were members and 37 per cent were members in the public sector (US Bureau of Statistics, 2011). The Taft-Hartley Act of 1947 in the USA established the 'right to work laws'. The Act gave individual States the option to pass a law prohibiting union membership as a condition of employment. So far 24 US States have passed such laws, the latest being Michigan (a former union stronghold) and Indiana in 2012. In Germany, trade unions are supported by a regulatory framework, that includes the law, relating to co-determination and employee involvement and, historically, have played an important role in decision-making on both national economic and corporate strategic issues. In many parts of Asia, trade unions have little power and are often linked to companies, as in Japan. Union membership also varies by employment sector. In countries such as the UK and the USA, membership is significantly higher in the public sector than the private sector (see Table 4.12).

The reasons for such differences are to be found in history, culture, politics, economics and the role of the state. Table 4.11 uses trade union density as a measure of membership. Density refers to the proportion of workers who are union members. The table shows significant variation between OECD countries, although all show a decline in membership. In Sweden (as with all Scandinavian countries) density is higher than most other countries, but still shows a recent decline. In France and Spain, density is low yet this may not reveal the full picture. In France, unions have a low density, but have a history of activism. Japanese unions have a higher density than those in South Korea, but the more independent Korean unions are more active than the company unions in Japan.

The reasons offered for the decline are many and varied. Several governments have passed laws restricting the action that unions can take as in the UK in the 1980s. More recently a number of US states have withdrawn public sector bargaining rights as part of the austerity measures following the banking crisis of 2008. In many countries there has been a decline of those industries and jobs that have historically been union strongholds such as coalmining and automobile manufacture. In manufacturing many jobs have moved to lower wage economies with little tradition of union membership.

For the remainder of this section we will examine the changes occurring in trade unions in the UK.

TABLE 4.11	Trade union density in selected OECD countries 1965-2011					
	1965	*1975*	*1985*	*1995*	*2001*	*2011**
Australia	47.9	50.1	n/a	32.6	24.3	18.0
Canada	28.1	36.6	32.6	33.8	28.2	28.8
France	19.5	22.2	13.6	9.8	9.6	7.6 (2008)
Germany	32.9	34.6	34.7	29.2	23.5	18.5 (2010)
Italy	25.5	48.0	42.5	38.1	34.8	35.1 (2010)
Japan	35.5	34.5	28.8	24.0	20.9	19.0
South Korea	11.6	15.8	12.4	12.5	11.3	9.7 (2010)
Spain	n/a	n/a	8.9	16.3	13.8	15.9 (2009)
Sweden	66.3	74.5	81.3	83.1	78	67.7
UK	40.3	48.3	46.2	34.1	30.7	25.8
USA	28.2	21.6	17.4	14.3	12.8	11.3

*or most recent figure available

Changes in UK trade unions

Trade union membership has both grown and declined considerably in the UK in the 20th century. The key changes have been:

- Membership fell during the depression years of the late 1920s, but from the 1930s there has been a continuous increase in membership reaching a peak of 52 per cent in the late 1970s. Since then there has been a marked decline. Between 1979 and 1991, trade unions lost 3.7 million members, a quarter of the total (Bird et al., 1993). In each year since 1979 there has been a consecutive fall in total membership. In 2011 union membership in the private sector was 14.2 per cent and in the public sector 56.3 per cent (BIS, 2011). In private sector manufacturing and services only 14 per cent of workplaces had any union members at all (van Wanrooy et al., 2014). Along with the decline in membership there is evidence that collective bargaining has also declined. This is the traditional mechanism used by unions to negotiate wages and conditions with management and many firms are clearly seeking other ways of wage determination. Van Wanrooy et al. (2013, 2014) found that only 16 per cent of employees in the private sector and 44 per cent in the public sector were covered by collective agreements. Emphasis appears to have shifted from collective to individual issues and in the UK, there has been an increase in the use of the courts and tribunals by individuals to pursue grievances with employers rather than using the union. In 1972 there were some 18 000 tribunal cases where action was taken by employees against employers. By 2006 the number had risen to 133 000 (Dix et al., 2008).

- Van Wanrooy et al. (2013, 2014) found that 17 per cent of managers were not in favour of unions and 80 per cent of managers would rather consult directly with employees than have to deal with unions.

- Within the overall decline, some groups have increased their membership levels. The largest increases have occurred among women, part-time workers and those of black and Asian origin. In 2006 a higher proportion of women workers were union members than were male workers. The respective densities were 27.8 per cent for women and 23.5 per cent for men (Grainger and Crowther, 2006).

- Union strongholds have shifted from traditional industries such as coal mining and shipbuilding to the public sector. Table 4.12 shows the differences in membership between private and public sector workers in the UK.

- The number of unions in the UK has declined from 1323 in 1900 to 393 in 1983 and to 275 at the end of 1991. This change is attributable to a mixture of amalgamation and

TABLE 4.12	UK union membership as percentage of the total workforce in the private and public sectors, 1993–2010	
	Private (%)	**Public (%)**
1993	24.0	64.4
2000	18.7	60.0
2006	16.5	58.5
2010	14.2	56.3

structural changes in the economy. De-industrialization has accounted for the loss of a number of specialist unions in manufacturing. For many years the largest union was the public sector union, UNISON, with around 1.3 million members. It was formed through the amalgamation of three unions, the National Association of Local Government Officers (NALGO), the National Union of Public Employees (NUPE) and the Confederation of Health Service Employees (COHSE). This has recently been overtaken by UNITE with 1.5 million members through an amalgamation of the Transport and General Workers Union (TGWU) with Amicus, itself the product of several mergers including the AEEU. For many unions, amalgamation has been the only way to survive and continue offering services to the membership.

- Trade unions are failing to secure members in many new areas of employment. They are also failing to attract young people. Almost half the union members are aged 35–49, while membership among the 16–24-year-olds is only 5.4 per cent (Grainger and Crowther, 2006).

Union growth and decline has mirrored economic, political and social changes. The reasons for the decline in membership of UK unions are the same as those given earlier. Two other developments may be noted. First, the influence of unions has been further weakened by the removal of unions from the political arena and from the development of national economic policy. Second, following the pattern set by US and Japanese multinationals, it is not unusual to find firms with no trade union representing the workforce.

Trade union power

Trade unions do have influence. For example, wage rates in general are higher in unionized firms than in non-unionized firms in the same industry. A 2006 survey revealed that the average hourly rate for union members was £12.43 while that for non-union members was £10.66 (Grainger and Crowther, 2006). Some groups, such as the Fleet Street print workers (see Case 4.2), were able to resist technical change in their industry for many years. The union supporter would doubtless claim that trade unions act as an important check and balance in management decision-making, preventing management from acting unreasonably, and improving the quality of the decisions made. However, the global decline in union membership, the decline in collective bargaining and the failure to attract younger members raises questions about the future effectiveness of trade unions.

SUMMARY

- Technology is viewed as both a determinant and as a product of business innovation and management choice.

- Most organizations have a technology strategy that focuses on internal controls, yet the key issue would appear to be the use of technology to gain competitive advantage through improvements in productivity, quality and cost reduction.

- Both ICT and e-commerce have transformed businesses as well as having an effect on people at work and on those who use business products and services. The impact of e-commerce has been greatest in business-to-business transactions.

- Technology changes job numbers and on job content, although the evidence is mixed, showing both job gains as well as losses and examples of both up-skilling and de-skilling.

SUMMARY (*Continued*)

- There has been a shift out of primary and industrial work to the service sector and generally there is a demand for increased levels of flexibility.
- Levels of unemployment and the total number of hours people work vary between countries and have changed over time. The effect of unemployment and changing hours of work on those affected has also varied between countries and at different times.
- Globalization has had an influence on the movement of jobs around the world but labour mobility in terms of people moving country remains very low.
- Trade unions have performed a useful role for members in terms of job protection and in establishing fair wages and conditions. However, trade union membership and union influence have declined in most countries.

DISCUSSION QUESTIONS

1 To what extent is technology a determinant or a product of management innovation and choice?

2 In what ways can technology be used to gain competitive advantage?

3 Identify the various types of change that are likely to occur from the introduction of business systems based around ICT. What opportunities and threats exist for management and the workforce? What problems will be created and how may they be overcome?

4 Assess the opportunities and constraints associated with e-commerce and e-business for a) the firm and b) customers.

5 Examine Tables 4.1 and 4.2. What conclusions do you draw?

6 Using Table 4.3 what conclusions do you draw from research on the impact of changing technology on job numbers and job content?

7 Examine employment trends in the global labour market over the past 20 years. What have been the drivers of change?

8 Examine Table 4.10 and the related comments made in the text. What conclusions do you draw about labour mobility in the EU?

9 Starting with Tables 4.11 and 4.12, assess the changes that have occurred in trade union membership over the past 30 years. What lies behind the data?

FURTHER READING

Useful accounts of technological change can be found in:

Castells, M. (1996) *The Rise of the Network Society*, Blackwell: Oxford.
Noon, M. and Blyton, P. (2007) *The Realities of Work*, 3rd edn, Palgrave: London.

A good review of global trends in the labour market is presented in:

ILO (2003) *Labour Market Trends and Globalization's Impact on Them*, International Labour Office: Geneva.
ILO (2013) *Key Indicators of the Labour Market*, 7th edn, International Labour Office: Geneva.
Rubery, J. and Grimshaw, D. (2003) *The Organization of Employment: An International Perspective*, Palgrave Macmillan: Basingstoke.

Specific data on UK changes in employment relations are in:

Grainger, H. and Crowther, M. (2006) *Trade Union Membership*, DTI: London.
van Wanrooy, B., Bewley, H., Bryson, A., Forth, J., Freeth, S., Stokes, L. and Wood, S. (2013). *Employment Relations in the Shadow of Recession: Findings from the 2011 Workplace Relations Study*. Palgrave Macmillan: London.

Useful websites include:

http://ec.europa.eu/eurostat: European Union statistics. www.ilo.org: the International Labour Organization.

CULTURAL AND INSTITUTIONAL FRAMEWORKS

5

made and influence business structures and behaviour.

In Chapter 3 in our discussion of the economy and the state we argued that economic and political structures and ideologies vary in different countries of the world and that the policies which business.... The....

LEARNING OBJECTIVES At the end of this chapter, you should be able to:

- Define culture and explain its different forms.
- Assess the relative effect of convergence and both cultural and institutional diversity on business practices and their relevance to the modern manager.
- Assess the links between convergence and globalization.
- Critically assess the contribution of Geert Hofstede and other writers to an understanding of culture and business.
- Assess the value of culture in explaining business behaviour.
- Explain institutional and regulatory differences that occur between nation states and identify their impact on business.
- Explain the various arguments related to the shift towards Anglo-Saxon systems.
- Assess the relative importance of convergence, and cultural and institutional diversity to the growth and decline of the Japanese economy.

INTRODUCTION

In the previous two chapters we have examined four aspects of the business environment. These were the economy, the state, technology and labour. In this chapter we focus on the fifth variable in our Business in Context model, culture and differences in regulatory and institutional frameworks. The use of institutional frameworks to explain differences in how business operates in different countries has grown in recent years. The notion of 'institutional' in this context covers a number of issues, including the operation of banking systems, stock market systems, educational systems, how the economy is managed by governments and the kind of regulations, legal and otherwise that affect the conduct of business. As well as distinguishing between state-controlled, free market and transitional economic systems, the institutional approach has been used to distinguish between arrangements in different free market countries. This is sometimes referred to as the 'varieties of capitalism' approach (Hall and Soskice, 2001). In Chapter 3 we introduced Anglo-Saxon, social market and Asian economic systems. These are examples of how institutional frameworks may be classified. Institutional frameworks have been used to challenge cultural explanations but have also emerged as explanatory frameworks in their own right.

In Chapter 2 we noted how globalization was changing cultures around the world. At a superficial level we are exposed to the same television programmes, films and music and our news is presented to us through media, controlled by a small number of large firms. At a more fundamental level we noted shifts in basic values. There is a tendency for people around the world to become more universalistic (guided by rules rather than relationships) and more individualistic. One interpretation is that cultures are converging. In the same chapter we noted the growth of the multinational firm and, through its operations, the increase in technology transfer and the transfer of business practices leading to a similarity in business operations in different parts of the world. Another view is that people in different parts of the world hold different values, which have a differential impact on the way business decisions are made and influence business strategies, structures and behaviour.

In Chapter 3 in our discussion of the economy and the state we argued that economic and political structures and ideologies vary in different parts of the world and that this influences how businesses operate. The economic, political and social fabrics of a nation have an influence on the institutions and the regulations operating in any one country. We refer to this as the institutional framework, which determines, for example, how stock markets operate, the extent to which jobs are protected and the relationship between the firms and banks, and the firm and its suppliers. As with culture, some see this institutional framework as a source of diversity, while some see convergence as with the spreading influence of an Anglo-Saxon approach typified by the USA and the UK.

This chapter will review these themes and issues and examine the relationship between business and culture and the relationship between business and the institutional framework within which it operates. Our discussion will be based around a theoretical model that examines the claims for both convergence and diversity. We will examine the theoretical basis and evidence for both positions looking at both culture and institutional frameworks. We will then apply our theoretical model to an examination of business operations and behaviour in post-war Japan. The closing case study looks at the contribution of differences in culture and institutional frameworks between the USA and Germany to the failure of Wal-Mart in the German market.

THEORETICAL OVERVIEW

The conceptual model identified in Figure 5.1. is influenced by Koen (2005). In her theoretical model she differentiates between universalistic theories which emphasize convergence, and particularistic theories which emphasize diversity. We used these concepts in Chapter 2 as illustrations of one aspect of cultural convergence as a consequence of globalization. In this chapter, to avoid any confusion of terminologies, we will use the broad headings of convergence and diversity.

FIGURE 5.1	Convergence-diversity model

Convergence

- As a product of globalization.
- As a result of the transfer of productive technology.
- As a result of the activities of multinational companies through the creation of global product markets, the transfer of technology, know-how and best practice.

Diversity

- Resulting from different paths of historical development. This is sometimes referred to as path dependency.
- As a product of different cultures.
- As a product of different institutional frameworks.

The contending views of convergence versus cultural diversity are sometimes referred to as the 'culture-free' versus the 'culture-specific' debate. A culture-free perspective suggests that culture has less influence over business practices and ideas than, for example, technology and economics. Culture-free advocates argue that practices and ideas across the world are converging and that businesses can borrow ideas from their counterparts in other nations. A culture-specific perspective suggests that business practices and ideas are rooted in specific cultures and that transference is only possible between nations displaying similar cultural characteristics. In our case we are reviewing not only the evidence for cultural diversity but also for institutional and regulatory diversity as well.

In the following sections we examine briefly the main points of the debate between convergence and diversity and attempt to draw some conclusions. In order we examine convergence, culture and institutional frameworks. It is important to note at the outset that convergence and diversity are not alternative models. We can find plenty of evidence of both convergence *and* diversity in businesses in all societies.

CONVERGENCE

The convergence hypothesis argues that businesses in the same sector in all countries are converging on similar types of technology, strategies, products and forms of business organization. Figure 5.1 represents convergence as a product of globalization, multinational companies and productive technology.

In our discussion of **globalization** in Chapter 2, we outlined the 'globalist' perspective, which proposed the benefits of globalization and convergence in terms of:

- Assisting developing nations to catch up, including improvements not just in economic prosperity but also in literacy, numeracy and health.
- An increase in the exchange of knowledge and ideas through developments in communications, particularly electronic communications and in travel. This has influenced the speed of convergence.

- The availability of a wider range of products on a global scale.
- Cooperation and coordination between nations via regional bodies and supranational organizations.
- The above assumes greater understanding between peoples and is in part due to the convergence of some cultural values notably universalism (a focus on rules such as contractual arrangements rather than building personal relationships as a means of doing business) and individualism rather than collectivism.

Many of the advantages perceived by the globalists have been achieved through the work of **multinationals.** These have been active in the development of global products and the creation of global markets, the transfer of technology between nations and the transfer of management know-how and the dissemination of best practice. The notion of best practice assumes that management problems are universal and that effective solutions exist that can be applied in different national contexts.

The argument for convergence based on **productive technology,** which refers to the nature of products and the way they are made, owes much to the work of Harbison and Myers (1959) and Kerr et al. (1973). They saw that the main imperative of all nations was efficient production and the key elements were developments in science and technology that were available to all. Businesses in all nations, faced with the same problems, adopted the same solutions. Productive technology was the key but was also linked to increasing size, increasing specialization and formalization, the development of similar systems of authority, occupational types and structures and the adoption of similar systems of education and training. To Kerr and his colleagues, the ultimate development was that 'industrialism', a form of democratic system based around industrialization. This would transcend differences formerly ascribed to culture and political economy. They predicted an end to the (then) ideological differences between the free-market western countries and the state-controlled system of the (then) Soviet Union.

Support for this approach may be found in the universality of similar forms of productive technology. A visitor to the Ford car plant at Niehl in Cologne, Germany will find many features in common with a General Motors car plant in the USA, a Renault factory in France, a Volkswagen operation in Germany, a Toyota plant in Japan, and the Proton factory in Malaysia. Such features include a common technology, similar types of organization structure, individuals with similar skills and job titles, and work being carried out in much the same way. In Chapter 11 we will explore how a system of manufacture known as lean production, developed by Toyota in Japan, has been adopted by different firms, not just manufacturing industry but the service sector as well.

Not everyone subscribes to the view of convergence based on productive technology. Hickson et al. (1969) argue that organization size is a more significant variable leading to both strategic and structural convergence.

KEY CONCEPT 5.1   CONVERGENCE

The concept of convergence has been applied to nation states as well as to business practices. Those who believe that globalization is taking place argue that there is evidence that the countries of the world are coming together economically, politically and culturally. In business there is a belief that firms in the same sector in all countries are converging on similar types of technology, strategies, products and forms of business organization. The drivers of convergence are technology transfer and the activities of multinational firms.

Implications of convergence for managers

For the manager, the implications of convergence are threefold:

- First, it enables manufacturing and services to take place on a global scale through the creation of global technologies, global practices and global products. This creates economies of scale to reduce costs and, in manufacturing, makes possible the global factory and globally integrated supply chains. We have discussed the twin concepts of the global factory and the global supply chain in Chapter 2.

- Second, managers and other staff of multinational companies can be moved around the firm's global operations and find themselves instantly at home with the operating systems.

- Third, ideas and techniques developed in one cultural or national setting may be transferred to another and used effectively. Furthermore, developing nations are able to learn from those more advanced countries and thus benefit from the mistakes of others. As Japan learned effectively from the UK, USA and Germany back in the 1860s to move rapidly from an agrarian to an industrial economy, so western firms in the 1970s and 1980s adopted methods successful in Japan. Belief in the transferability of techniques has led management to turn elsewhere for solutions to problems such as organization structures, new market entry, product and process design, controlling labour and cost reduction.

REFLECTION POINT

Examine a business with which you are familiar. What elements of that business and its operations can you find in similar businesses around the world? What differences might you expect to find?

The limits of convergence

The following two illustrations challenge the concept of convergence.

In the late 1980s, management at the (now closed) UK Ford car assembly plant in Dagenham wished to reduce the average time for resetting the car body presses and turned to international comparisons for assistance in tackling the problem. The time taken to change the set-up of metal presses at the beginning of the production process is a key element in the overall efficiency of that process. Such changeovers are frequently necessary given the large number and variety of metal parts in a car and delays at this stage hold back the entire process. It was found that Ford workers at the Genk factory in Belgium (also now planned to close in 2014) could, using the same machines and technology, achieve the changeover in approximately half the time of the Dagenham workers. As a result, a massive training exercise was undertaken and every member of the line-setting teams (those responsible for setting the presses) at Dagenham was sent to observe the Belgian operation. Lessons were learnt and the time was improved in the UK. However, the improvements did not match the time taken by the Belgian workers, which suggested that there were other factors accounting for the difference in the set-up times in the two countries. The differences could be the result of education and training or the influence of the trade unions. They could also be a product of differences in worker attitude and culture.

The Tower Records store in Kuala Lumpur, Malaysia, used to be located opposite an Islamic girls' high school. Pupils from the school could often be seen during their lunch break or after school in the store listening to the latest CDs or watching the latest music DVDs of western popular music. Young people in Japan have developed similar musical tastes and slavishly copy the casual dress sense of US teenagers. A western observer may be tempted to draw the superficial conclusion that, among young people at any rate, cultures are converging. While this may be true in terms of musical taste and dress preference among teenagers, there exists considerable diversity in underlying core values. An Islamic Malaysian girl and a Japanese boy may have some things in common with their US counterparts, but there are large cultural differences as well.

The above illustrations suggest that convergence and, in the case of Ford, the transfer of best practice, may be limited by cultural diversity. In Chapter 2 we challenged the notion of convergence through globalization by examining the views of the anti-globalists and the sceptics. Both perspectives argued that economic convergence was limited and that the gap between rich and poor nations was widening. The view of Kerr et al. (1973) was of convergence based around productive technologies and democratic systems. To some, their prophecy has been validated by the collapse of the Soviet Union and the shift in former state-controlled countries to free market capitalism. Others criticize their work as anti-Soviet Cold War propaganda; a claim for the superiority of US values.

Ultimately, we may question convergence on two points. First, what is converging? Is it culture, consumer behaviour, productive technology, management style, economic systems, or all of these? Second, is this convergence an amalgamation of different systems, practices and styles or are we converging on a dominant influence? For example, the analysis of globalization by Scholte (2005) identified a convergence on western values.

We now turn to explore explanations based on diversity.

APPROACHES BASED ON DIVERSITY

We have argued that the model based on convergence-diversity is not a model of alternatives and that both convergence and diversity can be identified in business practices. There is clear convergence in the nature and use of some technologies such as our use of computers and in manufacturing processes. However, as we saw in Chapter 4 and noted the low ownership figures for personal computers in Africa, our assumptions can be challenged.

There is evidence of diversity that is a product of culture, economic and political systems, individual variations in income, wealth, education and skills and historical differences. Historical differences have resulted in different paths of development. For example, we can see differences in the economic liberalization and subsequent economic growth patterns of transitional economies due in part to their different histories and historical links with other countries. In this way, Hungary, with its closer connections to Western Europe and its pre-1945 free market system can be contrasted with the Russian Federation, a state-controlled economy since 1917. In another example, Japan with its relatively late industrialization has developed a different approach to that found in the USA.

We examine these aspects of diversity by focusing first on cultural diversity and second by examining diversity that is a product of economic and political systems, often referred to as an institutional approach.

CULTURE

Management interest in culture would appear to stem from a growth in cross-cultural research in the 1960s and 1970s including the influential work of Geert Hofstede, published in the 1980s but based on earlier work; and from the idea that managers can make comparisons with the practices in other countries to solve problems. For example, there has been considerable interest in the 1970s and beyond in Japanese management practices following the post-war growth of the Japanese economy. Cultural differences were also used to explain differences in the competitiveness and economic growth of nations, including that of Japan and differences in management strategies and employment practices.

However, the focus of these problems has changed over time. Multinationals were originally concerned with preparing employees for international postings to avoid the problems associated with 'culture shock'. With the growth and geographical expansion of multinationals and the development of new forms of organization, such as joint ventures, the emphasis moved to solving the problem of managing cultural differences and cross-cultural teams. More recently, the emphasis has shifted to harnessing the diversity of cross-cultural teams to create a learning environment and synergy to develop improved solutions to problems (Holden, 2002).

In this section we will attempt to define culture and then examine the contribution of writers in the field.

Defining culture

Culture has been defined by many writers. We offer three quotations that attempt to define culture. The first is from the famous anthropologist, Margaret Mead, the second from the influential writer on the culture and business, Geert Hofstede, and the third is a comprehensive definition used by the ongoing GLOBE project.

Culture is a body of learned behaviour, a collection of beliefs, habits and traditions, shared by a group of people and successively learned by people who enter society.

(Mead, 1951)

Culture is the collective programming of the mind, which distinguishes the members of one group or category of people from another.

(Hofstede, 1994)

Shared motives, values, beliefs, identities and interpretations or meanings of significant events that result from common experiences of members of collectives and are transmitted across generations.

(Javidan and House, 2001, p. 293)

Schein (1992) views culture as evolving over time as the product of adapting to the environment and as a way of managing group relationships. As a result of this adaptation and attempts to manage relationships, there has developed in each society a set of beliefs and values (identifying what is desirable and what is undesirable) and a set of both formal and informal practices to support the beliefs and values. Schein's approach applied to both nations and organizations and influenced greatly members of GLOBE project team, whose findings are discussed later.

KEY CONCEPT 5.2   CULTURE

Culture represents all human activity that is socially, as opposed to genetically, transmitted. It includes norms, values and beliefs that manifest themselves in behaviour, practices and institutions. Culture pervades all areas of business life. Interest in culture and business has developed with the growth of cross border trade and investment and with the expansion of multinationals and the need to deal with a multicultural work force. A particular interest is the extent to which we can learn from the business experiences of other cultures and transplant ideas developed by one culture and use them in a different cultural setting.

Culture comprises ideas through which we perceive and interpret the world, symbols we use to communicate these ideas, and institutions, which enable individuals to become members of society and satisfy their needs. Several writers have used the analogy that culture is like an onion with several layers:

- At its most visible it represents those artefacts, goods and institutions that most readily distinguish one culture from another, such as architecture, food, ceremonies, language, and the different emphasis placed by different cultures on aspects of the educational system.

- At a deeper level it comprises our notions of 'right' and 'wrong', 'good' and 'bad', 'desirable' and 'undesirable'. These notions form the basis of our values, norms and beliefs. Many problems associated with the relationships between people of different cultures stem from variations in values, norms and beliefs.

- At its deepest level, however, culture comprises a set of basic assumptions that operate automatically to enable groups of people to solve the problems of daily life without thinking about them. In this way, culture is that which causes one group of people to act collectively in a way that is different from another group of people.

Culture is a complex subject and interacts with business in three ways. First, our socialization, the influences which shape our behaviour in a particular social setting, will determine our individual orientations to work. Second, we tend to see organizations as societies in microcosm with their own specific cultures and ways of transmitting these cultures to their members. In some companies, such as in the development and growth of Hewlett-Packard and many Japanese and Korean firms, the creation of a corporate culture is seen as a priority and a great deal of time, effort, and expenditure is given to induction and training. We use Hewlett-Packard to illustrate aspects of corporate culture in Chapter 6. Third, we use culture as an analytical device to distinguish one society from another.

We often tend to equate culture with nationality. Whilst most nation states have their own national cultural characteristics, some countries are typified by two or more cultural groups. A relatively small country such as Malaysia has two main cultural groups, Malay and Chinese, and several other smaller groups, including Indian. Each of these groups has its own customs and behaviour. In Italy, contrast is made between the cultures of north and south. Hofstede (1994) has identified six levels where cultural differences can be discerned. These are as follows.

- At the national level we can discern broad cultural differences between countries such as those aspects that make Americans think and behave differently to Japanese.

- Beneath this level we can discern differences; regionally such as between Northern and Southern Italians; between ethnic groups as in Malaysia; between religious groups such as Christians and Muslims, Catholics and Protestants in Northern Ireland or Calvinists and Catholics in the Netherlands; and between different language groups as in Belgium between the French- and Flemish-speaking populations. Different cultural groups within the same country are sometimes referred to as sub cultures.

- Cultural differences can occur between genders, leading in some countries to distinctive male and female roles, as in Japan, where there is a marked absence of women in senior positions within companies.

- Differences occur between generations, where the values of the older generation are challenged by those of the younger emerging generation. This is sometimes referred to as the generation gap.

- In some societies, social class determines differences in such things as attitudes to education and consumer preferences.

- Cultures can also vary between organizations as a result of differences in history, ownership patterns, technology, the type of work, leadership style and levels of employee skill. Such differences are often referred to as corporate or organizational culture.

We deal with the concepts of organizational and corporate culture in Chapter 6. In this section we focus on culture at the national and regional levels. Culture is the most pervasive of the five environmental factors in our model. Many aspects of the state, the application of technology, the nature of the labour force and their orientations to work are all culturally determined. However, influences are not just one way. Business organizations can and do influence cultures wherever they operate, as we can see from our analysis of multinationals operating in transitional and emerging economies.

As there have been many attempts to define culture, there have been many attempts to offer a theoretical framework to explain the influence of culture on business strategies, practices and behaviour. We have selected a number of writers and summarized their contribution. These are Edward Hall, Geert Hofstede, Fons Trompenaars and the contributions of the GLOBE project and the World Values Survey. We will also offer a critique of culture both generally in terms of its significance in business matters and more specifically in the case of some of our key writers.

The contribution of Edward Hall

Hall's main contribution to our understanding of the role of cultural differences in business has been his focus on communication, as depicted in his book *The Silent Language* (Hall, 1959) and followed up in further work (Hall, 1976, 1990). He distinguished between **high context cultures** and **low context cultures.**

High context cultures are found in Latin America, Southern Europe and in Japan and China. The main features are:

- Information is seen as an extension of the person.

- The content of the message is less important than the relationships of those communicating with one another.

- Agreements are based on trust and as a result negotiations tend to proceed at a relatively slow pace.

Low context cultures are found in the USA, UK and Northern Europe. The main features are:

- The message content is all important and expertise and performance are more important than relationships

- Negotiations take place in defined time frames and tend to be relatively quick.

- Agreements are based on legally binding contracts.

As we can see, Hall extended his view of culture to include perceptions of time. High context cultures were more likely to be polychromic, where time can be flexible to fit what was happening and where people were comfortable engaging in simultaneous events such as taking phone calls in meetings. Low context cultures on the other hand tended to view time as a resource with an importance placed upon timekeeping and timetables. Low context cultures were also likely to be monochromic and favoured dealing with events in sequence, an explanation often given for the British obsession for queuing.

Hall also noted differences between the two cultures in terms of how comfortable or uncomfortable people felt in terms of the physical proximity of others. For example, people in high context cultures were more comfortable with physical touching and a relatively small distance between people, whereas low context cultures favour greater personal space.

Hall offers insight into the role of communication, time and space in examining differences between cultures. However, with any classification that focuses on two categories there are bound to be differences between those countries within each category. For example, many relationships within Japanese firms, between employees, between the firm and its suppliers can be interpreted as high context, yet in inter-personal communication the Japanese are more comfortable with a large rather than small physical distance.

REFLECTION POINT

Examine your own culture in terms of Hall's classification of high and low context cultures.

The contribution of Geert Hofstede

Hofstede's major work was based on the findings of an attitude survey carried out at IBM between 1967 and 1973. Hofstede's analysis involved 116 000 employees in 40 countries (Hofstede, 1980a). The survey was an attempt to measure a number of cultural variables and hence determine the extent to which business activities were culturally defined. IBM is noted for its distinctive corporate culture and the deliberate strategy of developing that culture irrespective of national boundaries. Hofstede was dealing with an organization which had the same technology in all locations, the same organization structure and jobs and pursued the same strategies. The conditions were ripe for convergence. However, Hofstede found differences which could be explained by reference initially to four variables. Table 5.1 sets out these differences for a group of selected countries. The key differences related to values. Further work in South-East Asia with a colleague led to the development of a fifth variable, which explained more fully differences found between operations in the West and in Asia (Hofstede and Bond, 1988).

In recent years Hofstede has added a sixth dimension to his 5 existing variables. This dimension relates to the concept of indulgence versus restraint (Hostede, Hofstede and Minkov, 2010 and Minkov, 2012) and is based on data collected as part of the World Values Survey (see later).

Power distance This is the extent to which members of a society accept that power is distributed unequally. In all societies there is inequality between people, be it based upon physical, economic, intellectual or social characteristics. Hofstede found societies like France, Mexico and Hong Kong where the power distance is large and formed the basis of social relations. In those societies such as Germany, Sweden and the USA, the power distance was small and such societies were noted for their attempts to reduce inequality. For example, societies with a 'low' power

TABLE 5.1	Differences in cultural values for selected countries following Hofstede's findings				
	PD	**I**	**UA**	**M**	**LT**
Great Britain	35	89	35	66	25
Germany	35	67	65	66	31
France	68	71	86	43	na
Italy	50	76	75	70	na
USA	40	91	46	62	29
Canada	39	80	48	52	23
Brazil	69	38	76	49	65
Japan	54	46	92	95	80
China	78	10	38	44	118
Singapore	74	20	8	48	48
South Korea	60	18	85	39	75
Australia	36	90	51	61	31

Key:

PD **Power distance.** The larger score = more power distance. Highest score, 104 (Malaysia); lowest score, 11 (Austria)

I **Individualism.** The larger score = greater individualism. Highest score, 91 (USA); lowest score, 6 (Guatemala)

UA **Uncertainty avoidance.** The larger score = more risk averse. Highest score, 112 (Greece); lowest score, 8 (Singapore)

M **Masculinity.** The larger score = more masculine. Highest score, 95 (Japan); lowest score, 5 (Sweden)

LT **Long-term orientation.** The larger score = longer orientation. Highest score, 118 (China); lowest score, 0 (Pakistan)

distance usually have high rates of personal taxation as a means of redistributing wealth in the form of education and health care benefits for all. Employees in high-power distance societies tend to have a high level of dependence on their bosses and place importance on titles and status. The reverse is usually the case in low-power distance societies.

Individualism versus collectivism Individualistic societies such as the USA and the UK are depicted by a preference for looking after yourself or your immediate family group, a belief in freedom and a tendency towards a calculative involvement with work organizations. Social networks tend to be loose. Collectivistic societies such as India, Singapore and Mexico show concern for a much wider group and emphasize belongingness, which can extend to organizations.

Uncertainty avoidance This is the extent to which members of a society feel uncomfortable with uncertainty. Members of societies displaying strong uncertainty avoidance, as in Argentina, Switzerland and Japan, tend to be anxious about the future, have an inability to tolerate deviant ideas and feel threatened by ambiguity. In Japanese organizations, uncertainty avoidance is reflected in lengthy and detailed planning and decision-making procedures. Also in Japan, uncertainty avoidance may also inform the prevailing attitude towards innovation. Judged by the numbers of patents (see Chapter 10 for a full discussion) and by the success of Japanese products in export markets, Japanese firms are highly innovative. Yet much of that innovation is incremental indicating a slowly progressive methodical approach. Weak uncertainty avoidance as displayed in Hong Kong, USA and Thailand is associated with a willingness to accept ideas, speedy decision-making and a relaxed attitude to rules.

Masculinity versus femininity Masculine societies such as Japan, USA and Germany tend to display a preference for achievement, assertiveness and material success and display a strong belief in different gender roles. Feminine societies like Sweden and Holland place more emphasis on the quality of life, care for others and equality, more especially between the sexes. For example, Scandinavian countries were among the first to introduce paternity leave as an employment right.

Long versus short-term orientation Hofstede and Bond (1988) identified a fifth variable through their work in South-East Asia. They found that some societies, particularly those influenced by Confucian philosophy, were much more future-oriented, valued perseverance and savings and were much more adaptable than many societies, especially those in the west. They also called their variable 'Confucian dynamism'. It explains the difference between the long-term orientation of managers in Japan, Singapore, South Korea, Hong Kong as opposed to the more short-term strategies of the UK, USA and Canada. A long-term orientation was also found in Brazil and a short-term orientation in Pakistan and Nigeria.

Indulgence versus restraint This is a relatively recent addition to the Hofstede model and derives in part from the World Values Survey and Hofstede's work with Minkov (Hofstede, Hofstede and Minkov, 2012). The indulgence dimension is found to be relatively high in Latin America, Nordic Europe and in Anglo-Saxon economies. It places importance on the gratification of basic drives and emphasizes the importance of leisure, of free speech and is typified by relatively lenient sexual norms. The restraint dimension is found to be relatively high in East Asia, Eastern Europe and in Muslim countries. It places importance on the suppression of gratification and the need for individuals to control their desires and impulses. Restraint is often related to thrift and fairly strict sexual norms.

These variables shape the values and hence the behaviour of people operating in work organizations and enable us to explain differences in the way countries conduct their business affairs. They may also explain why work systems developed in one country will not work in another. For example, Hofstede reported that US car workers from Detroit working at the Saab-Scania plant in Sweden disliked the work system that placed a great deal of emphasis on group work. The Americans, with the exception of one woman, were much happier with a system that stressed individual achievement.

REFLECTION POINT

How would you assess you own culture in terms of Hofstede's five variables? Do you agree with the findings in Table 5.1?

Hofstede noted that many management theories originated in the USA (Hofstede, 1980b). The USA is typified by ratings that are below average for power distance and uncertainty avoidance, above average for masculinity, and has the highest rating on measures of individualism than any other country in Hofstede's survey. American motivation theory has been particularly influential and, in particular, the approaches of Maslow and Herzberg reflect typically US values. These are the need for individual achievement and performance (high individualism and masculinity) and involve the acceptance of risk (weak uncertainty avoidance). The implication is that such theories will not work so well in societies that are more collectivistic and feminine and whose people are risk avoiders.

Critique of Hofstede

The popularity of Hofstede's work has resulted in his theory based on five values being used as a basis of research in many areas of business and management. The same popularity has also attracted a number of critics. Criticisms of Hofstede's work may be summarized as follows:

- Hofstede's data was taken from an attitude survey carried out at IBM in 66 countries (a larger sample than the 50 countries Hofstede eventually used) over two periods, 1968–69 and 1971–73. The purpose of the survey was a company-based project. Javidan et al. (2006) describe Hofstede's work as a consulting project for IBM that has been re-interpreted.

- The original data is 40 years old. Many have questioned its relevance today, given that cultures do change and the political and economic state of the world in the 21st century is very different from that in the late 1960s.

- The overriding point made by McSweeney (2002) is summed up by the subtitle of his article, 'a triumph of faith – a failure of analysis'. He argues that the differences Hofstede attributes to culture might have been the product of other causes. This is a regular criticism of cultural research in general in that culture is cited as a causal factor when all other explanations have failed.

- Javidan et al. (2006) criticize Hofstede on his limited number of variables and suggest there are many other values that could have been considered, as they have done in the GLOBE project.

- The conclusions were drawn from a narrow sample from a single company. Yet Hofstede uses this data to put forward an entire theory to explain cultural differences, not simply in the work setting but in society as a whole. Indeed, McSweeney (2002), while acknowledging the relatively large samples from countries like USA, UK and Japan, refers to samples of fewer than 200 in 15 countries and fewer than 100 in 4 countries. Can such small numbers be representative of the national values of an entire culture?

- Hofstede's original study was based on behaviour at work. To what extent is this representative of all behaviour? For example, some US multinationals operating in Germany, such as Hewlett-Packard, insist on employees using first name terms when addressing each other. Such a practice was not common in German society, certainly at the time of Hofstede's original survey.

- McSweeney (2002) also believes that Hofstede has overstated the similarities in the culture and practices of IBM in different countries and that the answers to the questionnaires may reflect these differences rather than those ascribed to national culture.

Hofstede has always confronted his critics and challenged other 'theories', notably those of Trompenaars and the GLOBE project. This has led to some forceful exchanges in the literature, which have tended to focus on methodological details (see Javidan et al., 2006, for a flavour of this kind of debate). Hofstede (1999) has refuted the criticisms about the dated nature of the research by claiming that later findings have supported his theory and that while management practices may change, cultures and the core values remain constant. Furthermore, Hofstede claims that his work has developed through the ongoing collection of data, the addition of new country scores and the addition of the sixth dimension. However, he did acknowledge that movement had occurred on the individualism/collectivism dimension, as societies tended to shift from collectivism to individualism with increasing economic affluence.

The contribution of Fons Trompenaars

Fons Trompenaars (1993) produced his first book *Riding the Waves of Culture* and has continued to develop his ideas, working with Charles Hampden-Turner (Trompenaars and Hampden-Turner, 2004). Trompenaars, like Hofstede before him, believes that much of management behaviour is culturally determined and that the key to successful international management lies in the understanding of these cultural differences. Trompenaars uses an approach based on the earlier work of US anthropologists Kluckhohn and Strodtbeck and bases his work on a questionnaire which seeks people's responses to a number of scenarios. He establishes cultural differences:

- in the way we relate to others;
- in our attitudes to time;
- in our attitudes to the environment.

The few examples presented below offer a flavour of his approach.

In terms of how we relate to others, Trompenaars focuses on five variables relating to how we use rules, individualism, how public and private we are, the extent to which we show emotion and the extent to which we are achievement-oriented. For example, in countries such as the USA, Switzerland and Germany, the prevailing culture is much more universalistic and rules are applied irrespective of the situation. On the other hand, cultures such as those found in Malaysia and Indonesia tend to apply rules in a much more particularistic fashion and personal relationships can be more important in some situations than the rules governing conduct. In universalistic cultures, greater use is made in business of lawyers and contracts and in multinational operations, the head office plays a more directive role.

Cultures also differ in the way they display emotion. Neutral cultures such as those in Northern Europe and Japan tend to keep feelings hidden and debate and argument are seldom personalized. On the other hand emotional cultures such as those found in Italy or Latin America show their feelings and find it difficult to distinguish between issues and personalities. In some societies such as Japan much more emphasis is placed upon age, seniority, status and professional qualifications whereas in others, like the USA, respect tends to be earned on the basis of job performance. There may also be very different approaches to policies of pay and promotion.

Such differences can have a significant influence on doing business with people from a different culture, and on the operation of multinational corporations. Trompenaars believes that effective international management can only occur through the understanding of cultural differences and by being aware that problems can and do arise based on cultural differences. However, he believes that rather than trying to reduce the differences, cultural variations can be used by international firms as a strength to gain competitive advantage through cultural synergy. Different cultures offer new perspectives on problems and different approaches working together can find innovative solutions. This approach is vital to the concept of managing diversity.

The approach used is essentially a problem-solving one, aimed at the practising manager and deriving from Trompenaars' role as a consultant. Trompenaars' work has been accused of lacking academic rigour and of being little more than a training exercise to improve the effectiveness of global managers. However his conclusions are based on questionnaire data built up over a number of years and together with experience derived from cross cultural training in multinationals. Like Hofstede his data collection is on-going.

The contribution of the GLOBE project

GLOBE stands for the Global Leadership and Organizational Behaviour Effectiveness programme. A good overview of the project can be found in articles by the project leaders and main researchers (House, Javidan and Dorfman, 2001 and Javidan and House, 2011). A good summary of most aspects of the project can be found in French (2010).

The project sets out to study the impact of culture on leadership, on organizational processes and on the effectiveness of those processes. The focus on leadership is linked to the earlier work of one of the project leaders, Robert House.

In defining culture the researchers took Schein (1992) as their starting point and saw culture as the result of our adaptation to the external environment and how we manage relations between group members. They identified nine dimensions of culture that operate at both the societal and the organizational levels. These were:

- Power distance (using a similar definition to Hofstede).
- Uncertainty avoidance (again as Hofstede).
- Collectivism as a function of practices and institutions operating in society, which encourage collective action and collective rewards.
- In-group collectivism that focuses on how much individuals value being members of a group.
- Gender egalitarianism relating to the extent of equal treatment between genders and the extent to which roles are different or shared.
- Assertiveness and a competitive attitude.
- Future orientation involving the consideration of future actions.
- Performance orientation with a focus on results and outcomes.
- Humane orientation with a focus on altruism.

Despite Hofstede's criticism of the GLOBE research and the GLOBE team's criticism of Hofstede, it is clear that there is some overlap with Hofstede, a point acknowledged by the GLOBE researchers. However, the GLOBE team claim that 'it is time to move beyond Hofstede's approach and design constructs and scales that are more comprehensive, cross-culturally developed, theoretically sound and empirically verifiable' (Javidan et al, 2006, p. 898).

The research into these nine dimensions covered 62 countries, including some from the transitional economies of Eastern Europe. The survey focused on middle managers and involved over 17 000 participants from 950 firms. The firms were drawn mainly from three sectors, food, financial services and telecommunications, on the basis that these would be present in almost every country. Data was collected not just on cultural values but also on cultural practices.

The first results from the project identified the influence of culture as measured by the nine dimensions on values and practices of managers in the firms surveyed. Some of the results were similar to Hofstede but there were significant variations, e.g. the USA had a medium score on institutional collectivism and Japan did not have the highest score on gender differentiation. In general, the picture that emerged was more complex than Hofstede, perhaps understandable given the increase in variables employed, but like Hofstede the researchers were able to identify clusters of countries. An interesting finding relates to collectivism. Sweden scored the highest in terms of collectivism as encouraged by social institutions and processes and was illustrated by high rates of taxation. However, the Swedes scored lowest on collectivism as defined by membership of small groups, as illustrated by the high percentage who live in single flats.

The GLOBE project also examined leadership and the extent to which certain approaches to leadership were universally accepted, believed to be effective and also seen as the product of cultural values that themselves were fairly widespread. Not surprisingly they found that desirable leadership was associated with being motivational, honest and decisive and undesirable traits included ruthlessness and egocentricity.

The World Values Survey

The World Values Survey is an international non-profit making organization with headquarters in Sweden. It has been in existence since 1981 and comprises a network of social scientists in many countries, which has been responsible for five major surveys carried out between 1981 and 2008. A current wave of surveys is due for completion in 2014. The focus of the research has been to plot changing values and their impact on political, economic and social life. The organization claims to have surveyed 90 per cent of the world's population covering countries with highly diverse economic, political and social systems. A good summary of the work carried out by this organization can be found in www.worldvaluessurvey.org.

The focus of their study is to look at changing values (culture change) and their impact on individual beliefs. Despite its high profile in and use by organizations such as the United Nations it has largely been ignored by reviews of the relationship between culture and business. In part this is due to the apparent focus of the World Values Survey on political and social change often linked to the democratization process. However the Survey does deal with the impact of culture on business in a number of different ways:

- Their questionnaire seeks to obtain data on changing attitudes and beliefs about work motivations, gender roles, tolerance of diversity and subjective well-being, all significant issues in modern organizations.

- The surveys have been used to explain political change in the former Soviet Union and Eastern Europe in terms of changing values and beliefs. In Chapter 2 we noted how this change has played an important role in the process of globalization and the expansion of markets. The changing beliefs and values identified by the Survey are central to the globalization process and in the shift from state-run to transitional economies.

- Hofstede, as we have already noted, has incorporated findings of the World Values Survey to distinguish between those societies typified by indulgence and those by restraint, thereby extending his basic theoretical model.

- The Survey identifies a growing tendency towards individual expression which manifests itself at the workplace and is a key element in the shift from industrial to knowledge-based economies, in which the type of work people do gives them more freedom in terms of what they do and how and when they work.

The Survey identifies two major dimensions of cultural variation. These are:

- traditional versus secular-rational
- survival versus self-expression.

In **traditional** societies importance is placed on religion and on traditional family values, including the rejection of divorce and abortion. Religion and family values are less important in secular rational societies. In almost all industrial societies the survey notes a shift to more secular-rational beliefs and values.

In those societies where **survival** is important, it becomes a key aspect of life and is associated with traditional gender roles, a lack of tolerance to all forms of diversity and less concern for the environment. In those societies where **self-expression** is important, economic and physical security are taken for granted and a high value is placed on both individual freedom and freedom of speech. There is also a greater tolerance of diversity and gender roles are increasingly blurred. This shift towards the need for greater self-expression is linked to the shift towards the knowledge economy.

By combining these dimensions the Survey identifies clusters of countries as follows:

- Those countries scoring high on both traditional values and survival include the Islamic states of the Middle East as well as Bangladesh and Zimbabwe.
- Those countries scoring high on both traditional values and self-expression include the USA, much of Latin America and Ireland.
- Those countries scoring high on both secular-rational values and survival include the Russian Federation, Ukraine and Bulgaria.
- Those countries scoring high on both secular-rational values and self-expression include most countries in Northern Europe such as Sweden, Norway and the Netherlands.

REFLECTION POINT

How would you sum up the similarities and differences of the different studies and 'theories' of cultural difference?

The implications of cultural diversity for managers

First, managers need to be extremely cautious in the way business and management ideas are taken from a different cultural setting. A management technique developed in one country may only work in that country because it is based upon a particular set of cultural values. The failure in the UK and the USA of many attempts to introduce Japanese-style quality circles was due, in the main, to an incomplete understanding on the part of the adopters of the particular cultural values underpinning such an approach. The technique could be transposed but the conditions necessary for healthy growth could not.

Second, in dealing with people from other cultures managers must recognize that differences do exist and be prepared to adjust behaviour and expectations accordingly. This is the theme of many recent initiatives in training for international management.

Third, the policies of multinational corporations may well need to vary in different countries and managers operating out of their home environment need specific training in cultural differences.

Fourth, managers should be aware of the influence of culture on products, services and marketing. We examine the influence of cultural differences on business activities within each of the Chapters 10–14.

Difficulties in using culture as a variable

Culture remains a fascinating concept but a difficult analytical tool. The following points, which should be taken in conjunction with the critique of Hofstede, give some indication of the difficulties involved:

- Many studies, which use culture as a central concept, tend to define culture in rather broad, generalized terms. In many instances it is a kind of residual variable, a catch-all to explain away differences that cannot be explained by differences in the economy, technology, role of the state, size of the firm and so on.

- In many studies, there is an attempt to link culture and economic performance. Such links tend to be highly selective, ignoring evidence that does not fit. In this way, accounts of Japan may be biased, in that they focus on the successful but not the unsuccessful firms. The accounts also focus on large firms such as Toyota, and ignore the very important small firms sector of the Japanese economy.

- Many other explanations of behaviour based on culture use isolated examples and fail to explore other factors which may offer better explanations. Gladwell (2009) attributes the crash of a Korean Airlines plane to the failure of a co-pilot to contradict the captain and argued that this was an example of power distance in operation. This ignores other possible explanations of the same crash, which in any case was a rare incident. In addition, his analysis fails to explain why airlines in other high power distance societies such as Japan, have good safety records.

- Cultural comparisons tend to be made from the perspective of one culture only. We may make conclusions about another culture based on our own values. A study of the car industry worldwide showed that European and US manufacturers outperformed the Japanese on criteria they deemed most relevant: profitability measured by accounting ratios. The Japanese, however, laid greater store by market penetration and growth, and on these criteria easily outperformed the European and US manufacturers (Bhaskar, 1980).

- We have seen that we possess preconceived notions about other cultures, often expressed as stereotypes. These can creep into our analysis and become self-fulfilling prophecies; we see what we expect to see. Our ready acceptance of such stereotypes prevents us from digging more deeply. Such stereotypes are often deliberately used in training, when preparing managers for cross-cultural management. Clearly such approaches need to be used with caution.

- Cultures can and do change over time and our perceptions can become dated.

- Culture is often viewed as a problem when this may not be the case. Kanter and Corn (1994) concluded from studies of cross-national mergers and acquisitions that people from different cultures generally work together quite well and that cultural differences became less apparent over time. They found that differences in technical and educational background were often more significant than cultural differences. In other words, engineers get on with engineers and accountants get on with accountants, irrespective of differences in their culture. Moreover, they found that problems that were often attributed to culture were the product of strategic, organizational or political issues. For example, in the case of mergers between a USA firm and a German firm, the Germans were accused of being over-cautious and taking a long time to make decisions. In fact the delay was a product of German regulations that required such decisions to be referred to the works council.

This last point illustrates a further source of diversity that is rooted in the institutions and regulations of a specific country. It is to this we now turn.

REFLECTION POINT

Given these difficulties, is culture still a useful vehicle to explain differences in business?

INSTITUTIONAL FRAMEWORKS

Another approach to the use of culture to explain diversity of business strategies, practices and behaviours is the use of the institutional framework approach. Granovetter (1985) argued that economic and social activity is embedded in the contexts of the state, the financial system and the labour market. Key variations related to the extent of state intervention, the role of banks and to legal protection and representation in the labour market. Explanations based on institutional frameworks approach owe much to the 'variaties of capitalism' and 'business systems' approaches of academics such as Whitley (2000), Hall and Soskice (2001) and Amable (2003). Such approaches have identified that nation states have developed business systems that are a function of different institutional arrangements. A major role is played by the state and influences include the control of education, labour markets, finance and taxation.

Although the institutional framework approach to diversity is put forward as an alternative to cultural diversity, there are overlaps. The education system in any country is a reflection of cultural values. In both Hofstede's study and in that of the GLOBE project, issues relating to both power distance and collectivism were reflected in the taxation systems of some of the countries in the studies. We will first explain the model developed by Richard Whitley and then offer a simplified model based on the different economic systems we introduced in Chapter 3.

The business systems model of Whitley

Richard Whitley (2000) developed a complex model based initially on studies he carried out in Japan, South Korea and Europe. His model comprises actors and mechanisms for integration. The actors identified by Whitley are as follows:

- providers and users of capital, e.g. banks and firms
- customers and suppliers
- competitors
- firms in other sectors, i.e. those not in direct competition
- employees.

Variations exist in the type of relationships that exist between the actors and especially in the degree of integration. Such integration is exemplified, for example, in the closeness of the relationship between firms and banks and between firms and their suppliers or in the degree of involvement of employees in decision-making processes. Whitley goes on to explain how integration occurs and identifies a number of ways, including state direction, through ownership (e.g. by a firm of its supplier) and by non-ownership alliances.

As a result of differences in the relationship between actors and in the modes of integration, Whitley identifies six types of business system. We offer a simplified version of such models using the distinction between Anglo-Saxon, social market and Asian economies that we introduced in Chapter 3. We examine the extent to which those variations in market economies can explain differences in the way firms and managers operate. Variations can be found in, for example, the flexibility of labour markets, in the freedom of managers to make decisions, in the rights of individual workers, and in the relative importance of different stakeholders.

We examine the impact of Anglo-Saxon, social market and Asian systems before examining in more detail the alleged shift globally towards Anglo-Saxon capitalism, regarded by some as a form of convergence. We will also look at the model developed by Hall and Soskice (2001), known as the 'varieties of capitalism' approach featuring a comparison of liberal market economies and coordinated market economies.

The Anglo-Saxon model

The Anglo-Saxon capitalism model is sometimes called laissez-faire or competitive managerial capitalism. While all forms of capitalism see the market to be the ultimate arbiter and control of a well-regulated economy – and certainly preferable to state control – this form of capitalism, above all others, emphasizes the workings of the free market. Such a system can be seen best in the USA and the UK but is a feature also of Australia, New Zealand and Canada. We can identify its main features as follows:

- Markets are competitive and there is a belief that individuals should be encouraged to participate as entrepreneurs in an enterprise culture.

- The concept of private property is important and individuals are encouraged to own goods and capital as well as their own labour. Individualism is prized as a core value in society.

- Shareholders are viewed as the most important stakeholder in business, and thus managers see an important part of their role is to deliver profit and dividend for shareholders.

- A key role in business ownership is played by institutional shareholders such as banks, insurance companies, pension funds and investment companies. These take an interest in share price and dividend and seek returns on their investment.

- The system is typified by mergers and takeovers, many of them hostile, as share dealings result in rapid changes of ownership. For example, dividends paid to shareholders in the UK tend to be higher than those in Germany and Japan, and even higher than the USA.

- Managers are rewarded for maintaining share price and profits and part of that reward often includes shares. In the UK, senior managers have gained substantial pay rises in recent years as reward systems have tended to copy the USA.

- Trade unions are tolerated but their powers are often restricted by law.

- A response to changed economic circumstances is the flexible use of labour. For example, in a recession labour costs are cut to maintain profit levels, resulting in increased levels of unemployment. Other costs are also cut including training and R&D.

Whilst the above has underpinned the capitalist systems of the UK and the USA for some time, there has been an even greater shift towards the free market in the past 20 or so years with even greater deregulation in most areas of the economy and, especially in the UK, wholesale privatization of publicly-owned companies and utilities. However, as we noted in Chapter 3, the events of 2008–09 in the banking sector and with the dramatic falls in share prices have led some to question the workings of Anglo-Saxon capitalist systems.

KEY CONCEPT 5.3	ANGLO-SAXON CAPITALISM

Anglo-Saxon capitalism is a liberal market political economy found in the USA and the UK, but also in Canada, Australia and New Zealand. It is founded on a belief in the free market and a belief in individualism and the sanctity of private property. Markets are highly competitive and shareholders are seen as the main stakeholder of a business. As a consequence, stock markets have a tendency to frequent and significant changes and labour is often treated as a flexible commodity. Some believe that this system is developing as the predominant model of capitalism, although its utility was questioned by the banking crisis and 'credit crunch' of 2008–09.

The social market model

The social market model is also known as the German model and the Rhineland model and is typified by the system found in Germany. The model is also prevalent in France, the Netherlands and Scandinavia. However, there is considerable variation in the way the model operates. For example, much greater emphasis is placed on high-cost social welfare, funded by taxation, in Sweden and some other Scandinavian countries. In Germany and the Netherlands more emphasis is placed on the legal regulation of business decisions and trade unions play a significant role. In France, much more power lies in the hands of a centralist state.

The main features of the social market model are as follows:

- The free market is seen to be important but needs to be carefully watched and in some cases regulated by the state.
- Private and state ownership operate side by side.
- There are comprehensive and well-funded social welfare systems controlled by the state.
- Both markets and individual firms are regulated by law and by state bureaucracy.
- Shareholders are viewed as one among several stakeholders in business. The stakeholders also include the employees. As a result, corporate governance focuses on responsibility to society and not on shareholder interest.
- Generally, share markets are stable with few mergers and takeovers which, in any case, are regulated by law.
- Major companies in each sector are seen as national champions and are protected by the state.
- Banks tend to be integrated into the system and have a close relationship both with individual firms and the state.
- Reinvestment in the business is favoured over high dividends to shareholders and managers tend to be less well rewarded than their counterparts in the USA and UK.
- Trade unions play an important role in decision-making and there is considerable employee involvement. Where the state, business and unions come together to determine policy, as is often idealized in Germany, the system is referred to as corporatist.
- In general labour markets are less flexible than in Anglo-Saxon systems. First, the ability of managers to shed labour in response to an economic downturn is limited by greater

employee involvement, greater degrees of cooperation between management and labour and laws protecting employees. Second, specific and detailed training makes it less easy for employees to switch skills and jobs.

Amable (2003) identifies three variants of the social market model. These are:

- Social democratic: Sweden, Denmark, Finland.
- Continental European: Germany, Switzerland, Norway, France.
- Mediterranean: Italy, Spain, Portugal, Greece.

Key variants include the degree of employment protection, the degree of social protection and the flexibility of the labour force. For example, Germany has greater employment protection than Sweden but less labour market flexibility and a less well-developed welfare state.

In most social market systems, changes have been noted in the past 20 years. In many countries there has been a shift towards a freer market with deregulation and privatization. Some firms, particularly in Germany, have felt constrained by the system, leading them to acquire businesses overseas. In Germany, several firms have acquired USA companies, as with Daimler and Chrysler, Siemens and Westinghouse, and Bertelsmann and Random House. In France, Renault, a former state-owned company, has taken a major share of Nissan in Japan. In an increasingly global labour market for top executives, managers were attracted to better paid jobs in the USA and UK. This has resulted in substantial pay rises for senior executives in Germany and France in particular.

The Asian model

The Asian capitalism model is also known as the Japanese model, alliance capitalism or community capitalism. It is found throughout Asia but its core characteristics are best illustrated in Japan and the Asian tiger economies, especially South Korea. However, there are variations in the model across the various countries of Asia. Further insights into the model can be seen in Case 3.1 about Singapore. The elements of the model can be expressed as follows:

- The dominant belief is that of the free market but with strong state intervention where necessary.
- Business practices and working life are dominated by Confucian values, including discipline, hard work, duty, harmony, perseverance and the importance attached to savings.
- The state operates in a bureaucratic way, but for businesses rules tend to be applied pragmatically to smooth the way rather than hinder progress.
- Most states have weak social welfare systems and much is down to the individual and their family, hence the importance of savings.
- The firm and even its supply chain are viewed as a family. Organizations and large organizations in particular place great emphasis on developing strong corporate cultures (see Chapter 6 for a fuller discussion of corporate culture).
- Stock markets tend to be stable. Even between competing firms there will be collaboration to prevent a takeover by a foreign company. Where mergers do occur, much attention is paid to the harmonization of the corporate cultures of the respective firms.
- Managers tend to pursue long-term strategies and goals. Individual reputation is often based on the success of the firm in general.

- Trade unions tend to be weak and are often controlled by management or the state. They are, however, seen to be important in the protection of weaker employees.

- In a recession, every attempt is usually made to protect both employees and suppliers. As a consequence, firms have often been reluctant to restructure, and both managers and governments have been accused of reacting too slowly to economic problems.

The Asian system has been under threat in the past 15 years or more. Japan has suffered an economic slow down since 1992 and the tiger economies suffered badly in the crash of 1997. The limited industrial base of most Asian countries outside Japan was exposed in 1997 and continues to be exposed with each recession. Even stronger economies, such as Singapore, are not immune. Part of the problem has been the gradual move away from some of the core values that underpinned the Asian model. The slow growth of a strong manufacturing base was exchanged for the potentially richer and 'easier' returns from land and property speculation and international share trading. In tackling the recession in Japan, some firms have turned to some Anglo-Saxon practices such as performance-related pay.

REFLECTION POINT

What are the main differences between Anglo-Saxon, social market and Asian systems?

Varieties of capitalism: Liberal versus coordinated market economies

The 'varieties of capitalism' approach is attributed to Hall and Soskice (2001). They agreed with Whitley that the organization of production was linked to external institutions that were part of the political economy of a country. Hall and Soskice took this model a stage further and identified three factors that between them created variations in capitalist systems.

The state and institutions

Institutions included those concerned with finance and banking, with education, with labour markets and so on. They saw the role of the state as crucial as it had the power and the opportunity to influence all the institutions, especially through its legislative and regulatory framework and through its control of the economy.

Spheres of activity in which firms need to develop relationships to operate to the best of their ability. The five spheres they identified were:

- Industrial relations relating to issues of productivity and wages.

- Vocational training and education, which included recruiting people with skills and motivating them to use and develop their skills.

- Corporate governance which included relations with shareholders and access to finance.

- Relationships with other firms such as suppliers, buyers and joint venture partners.

- Relationships with employees.

These five spheres were seen as crucial to the success of any organization. Problems arose in all of these areas and the way the problems were solved varied according to the nature of the political economy. They identified those countries, which they called **liberal market**

TABLE 5.2	Liberal versus coordinated market economies	
Germany/Japan		**UK/USA**
• Coordinated market economy (CME) • Stable stock market • Stable and less flexible labour market • Employee involvement and commitment • Cooperation between competing firms and greater integration with supply chains • 'Patient capitalism'– a long-term approach to investment		• Liberal market economy (LME) • More volatile stock market • Greater labour mobility and flexibility • Top-down decisions and a more contractual relationship between employees and the firm • Competitive capitalism • A short-term approach to investment with an emphasis on return on investment

economies, where the market and competition were used to resolve problems and difficulties. They contrasted these with **coordinated market economies**, where there was much greater emphasis on relationships with banks, suppliers and employees to solve problems. They felt that such variations were influenced by both history and culture. The Hall and Soskice approach therefore acknowledges the interrelationship between cultural and institutional explanations.

The key differences between countries identified by Hall and Soskice can be seen in our definitions of Anglo-Saxon, social market and Asian systems.

As well as identifying differences between capitalist countries similar to those found by Whitley and by Amable, Hall and Soskice noted similarities between features of social market and Asian systems and in particular the systems of Japan and Germany. These coordinated market economies are contrasted with the liberal market economies of the UK and USA. Table 5.2 sets out the major differences between these two types.

The similarities between the UK and USA are acknowledged by most writers. There are also undoubted similarities between Germany and Japan based largely on the importance of social ties, collective obligations and moral commitments (Streeck, 2001). However, employee involvement and commitment take different forms, with more formal systems and a greater involvement of law in Germany and a greater emphasis on moral duty in Japan. There is also evidence of much greater state direction in Japan.

The success of Germany and Japan in the 1970s and 1980s has been attributed to the strong influence of the main features of the coordinated market economy. However, the economic rise of both countries has been followed by decline in 1990s, a decade which also saw the re-emergence of the USA. In Chapter 3 we questioned whether there had been a convergence towards Anglo-Saxon approaches and therefore a shift in the systems of both Germany and Japan.

REFLECTION POINT

Are Germany and Japan so similar?

A convergence on Anglo-Saxon capitalism?

A shift in Germany and Japan towards Anglo-Saxon capitalism has been identified based on a number of changes:

- It is seen as part of a wider trend involving economic liberalization and privatization.
- Globalization of German and Japanese firms and capital including their investment and acquisitions in other countries.
- Increased prioritization of shareholder interest above that of other stakeholders.
- Reduced involvement of banks in both shareholding and decision-making.
- Increasing focus by banks on short-term returns rather than long-term investment.
- Evidence of less protection for workers as jobs have been cut in recession and plants closed in major companies like Nissan.
- Increased adoption of 'US practices' including performance-related pay, increased job mobility and performance appraisals.

However, writers such as Streeck (2001) argue that the evidence suggests shift in kind and modification of some practices rather than total acceptance of the Anglo-Saxon approach. In Germany and Japan we can still find evidence of policies and practices such as:

- Greater involvement of banks together with their greater financial commitment towards firms.
- Cooperation between employees rather than self-interested individualism.
- Greater employee involvement in decision-making.
- The greater commitment of employees and strong corporate cultures (especially Japan).
- A more complex legal framework (especially Germany).

Institutional frameworks: Some conclusions

A key question that remains unanswered is whether a particular system results in superior economic performance. The Asian approach, or more specifically the Japanese approach, found favour in the West in the 1980s and western firms adopted Japanese practices relating to the organization of production. The shift to the Anglo-Saxon approach and its adoption, at least in part by China, implies certain advantages. However, do nations, particularly those that have undergone recent economic transition, have a choice of which path to follow or is their system so embedded in history and culture that choice is restricted? Rather than being an alternative explanation of differences in the organization of production, the institutional approach can be viewed alongside theories of cultural difference and theories of convergence to offer a richer picture that explains diversity and similarity in business practice. The next section uses Japan to illustrate how these various approaches fit together.

REFLECTION POINT

To what extent do you believe that differences between institutions and regulations in different countries are themselves products of differences in culture?

JAPAN: CONVERGENCE AND DIVERSITY

In this final section we illustrate the use of the convergence-diversity model by exploring the rise of the post-war Japanese economy and its comparative decline in the 1990s.

In Chapter 3 we noted that Japan emerged after the Second World War as the second-largest economy behind the USA and in Table 3.1 we showed that growth rates in Japan's GDP and industrial production were higher than the rates found in the USA, UK and Germany. In addition, Japan was dominating certain consumer export markets, notably cars and electrical goods. We also pointed to the economic crisis that befell Japan in the 1990s and persisted into the new millennium. This section will examine the relative impact on the Japanese economy of convergence, cultural and institutional framework.

Convergence

Convergence can be used to explain many features of the growth of the Japanese economy. Japan's relatively late start to industrialization in the middle of the 19th century enabled it to learn from the successes and mistakes of others, notably the USA, UK and Germany. It is clear that Japan borrowed heavily not just in terms of industrial processes but also in terms of business systems and supporting national institutions such as the civil service. Dore (1973) refers to this as the 'late development' effect, whereby developing nations can gain from the experience of more developed countries.

Convergence may also be used to explain the adoption of Japanese business methods by western firms in the 1980s. Japan became so successful as a late developer that its economic growth exceeded that of its mentors and in turn it became a focus of attention of would-be copiers. This is linked to the process sometimes referred to as 'Japanization' involving Japanese foreign direct investment and the adoption of Japanese business and management methods by firms in other countries. A classic example of such adoption is the widespread use of lean production and just-in-time methods in manufacturing and retailing industry across the world.

However, many would-be adopters of Japanese methods outside Japan have discovered limits to Japanization as a result of the influence of cultural and institutional factors. For example, there may be elements which are too embedded in the cultural values of the Japanese and which are difficult to transfer. These include the stability of employment, the strong company identification and work ethic and the ability of Japanese managers to employ a management style that is a mix of paternalistic, disciplinarian and egalitarian methods. This may explain why many UK and US firms found difficulty in introducing Japanese-style quality circles as a method of quality enhancement.

Convergence may also be used to examine the problems faced by Japan in the 1990s. The success of the Japanese economy was in part responsible for the availability of easy credit in the 1980s. This in turn led to speculation and the subsequent overvaluing of both equities and real estate. When the 'bubble-economy' burst in the early 1990s there was a dramatic fall in land, property and share prices. Companies, including some banks and individuals, were left with massive debts that they could not repay and the banking system was left with large amounts of bad debts. This could be interpreted as a convergence towards an Anglo-Saxon type of economy. This has been reinforced by other changes. There has been a growth of foreign companies operating in Japan either as joint ventures or having taken over Japanese firms as in the cases of Cable and Wireless and IDC, Renault and Nissan, and Ford and Mazda. Forty-five per cent of Sony shares are held by foreign investors and there has emerged a new type of chief executive in companies such as Nissan, Sony, Honda and Toyota, all with overseas experience. In companies such as Nissan, 'non Japanese' practices were introduced, including merit rather than seniority-based promotion and share options for senior management. Restructuring occurred in most major companies. In some cases this eradicated the over-staffing of many management hierarchies but it also resulted in job losses. In other words, Japanese companies were responding in much the same way as firms would in the USA and UK.

Cultural explanations

In our review of convergence related to the emergence of Japan as an economic power we noted how specific elements of Japanese culture undoubtedly gave fresh impetus to ideas and methods incorporated from other countries. In attempts to explain the growth of the Japanese economy, emphasis has been placed on the role of cultural values. These have been linked to broader Asian values including duty, obedience, teamwork and long-term orientation.

Using Hofstede's model we can assess the influence of culture upon Japanese business:

- The Japanese have moderately high **power distance** and consequently attach considerable importance to vertical relationships, which are typified by loyalty, dependence and a sense of duty. This is reflected in the average length of service of Japanese employees linked to the practices of lifetime employment, and the seniority principle.

- The Japanese score very high in terms of **uncertainty avoidance.** Their unwillingness to take risks is reflected in many aspects of business life. It explains both the time taken in the planning process and the detailed content of the plans themselves. It is also demonstrated in the lengthy decision-making processes in many Japanese firms. It may also explain the preference of the Japanese for incremental product development.

- **Collectivism** is a feature of the Japanese and is reflected in the importance placed upon harmony and teamwork in all aspects of working life. Peer group recognition is very important to the Japanese worker. Consultation is a feature of decision-making in Japanese firms and, with uncertainty avoidance, explains the time taken in the process. Collectivism explains the Japanese loyalty to the group, be it the country, the family, or their company.

- The **'Confucian dynamism'** or **'long-term orientation'** results in both conservatism and adaptability. This has resulted in the Japanese placing more emphasis on savings than their counterparts in other industrial nations, their willingness to adapt to changing conditions for survival and their preference for seeing things in the longer term. The planning horizons of Japanese firms tend to be much greater than those of their western counterparts.

All these cultural factors have at one time or another been put forward to explain the superior performance of Japanese firms. However, the difficulty in using culture to explain economic and financial success presents problems when the economy and firms are less than successful. The same cultural values that supposedly support success for both the national economy and individual firms are still present when a recession affects the economy and causes firms to change practices.

Institutional explanations

Unlike the cultural explanations these can be used in conjunction with both economic and decline. We will examine the role of the state, the role of banks, the relationship between firms and suppliers and the workings of the labour market.

The role of the state

Historically, the state has always had a significant role in the development of the Japanese economy. The state represents a network of influence between politics, the civil service and business operating a system of targeted development and trade protection at home, with selective investment overseas. Top civil servants often become top executives upon retirement in a process known poetically as *amakudari* (literally, descent from heaven).

A central feature of the state's influence is the role played by the civil service. The two most influential departments have always been MITI (Ministry of International Trade and Industry) and MOF (Ministry of Finance). Traditionally they have helped to coordinate and direct Japan's economic strategy. Undoubtedly the state has played a major role in the development of the Japanese economy, more especially by accelerating market forces. However, the role of MITI and MOF have been questioned during the economic changes of the 1990s, including recession and globalization. During the 1990s MITI came into conflict with the political parties and was blamed by some for the failure of government industrial policy since 1980, thereby contributing to the problems of recession (Berggren and Nomura, 1997).

The state, often blamed for over-regulation and over-protection in the boom years, was now blamed for its failure to regulate and control the economy and especially the financial sector. Porter et al. (2000) believed the state to be too concerned with export performance and failed to stimulate domestic markets.

Banks

The banks operate as shareholders of many companies. However, here we have a case of banks both as shareholders and a part of conglomerate empires in firms like Mitsubishi and Sumitomo. This not only gives such firms access to sources of investment, but also places them at the centre of a network of information. The relationship with subcontractors is further cemented in that the bigger firms, often through their banks, are big shareholders in the smaller companies.

The banking sector has come under both national and international scrutiny. Both a cause and consequence of the economic problems of the 1990s have been bankrupt financial institutions and bad loans. Financial companies such as Nomura, Yamaichi and Daiwa were found guilty of illegal trading. As a result, Yamaichi Securities was bankrupted in 1998. At best, the government through the Ministry of Finance was accused of weak control and at worst was implicated in the Daiwa scandal. Reforms of 1999 placed greater control of the banks with the government and MOF was effectively downgraded to a treasury ministry.

During the economic crises of the 1990s banks were mistrusted and people withdrew their savings. As a result, savings were not being channelled into the economy as previously. From 1992, bad debts held by the banks rose significantly, and in 1996 they outstripped operating profit. By 1998, total bad debts in the banking system were approximately the size of the GNP of Canada.

The relationship with suppliers

This is a major feature of Japanese manufacturing industry. Every large firm in Japan uses smaller firms as subcontractors. In this way a hierarchy of manufacture is built up, with larger firms subcontracting to smaller and so on. In every case, the relationship between the firm and its supplier is carefully specified, with deliveries being requested not by the week or even day, but by the hour. This is a central feature of the just-in-time system we discuss in Chapter 11. In general, the relationship is very close and 'parent' companies tend to be very loyal to their subcontractors. In recession, it is not unnatural for subcontractors to be supported and protected by the major company, which will often reduce its own labour force to cut costs rather than sever the link with its supplier. The idea of a close relationship between manufacturer and supplier is now embedded in much of manufacturing strategy throughout the world, a lead undoubtedly given by the Japanese.

The labour market

The traditional approach to subcontracting offers a competitive advantage for Japanese manufacturing industry. Smaller Japanese firms pay comparatively lower wages than their UK counterparts and a much larger percentage of Japanese labour operates in smaller firms (Williams et al., 1992). Given that the smaller firm predominates in the Japanese subcontracting network, there are substantial cost benefits derived from lower wage costs.

In addition, much publicity has been given to the Japanese concepts of lifetime employment, seniority payment systems and the use of temporary workers as a source of competitive advantage.

The above analysis has attempted to demonstrate the strengths and limitations in the use of convergence, culture and institutions to provide explanations for the rise and decline of the Japanese economy and Japanese firms from 1946 to the present day. The overriding conclusion is that, in part, all three approaches offer plausible explanations. There may also be factors which lie outside this model such as changes in the global economy, the behaviour of competitors, and the consequences of inappropriate management decisions. All these themes crop up in Case 5.1 examining the failure of Wal-Mart in Germany.

REFLECTION POINT

Which explanation best accounts for the growth of the post-war Japanese economy and its comparative decline in the 1990s?

CASE 5.1   WAL-MART IN GERMANY

The first Wal-Mart store was established by Sam Walton in 1962 in Rogers, Arkansas. At first expansion was steady with 24 stores by 1967. The initial focus for Wal-Mart operations was small town, rural America. The company grew to 276 stores by 1980 and the Wal-Mart empire reached 640 stores by 1984. The company currently has around 4100 stores in the USA and by 2003 it was the world's largest retailer, three times as large as its nearest rival, the French company, Carrefour. It was also the world's largest employer with 1.9 million employed worldwide in 2007. In 2009, Wal-Mart was ranked as the world's third-largest company by revenue in the Fortune 500.

Wal-Mart is noted for its large and diverse product range, which includes food, clothing, electrical goods, homeware, pharmaceuticals and so on. The USA business comprised four types of operation, 'supercenters', 'discount stores', 'Sam's Club' and a small number of convenience stores. The 'supercenters' carry the full range of goods, including food and a large variety of other types of merchandise. The 'discount stores' are like the 'supercenters' without the food and 'Sam's Club' is a membership discount warehouse for bulk purchases.

According to Knorr and Arndt (2003) the success of Wal-Mart is based on four factors:

- low prices;
- a focus on customer service;
- IT-driven logistics and inventory management involving large centralized warehouses;
- a strong corporate culture and employee commitment.

(Continued)

The 2007 company website described its core values as, "quality goods at low prices, responsible manufacturing, and opportunities for growth … dedicated to excellence in every part of our business". The company also prides itself on its service orientation. Staff are expected to be committed to the organization and all are expected to be positive and cheerful in their dealings with customers. The US operation developed a specific approach to customer service and staff were employed to greet customers on entry to the store, to assist them with packing their purchases into bags and to be proactive in assisting customers anywhere in the store.

Going international

A number of factors influenced Wal-Mart management to expand outside the USA. The company had perhaps reached the limits of expansion in the USA. There was strong competition from such as Target and K-Mart, both with similar strategies to Wal-Mart and both also started in 1962. Furthermore, management believed that the success formula of the US operation could be replicated elsewhere. The first international store was opened in 1991 in a suburb of Mexico City and the company developed rapidly in both Mexico, initially in a joint venture with the local firm Cifra, and in Canada, largely through the acquisition of Woolco. Mexico remains Wal-Mart's biggest international operation with over 900 stores. The company also opened stores in Puerto Rico, Argentina, Brazil, Japan, South Korea and Indonesia, and in Europe, in Germany and the UK. With the purchase of Asda, Wal-Mart owned around 500 stores in the UK by 2014, its largest European operation. The most recent developments have been in Central America with stores opening in Costa Rica, Guatemala, El Salvador, Nicaragua and Honduras, all in 2005. Wal-Mart opened its first store in India in 2010. The major international operations are listed in Table 5.3.

In 1993 Wal-Mart established a division to develop and manage its international operations, with the anticipation that these would soon contribute over a third of the company's profits. By 2007, the overseas operations contributed around 20 per cent.

Entry into the German market

Some analysts believed that Wal-Mart's decision to expand into Europe via Germany instead of the

TABLE 5.3	Wal-Mart stores outside the USA, October 2007	
Country	**Stores**	**First opened**
Mexico	919	1991
Japan	392	2002
UK	337	1999
Brazil	298	1995
Canada	290	1994
China	184	1996
Costa Rica	140	2005

UK was a strange decision given the cultural links between the USA and the UK. However, the German market was attractive as the world's third-largest economy with 80 million people, who were Europe's largest retail spenders. Furthermore, management saw Germany ideally located at the heart of Europe, and an important member of the EU. Unlike the UK, Germany was part of the euro zone.

Wal-Mart entered the German market at the end of 1997 with the purchase of 21 stores from Wertkauf and added to this in 1998 with the purchase of 74 Interspar stores from the French company, Intermarche. After only four years of operation in Germany it was clear that Wal-Mart was struggling with estimated accumulated losses at around €1 billion, although only estimates were available because the company published no accounts. The estimated losses continued at the same rate and by 2005 the company had cancelled its expansion plans, closed two stores and laid off 1350 staff. The failure was not unique to Germany. In Indonesia and South Korea all Wal-Mart stores had either been closed or sold. The company was not doing particularly well in Japan and Brazil, countries where it had large numbers of stores.

The problems

Many reasons have been given for the failure of Wal-Mart to establish itself in Germany. The main ones are:

- **The nature of the German market.** When Wal-Mart entered the German market, retail spending had stagnated and was about to enter

CASE 5.1   (Continued)

a period of decline as the German economy slowed down in 2000. In any case the German retail market was historically one where only low margins were possible and it was dominated by a small group of retailers notably Metro, Aldi, Rewe and Schwarz (with the brand Lidl). The acquisition of Wertkauf and Interspar gave Wal-Mart only a 1.1 per cent share, which many argued was too small to create a critical mass for expansion. Furthermore, acquisitions were difficult as no other firm wanted to sell. Some of the competitors, notably Aldi, had strategies and styles very similar to Wal-Mart with discounted goods, low prices, own brands and a diverse range of products.

- **The acquisitions.** Both Wertkauf and Interspar were generally regarded as second-class operators in the German retail market and both had relatively poor reputations. Wal-Mart bought the stores, but not the land on which they were located, giving the new company problems with leases and imposing limits on alteration and expansion. In any case, Wal-Mart was prevented from building big stores by German regulations which favoured small to medium stores such as Aldi and Lidl. The stores that were purchased varied in size, and layout and rarely were they in prime locations. As a result, the company had difficulty upgrading the stores to match Wal-Mart brand expectations. Wertkauf presented an additional problem in that all its stores were located in the south west, hardly giving Wal-Mart national coverage.

- **The senior managers.** The company employed four different chief executives in the first four years of its German operation; three American and one Englishman. None spoke German and Allan Leighton, formerly of Asda, preferred to conduct the German operations from a UK base. Although German CEOs were appointed later, the main language of business was initially English. Senior managers from Wertkauf and Interspar who transferred to Wal-Mart found the level of expenses cut and some were even asked to share rooms on overnight stays for company meetings. In general, middle and lower level managers felt that their pay was lower than average for Germany. Wal-Mart on the other hand was concerned about the high labour costs in Germany.

- **Corporate culture.** Wal-Mart USA prides itself on its strong corporate culture across all locations. The culture stresses customer orientation through a friendly, proactive and committed staff. This clashed with German expectations. As Jürgen Glaubitz of the HBV trade union stated, *'German workers do not like to be regarded as cheerleaders but as personalities with their own ideas and rights.'* In addition, the German operation was operating with three corporate cultures, the Wertkauf culture, the Interspar culture and that of Wal-Mart. Senior management had failed to integrate the three cultures.

- **Supply chain issues.** Wal-Mart USA was used to wielding considerable power over its suppliers. With only a 1.1 per cent share of the German market, the company found suppliers unwilling to tow the line. Nonetheless, the senior managers behaved as in the USA and demanded access to suppliers' premises to check their operations and the quality of the products. This did not go down well with German suppliers and as a consequence Wal-Mart failed to build good relationships and never established the supply and logistics network it wanted. Wal-Mart's US buyers made classic errors in Germany such as stocking US pillow cases that did not fit German pillows.

- **Employee relations.** In the USA, Wal-Mart is a traditional non-union employer and senior US managers failed to appreciate the role of trade unions in German business. The company failed to join the Employers Association, a key body in Germany, and refused to enter into industry-wide collective agreements. There was a failure to consult with the works council, as required under German law, and the union received no financial data such as profit and loss accounts and balance sheets. This led to strikes over pay and legal battles with the union over recognition and information disclosure. Wal-Mart was frequently in the courts and frequently fined.

- In February 2005, Wal-Mart issued employees with a code of ethics. The code forbade them

(Continued)

CASE 5.1 (Continued)

from accepting gifts from suppliers and barred them from having relationships with colleagues in a position of influence over them. Moreover, all employees were asked to report immediately any transgression of the code via an anonymous 'hotline'. The company argued that its stance was ethical and protected employees from sexual harassment. However, employees were annoyed, the unions and the works council objected and ultimately the German courts ruled that it was illegal for a company to impose restrictions on the nature of relationships.

- **Pricing issues.** Wal-Mart's simple strategy was to enter a new market and undercut all its competitors to build market share. In Germany, the competition, especially Aldi and Lidl, retaliated with their own price cuts and consumers felt that Wal-Mart was not offering the best deal. As one New York analyst put it, "the competition essentially out-Wal-Marted Wal-Mart". A tactic frequently used in the USA was the use of loss leaders, selling below cost price on a limited range of goods to attract people into the store. Such a tactic was contrary to German fair trading and anti-trust laws to protect smaller firms from unfair competition.

- **Customer relations issues.** In the USA, Wal-Mart stores open round-the-clock, every day. German law forbids shop opening beyond 80 hours a week and there is no opening on Sundays and public holidays. Germany has the most restrictive opening times in Europe; stores in the UK are allowed to open for 168 hours and those in France, for 144 hours. Wal-Mart's marketing strategy is based on the concept of customer service as a competitive edge. In a number of independent surveys Wal-Mart Germany was rated below average by its customers. Three related practices illustrate the problem Wal-Mart had with its German customers. Wal-Mart has always employed 'greeters' and 'baggers'. The 'greeters' engage customers as they enter the store and the 'baggers' help customers by putting their purchases into bags at the check-out. Throughout the store there is also a 10-foot (3-metre) rule, whereby employees are required to offer direct assistance to anyone within this

distance from them. German customers saw greeters as a form of harassment and did not like anyone else handling their purchases, especially where food was involved. In general, customers wanted to be left alone to get on with their shopping and saw the intervention of Wal-Mart staff as an imposition. In addition, some customers believed that these 'extra' personnel added unnecessarily to the cost of products in the store.

- **Financial reporting.** The company was fined repeatedly for failing to comply with German regulations on the disclosure of financial information and it was pursued by the unions through the courts, resulting in well-publicized legal battles.

- **Image and publicity.** All the above contributed to a generally bad press for Wal-Mart throughout its time in Germany. The national trade union organization issued warnings to all union members about the failure of Wal-Mart to comply with the law. In 2006 at the Berlin Film Festival, Germans watched the premier of a US film, *Wal-Mart: The High Cost of Low Price,* released in the USA the previous year. The film exposed Wal-Mart for behaving unethically towards employees and suppliers and for its corrupt dealings with local politicians. The film became a success in Germany. The operation of Wal-Mart in the German market coincided with widespread anti-US sentiments within Germany over the invasion of Iraq.

Wal-Mart pulls out

By 2006, Wal-Mart had 85 stores remaining in Germany. In July that year these were sold to a rival company, Metro. In typical fashion, no financial details were disclosed but the deal is estimated to have been concluded at less than the value of the assets with a loss to Wal-Mart of US$1 billion. Just after the conclusion of the deal in Germany, Wal-Mart sold all its stores in South Korea and by 2007 operated in only 13 countries. Its international rival Carrefour operates in 29 countries. Historically, Wal-Mart has always done best in markets closest to the USA, namely Mexico and Canada. In the UK, Wal-Mart trades as Asda, which is a rare success

CASE 5.1 (Continued)

contributing 43 per cent of Wal-Mart's international revenue.

The failure in Germany is summed up by two academics thus:

Wal-Mart's attempts to apply the company's proven US success formula in an unmodified manner to the German market, however, turned out to be nothing short of a fiasco.

(Knorr and Arndt, 2003, p. i)

Questions

1 To what extent can the failure of Wal-Mart in Germany be attributed to differences in cultural values in between Germany and the USA?

2 To what extent can the failure be attributed to the institutional and regulatory framework of Germany?

3 What other factors might have contributed to the failure of Wal-Mart in the German market?

SUMMARY

- This chapter develops themes introduced in Chapters 2 and 3, namely the view that national cultures, national economic systems and business practices are converging as a consequence of globalization. In this chapter we offer a different view, which stresses the influence on business and management policies and practices of cultural and institutional diversity.

- Convergence is explored as a product of globalization in general and as a product of technology transfer and the activities of multinational firms in particular. We conclude that convergence may be limited by cultural and institutional diversity.

- We acknowledge that culture is a wide-ranging topic and define it as a set of values, norms and beliefs that enable societies to cope with their environment and groups to integrate. As such it influences business policies and practices. We view culture and its effect on business through the work of contributors such as Hall, Hofstede, Trompenaars and the researchers of the GLOBE project. We reveal also the limitations of the use of culture as an analytical tool.

- We examine the significance of variations in social and state institutions and how these can influence business. At the same time we acknowledge the influence of culture on institutions.

- We explore differences in institutions and regulations and the relationships in the business system. We examine how these affect business through an analysis of the differences in the Anglo-Saxon, social market and Asian models of capitalism.

- We close the chapter by using convergence, culture and institutional frameworks to explain the changes in the Japanese economy and the impact on Japanese firms since 1945.

DISCUSSION QUESTIONS

1 What do you understand by the concept of convergence? What is the link between convergence and globalization?

2 What do you understand by the concept of culture? Identify the various forms of cultural difference (national, ethnic, age, gender, corporate, etc.) that you can see in your own environment.

3   How useful is the concept of culture in explaining the way businesses operate in different countries? To what extent can business ideas and management techniques developed in one cultural and national setting transfer to another?

4   Assess the contribution of Geert Hofstede to our understanding of business.

5   Based on the data in Table 5.1, what are the implications for joint venture activity between three firms from the UK, China and Japan respectively.

6   What do you understand by the 'institutional' and 'business systems' approaches and how can such concepts explain differences between business policies and practice in different countries?

7   What are the arguments for and against the convergence on the Anglo-Saxon system by countries such as Germany and Japan?

8   How can convergence and diversity be used to explain the development of and specific problems associated with the Japanese economy?

FURTHER READING

A useful overview to the theory behind most of this chapter can be found in:

Koen, C. I. (2005) *Comparative International Management*, McGraw-Hill: London.

An influential but particular approach to convergence can be found in:

Kerr, C., Dunlop, J.T., Harbison, F. and Myers, C.A. (1973) *Industrialism and Industrial Man*, Penguin: Harmondsworth.

An excellent overview of the relationship of culture and business and a summary of the main research can be found in:

French, R. (2010) *Cross-cultural Management in Work Organizations*, 2nd edn, CIPD: London.

Good accounts of specific approaches can be seen in:

Hofstede, G.H., Hofstede, G. J. and Minkov, M. (2010). *Cultures and Organizations: Software of the Mind – Intercultural Cooperation and its Importance for Survival*, 3rd edn, McGraw Hill: New York.

Hofstede has his own website that contains regular updates of his thinking and of country data. www.geert-hofstede.com

Holden, N.J. (2002) *Cross-cultural Management: A Knowledge Management Perspective*, FT/Prentice Hall: Harlow.

House, R.J., Javidan, M. and Dorfman, P. (2001) 'The GLOBE project', *Applied Psychology*, 50(4), 489–55.

Trompenaars, F., and Hampden-Turner, C. (2004), *Managing People Across Cultures*, Capstone: Oxford.

The institutional and business systems approaches are covered by:

Dore, R. (2000) *Stock Market Capitalism: Welfare capitalism: Japan and Germany versus the Anglo-Saxons*, Oxford University Press: Oxford.

Hall, P.A. and Soskice, D. (eds) (2001) *Varieties of Capitalism: The Institutional Foundations of Comparative Advantage*, Oxford University Press: Oxford.

Whitley, R. (2000) *Divergent Capitalisms: The Social Structuring and Change of Business Systems*, Oxford University Press: Oxford.

PART TWO
ORGANIZATIONAL AND STRATEGIC CONTEXTS

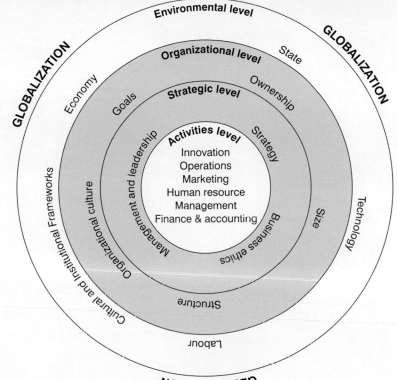

ORGANIZATIONAL ASPECTS OF BUSINESS

6

LEARNING OBJECTIVES At the end of this chapter you should be able to:

- Illustrate the interrelationships between goals, structure, ownership, size, and organizational and corporate culture.
- Explain the nature of goals, the role they play, and the causes and consequences of goal conflict in organizations.
- Identify the factors influencing organizational structure, explain the different types of structure and assess the suitability of different types of structure in different situations.
- Critically assess the factors that lead to structural change and the relationship between structure and performance.
- Explain the different forms of ownership and articulate the relationship between ownership and control.
- Assess the differences between management and control in the public and private sectors and the impact of privatization.
- Explain the impact of organizational size on business behaviour.
- Define the small firm and assess its role in relation to owners, customers and the economy.
- Explain the different approaches to examining company culture, and critically assess the contribution of company culture to organizational performance.

INTRODUCTION

In the previous four chapters we have examined aspects of the environment that interact with business. Such aspects constitute the outer level of our Business in Context model. In this chapter we examine a second level of interaction and influence belonging to the organization itself. We will consider five aspects in our model:

- goals
- structures
- size
- ownership
- organizational and corporate culture.

As with other aspects of the model, there is considerable interaction and overlap between these organizational issues. As well as pointing out the areas of overlap in each individual section, the way that issues relating to goals, ownership, structure and size come together is examined in more detail through the concept of organizational and corporate culture.

GOALS

In this section the nature of goals will be examined, the purposes they serve and how they emerge. The potential problem arising from a number of goals operating in the same organization will also be considered. We often speak of organizations like Wal-Mart and Microsoft or even our own college as having goals. In doing so we are ascribing behaviour to an abstract entity. In reality, goals are the product of some person or group, a theme which flows through this section.

There are cases where goals persist in organizations over time and assume a life of their own. A good example of this would be the goals and values set out by Bill Hewlett and Dave Packard in the early days of US electronics firm Hewlett-Packard, goals that persisted long after the two founders had retired. In Case 6.4 we explore the origins of these goals as part of HP's corporate culture and examine the changes in recent years. In Chapter 9 we will see that many companies have set out statements of ethical intent and corporate social responsibility, which are intended to have a meaning independent of the personnel involved. It is for this reason that we discuss goals in the context of organization rather than strategy. Nevertheless, we acknowledge the link between goals and strategy and return to this in Chapter 8. Managers often use goals with the assumption that a clear formulation of goals will influence performance. In the internal management of organizations, this assumption has been translated into a set of techniques aimed at influencing the behaviour of individual members, known as management-by-objectives or MBO (Drucker, 1964). Where MBO is used, the goals for the organization as a whole are generally broken down into individual goals or targets for each manager, forming a network of interconnected and internally consistent goals. The most effective MBO schemes tend to be those where there is some measure of negotiation between manager and subordinate over the precise nature of the goals to be achieved by the subordinate. This raises two points: that goal formulation is part of a political process and that goal achievement is undoubtedly related to the extent to which goals are shared by members of the organization.

However, the evidence on the influence of goals on performance is mixed, and even where such a relationship can be shown, it is unclear how it works. The use of goals to determine performance is easiest to understand where jobs are straightforward so that clear targets can be set and performance measured. Many jobs are more complex and performance measurement is difficult to achieve. Furthermore, employees may be expected to achieve goals that could conflict with one another or with those of other workers.

Not every company has clearly identified goals. For many small firms (as well as some larger ones), goals remain the unstated intentions of the owners; they may be thought of only in the vaguest of terms; employees may be unaware of them, and may give priority to their own personal goals, sometimes bringing them into conflict with management.

KEY CONCEPT 6.1   ORGANIZATIONAL GOALS

The stated goals of an organization exist to give direction to the activities of its members. In many companies, goals comprise both an overall statement of intent, sometimes referred to as a mission statement, and a set of more detailed objectives to guide strategic planning. Since many organizations are made up of different interest groups the formulation of goals can be a highly political process. This can cause conflict, but the goals of most businesses are generally accepted as being those of the senior management team. There has been a renewal of interest in the role of goals to shape the culture of an organization.

REFLECTION POINT

Examine the websites of some companies with which you are familiar. What can you learn from their mission statements and statements of corporate objectives?

The nature of goals

Allowing for the contention that organizations can engage in goal-seeking behaviour, this definition sees goals in terms of the future orientation of the company, but stated in rather loose, broad terms. A popular notion is that business firms should possess some superordinate goal, namely the maximization of profit. This view has been challenged. Some, like Handy (1993), see profit as a by-product of other goals like survival, market expansion and enhancing reputation. Marris (1964) sees profit as less important than growth. The reality is that the goals vary over time and can vary as a product of cultural differences. The variation of goals over time is best illustrated by reference to the public sector. Historically viewed as a public service organization, with the emphasis on service, more recent changes have widened the goals to incorporate notions of best value and the term 'new managerialism' is used to describe strategic shifts that have taken place in hospitals and universities. As we see below, the concept of goals is used differently by different writers. Some see goals as a generic concept, while others see them as part of a hierarchy of a generic concept that they define as strategic intentions. In this chapter we use the concept of goals in its broadest context.

Miller and Dess (1996) place concepts such as goals, objectives and mission as different forms of strategic intentions, in which goals are linked to vision, mission and objectives. These can be arranged in a hierarchy as follows:

- **Vision** relates to the future orientation of the organization and describes the kind of organization it ought to be.

- **Mission** is a statement of the key values, which define the purpose of the organization and, perhaps, its distinctive competitiveness.
- **Goals** are more specific statements of intent than mission statement, but are still broad and generalized.
- **Objectives** are the operationalization of the goals.

In Chapter 8 we locate strategy within this list as part of a 'hierarchy of intentions'.

How goals are developed

Our understanding of how goals develop owes much to the work of Cyert and March and their *Behavioural Theory of the Firm* (1963). They see organizations in terms of individuals and groups who combine to pursue mutual interests as coalitions. The interests need not be shared but the coalition is recognized by all participating interest groups as the most effective way of achieving their goals. This view of the firm reappears in Chapter 8 under our discussion of behavioural approaches to strategy formulation.

An interest group may be an entire department, such as marketing or research and development, or it might be a particular section within that department, such as a project team. It may even be a less formal grouping of managers within a department who collectively wish to pursue a specific policy. The creation of such interest groups may be a deliberate structural device. For example, senior management at Procter & Gamble felt that its interests could best be served through the creation of teams based around a single product or groups of products. The aim was the creation of healthy competition between product teams, and a competition and justification of resource allocation which would operate in the best interests of the firm as a whole. A more detailed discussion of the relationship between goals and structure may be found in the next section.

Interest groups can emerge owing to the complexity of the organization's task and/or its environment, requiring a degree of internal specialization to deal with specific problems, such as product development, or external bodies such as banks. Interest groups may also develop informally, cutting across formal structures.

Each interest group will determine its goals by reference to the information it collects. Such information generally includes comparative data on other organizations on such issues as price, product design and criteria for success. Many interest groups, for example, establish their goals in relation to competing groups in the same organization.

The important point made by Cyert and March is that groups deliberately limit strategic choice by selecting information from the range available and, having decided upon a course of action, often fail to consider other strategies. This is perfectly understandable given the range of information and the time available to make decisions. Such a process is sometimes referred to as **bounded rationality**.

Interest groups combine to form **coalitions** and in any one organization there will be a number of such coalitions. They are created by a process of influence, negotiation and bargaining between interest groups. It is out of this process that the goals that guide the behaviour of organization members emerge. However, in any one organization there is usually a group that may be identified as a dominant coalition. Once established, the dominant coalition will set up procedures to ensure that their goals are pursued by the organization as a whole. Such criteria will normally include establishing the procedures for staff selection, promotion and reward as well as laying down the rules of operation. The dominant coalition usually comprises, therefore, the senior management of an enterprise. However, certain groups align themselves with top management to ensure their goals are well represented. Even in those organizations where decision-making proceeds along more democratic lines, as in many universities, the various coalitions will compete for membership of committees at which decisions about such issues as resources are taken.

In short, the ability of groups to pursue their goals depends on the power they wield in the organization, which may depend on a number of variables. These may include their position in the hierarchy, the skills of group members, the resources they command and whether or not their role is seen as legitimate by the rest of the organization members.

It is inevitable that different coalitions will pursue different interests and that some will compete. The process of influence, negotiation and bargaining may be termed organizational politics. Such a concept tends to be viewed pejoratively and political activity in business firms is often seen as a problem. Yet, if we subscribe to the views of Cyert and March the process is an inevitable prelude to goal setting.

REFLECTION POINT

Are Cyert and March correct in their view of how goals develop?

Multiple goals

In any organization made up from different interest groups some conflict over goals is inevitable. Later in this chapter we examine goal conflict emerging from the separation of ownership and control, and the issues arising from the 'agency problem'. Handy (1993) presents several examples of goal conflict, including that between the sales and production departments. The goals of the sales department are normally measured by volume turnover, while those of the production department are measured by cost-efficiency. We return to this particular problem in Chapter 11, when we depict the classic dilemma of the production department as that of satisfying the twin demands of customer satisfaction and operating efficiency.

In some cases such conflict can be seen to operate against the best interests of the organization. A study by Selznick (1949) of the Tennessee Valley Authority is viewed as a classic of its kind. An emerging organization, formed to solve the problems of irrigating and redeveloping a vast area of the USA in the Tennessee Valley, tackled its job through delegation and specialization. In this case, each specialist division within the organization developed a greater commitment to its own goals than those of the organization as a whole. This fragmented the total effort and resulted in groups devoting a great deal of their time to legitimizing their activities and competing for resources. This set up conflicts with other groups, which strengthened the resolve of each to pursue its own goals. Burns and Stalker (1966) noted how conflict developed between the production and research and development departments in certain Scottish electronics firms, with the subsequent decline in their competitive standing.

In such cases, activities move away from dealing with customers or even coping with external changes in the market to focus on the resolution of internal tensions and management becomes the management of internal coalitions. Case 6.1 illustrates issues of goal conflict in London Zoo that were brought to the surface at the time of financial crisis in the early 1990s. In many organizations conflict often remains hidden, emerging only when problems get out of hand. In most situations conflict can be contained and managed. A similar situation occurred within the BBC during the summer of 1993. Viewing figures revealed that BBC1 was achieving only 29 per cent of the television audience against ITV's 41 per cent. This created a much-publicized debate about the future direction of BBC programming and there was a belief among senior managers at BBC1 that it was catering for an elite upper-income, middle-class audience and needed to widen its appeal. This debate led to allegations of autocratic management and a stifling of creativity, which led to conflict between factions within the organization. This would appear to be a continuing debate within the BBC, linked to the wider debate of publicly funded television versus television funded by advertising revenue.

We can see that it is normal for many goals to exist in most organizations. However, not all conflict of this kind is necessarily a problem. It would appear to be limited by four factors:

- Most groups in an organization will agree to those goals formulated by senior management as a means of achieving their own goals. This is the result of a bargaining and negotiating process between interest groups.

- Most organization members would appear to accept the goals of top management with little question. This would seem to be an implied element of the employment contract.

- The dominant coalition normally sets up controls to ensure compliance to their goals. Such controls have been alluded to earlier and include selection procedures, induction and training to ensure that rules are followed. In addition, management can use technological controls in the form of work design and job allocation, and financial controls in the form of budgets and reward systems. In such ways as these, the managers of organizations ensure at least a minimum level of compliance with their chosen goals.

- In many firms senior management acknowledge that different groups may have their own goals which need to be satisfied.

CASE 6.1   LONDON ZOO

London Zoo in Regent's Park, in the centre of London, faces many of the problems of urban zoos; relatively cramped and inappropriate conditions for keeping large animals in captivity, little prospect of expansion, falling attendance and increasing opposition from animal welfare groups. From its heyday in the 1950s when the zoo regularly attracted three million visitors a year, attendance figures fell to around one million in 2001. Furthermore, the zoo has pursued a policy of removing its larger animals to its sister zoo, Whipsnade. These were a particularly popular attraction. By 2012 attendances had risen with 1.6 million visiting the zoo in its London and Whipsnade locations, although London itself attracted 1.1 million of these.

This case study goes back to the events of the early 1990s when goal conflict was brought to the fore as different groups fought for control of the strategic direction of the zoo. In 1991, London Zoo faced a financial crisis and closure was imminent. The surrounding debate between the owners, the managers and employees was a good illustration of goal conflict within a complex organization faced with considerable external problems. The case also examines subsequent changes and their effect on the future of the zoo.

London Zoo and its sister zoo, Whipsnade, are the property and responsibility of the Zoological Society of London, a body made up of fellows elected on the basis of some special interest and expert knowledge in zoology and its related fields. The zoos had experienced financial problems for a number of years and, in 1988, the society commissioned a consultancy report. It recommended that the two zoos be run in a much more commercial way. The process began with the reduction in the number of animals, a marketing campaign to attract more visitors, the introduction of a more business-oriented approach and a number of organizational changes. Among these were wholesale changes in the terms and conditions of employees. Zoo employees were put on a consolidated pay scale and for the first time were faced with appraisal and performance-related pay. At the same time the problems facing the zoo were cushioned by government backing of £10 million.

Despite the changes, the recession in 1991 caused a decline in paying visitors and news of closure was leaked to the press. Paradoxically, this led to a sharp increase in visitors to the zoo, perhaps sensing their last chance to visit. An appeal was launched and the management embarked on fund-raising and cost-cutting exercises. A panda was borrowed from China in an attempt, amid much publicity, to mate London's own panda and a version of the popular television programme, *Blind Date,* was used to gain maximum coverage. It became particularly important to focus on specific attractions since parts of the zoo had been closed because they were unsafe and policies to reduce the number of animals kept were well advanced. Almost every day saw more animals leave the zoo for other destinations or to be destroyed. At the same time, the number of employees was cut by one-third. This necessitated jobs being combined and keepers, who were used to specializing in a particular area, were asked to take on a range of tasks with different types of animals.

These changes highlighted differences between various groups associated with the zoo. Goal conflict has never been far from the surface. As with any zoo there is a tension between those who see the zoo as a focus and means of academic research into zoological matters and those who see it primarily as a form of entertainment for the public. Some of the cruder attempts at commercialization were anathema to the former group. In general, the shift to a business management approach brought tensions to the surface and factions emerged. The members of the Zoological Society were one group, the management of the zoo another, and a third comprised those keepers and researchers who made up the majority of the zoo's employees. Within these groups there were differences. Some fellows saw commercialization as the only means of survival. Others, however, banded together as a 'reform group' opposed to blatant commercialism and questioned the policies of the zoo's management. There was a general debate about the role of zoos in society and the role governments might play. The £10 million grant was unusual for a UK government intent on creating a non-subsidized free market society. Despite this financial gesture, many of the fellows were openly critical of the government and cited a much greater financial backing given to zoos in other countries. There was a strong belief that no longer could zoos support themselves. The reform group formed a coalition with a group of employees who had established themselves as a 'survival group', and who were a useful source of information to the fellows on daily events at the zoo. Within the employees, a number of issues emerged. The primary concern of one group focused on changes in their terms of employment. Another group expressed the greatest concern at the loss of animals and the difficulties of providing adequate care for those remaining. Some researchers saw the crisis as an ideal opportunity to further their claim that greater attention should be paid to academic research and the furtherance of zoological knowledge.

The financial appeal and various marketing ploys were partially successful but the impact was essentially short term and when, in 1992, the zoo made further losses and failed to achieve its targets for the number of visitors, closure seemed inevitable once again. The zoo was saved by a donation from the Emir of Kuwait as a gesture of gratitude to the British people for their part in the first Gulf War. The publicity surrounding this donation and the plight of the zoo led to more donations. The basic divisions persisted. There were still those who wanted the zoo to become a profit-making theme park, and proposed that animals be placed in realistic sets to mirror their natural habitat, as well as the addition of a state-of-the-art aquarium. On the other hand, there were those who saw that the zoo's only chance for public support, and hence survival, lay in the preservation and breeding of endangered species. This battle for the ideological heart of London Zoo was dubbed by the media as the 'suits' versus the 'beards'.

In the event, the theme park and aquarium concept, at a joint estimated cost of £95 million, was deemed too expensive. The zoo focused,

(Continued)

CASE 6.1 (Continued)

instead, on conservation work and launched an extensive marketing campaign around the concept of 'Conservation in Action'. Part of the campaign was the introduction of an animal adoption programme, in which members of the public and organizations could sponsor particular animals. The campaign attracted a great deal of media attention through the support of national celebrities and through a BBC programme, *Zoowatch*.

In 1997, the zoo announced an operating surplus of over £1 million. Since then the zoo has attracted lottery funding and government support for special projects. Such funding has been relatively small and the zoo continues to be dogged by problems.

At the end of 2001, a keeper was crushed to death by one of the elephants during a public exhibition. The zoo came under attack from the Royal Society for the Prevention of Cruelty to Animals (RSPCA) and other animal rights and welfare organizations over its treatment of animals. They cited the reduced life expectancy of most zoo animals, which in the case of elephants was less than half that of animals in the wild. Part of the problem was the inappropriate nature of many of the buildings. Several of the buildings in Regent's Park are of considerable architectural interest and the zoo contains 12 listed buildings. For example, the penguin pool, designed by Lubetkin in 1934, is hailed as a masterpiece of modernist architecture, yet is far from the ideal habitat for penguins. Continuing attempts have been made to refocus the zoo around conservation but use this to attract the paying public. The key was the bringing together of entertainment, conservation and research. This was a clear attempt to move away from the image of a learned society to that of engaging the public in issues of conservation. The zoo, ever concerned for publicity and income from a variety of sources, was keen to stress the feature of the reptile house in the first Harry Potter book and film and its use as a location in the popular film *About a Boy*.

The conservation theme has persisted and the 2013 slogan of the Zoological Society was 'Living Conservation'. Research appears to have been strengthened by closer ties between the research arm of the Zoological Society and University College, London. Funding remains a constant theme and the focus has shifted to emphasize the Zoo's charitable status. Events using the animals have been staged to raise awareness and there have been fundraising galas involving celebrity hosts, charity concerts and charity runs such as the 'London Zoo 10km Stampede'. The financial status has improved and a surplus was achieved in the four years up to 2012. However, as in any organization where finances are tight, tensions are never far from the surface and the zoo struggles to balance commercialization and conservation research.

Questions

1 Identify the various interest groups in London Zoo and the nature and origins of the goal conflict between them.

2 To what extent are the financial problems affecting London Zoo since the early 1990s a product or a cause of the goal conflict? What other factors were at work?

3 What strategies may be most suited for London Zoo over the next ten years? What should be the main goal of the zoo and what issues of goal conflict may arise?

REFLECTION POINT

Are several goals necessarily a source of conflict?

This section has depicted the formation of goals as a complex process involving the resolution of external influences and internal politics. As such, the system is highly dynamic and changes in the goals will occur with changes in the external environment, such as market demand, technology and government policy, as well as changes that take place between interest groups within the organization. A change in ownership or top management may lead to a shift in emphasis of the firm's operations.

Goals are not formalized, meaningless statements but the products of an interactive and dynamic process. The changing of goals in the face of external and even internal changes is seen to be a prerequisite for the survival of the organization. Those managers who cling to inappropriate goals would appear to place their companies at risk. However, the assumption that the existence of explicit statements of intent, such as goals, is linked to superior company performance has not been widely researched and when it has been, the findings tend to be inconclusive. Bart and Baetz (1999) in their study of links between mission statements and performance among large Canadian firms concluded that there was no automatic connection between mission and performance. However, there was evidence of superior performance where a firm had a mission statement to which management subscribed and also where the mission statement had been produced as a result of some form of employee involvement. There would appear to be clear links here to issues of commitment and corporate culture, issues we deal with later in the chapter.

In much of our discussion of goals there are clear implications for organization structure and it is to this we now turn.

STRUCTURE

A theme in our discussion of goals was that organizations are made up of interest groups formed as coalitions. One of the factors that may facilitate or inhibit the way these groups pursue their goals and whether such goals may be achieved is the structure of the organization. In this section we will examine how structures develop, the variations that occur in structural type, and their impact on performance. You should note, however, that any discussion of structure is biased towards the large firm, and most of the studies in this area are of large corporations. This is inevitable in that structural problems tend to be associated with size and complexity.

A structure is concerned with the grouping of activities in the most suitable manner to achieve the goals of the dominant coalition. It is concerned with:

- the organization of work around roles;
- the grouping of these roles to form teams or departments;
- the allocation of differential amounts of power and authority to the various roles;
- job descriptions, mechanisms for coordination and control, and management information systems.

In Chapter 2 in our discussion of globalization we introduced issues of structure facing managers today, particularly those working in a global company. We examined outsourcing, alliances and joint ventures. These topics are concerned with structures.

Child (2005) recognizes the increased complexity of organizations. He identifies a number of choices that lie at the heart of structure. These are:

- The nature of the **hierarchy,** for example, whether it is tall or flat.
- The degree of **specialization.** In particular structures this will reflect the combined influence of hierarchy and specialization.
- The type of **grouping,** deciding which tasks should be placed together.
- **Rules, schedules and systems** and in particular how rigid or flexible working practices should be.
- **Integration** in terms of the mechanisms to be used to achieve effective coordination and operations throughout the organization.

- The nature of **control** mechanisms. In contemporary organizations the nature of both integration and control have changed as a result of developments in information and communications technology (see Chapter 4), more especially the use of email and more recently Facebook and Twitter. One effect of this has been the reduction in the number of managers, a theme we return to later in this chapter when discussing delayering.
- The nature of the **reward** systems. This is linked to structure in that reward can be based on hierarchy or, for example, more flexibly on performance.
- The extent of **cross-boundary** and **cross-border** activities, especially outsourcing, alliances and joint ventures.

Child speaks of choices, which assumes that managers have a choice and that structures can be deliberately created to affect overall performance. We will now examine those factors that can influence a firm's structure to determine the extent to which structures can be manipulated by management.

KEY CONCEPT 6.2   ORGANIZATION STRUCTURE

An organization structure is a grouping of activities and people to achieve the goals of the organization. Considerable variation is possible in the type of structure employed and the influences include management strategy, technology, size, the nature of the environment, the behaviour of interest groups, the firm's history and wider cultural factors. In general terms, a particular structure emerges to maximize the opportunities and solve the problems created by these influences. In practice, however, the evidence concerning the influence of structure and performance is very patchy.

Factors that influence structure

We can identify a number of factors that influence structure. We examine first the relationship between structure and strategy and in particular the seminal work of Alfred Chandler and then identify other influences: technology, size, changes in the environment, culture and interest groups.

Strategy and structure and the work of Alfred Chandler

The relationship of strategy to organizational structure owes much to the work of Alfred Chandler (1962) and his historical study of structural change in large US companies. The biggest change he discovered was the shift from functional to multidivisional structures as a consequence of changing strategies (the essential features of these structures will be identified in the following section). He presented a case study of the development of four companies, DuPont, General Motors, Standard Oil and Sears Roebuck. While he claimed that structure follows strategy, Chandler argued that the relationship between structure and strategy is complex (more so than many summaries of Chandler acknowledge). He found that structure did not automatically follow strategy and that managements often needed a crisis before they would agree to structural change. He also found that multidivisional structures were not without problems and that in some cases structures could influence strategy.

Chandler viewed the relationship between strategy and structure as dynamic and evolutionary. He identified several stages in the development of US capitalism. These were cycles of growth and consolidation, each with its own implications for the organizational structures of the emerging large corporations in his study:

- The growth of mass markets and the development of the techniques of mass production were accompanied by vertical integration to ensure the supply of materials and secure distribution channels, and by horizontal integration through takeovers to maintain growth. This was the classic strategy in the early days of Ford.

- Expansion brought its own problems of coordination and control and subsequent inefficiency. These were solved by the growth of professional management and the development of organizations structured around specialist functions, such as marketing and finance; a functional structure.

- As markets became saturated and the benefits accruing from organizational restructuring slowed down, new markets and products were vigorously pursued by overseas expansion and R&D respectively.

- Once again these developments brought their own problems of coordination and control. This time a new form of structure emerged. All four firms in Chandler's study had adopted a multi-divisional structure by 1929, with DuPont and GM leading the way.

For example, DuPont needed to search for new markets following its loss of military contracts and the crisis of financial loss. GM had expanded rapidly and developed the largest range of products of any car company, bringing problems of control and, like DuPont, it faced the crisis of financial loss. Sears was confronted by the need to switch from mail order to retail as population movement and concentration changed the nature of its traditional market, a large but scattered population in rural America. Standard Oil faced the restrictions imposed by anti-trust legislation and was forced to expand its already considerable overseas presence, adding greatly to problems of coordination and control.

In each case the solution was the creation of several divisions, with each division operating as a profit centre, almost a business in its own right. Divisions were either based around products or geography or both. By the early 1940s the multidivisional firm was common among US multinationals and was seen as a solution to the problems of coordination and control. Inevitably there were problems with the new structure, mainly a result of the tensions between a central headquarters and the independent divisions.

KEY CONCEPT 6.3   THE MULTI-DIVISIONAL COMPANY

A multi-divisional company comprises a number of business units, which may pursue markedly different types of business activity. The business units operate as profit centres and are centrally coordinated by a corporate headquarters, which may also control certain central services, such as research and development, and finance. This kind of structure was developed in the USA in response to business growth and complexity.

Stopford and Wells (1972) also noted a strong influence of strategy on structure. They too noted the shift from functional to multidivisional structures with expansion internationally. However, they identified that product divisions and geographical divisions resulted from different influences. The creation of product divisions was a function of increasing product diversity in foreign markets, while area or geographical divisions resulted as foreign sales grew in proportion to total sales. They noted that further expansion and complexity resulted in global matrix organizations (defined in the next section).

There would seem to be a logic that dictates the influence of strategy on structure. For example, a firm wishing to be a product leader in a technologically sophisticated product market will have a correspondingly large R&D department in terms of both investment and employees. A firm that places a great deal of emphasis on cost controls may have a larger than average accounting department. There are, however, complicating factors. We can see cases where structural change may not be necessary or at least delayed by the sheer market power of the firm, as in the case of IBM. The company was a clear technical leader and held a dominant position in the mainframe computer market throughout the 1960s and 1970s. Its functional structure was highly specialized and highly bureaucratic. As a result, IBM failed to respond to market changes and only did so with decentralization and divisionalization in the mid 1980s, enabling it to compete aggressively in the personal computer market.

There is also a case for arguing that structure can determine strategy. This was acknowledged by Chandler (1962) who saw that, with the switch to a multi-divisional structure, managers at HQ became less overloaded and could engage in more long-term planning. Furthermore, the multi-divisional structure meant that expansion was now relatively simple through the addition of other divisions. However, Chandler also noted that those firms that chose to expand through the acquisition of other firms once again overloaded HQ staff.

REFLECTION POINT

What problems do multi-divisional structures solve and what problems might they create?

Other influences on structure

Technology For some, technology is the most important, if not the sole, determinant of a firm's structure. This is part of the concept known as 'technological determinism'. Much of the work in this area is indebted to Joan Woodward's (1965) work on the impact of technology on a hundred manufacturing firms in south-east UK. She and her research team found that differences in manufacturing, from small batch to mass production to process technology, resulted in corresponding differences in a number of factors. These included the size and shape of the management hierarchy, the proportion of management to other employees, the proportion of direct to indirect labour, and the number of subordinates controlled by any one manager (the span of control). Technology has a clear influence in manufacturing industry. A car plant has departments created by the flow of the product through a number of processes. The press shop creates car parts out of rolled steel. The sub-assembly department then welds these parts together, from where they enter the paint shop to be sprayed. After this they enter the stage of final assembly where the car body is joined by engine and transmission parts.

Size Other researchers find size to be a more significant variable in influencing structure than is technology. This was a particular theme of a group of academics at Aston University in the 1960s and 70s (see, for example, Pugh, 1969). As firms increase in size, additional problems are created in terms of coordination and control, often necessitating structural changes. For example, as the business expands the owner of a small business often faces increasing pressures on his or her time. No longer is he or she able to maintain a close control of operations and act as the focal point for customers, as well as managing administration and wages. In such cases some formalization and delegation is inevitable and a stage is reached when small businesses take their first steps towards bureaucratization. Such changes in structure with increasing size can be viewed in large as well as in small firms. We can see with Dow Corning in Case 6.2 that structural changes were made as the company expanded its product range and its markets. The way firms respond to size may vary, resulting in different types of structure, which we identify in the next section. While there are obvious connections between size and structure, the complexity of an organization's operations may have a bigger impact on its structure than sheer size.

Changes in the environment Generally, organizations need to adapt to their environment to survive. An important feature of that adaptation is structural. Burns and Stalker (1966) noted that technological and market changes in the post-war electronics industry were best served by a less bureaucratic, more flexible kind of organization. Such organic structures were an essential element in the firms' ability to cope with a highly changing environment, and firms that retained their traditional bureaucratic or mechanistic structures were much less successful.

This concept of the structure fitting the dominant aspects of the firm's environment is the major theme in the work of Lawrence and Lorsch (1967). They believe that different tasks in the organization are confronted by different environmental problems and demands. These differences should be reflected in the structures of the departments carrying out those tasks. In their study of the plastics industry they found a highly uncertain technological environment that called for a flexible R&D function, while the demands imposed on the production department were more predictable, enabling a more traditional, bureaucratic structure to operate. The structural implications of Lawrence and Lorsch's analysis do not end with what they term the 'differentiation' of functions. To operate effectively, all organizations so differentiated must establish integrative devices, which might include a committee structure or designing special coordinating roles.

Culture The influence of culture on structure should not be underestimated. Firms in different countries often reflect different emphases. For example, US firms tend to stress the legal, finance and marketing functions, while those in Germany tend to feature operations. Studies on such aspects as the shape and extent of the management hierarchy have also noted differences between countries (Brossard and Maurice, 1976; Trompenaars, 1993). For example, the hierarchies in French firms tend to be steeper than in the UK, and much steeper than in Germany. Structure may also reflect specific organizational cultures; for example, those firms favouring the involvement of employees in decision-making may set up participative forums to facilitate this.

Interest groups The preferences of the dominant coalition can exert considerable influence on the structure, as can the demands of stakeholders. Those firms where the owners play a major role in management tend to be highly centralized. In the public sector, the pressure for accountability often results in elaborate financial control mechanisms and bureaucratic procedures. In some manufacturing firms, the pressure from banks on lending may in times of recession lead to reductions in development activities, with a corresponding impact on the size of the R&D function.

Two points emerge from our consideration of the six influences above:

- First, there is considerable overlap between factors. For example, the structural changes of firms like Dupont and GM link technology, size and strategy; the different structural routes taken by firms in different countries are a function of both cultural differences and variations in environmental factors. In short, the structure of an organization can only be explained by reference to a number of interrelated factors. This is illustrated in the Dow Corning case study.

- Second, our analysis raises the issue of management choice in determining the structure of an organization. Are structures creative innovations to implement changing strategies or are they the inevitable consequences of adaptation to prevailing influences?

Types of structure

In this section we present a brief review of structural types and examine some trends in organization structure.

Very few organizations conform precisely to a particular structural type. In some organizations a particular kind of structure predominates, while others display a variety of types. We will explain the basic characteristic of each type and present in Table 6.1 a summary statement of the supposed advantages and problems associated with each one. As mentioned earlier, structure does not emerge as an issue until a firm reaches a certain size. Many small firms have no apparent structure at all, beyond a centralized control system, but even this is not inevitable, as in the case of partnerships between professional people. We identify five main types of organization structure.

TABLE 6.1	A summary of advantages and problems associated with different types of organization structure

Advantages	Problems
1. Functional organization	
• Specialization	• Conflicting departmental objectives
• The logic of custom and practice	• Conflicting management values
• A clear chain of command	• A lack of coordination
	• A lack of consumer orientation
2. Divisional organization and holding company	
• The operation of businesses as profit centres	• Cooperation and interdependence
• The encouragement of entrepreneurship	• Accounting procedures, especially transfer pricing
• Reduces upward dependency on top management	• Increasing diversity of operations
• Economies of scale by centralization of common features like R&D	• Overall management control
3. Project teams	
• The ability to cope with an unstable environment	• A costly duplication of services
• The use of individual expertise	• Scheduling
• The ability to cope with diverse problems	• The participants have no functional home
• Deal directly with the customer	• What happens when the project is finished?
4. Matrix organization	
• Emphasizes the strengths of the functional and project types	• Coordination and control
• Flexibility of labour	• A proliferation of committees and meetings
• The ability to transfer expertise where it is most needed	• Too many bosses
• Dual control via function and project	• Conflicting loyalties for staff
• Closeness to the customer	• Can be slow to adapt

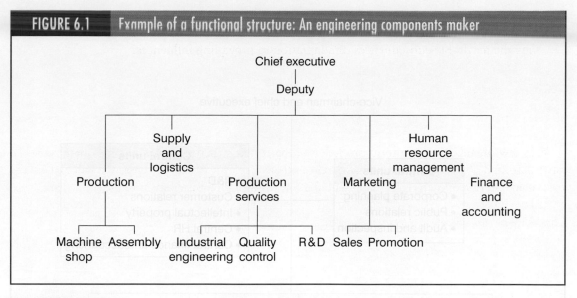

FIGURE 6.1   Example of a functional structure: An engineering components maker

Functional structures

The main criterion guiding this type of organization is functional specialization. There are clear links here with classic forms of bureaucracy. As we can see from Figure 6.1, employees performing related specialist tasks are grouped together under a single management structure. Of all the structural types, this reflects most clearly the relationship between hierarchy and specialization. Most firms, as they develop, adopt this form of structure and it is especially suited to single-product firms.

Multidivisional structures

We have explored issues related to multi-divisional structures in our discussion of the influence of strategy on structure and the contribution made by Alfred Chandler. The development of the multi-divisional company is associated with market expansion and product diversification. In both these cases traditional functional structures showed themselves to be inadequate in coordinating and controlling the firm's activities. Divisionalization was a particularly US development and is associated with such 'pioneer' companies as GM and DuPont in the 1920s and with the multinational expansion of US firms in the 1930s (Chandler, 1962). This form of structure has been hailed as a major management innovation (Birkenshaw and Mol, 2006).

An illustration of a multi-divisional structure is shown in Figure 6.2. Under such an organization structure each division is self-contained and operates as a profit centre. Divisions can be grouped around products or markets or a combination of the two. The activities of the divisions are directed by a headquarters unit which takes a global view of strategy. In many divisionalized structures, R&D and purchasing are often centralized activities to benefit from economies of scale, especially given the high costs associated with R&D. The dual existence of divisional profit centres and central units is a source of tension for many firms operating this structure, especially in the allocation of the costs of these central units to the individual divisions. In one case, a divisionalized engineering firm operated a central foundry, which also had to act as a profit centre in its own right. As well as serving the needs of its own organization, the foundry, having spare capacity, was encouraged to seek contracts outside the firm. This set up two sorts of tension. First, the various divisions complained about having to pay the 'going rate' for foundry products, and second, the divisions always demanded priority over external contracts, which hampered the foundry from achieving its own profit objectives.

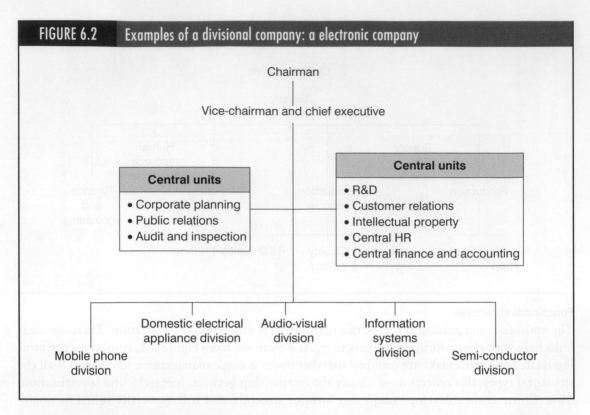

FIGURE 6.2   Examples of a divisional company: a electronic company

Once divisions have been established, a decision still has to be made about grouping within each division. In some cases this is done along traditional functional lines, whereas in others employees are organized around products.

The holding company

There are similarities between the holding company and the multidivisional structure. The holding company is a looser arrangement than the divisional company and may lack the focus. Holding companies are generally associated with the growth of the firm by acquisitions and a high degree of product diversification. It may comprise a group of independent companies controlled by a coordinating group, usually made up of the chief executives of the constituent companies. The holding company is the prevalent structural form for large, diversified Japanese and Korean companies. Figure 6.3 offers a typical illustration.

Project teams

These comprise units created to cope with a highly unstable environment. In essence they are temporary structures formed around a particular task or problem and reflect technical expertise rather than any notion of management hierarchy. Such structures are commonly found in high-technology firms and some types of service organizations, especially consulting firms. In advertising agencies, teams are usually created to deal with specific client accounts. In R&D departments the research work may be organized around teams, each handling a different problem. In construction companies project teams may be created to deal with a particular job such as the building of an office block. The membership of teams can be highly fluid; specialists may be brought in at different times and one employee may be a member of several teams.

The approach reflects a close identification with the needs of the client and is an extension of the kind of client-based structure found in professional firms such as solicitors, accountants and

FIGURE 6.3   The holding company: Hyundai Group

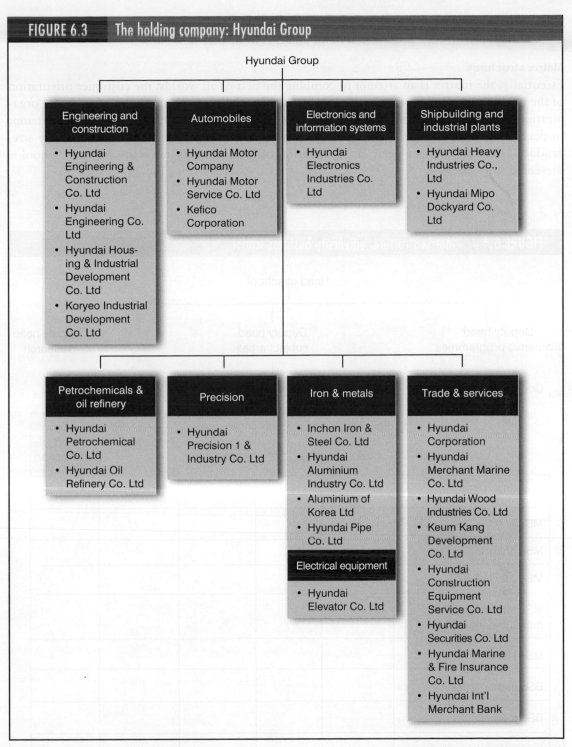

the like. However, the use of teams has become more common in firms of all sizes as they search for flexibility and responsiveness.

While focusing specifically on the needs of the client does have its advantages, there can be unnecessary duplication of resources and there may be scheduling and logistics problems. These become more severe as the organization gets larger, and a stage may be reached where project teams need to be supported within a functional or divisional framework. The matrix structure was developed with such problems in mind and it is to this we now turn.

Matrix structures

Essentially, the matrix is an attempt to combine the best of all worlds: the customer orientation of the project team, the economies of scale and the specialist orientation of the functional organization, and the product or market focus of the divisional company. The matrix is an attempt to devise a structure that can effectively manage at least two different elements, be they size, products, markets or customers. The illustration of a matrix in a university business school is presented in Figure 6.4.

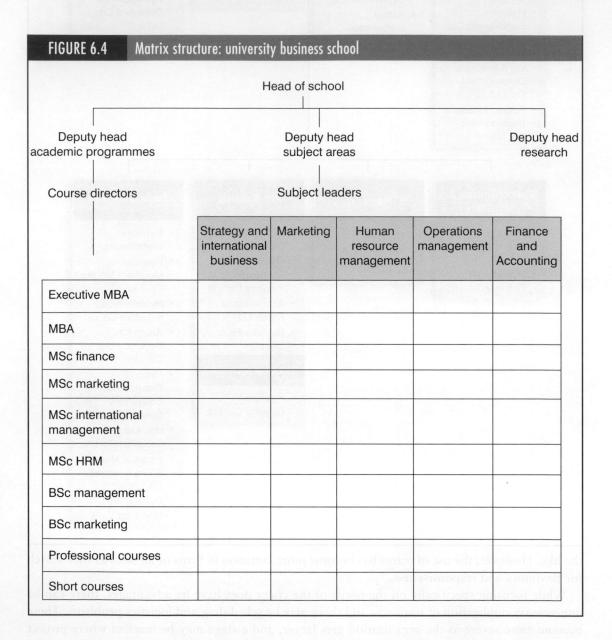

FIGURE 6.4   Matrix structure: university business school

	Strategy and international business	Marketing	Human resource management	Operations management	Finance and Accounting
Executive MBA					
MBA					
MSc finance					
MSc marketing					
MSc international management					
MSc HRM					
BSc management					
BSc marketing					
Professional courses					
Short courses					

The essence of the matrix is illustrated by Dow Corning in Case 6.2; the work was controlled originally in two directions, by a specialist function and by a product grouping. Committees were set up to coordinate the two orientations, and attention was given to training the staff towards goal congruence. Further developments in the matrix at Dow added a third dimension to the structure, that of geography.

The matrix became very popular in the 1970s and owed much to the work of Lawrence and Lorsch (1967) and Galbraith (1971). It was embraced by companies such as Dow Corning, General Electric, Ciba Geigy and Citibank. The matrix was developed to deal with increased complexity, especially technical complexity and the increased rate of change. A single manager was deemed to have insufficient knowledge to manage all aspects of a task and hence responsibilities needed to be split. Paul Lawrence in a later work (Davis and Lawrence, 1977) saw the advantages of the matrix in terms of:

- When two or more of a firm's dimensions, like products and markets, were especially critical to its performance. A stated advantage of the matrix is that it offers a greater focus on the customer.
- Where employees needed to carry out highly complex, interdependent tasks in an uncertain environment. A matrix brings together different skills to focus on a single project. In doing this, the matrix has the added advantage of breaking down bureaucracies and organizational barriers.
- When economies of scale were needed, especially in the use of scarce or expensive resources. Efficiencies can be gained by using employees flexibly.

However, the popularity of the matrix was short-lived and of all the structural types it has attracted most criticism. Even Paul Lawrence acknowledged that the matrix was an 'unnecessary complexity', which was only justified in certain situations (Davis and Lawrence, 1977, p. 21). Unless the demands facing the organization are very complex and unless employees are able to be flexible, then the matrix may cause more problems than it solves. Some of those problems are depicted in Case 6.2, which also illustrates the changes made by Dow to counteract such problems. Many employees find the system confusing and dislike reporting to two bosses. Managers representing different arms of the matrix can engage in inefficient power struggles and for some employees it gives them the opportunity to play one manager off against another.

CASE 6.2	DOW CORNING

Dow Corning was formed in 1942 out of part of Dow Chemical and Corning Glass in the USA. The company specialized in silicone products and made its name from the development of a silicone grease to prevent moisture in aircraft engines at altitude. The original focus of the firm was R&D, and it was highly centralized around technology and products. At this stage of its development the products were closely related and the firm operated under a traditional functional management structure.

By 1962, changes had taken place. The company had grown, largely through product diversity, and central control of product development was no longer appropriate. In addition, there had been a change in top management and the new chief executive established five product divisions as profit centres, each with its own functional structures. The new structure was seen as successful in integrating the functions, and a contributory factor in the firm's continued growth and increased profitability.

(Continued)

CASE 6.2   (*Continued*)

Within a short time, international expansion brought its own problems. There was conflict between the demands of the home and foreign markets. Conflict also arose over the central supply of raw materials and the mechanisms for transfer pricing. An economic recession meant that profit levels fell. These problems were met by another change in management along with a structural change to a matrix organization.

The ensuing matrix comprised two major elements: specialist functions and ten business profit centres created from the existing five divisions. Employees reported to a business centre manager and a functional vice-president. Each business centre comprised different product boards. Each product board was led by a particular functional manager and leadership tended to change with the product life cycle, from R&D at the early stages to marketing as the product moved through each stage of the cycle.

Structures and processes were developed within the matrix to enhance coordination and deal with conflict. The company used management-by-objectives linked to group goals. Goal congruence was helped by having a management dominated by chemical engineers. As the businesses developed it became clear that the firm needed to rethink the components of its matrix structure. In addition to organization by function and by business product, there was also organization by geography, to satisfy the increasing international dimension of Dow's business. In part the focus on area management was made to solve a problem attributed to the original matrix, that of building too many plants and failing to capitalize on economies of scale.

Problems with the matrix persisted. Area managers were seen to have too much power within the organization and were accused of empire-building; employees complained of too many bosses; and the matrix created a cumbersome bureaucracy with a great deal of time consumed in meetings. Dow, unlike many other organizations, did not retreat from the matrix in the face of these problems. An expansion into the pharmaceuticals sector through acquisitions meant that some form of flexible, semi-autonomous structure was required. Senior management decided to refocus the evolved matrix structure. A small team of senior executives was given the task of supervising all operations. They also had the responsibility of ensuring that only one of the three elements of function, business and geography took the lead in any venture, thus avoiding conflict and duplication of effort. In addition, considerable attention was paid to employee communication, with the result that the matrix was viewed as a more open, less secretive form of structure.

By the end of the 1980s the company operated in 32 countries and was responsible for the manufacture of 1800 products. The success of its flexible organization structure, particularly the growing interchange of ideas and practices across regions, gave management the confidence to seek out more areas for expansion. More business unit teams were created and were given autonomy to develop new products and encouraged to innovate.

One of the profitable growth markets had been in silicone breast implants. These were found to have caused health problems for many women and the company was sued in the US courts. The damages and potential future damages were so great that in 1995 the company filed for Chapter 11 bankruptcy in the USA. Under Chapter 11, a company may retain its assets but must develop a payment plan to the satisfaction of its creditors. In other words, the firm is pledging future cash flows against its debts.

Dow Corning was also hit by the financial crisis in Asia, which had a particular impact on its core silicone business. Despite this the company began to move out of Chapter 11 bankruptcy. It had closed plants in Asia, Europe and the USA and had begun to reorganize around product groups rather than geographical areas.

Dow Corning emerged from Chapter 11 bankruptcy in 2004 following a $3.2 billion settlement with recipients of the allegedly defective breast implants. The company has continued to use a complex matrix organization, although there is no mention of the matrix structure on its current website, except in the form of listing geographical and functional management staff. Dow Corning has regional vice presidents for Europe, Middle East and Africa, North America, Latin America, India, Japan/Korea and China, as well as business vice presidents on the functional side that oversee the company's business strategy and corporate governance on a global scale. For example, there are vice presidents for environment, health and safety, procurement and logistics, finance, strategic acquisitions and so on. The company is also split into 25 business sectors, alphabetically from Automotive to Textiles and Leather.

The site www.glassdoor.com provides a forum for past and current employees of companies to rate them and give their advice to the firm's management. There are many positive statements about Dow Corning as an employer and a place to work but there were some negative statements about the matrix organization. These include:

Decision-making process painstakingly slow, linked to an ambiguous matrix organization.
... organizational change is very frequent.
In four years, my bosses have been changed to six different people ....
Less reorganization would be nice.

Too many managers / levels between the individual contributors and the upper management.

Questions

1 What were the main factors involved in Dow Corning changing from a functional to a divisional and then to a matrix structure? How do these factors relate to the various influences on structure identified earlier in this section?

2 What problems did Dow Corning encounter with the matrix organization? How might such problems have been minimized?

3 What structure would be most appropriate for the company to aid its recovery post Chapter 11 bankruptcy?

For many years, matrix management was a by-word for inefficiency, conflict, delay and cost. However, it was seen by some companies in the 1990s as the structural form that was made for the company wishing to act globally and transnationally. In the case of Ford Motor Company, the creation of a matrix organization was an integral part of the Ford global strategy The structure was based around five vehicle centres, four in the USA and one in Europe. These vehicle centres are served by cross-national teams in most of the functional areas. In this way, a manager in the UK could report to a line manager in the USA and be part of a team embracing people in Germany and Spain. The system is supported by an extensive video-conferencing network, which facilitates regular meetings between team members. The structure was introduced by senior management, mindful of the problems of matrix organizations in other companies. Considerable attention was paid to setting clear objectives, having clear definitions of roles, appointing and promoting those people who could operate globally and investing heavily in public relations and training. The advantages of matrix management were stressed. The then chief executive, Alex Trotman, saw its advantage in breaking down the 'chimneys' of the functional structure, which act as barriers, and opening up people to new ideas.

Students should always remember that the structural types identified above represent fairly broad categories. In reality, a firm may display a mixture of structures. We have already seen how many divisionalized companies have functional specialisms within each division. In a functional organization we may find that departments are organized along different lines; the operations department may well extend the functional structure, while the R&D staff may well be organized as project teams. New structural forms are emerging all the time, adapting the traditional approaches to suit their own needs.

REFLECTION POINT

Why would a firm introduce a matrix structure and what difficulties might be associated with it?

Trends in organization structure

A cursory review of the management literature of the past 20 or so years will identify recurring themes and phrases. Numerous references are made to the flexible firm, the boundaryless organization, the flat organization, the lean organization, the down-sized organization, delayering, empowerment, outsourcing, networking and the virtual organization. These concepts represent two trends:

- Large organizations are being broken down into smaller units accompanied by a reduction in the number of employees (down-sizing) and a reduction in the numbers of level of management (delayering). There is a shift away from more rigid structures often associated with functional, divisional and even matrix organizations.

- Instead, the focus is upon the creation, through decentralization, of more flexible forms of organization, which empower employees and are more responsive to the needs of the customer.

We focus on two related trends; down-sizing and delayering and the flexible firm.

Down-sizing and delayering

If the flexible firm was the structural concept of the 1980s, down-sizing and delayering emerged as the key features of the 1990s. Down-sizing is the planned reduction of the workforce and delayering is defined as:

.... the planned vertical compression of managerial levels of hierarchy involving the wholesale removal of one or more layers of managerial or supervisory staff from the organization's payroll.

(Littler et al., 2003, p. 226)

While down-sizing can occur without delayering and vice versa, the two tend to go together. The group of employees that have been affected most is middle management. We referred briefly to this in Chapter 4 in our discussion on the impact of ICT on jobs.

The assumptions behind down-sizing and delayering are:

- Large bureaucracies are inefficient and ineffective. They are expensive, slow to respond to change, and focus on internal processes rather than on the needs of the customer.

- Delayering will result in better communication across the organization and improve the speed of decision-making.

- Delayering will create more flexible and responsive organizations that will empower employees and bring the firm closer to its customers.

- While cost-cutting is not a primary objective, this will be an added benefit as labour costs are cut.

The findings of a number of studies have been summarized in Littler et al. (2003), whose findings were supported by a study of 2964 firms in Australia, New Zealand and South Africa and in Ranjan and Wulf (2006) in a study of 300 US firms over 13 years.

- Delayering is happening in a high percentage of firms around the world and challenges the classical principles of organization and management, particularly with reference to the span of control (the number of employees effectively controlled by a single manager). In some cases the increase in the span of control through delayering and down-sizing makes the task of management more difficult with a larger number of employees to supervise.

- The reduction in the number of levels of management reduces opportunities for promotion and hence the career prospects of many managers. As a consequence there has been an increase in managerial job changes between firms.

- The subsequent redesign of those management jobs that remain has resulted in increased responsibility and increased workloads. While some managers are positive about this, others feel more stress and job dissatisfaction. In general, there are greater numbers expressing dissatisfaction than satisfaction.

- With the removal of management levels, employees are empowered and take on more responsibility. As with the management group, there are mixed views of enrichment versus stress and anxiety increases.

- Redundancies and increased labour mobility cause a reduction in the levels of loyalty and commitment to the organization.

- There is a certain cynicism about the real objectives of down-sizing and delayering. There is some evidence to suggest that in many organizations service levels have not improved, but have actually worsened. This reinforces the belief that cutting costs may be the primary objective.

The flexible firm

The concept of the flexible firm emerged from work carried out by the Institute of Manpower Studies and associated largely with the writing of Atkinson (1984). His article 'Manpower strategies for flexible organizations' offers an excellent summary.

The main assumptions behind Atkinson's model are that new forms of organization are required as a strategic response to the combined effects of market stagnation, job losses, technical change, increased uncertainty and reductions in the working week.

In the 1990s the focus shifted to emphasize flexibility as the key strategic response to globalization. The manipulation of labour costs are an easy option. The 1990s has also seen the growth of critical literature surrounding flexible labour market trends, with many of the critics focusing on issues of insecurity and exploitation.

Atkinson's original model identified three types of flexibility:

- **Numerical flexibility.** This is achieved through management's ability to make rapid alterations to the headcount of the firm to meet changes in demand. A growth in part-time work, temporary contracts and sub contracting were the expected consequences of numerical flexibility.

- **Functional flexibility.** This is achieved when employees are able to perform a range of jobs and can move between them as the need arises. In many organizations this will see an end to demarcation between different jobs and result in multi-skilling.

- **Financial flexibility.** This is required to reflect changes in the supply and demand of labour and to enhance the operation of functional and numerical flexibility. This can be achieved through the creation of differential rates of pay for full- and part-time workers, introducing the link between effort and reward for a greater number of workers and the use of incentives to encourage workers to become multi-skilled.

Sparrow and Marchington (1998) argue that there are not three but seven types of flexibility observable in modern organizations and that these flexibilities are both discrete and parallel. In addition to the three defined by Atkinson, they recognize temporal, geographical, organizational and cognitive flexibility. **Temporal flexibility** is concerned with changing the time patterns of work, as with the introduction of shift work. **Geographical flexibility** involves the increased mobility of groups of workers as in the introduction of transnational teams. **Organizational flexibility** relates to structural and systems changes and **cognitive flexibility** to the changing mindset of the workforce.

The introduction of such forms of the 'flexible firm' will break up traditional organization structures. For Atkinson, the outcome will be the establishment of two groups of employees; core and peripheral. Core employees are those on permanent or long-term contracts and who hold key skills and positions within the organization. Accordingly, core workers are well rewarded and often have the security of lifetime employment. Peripheral workers comprise two groups. It is envisaged that there will be a group of full-time workers, who will be less skilled and not enjoy the security of the core worker. The second group will comprise part-time and contract workers hired in direct proportion to the demand or to deal with non-core business such as cleaning and catering.

KEY CONCEPT 6.4   THE FLEXIBLE FIRM

Flexibility within organizations occurs in a number of ways. These include the employment of part-time workers, those on short-term contracts and the use of outsourced contract work. It also involves getting employees to do a range of jobs, introducing variations in pay and times of attendance and increasing the geographical mobility of labour. Such changes are seen to be on the increase as a result of globalization, higher levels of competition and the need for most firms to reduce costs. There is clear evidence that all forms of flexibility are on the increase. While the impact is often viewed positively from the perspective of the organization, disadvantages have been noted for the individual worker.

There has been a great deal of research into the impact of the flexible firm on organizations in the UK and the rest of Europe and good summaries can be found in Legge (1998) and Murton (2000). Some of the issues raised include:

- There is clear evidence of the increasing use of subcontractors across a range of public and private organizations, some of which is clearly linked to downsizing and delayering. There is increasing use of subcontracting in the production of parts in manufacturing, owing to both globalization and the development of modular manufacturing processes. Many large firms use subcontracting not only for cleaning and catering, but also for key HR functions such as recruitment, training and payrolling and in marketing for promotional and advertising activities.

- Multi-skilling has occurred but the weight of evidence suggests that much of this is as a result of job enlargement and the intensification of work as opposed to a focus on job enrichment for the individual.

Pollert (1987), in an early critique of Atkinson's work, accuses the Institute of Manpower Studies of offering vague concepts and of producing a model that is not supported by evidence. She argues that elements of the flexible firm model can be seen in many organizations, but they have been introduced as cost-cutting exercises rather than a strategic response to a changing market environment. This is particularly true of local authorities and other public sector organizations. She goes on to claim that many of the elements are far from new. In some industries, notably fast food, she cites core workers as anything but the skilled, highly paid elite of Atkinson's flexible firm. Finally, she fears that the adoption of the flexible model could lead to more problems than it solves. For example, the increase in part-time employment is seen as reducing job security and leading to reduced commitment on behalf of employees.

These themes reoccur in work throughout the 1990s. Dore (1997) sees flexibility in terms of a not necessarily appropriate response to increased shareholder pressures. Legge (1998) questions whether an increase in labour flexibility is a sound strategy and offers a clue as to her position in the title of her work, 'Flexibility: the gift-wrapping of employee degradation?' She argues that western cultures tend to associate flexibility with positive images, yet for the core worker the outcome is often work intensification and stress, and for the part-time or temporary worker it means insecurity. However, she does accept that there are advantages for employers in terms of cost reduction. For some employees there are advantages. In the case of parents, part-time work provides the opportunity of combining work and childcare and for some it has been an important route of re-entry into the labour market.

Ultimately, the links between the introduction of the different forms of flexibility and economic success at either the micro or macro levels is still unproven. We end this discussion of structure by extending this theme with a brief look at the relationship between structure and performance.

REFLECTION POINT

What kinds of flexibility can you observe in firms with which you are familiar? What are the drivers of flexibility in these cases?

Structure and performance

We can see from Table 6.1 and our discussion of the various structural types that some structures are more suited to some situations than others. Conversely, a firm that adheres stubbornly to a structure that is inappropriate to the contingencies that it faces may be creating problems for itself. However, the evidence on these matters is far from convincing. The difficulties in establishing a correlation between structure and performance would appear to be first, identifying appropriate measures of performance and second, proving causality. We can make some general points:

- Whatever the relationship between structure and performance, once a structure has been installed it is often very difficult to change it. Equally, frequent structural changes could be damaging in terms of the disruption that takes place and the requirement on the part of staff to learn new systems.

- It is extremely doubtful whether structure alone can lead to improvements in performance. Whatever the structure, it is unlikely that it can overcome problems created by staff incompetence or divisive internal politics. In some cases a high degree of specialization or divisionalization can lead to a worsening of relationships. We may even speculate that there is more evidence for suggesting that structure can damage performance than there is for its having a beneficial impact. There is some evidence that structure in harness with other variables can lead to improvements in performance.

- In our discussion of Chandler (1962) we noted his conclusion that structure can sometimes influence strategy. Elsewhere in this book we argue that performance can influence structure and systems (see the discussion on 'organizational culture' later in the chapter). More successful companies are likely to be less bureaucratic, while less successful firms tend to have more controls, particularly cost controls.

OWNERSHIP

We can assume, quite logically, that ownership is an important variable in that the owners of a business will wish to determine the goals and the way that business operates. In support of our assumption we could cite illustrations of influential founders, such as Henry Ford, Bill Hewlett and Dave Packard in the USA, the Sainsbury and Cadbury families in the UK, and the Botin family with Santander in Spain. We could also refer to numerous cases of small firms where the owner, often single-handedly, controls the destiny of the business. In the case of the small firm the owners can be clearly defined and their effect easily assessed. Discovering who actually owns and controls businesses becomes much more difficult with large corporations.

In this section we deal with three issues and their implications for business organization and operations. First, we identify the various types of firms that exist, largely from the perspective of their legal structures. Second, we examine the relationship between ownership and control. Finally, we examine the issue of the public ownership of organizations and the trend of privatization. Organizations that are wholly or partly state owned, or those that have been privatized, raise important issues of management control and public accountability. Issues related to privatization have become increasingly important in many countries in the 1990s. In countries such as the UK, France, Germany, Canada, Australia and South America, the state has divested itself of its public corporations, in some cases since the early 1980s. The changes were more dramatic in those economies in transition from state control to a market economy, as in many countries in Eastern Europe, the former Soviet Union and China.

Types of ownership

Sole trader

This defines the most common form of business ownership in the UK. A sole trader can, and often does, employ staff and a better term would probably be sole proprietor. This is a common route for entry into business and is found in most small business start-ups in most countries. Sole traders can be typically found as electricians, plumbers, hairdressers, shop owners and consultants. A feature of sole traders is that of unlimited personal liability, in that any debts accumulating are the responsibility of the owner. This is a common reason for small business failure. In most countries such firms are relatively easy to set up and have considerable attraction in that ownership and control are combined and, although personally responsible for all losses, sole traders take all the profits.

Partnership

Partnerships are generally found in the professions including law, accounting and medicine. In common with sole traders, a partnership has unlimited personal liability and partners may have their personal assets placed at risk to cover losses or if the firm is sued. This may be a particular problem in the case of professional malpractice, where sums can be large. As a consequence, some partnerships become companies with limited liability. This is not a popular trend, particularly among professional firms, and, in recent years, a new form of organization has emerged, the limited liability partnership. This is a hybrid organization with elements of both a partnership and a limited company and can be found in larger law firms and accountants in the UK. A similar type of organization exists in the USA. In essence, the firm must register its accounts and while individual members are liable, that liability does not extend to other members of the firm. Of course, to limit liability, most partnerships will take out professional indemnity insurance and, in some cases, this is a requirement of the profession.

Partnerships are essentially combinations for the mutual interest of partners. Ownership is shared on the basis of each partner putting capital into the firm, which is then taken out when the partner leaves or retires. Such input of capital is a means through which partnerships can expand. In most partnerships, income is derived by partners through a share of the profits. Not all partners may have an equal share of the business and the profits are divided according to the size of the share.

The role and responsibilities of partners tend to be controlled by law and many professional partnerships are controlled further by a professional body, such as the Law Society in the UK. Management and control issues in partnerships tend to be decision-making and the management of staff. Decision-making can be an issue where individual partners pursue their own interest rather than that of the firm as a whole. Managing staff becomes an issue in professional firms, where partners are the key practitioners and fee earners and, while technically skilled, are not necessarily trained managers. In many professional firms, a partnership or practice manager is appointed to manage the non-professional staff activities and usually the accounts, thereby creating a limited separation of ownership and control.

Limited companies

In the UK there are several types of limited company. The main types are **public limited company** (plc) and **private company,** which carries the suffix, limited (Ltd). The main difference between the two is that a plc has shares that are available for the general public to buy and the company is quoted on the stock market. In the private company the shares are not openly available and may be owned by the founders, family interest and/or the current management. A company limited by guarantee is owned not by shareholders but by a number of members, whose liability is limited to the amount of contribution. Companies limited by guarantee are most commonly found in the not-for-profit or the voluntary sector, but Network Rail is one such company that operates to make a profit (see Case 6.3).

Public limited companies tend to be larger firms and private companies are generally found among the small and medium-sized enterprises, although this is not always the case and some larger companies are still private. However, both forms of companies exist as legal entities that are separate from the people who own shares and all assets are owned by the company and not by individuals. In both cases the owner's liability is restricted to the amount they have invested in the company, usually in the form of shares. A common exception to this is found in the small business sector, where owners are frequently asked to give personal guarantees to banks for loans.

Limited companies in all countries are regulated by company law. Both public and private limited companies have directors elected by the shareholders. In general, the company is run on a day-to-day basis by a chief executive and a board of executive directors, who are normally paid employees. Non-executive directors may be appointed from outside if they have some special attribute to bring such as experience, skills or connections, or all three.

Some form of public limited company and/or private company exists in most other countries. In Germany, there are the exact equivalents in the form of an Aktiengesellschaft (AG), the equivalent of the UK plc, and a Gesellschaft mit beschränkter Haftung (GmbH), the equivalent of the UK private limited company. The GmbH predominates in Germany and forms most of the influential Mittelstand, a group of medium-sized companies, many of which are family-owned. In France, the distinction is made between a private limited company, SARL (société à responsabilité limitée) and a public limited company, SA (société anonyme).

All forms of limited company are governed by some type of board structure, but the nature of this varies. In the USA, UK and most southern European countries this is one governing board of directors. In Germany, Scandinavia, the Netherlands and some newer EU members such as the Czech Republic, Slovakia and Poland there is a two-tier board system comprising an overarching supervisory board and an executive board that is responsible for the daily operations. In France and Belgium, companies may choose to follow either a one- or two-board system. Such differences between the UK and USA and European countries including Germany and Scandinavia are features of the difference between Anglo-Saxon and social market systems of capitalism identified in Chapters 3 and 5.

REFLECTION POINT

What are the advantages of partnerships in professional firms?

Public sector organizations

Many variations in ownership and control exist in the public sector. This is a broad area that covers central government departments, local government departments, universities, schools, hospitals and public sector corporations. The final type is essentially business organizations that are nationalized. In most countries, the number of public corporations has declined significantly in the past few years with the increase in privatization in most countries and the liberalization of former state-controlled economies. Issues in both nationalized and privatized organizations alike include effectiveness, efficiency and public accountability.

Ownership and control

The issue of ownership versus control is a continuing debate. It is based on the assumption that those who own businesses do not control them and that there is a potential conflict between owners and managers. This is sometimes referred to as the 'agency problem'. A pioneering study by Berle and Means (1932) was in part motivated by the Wall Street crash of 1929 and the assumption that stock market losses by owners were the product of poor decisions made by managers. In 2008 and 2009 the blame for global 'credit crunch' and fall in stock market values around the world was once again laid at the door of managers of major companies, especially those in the financial sector.

The ownership and control debate raises questions for businesses in practice. How committed to the future of an enterprise are managers who have no stake in its ownership and how committed are shareholders who have no interest beyond a return on investment? Are the resulting strategies in the best interests of all concerned: owners, managers, employees, the state, the public at large? How much freedom do managers have in developing business strategies? The implications are not just important for the survival of organizations but also for jobs, the welfare of communities and the health of national economies.

The debate around these issues originates from the separation of ownership and control through the creation of the joint stock company and the subsequent dispersal of share ownership. With increased investment, businesses grew in size and complexity and control by professional managers became a necessity. The complexity of such growing businesses led to a specialization within the management group and the separation of the firm into specialist functions and activities. Bureaucratic rules and procedures were developed to coordinate and control such activities. Both the specialization and the bureaucratization reinforced the control of the management group with a supposed weakening in the power of the owner to influence decisions. The owner's main source of control was through the possession of capital stock.

KEY CONCEPT 6.5   OWNERSHIP VERSUS CONTROL

The ownership versus control debate is concerned with potential conflict of interests between the owners of business organizations and those who manage them on a day-to-day basis. The issue is a product of the creation of the joint stock company and the emergence of the professional manager to replace the owner-manager. The key issues are the extent to which managers make decisions in their own self-interest and the extent to which shareholders with no involvement with the firm act in their own self-interests rather than in the best interests of all stakeholders. This issue becomes especially significant in volatile share markets with a large proportion of institutional investors, where high levels of share trading can lead to large numbers of mergers and acquisitions. There is a fear that pressure from sharcholders for dividend leads to short-term management decisions that may not be in the long-term best interests of the firm. Current issues have also focused on high levels of pay and generous pension arrangements for senior managers of publicly quoted corporations.

The contribution of Berle and Means

In the early 1930s, Berle and Means carried out a study of the 200 largest non-financial firms in the USA ranked by assets. These included 42 railroad companies, 52 public utilities and 106 industrial firms. They discovered that management control was the dominant form of control and moreover this was particularly a feature of the wealthiest and more powerful firms and that it was a growing trend. In other words, the major corporations were controlled by managers and not shareholders. Their finding challenged a then basic premise of the US legal system, that those who own property have the legal right and the means to use it for their own benefit. This was clearly not the case, which led them to conclude:

> *The economic power in the hands of the few persons who control a giant corporation is a tremendous force which can harm or benefit a multitude of individuals, affect whole districts, shift the currents of trade, bring ruin to one community and prosperity to another. The organizations which they control have passed far beyond the realm of private enterprise – they have become more nearly social institutions.*
>
> (Berle and Means, 1932, p. 46)

Berle and Means used their data to develop and support their own view of a 'managerial revolution'. To them, management control was potentially a force for good in that it resulted in more effective decisions both for the profitability of the firm and for the general good of society; it was more professional and more socially responsible. According to Berle and Means, management control would be truly professional in that strategies would be guided more by scientific analysis and be more answerable to society than the potentially narrow self-interest of the owner-manager.

The 'agency problem'

This has been identified as an issue in the relationship between ownership and control and the conflict between owners and managers is seen as an example of the 'agency problem' (Jensen and Meckling, 1976). An agency relationship is a contractual relationship where a person (the agent) performs a service on behalf of someone else (the principal). In this case, the principal is the shareholder and the agent is the manager. The assumption is that there is an inevitable conflict of interests in that agents do not always make the best decisions in the interest of the principals. In the case of the relationship between managers and owners, the assumption is that managers will maximize personal benefit and act in their own short-term interests rather than the long-term interests of the organization.

This presents a potential cost to the owners and a reduction of their own benefits, apart from the costs of hiring and firing managers. As a result, managers (agents) have to be policed by a variety of expensive mechanisms which add to the costs. Such mechanisms include monitoring managers via accounts, audits, reports and frequent meetings. In many organizations such potential problems are tackled by a mixture of incentives, checks and balances. There are legal obligations of financial disclosure, senior managers can be removed by shareholder pressure, underperforming firms are inevitably sold and the incentive packages of managers can be tied to company performance that benefits the shareholders. Managers can even be incorporated as owners through bonus payments in the form of shares.

KEY CONCEPT 6.6   THE 'AGENCY PROBLEM'

An agency relationship exists when one person, the principal, instructs another person, the agent, to carry out work under contract on their behalf. With the separation of ownership and control, managers have become the agents of the shareholders. The relationship carries with it a potential problem in that agents, acting in their own best interest, may not act on the best interest of the principals. The 'problem' exists in other forms of agency relationship, for example between employers and employees or firms and their subcontractors.

The agency problem was raised as an issue in the global banking crisis of 2008. Senior managers at banks and other financial institutions were accused of making poor business decisions and maintaining insufficient control, while at the same time reaping huge financial benefits themselves. This eventually jeopardized the very existence of the banks they controlled and hence damaged the interest of the shareholders. In some cases, large respected global firms like Lehman Brothers ceased trading and others in both the USA and UK were effectively nationalized by their respective governments.

The agency theory can apply to any relationship requiring people to cooperate to get the job done, in which one party contracts another to do work on their behalf. Aspects of the agency problem can be seen in the relationship between employers and employees, suppliers and buyers and between managers and subcontractors. In the case of employees, the agency problem is about the extent to which the employee is motivated to achieve the employer's goals and what costs are incurred in offering incentives to the employee.

There is a tendency to view such debates as purely academic. This would be wrong, since the questions that emerge are central to the way businesses operate and the control of organizations has implications not only for the survival and prosperity of the organization itself but also for the people who work for it, firms who deal with it, and society at large. We therefore examine some key issues in the ownership and control and agency debate and raise questions around the conclusions drawn by Berle and Means.

Evidence and argument

Do managers really have more power and control than shareholders? Even with a dispersal of share ownership, shareholders' needs still have to be satisfied, which may place constraints on management decisions. There is always a danger that shareholders, in the face of what they perceive as unpopular management decisions, will sell their shares, creating instability in the firm's stock market position.

In any case, the distinction between managers and shareholders has become increasingly blurred. There has been an increasing tendency, especially in the larger firms, to offer senior management shares in the company as part of their annual remuneration deal. In this way, managers may well identify with shareholders' own aspirations. In addition to such arguments we can see that management freedom to make decisions is often held in check by government legislation and by banks.

There are significant differences between countries. For example, there is a much stronger regulatory framework in Germany that places restrictions on both the power of managers and shareholders to act in their own self-interest.

Many large and influential companies are both family-owned and controlled In such cases, no separation has occurred. The descendants of Sam Walton, founder of Wal-Mart own around 38 per cent of shares and occupy senior positions in the company. Members of the Ford family still own around 40 per cent of stock as well as being represented at the most senior level. One of Europe's largest banks, Santander, is both owned and controlled by the Botin family. Family ownership is also strong in firms such as BMW, Carrefour and News Corporation (See Case 4.2).

Are shareholders passive? Many individual shareholders are passive and neither vote nor attend meetings. However, in many countries in the world and certainly in the UK, USA and Japan, individual shareholders are the minority. A substantial shareholding of many of the major firms (some estimates quote around 80 per cent) are held by other companies, many of which are financial institutions, including banks, insurance and pension companies. Their presence changes the nature of the Berle and Means debate. There is an acknowledgment of a separation between shareholders and managers, but a challenge to the concept of the passive shareholder. Such financial intermediaries not only tend to hold a significant minority stockholding, which gives them both power and influence, but they also take an interest in important strategic decisions. Their credibility with their current clients and their ability to attract future investors rests upon the ability of their investment managers to ensure that yields are both attractive and secure. The sale of large numbers of shares by a bank or pension fund could well undermine the confidence of the stock market in a particular firm and result in a hostile takeover. Large financial investors have become the dominant type of strategic control in many companies around the world. They possess the mechanisms to be well informed and the power to make their views known to management. They become particularly active in crises and may be instrumental not just in dictating the policy of top management, but in determining the composition of that group.

Are professional managers more effective and more socially responsible? We have noted that Berle and Means saw managers as professionals acting beyond the narrow interest of shareholders. In most cases managers are more involved with the firm, its employees and its community and in some cases what is in the manager's best interests is also in the firm's best interests. Yet recent assessments of management behaviour across many firms have raised doubts about the competence of those managers and their social responsibility.

We can draw the following conclusions from the debate on ownership and control:

- In the light of events in 2008–2009 – the banking crisis, the destruction of shareholder value, the closure of firms, the erosion of private pension funds – management decision-making and management power are once again the focus of attention. The work of Berle and Means and the ensuing debate is as relevant today as it was in the 1930s.

- While the above would indicate the presence of significant management power, the involvement of financial institutions and other companies as shareholders suggests they have considerable influence. Their influence is far from being just financial. The representatives of financial institutions are elected or appointed to the boards of directors of those companies where they hold a substantial minority interest. The senior officials of a bank may each hold a number of such directorships, as do the senior officials of other financial institutions. A pattern is thus built up of interlocking directorships. Such directors will influence the recruitment of other directors and will inevitably favour those with access to vital information.

- The freedom of both managers and shareholders varies depending on the regulatory framework under which they operate. There is much more freedom in liberal market economies such as the UK and USA than in a more regulated market economy such as Germany.

REFLECTION POINT

Is there an agency problem in modern firms? How does it manifest itself?

Management and control in the public sector

We often refer to the public sector as if it were a homogeneous group of organizations. This is misleading, for the public sector in most countries encompasses a range of institutions. At least four types may be identified:

- **Industries that are wholly owned and controlled by the state.** These were the dominant type of business organization in the former communist countries of Eastern Europe and in China. In the non-communist world such industries comprised utilities such as gas and electricity, and former private industries that had been nationalized, such as the coal industry in the UK. In most parts of the world such state-owned industries have reduced in number as a result of economic liberalization and privatization.

- **Companies that the state controls as majority shareholder.** Such companies existed in many parts of the world, as with Volkswagen in Germany and Renault in France. In many cases such companies have since been privatized. As with wholly owned state enterprises, such ownership patterns are rare as countries adopt more market-driven systems.

However the banking crisis saw a reversal of the trend, where in the UK major banks such as RBS and HBOS became majority owned by the government. Similar patterns emerged in the USA with the government taking a majority holding in Citibank and General Motors.

- **Services to the population.** These include health, education and social services, where state provision is an historic duty and which are funded through the taxation system. Once again, in many countries, there has been a shift towards private provision in many of these areas. However, it is considered imperative that other services such as the police and armed forces remain under state control.

- **Other government departments at national and local levels.** Most governments have departments that oversee aspects of the economy such as the Department for Business, Innovation and Skills (BIS) in the UK and the Ministry of International Trade and Industry (MITI) in Japan. Local regions in most countries are controlled by departments serving local interests as with local authorities in the UK or the Beijing City government in China. Those employed in local and national government and in health, education and social services form a large proportion of the labour force in most countries.

The rationale for a public sector can be explained in political, economic and social terms, although we can make a broad distinction here between the business and nonbusiness institution. In terms of the provision for health, education, social services, and especially the police and armed forces, there is a broad consensus that public ownership and control is socially and indeed politically desirable. Even here there has been considerable debate about the extent of public provision in areas such as health and education. The political contention concerns a public sector business presence, brought sharply into focus by liberalization and privatization in the 1980s and 1990s in many countries.

Problems with the public sector

Traditionally the public sector has always faced problems arising from the tensions between public ownership, political control and day-to-day management. These tensions may be viewed in terms of goals and objectives, finance, control, management and organization. Here are some frequently held views about the public sector:

- **The goals of public sector organizations have often been ill-defined and conflicting.** Many public sector operations have found conflict between the provision of a service and the necessity to break even. A problem is the presence of a large number of stakeholders resulting in often conflicting goals. As a result, public sector managers may respond by being cautious and lacking in innovation. Procedures are seen as more important than customer focus and, as a consequence, strategy formulation tends to reinforce the status quo.

- **The superordinate goal of the public sector to operate in the public interest is itself open to question.** Who defines the public interest and is it possible to satisfy all elements of the public at the same time? For example, there has been a radical pruning of the coal industry and the wholesale closure of collieries in countries such as the UK and Poland. Such cuts have raised unemployment levels and damaged local economies. Governments in an attempt to balance the books and avoid raising taxes make cuts in public services having a negative effect on groups in the population.

- **Financially, the public sector operates under considerable constraints.** Pricing policies are often dictated by government in attempts to tackle budget deficits or to direct consumption, as in the case of energy use. Public sector enterprises may find investment difficult; they are often prevented from borrowing from the government and sources of external funding are severely restricted.

- **Excessive intervention** has been a frequent complaint among public sector managers. The very structure of the public sector means that it is answerable to different groups within government itself, to politicians, civil servants, appointed governing bodies, and consumer groups, all of whom may have differing expectations and impose conflicting demands upon management. The whole issue is invariably complicated by the organizational politics that develop in the relationship between the heads of public sector organizations and their respective government masters. Such relationships are rarely stable as a result of political change.

- **Decision-making is slow and complex.** This results from long chains of command and the constant need to refer upwards or to committees to satisfy the need for public accountability.

- **Management autonomy and motivation are limited.** Procedures can stifle initiative and pay is not linked to performance. As a result the public sector may attract less ambitious managers who see the job as 'safe'.

Such problems may well exaggerate the differences between the private and public sectors. Flexibility and inflexibility can be found in organizations in both sectors and that bureaucratic 'red tape' is more a function of size than it is of public versus private. Nonetheless, partly in response to such problems, and partly as a shift in ideology towards a more liberal system, many governments have embarked upon a policy of privatization, deregulation and the introduction of a commercial approach in the public sector, sometimes referred to as 'new public management'. It is to these issues we now turn.

REFLECTION POINT

How is managing in the public sector different from managing in the private sector?

Privatization

We introduced privatization in our discussion of liberalization and the change in the economies of Eastern Europe, the former Soviet Union and China in Chapter 3. In the UK we focus on the privatizations associated with the Thatcher Government in the 1980s and 1990s, yet the largest share issue privatizations have occurred in other countries (see Table 6.2). In several cases the share issues were released at different times over several years. The largest by far has involved NTT in Japan with 5 share issues over 12 years. In China, the privatizations have mainly involved smaller companies and large SOEs have remained in state ownership (see the section on China in Chapter 3).

The claimed advantages of privatization may be stated as follows:

- It creates increased competition, which leads to increased efficiency, higher productivity, quality improvement and, ultimately, growth and profit.

- Shareholders have a financial interest in the effective management of the enterprise. Managers' performance is therefore closely monitored and controlled.

TABLE 6.2	World's ten largest share issue privatizations as of August 2000		
Date	**Company**	**Country**	**Amount (US$ million)**
1987–99	Nippon Telegraph and Telephone	Japan	100 057
1996–2000	Deutsche Telecom	Germany	38 260
1997–99	Telstra	Australia	20 930
1999	ENEL	Italy	18 000
1998	NTT DoCoMo	Japan	18 000
1991–98	France Telecom	France	17 580
1991–93	British Telecom	UK	17 287
1997	Telecom Italia	Italy	15 500
1987	British Petroleum	UK	12 430
2000	ATT Wireless (tracking stock)	USA	10 500

- Since customers have a choice, there will be a focus on customer care and service levels will improve.
- Costs will be reduced as a result of competition. In particular there will be a reduction in labour costs as organizations seek greater efficiencies.
- There will be improved awareness of and adaptation to changes in local, national and global environments.
- There will be greater incentives for staff through more flexible pay arrangements and profit-sharing schemes. Managers will be encouraged through incentives to be more innovative and proactive.
- For the newly privatized organizations there would be greatly increased opportunity for raising revenue which could be reinvested in the operation. It was assumed this would stimulate innovation to the benefit of all.
- For the state there will be a reduced public sector deficit and borrowing requirement. Privatized businesses will attract more inward investment.
- Society will change as more people are given the opportunity to own shares.

KEY CONCEPT 6.7   PRIVATIZATION

Privatization refers to the government policy of selling off public assets to private ownership and control, usually by share issue. The policy was prevalent in the UK in the 1980s and 1990s, driven largely by an ideological belief in the workings of the free market. The policy extended to the deregulation of certain public services, thereby ending public monopolies over the provision of public transport and refuse removal. The process has also been pursued in other countries such as France, Germany, Japan, Australia and Canada as well as in former communist countries in Eastern Europe and in China. The policy is driven by the belief that private firms are both more effective and efficient, and free managers from the constraints of political control.

It is difficult to isolate privatization from its ideological and political agenda and as a consequence difficult to assess whether the claimed advantages have occurred and, if they have, benefited all parties. Privatization has been a key policy in the UK since the 1980s. It has also been a commitment of the EU, which saw privatization as a means of creating a competitive market across Europe that would reduce costs for the consumer. This was a particular aim of stipulating that the energy companies of member states had to be privatized.

Evidence is mixed both as to whether privatized companies deliver better products and services and on the effect on prices. In most cases privatized companies have reduced staffing levels significantly. In the case of most Western European countries, privatization took place in a market economy. Changes were much more radical in economies shifting from state control, the so-called transitional economies. In all cases however it is difficult to isolate the impact of privatization from other economic, political and social changes. Comparing the performance of a privatized company with that of its former state-owned company may be misleading as the goals of the company may have changed. A comprehensive review of studies was carried out by Megginson and Netter (2001) on privatizations across the world, including transitional and non-transitional economies. Their findings are summarized as follows:

- In non-transitional economies there was little evidence that privatization had improved the financial or operating performance of companies, although there was a marked decline in all countries of levels of employment. The findings varied widely. In Mexico, privatized firms quickly closed the performance gap with the private sector, although much was attributed to job cuts and the introduction of incentives. In the UK some studies have shown that fewer than 50 per cent of companies perform better after privatization.

- In transitional economies the results are more consistent and generally show improved performance. The greatest improvements have been found when companies move into foreign ownership and where the entire management is changed.

However, the restructuring that has taken place in transitional economies has created problems of adjustment. Many companies have been unable to compete against foreign competition when state controls and state protection were removed. There has been a subsequent rise in unemployment. This has been felt particularly in industries such a coal-mining, where job losses have been accompanied by regional decline and an increase in crime and social problems. Such problems are reinforced by the difficulties of obtaining investment and attracting sustainable new industries. Some countries, such as Hungary, Poland and the Czech Republic, have fared better than others. In Russia there was significant criticism of the sale of 12 state-owned oil and mining firms for low prices to certain individuals, now referred to as 'oligarchs'.

The economic changes in transitional economies brought by privatization have had an impact on individuals. The shift from state control to competitive markets requires a change in values and behaviour. For many, particularly the older workers and managers, such changes are difficult, resulting in feelings of increased insecurity.

CASE 6.3   NETWORK RAIL

In 1994 the UK government reorganized its state-owned railway system as a precursor to privatization. Railtrack was created and following privatization was renamed Network Rail in October 2002. The company was responsible for the running and maintenance of tracks, signalling systems, bridges, tunnels and level crossings on the UK rail system and 18 stations including the mainline stations in London and those in major cities such as Glasgow and Manchester. Twenty-five operating companies were formed as train operating units to run the trains, control the routes and set the timetables. These were organized on a regional basis.

The British government of the 1980s pursued a relentless policy of privatization and most publicly-owned companies and public utilities went into private ownership via share issues. However, the railway industry, under British Rail, emerged from the 1980s still in public control and was not privatized until 1996 and the shares were floated at an initial price of £3.80. The privatization was carried out on the same basis as those of the previous decade. Shares were offered to the general public, the company was to be run on profit lines and a regulator was appointed to safeguard the public interest. The train operating units were offered as franchises to companies who could demonstrate their competence to the newly-formed Office of Passenger Rail Franchising. The privatization was one of the last significant decisions of the John Major government before losing the election in 1997. Many consider that the privatization was rushed through and insufficient thought had been given to the new structures.

Railtrack's main source of funding was to come from the train operating companies who would pay to use the track, stations and so on. Railtrack also received income from its property portfolio, in addition to the funds it received from the government to assist with major projects. In 1998 all seemed to be going well. The share price had risen to £17, the company was valued at £17 billion and it was widely publicized that it was making £1 million a day profit. By May 2001, Railtrack announced losses of £534 million and from January to September that year the share price fell from £9.25 to £2.80. On 8 October 2001 the company had debts of £4.5 billion and went into administration at the request of the government. The transport minister, Stephen Byers, said:

> *Our action will see the end of Railtrack. In my judgement the time had come to take back the track and put the interests of the travelling public first.*

(*Guardian*, 8 October, 2001)

Ernst and Young, an accounting firm, was called in to act as administrator, run the company and effectively create the conditions for the launch of a new organization. The government decided that too much public money had already been spent on Railtrack projects and the company had shown itself ill-equipped to operate an effective service and manage its own budgets. It was thought at the time that any further money put into Railtrack would jeopardize plans for increased spending on health and education. The action of the government was seen by some as re-nationalization.

The problems that led to the demise of Railtrack were several:

- Throughout the five-year existence of Railtrack as a private company there had been continuous requests for government funding and it was seen by the government as a company that had no effective strategy for controlling costs. Major projects were out of control. The modernization of the west coast mainline was budgeted at £2.2 billion and was eventually completed at a cost of almost £10 billion, which some noted was £3 billion more than NASA's plans to revisit the moon under the second Bush presidency.

- Despite the publicity given to major projects, there was a lack of investment in the infrastructure. The company was criticized for the high amounts of dividend paid to shareholders and for ignoring the public interest. Indeed, lack of investment was seen as the cause of the Hatfield rail crash in 2000 (see below).

- There were several well-publicized disasters, all of which implicated Railtrack. In September 1997, seven people were killed in a rail crash at Southall, when safety equipment was found to be at fault. In October 1999, two passenger trains collided as they approached Paddington station in London, with 31 deaths. The main cause of the collision was signal failure. In October 2000 a train crash at Hatfield killed four people. The cause was found to be a disintegrating track, which had been scheduled for renewal 12 months earlier.

- There were frequent customer complaints about delays and Railtrack was invariably blamed by the train operating companies. Railtrack acquired a reputation for unreliability and had to make large penalty payments to the operating

(Continued)

CASE 6.3   (Continued)

companies. Customers were also critical of the increased cost of rail travel and placed some of the blame for this with Railtrack.

- During the late 1990s many key staff left the company. A criticism was that they were replaced by people with little or no experience of running railways. In addition there was criticism of the large salaries paid to top management, a frequent complaint in newly privatized companies.

- The regulatory mechanism was accused of weakness and of ignoring the lack of investment and consequently blamed for the poor safety record. In an attempt to sort out the regulatory system, the government appointed Tom Winsor as the new regulator just before putting Railtrack into administration. One of his first acts was to commission an independent report, which exposed the lack of investment, while the state of the track was deemed to be in a worse condition than it was before privatization.

The administration led to a bitter dispute between Railtrack and the government. The chief executive of Railtrack, Steve Marshall, resigned and accused the government of unacceptable behaviour and going back on its promises. This accusation was directed partly at the government's refusal to back the company with funds and partly to the government's attempt to freeze £350 million, which Railtrack had in its bank accounts. Railtrack insisted this was income derived from its property activities and not directly related to the rail business. In the end, the government relented and much of the money was paid to existing shareholders. Many of the institutional shareholders saw the administration as a government takeover tantamount to re-nationalization. However, the government was keen to avoid this because of the cost involved in paying off the shareholders (which, by law, had to be based on an average share price of the last few years). Shareholders did receive some compensation, mainly from the sale of assets and the bank account of the Railtrack Group. However, investors considered their compensation of £2.50 a share to be insufficient and launched a class action against the government, accusing it of pushing Railtrack into administration, an action which took several years and was ultimately lost by the former shareholders.

The collapse of the company had an immediate knock-on effect in other sectors. Many construction companies, such as Balfour Beatty and Jarvis, were reliant on Railtrack for much of their revenue, e.g. Railtrack contributed 40 per cent of the turnover of Jarvis. Share prices in the construction industry fell immediately and many companies feared that work would slow down and that outstanding payments would not be made.

The process of administration led to the creation of a new company and a new brand, Network Rail. The new company would assume all the responsibilities previously undertaken by Railtrack. Network Rail was set up as a private company to operate on a commercial basis. However, it was established as a company limited by guarantee (CLG). Such a company is often found in charitable organizations. A CLG has no shareholders but is owned by members, who hold the board accountable. The liability of the company is limited to the amount each member guarantees. Network Rail has 116 members drawn from industry partners and from the general public. As there are no shareholders, no dividend is paid and all profits are reinvested. All the senior management of Network Rail had either engineering experience or experience of railway operations in the UK or overseas.

However, the problems continued.

- At Potters Bar in 2002, poorly maintained points were found to be the cause of a train derailment, which killed seven people and injured 81, seven of them seriously. In addition, the company received bad publicity as a result of its contractor Jarvis falsely claiming that the accident was the result of sabotage. On the new west coast mainline a high speed train was derailed with one death and 88 injuries, again caused by the deterioration of points. In 2011 Network Rail admitted criminal liability for the points failure at Potters Bar and was fined £3 million.

- Network Rail continued to be dogged by train delays, although its record was improving.

- As a result of the Hatfield crash, both Network Rail and Balfour Beatty were accused of corporate manslaughter. While these charges were dropped, the two companies were found guilty of health and safety offences. Network Rail was fined £3.5 million and Balfour Beatty £10 million, the latter for what the judge described as 'the worst example of sustained industrial negligence in a high risk industry'. This was later reduced to £7.5 million. Network Rail was also found guilty of breaches of health and safety relating to the Paddington crash and fined £4 million. Private cases were taken against Network Rail by relatives and survivors of the Potters Bar crash. However, a key issue in the fines levied on Network Rail is that the courts are effectively fining a public company and ultimately the money comes from the taxpayer.

A 2009 poll showed that 51 per cent of the public were in favour of re-nationalization. Network Rail were criticized for excessive public subsidies, the highest fares in Europe, a complex pricing system and overcrowding. A 'Value for Money Study'

was commissioned by the government in 2011 (The McNulty Report). The report found that the nationalized rail systems in France, Holland, Sweden and Switzerland were 40 per cent more efficient and fares were 30 per cent cheaper than in the UK. The report also noted that 90 per cent of trains arrive on time and there has been no fatal accident due to maintenance error since 2007.

Questions

1 What rationale can you give for the privatization of British Rail?

2 What, in your view, were the key factors that created the problems in Railtrack?

3 In what ways does Network Rail differ from Railtrack? What similar problems does it face?

4 What does the case tell us about privatization of industries such as the railways?

SIZE

There have been a number of attempts to define small businesses, largely through the need to establish criteria as a basis for government funding. Defining what we mean by big business is somewhat more illusive. By size, do we mean revenue, profit, number of employees or even the extent of global operations? We can see from Table 6.3 that the world's largest corporations vary according to the criteria used.

Whatever the definitional problems, the influence of size as an organizational variable interacts across all levels of our Business in Context model. Many of the issues relating to size are dealt with elsewhere in this book and in this section we simply present a summary of those issues. We do, however, develop the concept by examining the issues relating to small businesses.

We have already seen in this chapter how size is an important determinant of structure. Hickson et al. (1969) noted that, with increasing size, the technological imperative gives way to the size imperative. Increasing formalization and bureaucratization are inevitable consequences of the growing firm, and the organization structure and management procedures are shaped by the need to coordinate and control large numbers of people. In our earlier discussion we saw how the growth of firms, especially through diversification, was an important element in companies such as GM adopting a divisional structure.

With size comes the development of specialist activities. In Chapter 13 we see how the development of human resource management as a specialist function is closely related to the increasing size of organizations. In Chapter 10 we see a relationship between size and innovation.

TABLE 6.3 The world's largest corporations in 2011–2 ranked by revenues, foreign assets, employment and profits

Company	Revenue (US$ millions)	Company	Employees	Company	Foreign Assets (US$ millions, 2011)	Company	Profits (US$ millions)
1	Royal Dutch Shell (Netherlands, UK)	484 489	Wal-Mart (USA)	2 200 000	General Electric (USA)	502 612	Gazprom (Russia)	44 596.6
2	Exxon Mobil (USA)	452 926	China National Petroleum (China)	1 668 072	Royal Dutch Shell (Netherlands, UK)	296 449	Exxon Mobil (USA)	41 060
3	Wal-Mart (USA)	446 950	State Grid (China)	1 583 000	BP (UK)	263 577	Industrial & Commercial Bank of China	32 214.1
4	BP (UK)	386 463	Sinopec Group (China)	1 021 979	Exxon Mobil (USA)	214 231	Royal Dutch Shell (Netherlands, UK)	30 918
5	Sinopec Group (China)	375 214	Hon Hai Precision Industry (Taiwan)	961 000	Toyota Motor (Japan)	214 117	Chevron (USA)	26 895
6	China National Petroleum (China)	352 338	China Post Group (China)	889 307	Total (France)	211 314	China Construction Bank	26 180.6
7	State Grid (China)	259 141.8	US Postal Service (USA)	601 601	GDF Suez (France)	194 422	Apple (USA)	25 922
8	Chevron (USA)	245 621	Volkswagen (Germany)	501 956	Vodafone Group (UK)	171 941	BP (UK)	25 700
9	ConocoPhillips (USA)	237 272	China Telecommunications (China)	491 447	Enel (Italy)	153 665	BHP Billiton (Australia)	23 648
10	Toyota Motor (Japan)	235 364	Aviation Industry Corp of China	48 147	Telefonica (Spain)	147 903	Microsoft (USA)	23 150

Size is also related to dominance in the marketplace, as illustrated by the international brewing industry, dominated by firms such as InBev (Belgium, USA and Brazil), SABMiller (South Africa) and Heineken International (Holland).

The ability of the large firm to dominate the marketplace is only part of its relationship with its environment. The size of a firm may be an important buffer in dealing with the demands imposed by its environment. We saw in Chapter 2 how the multinational corporation is able to dominate its environment, including influencing and in some cases over-riding the policies of nation states.

An important rider to this discussion is the influence of technology. Developments in technology, and more specifically information technology, have meant that, in some industries, size becomes less important. Business activities can be concentrated in smaller units and smaller firms can have access to larger markets through online sales.

Size, structure and market position are themselves important variables in the determination of organization culture, which we deal with in the next section. At the micro-level there has been a great deal written about the impact of organizational size on the individual by focusing on the concepts of bureaucracy and alienation. Large organizations can undoubtedly present behavioural problems in terms of both management control and individual motivation. Despite such behavioural problems it should not be forgotten that, at the management level at least, many employees seek out large firms for the career opportunities they offer.

We now deal with the specific issues and arguments surrounding small firms.

Small businesses

The small firm has played a key role in the development of the business enterprise, particularly in the 19th century when economic growth owed much to the activities of individual entrepreneurs. The role of the small firm was overtaken by the development of mass production, mass markets and, above all, the creation of the joint stock company, which created investment and removed a constraint to the growth of businesses. There was renewed interest in the small firm in the 1970s. For example, in the UK this emerged with the publication of the Bolton Report, which concluded that the small firms' sector was in decline and this was more marked in the UK than elsewhere. The report stressed the importance of small firms to the economy and to society (Bolton, 1971).

Definitions

The Bolton Report's working definition included those firms employing fewer than 200 people. The EU classifies small and medium-sized enterprises (SMEs) as having fewer than 250 employees. Bolton identified three characteristics of a small firm. These were: having a small market share; being owner-managed; and being independent of any larger concern. Ultimately some kind of quantitative definition is essential to the effective administration of government support and the law, small firms being exempt from certain aspects of employment law. However, there are still difficulties because what is a small firm in one industry may not be a small firm in another.

Because of the difficulties with quantitative measures, some have attempted to distinguish small businesses by identifying characteristics that are special to them (Bolton, 1971; Bridge et al., 1998; Burns, 2001):

- Small firms generally operate with a limited range of products and have relatively few customers in relatively small markets. They tend to have limited market share and have little influence on price. However, some small firms operate in niche markets with a wide customer base and have considerable influence on price.

- Small firms are independent and have little in the way of outside controls.
- Small firms are influenced greatly by the owner-manager and owner values tend to dominate. Management is carried out, in many cases, by one person, who performs all or most of the functional roles. Most small firms have an absence of functional managers and specialists.
- Small firms tend to be perennially short of cash. They are reliant on personal investment and are unable to raise capital as easily as large firms. This results in a lack of investment in new technology and in training and development.
- Strategies tend to be reactive and short-term, the latter often being a function of cash-flow problems.
- Business systems are rarely formalized and tend to be based on the experience of the owner-manager.

The extent of the small firms sector

In most countries this is difficult to ascertain because there is a marked preference on the part of some small business owners to remain outside official statistics for the purposes of tax avoidance. Because of these problems, the estimates of the extent of small business activity and the contribution to the economy can vary considerably. However, in all countries there does appear to be an increase in the number of small firms. Two main reasons are given for this growth:

- There has been a shift from manufacturing to the service economy in most countries. Small firms tend to predominate in the service industry.
- Developments in information and communications technology and the reducing price of that technology have enabled smaller business units to function independently and it is now viable to operate as a small firm in many sectors of the economy.

It has been estimated that 95 per cent of all businesses in the EU come under the definition of small and that they generate 66 per cent of employment across the EU, with 62 per cent in the UK and 79 per cent in Italy. Estimates of the USA economy suggest that firms employing fewer than 20 people contribute half of the GDP and account for half of exports (Burns, 2001).

International figures confirm the view that the small business start-up is a risky venture. A survey of small firms across the world from 1980 to 1990 revealed that, on average, 50–60 per cent of start-ups failed within the first five years (El-Namiki, 1993). In general, the main reasons for failure would appear to be finance, including cash flow problems, poor products and inadequate marketing and market research. However, small business owners are not always the best people to offer an objective analysis of the failure of their own business. It must be acknowledged that not all small firm closures are the result of failure. The success of some firms means that they are bought by larger concerns. Other reasons for closure can be related to the retirement or death of the owner.

Types of small firm

Burns (2001) identifies two types of small firm:

- **The lifestyle firm** typifies most small firms. It is the preferred alternative for many to working for someone else. It is not seen as a route to growth and fortune and operates to provide an adequate level of income. Such firms are rarely dynamic and the owners wish them to remain small. Examples of such businesses would include the neighbourhood newsagent, the local plumber or jobbing builder.

- The growth firm represents those entrepreneurial businesses that offer innovative products and services or those businesses seeking rapid growth. The most successful of these rapidly move out of the small firm category. Examples of such businesses include those developed by entrepreneurs such as Bill Gates and Microsoft, and Steve Jobs and Apple.

Others have distinguished between the family firm and the non-family firm. The **family firm** has been the source of considerable academic interest. Typically, it is a firm established within a family and managed by family members. A Barclays Bank survey (2002) found that 60 per cent of all businesses in the UK with a turnover of less than £5 million were owned and managed as family firms. Their survey indicated that family firms were both smaller than most small firms and generally more productive. It should not be forgotten that family-owned businesses can also be large as is the case with Wal-Mart, Carrefour, Santander and BMW.

The value of small businesses

The value of small businesses may be viewed in terms of the benefits to the owners, economic growth, the number of jobs they provide, and their service to the consumer. We will deal with each of these aspects in turn.

Benefits to owners

- Self-employment offers the individual far greater opportunities for control, and perhaps greater satisfaction through direct involvement, than working for someone else.
- The small business has for many been the pathway to real wealth, social mobility, and perhaps political power in the local community.
- Some owners doubtless see their own business as a source of security for their family and as a kind of immortality via family succession.

Against such values is the very real risk of failure and financial loss for the owner and his or her family. Romantic tales of individualism, wealth and job satisfaction should be set alongside the long working week, the frustration and the stress that many small business owners inevitably experience. The reality for many is that self-employment is less lucrative than working for someone else, and those that are successful either become prime candidates for a takeover bid by a larger firm or fear the loss of control that inevitably comes with growth.

Contribution to economic growth

We have already noted that many governments see the small firm as an essential ingredient of a healthy economy.

- The most obvious role for the small firm in this respect is to act as a 'seedbed' for future big business and in so doing secure the future of the economy.
- The small firm is seen as filling gaps in the marketplace by offering specialist products that would be uneconomic for a large firm to offer.
- More significantly, the small firm is seen as a force for change by being inherently more flexible and innovative than the larger business. This image of the small firm was strengthened by the publicity given to the success and growth of certain small firms in the computer industry, although the majority of small businesses are decidedly 'low' rather than 'high' tech.

- In particular, the small firm is seen as a useful vehicle in a recession; small firms are seen as price-takers and therefore offer no threat to inflation rates, and they are able to plug the gaps left after larger firms have rationalized their operations.

However, the small firm can be exploited by big business and the main economic advantages of a small business presence accrue to the larger company. Certainly large manufacturing concerns could not survive without the components supplied by a host of smaller companies, and the extension of subcontracting in manufacturing has been a factor in the growth of the small business sector. There is evidence of larger firms taking over markets created by smaller companies when those markets prove successful. For example, IBM only entered the PC market once the market had been established by a number of small firms. IBM then dominated that market for several years.

A high proportion of small business start-ups do not involve new products but involve the owner in replicating his or her previous employment. This trend becomes critical where buy-outs are concerned and may be a primary cause of small business failure among buy-outs. In this case an ailing firm either sells out or divests part of its operation to a group of employees, usually management. Their experience and skills give them the optimism to continue operations in the same product market, perhaps ignoring the lack of demand or excessive competition operating in that same market, and they merely repeat the failure of the original firm.

Job creation

We have noted that the small firm sector employs a large percentage of the workforce in most countries. The small firm makes a number of contributions towards job creation

- Redundancy and unemployment are big push factors towards self-employment.
- Self-employment is a valuable source of work for those groups, such as ethnic minorities, who are discriminated against in the labour market.
- In certain communities an over-dependence on a few large firms for employment can be damaging when those firms close. More diversity is offered by a healthy small firms sector.

Benefit to the consumer

- The small firm can benefit by filling the gaps left by the larger company. A good example of this was the deregulation of the UK bus industry.
- There is also the argument that the smaller firm is closer to its customers and can provide them with a more personalized, responsive and specialized service.
- There are certain highly specialized product markets, such as precision scientific instrumentation, which tend to favour the smaller concern.

Whether the smaller firm offers a 'better' service to the consumer is impossible to judge. When buying expensive wine for 'laying down' for several years, a small specialist firm may be the most appropriate consumer choice, while a supermarket chain may offer the best value on less expensive purchases. The situation becomes particularly blurred when you consider that a number of larger firms of all types pay particular attention to customer sales and after-sales service.

REFLECTION POINT

What advantages and disadvantages do small firms have compared with large firms?

ORGANIZATIONAL AND CORPORATE CULTURE

We encountered the concept of culture in Chapter 5. There, we focused on broad cultural distinctions between groups of people, and focused on culture and business at the national level. In this section we focus upon culture in a more localized setting, that of the organization itself. The goals, structure, patterns of ownership and size of an organization both reflect and are reflected in its culture. Organizational culture influences both strategy and operations and is therefore a key element in our model of business.

The terms 'organizational culture' and 'corporate culture' are used interchangeably in the literature. In our review we draw a distinction between them. In this section we will define culture at the level of the firm and investigate our concepts of organizational and corporate culture. We examine the concept of a strong culture and its relationship to notions of the 'excellent company'. We assess its value as a business tool and offer a critique. We will illustrate these points by reference to Hewlett Packard, the US computer and electronic instrument firm, presented as Case 6.4.

The terms defined

Culture at the level of the firm has been defined as:

The way we do things around here.

(Deal and Kennedy, 1982, p. 4)

The pattern of beliefs, values and learned ways of coping with experience that have developed during the course of an organization's history and which tend to be manifested in its material arrangements and in the behaviour of its members.

(Brown, 1998, p. 9)

a) A pattern of basic assumptions, b) invented, discovered or developed by a particular group c) as it learns to cope with problems of external adaptation and internal integration, d) that has worked well enough to be considered valid, and e) is to be taught to new members as the f) correct way to perceive, think and feel in relation to those problems.

(Schein, 1990, p. 111)

The quote from Deal and Kennedy is frequently used in both managerial and academic treatments of the subject. It is in fact not the authors' own, but a quote from Marvin Bower, then managing director of McKinsey, for whom Deal and Kennedy were consultants. Their definition is typical of the language used in many of the managerial texts and is sufficiently broad to add little to our understanding of the concept. Brown and Schein attempt to detail the key elements, which are:

- beliefs and values that are developed in an organization over time;
- learned by its members;
- used to guide their behaviour and solve their problems;
- manifested in the language used and in every aspect of organization life.

In this book, we make a distinction between organizational culture and corporate culture. We explain that distinction as follows.

Organizational culture This sees organizations in terms of a unique combination of variables. These include history, technology, product market, type of employees, type of ownership, leadership and strategy. Other influences include the broader culture of the country or region, the prevailing political economy and the behaviour of the stakeholders. Many attempts have been made to simplify this range of variables through the use of models attempting to draw distinctions between generic types of organization. An early and highly simplistic attempt was made by Harrison (1972) who classified the character or ideology of organizations under four categories: power, role, task and person. This same classification was popularized by Handy (1993), who referred specifically to these categories as cultures.

Corporate culture This focuses on the use of culture as a control device to enhance performance through the development of greater commitment and the integration of all employees at all levels in the organization. It is this perspective on culture at the level of the firm that attracts the greatest critical attention. Some writers, notably Willmott (1993), view the manipulation of culture in this way as highly questionable, referring to it as the 'dark side of the force'. Others, such as Thompson and McHugh (2003), while offering similar criticisms, also see some benefits to employees through the more paternalistic strategies of employers. The idea of a management-led corporate culture lies at the heart of the notions of a 'strong culture' and 'the excellent company', to which we now turn.

KEY CONCEPT 6.8   ORGANIZATIONAL AND CORPORATE CULTURE

These two terms are often used interchangeably, but in this book they are defined differently. Organizational culture represents the collective values, beliefs and practices of organizational members and is a product of such factors as history, product market, technology, strategy, type of employees, management style, national cultures and so on. Corporate culture, on the other hand, refers to those cultures deliberately created by management to achieve specific strategic ends. The concept came to prominence in the 1980s with interest in so-called excellent companies and the idea that specific types of corporate culture were a template for success. Such views have been challenged by much of the evidence, although certain cultures can make a significant contribution to coordination and control and levels of employee satisfaction.

REFLECTION POINT

Do you think we can differentiate between organizational and corporate culture as we have done or are they really the same thing?

Strong cultures and the excellent company

The concept of corporate culture is most apparent when we examine those companies with strong cultures. Strong cultures are associated with those organizations where the guiding values of top management are clear and consistent and are widely shared by the employees. Such cultures are typified by a set of strong values passed down by senior management. The values are strengthened by rituals, which emphasize and reward appropriate behaviour, and a cultural network, comprising a system of communication to spread the values and create corporate heroes. A feature of strong cultures is their association with hero figures, who exemplify such values. Bill

Hewlett and Dave Packard of Hewlett Packard and Bill Gates of Microsoft and Herbert Kelleher of Southwest Airlines are examples of such corporate heroes.

The processes of creating such a 'positive' organizational culture would appear to operate as follows:

- The senior management of a company sets goals and issues guidelines, which promote strongly held shared values; common emphases are enthusiasm, diligence, loyalty, quality and customer care.

- To ensure that such guidelines are passed on to all employees there is usually a high level of investment in the procedures of communication and integration.

- Several techniques are used to create and maintain a specific corporate culture. Some firms pay particular attention to the physical environment, and some like HP, attempt to create a corporate style that is recognizable wherever they operate. In IBM, a layout that facilitates communication is equally important, as is the use of a corporate colour: blue.

- The goals of the company are invariably written down, explicit, communicated to all employees and tend to stress the contribution that employees can make to the firm. Heroes and myths play an important role in communicating the core values as illustrated by the 'Bill and Dave stories' in Case 6.4.

- The same importance is ascribed to rituals, which take the form of team meetings or out-of-work social activities, where participation is the norm.

- Recruitment and selection methods tend to be rigorous to screen out unsuitable candidates and ensure a fit between the recruit and the prevailing culture.

Considerable emphasis is placed on induction and training as primary vehicles for cultural socialization. All these processes and procedures can be found in firms such as IBM and HP and in Korean firms such as Hyundai, Samsung and LG. Such strong cultures are a central feature of the so-called excellent company. Peters and Waterman (1982) may not be the only writers to attempt to identify the features of the excellent company, but their attempt proved to be the most successful by far with their book *In Search of Excellence*. Peters and Waterman carried out an investigation of 62 top-performing US companies. Six measures of long-term productivity were devised and only those firms that ranked in the top 20 of their industry on four out of the six criteria were included in their in-depth study. Their final sample numbered 43 firms, including IBM, HP, Boeing, Digital, Caterpillar, Eastman Kodak, Walt Disney and 3M. In all, eight attributes of excellence were identified. These were, using Peters and Waterman's own terminology, as follows:

- 'Bias for action', being typified by clear objectives and a marked absence of committee procedures.

- 'Closeness to the customer', typified by processes and procedures aimed at identifying and serving the customer's needs.

- 'Autonomy and entrepreneurship', which were best achieved through the creation of small, cohesive teams.

- 'Productivity through people', with workforce involvement at all times.

- 'Hands on; value driven', involving the fostering of a strong corporate culture by top managers who are seen to be in touch with all employees.

- 'Stick to the knitting', which involves limiting activities to what the firm does best and avoiding diversification into unknown territory.

- 'Simple form, lean staff', avoiding complex hierarchies and large administration sections.
- 'Simultaneous loose-tight properties', which means that an organization's structure should display a combination of strong central direction with work group autonomy.

Throughout their work, Peters and Waterman stressed the importance of socializing and integrating individuals into a clearly defined corporate culture. The firm becomes much more than a place of work.

By offering meaning as well as money, the excellent companies give their employees a mission as well as a sense of feeling great.

(Peters and Waterman, 1982, p. 323)

REFLECTION POINT

What do you need for a strong culture to work?

Culture and performance

Those who subscribe to this kind of vision of organizations argue that companies displaying such characteristics are invariably more successful than those that do not (Peters and Waterman, 1982; Deal and Kennedy, 1982). We examine this claim by reference to studies that have been carried out examining the effect of culture on strategy and on performance.

Brown (1998) sees the link between culture and strategy as inevitable. He argues that the culture of an organization will determine key strategic elements, including how the environment is perceived and interpreted, how information is analysed, and how the main players react. The notion of a culture-strategy fit also underpins many studies on culture change, where culture is manipulated to achieve the desired strategic ends. At best, this represents an understanding by management that successful implementation of a strategy requires consideration of behavioural and culture change and a corresponding investment in training and other processes. The case of British Airways is a good illustration of this kind of change process (see Case 13.1). At worst, however, it represents a vague hope on the part of management that simple exhortations to culture change will bring about the desired strategic change.

Links between culture and performance were examined by Gordan and Ditomaso (1992), who found some correlation between the strength of a widely shared culture and short-term financial performance. In Whipp et al. (1989) an analysis was made of Jaguar, a high-end car producer with a sought-after product and strong export market. The placing of Jaguar under British Leyland (BL) management in the 1970s resulted in a performance decline, explained as a clash of cultures between Jaguar employees and BL management. It was a case of a specialist versus volume car manufacturer, where energies were diverted as Jaguar management engaged in political battles to retain a distinctive corporate identity. Performance at Jaguar improved dramatically in the 1980s when, free from the restrictions of BL, a new management team attempted to recreate the values of the company's most successful era through a focus on costs, quality and incremental quality improvements. When Ford acquired Jaguar in the late 1980s, Jaguar was allowed to operate with considerable independence and the relationship and integration was carefully planned to avoid the earlier mistakes.

Yet such studies also point out the dangers of linking culture and performance too directly. Both acknowledge the likely interference factor of a range of variables. In the case of Jaguar, the performance of the company, especially in its main export market, the USA, was aided by a favourable sterling-dollar exchange rate. Such limitations have led many to question its utility as a concept. It is to these issues we now turn.

How useful is organizational culture as a concept?

The more analytical perspective of organizational culture attempts to view culture as a complex collection of many variables. The problem with such analyses is the isolation and measurement of variables. It is hardly surprising that so many articles and books are dependent upon anecdotes from key participants as the major form of data. However, an attempt at such an analysis may be useful to management attempting a strategic change. An assessment of the prevailing influences on the culture of the firm may indicate the likely success of a strategic initiative in terms of its fit with the culture.

An analysis of organization culture can assist us in gaining insights into the realities of organizational life and obtaining a richer picture. For example, a focus on culture and, in particular, subcultures, as large public organizations, such as universities and hospitals, undergo change, may lead to a greater understanding of the underlying issues. In hospitals, there are tensions between the medical staff and budget-conscious administrators. In universities, similar tensions exist between academics and senior management. Academics see traditional freedoms being eroded by management initiatives responding to financial cuts and the increased use of performance indicators.

How useful is corporate culture as a concept?

Problems have been identified with the use by managers of a strong culture to guide and control the behaviour of organization members as indicated below.

Official versus unofficial cultures
The exhortations of corporate literature and of top management can appear markedly different from the realities of organizational life.

The rigour of the research
The result of studies, particularly into the so-called excellent companies, is challenged. For example, Hitt and Ireland (1987) argue that the excellent companies of the Peters and Waterman study performed no better on stock market valuation than other 'non-excellent' companies appearing in the 'Fortune 1000' listing.

Corporate culture is not an effective management tool
Limitations in the management use of culture have been identified:

- Some authors believe that the significance of culture is overstated, and that variables such as product/market, size and monopoly power are more important (Carroll, 1983). The case of IBM frequently appears in the literature where it is questioned whether their dominance of the market was a function of culture or monopoly power. Willmott (1993) argues that changing economic conditions have much more impact on a firm's performance than culture. The strong culture of the three Korean electronics companies, Hyundai, Samsung and LG, made little difference in the face of the economic crisis in Asia in 1997 (Needle, 2000).

- The kind of culture seen in firms such as HP and IBM may only be found in certain types of organization. Dawson (1986) argues that Peters and Waterman have not uncovered a set of universal principles, but strategies that only work under certain conditions.

Their 'slim, consensual organizations' of the future are probably applicable to firms employing professionals and technicians from the primary labour market in the development and operation of new technology or highly fashionable products and processes. They may, however, be less successful in other technological, product or labour market conditions.

(Dawson, 1986, p. 137)

- It may be difficult to establish corporate values and gain commitment among a growing number of part-time and contract employees. Labour market issues are clearly important here, particularly when combined with employee characteristics related to job mobility. Even where conditions are 'favourable', cultures may be very difficult to change. Scholz (1987) maintains that culture change can take anything from six to 15 years. This is in stark contrast to those managers who regard instant culture change as the panacea for all that ails their company.

- Ultimately, as we have shown, there is the continued difficulty in establishing any meaningful links between culture, strategy and performance. Dawson (1986) raises the fundamental question as to whether culture is a cause or a consequence of a firm's success. In other words, is a firm like HP successful because it has a particular kind of culture, or does it have a particular kind of culture because it is successful? It is much easier to gain employee consensus when profits are healthy, bonuses are good and job security is guaranteed.

Use of corporate culture as a management tool is not desirable

- The issue here is one of ethics. At worst, corporate culture is seen as a form of brainwashing or conditioning and at best it sends out conflicting messages to employees. It is true that in companies such as HP, employees are encouraged to be creative, yet are expected to conform; to be individualistic within a corporate image of a vast collective; to exhibit freedom, yet be subject to considerable expectations as to appropriate behaviour.

- A number of writers, notably Silver (1987), are concerned about the exploitative potential of corporate culture. The essence of such criticism is that the emphasis on the moral commitment of the workforce is simply a means of achieving high productivity on the cheap. Silver singles out McDonald's for particularly harsh criticism.

The lively, people-oriented culture is but a complement to the speeded-up, Taylorized assembly line production of food . ... grease burns, irregular hours, autocratic bosses, sexual harassment and low wages all come with the quarter pounder.

(Silver, 1987, pp. 109–10)

- Ethical or exploitative, corporate culture may be undesirable simply because it prevents change. In Rank Xerox, middle managers were so cast in an identical mould of strong corporate values that they were dubbed 'xeroids'. Their programmed thinking and successful company, built on the patent protection of the photocopying machine, rendered them impervious to a changing business climate and, ultimately, unable to respond to increased competition (Williams et al., 1989).

CASE 6.4   HEWLETT PACKARD

Hewlett Packard (HP) is a large US multinational operating in around 170 countries. It specializes in computers and related products and services and was one of the original companies in 'Silicon Valley'. It was founded in 1939 in Palo Alto, California, by Bill Hewlett and Dave Packard, both of whom have had considerable influence on company philosophy and culture. Their influence extends today, although Dave Packard died in 1996 and Bill Hewlett died in 2001. The company describes itself as:

... a leading global provider of products, technologies, software, solutions and services to individual consumers, small- and medium-sized businesses and large enterprises.

The firm operates in several product areas. These are:

- Personal systems: business and consumer PCs, mobile computing devices, workstations, calculators and supporting software.
- Imaging and printing: inkjet and laserjet printing, digital photography and entertainment.
- Services including technology outsourcing and consulting
- Server, storage and networking products
- Financial services.

The company places an emphasis on product innovation and development and operates R&D centres in seven countries. As well as the main one in Palo Alto, R&D centres are in the UK, Japan, Israel, China, India and, most recently, in Russia. The last three are indicative of the importance placed upon emerging markets.

In terms of performance, the imaging and printing group has become the most profitable as competition has driven down the cost of PCs, thereby reducing margins. Consulting has become a major feature and in 2008, HP acquired Electronic Data Systems (EDS) a global IT systems consulting firm. The company now employs around 317 000 people.

The HP Way

A key element historically of the company's corporate culture is known as the 'HP Way'. This was set down in writing by the two founders. It comprised a set of beliefs, objectives and guiding principles, and is described by Bill Hewlett as follows:

... the policies and actions that flow from the belief that men and women want to do a good job, a creative job, and that if they are provided with the proper environment they will do so. It is the tradition of treating every individual with respect and recognizing personal achievements ... You can't describe it in numbers or statistics. In the last analysis it is a spirit, a point of view. There is a feeling that everyone is part of a team and that team is HP. As I said at the beginning it is an idea that is based on the individual. It exists because people have seen that it works, and they believe that this feeling makes HP what it is.
(Quoted in Peters and Waterman, 1982, p. 244)

The founders believe that these same values have guided the company since its foundation in 1939. Indeed, history plays a big role in HP. The company began life in the garage of a house in Palo Alto, bought by Bill Hewlett and where Dave Packard rented the ground floor. Their first product was an audio oscillator, bought by Disney and used in making the film *Fantasia*. Such stories form part of the induction of employees in HP. In 1989, the garage was designated as a Californian historical landmark and 'the birthplace of Silicon Valley'. The property and garage were bought by the company in 2000 and work was undertaken to recreate the house and garage as it was in 1939. The house and in particular the garage are important symbols and feature prominently on the company's website.

The shared values and corporate objectives display a strong concern for people and a strong focus on results and are currently expressed in corporate literature as in Table 6.4.

It is not just the statement of values and objectives that were important in HP but that they appeared to be shared by a majority of employees. The values and objectives were reinforced by a set of processes and procedures that clearly operated through the 1980s and 1990s. These are set out below:

- Communication is the underlying theme and is an important ingredient of the company's

(Continued)

CASE 6.4   (Continued)

TABLE 6.4   Values and objectives at HP

Shared values	Corporate objectives
• Passion for customers • Trust and responsibility for individuals • Results through teamwork • Speed and agility • Meaningful innovation • Uncompromising integrity	• Customer loyalty • Profit • Market leadership • Growth • Employee commitment • Developing leaders to achieve business results and exemplify values • Global citizenship and expression of corporate social responsibility

attitude towards innovation and quality. Informal communication is encouraged between all employees. The layout of the offices and work stations has been designed to encourage ad hoc meetings and brainstorming. The use of first names is almost obligatory and is the norm. Management assists the informal processes by engaging in what HP term MBWA (management by wandering around). At a more formal level there are frequent announcements to the workforce on such matters as company performance and all employees are given a written statement of the company goals stressing, as they do, the contribution that individuals can make. Regular team meetings are obligatory for groups within the organization and once a week all employees meet for a briefing session by senior management. Less formal channels of communication are still guided by the company, in that employees are encouraged to participate in coffee breaks signalled by a bell. The communication policy is assisted by the company's commitment to decentralization.

• Stories and myths play an important role and are a feature of management training, retirement parties, company speeches and in-house journals. These stories generally tell of key moments in the company's history, or recount the exploits of the corporate heroes, usually Bill

Hewlett and Dave Packard. This is reflected in the importance of the garage in Addison Avenue. These stories serve an important purpose of stressing a collective identity and underlining the goals of the founders.

• The company sees its objective as a commitment to the design, manufacture and marketing of high-quality goods. Commitment to quality is viewed as ongoing with continual product improvement as a major goal. All employees are involved in the definition and monitoring of quality, a process reinforced by ceremonies to recognize, reward and publicize good work. The company has a stated policy and associated methodologies of continuous improvement.

• Innovation, like quality, is regarded as the responsibility of all employees. Openness is encouraged and prototypes are often left for other employees to test and criticize. Employees are free to take company equipment home. A central strategy in R&D is the design of products to customer specifications and regular consultation with customers. Such procedures stress the strong emphasis on customer service. The move into consulting is a further attempt to link new developments with the needs of customers.

• Human resource policies are designed to reinforce the HP Way as well as ensuring that it works.

Most HP employees have no requirement for clocking-on and many operate on flexible working hours. All employees attend a detailed induction programme with communication of the HP Way as a key ingredient. In terms of selection, care is taken to select only those who meet the criteria of being high calibre and possessing flair, adaptability and openness. Most recruits are young. As we have seen, considerable attention is paid to the environment and the general well-being of employees is a major consideration. Employee commitment is reinforced by a highly structured system of setting objectives. Objectives are mutually set at all levels and are fed throughout the organization. Salaries are reviewed every three months for each employee through an evaluation based on the achievement of objectives.

The overall impression in the 1980s and 1990s was that HP was too good to be true.

We tried to remain sober, not to become fans. But it proved impossible.
                    (Peters and Waterman, 1982, p. 246)

Certainly, on most measures of performance and employee satisfaction, HP emerged as a highly successful company. Until the 1990s the net profit was never less than 3 per cent of net turnover and R&D expenditure never less than 10 per cent of turnover. More than half of the turnover was generally attributed to products developed in the previous two years. A measure of the employees' commitment occurred in 1970 when, in the middle of a recession and bad time for the company financially, a 10 per cent pay cut was agreed rather than lay people off.

1990s to the present

Since the end of the 1990s there have been significant changes.

- The downturn in the computer industry towards the end of the 1990s and the early part of the new millennium cut HP sales and profits. The company shed 10 per cent of its workforce in 1999, over 14 000 jobs.
- HP announced a merger/acquisition with Compaq in 2002 at a cost of US$25 billion. The

enhancement of the consulting group resulted in the acquisition in 2008 of EDS in an attempt to break into the analytics market. Most financial analysts believed HP grossly overpaid for EDS at $13.9 billion. The company acquired Palm for $1.2 billion to get into the tablet market. The company launched its own tablet but withdrew the product after only 7 weeks.

- Hewlett and Packard led the company themselves until 1978. The company had only 3 CEOs from 1978 to 2005. From 2005 to 2014 there have been 7 CEOs and the job changed hands four times in 2010–2011. Carly Fiorina, who moved from AT&T in 1999, was appointed to revitalize HP but her time was turbulent and she left in 2005. The share price halved during that time and the company became embroiled in scandals of industrial espionage. Consultants, hired to discover what rival companies were doing and who they were dealing with, were accused of using fraudulent and underhand methods to gather information. Fraudulent methods were used against the media including the *Wall Street Journal,* including phone hacking and infiltration. Her replacements from 2005–2011 fared little better in terms of their reputations in the media. As a result of the recession and 'credit crunch' of 2008, there was a drop in profits. Job cuts of 24 600 were announced in 2008 and in the USA a paycut of 5 per cent was announced for all staff, and executive pay was cut by 10–15 per cent. With the appointment of Meg Whitman as CEO in 2011 the company was appearing to recover but in 2014 a further 29 000 job cuts were announced as HP lost its market leadership in PC production to Lenovo, the Chinese company that had acquired IBM's PC business.

- HP had difficulty merging its own culture with that of EDS. Internally there were signs that the spirit of the 'HP Way' was disintegrating. Its own product divisions were being run as separate entities with little cooperation between them.

The decline in the company's performance, its poor acquisitions, its frequent changes in top management positions and its widely publicized ethical problems appear to have had an impact on

(Continued)

CASE 6.4   (Continued)

the culture of HP. The 'HP Way' appears to have disappeared from corporate literature to be replaced with phrases such as 'our shared values' and 'our corporate objectives'.

Questions

1 What are the key elements of the HP culture and how are they implemented?

2 What are the strengths and weaknesses of this approach?

3 Assess the impact of the HP culture on the performance of the company. What other factors may be significant?

4 Can the HP culture survive mergers and acquisitions and the scandals, competition and job cuts of the early 21st century? Can the original 'HP Way' be revived?

5 To what extent will the expansion of HP into emerging and transitional markets require changes to the culture of the company?

Culture as a useful concept

Thus far in the critique we have focused on the problematic aspects of organizational and corporate culture, yet even some of the more critical writers have identified some benefits. Of course, one must always add the rider, benefits for whom and at what cost?

- For Ray (1986), corporate culture offers management coordination and control via a moral involvement of the workforce. It is also claimed to reduce conflict and uncertainty, particularly through the emphasis on clear guidelines and effective training (Deal and Kennedy, 1982).

- Peters and Waterman (1982) stress the benefits to employees, notably a sense of belonging and good pay.

- Culture has also been viewed as a vital link between the rational and the subjective aspects of determining strategy and is seen as the element that turns strategy into a reality (Whipp et al., 1989).

- The continued success of firms with strong cultures is used as evidence that strong cultures are not necessarily as dysfunctional as the critics suggest. A good example would be Southwest Airlines (see Case 8.1)

SUMMARY

This chapter examined the organizational elements of business which we identified as goals, structure, ownership, size and organizational and corporate culture. All these elements interact not just with each other but with aspects of the environment, business strategy and business functions.

- **Goals** are viewed as the products of a highly interactive, dynamic and political process, involving influence, conflict and compromise between different interest groups. Goals give a sense of direction to a firm's activities but a number of goals may operate at any one time and may conflict.

- We identify the factors that influence **structure** and examine a number of structural types, including the significance of the multi-divisional firm to the global company. The relationship between structure and performance is of obvious interest to managers, but as yet the evidence is inconclusive.

SUMMARY   *(Continued)*

- **Ownership** is seen as important because of its potential effect on the way businesses are managed and we examine the relationship between ownership and control in terms of the agency problem. The relationship between **public and private sector management** is explored including a review of the issues relating to **privatization.**

- We examine the influence of **size** on such factors as structure, market power, relationship with the state, and the impact on the individual. We assess the case for government support of the **small firm** in light of the potential contribution of small businesses to the economy and society.

- **Organizational culture** is viewed as the product of a number of variables that distinguish organizations from one another. **Corporate culture** is viewed as a strategic device created by top management. In terms of the relationship between culture and performance, culture may be less important than technology or the product-market and we question its usefulness in terms of the feasibility and desirability of culture change at the level of the firm.

DISCUSSION QUESTIONS

1 How are goals formed and what are the main difficulties encountered in goal formulation and implementation?

2 What are the major causes of goal conflict and how may they be resolved?

3 Assess the relative importance of the various strategic, organizational and environmental factors that influence organizational structures.

4 Why did firms adopt multi-divisional structures? What advantages do they have over functional structures?

5 Assess the advantages and disadvantages to both management and employees of flexible forms of organization.

6 How significant is the separation of ownership and control to the way businesses operate? Is the agency problem an issue today?

7 Examine the advantages and the prime beneficiaries of privatization. To what extent does privatization solve the problems of managing public sector organizations?

8 To what extent and in what ways are small firms economically relevant today?

9 What influences the type of culture found in an organization?

10 What is the relationship between the type of corporate culture envisaged by Deal and Kennedy and by Peters and Waterman and company performance in terms of profitability and job satisfaction? Can the internal culture of an organization act as a buffer against environmental influences?

FURTHER READING

A number of the issues raised in this chapter can be found in more general texts on organization, management and organizational behaviour. The following cover many of the issues.

Child, J. (2005) *Organization: Contemporary Principles and Practice*, Blackwell: Oxford.
French, R., Rayner, C, Rees, G. and Rumbles, S. (2008) *Organizational Behaviour*, John Wiley: Chichester.
Dawson, S. (1996), *Analysing Organisations*, 3rd edn, Palgrave Macmillan: Basingstoke.

A classic and historical perspective on structural issues can be found in:

Chandler, A.D. (1962) *Strategy and Structure: Chapters in the History of American Capitalism*, MIT Press: Cambridge, MA.

Ownership, control and the agency theory can be found in:

Berle, A.A. and Means, G.C. (1932) *The Modern Corporation and Frivate Property*, Macmillan: New York, (old but a classic study).
Child, J. (1969) *The Business Enterprise in Modern Industrial Society*, Collier-Macmillan: London.

Issues relating to small firms can be found in:

Johnson, P. (2007) *The Economics of Small Firms: An Introduction*, Routledge: London.

Organizational culture is dealt with extensively in:

Brown, A. (1998) *Organizational Culture*, 2nd edn, *Financial Times*, Pitman: London.

A particular approach that became a popular management read was:

Peters, T.J. and Waterman, R.H. (1982) *In Search of Excellence: Lessons from America's Best Run Companies*, Harper & Row: London.

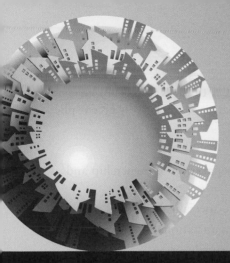

MANAGEMENT AND LEADERSHIP

7

LEARNING OBJECTIVES At the end of this chapter you should be able to:

- Define management and explain the difficulties with such definitions.
- Assess the wide range of management roles and managerial behaviour.
- Explain the reasons for the 'manager's right to manage'.
- Recount the various models of management and explain the reasons for their change over time.
- Explain the contribution of key writers and offer a critique of the main theoretical models.
- Assess management activities and explain their link to the theoretical models.
- Articulate the differences between management and leadership.
- Explain the significance of leadership to modern management.
- Assess the different theories of leadership in the context of modern organizations.

INTRODUCTION

The authors of several management texts are fond of telling us that management can be traced back to the building of the pyramids and even earlier. It is undoubtedly true that many management functions we see today were performed by those responsible for projects like the pyramids and for raising the money to sail a ship to discover and exploit the resources the New World. However, none of the people performing these tasks in historical times was recognized as a manager. The emergence of the manager as an identifiable occupation is a relatively recent phenomenon and is related to a number of factors:

- industrialization;
- the creation of the joint stock company and the subsequent separation of ownership and control;
- the increasing size and complexity of organizations leading to specialization;
- the growth of bureaucracies leading to the development of organizational hierarchies;
- notions of professionalism and the development of management education.

Caulkin (2005) reported that managers form the largest occupational group in the UK, comprising 15 per cent of the working population compared with 14 per cent in the professions and 12 per cent in skilled trades. The numbers of managers has grown in the UK and elsewhere despite widespread delayering of many organizations. This is due to the growing complexity of work and the growth of management specialists, especially in analysis, planning and IT; to the creation of management functions in the public sector such as marketing and public relations; and to the growth of outsourcing, where two managers now control the work formerly done by one.

REFLECTION POINT

Why would outsourcing lead to an increase in the number of managers?

This chapter will explore several dimensions of management and leadership. We will attempt to define management and explore the basis upon which managers can claim the right to manage. We will contrast the classical theories of management with what we know about management behaviour and attempt to link the two. We treat leadership as a separate section, acknowledging its popularity among those who seek to influence management development. The various theories of leadership are examined in the light of the needs of modern organizations.

MANAGEMENT

What is management?

You know, you start off doing a real – I mean a – you know, an actual job and then you end up getting promoted. And then you're the manager.

(Manager quoted in Watson, 1994, p. 29)

This is similar to the view of Charles Handy, who once said at a presentation that 'management was something that happened to nice people at a certain stage of their lives, like getting married and having children'. These quotes highlight the vague nature of management to many people. That vague nature is due to the difficulty of identifying the role of the manager. There are obstacles to finding out what management is, many of which are related to the broad and varied nature of managerial work:

- Many definitions of management are prescriptive and idealized and can be challenged by research studies into what managers actually do.
- Managers control access to information about their role in organizations and many are defensive and secretive. As a result it is difficult to find out what they do.
- We can see management roles in different contexts. A public sector manager may take a different approach from a private sector manager. Managing a small business is different from managing a large global company. A section manager in a bank may have different priorities to a section manager in a public sector housing department.
- Within the same organization there are differences between managers. Such differences exist first at different levels. A chief executive has a different role to a manager in charge of a small administrative team. Managers in one function, such as operations, may have different objectives and display different behaviour from a manager in accounts or human resources.
- Some managers are effective by performing their role in an assertive, extrovert fashion, while others are equally successful 'leading from behind'.
- In the discussion in Chapter 5, we have seen how management priorities vary across cultures, affecting the way managers choose and plan their strategies.
- In our discussion of organizational culture in Chapter 6 we have seen how management style may vary between companies as a result of the prevailing culture.
- Different influences at different stages in the life of an organization will alter the way managers behave. Managers in start-up businesses will operate differently from those in mature organizations.
- In general, managers in different environmental and organizational contexts will act differently. The management role will thus be affected by economic and political situations, by the size of the organization, in family firms versus those owned by a variety of shareholders, and so on.

REFLECTION POINT

How would you find out what the role of a manager entails? What are the difficulties you would face?

Nevertheless, if we are to make sense of management and what managers do, a definition is needed. A popular definition is 'getting things done through other people', ascribed to various people from Mary Parker Follet to Rosemary Stewart. It is a succinct definition and links management clearly with a leadership role.

A more detailed definition is offered by Tony Watson:

Managing is organizing: pulling things together and along in a general direction to bring about long-term organizational survival.

(Watson, 1986, p. 41)

To support this definition Watson speaks of 'strategic exchange', in which the manager shapes a team of people to result in efforts to match and meet the external demands placed on the organization. In this sense, the strategic exchange takes place both within the firm and between the firm and its environment. Within the firm the exchange occurs between individuals in the same department, and between managers of different departments. The exchange occurs externally between the firm and its suppliers, the firm and its customers and the firm and its shareholders. In this way management lies at the heart of our Business in Context model. First, managers shape the functional, strategic, and organizational contexts and, at the same time, are constrained by them. Second, they cope with the demands of the external environment.

We can illustrate this by looking at some of the jobs performed by a university head of department. He or she must shape and organize the academic staff to address the teaching requirements for the academic year and ensure that their research and scholarly output meets the objectives of the university in terms of funding and reputation. The head is also ultimately responsible for the work of administrative support staff in the department. He or she must liaise with other departments, where courses are shared by students or where there are joint projects in research and consulting. He or she must also work with the senior management of the university to meet targets set on student numbers, income generation and research outputs and with central service staff in finance, human resources and estate services. He or she may talk to school and college teachers and heads about student recruitment and to employers about research projects, job opportunities for students and to involve them as advisors for the department. He or she may negotiate with organizations to provide in-company courses, with other colleges, both home and overseas, about international research projects and collaborations such as the franchising of a degree programme. All this is done within a framework of a strategic plan informed by student target numbers, research targets and an income generation target set by the vice-chancellor. Not all these activities will be performed directly by the head of department, but he or she will have ultimate responsibility for them.

The overall aim is the satisfaction of the various stakeholders and the long-term survival of the institution.

KEY CONCEPT 7.1   MANAGEMENT

Management is a broad term that is applied to a range of people in different types of organization and in different contexts. In essence, management is the balancing of external and internal influences, the coordination of activities and of people to achieve the goals of the organization. There is often some discrepancy between definitions of management in theory and management practice.

According to Child (1969) and Watson (1994) we can view management in a number of ways:

- Management is an economic resource that performs functions to direct the work of an organization.
- Management is a set of activities designed to achieve a function.
- Management is a system of authority within an organization.
- Management is a team of people within an organization.
- Management is an elite group within society.
- Management is an employee group within the organization.

A key aspect of the manager's role is the legitimacy they have to do their job.

The manager's right to manage

The legitimacy of the manager rests upon several factors:

- The manager may own the business and the right to manage is legitimized through property ownership. The majority of managers do not own the business, but control the capital assets of those who do. We have explored this theme in more detail in Chapter 6 in our discussion of Berle and Means and of agency theory.

- The manager's right to manage is enshrined in law. Managers of public limited companies have a legal duty towards their shareholders. All managers have a set of legal duties towards their employees but, more significantly, employees have a legal obligation to obey reasonable orders and meet the requirements of their contracts.

- The right to manage is reinforced by the various types of power in the possession of the manager. These are:

  - **Position power**, sometimes known as legitimate power and is derived from the manager's formal position in the organizational hierarchy.

  - **Reward power** derives from the ability of the manager to reward subordinates for obeying orders, performing the task and achieving the goals. The reward can be direct in the form of payment or bonus or less obvious in giving employees time, freedom or access to interesting jobs. There is a negative side to this in that the manager can withhold such rewards from those employees not performing as required and the ultimate sanction is dismissal. The negative side is sometimes referred to as coercive power.

  - **Charisma power**, sometimes referred to as referent power, relates to the ability of the manager to get subordinates to follow him or her by virtue of the strength of his or her personality.

  - **Political power** is sometimes known as connection power. Here, the right to manage rests on the ability of the manager to create a favourable situation for employees and the organization by negotiating with others inside the organization as well as external stakeholders. Managers are often seen in a favourable light by their subordinates if they can access scarce resources or win contracts.

  - **Expertise power** rests on the manager's specific knowledge of the technical aspects of the job or on the know-how to get things done within the organization. Linked to these aspects is the access to information to enable the group to complete their task. This is sometimes known as information power.

- The right to manage is part of a widespread value system and is accepted by the workforce and rarely questioned. This view has been supported in more radical accounts of management (Nicholls, 1969) and in accounts of industrial relations at a time of widely publicized strikes in the UK (Hawkins, 1978). The conclusion of such authors is surprise that there is so little conflict and challenge to the manager's right to manage.

We can therefore see that the legitimacy of management rests upon a number of factors, most of which lend considerable support to the manager's position and actions. Despite the view that there is little challenge to the manager's legitimacy a number of points should be made:

- Surveys of UK managers have uncovered a widespread belief that the majority of their managers lack competence and certainly lack leadership skills (Horne and Stedman-Jones,

2001; Council for Excellence in Management and Leadership, 2002). A traditional view of UK managers is that they spend too much time on person mismanagement and insufficient time on strategic issues.

- The delayering that has occurred in many organizations throughout the world, creating flatter structures has undermined the manager's position power.

- The global competitive environment has given managers problems in just keeping up with the changes that are occurring. Many lag behind and, as a consequence, their expertise and knowledge power is undermined. However, this situation may favour those managers who are adept at managing through their connections within and outside the firm.

- The stakeholders of the firm may restrict the manager's freedom to act in a number of ways. Banks to which the firm owes money may dictate strategic direction. Shareholders can block management decisions. The state through its legislative devices can restrict the freedom of managers to act as they wish. In some organizations there is the countervailing force of the trade unions.

REFLECTION POINT

Which of the above reasons best legitimizes the manager's role?

What managers are supposed to do

A review of most management textbooks will offer us a list of activities that purport to define the role of the manager. As we shall see in the next section, studies of management reveal a different picture. Nonetheless, we continue our exploration of management by examining those activities and the various historical models of management that underpin them.

The most frequently identified activities of management are:

- forecasting
- planning
- organizing
- coordinating
- communicating
- motivating
- controlling.

The sequence of these is deliberate, implying a logical progression. A manager must forecast before a plan can be made and planning must precede organizing and so on. These activities derive in the main from the earlier models of management that focused on rational approaches. It is to these we now turn.

Models of management

In examining the models of management, we will use the classification set out by Boddy (2002) with some modifications. These are:

- rational goal models
- internal process models

- human relations models
- motivation models
- open systems models
- responsive management models
- fashions, fads and gurus.

Our treatment of these models is selective and more detailed accounts, especially of 'scientific management', 'bureaucracy', 'human relations' and 'motivation theory' can be found in textbooks on organization theory and behaviour. We close the section by offering a critical reflection on such models of management.

Rational goal models

These models assume that management is a scientific and rational process moving employees and the organization towards some stated goal. Its chief exponent was **Frederick Winslow Taylor** (1947), whose work in the earlier part of the twentieth century changed the way organizations, more especially manufacturing operations, worked. As with many management models, Taylorism was a product of its time. Taylor (1856–1915) was, for most of his working life, an engineer and manager. His later life was spent promoting his ideas on scientific management. In the USA, in the early part of the twentieth century, there was a shortage of skilled workers and a need to increase efficiency. Methods were needed to coordinate the work in organizations that were growing ever larger. At the same time trades unions were recruiting members and becoming more active. In essence, Taylorism encompasses:

- The use of scientific methods to find the best way of doing the job and the best equipment to do it with. If possible, jobs should be reduced to a series of routine, predictable tasks.
- The need to ensure that the best person to do the job is selected.
- The training of those selected to follow the procedures derived scientifically.
- The provision of financial incentives for following the procedures and achieving targets.
- The separation of 'doers' (the operators) and 'planners' (the managers).

The introduction of scientific management under these principles was shown to increase efficiency in many organizations, although initially it met with opposition from both the US government of the day and trade unions. Its widespread acceptance as a set of guiding principles, particularly in manufacturing industry, around the world was an important part of the process of the creation of the semi-skilled worker to replace the craftsman and the introduction of a new breed of planner/managers. Taylor's ideas were also influential in the organization of work in large offices.

Taylor's work was extended by contemporaries such as Frank Gilbreth (1868–1924), in the field of work study and by Henry Gantt (1861–1919), a one-time colleague of Taylor, in the field of incentive schemes.

REFLECTION POINT

What elements of the rational goal model do you see in organizations today?

Internal process models

Internal process models are sometimes referred to as administrative management or classical organization theory and, like Taylorism, are based on rationality and the scientific method.

Indeed, the applications of the ideas of Weber and Fayol, as outlined below, were intended to complement scientific management.

Weber and bureaucracy Max Weber (1864–1920) was German, initially an economist, his later work was sociological in orientation. He was interested (among other things including religion and the development of capitalism) in the difficulties of managing large complex organizations, particularly government organizations. He felt that the problems found in large organizations, a relatively new phenomenon at the turn of the century, could be solved by the application of bureaucracy. This involved:

- The application of rules governing the conduct of all workers in carrying out their duties.
- A division of labour allowing individuals to specialize and become expert in a particular field.
- An authority structure arranged in a hierarchy of jobs ranked on the basis of the authority needed to carry them out.
- Rationality and scientific method.
- Impersonality, particularly in choosing strategic options and in the selection and promotion of staff. All these activities should be done scientifically.

Fayol and administrative management Henri Fayol (1841–1925) was born in France and, like Taylor, was a practising engineer for much of his life but spent his later years promoting his management ideas. His original work, *Administration, Industrielle et Générale* was published in 1916, but the English version did not appear until 1949 as *General and Industrial Management* (Fayol, 1949). The work was influential and taken up in the UK by Lyndall Urwick (1891–1983), who assisted in the UK publication of works of not just Fayol, but of Taylor and Follett as well. Fayol's chief contribution to the development of management lies in the identification of the basic management tasks and in the creation of principles of management. He identified the core management tasks as:

- planning
- organizing
- commanding
- coordinating
- controlling.

His principles of management are presented in Table 7.1. They were written at a time when there was a theoretical void in management, which was to be filled partly by Fayol and partly by Taylor. His principles were an important guide to practising managers and formed the basis of management training for many years. In contrast to Taylor's machine approach to management, Fayol viewed the organization much more as a living organism and, in some ways, prepared the way for a systems view of organizations.

Human relations models

Like the rational goal models, human relations models emerged at the beginning of the twentieth century and were a response to a particular social and economic context, particularly in the USA. It was a time of rapid industrialization and increased mobility, which was breaking up traditional society. As a consequence, there was a search for an element of stability and security through work organizations. The work group was identified as the stand-in family. It was also a time of

TABLE 7.1   Fayol's principles of management

Division of work
Essentially greater specialization would lead to greater effectiveness

Authority
Should always be linked to responsibility

Discipline
Could take different forms but all involved the agreement between the firm and its employees. Employees should be obedient within the terms of the agreement and managers should impose sanctions where necessary

Unity of command
Orders should come from one manager only and there should be no conflicting instructions

Unity of direction
There should be one plan led by one head

Subordination of individual interest to general interest

The interest of the firm should be paramount at all times

Remuneration of personnel
A fair price for services rendered and paternalistic considerations such as health, education and social welfare

Centralization
The organization is like a living organism and the degree of centralization versus decentralization depends on the organization's needs

Scalar chain
The hierarchy of authority and the line of communication. Speed of decision is important and delegated authority may be needed to avoid delay

Order
Essentially 'a place for everything and everything in its place'; includes the right place for materials at the right time and the filling of posts by the right people

Equity
Treating people fairly on the basis of both justice and kindliness

Stability of tenure of personnel
A particular problem in large organizations and needed to be addressed by attention to induction, staff development and motivation

Initiative
The ability to develop plans and see them through to success. This was seen as a key ingredient in the motivation of employees

Esprit de corps
Team-building based on harmony

increasing organizational size, inexperienced managers and growth of trade union opposition. Management was seeking ways to ensure the compliance and commitment of their workforce. The advocates of human relations at the time of the publication of F. W. Taylor's *Scientific Management* saw little that was contradictory in Taylor's ideas and saw human relations as adding to the theory provided by scientific management. Interest in human relations developed strongly throughout the 1950s and 1960s, due largely to the late publication of the findings of the Hawthorne Studies, particularly in the UK, and subsequent work by Likert and his team at the University of Michigan, encapsulated in his book, *New Patterns of Management* (Likert, 1961). The human relations model influenced the training of managers, particularly at supervisory level.

We can identify two influences behind the human relations school, Follet and Mayo:

- **Mary Parker Follett** (1868–1933) started from the assumption that, for the good of society, the group was more important than the individual. Much of her thinking on the subordination of the individual to the needs of the group had echoes of early socialism. For the management of organizations, she emphasized the importance of teams to get the job done and in particular their contribution to the creative process. She was supportive of many elements of scientific management but was critical of the concept of the division of labour, as this could break up teams.

- **Elton Mayo** (1880–1949) was born in Australia (where he was mainly educated), and where his earlier works on the political and social problems of industrialization were published. His move to the USA, in the 1920s, coincided with his developing interest in the application of psychotherapy to problems of conflict at work (a theme taken up by the Tavistock Institute later). His fame, however, derives from his time at Harvard University and his membership of the team that carried out the Hawthorne studies. These were carried out at the Hawthorne plant of Western Electric in Chicago. Experiments were set up between 1927 and 1932 that led to the discovery that favourable social relations and social situations were more significant to workers and had more of an influence on performance than physical conditions. The work stressed the importance of the work group, leadership and communication. The main findings were published by others but Mayo emerged as the chief publicist and has been forever associated with them.

Motivation models

The human relations researchers continued their work on groups and communication, some of which we discuss in the section on leadership later in this chapter. In the main, the focus of human relations models was the group. An approach to human relations emerged that based its approaches on the individual. This owed much to the work of Abraham Maslow (1908–70) and his theory based on a hierarchy of needs. His work was echoed by Frederick Herzberg (1923–2000), whose motivation-hygiene theory led to the development of job enrichment techniques.

The essence of these theories and much of the motivation theory that followed (expectancy theory, for instance) is the importance of the individual. To Maslow and Herzberg, good group relations and good relations with supervisors are seen only as the rock upon which real motivation occurs. Real motivation lies in goal-seeking behaviour that stretches the individual in a sense of personal achievement. Such theories, which focus on the individual, are often criticized for being culturally biased and specifically American.

Open systems models

This approach to management argues that management can only be understood in terms of the context within which it operates. This is a theme of this book. Management activities are a product of:

- Interaction with the external environment including suppliers, customers, labour supply, banks, prevailing technology, governments, culture and so on.
- Interaction with the organizational environment, including influences relating to size, structure, organizational culture, interaction with employees and other managers and so on.

As a consequence, management is part analysis, part negotiation and part adjustment.

Responsive management models

There has been increasing uncertainty as a result of rapid technological and social change, increasing global competition, globalization, more demanding customers and employees and so on. As a result of this uncertainty management can respond in two ways:

- By recognizing that there is no magic formula for management in all situations and management is essentially an iterative process. Effective management is what works in a particular situation at a particular time and managers build up a repertoire of appropriate behaviours as they encounter each situation.

- By being flexible and adaptable and by developing skills in communication and in their handling of uncertainty.

The former is similar to the 'science of muddling through' that we introduce as an approach to strategy in the next chapter. This presupposes that managers can be flexible and adaptable and that the ability to deal with uncertainty can be trained. This may not always be the case.

Fashions, fads and gurus

In the past 30 or so years, book stores (in particular those at airports) have been dominated by a new wave of management books, which offer advice and above all solutions to the practising manager. New titles emerge each month. Some of these books are sold in millions and authors like Tom Peters and Peter Senge assume the status of gurus, enjoying lucrative careers as consultants and speakers at management conferences.

The problem with most of these books is that they present ideas that are very much the fashionable product of their time. The effectiveness of the ideas is almost impossible to prove and most lack any critical reflection. At best, they present common sense in an embellished form. Nevertheless, the influence of such works should not be underestimated. Senge's ideas on the learning organization were embraced by the top management of many organizations, including Ford, and used as part of management training. Ultimately, however, many such ideas are transient and are influential only until the next fashion comes along.

Critique of management models

In general, there is no real body of scientific knowledge to underpin so-called management theory. This questions both the value of any model to the practising manager and also claims that management is indeed a profession.

- Many of the approaches have come under severe criticism. Taylor's system of specialization, prescribed tasks and payment by results, has been criticized as 'deskilling' and even inhuman. The Hawthorne studies have been criticized for their flawed methodology and poor science. Weber's principles of bureaucracy have been shown in many situations to be counter-productive to the effective achievement of goals. The fashionable theories of the modern era are seen to lack substance.

- Many of the models (Fayol excepted) have their origins in the USA. As such they reflect USA culture, which is individualistic, risk-taking, fairly assertive and is more likely to accept authority than those cultures in other advanced industrialized nations (Hofstede, 1980b). As such, these models may not apply to management in other cultural settings.

- The manager is neither scientific in his or her approach nor is he or she a disinterested professional. The Marxist argument is that the manager is the agent of capital and will always take the side of the owners. Even if one disagrees with this perspective, there is plenty of evidence to suggest that managers pursue behaviour and strategies that are in their best interests and not necessarily those of their employees or organizations. For example, studies reveal that managers favour takeovers where their position will be secure (not unnaturally) and resist takeovers that would threaten their position, even though it may be in the interests of the long-term survival of the organization. This is supported by the banking crisis of 2008–09 when large bonuses were paid to senior staff in failing companies. Managers do not always behave in an objective, rational and scientific fashion. They operate politically, balancing conflicting interests, negotiating, persuading and selling ideas to others. In this respect the 'open systems' and 'responsive' models come closest to incorporating this kind of reality.

- Thomas (2003) believes that managers have developed sets of techniques, which have the appearance of science, but are in fact no such thing. He argues, controversially, that much of what managers do is more like magic and religious symbolism.

- There is little evidence to suggest that managers perform their tasks as depicted by the models and it is to this we now turn.

What managers actually do

There have been many frequently cited studies about the work that managers do. These include studies by Carlson (1951), Stewart (1967), Mintzberg (1973a), Luthans (1988) and Watson (1994). They have much in common in that they all conclude that management rarely conforms to the kind of models we have just discussed.

Rosemary Stewart, for example, asked 160 senior and middle managers to keep a diary of their work lives. Henry Mintzberg drew heavily on the work of Carlson and Stewart and added his own in-depth study of five senior executives. Fred Luthans, and his team of researchers, observed 292 managers in four organizations over two weeks. Tony Watson spent some time among managers at a firm in the Nottingham area.

The conclusions drawn from all these studies may be summarized as follows:

- The managers displayed a variety of behaviours, and their roles varied greatly. Equally, a variety of styles was identified. If this is the case, can we identify transferable behaviour in managers that can be carried over into the next job? Does this also question the value of generic courses such as the MBA?

- During the week, and even during the day, managers play a large number of roles and engage in many activities. Many of these are not planned and seldom do they follow any logical sequence.

- Managerial work is highly fragmented, typified by constant interruptions.

- Managers spend most of their time talking to others, giving and receiving information; in formal meetings, telephone calls and informal, social interaction. The studies found that managers show a distinct preference for verbal over written communication. However, managers also considered that they spent a great deal of time on paperwork. Were such a study carried out today, the use of email might be a feature.

- Managers see themselves as part of a network of relationships both within the organization and outside. As such, political and networking skills are viewed as essential.

- Managers tend to rely on habit and intuition rather than theory.
- Managers are reactive and engage in firefighting rather than follow carefully formulated strategic plans.
- More senior managers perform a great quantity of work at speed.
- Managers have a preference for current, specific and non-routine tasks.

Based upon such studies some of the writers have attempted to classify management behaviour.

Rosemary Stewart (1967) in her account of the work of 160 managers identified five types of manager:

- Emissaries were outward-facing and spent a great deal of time with customers and other organizational stakeholders.
- Writers adopted a solitary approach and either spent most of their time on their own with their paperwork or in one-to-one situations.
- Discussers, on the other hand, spent most of their time with others.
- Troubleshooters tended to operate in a highly fragmented way, spending little time on any one task and moving between them quickly.
- Committee members were mostly seen in formal meetings.

Henry Mintzberg (1973a) from his in-depth study of five senior executives identified ten manager roles, which he placed in three categories as presented in Table 7.2. Mintzberg argued that all managers play a combination of these roles, although their importance varies with the level of the manager in the hierarchy, the type of business and the personality of the manager. In addition, he identified 13 fairly precise propositions about management behaviour such as the fragmentation and relentless pace of management work and the preference managers showed for face-to-face communication. Some of these propositions are incorporated in some of the

TABLE 7.2	Mintzberg's manager roles
Roles	**Function**
Informational roles	
Monitor	Seeks out and analyses information to understand the organization and its environment
Disseminator	Shares information with members of the team and others in the organization
Spokesperson	Represents the organization to the rest of the world. Outward-facing communicator
Interpersonal roles	
Figurehead	Symbolic representative of the organization
Leader	Focuses on communicating with and motivating subordinates and colleagues
Liaison	Focuses on making contacts outside the organization
Decisional roles	
Entrepreneur	Initiates change
Disturbance handler	Deals with unexpected changes
Resource allocator	Chooses between competing demands for resources
Negotiator	Reaches agreement particularly over the allocation of scarce resources

conclusions above about what managers actually do. His study was replicated by Kurke and Aldrich (1983) with almost identical results.

Fred Luthans (1988) argued that the problem with classifications, such as those of Stewart and Mintzberg, is that they may add to our knowledge of what managers do and what roles they play, but they offer little guide to managers themselves on the activities that may make the difference between success and failure. As well as classifying activities, Luthans measured managers' performance in terms of success and effectiveness. Success was measured in terms of whether managers had been promoted. Effectiveness was measured by reference to the team's performance and their level of satisfaction.

Luthans identified four types of activity:

- Communicating.
- Traditional management seen in terms of planning, decision-making, controlling and so on.
- Networking, especially outside the organization and engaging in organizational politics.
- Human resource management in terms of staffing, motivating, handling conflict and so on.

Luthans concluded that successful managers, those that got promotion, spent most of their time as networkers and least of their time dealing with staff issues. Effective managers, on the other hand, spent most of their time communicating and engaging with staff.

Reality versus theory?

Hales (1986) was critical of the studies of Stewart, Mintzberg and Luthans. He believed that they were based on the flawed assumption that we could learn about managers from observable behaviour or even diaries. To Hales, the missing piece was how the managers themselves interpreted their behaviour. He felt that the activities identified by managers could be reclassified in terms of the classical principles of writers such as Fayol. This position is admirably summed up by Thomas:

> When the findings of studies of managerial behaviour are recast in terms of the categories defined by classical writers, their much maligned analysis turns out to be surprisingly robust.
>
> (Thomas, 2003, p. 42)

Watson (1994), in his study of managers at Ericsson in the UK (he used the name ZTC Ryland for the company), concluded that managers rarely conformed to the classical interpretation of their role, yet he accepted that the survival of any organization does depend on someone planning, organizing, coordinating and controlling, and needs the compliance of its employees. He argued that the classical writers should not be dismissed, rather that they provide a broad template for managerial activity.

Tengblad (2006) replicated Mintzberg's study in carrying out a detailed examination of four chief executives in Sweden. His findings were similar to Mintzberg's on eight out of the 13 propositions set out in the original study. Like Mintzberg's executives, the Swedish ones worked at an unrelenting pace and dealt with administrative tasks such as mail very quickly. They also shared a preference for face-to-face verbal contact. However, the work of the Swedish sample was not as fragmented, nor were there so many interruptions. Tengblad found that his executives worked longer hours and travelled much more. They tended to be involved in much longer meetings with more participants and spent more time with subordinates, both communicating strategic intentions and delegating responsibilities.

Tengblad concluded that, even allowing for cultural differences between US and Swedish managers, a change had occurred in the behaviour of managers due largely to the greater international nature of business, the emergence of decentralized structures and a greater number of independent subsidiaries. He rejected, however, a view that the shift was radical or that managers were operating in a post-bureaucratic environment. He identified the change in terms of a shift from 'administrative management' to 'institutional leadership'. Indeed, the focus on leadership is a recurring theme of the past 25 or so years.

LEADERSHIP

The shift from administrative management to institutional leadership that Tengblad (2006) saw in his Swedish study of executives reflects what he described as a change in management discourse in the 1980s. The change was dubbed by Bryman (1992) as the 'new leadership approach'. The change was attributable to globalization, increased competition and increased customer focus and called for greater flexibility, greater vision, shared values and empowerment. It called for managers to be leaders and leadership was placed firmly on the agenda. Accordingly, there was a growth of books on leadership, journals about leadership and government initiatives, the latter especially in the UK.

What is leadership?

Management and leadership have often been used to mean the same thing. However, in recent years leadership, while part of the job of management, has been identified as the determining factor in the success of the organization. In this section we will examine this contention as well as looking at the approaches and theories to leadership that have developed over the years.

There are a large number of definitions of leadership. Each book and article dealing with the subject seems to come up with its own definition. There are however some common themes.

Most definitions of leadership reflect the assumption that it involves a process whereby intentional influence is exerted over other people to guide, structure, and facilitate activities and relationships in a group or organization.

(Yukl, 2013, p. 18)

A similar view is taken in the GLOBE project described in Chapter 5, House et al. (2004) define leadership as:

... the ability to motivate, influence and enable individuals to contribute to the objectives of the organization of which they are members.

(House et al., 2004, p. xxii)

KEY CONCEPT 7.2   LEADERSHIP

Whereas management focuses on coordination, leadership is concerned with influencing the performance of individuals and groups and inspiring them to higher levels of performance. There are links between leadership and innovative thinking, and leadership is currently thought by many to be the determining factor in the success of the organization.

The differences between management and leadership

Several writers have made the distinction between management and leadership. Martin (2001) distinguishes between management and leadership in a number of ways and the following classifications draw heavily on his work:

- In terms of the **role,** he views leadership as a component of management and argues that leadership is what managers do to be effective. A person can be a leader and not the manager. In certain situations, as in the work of a team on a highly technical project, the leader of the project may not be the most senior person in the team in terms of hierarchy. In terms of role, Martin argues that managers tend to be outwardly focused, while leaders tend to be inwardly focused.

- In terms of **situation,** leaders tend to be more situation-specific. Whereas managers are appointed to a position in the organization and their job is defined by contract and job description, different leaders may emerge at different times as the situation demands. In a complex project over some time, the leader can change as the situation calls for different skills or different approaches.

- In terms of **context,** some organizations place more emphasis upon leadership than on management as such. Martin cites the armed forces as one such context, in which roles are so clearly defined and role holders drilled in the tasks required that the main role for officers is to lead.

- In terms of **what managers and leaders do,** management activities tend to be focused more on routine procedures. Leadership skills, on the other hand, are necessary under conditions of change.

The above classifications have been reinforced by writers such as Kotter (1990). Katz and Kahn suggest the difference between management and leadership as follows.

> *We consider the essence of organization leadership as the influential increment over and above mechanical compliance with the routine directives of the organization*
>
> (Katz and Kahn, 1978, p. 528)

Katz and Kahn see leadership as the 'influential increment' and management as 'routine directives'. A similar approach is taken by Kotter (1990). While managers plan and budget, find and allocate resources and monitor performance against plans, leadership establishes a direction through a vision that motivates and inspires followers. Zaleznik (1977) sees leadership in terms of the traits, skills and preferences of leaders. He sees leaders as self reliant, imaginative and communicative, empathetic and emotionally intuitive, and interested in change.

A summary of the differences between management and leadership is presented in Table 7.3.

However, the creation of such lists can be misleading in that they set up artificial distinctions between management and leadership. The findings of such as Kotter and Zaleznik and even Table 7.3 tend to polarize the difference between management and leadership. It could be argued that effective leaders need to be outward as well as inward-oriented. Spotting an opportunity in the market before everyone else fits many of the above characteristics of a leader. Managers cannot only be concerned with the routine. We therefore return to the view that leadership is an essential ingredient of successful management.

TABLE 7.3	Differences between management and leadership	

Management	**Leadership**
• Concerned with formal authority in an organization	• Concerned with influencing the performance of a group within an organization
• Balances the complexities of the external environment with the availability of internal resources	• Inward orientation on the performance of individuals and teams
• Solving organizational problems	• Focus on bringing about change
• Operation of current procedures	• Vision and innovation
• Setting tasks and achieving goals	• Inspiring people towards a higher level of performance
• Control	• Motivation and empowerment

Why leadership?

Many argue that leadership is an essential ingredient of modern management and the difference between an organization is success and failure. Several reasons are offered for this. First, through downsizing and delayering, old hierarchies have been changed radically. Most organizations are now much flatter and old systems of power and authority, based on a manager's position in the hierarchy, are no longer appropriate. Second, most organizations face rapid and constant change. Managers need to respond by being creative, visionary and, above all, leading. Third, the control of staff can be effective through a set of strong values within the creation of a corporate culture. Leaders have an important role to play in this process, by embodying the core values of the organization. Fourth, employees have become more demanding and require strong leadership.

Such changes, especially those within the competitive environment, have been at the heart of initiatives to place leadership at the centre of the management agenda.

Theories of leadership

A brief review of texts dealing with leadership reveals a remarkable consistency in their approach to leadership theory. We can identify several types of theory: theories based on traits and/or skills; those based on the leader's behaviour or style; situational or contingency models; transformational versus transactional leadership; charismatic and ethical leadership; and shared or distributed leadership. In looking at theories we need to consider that leadership can be **indirect** as well as direct. A CEO can influence people at all levels of the organization by cascading values downwards through various management levels. This can be strengthened via selection procedures that seek certain types of individual; by training programmes; and by creating the kind of corporate culture we saw in Hewlett-Packard in Case 6.4.

Theories based on traits and skills

These are some of the earliest attempts to define and identify leaders and have their origins in the notion that leaders can be selected on the basis of some personal characteristic. Early attempts to identify leaders even took into account physical characteristics, particularly height. Such theories

CASE 7.1   THE INSTITUTE OF MANAGEMENT STUDY

The study was based on a survey of 1500 practising managers and a number of interviews, involving 10 established leaders from different organizations, 10 middle-managers and 10 who were part of the government scheme to support voluntary involvement of young people.

Horne and Stedman-Jones (2001) point to the context of the need for organizations in the UK to recruit 400 000 managers by 2006 and that such managers would need to operate in an internal and external environment of growing complexity. Such complexities include continuous change, increasing competition, more demanding employees and customers, and flatter organizations. They argue that such changes challenge traditional notions of management and leadership, and the new focus needs to be around vision, values, communication and interpersonal relations.

Their survey of UK managers revealed the following:

- UK managers are generally unimpressed with the qualities and the abilities of their leaders, in particular, although viewed as knowledgeable, they are seen to lack the ability to inspire others. A follow-up survey to find out more about this 'inspiration gap' was carried out in 2005. The respondents in this survey identified vision, trust and respect as the three most important leadership qualities, yet out of 568 surveyed only 40 per cent saw these demonstrated in their companies.

- There is a link between increased turnover as a measure of organizational performance and the priority given by organizations to leadership development. In general, however, low priority was given to leadership development.

- A strong emphasis was placed on a leader's role to shape goals and unlock the potential of their people to achieve them. Relationships with others were seen as the key to leadership success.

- UK managers' preferred characteristics of ideal leaders were identified as follows:
  - inspiration (identified by 55 per cent of respondents)
  - strategic thinking (41 per cent)

- forward-looking (36 per cent)
- honesty (26 per cent)
- fair-mindedness (23 per cent)
- courage (21 per cent)
- supportiveness (20 per cent)
- knowledge (19 per cent).

The recommendations of the report urged organizations and their managers to take a proactive approach to leadership development, which included:

- The recognition that leaders need to take action to make managers feel they are well led and, in this respect, the survey reveals they have much to do.

- There should be a systematic and consistent framework for reward, promotion and leadership development.

- The focus should be on forms of leadership development suitable for flatter organizations. In particular, there should be an emphasis on 360-degree appraisal (where subordinates are not only appraised by their line manager but line managers are also appraised by subordinates) and on self-managed careers.

- All people at all levels need mentors.

- Leadership opportunities can be given to all as through project leadership.

- Leadership should be based on acceptance and participation and not authority systems.

- Leaders should take control of their own learning and development.

Questions

1 Can you sum up the approach to leadership taken in this report? To what extent do you agree with this approach?

2 To what extent do you agree or disagree with the list of leader qualities and skills identified by the report?

3 Assess the recommendations of the report.

have tended to be discarded for many years, yet the identification of traits and skills has been an important feature in more recent attempts to identify leadership development as a priority. See, for example, Case 7.1 and the report of the Council for Excellence in Management and Leadership (2002). The latter identifies 83 factors, a combination of traits, skills and tasks that contribute towards leadership excellence. Commonly cited traits and skills include:

Vision	Intelligence	Initiative
Decisiveness	Creativity	Enthusiasm
Courage	Dependability	Sensitivity to people's needs
Self-confidence	Inspirational	Being well organized
Tough-mindedness	Leading by example	Emotional stability

In terms of **traits**, Kirkpatrick and Locke (1991) identified six traits, which they found to differentiate leaders from non-leaders. These were:

- ambition and energy
- desire to lead
- honesty and integrity
- self-confidence
- intelligence
- job-relevant knowledge.

However, they added a warning that the possession of such traits did not guarantee success as a leader and were merely an indication.

In more recent times there has been an emphasis on emotional intelligence as a prerequisite for successful leadership. Goleman (1995) defines emotional intelligence in terms of:

- Self-awareness in terms of knowing your own emotions, your values and goals and knowing how they impact on others.
- Self-regulation in terms of controlling those emotions that would have a negative impact on a situation and being able to adapt as situations change.
- Motivation in terms of being achievement oriented.
- Empathy with the feelings of other people and being aware of these in communications and decision-making.
- Social skills which are used to persuade and inspire people to pursue the desired goals of the organization.

Goleman believes that emotional intelligence can be acquired, especially by people that have a strong desire for personal development. Emotional intelligence depends on being sensitive to the kind of behaviour that will be effective in a given situation. Given that situations, groups and individuals will vary, then the behaviour of leaders may have to vary. There is then a danger that the leader will appear manipulative.

Approaches based on **skills** are similar to those based on traits in that a number of relevant skills can be identified, although there seems to be more agreement on the core skills of leadership. We can summarize these as:

- Technical skills which can be classified as internal and external. Internal skills are those related to the predominant technologies used by the organization and knowledge of the products, processes and procedures. External skills involve knowledge of the market and market trends and in particular, knowledge of the competitor product market. This latter point is often cited as one of the great strengths of Steve Jobs in his leadership role at Apple.

- Conceptual skills, particularly those related to analysis and problem diagnosis.
- People skills including emotional intelligence, concern for the needs of others and communication skills.

In many modern organizations the complexity of operations can mean that technical skills are less important. For example, does the senior management team of a pharmaceutical company need to know the biochemistry of all their products? In such organizations leaders can still be effective by relying on others who possess such detailed technical skills. There are links here to distributed or shared leadership that we deal with later in this chapter.

One of the major differences between traits and skills is that most skills can be learnt and therefore leaders can be trained. Those approaches, based on personal traits or characteristics, assume that the selection of leaders is more important than their training (leaders are born and not made). Approaches that combine both traits and skills at least allow some scope for leadership training. With all such approaches, however, there would seem to be difficulties:

- The lists appear to be endless and it would be impossible to find all the characteristics in any one person.
- We do not know which traits are more important than others and which work best in what situations. Many believe that there are no universal traits for all leadership situations.
- Some of the lists appear contradictory. For example, can leaders be tough-minded and sensitive to the needs of others at the same time?
- Is leadership a product of these characteristics or do these characteristics develop with experience of leadership? For example, some people grow in self-confidence and their ability to make decisions when given leadership responsibility.

Despite such criticisms we can still see trait and skills approaches being used today. They are often used by the media to describe management success or failure and they feature heavily in the person specifications, which guide many management selection processes. There is some evidence linking traits to leadership effectiveness. For example, Judge et al. (2002) found a strong relationship between leader effectiveness and leaders who were extrovert, conscientious and open. However, most studies are descriptive and lack real evidence. Traits and skills have reappeared under the more fashionable heading of 'management competencies' and form an important part of what is referred to as 'charismatic leadership', which some see as trait theory in modern form.

REFLECTION POINT

What do you believe to be the characteristics of an effective leader? Compare your list with those of fellow students. What similarities and differences can you find in your perception of a leader?

Theories based on behaviour and style

The early rejection of the trait theories led researchers to seek other factors to explain leadership. Theories based on behaviour and style look at what leaders do and how they interact with their employees. Much of this research was conducted in the USA from the 1930s onwards in the universities of Iowa, Ohio and Michigan. The appeal of this approach was that if a style or type of behaviour could be identified that was associated with effective leader behaviour then managers could be trained to behave accordingly. Much of the work is associated with the 'human relations' school of management.

The impetus for much of the work came from researchers at the **University of Iowa** who studied leadership styles in boys clubs. Leaders were identified as authoritarian (directive, impersonal and non-participative), democratic (discussion and contribution from the group) and laissez-faire (complete freedom given to the group). The democratic style was found to be the most successful.

The Ohio studies were carried out in the immediate post-war period and involved both military personnel as well as managers from a range of organizations, including student leaders. The studies are presented in Stogdill and Coons (1957). Two leadership styles emerged:

- The **considerate style** emphasized concern for the employee's well-being and the building up of respect and rapport.
- The **initiating structure style** focused on getting the job done and emphasized goal attainment by setting standards and allocating resources.

The studies found that leaders could score high on both styles, low on both styles, or high on one and low on the other. It is generally agreed that scoring high on both consideration and initiating structure was the most effective form of leadership. However, the researchers acknowledged that other combinations could be equally effective depending upon the situation. The study therefore ushered in the situational or contingency approach to leadership, discussed in the next section.

The Michigan studies initially took a similar approach to the Ohio team. Here, also, two factors were identified:

- The **employee- or relationship-oriented** leader was concerned for people and demonstrated a broad rather than a detailed approach to supervision.
- The **task-oriented** leader was concerned for task completion and was involved in planning, organizing and controlling rather than doing.

The studies found that dissatisfaction and labour turnover were highest where managers saw the task as more important than people and on the whole favoured the employee-centred style. However, as with the Ohio studies, the researchers acknowledged that there were some situations in which a task-oriented style might be more effective.

The Ohio and Michigan studies were highly influential in the development of the human relations school of management thinking. A good summary of the Michigan studies can be found in Likert (1961). Likert himself took the studies a stage further in his development of the four systems of management/leadership. These were:

- **System 1: exploitative autocratic.** The leader has no confidence and/or trust in subordinates.
- **System 2: benevolent autocratic.** The leader has some confidence and trust and will occasionally seek opinions but ultimately makes all decisions.
- **System 3: participative.** The leader shows confidence and trust in subordinates and seeks their opinion before making the decision.
- **System 4: democratic.** The leader has complete trust in subordinates, seeks their views and makes use of their opinions in formulating decisions.

Likert's research in successful and unsuccessful teams concluded that systems 3 and 4 were more likely to be associated with successful teams.

The work of **Blake and Mouton** (1964) was an extension of the Ohio studies. Their work culminated in the production of the managerial grid, identifying management styles according to concern for people and concern for production (see Figure 7.1). Blake and Mouton argued that managers had one dominant style but that style could be varied and most had a back-up style if their preferred style failed to work. They argued that the preferred style was a function of the manager's own beliefs, their background and experience and the organization structure and processes. As such, Blake and Mouton's grid could be classed as situational theory, which we introduce in the next section.

The conclusion drawn from Blake and Mouton was that the most effective leadership style was 9.9; the team management approach. Moreover, they developed training techniques to move managers towards a team management style. However, there is little hard evidence to suggest that the 9.9 approach is the best for all situations and certain situations may favour a concern for people while others a concern for production.

While the focus on behaviour and style broadened the focus to examine the task and those with whom the leader interacts, there are some issues:

• The types of leadership identified are somewhat broad and even broader are such categories as 'people orientation' and 'task orientation'.

• The studies are mainly descriptive and correlation with performance outcomes is weak.

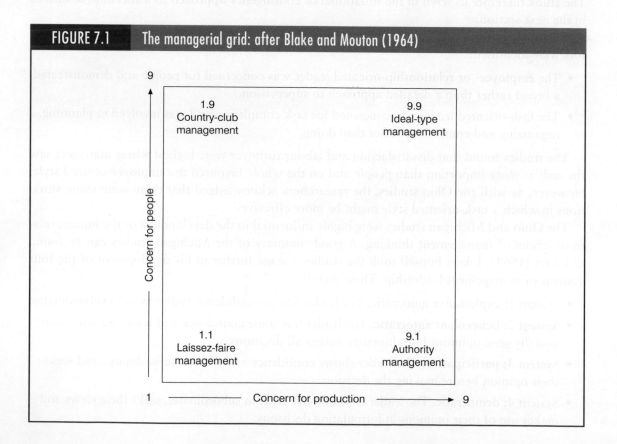

FIGURE 7.1   The managerial grid: after Blake and Mouton (1964)

- There are problems in showing causality between leader behaviour and organizational performance. For example, Yukl (2013) suggests that leaders are more supportive of high performers than poor performers, and the outcomes are therefore self-fulfilling prophecies.

Situational or contingency approaches

Almost all the work of the behavioural or style 'school', while suggesting that one approach to leadership may be the best for most situations, acknowledges that situational variables play an important part. The situational or contingency approach takes this a stage further by suggesting that leadership style and effectiveness may be contingent upon the factors in the situation within which it is practised. This means there are no universal traits, skills, styles and behaviours. It all depends on the situation. This does illustrate the difficulty of fitting theories into neat classifications.

Tannenbaum and Schmidt (1973) took the classification of leadership styles identified in the Iowa studies, namely autocratic (authoritarian), democratic and laissez-faire, and identified how each approached decision-making in a different way. Autocratic leaders make the decisions and announce them to the groups. Democratic leaders involve employees much more in the decision-making processes. Laissez-faire leaders give employees complete freedom of action.

The researchers argued that there were three main influences on this process:

- The background, experience and confidence of the manager.
- The characteristics of the employees.
- The nature of the task, the time available for its completion and the culture of the organization.

The introduction of situational variables extends the work of the behavioural/style school and this study is really a cross-over between that theoretical school and the situational/contingency approach. Tannenbaum and Schmidt's argument was that the most effective leadership style was a function of the situation. However, their approach has its critics. A common criticism accuses the model of being a self-fulfilling prophecy, in that an autocratic leader may behave that way because he believes the employees to be incapable of contributing to decisions. This has the result of de-motivating employees, their performance drops still further and the opinion of the manager is confirmed.

Fiedler's contingency theory (Fiedler, 1967) argued that effective leadership was a combination of four factors:

- Fiedler believed that the **leader's preferred style** was a function of his or her view of the least preferred co-worker (LPC). If this view was favourable then the preferred style was a concern for people, and if unfavourable the preferred style was a concern for the task. Fiedler believed that the style was a function of the leader's personality and could not be changed.
- **Leader-member relations** were identified as either good or poor. Good relations exist when the leader is confident, accepted by the group and has their loyalty. This places the leader in a strong position to influence group members. When relations are poor the leader resorts to getting things done by using his or her authority or position within the organization.
- **Task structure** was identified as being either structured or unstructured. Structured jobs tend to be routine and simple and offer considerable power to the leader. Unstructured jobs tend to be more complex and favour a more democratic leadership style.
- **Leader position power** was identified as being either strong or weak. In general, the stronger the position power the more autocratic behaviour is tolerated by the group.

Fiedler believed that different kinds of leaders performed best under certain situations. For example, the leader has most control when leader-member relations are good, when the job is highly structured and when position power is strong. Fiedler identifies such situations as 'favourable'. On the other hand, when relations are poor, the job is unstructured and position power is weak, the leader struggles to maintain control and the situation is 'unfavourable'. Fiedler believed that task-oriented leaders performed best in situations that were either very favourable or very unfavourable to them. People-oriented leaders were most successful when the situation was neither favourable nor unfavourable. However, given that the leader's style is fixed, if the style does not match the situation then either the leader must be changed or the situation must be changed, generally by attempting to change the relations between leaders and their groups. Fiedler's theory has been supported by research but, in common with many contingency theories, it is difficult for the practising manager to apply.

The path-goal model was developed by House and Mitchell (1974) as an attempt to add to the work of the style approaches. It is based on the belief that effective leaders assist their subordinates to learn appropriate types of behaviour, so that the subordinates are able to gain rewards for the satisfactory completion of a task. Four styles of leadership are identified:

- **Directive.** Group members are offered specific guidance, given specific targets and a set of rules for the completion of a task.
- **Supportive.** Group members are shown concern and friendliness by the leader and assistance in achieving the task.
- **Achievement-oriented.** Group members are persuaded to accept challenging goals. The leader expresses confidence in the group.
- **Participative.** The leader consults with the group about what to do and how to do it and takes the group's views into account.

The appropriate style under this model depends upon:

- the group members' abilities and personal needs;
- the nature of the task and the authority structure of the organization (termed as the 'environment').

Different styles work best in different situations. For example, directive leadership works best where the task is ambiguous or stressful and the group is generally inflexible. It works less well with high ability groups. A supportive style tends to work best where jobs are boring and repetitive or unpleasant. A participative style works best where the group is confident in their own abilities and the task is complex. However, House and Mitchell are keen to point out that there is no magic formula and managers must work out their most effective style given the prevailing situation.

Contingency approaches give a more complex, and some would argue, a more realistic view of leadership. Compared with other theories of leadership there tends to be more empirical evidence supporting the studies. However, some believe this to be less of a theory and more a reliance on the manager's own intuition. Is it practical? Can leaders diagnose situations and behave accordingly, especially when some behaviours may be a function of their personality. In addition, if managers change the way they treat different people, then they may be viewed as manipulative.

Transactional and transformational leadership

The difference between transactional and transformational leadership owes much to the work of Burns (1978) and Bass (1985, 1990). Transformational leadership in particular focuses on the need for leadership in complex, competitive and changing environments.

Transactional leadership is seen as the standard management approach. It is so-called because it is an exchange process. Employees are told what is expected of them and what rewards will follow if they meet these expectations and what punishments will follow if they do not. Transactional leaders allocate work, make routine decisions and monitor performance. The approach tends to work best where conditions are relatively stable, tasks are unambiguous and the employees have fairly traditional orientations to work. It could be regarded as management rather than leadership. Bass (1990) argues that, 'In many instances such transactional leadership is a prescription for mediocrity' (p. 20). He further argues that many managers only intervene when events are not going to plan and that such an approach requires rewards and penalties both to be under the control of managers and valued by employees.

Much of traditional leadership theory has focused on transactional situations whereas the argument is that modern organizations operating in rapidly changing environments require a transformational approach.

Transformational leadership is suited to conditions of uncertainty and change. Burns (1978) introduced the concept of transformational leadership, which he summed up as occurring when, '. . . one of more persons engage with others in such a way that leaders and followers raise one another to higher levels of motivation and morality' (Burns, 1978, p. 26). It is associated with charisma, vision and inspiring the group to change and achieve exceptional performance. It involves the following (taken largely from Burns, 1978 and Bass, 1985, 1990):

- The employees accept the vision of the leader as to the meaning and purpose of the organization.
- The vision and its appeal raise the aspiration levels of employees and broadens their interest in and commitment to the organization.
- Getting employees to look beyond their own self-interest and putting that of the organization first.

All the above result in performance that is beyond the expected and is achieved by the following:

- The leader uses his or her charismatic qualities to appeal to employees' own ideals, values and emotions. This has the effect of inspiring them.
- Through interaction with the leader, employees are stimulated intellectually so that they are motivated to find new ways of solving organizational problems.
- The leader ensures that he or she addresses and meets individual employee's needs including their emotional needs.
- The leader gets employees to think differently about their jobs. Piccolo and Colquitt (2006) found that employees with inspirational leaders saw their jobs as more challenging and as being more important. As a result, motivation and commitment levels rise.
- Transformational leaders have the skills and personal qualities to recognize the need for change and identify the appropriate course of action.

The findings of the GLOBE project (House et al., 2001, 2004) supported the view that effective leaders conformed to the model of transformational leadership. The study (introduced in Chapter 5) looked at leadership patterns of 17 300 managers in 951 organizations in 62 countries. The project found two important similarities across all countries. First, there would appear to be a universal acceptance of charismatic leadership (an important element of transformational leadership). Second, highly effective leader behaviour in all societies involved the communication of specific values, a vision for the organization and the ability to inspire confidence in followers.

Despite his claim for the superiority of transformational leadership, Bass (1985) was clear that effective leaders used both transformational and transactional approaches to leadership. Both approaches can be seen in the work of the Council for Excellence in Management and Leadership (2002), a body established in 2000 by the UK government. The council recognizes that the effective performance of organizations depends on having management systems to deal with the complexities of the internal and external environments and having leaders to motivate and inspire employees to improved performance levels. The council has established a framework of 83 management and leadership abilities and has set out to establish research to uncover an improved theoretical base and a framework for leadership education and training that involves secondary schools, business schools and business organizations.

We can see that transformational leadership has featured prominently in leadership studies since the early 1990s. The image of the leader as a charismatic figure with a vision that leads the organization through turbulent times appeals to employees and the media alike. However, the approach can appear somewhat idealistic and evangelical. Moreover, many of the studies can be criticized for their lack of any real measurement and they lack real evidence beyond the descriptive and anecdotal that links elements of transformational leadership with organization performance.

REFLECTION POINT

Both the responsive manager (see the definition in the section on management) and the transformational leader are ideally suited to complexity, change and a competitive environment. Are they the same? What does this tell us about the difference between management and leadership?

Charismatic and ethical leadership

Aspects of both charismatic leadership and ethical leadership feature significantly in any discussion of transformational leadership.

Charismatic leadership is about inspiring others to follow and focuses on the characteristics and behaviour of the leader. There are obvious links with trait theory. The key traits include being a strong role model, having a vision, displaying confidence and optimism, and having strong self-belief and self-confidence. Charismatic leaders are often risk-takers, often have a high need for power and can have unconventional views and use unconventional methods. As a result they can polarize those who follow them into supporting and opposing camps (Yukl, 2013). Weber (1947) found that the charismatic leader tends to emerge at a time of social crisis and fear about the future. The charismatic leader has the radical vision to solve the crisis and gain the confidence of followers. However, as crises pass then such charismatic leadership can be temporary. Churchill was recognized as a great UK leader during World War II but was ousted as prime minister in the first post-war election (Yukl, 2013).

REFLECTION POINT

Why do you think the GLOBE project concludes that there is universal acceptance of charismatic leadership?

The focus on business ethics and corporate social responsibility that we discuss in Chapter 9 has resulted in an interest in **ethical leadership**. Burns (1978) was clear that transformational leadership should have a moral dimension. The focus here is on the leader's character and conduct. The ethical and socially responsible policies and statements of the organization need to be backed by ethical and socially responsible actions on behalf of its leaders.

Evidence suggests that both charismatic and ethical leadership have what Conger (1990) refers to as the 'dark side of leadership'. He cites a number of examples of such behaviour; the leader's vision is a manifesto for their own personal gain rather than that of the organization or its employees; the leader restricts information, especially negative information; and often creates internal rivalries to achieve his or her own goals. History is littered with examples of such leaders who ruin countries for their own personal gain. In organizations we see in Case 9.1 about Enron how the primary reason for the company's downfall was the greed of its most senior managers.

Shared or distributed leadership

There is a view that in highly complex and competitive businesses, especially where the knowledge base of the business is rapidly changing, that it is unrealistic to assume that leadership can be vested in one person or even a small group. There are two main reasons for this. First, it is difficult for one person or even a group of senior managers to have all the knowledge, skills and abilities for all situations. This is particularly true for work in such organizations as large multinationals operating in many countries or organizations at the cutting edge of pharmaceutical or telecommunications research. This has become particularly apparent with the growth of knowledge work. Second, traditional leadership focusing on one individual (sometimes referred to as vertical leadership) can slow down the decision-making process by the need to get expert opinions and consult with colleagues when a fast response is required, especially in highly competitive sectors.

Under such conditions, as an alternative to traditional hierarchical leadership, the locus of leadership changes whenever a particular type of knowledge or skill or expert power is required. In this system the hierarchical position of the key decision-maker is less important than their specific contribution to the task.

Pearce (2004), an advocate for shared leadership believes it is not appropriate for all organizations. He believes that it is more suited to knowledge work under conditions where the jobs that people do are interdependent, where there is a strong need for creative solutions and where the organization, its product market and its work are complex. He emphasizes that the role of the vertical leader is critical to the effectiveness of shared leadership. Someone is needed to design the team and to manage their interdependent efforts. He further acknowledges that shared leadership is incompatible with traditional pay systems rooted in rewarding individual contributions. Alternatively, paying people as a team has its drawbacks in that some individuals can act as 'free riders'. For shared leadership to work, new systems of reward are needed that combine individual and team contributions.

There is little empirical evidence on the superior effectiveness of shared leadership systems. In many ways it harks back to more traditional forms of management that involve effective delegation and motivating people by empowering them.

Some concluding thoughts on leadership

Thomas (2003) concludes that from all the many studies on leadership there is little in the way of useful conclusion and there is no real evidence that any of the researchers have demonstrated the key to leadership effectiveness. He feels that too much emphasis has been placed on groups and their performance and insufficient attention has been paid to the organizational and social context within which leaders operate. While his conclusions may be sweeping, he raises issues that lie at the heart of the Business in Context model, namely the organizational and environmental contexts.

A number of such factors can be identified. The **age** of the organization may inhibit change. Leaders tend to be most effective in the early stages of an organization but those that follow later have difficulty in changing entrenched views and attitudes. We have seen in Chapter 6 that many of the policies of Hewlett Packard are directly attributable to its founders, Bill Hewlett and Dave Packard. The **size** of the organization affects the extent of the leader's influence. Large organizations are much more difficult to influence and change than small ones. Large complex organizations tend to have a complexity of tasks in different locations and requiring different expertise. These may all limit the ability of the leader to influence performance. The **structure** may facilitate or inhibit a leader's influence. In highly centralized structures, local leaders may have difficulty bringing about change or influencing performance, but those at the top may wield considerable influence on procedures throughout the organization. The **operating situation** can vary between stability and crisis. Thomas argues that leaders are seldom needed in stable situations and are most needed in times of crisis. The need for leaders in times of crisis accords with the transformational view of leadership necessary in complex, changing organizations. However, leaders may also be needed in stable situations where the motivation of the employees is an issue. Employees can resist attempts by leaders to influence them. This can be done through absenteeism, group or trade union action but most commonly through inertia.

In terms of the **environmental context** many factors lie outside the control of leaders. This was discussed in Chapters 3, 4 and 5, when we examined the manager's ability to influence the environment of the firm. Our conclusion now is the same. The environment can be difficult to change, but managers can lead the organization in its adaptation to its environment and may even be successful in shaping the environment to the advantage of the organization.

Leadership may also vary **geographically and culturally**. The GLOBE project found wide variation of effective leadership in different countries. For example, autonomous leadership, including independence from superiors was very effective in Eastern Europe, Germany and Austria but less effective elsewhere; and self-protective leadership involving leaders being self-centred and status conscious was less effective in most countries with the exception of Taiwan, Egypt and Iran (House et al., 2001, 2004).

CASE 7.2   EXECUTIVE PAY IN THE UK: A REVIEW OF RECENT ISSUES

In 2003, GlaxoSmithKline (GSK) decided to increase the remuneration of its chief executive, Jean-Pierre Garnier, by 70 per cent a year and to guarantee him a pay-off on leaving of a package worth £22 million. The GSK case made the headlines because, in an unprecedented move, the shareholders voted against the proposals at the annual general meeting (AGM) of the company. The vote was part of a new procedure requiring shareholders to vote on remuneration issues. Opposition was also voiced at the AGMs of HSBC, Barclays, Reuters and Granada, but in none of those cases was there a 51 per cent vote against, as in the case of GSK. The GSK

shareholders were angry that the share price of the company had fallen and that it had under-performed alongside its competitors. However, their vote could not force the company to change since the decision and policy had already been made. The purpose of the vote appeared to be intended simply to ratify a board decision. The force of the rejection did, however, make the company review its pay policy for top executives.

There are arguments why senior executives should be paid such large amounts. The remuneration packages are not out of line with those paid to USA executives. This was an argument used by

GSK in comparing itself with Merck and Pfizer. It is argued that high levels of pay are required to recruit the best international talent, which is in short supply, and to prevent the best UK talent from being poached by overseas competitors. An argument, often put by chief executives themselves, is that innovative inspirational leadership with responsibility for shareholders, employees and customers is high pressure, high risk and should be commensurate with high rewards. Garnier of GSK did not consider himself overpaid. In an interview with the *Daily Telegraph* on 21 May, 2003, he stated: 'I didn't seek this contract ... I accepted it ... I'm not Mother Teresa. This is a highly competitive business.'

Since then, GSK has taken steps to put its house in order. Some non-executive directors were removed and Deloitte Touche was asked to review the issue of executive pay. Andrew Witty, chief executive of GSK, on appointment in 2008, promised shareholders a new approach. He declared that pay would be based on the performance of the company rather than on the pay policies of its US competitors; bonuses would be reduced; and overall rewards would 'not be out of bounds'. The company's remuneration report was approved by 97 per cent of shareholders at the 2009 annual meeting.

In 2003, the GSK case reflected the general trend in executive pay in the UK. Chief executive pay and other rewards such as bonuses and shares rose by 77 per cent between 1997 and 2003, largely to catch up with US executives. Even so, such pay in the UK still trailed the US by some 40 per cent. *The Guardian* annual pay survey of FTSE 100 companies in 2007, based on data for 2006, revealed that while inflation was 2.3 per cent and average pay rose by 4 per cent, executive pay, bonuses and share payments rose 37 per cent. The average CEO reward package was £2.9 million, more than a hundred times the average wage. The highest paid UK executive received £23 million. The highest paid female executive received £2.1 million.

The argument over top executive pay raises a number of issues. First, there is the size of the pay award compared with that received by others in the organization. Second, there are the pay-offs made to directors of poorly performing companies. Third, there is the amount companies invest in the pension pots of existing and retired directors. Such pension payments are approved by existing directors, who are doubtless seeking such payments when they retire. Finally, there is an issue of principle. Should anyone receive a pay package of several million pounds?

Some UK academics noted that 'in recent years the literature on executive remuneration has grown at a pace rivalled only by the growth of executive pay itself' (Bruce et al., 2005, p. 1493). The same authors identify a number of perspectives. An agency theory perspective would argue that remuneration systems appeal to managers' self-interest and benefit shareholders by rewarding managers who increase shareholder value. It is claimed that the agency approach typifies the situation in the USA and UK. Stakeholder theory argues that decisions on pay are generally made in the interests of the firm and all its stakeholders, a position generally accepted to reflect more the situation in Germany. Bruce et al. (2005) identified a third perspective, where managers now have the power to award themselves pay packages as they like, constrained only by the 'avoidance of provoking outrage' (p. 1495).

The social outrage that had emerged over GSK in 2003 became widespread during 2008–09. The problems, which had their roots in earlier years, were focused initially on the banking sector but soon spread. The banks had been highlighted because senior staff in banking had traditionally been paid more than those in other sectors and the level of reward continued to rise as profits and share price fell. For example, the chief of HBOS received £787 000 in 2006, £940 000 in 2007 and just over £1 million in 2008. The problems in the banking sector were identified as too much reward for taking too many risks with depositors' and investors' money, short-term strategies and even greed. A series of complex financial products had emerged that obscured the risk and resulted in the sub-prime loan and mortgage problem in the USA that soon created problems in other countries. At the heart of these problems were the bonus payments to staff. John McFall, chairman of the UK Treasury select committee, an influential committee made up of members of parliament, described the bonus culture in banks as a 'lethal combination of reckless and excessive risk-taking'. As an example, Morgan Stanley's pay

(Continued)

CASE 7.2   (Continued)

during 2007–08 was greater than the value of the bank; the staff could technically pool their salaries and bonuses and buy the bank!

The crisis in banking was highlighted in the UK by the case of Sir Fred Goodwin, the departing chief of the Royal Bank of Scotland (RBS). He received a pension fund of £16.9 million, the equivalent of over £700 000 a year for life. The pension fund had been doubled in October 2008 at the same time as the bank had to be rescued by the UK government. During his reign the share price had fallen from a high of 345 pence to just 28 pence. The dramatic fall was attributed to a rights issue in 2008 to raise capital and the acquisition of ABN Amro at a price most considered to be highly inflated. At its AGM, shareholders considered Goodwin's stewardship a failure and 90 per cent of investors opposed the remuneration plan. A large proportion of the vote came from UK Financial Investors, an organization set up by the UK government to oversee its 58 per cent share in RBS and its shareholding in other banks. In 2009, RBS, which had already cut 2700 jobs planned further cuts of 9000 jobs, half in the UK. Goodwin, whose family had been threatened and whose addresses both in the UK and the south of France had been disclosed, agreed to reduce his pension demands to £342 000 a year. In addition, he had received a retirement lump sum, with tax paid by the bank and a bonus, both in excess of £2.5 million.

The shareholder revolt at RBS, echoing the events at GSK some six years earlier, was one of many such revolts in 2009. Shareholders are historically passive. They have always been able to vote against the annual report and accounts but have rarely done so. The majority, the institutional shareholders, have rarely been concerned with corporate governance and executive pay, preferring the direct route of selling their shares when there is something they do not like. The banking crisis had clearly made shareholders more militant. Opposition was voiced by shareholders to remuneration plans at BP, Provident Financial, Next, Rightmove, Tesco, Cable & Wireless and Nationwide. At Royal Dutch Shell, 59 per cent of shareholders at simultaneous AGMs in London and The Hague rejected a plan to pay bonuses to senior executives. Bonuses had been agreed if the company's performance among the big five oil companies was third or better. The

company came fourth but the remuneration committee recommended that bonuses should be paid. The shareholders argued that the executives had a moral duty to pay them back.

By mid-July 2009, banks such as Morgan Stanley, Goldman Sachs, Credit Suisse and Deutsche Bank were predicting large profits. The finance chief of Goldman Sachs claimed that it was all down to the staff and, since it was company policy for pay to follow performance, bonuses should be paid, especially as staff had lost out in 2008. Other banks planned to do the same. In the US, Stephen Lerner, director of the Financial Reform Campaign of the Service Employees International Union, commented on the banks plans to restart the bonus round:

They have some kind of moral and economic amnesia. After we bail them out with tens of billions of taxpayers' funds they go back to exactly the same practices as before.

In 2010–11 Barclays Bank in the UK gave out reward packages to its top five earners to a total of £110 million, with two staff getting in excess of £40 million, more than that paid to the CEO. The UK High Pay Commission set up by the government to review pay of senior staff in the public and private sector found in 2011 that top salaries were 145 times the average salary and that the gap had widened. Data from the Centre for Global Research on CEO pay in Standard and Poor's 500 companies on the US stock exchange found that CEO pay has increased by 50 per cent in three years since 2010 and in 2013 stood at 257 times the average US salary. In 2013 the top CEO reward package as reported by the compensation consultants Equilar was US$142 million.

The 'Occupy Wall Street' movement began in 2011 and expressed general discontent about the weakening of democracy and the undue influence of big business on governments, but a key focus was that of income inequality and the financial sector was specifically targeted. A large group set up a protest camp in a park next to Wall Street in New York. The camp was broken up by state and New York City authorities after two months. The movement spread to a large number of cities worldwide and the equivalent camp set up outside St Paul's Cathedral in London was in occupation for 4 months.

CASE 7.2   (Continued)

As initiated by GSK shareholders, in 2003 the shareholder backlash continued. In 2012 the CEO of Aviva resigned when 50 per cent of shareholders rejected his pay plan and 50 per cent of William Hill shareholders also rejected the proposed pay deals for directors. The UK media were active in publishing widely such shareholder revolts as well as on the remuneration of top managers, especially those involved in banking and the financial industry generally. Considerable exposure was given to the case of the five Barclay executives awarded large reward deals in 2011 and most of the coverage was critical from newspapers of widely differing political perspectives. Stephen Hester replaced Fred Goodwin as CEO of RBS with a brief to restructure the bank whose major shareholder was the UK government. Although his salary was lower than many in the sector there was a public outcry against his bonus payment of £1 million in 2011–12. Will Hutton quoted at the time:

Incentives designed with no sense of proportionality, no eye on the role of sheer good luck in the outcome, nor any care to design a process that is rigorous and legitimate, bring the whole apparatus of incentives into disrepute
(Will Hutton, *The Observer*, 29.01.12)

Following the public and media outcry, Hester declined his 2011–12 bonus and offered to forego that of 2012–13 as well.

Since the banking crisis there have been a number of government initiatives. The Troubled Asset Relief Program (TARP) in the USA reviewed the compensation levels for senior executives in seven companies receiving assistance, including Bank of America, Citigroup and General Motors. Their first action in 2009 was to reduce by 50 per cent the compensation for 175 employees. In the same year the UK government established a one-off windfall tax of 50 per cent on all bonuses of over £25 000 paid in the banking sector, irrespective of whether the bank had been bailed out or not. The government, however, acknowledged that the action was largely symbolic as the money raised would be an insignificant percentage of that paid out to banks.

In 2014 the EU parliament approved a law aimed at controlling bonuses paid to senior bank employees. Rules were set restricting bonuses to the equivalent of the annual salary. This could be increased to two year's salary but only with a minimum shareholder vote in favour of 66 per cent. The EU law covers senior managers and 'material risk takers' whose salaries exceed Euros 500 000. It applies to all banks of EU countries anywhere in the world and also applies to foreign banks with respect to their operation in the EU. The UK government sided with the UK banking community in its assessment of the new law. They believed that the net effect would be that salaries would be raised to retain top staff, with the result that the banks would lose the financial flexibility that an unrestricted bonus payments system would give them, in that fixed salary costs would rise. They claimed also that the banking sector in EU countries would lose out to competition from the USA, Asia and Switzerland, with a substantial loss of tax revenue.

Following the introduction of the law, the EU accused the UK banks with the support of the UK government of sidestepping the law by manipulating pay packages to get around the restrictions.

Questions

1 If leaders are to inspire and innovate and are in short supply should not the salaries of top executives reflect this? What arguments can you give in terms of management and leadership roles and functions to support the claim that senior executives should be well rewarded?

2 To what extent is it fair that the price of shares should be used as an argument in the determination of executive pay? Examine the issue of executive pay from the perspective of agency theory (see Chapter 6 and the section on 'ownership and control' for background on this).

3 How much do you attribute the banking crisis of 2008–09 to executive pay? Do you agree with the statements of Lerner and Hutton quoted in the case.

4 What conclusions do you draw about 2014 EU law on bonuses for the banking community and the UK response? Why has the banking community been singled out?

SUMMARY

- While management is 'getting things done through other people' and 'pulling it all together' to meet organizational and environmental **demands**, there are difficulties associated with any definition. This is because of the weak body of knowledge and the large variation in the types of management work.
- The legitimacy of the manager is based on a number of things including property rights, law, various forms of power and an underlying value system.
- Several theories and models of management have emerged at different times. However, for the most part we can question their rationality and their utility.
- There have been many attempts to identify what managers do and construct models around this, but several linkages can be found to the more classical approaches.
- Leadership is considered a key element of modern management and is especially important in times of rapid change and intense competition.
- There have been attempts to develop an appropriate theory of leadership, most of which have only limited application.
- In keeping with the Business in Context model, we may conclude that both management and leadership are best viewed within an organizational and environmental context.

DISCUSSION QUESTIONS

1   Consider the roles of the chief executive of a global company, the canteen manager at a manufacturing plant and a university head of department. To what extent can these three be called managers? What roles and activities do they have in common and how do they differ?

2   Why should we do what managers tell us to do? What kinds of power do the three examples in question 1 possess?

3   Critically examine the various models of managers. Which do you consider the most relevant and why?

4   Why do managers seek gurus and follow fashions in management practice?

5   What conclusions do you draw from the studies on the work managers do? Contrast these findings with Fayol's principles of management in Table 7.1. Do such studies invalidate much of management theory?

6   To what extent is leadership different from management?

7   Why is leadership such a focus of concern among management professional bodies and with governments?

8   Critically assess the various theories of leadership. Which do you find most relevant and why?

FURTHER READING

An excellent tour through management writers and their models and theories can be found in:

Sheldrake, J. (2003) *Management Theory*, 2nd edn, Thomson: London.

An interesting study of management with some excellent illustrations and thought-provoking comment is found in:

Watson, T.J. (1994) *In Search of Management: Culture, Chaos and Control in Management Work*, Routledge: London.

A critical account of most aspects of management and leadership can be found in:

Thomas, A.B. (2003) *Controversies in Management: Issues, Debates, Answers*, 2nd edn, Routledge: London.

An excellent general review of leadership is provided by:

Yukl, G. (2013) *Leadership in Organizations*, 8th edn, Pearson Education: Harlow.

Insights into leadership can be found in:

Council for Excellence in Management and Leadership (2002), *Managers and Leaders: Raising our Game*, Council for Excellence in Management and Leadership: London.

House, R.J., Javidan, M. and Dorfman, P. (2001) 'The GLOBE project', *Applied Psychology*, 50(4), 489–55.

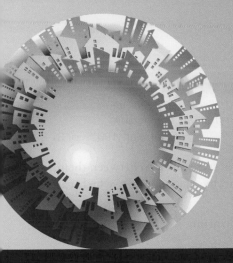

STRATEGY

8

LEARNING OBJECTIVES At the end of this chapter you should be able to:

- Explain the strengths and weaknesses of the various approaches to strategy and how they interact.
- Assess the uses of strategy in different organizational contexts.
- Use simple models to assess the general and immediate competitive environments of an organization and demonstrate the limitations of such models.
- Illustrate the links between strategy, goals, structure, ownership, size and culture at the level of the firm.
- Explain the concepts and assess the value of resource analysis, core competence, value chain and portfolio analysis.
- Explain the various kinds of strategic option and demonstrate the basis for the selection of a particular strategy in different situations.

WHAT IS STRATEGY?

Strategy has been defined as simply:

> ... the long-term direction of the organization.
>
> (Johnson, Whittington and Scholes, 2012, p. 2)

and as:

... the determination of long-run goals and objectives of an enterprise and the adoption of courses of action and the allocation of resources necessary for carrying out these goals.

(Chandler, 1962, p. 3)

In Chapter 6 we examined organizational goals. Although there is some overlap between them, strategies and goals are linked in what some refer to as a hierarchy of intentions, which can comprise:

- A **vision** setting out the overall future intentions of the organization.
- A **mission statement,** which sets out the organization's core values.
- **Goals** as broad statements of intent.
- **Strategies** refine the goal setting process by determining what needs to be done to achieve the goals.
- **Objectives** are the specific intentions identified by the strategy, the level of achievement of which can be measured within a specific time.

Strategy contains a number of interrelated elements:

- It involves consideration of environmental changes that bring about opportunities and pose threats.
- It is concerned with the assessment of the internal strengths and weaknesses of the institution and, in particular, its ability to respond to those opportunities and threats. In this way strategy can be seen as a linking process between the environmental, organizational and functional components of the Business in Context model.
- It is the product of a decision-making process influenced by the values, preferences and power of interested parties. We examined some of the issues involved in this in our discussion of management in the previous chapter.
- It is concerned with generating options and evaluating them.

Strategy is, therefore, an all-embracing term dealing with goals and objectives, the firm's environment, its resources and structure, the scope and nature of its activities and ultimately the behaviour of its members. Given the large number of variables involved and the considerable subjectivity of the decision-making process, strategy formulation is a very complex process. The approach used by management texts (including, to a certain extent, this book) is to reduce such complexity to a series of steps. While this is understandable, it can both oversimplify and give the impression that strategy formulation is a logical process.

In this chapter we deal with the elements of strategy and attempt, wherever possible, to draw attention to the more subjective and political aspects. We begin by examining the nature of strategy, through the way strategy is formed. We refer to this as the strategic process. We then look at the contexts in which strategic decisions are taken, and go on to identify the environmental and organizational aspects of management strategy. We end the chapter by examining common strategic options, with a brief look at the criteria for strategic choice.

Most strategies in most organizations originate from the management group. The concept crops up in many guises and is sometimes referred to as 'business policy', 'corporate strategy', 'business strategy', 'corporate planning', and so on. While there is significant overlap between such concepts and similar approaches are used, we can differentiate between corporate strategy, business strategy and functional strategy.

- **Corporate strategy** deals with decisions about the organization as a whole. In diversified multi-product companies, it is the overall strategy that covers all activities. The corporate strategy of a firm like Samsung or a university such as King's College London will give direction and aim to add value to the entire organization. Corporate level decisions can include whether to enter a new market, whether to expand the organization by acquisition and decisions about the total range of products and services.

- **Business strategy** deals with decisions that are linked to specific products and markets that can be differentiated from other products and markets in the same organization. Decisions at this level are about competing in a specific product market. Such strategies can apply to stand-alone businesses as **strategic business units** (SBUs). Business strategies in Samsung would apply to specific product areas such as televisions or mobile phones or even specific geographic markets. In King's College, each department such as dentistry or management would have its own business strategy. Obviously, business strategies should relate to the overall corporate strategy.

- **Functional strategy** is concerned with the various activities of business; innovation, operations, marketing, HRM, and finance and accounting. The functional strategies of each of these activities determines how they will deliver the corporate and business strategies.

THE STRATEGIC PROCESS

Approaches to strategy

An examination of how strategy is formed gives us insights into the nature of strategy itself. We identify five approaches, which we have termed rational, flexible, creative, behavioural and incremental, and a sixth which suggests that some managers operate without a conscious strategy. We deal with each in turn.

KEY CONCEPT 8.1   THE STRATEGIC PROCESS

The strategic process refers to the way in which management strategy is formed. In most organizations this involves a mixture of scientific and rational analysis together with more subjective and political considerations.

The rational approach

This is the classical approach to strategy and is typified by the work of Ansoff (1968), Andrews (1971) and Porter (1980, 1985). Strategy formulation is portrayed as a scientific and rational process, assisted by techniques such as technological forecasting, portfolio analysis, environmental impact analysis and sensitivity analysis. The aim of such techniques is generally profit maximization. The rational approach owes much to the development of contingency theory. In Chapter 1 we noted that the contingency approach stressed the importance of a strategic fit between the firm and its environment. Analyses are made of a firm's environment to assess likely opportunities and threats, and of its internal resource position to identify strengths and weaknesses. This process is sometimes referred to as SWOT analysis, an acronym for strengths, weaknesses, opportunities and threats. The development of SWOT is attributed to Kenneth Andrews of Harvard Business School (Andrews, 1971). An illustration of the kind of analysis that can be made is offered in Figure 8.1. There are disadvantages with this kind of approach:

- Assumes that information is readily available to the strategist and an accurate assessment can be made of its likely effect on the firm. In reality, knowledge is often imperfect.

- The environment of modern business is often complex and dynamic. This makes assessment of opportunities and threats difficult.

- Complexity and lack of information do not just apply to the environment. Managers can often be unaware of the real strengths and weaknesses of their own organization.

FIGURE 8.1	An analysis of the strengths, weaknesses, opportunities and threats of SWOT United, a Second Division football club

Opportunities	Threats
Promotion to other divisions Increased revenue from success in cup competitions Sale of town-centre site and redevelopment on the outskirts Development of a membership squash and rackets club and fitness centre attached to the ground Use of ground for other functions, e.g. rock concerts Development of retailing activities	Seven other professional clubs operating in a 25-mile radius Rising costs of wages and transfer fees, bank interest charges, policing, equipment Local authority refusing planning permission for a new ground and any other development Best players may leave Competition for spectators' time and money from other sources, e.g. TV, cinema, shopping, DIY Increased levels of unemployment in the area and less disposal income

Strengths	Weaknesses
The club owns its own ground and car parks in a good town-centre site Good housekeeping and relatively low wages 2000 loyal supporters A successful and well established youth development policy The image of a 'friendly' club with good connections	Cannot break even. Losses are supported by donations and loans from the chairman and a large bank overdraft Ground facilities in poor order, especially seating and toilets Insufficient funds to invest in higher wages and transfer fees A relatively small population to support so many clubs in close proximity Poor image compared with many other clubs in the area especially a recently promoted Premier League team

- In scanning the environment, managers are often collecting the same information as rival firms. As a result, similar strategies occur and there may be a lack of truly innovative solutions. The focus is on the environment rather than on the creation of distinctive competences and on the needs of the individual customer.

- The process of making decisions becomes both subjective and political, attracting the criticism of 'pseudo-science'.

Despite these criticisms, the rational approach can be useful in that it collects relevant data, it can give direction, it has face validity and, as Whittington (2000) argues, it can serve as a form of group therapy. The approach is popular and is the basis of many texts. It can be a useful starting point, provided managers are aware of its limitations.

KEY CONCEPT 8.2   SWOT ANALYSIS

SWOT stands for strengths, weaknesses, opportunities and threats. It is normally associated with more rational approaches to strategy formulation but perhaps its greatest contribution lies in providing the management strategist and student of business with a framework for analysing the position of a firm at a particular time. It can also be useful in the development of strategic options which attempt to tackle opportunities and threats, build on corporate strengths and avoid weaknesses. An important consideration is that for most management there is a choice of strategy.

In the 1960s and 1970s the emergence of an increasingly complex and turbulent business environment called for modifications in the rational approach.

The flexible approach

The complexity and volatility of the environment may mean that a detailed SWOT analysis is both difficult and inappropriate and profit maximization may be an inappropriate strategy. The environment may be changing so rapidly that many of the historical and current data are meaningless. This kind of situation led the oil companies, such as Shell, to adopt a different approach to strategy formulation known as **scenario planning.** The approach recognizes that uncertainty can never be eliminated, but it can be reduced by plotting scenarios, each responding to different visions of the future. Managements are therefore prepared for a number of possible changes that may occur. Writers such as Williamson (1991) argue that, under such conditions, the best that managers can hope for is to maximize the chances of survival by cutting costs to become more efficient (survival of the fittest) and by playing the market. A good example of the latter is offered by Whittington (2000) citing Sony, who, in the 1980s, produced 160 different models of the Walkman for the US, but kept only about 20 models on the market at any one time (survival of the most popular).

The creative approach

This takes the flexible approach one step further by stressing the importance of imagination in the strategic process. The idea that such an approach to strategy formulation is actually better has been taken up by management writers in the 1980s. Peters and Waterman believe that the more formal approaches to strategy formulation with the emphasis on complex environmental and organizational analysis can lead to 'paralysis through analysis' (Peters and Waterman, 1982, p. 31). Managers using the rational approach to make strategic decisions in a specific product market will invariably have access to precisely the same information as their competitors.

The resulting strategies are often too conservative, insufficiently adventurous and are similar to those of competitor companies. A creative approach offers more chance of achieving competitive advantage. Moreover, the more complex and changing the business environment and the more difficult the problems facing managers, the more creative they need to be.

The behavioural approach

There is strong support for the view that strategy formulation is far from being a rational, logical process (Cyert and March, 1963; Mintzberg and Quinn, 1991). Instead, strategic choice is the product of the organization's dominant coalition, invariably senior management, and is based upon its values, ideologies and personalities, and upon organizational power and politics. The process invariably involves negotiation between senior management and other groups. The most overt of these processes take place at shareholders' meetings. However, the most significant negotiations generally take place between competing factions within management itself, over such issues as the allocation of scarce resources, and are consequently much more difficult to observe. Behavioural analyses of the strategy formulation see management values and objectives as more than individual inputs to the planning process. They influence the way the environment is perceived and, hence, the choice of opportunities and threats and the assessment of strengths and weaknesses. Because of the bargaining processes involved, the outcomes of the behavioural approach to strategy are likely to be satisfactory rather than seeking to maximize the result.

The incremental approach

This approach has much in common with the behavioural approach. Strategy is not a carefully prepared plan with clear goals, but a process by which managers in the organization gradually come to terms with the environment. Limited objectives are constantly modified in the light of experience and through the process of negotiation between interested parties. As a consequence, strategies are continually being changed. The incremental approach has been put forward as a more realistic and more effective method of dealing with complex and changing situations. The concept originated from the work of Lindblom (1959) in an article appropriately titled 'The science of muddling through'. Although his work was mainly concerned with large public sector organizations such as hospitals and universities, there are strong parallels with larger private sector firms. Mintzberg (1990) has sympathy with this perspective and sees many strategies emerging as opposed to being consciously planned. This gives rise to notions of strategic learning as management builds up a repertoire of strategies based on what has worked in the past.

An absence of strategy?

Finally, we present the view that strategy formulation is not a conscious management activity. Strategy is not an issue when firms appear to be operating to the satisfaction of management. It becomes an issue only in times of crisis when any attempt at strategy formulation may be too little and too late. There may be several reasons for this. In some cases managers may have a simple view of what the organization does. If it produces good quality, reliable products that sell and make profit then there may be no incentive to develop a strategy to do things differently. Porter (1996) argued that apart from Sony, Canon and Sega, most Japanese firms lacked a strategy beyond firms imitating and emulating each other. Japanese firms had grown in global markets on the basis of operational efficiency through such approaches as lean production. However, as global competitors adopted similar methods, the competitive advantage of the Japanese was eroded. Porter's view was that such firms had no unique strategic position. It may be the case that managers are complacent and reluctant to rock the boat or they may have myopic vision and hence a limited view of options (see Levitt, 1960, and a discussion of the concept of 'marketing myopia' in Chapter 12). It may be that managers are too distracted by the daily business of survival and see themselves too weighed down by resource constraints to contemplate strategic options. In the last scenario, management becomes an endless round of firefighting with no time for strategic contemplation.

The various approaches we have identified reveal a mixture of rational and non-rational approaches to the formulation of management strategy. Nevertheless, strategies are more than management hunches played out in an information vacuum. More likely, managers select what information is appropriate for their purposes, and this invariably involves consideration of both environmental and organizational variables. Management values and organization politics are important not only in the choice of strategy but in the selection of information upon which that strategy is based. All six of the approaches we have identified may operate together in the same firm. The following illustration reveals this mixed approach to strategic decision-making.

Example of a mixed approach

Partners and office staff in a firm of solicitors have had problems with their computerized client record and accounts system. The firm was one of the first to buy such a system, but the increasing complexity of its expanding international business has meant that the software cannot cope. One of the newer partners joined the organization from a rival firm, and he was impressed with the system used there. He spends several months persuading his fellow partners that it may be a good idea to change systems. The process of persuasion is accompanied by the gathering of information to show the growth of the firm over the past few years and illustrations are well chosen to show the advantages of the new system in terms of faster information retrieval and better management information on the current status of client accounts. Information is also collected on the cost of the proposed software and the hardware needed to support it. The office practice manager also presents information on the cost, strengths and weaknesses of rival systems. Quotations are sought from computer firms with experience of installing such systems and in servicing professional firms. The partners agree to go ahead with the proposal. A more recent convert to the idea, one of the senior partners, uses his influence to promote and eventually engage a firm of computer consultants. This firm has been set up by the brother of a senior partner in another law firm and he has installed the chosen system in that firm.

The above illustration reinforces the notion of strategy as both an intellectual exercise in information gathering and presentation and a political exercise involving values, power and influence. In this case, the situation was a relatively straightforward investment decision with implications for office practice. Strategic decisions to enter a new product market or change radically the structure of the organization involve far greater complexities.

Apart from these six approaches, we can identify three broad planning styles: formalized planning, negotiation and consultation, and entrepreneurship (a similar model is offered by Mintzberg, 1973b). Figure 8.2 shows how these planning styles interact with the first five of the strategic approaches.

The suitability of a particular planning style may depend on the size and nature of the firm. For example, a formal planning system is more likely to be found in a large firm. Smaller firms by their very nature will favour an entrepreneurial style, and a high degree of consultation will be found in larger public sector organizations. Moreover, different styles may be appropriate for different functions. While formalized planning may be a key feature of operations strategy, an

FIGURE 8.2	Approaches and styles of management strategy

Approach	Style		
	Formalized planning	Entrepreneurial	Negotiation and consultation
Rational	X		
Flexible	X	X	
Creative		X	X
Behavioural			X
Incremental			X

R&D strategy may benefit more from an entrepreneurial approach. Where trade union influence is considerable, management may need to proceed more through consultation.

Both the approaches and styles may change over time. A university which has operated through a mixture of an incremental approach and a consultative style may, when faced with increased competition at the same time as budget cuts, need to operate in a much more entrepreneurial way.

REFLECTION POINT

Using the approaches to strategy identified above consider the types of organization and the types of situation where each of the approaches would be more suitable than the others.

Strategic contexts

We have identified how managers may employ different approaches to the task of strategy formulation. In addition, we can identify various contexts in which the strategic process operates:

- Strategy is not the sole preserve of the profit-making organization. All organizations have strategies, formalized to a greater or lesser extent. We can see strategies at work in such diverse organizations as schools, the police, charities, professional football clubs and the church. In recent years there has been a focus on management strategies in the UK public sector. For example, the health service has recruited its area managers from industry and commerce in an attempt to introduce a more businesslike approach, including a greater emphasis on strategy formulation.

- We may differentiate between those strategies pertaining to entire industries, strategies employed by firms operating in a number of business markets, and strategies pertaining to those operating in a single or restricted product market.

- We have already made the distinction between a corporate and business strategy. A corporate strategy relates to the whole business, whereas a business strategy relates to a specific product group or market. A multi-divisional firm like Samsung therefore operates both corporate and business strategies.

- We may identify strategies operating at different levels of the organization from broad strategies at the top, moving through stages towards strategies for specific functional areas like HRM or marketing, and finally to individual targets and budgets.

The uses and value of strategy

We can identify reasons for management to engage in strategy formulation:

- Strategy assists in the formulation of goals and objectives and enables them to be modified in the light of information and experience.
- Strategy is a form of management control. It is a plan that guides behaviour along a predetermined route. At the operational level it results in budgets and targets.
- A clear strategy both assists in the process of allocating resources and may provide a rationale for that allocation so that it is perceived to be fair by organization members.
- It enables management to identify strategic issues that the firm may face in the future and prepare appropriate action.
- Strategy performs a useful role in guiding the action of the constituent parts of the organization as well as acting as an integrating mechanism ensuring units work together. The integrating power of strategy is a central feature of 'strong' corporate cultures as illustrated by firms such as IBM and HP.
- Leading on from that, strategy formulation can be an important element in the process of social change. Strategic objectives are achieved by changing the behaviour of employees. This is the essence of organizational development programmes used by such companies as Shell.
- The formulation of strategy is seen as a training ground for the development of future managers.

We have already questioned the extent to which formalized strategy is used by firms. An even more important consideration is the extent to which the existence of a formalized strategy contributes to organizational success. There is mixed evidence on strategy and performance. There would appear to be two problems. First, there is the difficulty of isolating and measuring the effect of strategy on performance, be it return on investment (ROI), market share, or some other criterion. A firm's financial and market performance, even over time, may be influenced by so many variables outside the control of management that causal links between strategy and performance may be difficult to show. Second, the relationship is complicated in that performance may well influence strategy rather than the other way around. A firm that has been highly profitable may be stimulated into seeking investment opportunities either through product development or acquisition. Conversely, a firm incurring losses may well be limited in its strategic options and have them determined by people external to the firm such as bank managers or liquidators. In this case the firm's performance is the reason for pursuing a divestment strategy, involving the closure or sale of the least profitable parts.

REFLECTION POINT

What do you think is the most important use of strategy?

ENVIRONMENTAL ASPECTS OF STRATEGY

In the last section we suggested that it was often difficult to establish a clear link between strategy and performance because of the great number of influences at work. Much of that complexity may be attributed to the firm's environment.

The firm's environment is, of course, a key aspect of our Business in Context model. In Chapter 1 we introduced the notion of contingency theory and the belief that a firm's performance was dependent upon it achieving a strategic fit between itself and the environment in which it operates. In Chapters 3, 4 and 5 we identified, with the use of selected examples, aspects of the business environment. We suggested that these elements not only interact with business but with each other, resulting, for most firms, in an environment that is complex and changing. In this and the previous two chapters we have noted how that complexity is further complicated by the values of decision-makers and the internal structures and politics of organizations. The manager's task of making sense of the environment is therefore a very difficult assignment.

We can identify two aspects of the environment that may influence strategy as follows:

- There are those issues that affect all firms operating in a given business environment. These are many of the issues we raised in Chapters 3, 4 and 5 and may include the state of the economy, the labour market, changing technology, government policy and social and cultural influences. This is called the **general environment.**

- There are those factors that have direct bearing on the firm's competitive position, which we will call the **immediate competitive environment.** An analysis of both these environments will enable management to arrive at some assessment of the opportunities and threats facing the organization.

The general environment

An analysis of a firm's general environment is sometimes known as environmental scanning, and usually comprises some sort of assessment of environmental influences, how they interact with the firm and with each other and how they change over time. There are many difficulties with such an analysis. Some managers tackle the sheer complexity of the environment by generating masses of information, not all of which is relevant and not all of which is accurate. The use of computers has increased the capacity for information handling and, in some firms, managers can be submerged in a sea of data, much of which has only marginal relevance to their needs. At the other extreme there are those who either ignore the environment or who have a blinkered perception of the firm's relationship to it. In such a situation trends can be missed, and the firm either cedes opportunities to its competitors or is unprepared for changes when they occur.

Johnson et al. (2013) identify the problems with the environment facing all organizations in terms of its diversity, complexity and speed of change. Of course, some firms operate in environments that are less diverse, less complex and where change, in some respects, is less rapid than in others. For example, a firm making chocolate products in the UK knows that peak demand for its products will occur around Christmas and Easter and must gear up its entire organization to meet those periods. However, seemingly simple and relatively static environments can change. For example, a company that produced Christmas cards knew precisely that demand would peak at the end of the calendar year and would have a good idea of the size of that demand. However, the Christmas card market has become highly competitive, with many new entrants, including charities and societies. Moreover, the card market in general has grown with specialist cards demanded for other occasions throughout the year.

The environment facing most organizations is dynamic, changing quickly and frequently. Managers need to be sensitive to the environment and predict changes that are likely to occur. The UK home computer industry of the 1980s was particularly dynamic. Sinclair was first to launch a mass-market personal computer, but failed to maintain product development. The company was challenged by Acorn's more upmarket BBC Micro, and these and other rivals found buyers switching to Amstrad, which was sensitive to, and even helped create, changing consumer needs, and ushered in cheap IBM-compatible PCs. In its turn, Amstrad was replaced by companies such as Packard Bell, offering attractive all-in packages and forging alliances with computer superstores. New entrants then emerged and, in the case of Dell, based their rapid growth on selling directly to the customer through mail order. In such a dynamic market, household names quickly come and go. Businesses that fail in dynamic environments are generally those where managers have failed to see the changes which are occurring or are either unable or unwilling to take appropriate action.

The case of professional soccer in England and Wales is one where an entire industry lost ground to a variety of competitors for its customers' time and money, and the general trend towards declining attendance and hence revenue seemed irreversible 20 years ago. The football authorities tackled the problem, in part, by the creation of an elite Premier League and by insisting on ground improvements for the top clubs, including the creation of all-seater stadiums. A lucrative television deal for the Premier League was struck with a leading satellite television company and the clubs imported stars from other countries. The result has been a turnaround for the leading clubs, with capacity attendances for most matches, a corresponding rise in ticket prices and a vast increase in profits. This, in turn, has led to a rise in wages and much greater mobility among players. Increased mobility is a function of an EU ruling giving players freedom of movement at the end of a contract, where previously clubs could demand a transfer fee. In the main, clubs have had to make rapid adjustments to rising costs through increased prices and the growth of selling club shirts and other products. Some of the larger clubs have shops of the size of small department stores. In Chapter 14 we examine football finances as a case in accounting and finance.

Dynamic environments require more creative approaches to strategy. However, there may be a danger that managers may respond unnecessarily to changes. For example, some firms, when threatened by entrants offering much cheaper products in the same market, respond by launching a cheaper version of their own product. This not only shows a lack of faith in the quality of the firm's original product, but it will inevitably take sales away from that product and have a potentially damaging effect on the firm's reputation.

Not only has the environment become more dynamic, it is also more complex in that different demands are placed upon different aspects of the firm's operation. A firm producing a range of products for different markets could be said to be operating in a complex environment. Most firms in such situations reflect this complexity in their organizational structures. We saw in Chapter 6 how the development of the multi-divisional firm was a direct response to the problems faced by emerging multinational corporations like General Motors in the 1920s. The problem facing firms in a complex environment is the extent to which the complexity needs to be accommodated by organizational changes. Some firms attempt to reduce complexity by restructuring, which may include selling off some units. Such action is a common feature of mergers and acquisitions and will be dealt with later in this chapter.

We can see that most organizations face interconnected problems related to the degree of change, the speed of change, the complexity of its environment and the corresponding complexity of the organization. Managers tend to seek to reduce such uncertainty as much as they can by a variety of measures:

- Uncertainty may be reduced by collecting relevant information. We have already noted the problems associated with collecting accurate information and with information overload.

- As we saw in Chapter 3, managers will attempt to influence and control the environment. This can be done by measures such as technological innovation, forming coalitions with other organizations, political lobbying, acquiring raw material suppliers, retail outlets and even competitors, and training staff in rare skills.

- Structures and procedures, such as planning and forecasting, may be set up to cope with uncertainty. There are, however, dangers with setting up new structures. Specialist units can lead to problems of cooperation and integration. In the early days of computing in business, the creation of specialist groups of programmers and analysts led to tensions and conflict (as identified in a classic study by Pettigrew, 1973).

The immediate competitive environment

We will attempt to locate a business in its immediate competitive environment using the model devised by Porter (1980, 2008). Porter has identified five forces, which have immediate bearing on a firm's competitive position. The forces he identifies are: the threat of new entrants; the threat of substitute products; the bargaining power of suppliers and that of buyers; and competitive rivalry. Porter argues that these five forces operate in every sector but vary in each case. They tell us much about the industry structure and how the operation of the forces affects profit. We explain and illustrate these forces in turn.

The threat of potential entrants

The threat of entry is often related to the ease with which a new business can establish itself in the same product market. This is sometimes referred to as low barriers to entry. The relative ease with which new restaurants emerge in large cities such as London and New York suggests that the threat to existing restaurants is very real. However, the ease of entry means increased competition and can result in a highly volatile market, to which the death rate of new restaurants will testify. The closure of restaurants provides in turn opportunities to acquire premises with fully fitted kitchens and the opportunity to acquire bankrupt stock such as furniture, crockery and cutlery at bargain rates. Other sectors where there are relatively low barriers to entry include estate agents and housing management services in the property market.

The threat of entry can also be high if new entrants come into the market with a strong brand and a success in other markets. Porter (2008) cites the example of Apple entering the music distribution market. In a similar way Virgin has used its brand to enter a range of markets including TV and media, mobile phones and financial services

The threat posed by potential entrants is reduced if there are **barriers to entry.** These can operate in a number of ways:

- Equipment and associated capital requirements place burdens on investment and firms may have to withstand considerable unit cost disadvantages initially. Such difficulties would be presented to firms attempting to enter mass car production or oil refining.

It would be difficult for newcomers to achieve sufficient economies of scale to recover their outlay in a reasonable time.

- These difficulties can be increased where access to raw materials is an additional problem.

- In some types of industry, breaking into a market is difficult owing to the considerable customer loyalty to existing products and brands. A soft drinks manufacturer attempting to launch a cola drink would have considerable difficulty persuading the market to switch from Coca-Cola or Pepsi Cola.

- In the industrial components industry, getting customers to switch may pose the additional difficulties of part compatibility.

- Such barriers may be compounded by the difficulty of obtaining access to channels of distribution. A producer of a new brand in the food and drink industry may have difficulty persuading supermarket chains to stock its products. Getting supermarket shelf space is especially difficult for small independent producers

- Patents held by manufacturers can block those wishing to enter the market with imitative products. Patents held by Polaroid posed difficulties for Kodak in entering the instant camera market. This is also linked to the need for high investment in R&D and where the need for high investment and existing patents have been particular barriers to entry in the pharmaceutical market.

- In a more general way the operating experience, which may include economies of scale gained by existing firms over a number of years, can place the newcomer at a disadvantage.

We should not forget that there are barriers to exit as well as barriers to entry. A large manufacturing company with considerable operating losses, but with many employees and a significant investment in plant and machinery, will undoubtedly face pressures to stay in business. Such pressures will be related to the extent of the firm's assets, which may not be recoverable if the firm closes. This fear of lost investment may only be one factor. Senior managers may be particularly attached to the company, emotionally as well as financially, and place a high value on its survival, despite market and financial evidence to the contrary. Pressures will undoubtedly come from the local community and, in the case of some firms, from the national government, fearing the effect of closure on local and national economies and on levels of unemployment. Barriers to exit operate in small firms as well, where there is likely to be an even greater ego involvement on the part of the owner-managers and a subsequent reluctance to accept forced closure in the face of market forces.

REFLECTION POINT

Consider a range of businesses. What are the barriers to entry? How do they vary between the businesses you have chosen?

The threat of substitution

A substitute performs the same or similar function as an industry's product by a different means.

(Porter, 2008)

The threat is greater where the substitute offers a real price or performance advantage. The cotton textile industry in Britain was not only threatened by cheap labour economies but also by the development of substitute products in the form of man-made fibres selling at a cheaper price to cotton goods. The introduction of digital photography to replace film in cameras was the main reason for the bankruptcy of Kodak. Rail travel in the USA declined as airlines opened up local networks and assisted in the establishment of local airports. The size of the country meant that air travel was perceived as a more effective means of covering large distances. Distances are less of a problem in the UK, yet rail companies face competition from bus companies, competing on price, and from a growing network of local air traffic, competing on the basis of speed and comparative price. The travel business has changed significantly as high street travel agents have been replaced by online booking. However, travel agents can and do prosper by offering a service based on detailed specialist knowledge of a particular country and its travel and hotel networks.

REFLECTION POINT

Identify several products. In what ways and by what could they be substituted?

The bargaining power of buyers

Buyer power increases where there is a wide choice of suppliers offering the same or substitute products, especially where there is little or no cost involved for the buyer in switching from one supplier to another. For the industrial components industry, particularly where specialist components are involved, the relationship may be different. There may have been a mutual accommodation of product changes over a number of years and such a strong relationship forged that the cost of switching would be high. Components suppliers often invest time and energy building up such relationships with customers.

The buyer–supplier relationship is highly complex. The complexity of the technology plays a major part, as does the competitiveness of the market. A mix of cultural and economic factors can also be significant. As part of their normal business strategy, Japanese industrial firms rely on subcontractors to supply components, and tend to build close relationships with these suppliers. When Japanese firms moved into the UK they tended to locate in areas of low economic activity. This placed the Japanese in a strong bargaining position to drive down costs.

The power of a buyer generally increases with the volume bought. This power can be exercised in the demand for discounts or the expectation of preferential treatment in the supply of goods. A factor to consider here is the relative size of the two parties. Buyer power normally exists only if the volume purchased forms a high proportion of the selling company's total sales. The larger supermarket chains like Wal-Mart in the USA and Tesco in the UK have considerable buyer power, particularly over the smaller food suppliers. The cost of special offers to supermarket customers, especially 'buy-one-get-one-free', is generally borne by the supplier and not the supermarket. In general, the stronger the bargaining position of buyers then their ability to bring down prices and demand improved services increases. Profits are therefore transferred from the supplier to the buyer. In certain circumstances, buyer power can be reinterpreted as consumer choice. A restaurant in central London faces considerable competition from other restaurants operating in that area. Buyers have a wide choice and switching is easy. In such situations the product/market strategy of the restaurant becomes of utmost importance. Such strategies will include considerations of product differentiation and quality, market segmentation, price and promotion (Chapter 12 has a fuller account of these strategies).

The bargaining power of suppliers

The illustration of the bargaining power of buyers in the industrial components industry works equally well for suppliers. In this and other cases, supplier power is stronger where the component is specialized and few suppliers exist. Supplier power is also strong where the cost to the buyer of switching allegiance would include costly product adaptations. A computer manufacturer can gain additional market power where it develops popular software that can only be used on its own machines. A case of supplier power in the computer industry emerged in the late 1990s around the monopoly power of Microsoft, the creator of the Windows Operating System for PCs. The system is sold as the standard operating environment with most PCs and Microsoft has a 90 per cent share of the market. However, Microsoft came under criticism and was eventually taken to court under USA anti-trust laws. The company was accused of abusing its monopoly power in its attempt to control the market for access to the Internet via its web browser, Internet Explorer. Porter (2008) describes the computer industry as the classic industry structure favouring suppliers, Firms like Microsoft and Intel occupy monopoly positions, while, by comparison, the computer manufacturing sector is split between a relatively large number of firms.

The power of suppliers can also be seen in labour markets. Those with rare skills or where supply is scarce can command high salaries. University professors in business, finance and medicine can command higher salaries than those in the liberal arts. This is particularly true in USA universities.

Most firms act as both suppliers and buyers and the bargaining power can be a two-edged weapon. The cost of switching is also a factor in determining the relative power of buyers and suppliers and also the threat of substitutes.

REFLECTION POINT

Identify a particular business. Assess the relative bargaining power of that business as both a buyer and supplier.

Competitive rivalry

Competitive rivalry lies at the heart of Porter's model and is depicted by Porter as firms jockeying for position. Particularly intense rivalry is found in such situations as a large number of competitors of equal size, where the market has slow growth or where exit barriers are especially high. Such situations exist in the European car industry. Intense rivalry can also be found among UK supermarkets, particularly those like Sainsbury, Tesco, Asda and Waitrose, operating in the same general market segment. Such companies employ staff whose sole job is to monitor the competition through regular product and price checks. Intense rivalry in the IT industry often takes the form of poaching staff.

Rivalry can be especially damaging if rival firms all attempt to compete on the same basis. Porter (2008) sees price rivalry as especially damaging as it is easy to copy and dilutes profits. On the other hand, product innovation or improving customer relations by improving delivery times or offering a customized service can justify price increases even in highly competitive markets.

Assessment of Porter's model

In a later reflection of his original work Porter re-affirms the value of his five forces model.

Industry structure as manifested in the strength of the five competitive forces determines the industry's long-run profit potential because it determines how economic value created by the industry is divided – how much is retained by the companies in the industry versus bargained away by customers and suppliers, limited by substitutes or constrained by potential new entrants.

(Porter, 2008, p. 86)

The strength of a model like Porter's is that it focuses on the immediate operating environment of the business and avoids prescription by enabling managers to examine the forces acting upon their firm. Porter also intended managers to consider how the forces might change over time. The five-forces model has been very influential. However, a number of questions have been raised:

- The analysis depends upon a level of knowledge about competitors, which may not be so easy to obtain, as with competing supermarkets.

- As we have seen earlier in the chapter, the model portrays a rational approach to strategy that may not match reality.

- The model sees customers as one of several factors, when several current approaches elevate the customer to a more central role.

- Porter also views buyer–supplier relationships in terms of power and that they pose a threat, when, in some industries, the prevailing trend is towards greater partnership and long-term relations.

- The model assumes that once the analysis has been made, an appropriate strategy can be found. We have already noted that strategy is much more complex.

Managers can make use of Porter's model by establishing a position for their firms in the market to maximize defences against competitive forces and, where possible, turn them to best advantage. Porter identifies three generic strategies of particular advantage in this respect. These are product differentiation, market segmentation and seeking to obtain the lowest costs and are explored later in the chapter.

Environmental threats and opportunities

An assessment of the general environment and the firm's immediate competitive position should enable management to identify the major threats and opportunities facing the firm. Table 8.1 gives an illustrative list of the environmental opportunities and threats using the elements of the Business in Context model. This is usually the first stage in selecting appropriate strategic options and is a key part of SWOT analysis. For a firm like Orlake Records (Case 11.2), producing vinyl records in a declining market, or a restaurant owner opening in central London, the threats and opportunities may be very clear. However, we can identify several complicating factors:

- A threat to one part of an organization may represent an opportunity to another. Thus in the 1970s, when the post and telecommunications services in Britain were part of the same organization, a postal workers' strike led to increased revenue through telephone calls. The closure of some courses in a university, owing to falling student demand, may divert resources to other areas.

- Defending yourself against a threat or capitalizing upon an opportunity is a function of both the firm's standing in its environment and its internal resource position. Survival in a declining market may be easier if you have a large market share to begin with and raising finance to invest in new products is often easier for larger established firms than the small business. Small firms often face the particular dilemma of spotting a market opportunity

TABLE 0.1	Examples of environmental opportunity and constraints using the Business in Context model, as they affect a small manufacturing firm	
Aspects of the environment	**Opportunity**	**Constraint**
Economy	Market growth with increased demand in the BRICs economies and in emerging markets	Increased competition plus 'difficult' politics in emerging markets
State	Tax concessions for small firms	New laws on health and safety requiring the redesign of the product and costly investment in changes in the building and processes
Technology	Substitute raw materials become available at low prices	High levels of investment needed to convert existing machinery to process the new materials
Labour	Local labour supply exceeds demand together with a good supply of part-time and contract labour	Labour shortages in key skills together with the rising costs of hiring labour with those skills
Culture and institutions	A community with a strong tradition of working for small firms. A tradition for hard work and company loyalty	Labour market changes through an influx of new firms and labour from outside the region. Restrictions imposed by local laws on expansion plans and changes in working practices

but lacking the resources to take full advantage. Even if smaller firms are successful they face a backlash from established firms. For example, new entrants into the airline business usually offer flights at lower prices. They can have difficulty expanding their market share if the major airlines respond in kind or use their relationship with airports to prevent newcomers gaining landing rights.

- Managers differ in their ability to identify opportunities and threats. The management of a firm doing particularly well in a declining market may ignore the longer-term implications of their position. Even when opportunities and threats have been identified, managers may differ as to their relative importance and may develop different perspectives, based perhaps on their attitudes to risk. Careful analyses of market opportunities may come to naught in the face of a preference for inaction rather than entrepreneurial risk-taking. Failure to take action in the light of environmental change is one form of management myopia. Some managers can miss opportunities by perceiving the environmental constraints as greater than they really are.

We can therefore see that the perception of an opportunity or threat is a subjective process. It is partly for this reason that strategy formulation is as much a behavioural and political process as it is analytical. There is another important point. We have tended to focus on the environment as offering the management decision-maker opportunities or constraints. A major contention in this book is that the manager can influence and shape the environment. It is not simply the analysis of the environment that provides the answer but the ability of managers to see more in that environment than their competitors and in so doing create their own opportunities.

ORGANIZATIONAL ASPECTS OF STRATEGY

In this section we will explore the relationship between management strategy and the organizational aspects of the Business in Context model, and focus on issues related to an organization's resources. We look in detail at the resource-based view and follow up with a review of dynamic capabilities, core competences, value chains and portfolio analysis. Organizational analysis is traditionally an integral part of strategy formulation and serves a number of related purposes for managers.

- Some kind of resource profile is needed to establish whether the various opportunities, threats and management expectations can be met by the organization in its present state. A knowledge of the resources an organization possesses, and what can be done with them, is a prerequisite for determining future plans and establishes whether a gap exists between what management would like to do and what they can do. This is sometimes referred to as **gap analysis.** For example, the management of a manufacturing firm would need to know if it could accept and meet a large order using its existing product range and its existing machine and labour capacity. A gap analysis would identify resources that might be lacking and must be made good if opportunities are to be realized or threats are to be fought off. The completion of new orders by the manufacturing firm may be dependent upon product modification, purchasing equipment and hiring staff. This, in turn, may involve raising loans from a bank and setting up programmes to recruit and train staff. Expansion of this nature has further implications for the size of the supervisory and maintenance teams.
- The way resources are used by managers and how resource elements of the organization link together can create competitive advantage. Examples of this include focusing on efficient low-cost internal systems or a niche market producer developing and maintaining good customer relations. An internal analysis will enable managers to assess the attractiveness of the organization, its activities and its products in its current markets and assess their potential for future investment. This is the particular contribution of portfolio analysis.

A rather narrow, traditional view of strategic planning sees strategy as the result of environmental analysis and the organization factors are seen either to facilitate or inhibit the chosen strategy. Such a view runs counter to the contention of our Business in Context model, which sees all elements as interacting with one another. Organizational changes are brought about by changes in strategy, but strategic changes are also the product of aspects of the organization. In this way strategy influences structure but structure can also influence strategy. We can also see that expansion plans will undoubtedly build on strengths or core competences, a case of the firm focusing strategy around a key resource, such as the skills of a particular group. For example, a university may decide to invest and encourage growth in a small number of 'star' departments and allow others to run down.

We examine more general issues of strategy and organization before turning to the more practical questions of resource analysis, core competences, value chains and portfolio analysis.

Interaction of strategy and organization

All the organizational elements of our model – goals, ownership, structure, size and culture – interact with the process of strategy formulation.

The **goals** of an organization set targets for strategy to follow. We have also emphasized the behavioural nature of this process in that both goal and strategy formulation are the products of management values, and the processes of organizational power and politics, which have a major influence upon management decision-making.

The process of goal-setting and strategy formulation is greatly influenced by **ownership** variables. Professional accountants in partnership may each have their own views about the growth of the firm, the recruitment and training of staff and so on. In a partnership these views are generally resolved by discussion or through the dominance of a particular partner. The discussion of ownership and control in Chapter 6 showed that for larger companies, with diffuse share ownership and professional managers, strategy formulation was more complex and often dependent upon the influence of some shareholder groups. There are numerous illustrations where small business owners may deliberately resist growth strategies to retain personal control over the firm. However, the reverse is also true in that strategies involving merger and acquisition affect patterns of ownership and control. Managers may actively pursue acquisitions which give them more power and enhance their own career aspirations.

We also noted in Chapter 6 that, according to Chandler (1962), **structure** followed strategy, and this was a dominant feature in the expansion of American multinationals and in particular the development of multi-divisional structures. It was also suggested that strategy might be influenced by structure. For example, a company with a large and active R&D department would almost certainly pursue vigorous strategies of new product development. Burns and Stalker (1966) studied the post-war electronics industry and saw differences in the strategic responses of firms to changing market conditions. Those firms that had responded most effectively to changing market demand were typified by a more flexible, open structure, which they termed organic. The firms that struggled in the changed environment and failed to adapt were by contrast more bureaucratic, with often lengthy and inappropriate procedures for making decisions, and where structural divisions between departments inhibited cooperation. Organizations, particularly those in the public sector, which rely heavily on committees for the formulation of important decisions, may find the process too cumbersome when a quick strategic response is needed. In a similar way, participation, which can facilitate employee motivation and commitment, may inhibit decision-making through the inherent slowness of the procedure. This, in part, accounts for the slowness of the decision-making process in some Japanese firms. In some cases structural change is so difficult that the disruptive effects may be counterproductive in achieving strategic goals. In other cases, strategic change in a highly competitive environment may only be possible by radical organizational change, which could involve replacing the management team or selling off parts of the business.

Such considerations of structure are inevitably linked to size. In very large organizations strategy formulation may be cumbersome due to the number of people and processes involved. There is also a danger that strategy can become fragmented through the diverse nature of operations and locations. Another handicap of large size involves the control of a strategy once it is formulated. The larger the organization, the more filters there are to interpret and perhaps distort a central strategy.

An important element in the core management strategies of firms such as IBM, Southwest Airlines and Hewlett Packard is the creation of an **organizational culture**, with an emphasis upon shared values. We have stressed the importance of management values in both formulating and evaluating strategy. In this case the creation of a value system to embrace the entire organization is seen by some to be more significant than strategy itself.

Resource analysis

At the beginning of this section we explained the importance of the current resource position to the formulation of management strategy. The resource-based view developed by Barney (1991) goes further and sees the way in which a firm uses its resources as a source of significant competitive advantage. Resource analysis clearly covers physical resources such as land, plant and machinery, financial resources and human resources. The analysis should also cover the key relationships in the operating system. These exist between the firm and its suppliers and the firm and its customers as well as the relationship between parts of the same operating system. Barney (1991) calls the latter organizational resources.

In many firms, resource analysis is accompanied by the use of a variety of accounting ratios such as return on capital employed, profitability and so on. Different ratios have more relevance at different stages of the firm's development than at others, so that while profitability may be appropriate for established firms, productivity and sales may be more useful for newly established companies and cash flows may be more significant when firms are in decline. A fuller discussion of accounting ratios can be found in Chapter 14.

The value of resource analysis lies not only in assessing the viability of a strategic proposal but also in assessing the ability of the organization to adapt to change. Can the firm deal with changes in demand or can it withstand increased competition on a global scale? Has it the financial backing to invest in new technology? Do employees possess the necessary skills and is the age profile of its staff sufficiently balanced to ensure succession? Competing through resources is a dominant theme in the resource-based view.

Resource-based view (RBV)

Traditional approaches to organizational analysis have tended to consider resource analysis as of secondary importance to environmental analysis. Firms in the same industry have similar products with similar functions selling to broadly similar markets. Yet some companies do extremely well, while others struggle to survive even though they operate in the same environment and have access to the same information. This has led a number of writers to focus on resource and organizational analysis as a source of sustainable competitive advantage. In this section we will deal with the resource-based view of the firm and follow this with a brief look at dynamic capabilities and core competence.

The resource-based view of the firm was brought to the forefront by Jay Barney and in particular an article published in 1991 (Barney 1991). The article is highly theoretical and offers few illustrations. A more accessible version of his approach can be found in Barney and Hesterly (2012). In his original article Barney identified three key resource elements but later added a fourth in the form of financial capital. The four key resource elements are therefore:

- **Physical capital.** This includes products and brands, patents, plant and equipment, location and access to raw materials and other supplies.

- **Human capital.** This includes the experience, skills and talents of the workforce, their judgement and insights and the training and development they receive. It can also include the specific talents of individuals in the form of entrepreneurial and leadership skills.

- **Organizational capital.** This includes the organization structure, planning procedures, mechanisms for coordination and control and the nature of relationships between groups both internally between operating teams or different departments and externally with various stakeholders.
- **Financial capital** relates to the firm's abilities to raise, create, use and manage funds.

Barney (1991) explored conditions under which a firm's resources can be a source of sustainable competitive advantage. He argued that different firms have different bundles of resources and capabilities. He believed that some forms are more skilled at using their resources than others. He called this **resource heterogeneity.** In some cases the advantages derived from a firm's resources and capabilities tend to be long lasting because they are difficult to copy or it would take a competitor a long time to develop them, almost certainly at great cost. He called this **resource immobility.** This explains why Ford dominated the early mass car industry until it was overtaken by GM and then both were outperformed by Toyota. It also explains Apple's dominance despite competitor attempts to replicate their products.

Barney and Hesterly (2012) have developed a framework to assess a firm's competitive advantage through its resources based on the concepts of heterogeneity and immobility. Their framework is VRIO representing value, rarity, imitability (can it be copied?) and organization.

- **Value** represents those activities that add value for the customer. This is linked to the notion of the value chain that we deal with later in this section. At different stages of the chain, a firm can make choices that add value to the final product.
- **Rarity** relates to those elements and qualities that are only possessed by a few companies. Barney and Hesterly accept that only a small number of firms have real rarity and even without it, the efficient use of resources can ensure survival in competitive markets.
- **Imitability** exists when the value and rarity elements can be copied. The key to competitive advantage is where such elements cannot be copied or that the cost of doing so is too high. The difficulty in copying a particular factor may be the product of a number of factors. For example, the firm may have been able to develop unique resources because it was the first to do so. We discuss such first mover advantages in our review of innovation strategy in Chapter 10. A particular advantage may be difficult to copy because it is unclear as to what specific element or group of elements actually create competitive advantage. The advantage could be based on corporate culture, which as we saw in Chapter 6 is difficult to copy, or upon a unique set of social relationships. While physical capital is sometimes easier to copy this can be protected by patents.
- **Organization is** seen by Barney and Hesterly (2012) as the route to realizing potential. Whereas physical capital is relatively easy for competitors to understand, organizational capital especially the less tangible aspects of organizational culture, tacit learning and relationships are more difficult to define and copy. The importance of organizational and management innovation is highlighted in Chapter 10.

The resource-based view of competitive advantage is appealing and lends itself to the creation of a unique strategic position. Its critics argue that it is largely descriptive and evidence is difficult to find as to how RBV can be turned into competitive advantage. For example, we assume that investment in human capital through training and other HR interventions is 'good' policy, but it is very difficult to show links with improved performance.

RBV has much in common with dynamic capabilities and core competence.

Dynamic capabilities

This is a concept associated with the work of Teece et al. (1997). Dynamic capabilities relate to the ability of the firm to recreate its resources and capabilities to meet the needs of a changing environment in ways that are different to its competitors. Teece and his colleagues argue that such capabilities can be built into formal structures and processes such as R&D and training. However, like Barney he associates them more with less formal aspects such as organizational culture, tacit learning, social networks and leadership.

Core competences

The idea of core competences is associated with the work of Hamel and Prahalad (1990, 1994) and Kay (1993). Core competences refer to those activities of a firm that make a difference and give the firm a competitive edge. This could be the development of efficient and effective internal operating systems, as with Toyota and the Toyota production system, whose core competences became a model for other car manufacturers to follow. In certain specialist markets, such as fine wine, a merchant may build its reputation on good customer relationships and continuing business. A university may develop a reputation in particular subject areas. It can build on that reputation through the attraction of students, bringing increased revenue, and maintain that reputation through the attraction of leading academics in the field.

To Hamel and Prahalad, core competences represented the integration of knowledge, skills and technology to give the customer added value in terms of cost and customer value, differentiation from competitors or innovation of new products and processes. They also argue that the core competences should not be tied to a specific range of applications such as an existing product range. They should be extendable beyond their current application to give the firm a sustainable competitive advantage over time.

Kay (1993) identified three areas of core competence. First, architecture refers to relationships both within and around the firm, including those with customers and suppliers. A key component of architecture is information exchange between the various parties. Second, reputation refers to the quality of a firm's goods and services and for such qualities as the dependability and speed of delivery. The third area of core competence is innovative ability, defined as the ability to develop products and processes to gain competitive advantage through differentiation.

The notion of core competences enables a firm to focus its competitive advantage around its resources rather than focusing exclusively on the market. However, it is important that such core competences are difficult to copy by a rival firm, otherwise the basis for competitive advantage is eroded. Toyota maintained a competitive advantage for many years despite attempts by its competitors, both inside and outside Japan, to copy its production system. While some core competences do lend themselves to measurement and analysis, as with stockholding and retention, many others are vague and may only be assessed subjectively.

KEY CONCEPT 8.3   CORE COMPETENCE

Core competences refer to those activities of an organization that give it an advantage over its competitors. Such advantages could derive from such as an effective R&D department, an efficient operating system, good internal and external communications, the presence of key individuals, reputation and a loyal customer base. The strategic relevance of core competences is the opportunity they provide management to build upon such specific advantages.

REFLECTION POINT

Select a number of organizations with which you are familiar. Does each of them possess core competences? What are they?

CASE 8.1 — SOUTHWEST AIRLINES

Having achieved 41 consecutive years in profit, Southwest Airlines is the most consistently profitable airline in the USA, if not the world. Southwest Airlines started in 1971 out of Dallas and initially flew just three routes between three cities in Texas: Dallas, Houston and San Antonio. It began with just three Boeing 737 aircraft and its ability to operate at all was due largely to the credit terms offered by Boeing for these planes. Boeing's generosity has paid off. Southwest has only ever purchased Boeing planes and the company has become the US largest domestic airline and the world's largest low-cost airline. It has carried more domestic passengers in the USA than any other airline since 2001 and had 24 per cent share of the US domestic market in 2013. In 2014 it flew to 96 destinations in 41 US states, plus Washington DC and Puerto Rico as well as serving 5 international destinations. There are more than 200 Southwest departures per day from Chicago Midway, Las Vegas and Baltimore/ Washington airports. According to the US Department of Transportation it is the number one airline for customer satisfaction and Fortune ranked Southwest 7th in a list of the world's most admired companies in 2013.

The final performance of the company in 2012–13 is set out in the following table.

	2012	2013
	(US$ millions)	
Operating revenues	17 088	17 699
Operating expenses	16 465	16 421
Operating income	623	1 278
Operating margin	3.6%	7.2%

(Source: 2013 Southwest Airlines One Report)

The numbers of passengers carried is shown in the following table.

	2004	2006	2008	2010	2012	2013
Revenue passengers carried (millions)	70.9	83.8	88.5	88.2	109.3	108.1
Average capacity per aircraft	69%	73%	71%	79%	81%	80%

(Source: 2013 Southwest Airlines One Report)

In its Annual Report for 2013 the company set out its strategic vision and purpose as follows.

Our vision is to become the world's most loved, most flown and most profitable airline.

Our purpose is to connect people to what's important in their lives through friendly, reliable, and low-cost air travel.

A number of factors have been related to the company's growth and success in an industry that has suffered through global recession and competition. These same factors are seen by the company itself as helping it achieve its vision and purpose.

Operations

Southwest Airlines operations strategy is built around cost. The company has made a conscious decision to fly only Boeing 737 aircraft, although it has a smaller number of Boeing 717-200 jets. At the end of 2013 the company had 680 Boeing jets, including 425 737-700 with a maximum capacity of 143 passengers, and 52 737-800 carrying 175 passengers. By using only one type of aircraft, maintenance costs and the need to stock a wide variety of parts are reduced. It also means that staff training requirements are simplified, not only for maintenance workers but pilots, cabin crew and other staff.

(Continued)

CASE 8.1   (Continued)

The company has created effective systems of cleaning, baggage handling and restocking of catering products, all of which contribute to a fast turnaround of aircraft at the gate. The time is variously reported between 15 and 18 minutes compared to an average time taken by other airlines of 45 minutes. This ensures that the aircraft spend more time in the air which enables Southwest to run more frequent departures with fewer aircraft than their competitors. The average flight distance is less than 500 miles, fewer than its competitors and enabling the airline to use its planes for more trips per day.

The standard routing used by most carriers is known as a hub and spoke system in which carriers will fly passengers to a given centre where they can then connect to other flights. Southwest only operates on a point-to-point system with no scheduled connecting flights either within Southwest or with other airlines. This arrangement cuts out the cost of baggage transfers. Further costs are reduced by the policy of favouring smaller airports with lower-cost landing fees. There are some exceptions, most notably the recent use of New York's La Guardia airport.

Southwest has deliberately set out to be a 'no frills' airline. The airline was one of the first to offer customers the option of using an automated ticketing system at the gate, thereby reducing the need to pay commission to intermediaries. The flights do not offer free catering and passengers must pay for food and drinks. However, paying for food and drink is not uncommon on US short haul flights even among the major airlines like American and United. Although many airlines seek increased revenues from first and business class fares, Southwest offers the same service to all passengers. This simplifies its operations and avoids the need for airport lounges and alternative checking-in facilities.

In recent years the key focus has been to reduce fuel usage. The average fuel cost per gallon has risen from US$ 0.92 in 2004 to US$3.30 in 2013. An attack on fuel usage not only reduces overall costs but savings on fuel helps the airline maintain low ticket prices as well as them being seen to be environmentally friendly. Fuel efficiency is a key element in their purchase of new aircraft and airline staff are encouraged and rewarded for developing ideas on fuel saving.

The airline has a close relationship with its suppliers and provides them with training. Through its policy on ethical suppliers the company is particularly keen to ensure that its suppliers are 'accountable for their social and environmental performance'. For its part, Southwest has a policy of extending the opportunity for suppliers from small businesses and from businesses in designated deprived areas and those that are owned by minorities, women, disabled and military veterans.

Barney and Hesterly (2012) have claimed that Southwest Airlines' operational model is relatively easy to copy. However, the company has had few successful competitors that have stayed in business or even come close to the financial success of Southwest. Jet Blue have been fairly successful as have AirTran Airways (subsequently acquired by Southwest). Major carriers such as Continental, with its budget offshoot Continental Lite, have tried and failed. In Europe, Southwest has been a model for such airlines as Ryanair and easyJet. Mike O'Leary, the current CEO of Ryanair, spent some time at Southwest in the 1980s to learn about operating a low-cost airline at a time when the newly formed Ryanair was losing money.

Leadership and culture

Much of the operating policy of the current company was set out by one of the company's founders and its second CEO, Herb Kelleher. Although retired, he still acts as an advisor and a teacher in Southwest's learning and development centre. A key induction tool is a video that features Kelleher and some of the original employees. The video sets out the company's core values. All employees receive a weekly recorded telephone message from the CEO informing them on what the company is doing and of any future plans. They are also encouraged to communicate with senior management on any matter by email. As well as naming planes after US states, they are also named after senior managers and those employees the company feel have made a significant contribution. The plane 'The Fred J. Jones', is named after one of the original employees. Such employees and ex-employees are referred to as 'Heroes of the Heart'. The company is fond of giving titles such as this to many of its activities and policies. For example, all employees are encouraged and rewarded for contributing ideas to improve efficiency and effectiveness under the heading, 'Together we make it great'.

Humour plays an important role in culture. The company speaks of a 'fun-luving attitude' (in Southwest Airlines 'love' is always spelt 'luv'). The airline has been known to hold on-board competitions to find the passenger with most holes in their socks, with a free flight as a prize. For its inaugural flight to California, boarding passes were issued in the shape of the state.

An important part of Southwest's cultural agenda is the importance placed on links with the local community. The following is an extract from the 2013 Annual Report:

We understand the powerful impacts our company can have on the social systems in which we operate.

In 2013 the company donated US$19 million in the form of tickets to organizations it identified as being worthy of its support in the local community. In the same year Southwest employees gave over 144 000 volunteer hours to community projects. The airline operates an emergency response team that is ready to mobilize support for disasters such as the tornado that swept through Oklahoma making many people homeless.

Employees

In its 2013 Annual Report Southwest claimed:

We believe in creating a secure environment where our employees have opportunities to grow, live well and make a positive difference.
Our people are our greatest strength and competitive advantage.

The company calls its employees 'people' and employs around 45 000 in the following categories:

	%
Flight division (Pilots and cabin crew)	42
Ground, customer and fleet services	35
Management, accounting, marketing and clerical	17
Technical operations (Maintenance)	6

The company claims high levels of employee loyalty and commitment based on its corporate culture and style of leadership and management, both built over 40 years. In several of its statements the company states that its people are more important than either customers or shareholders, Annual labour turnover in the company is low at less than 2 per cent. The company holds an employee survey every two years. The results of this and of external ratings of employee satisfaction reveal that the airline is regarded highly by its employees.

Trade union membership in Southwest is 83 per cent, making it the most unionized of all US airlines. The company enjoys good union relations in an industry that has historically been dogged by bitter disputes. The company has never had a strike and no employee has ever been laid off. There have been voluntary pay freezes to avoid lay-offs and in the business downturn following 9/11 the employees agreed to take a pay cut to avoid anyone losing their job.

Overall, rates of pay are above average for the industry and the company operates a stock option scheme for employees. There is an annual profit share plan which, in 2013 was 88 per cent up on the previous year. Employees are entitled to free stand-by flights for themselves, their partners, children and parents. The company offers a range of other benefits, including health insurance and health care for employees and partners, life insurance, wellness and fitness programmes, including helping staff give up smoking and lose weight and retirement planning.

Training is seen as important, especially in health and safety, but there are many other training and development opportunities. In 2013 the company integrated its training and development facilities under the banner of 'Southwest Airlines University'. Its training programme involves comprehensive diversity and inclusion training. The company operates a comprehensive employee recognition scheme, referred to as SWAG (Southwest Airlines Gratitude). Under this scheme all employees have a profile that records all recognitions they have received during their employment. Points are collected that may be exchanged for free flights, merchandise or gift vouchers.

(Continued)

CASE 8.1   (Continued)

Customers

Throughout its history Southwest has focused on creating new markets rather than compete with other airlines for existing passengers. They have focused on low ticket prices to get bus travellers to switch to air travel and persuade others to take trips they have always considered too expensive. Despite labelling itself a 'no frills' airline Southwest does offer a frequent flyer programme, called 'Rapid Rewards'. Unlike schemes of other airlines that are based on miles flown, the Southwest scheme was initially based on the number of trips taken and then changed in 2011 to a points system based on the ticket price. The airline is rated highly by its customers on numerous surveys and has the lowest number of passenger complaints. In 2013 it received 0.34 complaints per 100 000 passengers. This compares to 0.64 complaints on Jet Blue, a rival low-cost airline and 1.99 on American and 2.14 on United, the two largest airlines in the USA.

International expansion

In June 2014 Southwest Airlines made its first international flight under the Southwest brand. The change in strategy to expand into the international market was linked to the acquisition of AirTran Airways in 2011. AirTran had a few international routes which Southwest had kept running under the AirTran brand. There were fights from a number of US cities to the Bahamas, Aruba and Jamaica. Southwest has plans to extend its range of international flights to Mexico City and the Dominican Republic. This is seen by Southwest as an important strategy to counteract the effects of rising costs and slower growth in its domestic business. Investment was necessary to upgrade the Boeing fleet and in IT systems to enable international flights to take place. The expansion plans however are limited to what the airline calls near-international destinations, which are defined as the Caribbean, Central America, only the northern part of South America and to Canada.

Strategic plan 2014 and beyond

The company has identified the following objectives as the most important:

- The full integration of AirTran with the conversion of all domestic and international flights and all personnel to Southwest.

- Fleet modernization with interior refits scheduled to existing aircraft. There are plans to increase the proportion of flights using 737-800 planes as these are more fuel efficient. The company has 170 firm orders for the new 737-MAX that is even more fuel efficient and environmentally friendly than existing 737 aircraft. These will be delivered in stages between 2017 and 2024.

- The introduction of a new reservation system to support its new international operations.

- An increase in the frequency of flights to the most popular domestic destinations and an increasing use of New York's La Guardia airport.

Questions

1 What are Southwest Airlines' resource-based advantages and core competences?

2 Which of the resource-based advantages and core competences do you consider have made the greatest contribution to the airline's success?

3 The company's culture has been described as 'goofy'. To what extent do you agree?

4 What additional complexities are presented by the decision to fly international routes?

5 What are the key opportunities and threats facing Southwest Airlines?

The value chain

The value chain describes the full range of activities which are required to bring a product or service from conception, through the intermediary phases of production ..., delivery to final customers and final disposal after use.

(Kaplinsky, 2000, p. 8)

We introduced the concept of the value chain in our discussion of global value chains and the global factory in Chapter 2. The significance of the value chain concept owes much to the work of Porter (1985) and in essence is about the way resources are organized to give value added to the end user. Porter's value chain is illustrated in Figure 8.3. The key element of the value chain is not just the added value that the various resources bring to the whole, but added value that derives from the linkages between them, which to gain competitive advantage should be greater than the sum of the parts.

KEY CONCEPT 8.4   VALUE CHAIN

The value chain offers a view of the organization as a cumulative build-up of added value for the customer through the interaction between key operations activities. The end result is greater than the sum of its parts and, for profit-seeking organizations, means increased margins. Porter identifies elements of the value chain in terms of primary and support activities. Like the Business in Context model, the value chain sees organizations in terms of interactions between the various parts.

The value chain thus views the firm as a system and a process. Porter identifies five primary activities, which individually and, more importantly collectively, contribute towards adding value for the customer. The end result for Porter is defined as margin, which is the difference between the cost of providing the activities and the total value they generate. For the company, margin may be translated into profit while the customer may see it more in terms of value for money.

FIGURE 8.3   Porter's value chain

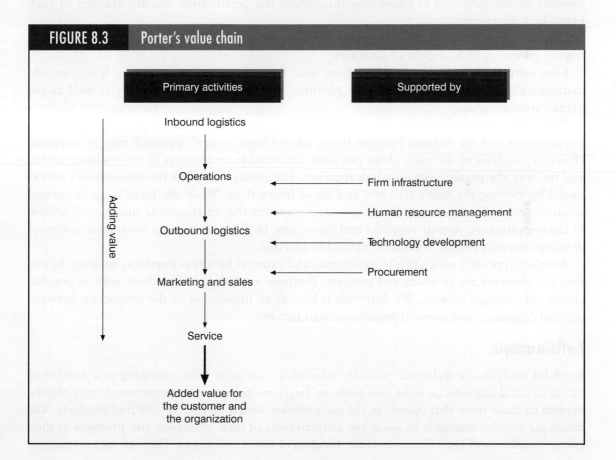

Inbound logistics refers to those activities concerned with the receiving and handling of goods from suppliers and transporting them within the organization.

Operations transform the goods into the final product and may comprise a number of different stages and extend across a number of specialist departments.

Outbound logistics deal with storing finished items and distributing them to customers. In the case of services it is concerned with all those processes involved in bringing the service to the customer or the customer to the service.

Marketing and sales help to identify customer needs and, through advertising and promotion, make potential customers aware of products and services.

Services cover all those processes involved in before- and after-sales activities such as requirements planning and the provision of customer help lines.

The five primary activities are supported by four other types of activity, referred to by Porter as support activities.

Procurement deals with those activities engaged in the acquisition of the resource inputs to the primary activities. In manufacturing this can occur at a number of stages. Buyers are responsible for obtaining dependable supplies at high quality and at the best possible price. The transport department is responsible for ensuring the most cost-effective delivery of goods to customers, which may involve subcontracting to another firm, or using the post or rail services.

Technology development occurs in all primary activities. It covers product and process development, which can occur in inbound and outbound logistics as much as in operations. It also involves the development of know-how throughout the organization and the transfer of such know-how via training.

Human resource management is concerned with the recruitment, selection, training and reward systems which support all activities.

Firm infrastructure relates to the systems used throughout the organization. It can include materials planning, logistics, operations planning, finance and budget systems as well as the overall strategic plan.

The value chain has drawn criticism for focusing attention on the improvement of existing resources and the linkages between them, when a more radical approach may be required. However, analysis of the value chain can draw attention to weaknesses in the resource profile and the way the primary activities link together. The concept supports the Business in Context model by viewing the firm's activities as a set of interactions. While the focus is upon internal resource arrangements, the model incorporates elements that exist outside the internal system of the organization, namely suppliers and customers. In doing so it raises the impracticality of defining elements purely in terms of internal or external.

Another approach which combines internal and external factors is portfolio analysis. In this case the elements are products and markets. Portfolio analysis could be dealt with in our discussion of strategic options. We deal with it here as an illustration of the interaction between internal (resource) and external (environmental) factors.

Portfolio analysis

Portfolio analysis is a technique normally associated with those firms operating in a number of businesses and markets, as is the case with the larger multinational corporations. It may also be applied to those firms that operate in the same market with a number of different products. The technique enables managers to assess the attractiveness of their businesses and products in their current markets and assist decisions on the direction of future investment. Through such an analysis the manager may reach conclusions on the particular mix of products and markets, the growth and profit potential of those products and markets and the level of risk involved with each one. As a result, a clearer idea emerges regarding priorities for corporate effort and resource allocation.

There are several models that may be used in portfolio analysis and two are illustrated in Figure 8.4. The most famous portfolio technique is the matrix developed by the Boston Consulting Group (BCG). The BCG matrix was designed to analyse individual businesses in a company with a range of business interests. The matrix enables the analyst to plot the position of that business (or product) with reference to the growth of the market and the company's share of that market. We can see from Figure 8.4 that the matrix has been divided into four sectors, each with different product/market characteristics. The products located within these sectors have been labelled Question marks, Stars, Cash cows and Dogs respectively. We will deal with the characteristics of each:

KEY CONCEPT 8.5   PORTFOLIO ANALYSIS

Portfolio analysis is a technique that can be used by firms operating in a number of markets and/ or with a number of different products. The technique enables management to assess the relative attractiveness of products and markets to assist decision-making on future directions and resource allocation. There are several methods and models available, the most famous of which are probably the Boston Consulting Group matrix and the General Electric business screen.

FIGURE 8.4   Illustrations of portfolio analysis

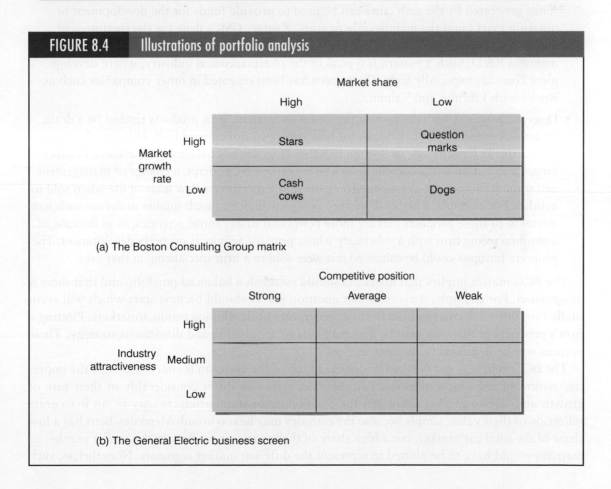

(a) The Boston Consulting Group matrix

(b) The General Electric business screen

- **Question marks** represent products that have a low market share in a market of high growth. The market offers clear potential but the firm invariably needs significant financial and other resource inputs to compete. This may involve product modification, increasing output capacity, increasing promotional activity, recruiting staff and raising the level of bank borrowing. Investing in question marks carries a high level of risk. The gains may be significant but the market tends to be highly competitive and the costs of improving market position are invariably high.

- **Stars** are those products that have achieved a high share of a still expanding market. A company with a number or even one of such stars is generally envied by its competitors. Nevertheless, the cost of maintaining this position is usually high. A growing market tends to attract competitors and stars usually need continuing investment in product development and promotion. The PC market in the past few years has maintained a high growth but the increased competition, particularly in terms of product development and price, has meant that several of its stars have risen and fallen in a relatively short time. Other markets where stars have risen and fallen rapidly include cameras and video cassette recorders.

- **Cash cows** are products with a high market share but market growth has stabilized. These provide the firm with its greatest return on investment. The market is generally much less competitive and the market position is generally less costly to maintain than with stars. Overall costs are generally lower and economies of scale can be achieved. The surplus funds generated by the cash cows can be used to provide funds for the development of question marks and the maintenance of stars. Zantac, GSK's drug for the treatment of ulcers, was for many years the cash cow that enabled the company to maintain high investments in R&D. Such a pattern is typical in the pharmaceutical industry, where development costs are especially high. The pattern has been repeated in other companies such as Roche with Librium and Valium.

- **Dogs** are products with the poorest profile on the matrix. Such products tend to be a drain on resources and can be candidates for being dropped or being sold off. This was the reason behind the TI Group's sale of Raleigh Bicycles. Dogs are not necessarily worthless. Product ranges and indeed entire companies can be revitalized by, perhaps, a change of management and some fresh ideas. A dog to one company may experience a new lease of life when sold to another. For example, a highly diversified company may find itself unable to devote sufficient attention to those products that are more peripheral to its central activities, as in the case of a manufacturing firm with a subsidiary whose primary activity is property development. The property business could be enhanced if it were sold to a firm specializing in that area.

The BCG matrix implies that managers should establish a balanced portfolio and that there is progression. For example, it assumes that question marks should become stars which will eventually turn into cash cows to fund the next generation of developing product/markets. Plotting a firm's products in this way may be a useful guide to acquisition and divestment strategy. These options will be discussed in the next section.

The BCG matrix is not without its critics. Much of the criticism is concerned with the imprecise nature of the four categories. For example, stars can differ considerably in their rate of growth and size of market share and the positioning of some products may be an inaccurate reflection of their value, simply because the category may be too broad. Mercedes-Benz has a low share of the total car market, but a high share of the luxury car market. In this case a number of matrices would have to be plotted to represent the different market segments. Nonetheless, such an analysis is perhaps the reason for Mercedes Benz broadening its market appeal through the production of the smaller, lower-priced A series and the launch of a competitively priced sports model, the SLK. More complex matrices have been developed so that products can be plotted more usefully. An illustration of the General Electric business screen is shown alongside the BCG matrix in Figure 8.4. In this case the concept of industry attractiveness is used instead of market growth and nine categories have been identified to achieve greater accuracy.

REFLECTION POINT

Can the BCG matrix be applied to university courses at a single university? What courses would you place in each category?

In spite of the problems of plotting and measurement, such methods of portfolio analysis are not only of use in planning future product/market strategy but also in raising important questions about how business interests are handled. We have already seen that by analyzing a dog changes may be made to improve its position. One company to make use of this type of analysis is 3M. It developed a matrix to analyze both products and markets, as illustrated in Figure 8.5. The management of 3M is concerned that each of its products and markets are capable of being maintained or improved. It was this method of analysis that led the company to sell off its photocopying equipment business (Kennedy, 1988).

STRATEGIC OPTIONS

So far in this chapter we have discussed the components of strategic analysis: the environment, resources and dominant values. We have also suggested that strategy may be formulated by a

FIGURE 8.5   3M product and market portfolio matrix

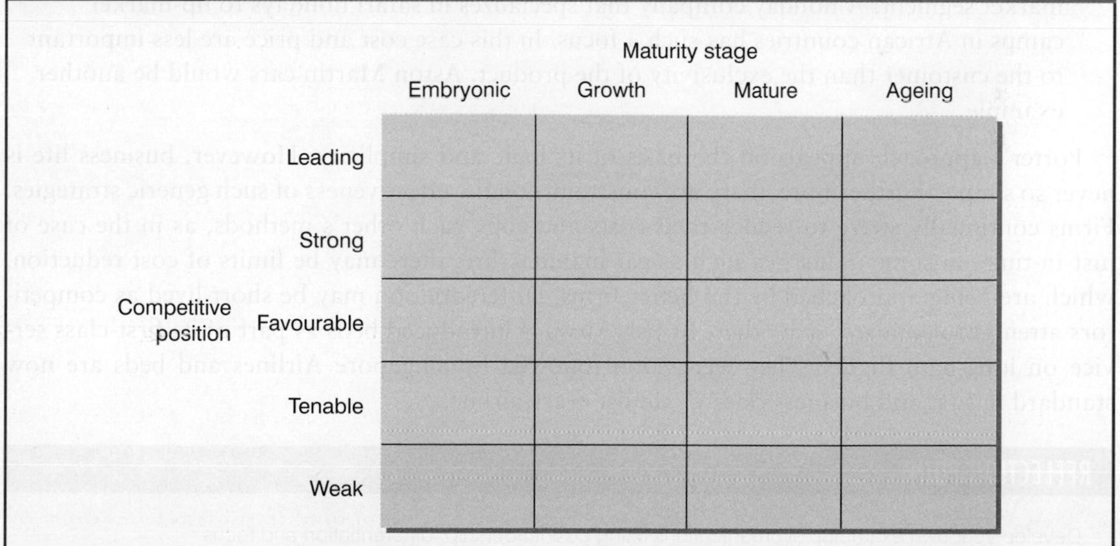

variety of methods, which may involve a highly formalized planning procedure or may simply be no more than the stated preferences of the chief executive. Whatever the process, the outcome is a particular strategic option or range of possible options. In this section we examine a number of strategic options. Earlier in this chapter we made a distinction between corporate strategies which change the position of the entire organization, and business strategies which change the competitive position in a specific product market. We examine strategic options in each of these cases.

Business level strategies

Porter (1980, 1985) focuses on competitive strategies and presents a relatively straightforward view of competitive options within its product markets. He identifies two generic strategies:

- The first of these is competing on the basis of **cost leadership.** Firms pursuing this must aim to be the lowest-cost producer, but still be able to compete in terms of product function and quality. A good example of firms achieving this would be Toyota through its entire production system, one of the first to incorporate just-in-time methods as part of its lean manufacturing strategy.

- The second of Porter's generic competitive strategies is **differentiation.** Firms pursuing this strategy must aim to produce goods and services that have certain unique dimensions that make them attractive to customers. In aiming at product differentiation, competitive advantage can only be achieved by maintaining cost parity or cost proximity. Dyson developed a new form of carpet cleaner that challenged and outsold traditional vacuum cleaners.

Both these strategies have a broad scope and can apply to a range of products and markets, However, when cost leadership cannot be achieved because costs are simply too high or when product differentiation is difficult across a range of products, Porter offers a third strategic option:

- **Focus** is a strategy relating to niche products and niche markets and occurs when the organization focuses on a single or set of related niche products or aims for a specific market segment. A holiday company that specializes in safari holidays to up-market camps in African countries has such a focus. In this case cost and price are less important to the customer than the exclusivity of the product. Aston Martin cars would be another example.

Porter's approach appeals on the basis of its logic and simplicity. However, business life is never so simple. Furthermore, there are constraints on the effectiveness of such generic strategies. Firms continually strive to reduce their costs and copy each other's methods, as in the case of just-in-time. In some industries such as car manufacture, there may be limits of cost reduction, which are being approached by the better firms. Differentiation may be short-lived as competitors attempt to emulate each other. British Airways introduced beds as part of its first-class service on long-haul flights. They were soon followed by Singapore Airlines and beds are now standard in first and business class in almost every airline.

REFLECTION POINT

Develop your own examples of organizations using cost leadership, differentiation and focus.

Bowman and Faulkner (1996) expanded on Porter's ideas and developed the 'strategy clock', which is based on two variables, price and the perceived value of the product or service to the customer. The relationship of these two variables produces a range of eight different options.

A **'no frills'** strategy would be the kind of product and service offered by a low-cost airlines such as Southwest Airlines in the USA and copied by such as Ryanair in the UK. Ryanair offers a minimum service at a minimum price, although there are options to increase the level of service by extra payments. A **'low price'** strategy is followed by supermarkets such as Wal-Mart and Lidl, where the same products are offered at a lower price than competitors. This can lead to price wars. However, the volume sales of a firm like Wal-Mart usually means that they can under-price the competition to gain market share and, in some cases, force competitors out of business. With such a strategy margins are low but sales and turnover are high to compensate. A **'hybrid'** strategy emphasizes differentiation and low price. Johnson et al. (2013) suggest that a 'hybrid' strategy needs high volume turnover to cover the cost of differentiation and cite Ikea as an example. A **differentiation** strategy offers something different to competitor offerings that add value to the customer and gains market share. The added value may be sufficient to charge higher prices. **'Focused differentiation'** on the other hand enables the organization to charge a high price for an innovative and exclusive product aimed at a specific market segment. **Strategies 6, 7 and 8** on the strategy clock are destined to fail and Bowman and Faulkner (1996) claim they should be avoided. In all these cases the organization is offering a standard or low value product at an average of above average price. The conclusions are fairly obvious. Increasing the price while offering a low value product is only possible where the organization holds a monopoly position.

The strategies identified above all attempt to improve market position of existing products and services. We revisit these strategic options in our discussion of functional areas in Part Three. New product development is explored in the chapters on innovation and marketing (10 and 12). Improving products and services with an emphasis on product quality is discussed in Chapter 11. The same chapter deals with cost reductions through better use of resources and improvements in productivity. Improved market penetration, by deploying the elements of the marketing mix, such as promotion or price strategies, is explored in Chapter 12. The same chapter also deals with seeking expansion through new market segments or by export.

Corporate-level strategies

One of the early models of corporate strategy options was offered by Igor Ansoff (Ansoff, 1968). He presents a number of growth options based on products and markets (which he refers to as missions). This is presented in Figure 8.6.

- Growth based on existing products in existing markets requires a **product penetration** strategy.

- Growth based on new products in an existing market requires a **product development** strategy.

- Growth based on seeking new markets for existing products requires a **market development** strategy.

- Growth based both on new products in new markets requires a **diversification** strategy.

There is an assumption that the overarching goal of most businesses is survival and this may only be achieved by pursuing strategies of growth. While it is difficult to argue against the

FIGURE 8.6	Ansoff's corporate strategy matrix	
	Existing products	**New products**
Existing markets	Product penetration strategy	Product development strategy
New markets	Market development strategy	Diversification strategy

first assumption, it is clear that not all businesses pursue growth strategies. Some companies spend most of their time maintaining or consolidating existing positions, and, for those such as coalmining as in the UK or Poland, drastic contraction may be the only chance of survival.

The following classification of strategies depicts approaches to growth and contraction. These options are not discrete categories and in many cases the distinction between them can be blurred. They also recognize the complex nature of the strategic process and incorporate discussion of both rational and more subjective factors. We examine diversification in some detail before looking briefly at other types of strategy.

Diversification strategies

As a corporate strategy, diversification is one of the most far-reaching growth strategies open to management, in that it represents an attempt to change the nature of the business by increasing its portfolio of products and/or markets. We can identify two types of diversification: related and unrelated. Related diversification can be classified into backward, forward and horizontal integration.

KEY CONCEPT 8.6   DIVERSIFICATION STRATEGIES

These are strategies that move the organization in different directions involving products or markets or both. Related diversification refers to new activities that are directly related in some way to existing operations, such as a hotel acquiring a catering business. Unrelated diversification moves the organization in a new direction, such as a hotel chain acquiring a newspaper. Highly diversified firms can spread risk across a number of products and/or markets. However, there may be problems associated with coordination and control. Related diversification can lead to benefits of economies of scale and scope.

Related diversification occurs when the new business is related in some way to the old one. Several firms have sought to gain greater control over the source of raw materials or the supply of components by some form of **backward integration.** Japanese manufacturing firms depend on a network of subcontractors for the supply of components. In many cases the larger company has a controlling financial interest in the supplier. In the restaurant business it is becoming more common for some restaurant owners to grow their own herbs and vegetables and bake their own bread, to ensure both the quantity and the quality of the supply. This also provides the restaurant with an additional promotional strategy. Some universities have widened access by setting up pre-degree courses, giving students without the traditional entry qualifications the opportunity to feed into the mainstream degree programmes.

Forward integration occurs when producers diversify to control the onward processes of delivering their goods to the consumer, as in the case of a manufacturer setting up a transport or retail operation or a group of actors leasing a theatre to stage their own work. In the UK, Post Office letters and parcels were always transported by rail. Before privatization, British Rail extended its own delivery service, Red Star, and took business away from the Post Office by offering a speedier and guaranteed delivery service.

An integrated system of backward and forward integration is known as **vertical integration.**

KEY CONCEPT 8.7   BACKWARD AND FORWARD INTEGRATION

Backward integration is a diversification strategy to gain control of activities and/or firms further back in the supply chain, such as raw material or components suppliers. Forward integration is a strategy to gain control of activities further forward in the supply chain, such as distribution and retailing. Both backward and forward integration can be achieved by acquisition, joint venture or strategic alliance. Backward and forward integration, either singly or together, is often referred to as vertical integration.

Horizontal integration occurs most commonly when a firm adds to its portfolio of products by acquisition. A related strategy to horizontal integration is the move for economies of scope. This occurs when the product range is extended to incorporate similar items, as with the case of a firm supplying fitted kitchens diversifying its operation to include fitted bathrooms and bedrooms as well. Ralph Lauren began by selling sports shirts for men but extended its range into all types of casual clothes for men and women, into soft furnishings and then furniture. The fibreglass operations of Pilkington Glass found that the waste created in cutting standard widths of fibre-glass could be put to good use through the setting up of another operation which compressed the material into insulating bricks, thereby creating a different but related product. Case 11.2 shows how Orlake Records has used related diversification into specialized products as a strategy for survival in a declining market.

Kwik-Fit presents a good example of a number of kinds of related diversification. The company was formed to offer a speedy, low-cost service to motorists by fitting tyres and replacing exhaust systems. The opportunity presented itself as a result of the modular manufacture of cars and the ready availability of standardized parts. The reduction of operations to highly specialized routines meant that low levels of skill were needed and hence labour costs were low. Central buying and computerized stock control were other contributory factors to low costs. As a result of low costs and a while-you-wait service the company became very successful and expanded geographically. The company also expanded its product and service range to include shock absorber and brake replacement. The success of the company in terms of profit and market share made it an attractive acquisition for Ford, which thus diversified into after-sales service and parts sales, although it sold the company on in 2002.

Unrelated diversification

Unrelated diversification occurs when management expands its business into a different product market. Supermarkets have moved into financial services, a totally different operation from their core business. Many diversified companies have a mixture of both related and unrelated products. As with many forms of classification, the difference between related and unrelated diversification is often a matter of degree. Minnesota Mining and Manufacturing (3M) switched from the mining of corundum (an abrasive) to the manufacture of sandpaper (using abrasives as a raw material). The company then began producing masking tape, which led to the related products of adhesive tape and all other kinds of tape and adhesive products, such as Post-It notes. In recent years the most profitable arm of Ford in the UK has been Ford Credit, a company formed to provide finance for car buyers. A similar picture emerges with most car producers.

The concept often associated with unrelated diversification is synergy. This refers to the collective influence of the various activities of the company producing an overall effect that is greater than the sum of the parts. Synergy is often cited as a benefit of diversification, although its effect is often difficult to identify and measure.

We have seen how diversification can provide managers with greater control over supplies and distribution and exploit resources. A highly diversified firm may also be one where risks are spread across products and markets. The motives for diversification may be complex and may include the desire of senior management to extend its power and influence as the firm grows larger. In the USA, the diversification of many companies into different areas of business was a direct response to anti-trust laws, which put severe restrictions on the creation of monopolies. There are problems with diversification strategies. A highly diversified company often presents special problems of communication and control and resources may be duplicated. It is for this reason that many diversified companies have adopted a structure involving a mixture of autonomous units sharing some central services, as in the case of multidivisional companies. (A fuller discussion of such structural devices may be found in Chapter 6.) While extra efficiency gains can result from related diversification, unrelated diversification brings extra costs associated with coordination and control.

Joint ventures, mergers and acquisitions

Many of the illustrations of diversification presented above represent activities that have grown out of a firm's existing business. Firms may also add new products and markets through joint ventures and through mergers and acquisitions. This has the advantage of being a much faster method of diversification than internal development. The company is gaining an 'off-the-peg' business with the experience, knowledge, resources and markets already in existence. Much has been written about acquisitions and mergers and such activity presents consistently good copy for financial journalists, particularly when it is accompanied by boardroom battles and accusations of insider dealing on the stock market. While referred to as mergers and acquisitions, most could more accurately be described as acquisitions. Joint ventures include licensing agreements, particular arrangements with suppliers, joint R&D projects and the creation of a new company as an offshoot of two or more independent parent companies. A fuller account of joint ventures is presented in Chapter 2, where we identify joint ventures as an increasing trend that is directly related to globalization. In Figure 8.7 the differences between mergers, acquisitions and different forms of joint venture in terms of ownership are shown. These various forms of ownership also reveal possibilities for variations in control.

Haleblian et al. (2009) carried out a comprehensive review of studies relating to mergers and acquisitions. They cite the findings of several studies, which indicate that, in terms of shareholder value, acquisitions are rarely successful. They then go on to offer reasons why acquisitions take place and identify some influencing factors. Some of their findings are:

- Global investment in acquisitions has grown in recent years.
- Most acquisitions did not enhance shareholder value in either the short- or the long term and in fact were often seen as eroding value or producing volatile returns.

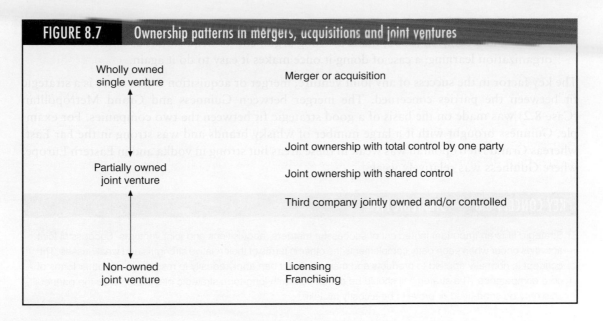

FIGURE 8.7 Ownership patterns in mergers, acquisitions and joint ventures

- Shareholders of target companies, i.e. those being bought, benefited from the sale of their shares above their true value as an incentive to sell.

Given such findings it is perhaps surprising that acquisitions happen at all. Haleblian and his colleagues found evidence to support the following reasons:

- Firms are acquired to achieve greater market power on the part of the buyer and enable it to charge higher prices.
- Acquisitions enable firms to reduce costs by consolidating some operations and achieving economies of scope. As a result, staff cuts are made and the process has the added advantage of getting rid of ineffective staff.
- Some acquisitions are clearly motivated by senior managers wishing to increase their salaries and other benefits. This would contribute to a fall in shareholder returns and lies at the heart of the agency problem outlined in Chapter 6 and the debate over executive pay in the case study at the end of the previous chapter. Some studies have even found links between acquisition behaviour and managers wanting to build up their egos.
- Acquisitions are linked to a firm seeking a better fit with its operating environment. For example firms in tobacco, alcohol and gambling may seek to diversify in the face of increasing state regulation limiting their activities.
- There is some evidence of imitative behaviour. Acquisitions occur because it is happening elsewhere. In a much earlier study in the UK it was found that acquisitions and mergers tend to occur in cycles (Channon, 1973). Why such cycles occurred could only be explained by imitation or fashion.
- Acquisitions also occur as a result of network behaviour. The pattern of governance of so many firms involves directors in a series of interlocking directorships. This gives them access to information and both contacts and opportunities to make acquisitions.

- Some studies suggest that acquisitions become a way of life for some organizations. Barkema and Schijven (2008) make a strong argument for acquisitions as a form of organization learning; a case of doing it once makes it easy to do it again.

The key factor in the success of any joint venture, merger or acquisition is that there is a strategic fit between the parties concerned. The merger between Guinness and Grand Metropolitan (Case 8.2) was made on the basis of a good strategic fit between the two companies. For example, Guinness brought with it a large number of whisky brands and was strong in the Far East, whereas Grand Metropolitan was weak in these areas but strong in vodka and in Eastern Europe, where Guinness was relatively weak.

KEY CONCEPT 8.8   STRATEGIC FIT

Strategic fit is an important ingredient of successful mergers, acquisitions and joint ventures. Successful joint activities occur when each party complements the other in terms of their relative strengths and weaknesses. The concept is normally applied to products and markets, but it can apply equally to resources and other forms of core competence. The strategic fit should be compatible with long-term strategic plans, otherwise the partnership may be short-lived or prove to be a costly mistake.

The evidence concerning joint ventures is very mixed. Medcof (1997) cites evidence that successful alliances outperform single businesses, but he does point to a high casualty rate among joint ventures. Peters and Waterman (1982) present a rather negative view, especially of acquisitions. They cite the case of ITT and the difficulties the firm encountered when it diversified out of telephones by acquiring banking and hotel interests. They claim that synergy rarely happens through acquisition, and the whole exercise takes up a disproportionate amount of management time and effort. Peters and Waterman see great difficulties in achieving a cultural fit between two different enterprises and advise managers to 'stick to the knitting'. The negative views of acquisition support the conclusions of Haleblian et al. (2009).

Gomes et al. (2013) have examined numerous academic studies of mergers and acquisitions, but the conflicting evidence led them to the conclusion that it is difficult to pinpoint reasons for their future poor share price and poor performance generally. They do however identify a number of possible causes of underperformance, some stronger than others:

- The choice of partner and the detailed evaluation of partners seems to be important. A recent series of studies involving the Cass Business School London and the consultants Towers Watson, of European companies in completed deals of US$100 million or more and also in the insurance industry have found that average share price returns are higher than the industry average and contradicts earlier studies (Johnson, 2011, Towers Watson, 2014). Although these findings represent a very short timeframe and may be unrepresentative, they do point to the importance of firms doing their homework and due diligence before merger of acquisiton and only proceeding when they are optimistic about the outcome.
- Paying more than a company is worth.
- Where there is a mismatch in size. Better results post merger seem to be found when the partners are of a similar size.
- Failure to pay sufficient attention to integration strategies and to management and organization factors seems to be a significant factor in underperformance. This involves

effective communication to deal with stakeholder anxieties, managing cultural differences at corporate and national levels and ensuring there is effective leadership post acquisition or merger.

We can also see variations in acquisition behaviour as a result of different **institutional frameworks**. In the UK there is a large number of mergers and acquisitions compared with other countries. This is explained in part by the behaviour of the stock market and the massive turnover in shares. Germany has a much more stable stock market, yet mergers and acquisitions are on the increase, particularly with overseas companies. Some of the acquisitions have represented very high stakes indeed, as with the acquisition of the USA publishing company Random House by Bertelsmann and of the Westinghouse Power Generation business by Siemens. The drivers for German companies include high labour costs, high rates of taxation, a business climate that is highly regulated in Germany and shareholder pressure for increased dividend. Firms in some countries appear more at risk from takeover, especially when they are seen to be in financial trouble. Owen (2010) notes that Courtaulds, a UK textile company founded in 1794, became a leading global player yet lacked investment in product development, lost out to foreign competition and was eventually broken up in 1990. He compares this with the more patient approaches used in Japan and Austria and the resistance to takeovers in those countries. This has led to the long-term development of the synthetic fibre industry led by such companies as Toray (Japan) and Lenzing (Austria). Such issues were presented in our comparison of Anglo-Saxon and social market economic systems and were discussed more fully in Chapters 3 and 5.

Mergers and acquisitions: political and stakeholder issues

As we can see by the SABMiller case later in this chapter, the political history of South Africa had a great influence on the acquisition patterns and strategies of South African Breweries. In addition, a number of mergers and acquisitions have failed to materialize due to various political and stakeholder issues as the following three illustrations show.

The proposed merger between Renault and Volvo in the early 1990s failed after several years of joint venture activity, although the strengths of each company were complementary. Volvo was strong in large cars, Renault in small; Volvo was strong in North America, while Renault had a larger market share in South America. In this case, strategic fit was not sufficient to sustain the relationship in the face of other constraints, which included issues of ownership share and pressures from Swedish politicians and trade unions, fearing French dominance of the newly merged company and job losses in Sweden.

In 2012 there was a proposed merger between BAE systems, the defence contractor and the largest manufacturing company in the UK, and EADS, the company making Airbus with the French and German governments having a significant share of the ownership. BAE systems used to own part of EADS but sold off its 20 per cent stake to fund its defence contract expansion in the USA. The proposed merger was called off after a few months of negotiation for a number of reasons. The merger was supported by the UK government, especially since it secured UK jobs, but they blocked political representatives of France and Germany from taking a seat on the board. For its part Germany feared their influence over EADS would diminish and objected to the proposed size of share ownership by France and the UK. The USA also expressed concern that one of its largest defence contractors (BAE) was to be part of a company involving Germany and France as partners. Finally BAE's largest investor, Invesco, was unhappy about the forecasted impact on the share price if the merger went ahead.

In May 2014, Pfizer, one of the largest American pharmaceutical companies withdrew from a bid to merge with AstraZeneca, a British-Swedish company with its HQ in London, and the second largest pharmaceutical company in the UK behind GSK. Pfizer had increased its bid from £60 billion to £69 billion, but this was deemed insufficient by the AstraZeneca board. Both Pfizer and AstraZeneca were politically significant in the UK as the suppliers of £3 billion worth of drugs to the NHS between 2010 and 2013. The rejection of the bid was strongly defended by both the chairman and the CEO of AstraZeneca for a number of reasons linked to the company's relationships with a range of stakeholders. Further, both the chairman and the CEO of AstraZeneca saw a merger as of little strategic value to the company and at odds with their own strategic vision.

Employees were seen to be at risk in the UK and Sweden and in the company's R&D establishment in Delaware, USA. Pfizer were vague about job cuts, although consolidation of the two companies would make this inevitable. Pfizer had already closed its R&D establishment at Sandwich in the UK in 2011 and had made 68 000 job cuts globally since 2005. Whatever pledges they made about the retention of jobs in the UK, the UK government were sceptical following Kraft reneging on its pledges after acquiring Cadbury in 2010.

There was a fear within AstraZeneca and in UK political and academic circles that the merger would reduce significantly the UK presence in pharmaceutical research specifically and scientific research generally. AstraZeneca had planned to move its R&D centre to Cambridge to assist in the development of a new cancer drug based on immunotherapy as an alternative to treatments based on chemotherapy. Despite assurances to the contrary by Pfizer, there was a fear that both the move and the development of the drug would be delayed.

Pfizer's proposal to move its HQ to the UK was seen to be motivated entirely by the opportunity to reduce its corporation tax bill (20 per cent UK versus 39 per cent USA) and to make savings via consolidating research and other activities with related job cuts. The move for tax purposes was criticized by some US senators, who planned to introduce a bill to prevent such moves by Pfizer and other companies.

AstraZeneca believed that the bid was not in the long-term interests of its shareholders, although some of the larger shareholders urged the company to accept. As a consequence of the bid being rejected the share price of AstraZeneca fell. Pfizer claimed it would not make another bid and the deal can only be resurrected on the request of AstraZeneca shareholders.

Other strategic options

Other options include outsourcing, licensing, deleting operations and even closure. We have dealt with outsourcing in some detail in Chapter 2 in relation to globalization. However, outsourcing takes place in domestic markets as well. Through franchising its products or services to other businesses, a firm can reach a wider market and, at the same time, spread the risk of that expansion.

The decision to cut back and/or sell off part of the operations of a firm is referred to as rationalization or divestment. At its ultimate level this will include liquidation and closure. Such strategies can pose enormous difficulties for the firm involved. The cutting back of activities such as R&D and training to achieve short-term savings may have damaging long-term repercussions. Reducing product lines and services may alienate customers. Cutbacks and closures have significant implications for whole communities. Nevertheless, for some firms, rationalization is the only viable option and may, as successful management buy-outs have shown, offer a new lease of life to part of an organization.

STRATEGIC CHOICE

Faced with a number of strategic options a manager must make a choice. We have already indicated that the process involves consideration of several factors, which we may summarize as follows:

- analysis of environmental threats and opportunities;
- analysis of company resources;
- stated objectives of the company and those of the management team;
- values and preferences of management decision-makers;
- realities of organizational politics.

The options must be tested for their suitability, feasibility and acceptability. The suitability of a strategy would include such considerations as its ability to tackle problems, improve competitive standing, exploit strengths, and the extent to which it meets corporate objectives. The feasibility of a strategy is the extent to which that strategy can be achieved given the financial, physical and human resource base of the company. Even if a strategy is both suitable and feasible it must still be acceptable to interested parties, such as management, employees, shareholders and customers. As we have seen stakeholders can be particularly sensitive to strategies of acquisition. The acceptance of a particular strategy may also depend on the attitude of senior management to risk.

The way a strategic choice is made will depend on the power and authority structure of the organization. In some firms, the strategy may be highly detailed with little scope for interpretation by functional managers. In other firms, a great deal of freedom is given to functional management to develop appropriate strategies within broad guidelines. We deal with specific functional strategies in Chapters 10–14. A theme stressed throughout is that R&D, production, marketing, HR and financial strategies should achieve a high level of internal consistency, irrespective of where in the firm the strategy was formulated.

A factor often overlooked in the choice of strategy is its sustainability. This refers to the extent to which the strategy will last and the extent to which it is difficult for others to copy. Such a concept has much in common with the resource-based view and with notions of core competence, discussed earlier in this chapter. Product and process innovation can lead to a sustainable competitive advantage that persists for many years, especially when protected by patents and trademarks, as in the case of Rank Xerox. Toyota achieved sustainable advantage over rival car manufacturers both within and outside Japan through continuous refinements in its system of lean production. Coca-Cola's sustainable advantage lay in its secret formula and branding policies. However, the history of strategic initiatives is littered with examples of non-sustainable advantages. An excellent illustration of this may be found in the rivalry between UK supermarkets. Each chain rigorously monitors its rivals so that any product and price advantage is quickly countered. All followed one another to introduce petrol stations, cafeterias and loyalty cards and as one announced diversification into financial services, it was followed quickly by the others.

CASE 8.2   SOUTH AFRICAN BREWERIES/SABMILLER

In 2002, South African Breweries bought Miller Brewing Company in the USA to become SABMiller. By 2007, SABMiller had overtaken InBev of Belgium to become the largest brewer by volume in the world. The company is active in 60 countries with brands such as Castle Lager, Miller Genuine Draft, Miller Lite, Peroni Nastro Azzuro and Pilsner Urquell. In addition to beer, SABMiller is one of the world's largest producers of Coca-Cola under licence, as well as other soft drinks. In 2008 InBev regained the top brewer spot through its acquisition of Anheuser Busch in the USA. By 2013 SABMiller was the world's second-largest producer of beer by volume and the largest brewer in terms of sales. Globally the company has over 200 different brands of beer and is one of the largest bottlers of Coca-Cola products. The company employs 70 000 people in 75 countries,

South African Breweries was founded in 1895 as Castle Brewery producing Castle Lager to supply a growing market in the newly established goldfields around the mining town of Johannesburg. By 1902 the company was the most valuable non-mining company in South Africa. In 1910 the Union of South Africa was formed as part of the British Commonwealth. The company expanded into Rhodesia forming Rhodesian Breweries. Over the next 30 years the company diversified by acquiring a stake in Schweppes, and along with its rival brewer Ohlsson's, created a joint venture to grow hops and barley, thus securing important supplies. During WW I the company acquired Union Glass to secure bottle supply at a time when glass was in short supply.

In 1948, the South African government introduced apartheid, a system of 'separate development' for different racial groups that was effectively discrimination favouring the white minority. Black South Africans were removed (in some cases, forcibly) from their homes and placed in townships outside cities, such as Soweto near Johannesburg. They were denied the vote and their movement restricted to designated areas.

The years immediately following apartheid were years of expansion for the brewery. Breweries were acquired and built in South Africa and Namibia and the company greatly extended its network of pubs and hotels. There was new investment in Zambia and Castle built the largest brewery in South Africa just outside Johannesburg. In 1955, the government placed significant taxes on the purchase of beer in South Africa. Beer was the favoured drink of black South Africans, who were prevented by law from buying spirits. A year later South African Breweries was formed when the company bought its two main rivals, Ohlsson's and Chandlers Union. This gave SAB effective control of the beer market in South Africa. In 1960 the company acquired Stellenbosch Farmers Winery and diversified into wine and spirits manufacture.

In 1961 South Africa broke from the British Commonwealth and became an independent country. Prohibition on liquor for black South Africans was lifted, opening up a new commercial market. However, high taxes were maintained on beer and these were raised even higher by the mid-1960s. The 1960s was a period of expansion for SAB in a number of directions. The company obtained licence agreements to brew Guinness, Amstel and Carling Black Label from the respective owners of those brands. SAB expanded its interests in wines and spirits through acquisition, moved into the food industry, the property development industry and took a much bigger stake in the hotel industry. In addition, the company formed a venture with an investment company to maximize investment opportunities outside their core business in the South African industrial sector eventually controlling the company's shoe and furniture business. Outside South Africa, the company established breweries in Angola and Botswana.

In 1974, South Africa was excluded from the United Nations over its apartheid policies. This did not halt SAB's expansion within South Africa. SAB moved into mass market retailing and set up joint ventures with Schweppes for soft drinks and with Pepsi, the latter for bottling. Swaziland Breweries was bought. At the end of the 1970s, Pepsi Cola was dropped as the company acquired the franchise for Coca-Cola. Around the same time food, coffee, tea and property interests were sold in an attempt to focus on the core business and SAB expanded its hotel interests by opening a casino and hotel complex at Sun City. By 1979 the company had bought out its only rival in South Africa, the Rembrandt Group, and SAB thus acquired 99 per cent of the South African market. The next two years saw expansion in Botswana and the acquisition of a controlling interest in Lesotho Brewery. There were acquisitions in clothing retail and for the first time the company invested outside Africa by buying interests in the USA, specifically in soft drinks and Rolling Rock beer. In the hotel business, the Holiday Inn franchise was obtained for South Africa.

In 1985, through the United Nations, trade and cultural sanctions were imposed on South Africa for its continued allegiance to apartheid. Some countries, such as the UK, had already imposed trade bans and had broken off sporting connections in cricket and rugby. South Africa had also been shunned by many African leaders, effectively ending SAB's interest in many African countries. As a result of the UN sanctions, SAB's interest in the USA ended.

In 1990 a new political era was ushered in with the release of Nelson Mandela, leader of the African National Congress party (ANC) and anti-apartheid campaigner, after 27 years as a political prisoner. Bans on opposition political parties, such as the ANC, were lifted, although the first wholly democratic elections were not held until 1994. At that election the Government of National Unity was formed and black South Africans were, for the first time, represented in government.

Political change coincided with expansion for SAB in three directions. The company expanded in emerging economies including Russia, Hungary, Czech Republic, Slovakia, Romania and China, mainly through acquisition including that of Dreher, the largest brewing firm in Hungary, but also forming a joint venture with China's second-largest brewery. Second, the company was welcomed back by African nations. It was chosen to revitalize the Tanzanian brewing industry and re-established itself in Angola, Mozambique and Zambia. Third, the company continued its policy of diversification through acquisition of manufacturing interests in plate glass and board and automotive products. This third policy was reversed towards the end of the 1990s with the closure or sale of several non-core businesses.

By 2001, SAB's international operations contributed 42 per cent of turnover. This expansion offset a fall of sales in South Africa and reflected a strategic focus of investment in the growing transitional economies of Eastern Europe and China.

Transitional economies were favoured for a number of reasons. China was a beer drinking market of huge potential. In many Eastern European countries the beer drinking tradition was strong, as in Poland and the Czech Republic, where SAB had acquired brands in Tyskie and Pilsner Urquell respectively. The opportunity for SAB lay not just in market size but in the nature of those markets. In general, the markets tended to be fragmented and dominated by cheap, lower quality products. Marketing and distribution tended to be weak, as did the management and organization of the companies. SAB saw two types of opportunity. Its experience of product development, and of operations and distribution management in Africa, allied with the political skills honed over years of dealing with African governments, meant SAB was ideally placed to develop those companies. Second, the changing market itself presented an opportunity. As the transitional economy developed then consumer spending would increase. This meant not only increased sales but the opportunity to replace lower quality local products with premium beers at higher prices. SAB was aware that transitional economies offer threats in the form of unstable economies and political systems, volatile currencies and variable returns. For this reason the company favoured a broad portfolio of acquisitions across many countries as well as seeking expansion into a major economy.

The acquisition of a company in a major economy took place in 2002 when SAB paid US$5.6 billion to acquire Miller Brewing Company of Milwaukee. The acquisition offered a number of advantages to SAB. It gained premium brands such as Miller Genuine Draft and Miller Lite and a direct presence in the world's largest economy. It reduced the company's dependency on emerging markets and on the rand as its main currency; now it was operating in a dollar economy. The new company would give more clout for acquisitions, especially in Western Europe.

As SABMiller, the company has pursued its aggressive acquisition policy. The company took a large stake in Colombia's Bavaria Brewery and in so doing became South America's second largest brewer. Acquisitions were made in North Africa, India, Holland, Argentina, Australia, Poland and China, although the company lost out to Anheuser

(Continued)

CASE 8.2   (Continued)

Busch in a major deal with the Chinese Harbin Brewery. Nonetheless in 2013 seven breweries were bought in China in a joint venture with CR Snow Breweries, the Chinese market leader with 22 per cent of the Chinese market, currently the largest market in the world by volume. Two years earlier SABMiller was engaged in a highly contentious hostile takeover of Fosters, the Australian brewer, with 50 per cent share of the domestic market. The acquisition gave them seven of the top Australian brands including the brand leader, Victoria Bitter.

Currently SABMiller emphasizes four strategic priorities:

- Creating a balanced and attractive spread of global businesses.
- Developing strong, relevant brand portfolios in the local market.
- Constantly raising the performance of local businesses.
- Leveraging the company's global scale by global learning.

In 2013, SABMiller's financial statements showed the following revenue and profit:

	2013 revenue (US$ million)	2013 profit/ EBITA (US$ million)
North America	5 355	771
Latin America	7 821	2 112
Europe	5 767	784
Africa and Asia	3 853	838
Asia Pacific (inc. Australia)	5 685	855
South Africa	5 540	1 263

Questions

1 To what extent do changes in the strategies of SAB and SABMiller reflect changing economic and political changes?

2 What are the main issues before 1990 and after 1990?

3 Is the acquisition of Miller a good move for SAB?

4 What conclusions do you draw from the strategy statement and financial statements of 2013?

CASE 8.3   GUINNESS AND GRAND METROPOLITAN CREATE DIAGEO

In June 1997, a merger was agreed between Guinness and Grand Metropolitan (Grand Met) to create the world's largest drinks company to be called Diageo. At the time of the merger the two companies could claim 24.7 per cent of the world market, with the nearest rival, Allied Domecq, coming in at 10.8 per cent. The 1996 sales of both companies combined amounted to £12.9 billion with profits of £1.6 billion, 60 per cent of which came from the manufacture and sale of spirits. The merger was completed in December 1997 after approval from the UK government, the EU Commission and the US Federal Trade Commission. The terms of acceptance required the companies to sell Dewars Whisky and Bombay Sapphire Gin and reduce their market power in some smaller European countries. The company surprised everyone by announcing the new company name as

Diageo, when the expectation was for the more obvious choice of Grand Metropolitan Guinness.

Ownership was split 52.7 per cent and 47.3 per cent in favour of Grand Met and four divisions were created: Guinness Brewing Worldwide; Burger King; Pillsbury; and United Distillers and Vintners, the last being the largest division by far.

There was a clear strategic fit between the two partners. Guinness brought considerable strength in whiskies, with such brands as Bells, White Horse and, the world's best-seller, Johnnie Walker. In addition to whiskies, Guinness possessed brands such as Gordon's Gin, Harp Lager and Kilkenny Beer, as well as its famous dark stout. Its 34 per cent stake in LVMH, the French luxury goods firm, incorporated Hennessy Cognac and Moet and Chandon Champagne. Grand Met's strengths lay

CASE 8.3   (Continued)

in vodka and white spirits generally. It owned the world's best-selling vodka brand in Smirnoff and had led the market in the production and sale of popular spirit combination drinks such as Malibu and Baileys. Whereas Guinness was predominantly a drinks firm, Grand Met owned Pillsbury, the US-based dough and cake makers, Burger King and Haagen-Dazs ice cream. Guinness had particular strengths in the Far Eastern markets where Grand Met was weak, and Grand Met was strong in Eastern Europe, where Guinness was weak. Grand Met also brought strengths in the USA market through its vodka sales and its food interests. The joint venture served both interests in a declining world spirits market and growing competition from supermarket and retail chain own brands. Global sales teams now had more to offer their customers.

Neither party was new to mergers and joint ventures. Grand Met has had a fairly volatile history in this respect. The company began life as a hotel chain, which it then sold off. Most of its brands were acquisitions such as Burger King and Pillsbury. The company has owned and subsequently sold Watney Mann Truman, Mecca Bingo Halls and Express Dairies. Guinness, for its part, acquired the Distillers Company and Cruz Campo and obtained a large share in LVMH (Louis Vuitton Moet Hennessy). The merger was initially opposed by Bernard Arnault, the head of LVMH, whose company owned a 14 per cent share in Guinness. He was a member of the Guinness board and feared losing his place in the new order of things.

The drinks industry has a history of merger activity and the deals that preceded and followed the creation of Diageo illustrate the volatile nature of merger activity in the UK and beyond. When Watney Mann Truman was sold by Grand Met it became part of the Courage group. Courage then merged with Scottish Newcastle Breweries to form Scottish-Courage. A rival company, Carlsberg Tetley, wanted to merge with Guinness. The strategic fit was good in that Carlsberg Tetley brought with it a large number of public houses and strength in bitter and lager beers. However, the company's interest in Guinness came after an unsuccessful attempt to merge with

Bass. That proposed merger was blocked by the government as being against the public interest on the forecast of price rises and job losses. This had a knock-on effect for Allied Domecq, which saw any merger involving Carlsberg Tetley as a means of extricating itself from an expensive supply agreement with the company. Bass, unsuccessful in its attempts to merge with Carlsberg Tetley, then turned its attentions to the bookmakers William Hill, given that Bass already owned another major betting firm in Corals. In the event, William Hill was bought by the Japanese firm, Nomura.

In 2013 Diageo retained its position as the world's largest distiller and producer of alcoholic spirits. It sold off its food businesses, including Pillsbury and Burger King to focus on its core business of alcoholic drinks. Diageo produces a large number of brands worldwide but around 80 per cent of its revenue is attributed to what it terms 'strategic global priority brands', of which it currently lists 13. These include world leaders in scotch whisky (Johnnie Walker), Canadian whisky (Crown Royal), vodka (Smirnoff), liquer (Baileys), stout (Guinness) and the top imported gin in the USA (Tanqueray). In terms of revenues, 33 per cent come from the USA, 26 per cent from Europe and 40 per cent from the rest of the world. There has been significant marketing investment in fast growing emerging markets especially China, India, Turkey, parts of Africa and Central and South America.

Sources: Financial Times, Guardian, Observer, various editions 1997–2000, Bloomberg News 2012, Diageo.com, Diageo company Reports 2010–12

Questions

1 What are the strategic advantages gained from the creation of Diageo?

2 What issues does the merger raise for the management of the company and for the state?

3 What reasons can you give for the large number of mergers in the food and drinks industry?

4 Identify future strategic directions Diageo might wish to take.

SUMMARY

In this chapter we have portrayed the formulation of strategy as a complex process involving environmental and organizational factors as well as management values and organization politics. As a result, the process is a mixture of rational techniques and subjective decision-making processes, including a consideration of management values and negotiations between interested parties.

- We have identified a range of approaches and styles, which may operate at the same time, although at different stages of the firm's development one type of strategy may be more appropriate than another.

- The formulated strategy has several functions, not least of which is to anticipate the future by coordinating activities and focusing resources towards chosen objectives.

- We note that the links between strategy and performance are difficult to prove.

- An analysis of the general environment and a focus on the immediate competitive environment will enable management to identify opportunities and threats, although how these are interpreted is a function of the values and creative ability of management.

- We identify four kinds of resource: product, physical, financial and people. All are important in enabling management to formulate strategy around the organization's strengths. These strengths may be examined through an analysis of a firm's core competences and its value chain. Portfolio analysis offers both an analysis of resources and an insight into strategic options.

- We examine a number of strategic options, and suggest that each option should be assessed in terms of its suitability, its feasibility and its acceptability to managers, employees, shareholders and customers.

DISCUSSION QUESTIONS

1 Examine the role of the scientific method in the process of strategy formulation. Is there a place for subjectivity and creativity?

2 What is the purpose of strategy and how might a particular strategy be evaluated?

3 Identify the environmental opportunities and threats faced by a city centre restaurant, a large retail store, a high street bank, a university, and a firm manufacturing television sets.

4 Using Porter's five-forces model, identify the specific competitive forces operating in the five situations defined in the previous question.

5 In what ways can management use resource analysis and portfolio analysis to guide strategy? What are the strengths and weaknesses of the models for portfolio analysis identified in this chapter?

6 Assess the usefulness of core competences and the value chain in analysing resources and developing strategy.

7 Make a critical analysis of the different approaches to diversification.

8 Identify the opportunities and threats associated with a merger.

9 What strategic approaches, styles and options would best fit your college or your firm for the 21st century? What problems do you foresee with these approaches, styles and options?

FURTHER READING

There are several popular texts, all of which have features to commend them. An excellent coverage and good cases is provided by:

Johnson, G., Whittington, R., Scholes, K., Angwin, D. and Regnér, P. (2013) *Exploring Strategy: Text and Cases*, 10th edn, FT Prentice Hall: Harlow.

A condensed version of the above focusing on key issues and techniques can be found in:

Johnson, G., Whittington, R. and Scholes, K. (2012) *Fundamentals of Strategy*, 2nd edn, FT Prentice Hall: Harlow.

The following book covers much of the same ground but it approaches the subject in a slightly different way. It has the added feature of including a number of classic journal articles.

de Wit, B. and Meyer, R. (2010) *Strategy: Process, Content, Context: An International Perspective*, 4th edn, Cengage Learning: Andover.

A number of key articles can also be found in:

Mintzberg, H., Lampel, J.B., Quinn, J.B. and Ghoshal, S. (2003) *The Strategy Process: Concepts, Contexts and Cases*, 4th edn, Prentice Hall: London.

A different and interesting view of strategy is taken by:

Whittington, R. (2000) *What is Strategy – And Does It Matter?* Cengage Learning: Andover.

At a more specific level, a good analysis of the competitive environment is offered by:

Porter, M.E. (1980), *Competitive Strategy: Techniques for Analyzing Industries and Competitors*, Free Press: New York.

The following contains an excellent summary of the above with updated examples:

Porter, M.E. (2008) 'The five competitive forces that shape strategy', *Harvard Business Review*, January, 79–93.

BUSINESS ETHICS AND CORPORATE SOCIAL RESPONSIBILITY

LEARNING OBJECTIVES At the end of this chapter you should be able to:

- Define business ethics and corporate social responsibility and explain the relationship between them.
- Explain the historical and theoretical origins of business ethics.
- Explain and illustrate the complexities involved in doing business ethically.
- Identify and assess the issues involved in corporate social responsibility between the firm and its numerous stakeholders.
- Assess the moral and business arguments for doing business ethically.
- Identify and explain the various mechanisms used in organizations for ethical business and corporate social responsibility.

INTRODUCTION

Some companies have acknowledged that there is enhanced corporate reputation to be gained through recognizing that capitalism will be most successful when it cares for its customers, its producers, the environment and the communities in which it operates.

(McIntosh, 1998, p. 3)

The quote by McIntosh represents a growing concern by commentators from inside and outside business that the goals and activities of business should be concerned with:

- Conducting business honestly.
- Treating people who come into contact with the business (suppliers, customers, employers, etc.) fairly and in a socially responsible manner.
- Being accountable. For example, corporations are accountable for their actions to the general public. In this case companies that transgress socially acceptable standards can expect to be punished, usually by the imposition of fines. In some cases board members can be held responsible and prosecuted as individuals.
- Looking after the environment.

A number of labels have been attached to such intentions, including business ethics, corporate social responsibility (CSR) and green business. In this chapter we will address the issues under the twin headings of business ethics and corporate social responsibility. We consider business ethics to be the broader of the two concepts. It is concerned with establishing values and making choices about right and wrong courses of action. The values that are embodied in the bullet points above include honesty, fairness and transparency and accountability. Business ethics has been defined as:

A study of business situations, activities and decisions where issues of right and wrong are addressed.

(Crane and Matten, 2010, p. 5)

Corporate social responsibility focuses on issues in the relationship between the firm and its stakeholders and the firm and its environment. As well as links with broader issues of morality, there is an overlap with the law as many ethical issues in business are covered by laws. In Chapter 6 in our discussion of corporate governance and the agency theory we noted that definitions of corporate governance often incorporate reference to social responsibility. There are strong links with stakeholder theory. Treating stakeholders fairly involves paying employees and suppliers as agreed and on time and only making promises that can be met. An example of social responsibility cropped up in a study of the corporate culture of Korean electronics firms Hyundai, Samsung and LG. The firms placed considerable importance in corporate literature on the dignity of the individual, their life outside work and on the aim of creating a better world for all (Needle, 2000).

The issues covered by business ethics and corporate social responsibility are wide-ranging. The issues include pollution reduction, the responsible exploitation of raw materials, the exploitation of child labour, corporate fraud, bribery and corruption, fair pay, sexual harassment and even an individual cheating on expenses. Issues such as these cover every business activity.

- In R&D, larger pharmaceutical firms have established committees to oversee the ethical aspects of testing drugs. In the cosmetic industry, countries such as the UK and Japan have banned the testing of products on animals.
- In terms of product development and operations, the emphasis has been on safe, non-polluting products and working environments. The Ford Pinto was withdrawn from production in the USA after several accidents involving the explosion of the petrol tank. The Pinto was launched in 1971 and the design, while conforming to the standards of the day, failed to anticipate incoming legislation that cars should be able to withstand a collision at 30 mph. Exhaust emissions from car engines have been the subject of legislation, leading to the development of new technologies.

- In marketing, many countries have banned or restricted tobacco advertising and set up commissions to monitor advertising and sales promotions to ensure honest representation. Both in terms of products and marketing, the focus in recent years has been less on manufactured goods and more on the products and marketing of financial services focusing on such issues as misrepresentation and the activities of high interest loan companies.
- HR policies have been designed to improve working conditions and enhance the involvement of employees in the decision-making process. The banking crisis of 2008 and 2009 has focused on the pay and bonuses made to senior managers.
- In finance and accounting, standards have been established about public accountability and, for multinationals, their contribution to the local communities in which they operate.

Undoubtedly, interest in ethical issues and responsible business stems from public and corporate disquiet about a number of disasters and scandals. In 1984 in Bhopal, India, at the Union Carbide plant there was a leakage of toxic pesticide gas. This resulted in an estimated 2500 deaths and 200 000 injuries. Later reports offer conflicting data and some estimate that as many as 8000 were killed and up to 10 000 have since died as a result of the accident. There was also considerable damage to the environment including the death of animals and the destruction of plants and trees. A resulting criminal case for culpable multiple homicide was brought against the company executive. The company has since been sold to Dow Chemicals.

The Chernobyl nuclear reactor disaster in the Ukraine attracted similar attention, as did the massive oil spillage from the Exxon Valdes in Alaska. In 2013 at Rana Plaza in Dhaka, Bangladesh, a garment factory collapsed killing 1133 and injuring over 2500 workers. The factory was part of a global clothing industry supply chain and produced goods for high street multinationals. The incident raised awareness of the poor working conditions in many such factories and questioned the responsibilities of western companies utilizing cheap overseas labour. Many well-known names and figures have hit the headlines. Guinness executives were tried and found guilty of corporate fraud. The Maxwell publishing empire collapsed as a result of the illegal misappropriation of pension funds, leaving many thousands in danger of losing their pensions. The established bank, Barings, was brought down by the illegal activities of one of its traders in Singapore. In Japan such established firms as Nomura, Daiwa and Yamaichi were found guilty of fraudulent and illegal operations both at home and overseas. We examine one such major case, Enron, and the issues involved at the end of this chapter (see Case 9.1).

In this chapter we will define business ethics and corporate social responsibility, examine the historical background and related theoretical perspectives. We will then put the case for ethical and socially responsible business and examine a number of problems and issues. Finally, we will look at some mechanisms used by companies to support doing business ethically.

DEFINING BUSINESS ETHICS AND CORPORATE SOCIAL RESPONSIBILITY

Ethics is a branch of moral philosophy and there is considerable debate within philosophy over its true nature. In simple terms, it is the study of morals and principles governing the rights and wrongs of human conduct. We can identify a number of approaches:

- **Transcendental ethics** or **ethical absolutism** assumes that there are absolute concepts of right and wrong, which apply across all societies. Most world religions claim a universal moral code, albeit with variations between them, which is a form of transcendental ethics.

- **Utilitarianism** is a pragmatic approach to transcendental ethics and is a position that argues that an action is morally right if it produces the greatest good for the greatest number of people. Supporters of the utilitarian position would argue that it is justifiable to lay-off a proportion of the workforce to save the company from bankruptcy and protect the jobs of the other employees. Opponents would argue this is an unfair and unethical action upon those losing their jobs.

- **Ethical relativism** or **social ethics** assumes that ethical standards will vary between societies reflecting their histories and influences. Hence, ethical relativism can be demonstrated by the fact that the death penalty is acceptable in some societies but not in others. In some countries paying bribes or offering gifts to government officials is a necessary precursor to doing business in that country, while in others it is illegal and potentially damaging to successful business outcomes. There are those who maintain that all ethical standards are socially constructed and that no absolute standards exist. Others would argue that just because a practice like child labour is acceptable in some societies does not make the practice ethical. In business, ethical issues have become more complex as multinational firms operate in countries with different cultures, laws and institutions and there are few universals. There are strong links here with globalization.

- **Tactical ethics** assumes that people pursue ethical standards because it suits them so to do. Drivers who slow down when they see a speed camera not out of any belief in the speed limit but to avoid getting caught and paying a fine are practising tactical ethics. In business, managers can make rapid improvements to work places prior to a health and safety inspection but ignore health and safety issues thereafter. Many companies produce codes of practice and corporate statements identifying ethical intentions, yet for some this is simply a public relations exercise to gain reputation, when the reality is that such issues are ignored in the practices pursued by the company.

These different perspectives on ethics illustrate the difficulties and potential conflicts of operating as an ethical business.

REFLECTION POINT

Which of the above approaches to ethics is the most applicable to business and why? To what extent can businesses pursue a utilitarian approach?

Business ethics

Business ethics is concerned with those moral issues and individual choices of right and wrong and values of what is good and bad within the conduct of business affairs. The relationship of ethics to business is complex and incorporates all the approaches identified above. It has become much more complex with globalization. We can illustrate some of the complexities in a number of ways:

- Within business there are widespread beliefs about how customers or employees should be treated. However, we can see from examples around the world, and even between firms in the same area, that practices vary. As a consequence, we may conclude that the approach used by many companies to business ethics is one of ethical relativism, identified above, in that standards in business are a function of:

- the values of individuals working in organizations;
- the corporate culture created by top management;
- codes of conduct operating in individual organizations;
- the social norms of the society within which the organization is located;
- the prevailing laws, which may vary from country to country.

- Values vary across societies. In some societies the use of bribes is an essential part of getting business done, while in others it is considered unacceptable behaviour. The dilemma occurs when employees of an organization in a country where bribes are unacceptable must do business in a country where bribes are expected. Often, such bribes are dressed up as gifts and in many situations there is a fine line between a gift as a token of cooperation and goodwill and a bribe. In some organizations many business people adopt a stance of 'moral relativism', in that they acknowledge things are done differently elsewhere and it is acceptable to operate to those standards in that setting. In other organizations there are strict codes about the giving and receiving of presents.

- Bribery in business is a good illustration of the complexities of business ethics. The World Bank estimates that US$ 1 trillion is paid annually to officials of foreign governments by companies to secure government contracts and other trade deals (Wayne, 2012). Laws preventing such bribery have existed in the USA in the form of the Foreign Corrupt Practices Act 1977 and in the UK as the Bribery Act 2010. In the USA there were very few prosecutions until 2009, yet there appears to have been a backlash since the 2008 financial crisis and in 2012, 78 companies, including large, well-known corporations were under investigation. This was seen by many in business as an over-zealous reaction by the US Government (Wayne. 2012). In the UK the Bribery Act was held up while the business community debated with the government the type and level of business entertaining permitted to smooth the deal-making process. Transparency International has been established as an independent global watchdog on bribery and corruption since 1993 and publishes an annual 'Corruption Index' listing those coutries where bribery is rife and those where every step is taken to avoid it. Transparency International regularly publishes reports on a variety of issues relating to bribery and corruption. In 2013 a report highlighted problems at all levels of education globally. They identified 'ghost' schools in Pakistan, where schools are funded by the state, teachers receive salaries but no teaching takes place and buildings are used for other purposes; fake diplomas; undue corporate influence in university research; universities obtaining funds from dubious sources; bribes for places at universities and so on (Transparency International, 2013).

- We can also see that such standards change over time. People in the West decry the use of child labour in such countries as Indonesia and India, yet it was commonplace in the mining and textile industries of 19th-century Britain. Our attitudes, and hence our standards, have also changed on issues such as equal opportunities although, some would argue, not nearly enough.

- Managers are presented with many dilemmas. We have already seen that to save the business and hence jobs in one location, it may be necessary to close operations and shed jobs elsewhere or even in the same location. In many situations such dilemmas are resolved by behaving fairly towards those adversely affected. In this case there would be redundancy, early retirement, and retraining packages and counselling for those losing their jobs. Nonetheless, there are many decisions in business, while favourable to one group are less favourable to another.

REFLECTION POINT

What are the ethical dilemmas facing managers who close down operations and make employees redundant to save the whole business from bankruptcy?

KEY CONCEPT 9.1   BUSINESS ETHICS

Business ethics is the concern for moral standards and individual choices of right and wrong in the conduct of business affairs. Business ethics is a function of individual values, corporate culture, prevailing social norms and the laws of the land. As a result we can see variations across cultures and changing standards operating at different times. Business ethics sets the framework for the operation of corporate social responsibility and attention to both are believed to contribute towards business success, although causal links are difficult to prove.

Corporate social responsibility

Corporate social responsibility (CSR) highlights ethical issues in business by defining those activities and those groups to whom the company and its representatives are responsible and those areas for which responsibility is taken. CSR is linked closely to stakeholder theory, which views business in terms of its relationship to a number of groups, in this case acknowledging some responsibility. Part of that responsibility is a legal requirement. However, the intention of much of CSR goes beyond legal compliance. McWilliams et al. define CSR as:

... a situation where the firm goes beyond compliance and engages in actions that appear to further some social good beyond the interests of the firm and that which is required by law.

(McWilliams et al., 2006, p. I)

Areas of activity in CSR

Blowfield and Murray (2011) identify the following activities which they see as part of corporate social responsibility, although they refer to it as simply 'corporate responsibility'.

- Business ethics
- Legal compliance
- Philanthropy and community investment
- Environmental management
- Sustainability
- Animal rights
- Human rights
- Employee rights and welfare
- Market relations
- Corruption
- Corporate governance

The authors note the rise in prominence of CSR, which they link, in part, to the financial crisis of 2008. They see increased interest by companies themselves, a rise in the number of CSR consultancies and standards watchdogs and increased media attention. Their list of activities is fairly comprehensive. The inclusion of animal rights is interesting, reflecting the debate surrounding the use of animals in drug and cosmetics testing. They also distinguish between employee rights and human rights, the latter relating to businesses responsibilities to wider society. They see the core characteristics of CSR as follows:

- It is voluntary in that it goes beyond legal requirement.
- It is about managing external impacts of business. This is not just about the environment (as with pollution, waste and the use of energy) but also about the impact on people and on the market place as it affects suppliers and competitors.
- CSR works best when it operates within a framework of ethical values.
- CSR takes the view that business is about all stakeholders and not just shareholders.
- CSR is more than philanthropy and carrying out good deeds, it is recognizing that business activities have an impact on society and structuring policies and practices accordingly.
- CSR is where economic and social responsibilities can be aligned. We return to this theme when we discuss the strategic approach to CSR later in the chapter.

Much of the above echoes the work of Carroll (1991) who identifies 'the pyramid of corporate social responsibility' with economic responsibility as the basic requirement and philanthropic responsibility at the peak as something that is desirable. This can be set out as follows:

- Philanthropic responsibility. This is deemed to be **discretionary** and involves contributing company resources to the community to improve the quality of life. This can include making donations to charities and educational causes, sponsoring the arts and managers and employees engaging in charitable work in local communities.
- Ethical responsibility is that which goes beyond legal requirements and, according to Carroll, is expected. This involves achieving corporate goals by behaviour that is consistent with the ethical values of society.
- Legal responsibility through adherence to the laws of a particular country or, in the case of global firms, different countries is **required.**
- Economic responsibility to such as shareholders for a return on their investment, to suppliers, customers and employees is also **required.** This involves being profitable, maximizing earnings per share, maintaining a strong competitive position and being efficient. Carroll recognizes that it is only through these outcomes that an organization can satisfy the needs of its various stackholders.

Carroll goes further and uses this framework to identify three types of manager. The immoral manager 'exploits opportunities for personal or corporate gain' (Carroll 1991, p. 45). Case 9.1 contains some good examples of Enron managers that Carroll would undoubtedly classify as immoral. The amoral manager is insensitive to the fact that decisions and actions can have a negative impact on others. Moral management on the other hand is the embodiment of good organizational citizenship, which demonstrates an awareness for stakeholder, community and environmental needs.

KEY CONCEPT 9.2   CORPORATE SOCIAL RESPONSIBILITY

Corporate social responsibility (CSR) involves the application of business ethics. CSR is concerned primarily with the firm and its relationships with its various stakeholders. These include shareholders, employees, customers, suppliers, the community and society and government. There is also a responsibility towards the sustainability of the environment. The assumption is that such relationships are conducted morally and ethically.

REFLECTION POINT

What philanthropic responsibilities might it be desirable for a company to have? What ethical responsibilities are expected of modern firms?

Stakeholders

A key approach to examining corporate social responsibility is to identify groups or stakeholders to whom the firm is responsible to various degrees. In this list we include also the environment. However, as the following examples show, there are dilemmas in exercising such responsibility.

- **Shareholders.** Some, like Friedman (1970), argue that shareholders are the prime responsibility of companies. However, there are important issues. We discussed this issue in Chapter 6 when we looked at the agency problem between managers and shareholders. One issue is that of the amount allocated to share dividend versus the amount allocated to reinvestment. Many shareholders, particularly institutional shareholders, are concerned above all for a rising share price and a good dividend. In some cases this leads managers to focus on short-term gains over long-term growth, possibly to the detriment of the company and its responsibility to other stakeholders. Moreover, in volatile stock markets, such as in the UK, shares change hands frequently. It is, therefore, sometimes difficult to identify the shareholders and their motives. In contrast to the view of the selfish and fickle shareholder, there is evidence of the growth of shareholders who are concerned to invest only in those businesses with clear ethical standards and which demonstrate social responsibility.

REFLECTION POINT

Should shareholders be the prime focus for companies?

- **Financial institutions.** Many of these are shareholders but some, like banks, lend money to companies. They have an expectation that their money will be paid back in a timely fashion. In cases of corporate insolvency, decisions must be made about the relative priority of stakeholders in terms of receiving payments owed to them. In this respect banks tend to have priority. Banks can also have considerable influence on management decisions, which may conflict with the needs of other stakeholders. In UK soccer, many teams are financed by bank borrowing. The terms of such borrowing often forces clubs to sell their most valuable assets (usually young, talented players) in an attempt to balance the books. This conflicts with the wishes of the fans, the paying customers.

- **Customers.** In most cases a customer wants quality goods and services at reasonable prices. Customers also expect transparent pricing and honest sales promotions and advertising. For firms to keep prices down, costs must be cut. In some cases this has resulted in the firm cutting out safety features to keep costs down. In the case of the Ford Pinto, managers made the decision that the alteration of the design to accommodate proposed changes in safety law would be too expensive once production had begun. Cost reduction often means making people unemployed or, in the case of global companies, switching operations to low-cost economies, creating problems of unemployment at home and facing accusations of exploitation overseas. As with shareholders, not all customers are selfish and calculating and there is evidence to suggest that customers will actually choose and pay more for those goods and services produced ethically.

- **Employees.** If we view employment as a calculative arrangement then employees offer their services in return for wages. However, the modern employee expects much more from employers. Employers are expected to provide not just a means of making a living but a safe working environment, job security, rewarding work, fair treatment, equal opportunities and so on. Many of these are human resource management issues, such as how long should employees be expected to work and how much should they be paid. The relationship between HRM and ethics has changed as a result of globalization in that labour is sourced globally. A further change is that, with the decline of trade union membership, employee rights are less protected by collective agreements. As with other stakeholders there are dilemmas. For example, take the case of a firm that pays for the private medical care of its employees, including an annual medical check. If the medical reveals that the employee is HIV positive has the firm the right to know or has the employee the right to privacy?

- **Suppliers.** In recent years there has been increased focus on treating suppliers not just fairly but as members of the corporate family. Cut-throat competition between suppliers has, in many instances, given way to the emergence of a small number of suppliers enjoying close working relationships with their customers. Much of the lead for this has come from the practice of firms in coordinated market economies such as Japan and Germany (see Chapter 5). In times of recession a Japanese firm is keen to behave honourably to its key suppliers and maintain contracts, seeking to cut costs in other areas. The relationship works both ways. When Mazda experienced difficulties in the 1970s, it benefited from suppliers extending credit for several months (Pascale and Rohlen, 1983). The 2013 clothing factory collapse in Bangladesh elicited an immediate response from some suppliers. Primark sent a team to Dhaka, established a worker compensation scheme, guaranteed salaries of existing workers for 3 months and liaised with trade unions and food agencies (Siegle 2013). There are also examples of major firms making life more difficult for suppliers. In 2014 the US food company Mars changed its payment policy to suppliers from 60 days to 120 days, with many smaller suppliers feeling that the impact on their cash flows would drive them out of business. When the Belgian brewer InBev took over the US firm Anheuser Busch, it changed unilaterally the payment terms from 30 days to up to 120 days. Similar changes have been made by Procter and Gamble and Johnson and Johnson (Schultz, 2014).

- **Competitors.** These are also seen as a group to whom the firm has a responsibility. Issues here relate to the abuse of monopoly power, aggressive promotional or pricing tactics or even dirty tricks in some cases. Much of the debate here involves the power of big business over smaller firms. Fishman (2006) examined the impact of Wal-Mart on other stores and noted that, since 1991, 27 supermarket chains that had been bankrupted in the USA cited Wal-Mart's growth as the main reason. The same author also cites studies that show that while competitors lose out, customers can save up to 15 per cent on their grocery bills by shopping at Wal-Mart and even benefit from price cuts in other stores as they respond to Wal-Mart's competition.

- **The community.** The relationship between firms and their local community can be significant. A big employer not only provides jobs for many people in the community, but indirectly supports the local housing market and provides revenue for shops and local services. In many parts of the world, a single firm dominates a community. This happens in such industries as mining, steel, shipbuilding and with some car plants. In such circumstances does the firm have a responsibility to the community to stay in business in that location? The effect on communities of coal mine closures in the UK in the 1980s has been significant, not just in terms of rising unemployment at a local level but in terms of the prosperity of other businesses, such as suppliers, outsourcers and local shops. Similar experiences have been noted in Poland and the Czech Republic. Some argue that the reliance of communities on single employers has diminished with increased geographical and labour mobility and community policies of economic diversity.

- **Society in general.** A company, its managers and employees must conform to prevailing social norms. However, we have already seen how these vary with cultural differences as well as over time. Moreover, there would seem to be a remarkable tolerance within society to a range of permissible business behaviour.

- **Government and the law.** In many cases, social norms are codified in law. In this way we have laws controlling the safety of products, permissible forms of advertising, the disclosure of financial information and conditions of employment. In addition, governments may set policies which it expects firms to follow. Such policies may restrict the firm doing business in certain countries, as was the case of many governments during apartheid in South Africa, or it may set voluntary limits on pay awards.

- **The environment.** Although not an individual or a group in the sense of the above, most believe that the firm has a responsibility not just to the environment in which it operates but also to the global environment. To many, this area is the most obvious and visible face of corporate social responsibility. It involves the environmental impact of the firm's activities and, as we shall see in subsequent sections, often carries the highest public profile, is used as a focus of public relations and carries the highest risk in terms of cost. For example, the oil spillage from the tanker Exxon Valdes is estimated to have cost Esso over US$7000 million in clean-up costs and compensation. More recently, there has been recognition that environmental concerns are global rather than local, as with the emission of greenhouse gases causing global warming. There is a clear emphasis on sustainability defined by the World Commission on Environment and Development (1987) as '(meeting) the needs of the present without compromising the ability of future generations to meet their needs'. This definition of sustainability was adopted by the United Nations.

- The Kyoto Summit of 1997 illustrates some of the dilemmas facing both firms and governments in acting responsibly towards the environment. The disagreements were between the USA, the EU countries and emerging industrial nations such as China and India. The EU nations favoured restricting the emission of greenhouse gases to the same level for all. Emerging economies, such as China, argued that such a proposal was unfair since it penalized poorer countries by forcing them into high-cost remedial action, when richer countries had been emitting greenhouse gases at unacceptable levels for decades. The USA argued that rich countries should give technological assistance to poorer nations and gain 'carbon credits' for so doing, which would count towards their reduction target. The debate is still ongoing.

As we can see from many of the illustrations above, there are problems with the stakeholder approach to corporate social responsibility, many of which are recurring themes throughout this chapter:

- Which groups have a legitimate right to be considered as stakeholders? Managers would probably have little difficulty identifying shareholders, customers, employees, suppliers and banks as stakeholders but how broad should the concern for social responsibility be?

- There are so many stakeholders that conflicts can and do arise with the conflicting priorities of different groups. Do consumers pay more to keep local workers in a job? Do banks forgo what is owed them so that suppliers can get paid? When such conflicts occur, which stakeholder has the priority?

- Many of the stakeholders, such as community groups and even shareholders and employees, represent very broad groups. Within each group there will be different needs, which are likely to set up conflicts.

- Satisfaction of the needs of stakeholders requires their representation in company affairs and adequate disclosure of information. In many cases, managers have shown reluctance to provide detailed information or allow involvement in decision-making.

- The stakeholder approach becomes even more complex in global companies, when the number of stakeholders is likely to multiply, as are the differences between them. In such situations companies either follow an ethical code of the home nation, irrespective of setting, or adopt a position of ethical relativism. For many years, firms in several countries did not trade with South Africa while apartheid was practised. US firms were prevented from trading with Vietnam for many years following the Vietnam war. Such ethical positions of the home nation were reinforced by legal sanctions imposed by the respective governments for transgressions. However, before China joined the WTO, many western and Japanese firms embraced the Chinese in joint ventures, despite expressing reservations about China's record on human rights violations. The argument used here could be one of ethical relativism and an acceptance of different practices in different societies. However, in some of these examples it could be a case of business goals superseding ethical goals.

REFLECTION POINT

Which groups can justifiably be included as stakeholders as far as CSR is concerned? Should any of the groups listed above NOT be considered?

HISTORICAL DEVELOPMENT OF ETHICAL CONCERNS IN BUSINESS

In the last section we noted how notions of ethical behaviour can change over time. In this section we examine the development of business ethics and corporate social responsibility, linking that development to prevailing philosophies, to political and economic decisions and to social trends.

- There are links with western Christian values but the growing importance of Islamic banking and its ethical stance on fairness demonstrates that ethical values are not confined to any single religion. In the UK, ethical approaches to business can be traced back to the early paternalism of Quaker employers such as Cadbury and Rowntree, although the focus was mainly on the treatment of employees. Many of these paternalistic employers established model villages to house their workers. One of the earliest was at Saltaire, around the textile mills of Titus Salt, near Bradford. Cadbury established Bournville and Lever, Port Sunlight.

- Such paternalism was threatened by the separation of ownership and control (see Chapter 6). The early paternalists were both owners and managers. The growth of the size of the firm with the emergence of the joint stock company created a new breed of 'professional' managers, with the need to keep shareholders happy.

- In the 20th century, concerns arose out of the growth of big business and the need to curb the power of large corporations, as with the anti-trust legislation in the USA, and as a reaction to the depression of the 1920s and 30s. Lobbying for improved terms and conditions at work arose from the growth of the trade union movement around the same period.

- The Bretton Woods Conference of 1944 was a response to the experience of two world wars and a global depression and the need to control the future global economy. Markets were seen as providing insufficient protection and both laws and institutions were needed. The conference set the scene for the development of the United Nations, the IMF and World Bank and associated organizations, most fairly central to ethical concerns with business.

- In the post-war era, interest in ethical business was related to the 1960s reaction to materialism, the activities of some multinationals in the Third World and increasing concern and publicity about pollution.

- In the 1970s the shock of oil price rises, and, in many countries, rising unemployment, poor outcomes of government intervention and problems related to industrial relations created a backlash with a renewed belief in the market. The political and economic ideologies of Margaret Thatcher in the UK and Ronald Reagan in the USA emphasized a self-regulating market. This in turn created its own backlash and placed business ethics back on the agenda.

- In the late 1980s and early 1990s business ethics entered the political agenda through issues related to globalization, sustainability and fears for the future of the planet. At the same time the public agenda was stimulated by increased news coverage of environmental and other issues. Consumer groups emerged demanding environmentally friendly products made by employees working under fair conditions.

- More recent concerns have focused on the collapse and associated scandals associated with firms such as Enron and Worldcom in the USA and Parmalat in Italy. In the USA, the fraudulent behaviour of large firms such as Enron led directly to legislation such as the Sarbanes-Oxley Act of 2002 to prevent such things happening again. More recently, attention has shifted to the ethics of paying large salaries and bonuses to the managers of failing companies. As we have seen in Chapters 3 and 7 the focus on the latter in 2009 has been very much on the banking sector.

REFLECTION POINT

Which contemporary factors do you feel have the greatest influence on a firm operating ethically?

WHY SHOULD BUSINESSES BE SOCIALLY RESPONSIBLE?

In this section we offer four perspectives: the moral argument; the business case; the strategic case; and a critical perspective.

The moral argument

The moral argument is based on the belief that business organizations have a responsibility for the public good. The argument has been summed up by Crane and Matten (2010) as follows:

- Organizatons are part of society and should therefore behave in a responsible manner as all good citizens should. An element of this involves treating stakeholders fairly.
- All activities of business have social effects. Firms use resources, they employ people, they provide essential and non-essential goods and services and they often support a network of suppliers and other types of activity such as local food outlets and shops.
- Business activity can and does cause problems. We have already noted examples of community and environmental disaster as in the cases of Bhopal and the Exxon Valdes and Case 9.1 examines the impact on a wide range of stakeholders of the collapse of Enron. Crane and Matten argue that solving such problems is of benefit to society.

There are links here with both Christian and Islamic principles. Indeed, most religions make assumptions about how business should be conducted. Such principles lie behind the activities of the early Quaker employers in the UK such as Cadbury and Rowntree and can be seen in the principles that underpin Islamic banking. The moral argument clearly guided such firms as Lush, the manufacturer and retailer of soaps and cosmetics embodies many of the values we associate with ethical business. The founder of the company began as a supplier of cosmetics to the Body Shop, an earlier embodiment of ethical business, that ultimately became part of the French cosmetic giant, L'Oréal, losing a good deal of its ethical image in the process. Lush was officially launched in 1994, extended its range of products and opened its first store in 1999. By 2014 it had over 900 stores in 50 countries, with 190 in the USA. It was voted the best UK high street store in the 2014 *Which* Magazine annual survey. All its products are handmade from natural ingredients and its uses no animal fats and has never used products that have been tested on animals. In 2014 it opened its first store in Brazil in São Paulo just after the São Paulo state government had banned animal testing. Lush employs a maximum salary gap of 17 to 1 between the highest and lowest paid. The company invests 2 per cent of money spent on raw materials in the communities that supply them, as is the case with small collectives of aloe growers in Kenya. The company regularly donates to anti-aviation, animal rights and anti-fracking groups and has campaigned for the release of Guantanamo Bay prisoners.

However, many would argue that ethical principles and corporate social responsibility are not incompatible with being a successful business by making profit.

The business argument

For business managers, government officials, academics, consultants to name but a few, making the business case has become the Holy Grail. There is a simple reason for this: demonstrating a positive correlation between corporate responsibility and business performance (especially financial performance) is seen as giving social and environmental issues legitimacy in the world of mainstream business.

(Blowfield and Murray, 2011, p. 131).

Ethical business is profitable business

A few years ago, Nike linked its worsening financial performance to a fall in sales, which it attributed directly to well-publicized allegations of the mistreatment of workers in its operations in developing countries. In particular, a *New York Times* account of Nike's use of child labour in Indonesia resulted in protests and boycotts of Nike products.

We summarize the reasons put forward to support the claim that ethical business is good for business and examine a number of arguments related to bad publicity, costs, the involvement of governments and the potential benefits in using ethical suppliers and in attracting ethical investors and employees:

- Blowfield and Murray (2011) cite cases of major companies such as Ford, Dupont, Dow and Phillips where their focus on energy saving has had a major impact on costs.
- Ethical business gains favour with consumers, gives them satisfaction and is likely to result in repeat purchases.
- The highlighting of corporate social responsibility attracts the interest of the media. The coverage attracted is not only good public relations, but may be more effective than costly advertising campaigns.
- In the same way, the branding of goods as 'ethical' or 'socially responsible' is good public relations and can lead to greater awareness and increased sales. Increased sales can mean increased profits.
- There is the argument of long-term self-interest that ethical behaviour is conducive to good performance. For example, numerous studies of motivation have shown that if workers are paid minimum wages and have to work in poor conditions then the quantity and quality of their output will fall.

However, with most of these points there are problems of measurement and correlation. In addition there is the presence of strong countervailing forces. Many managers face considerable pressure to cut costs to stay competitive and to focus on profit, growth and dividend. Such pressures can push ethical issues into the background.

Attracting bad publicity

While good practice in corporate social responsibility can attract publicity that is good for business, companies can attract bad publicity and become the target of action groups such as Greenpeace. We have already noted the impact on Nike of articles in the *New York Times*. There was considerable adverse publicity directed at major clothing retailers and their use of low cost manufacturers in developing countries following the factory collapse in Bangladesh. Shell suffered a particularly bad press over its attempt to dispose of Brent Spar, a North Sea oil platform, in deep water in the North Sea. The company admitted that, whatever the rights and wrongs of the issue, it could have been better handled.

The cost argument

Cutting energy usage can both reduce costs and demonstrate responsibility towards the environment. The costs of not behaving responsibly can also be considerable. It is claimed that 22 per cent of the total operating costs of Amoco are attributable to environmental costs (Thomas and Eyres, 1998). The oil spillage from the tanker Exxon Valdes cost Esso a reported US$7250 million. The tragedy at Bhopal cost Union Carbide an estimated US$4700 million. Civil actions over the loss of life resulting from accidents in Ford Pinto cars cost Ford US$250 million, although had the actions been taken today the sum would have been considerably higher. The cost to Ford was not just in civil action. All Ford Pinto cars built and sold in 1971–76 were recalled and had their petrol tanks refitted at considerable cost to the company. It is interesting to note that the case arose from a company decision that a change in the design at a late stage in the development of the car would be too expensive.

Government influence

There are increasing government pressures on firms to conform to national and international standards on social and environmental matters. The UK government launched an ethical trading initiative, and an international standard, SA 8000, covers such areas as working hours and the use of child labour. In some cases the pressures are backed by legislation. There are links here to the cost argument for ethical business, in that failure to comply with laws on pollution or conditions of employment may result in prosecution and subsequent fines. There is also a view that, when cases are brought, courts are more lenient if a strong ethical stance has been demonstrated by the company. Another view of the relationship with governments suggests that firms that operate ethically not only gain the support of governments but also achieve greater independence by keeping governments 'at arm's length'.

The ethical supply chain

To do business with some companies, such as Toys 'R' Us, Timberland and Levi Strauss, suppliers must comply with a code of ethical conduct. There is also a belief that doing business ethically attracts both buyers and suppliers. In broader terms, the relationship between buyer and supplier has become an important ingredient of business success, especially in manufacturing. An important element in that relationship is trust and the need to behave openly and honourably towards each other.

Ethical consumers

Wilson (1997) argues that, even during a recession, there are consumers who seek out goods and services that are both environmentally friendly and have been produced ethically. He cites the example of the Cooperative Bank, which announced that it would not be involved with tobacco companies, firms with poor environmental records or those engaged in factory farming and animal testing. As a result, the bank claimed an increase in the number of new accounts. In 2014 the same bank was losing customers as a result of accusations of poor management decision-making and the arrest of a former chairman on drugs charges, Research by Mintel (1994) demonstrated that consumers were willing to pay more for ethical products.

Ethical investors

Such investors seek out ethical companies in which to invest, and some investment companies have responded by establishing investment portfolios of ethical companies. In general, ethical investors view companies in either positive or negative terms. Investment opportunities frequently viewed as negative include firms involved in pornography, tobacco, gambling and those with a history of using child labour. Stock markets have responded. FTSE4Good was established in the UK in 2001. The listing excludes companies involved in tobacco, defence and nuclear power but includes oil companies and airlines (to the dismay of some in the environmental lobby). To be included in FTSE4Good, companies must demonstrate that they are working towards environmental sustainability, that they are developing positive relations with stakeholders and that they uphold and support universal human rights. These are broad and somewhat vague criteria. In the USA, the Dow Jones Sustainability index, established in 1999, lists companies that have demonstrated a positive attitude towards 'good' corporate social responsibility with special reference to the environment.

However, there are difficulties. Who decides which company is ethical and which is not, and on what criteria? Many investors lack detailed knowledge of the ethical code and behaviour of the companies in which they seek to invest and focus on financial performance as a priority.

Ethical employees

In general terms, most firms will seek to establish some sort of match between corporate values and those of employees to gain commitment from them and to retain their services. Many firms use induction and employee development programmes to reinforce corporate values. Employees are clearly attracted by fair pay, security of employment and benefits such as travel season ticket loans and child-care provisions. There is some evidence to suggest that an ethical stance taken by an employer contributes towards the job satisfaction of its employees (Koh and Boo, 2001). Equally firms have noted an increase in job seekers who are concerned about ethical issues and social responsibility. Many firms now highlight such issues in their recruitment literature. Shell identifies seven principles, which address financial, economic and social goals within an ethical framework. The company recognizes that it has a responsibility to shareholders, customers, employees, those with whom they do business and society at large. Shell and other firms seek both ethical and socially responsible behaviour and profit-seeking behaviour.

REFLECTION POINT

Is ethical business profitable business?
  Do most people consider the ethical position of a company in buying goods and services or in making a job choice?

The strategic argument

The business case for ethical business is further strengthened and expanded by a strategic argument. Many of the points put forward under the business argument use cost, or the avoidance of costs, as a theme. The strategic argument is more positive and, perhaps, offers a more persuasive argument for managers. Writers such as McWilliams, Siegel and Wright (2006) and Porter and Kramer (2006, 2011) argue that ethical business and CSR can be sources of competitive advantage and a strategic investment.

In particular, Porter and Kramer (2006) argue that many companies view CSR as a form of cost, when if viewed strategically it can be a source of benefit both to the company and to society.

The same authors question the response of many companies, where CSR is confined to press releases and glossy brochures, which cite isolated examples and sketch over mainstream activities that add little to the CSR agenda. They argue that the corporate response is often inadequate, fragmented, uncoordinated and tends to focus on the tension between business and society. In their later article they argue that business mistakenly seeks short-term solutions to competition by shifting jobs overseas, ignoring the needs of customers and depleting natural resources. They also blame governments for ignoring the business community in finding solutions to social problems (Porter and Kramer, 2011). They conclude that, as a result, both business and society lose out. Porter and Kramer (2006, 2011) see effective and strategic CSR as:

- Integrating the needs of business and society to benefit both. In their second article they introduce the principle of 'shared value', where economic value for the company creates value for society,

- Prioritizing issues that mean something to the company. While the Aids pandemic in Africa is a global human tragedy, in business terms it has a greater relevance for some firms more than others. In the case of GlaxoSmithKline, the development of effective drugs to combat Aids enhances the profitability of the company while at the same time offering society a solution to a problem. In the case of Anglo-American Mining, a solution to the problems caused by Aids will also tackle labour shortages caused by the disease.

- Choosing a unique position that goes beyond the normal response to offer a competitive advantage. The authors offer examples to illustrate this point. Toyota has become the world market leader in hybrid cars through developing the Prius. As well as offering environmental benefits, Toyota has a competitive advantage and not only gains profit from sales but also through licensing the technology to companies such as Ford. The French bank Credit Agricole differentiated itself by offering financial products linked to environmental measures such as special deals for energy saving projects and for organic farming. This attracted business to the bank. Nestlé works with local communities in developing countries to source milk, coffee and cocoa, offering both a competitive advantage to the company and benefiting the community.

- Following on from their examples above, they feel that the demand for products that meet social needs is growing. They feel that both companies and society can gain significantly by businesses 'reconceiving products and markets' (Porter and Kramer, 2011). One of their key examples is General Electric (GE) and its range of 'Ecomagination' products with sales of US$8 billion in 2009. GE's corporate website defines these as products that are 'creating value for customers, investors and society by helping them solve energy, efficiency and water challenges' (www.ge.com/uk/company/ecomagination). GE have developed products such as: energy efficient air-conditioning units, dishwashers and washing machines for the home; more efficient and effective digital X-ray and ultrasound systems for hospitals; and at the country level, desalination plants and energy efficient locomotive systems now used in Brazil, China and Kazakhstan. Both Porter and Kramer (2011) and Crane, Matten and Spence (2014) cite the example where, in both developed and developing markets, there are opportunities to develop products for lower income markets such as lower priced cell phones. Vodafone with 65 per cent of their customers in emerging markets saw the opportunity to make money and have a social impact. In Africa they launched 'mHealth' using their cell phone network to provide remote medical assistance in 26 countries, backed up by a system for tracking and monitoring the supply of medicines. Also using their cell phone system they introduced 'M-Pesa' which offers a range of financial services including paying suppliers and wages where people do not have a bank account. In higher income markets like New Zealand, Vodafone has developed a system for the remote monitoring of gas, electricity and water usage.

- Porter and Kramer (2011) also feel that much more can be done through 'redefining productivity' in the value chain. Costs can be saved by redesigning supply and delivery transport
networks, by sharing technology with suppliers instead of exploiting them, and by reducing
energy costs across the whole supply chain, all of which can reduce overall environmental
impact, improve quality and reduce costs for everyone. They also see productivity increases
stemming from greater concern for the health and safety of employees and their working
conditions. Johnson & Johnson reduced time off work by employees by launching an initiative to help them quit smoking. Many UK supermarkets now make a small feature of locally
grown food stuffs thereby boosting local economies and cutting back on transport costs.

The critical perspective

In previous sections we have noted difficulties and potential dilemmas facing managers wishing
to operate ethically and in a socially responsible way. In this section we reinforce those points by
identifying arguments, problems and issues.

The alternative debate

Several authors have questioned the need for an ethical debate at all. Levitt (1958) wrote about
the dangers of social responsibility and argued that it was the government's responsibility via the
law and not that of business. Friedman (1970) challenges the business case for ethical operations
as identified above by re-interpreting it as the use of ethical arguments to support profit maximization, which he saw as the primary purpose of business. He believed that the real social benefit
of business was in its wealth creation and that any other concern was not in the best interests
of the shareholders. However, Friedman also believed that managers should operate within the
law and adhere to basic social norms. More forthright views than Friedman were expressed by
Carr (1968). He compared business with a poker game and even a Wild West shoot-out, where
ethics mattered less than winning. He felt that managers could separate business and private life
in terms of behaving ethically. Both perspectives are the products of a traditional US view of
the sanctity of the free market and, like Levitt, favour the use of law to police the transgressors.

The misuse of resource argument

Friedman (1970) argued that CSR was a misuse of resources that should be aimed at maximizing
shareholder value. This view was upheld many years earlier in US law in the landmark case of
Dodge v *Ford Motor* in a ruling of the Michigan Supreme Court in 1919. Ford wished to withhold dividend from shareholders, and were taken to court by Dodge who owned shares in Ford.
However the court ruled that the corporation exists for the sole benefit of its shareholders and
concerns for other groups were not relevant.

Ethical behaviour is no more than good management practice

If a company enhances the attractiveness of the product by stressing its environmental credentials or changes its practices to avoid being taken to court, does this represent a change in the
ethical values of the company or is it a strategy aimed at profit and shareholder value maximization? Has business ethics simply jumped on the bandwagon of sound business practice?
In Chapter 12 we examine the growth of relationship marketing which focuses on the benefits
of a close relationship with customers to understand their needs. Is this driven by corporate
social responsibility to a significant stakeholder or is it a means of increasing sales by enhancing
customer satisfaction? Is paying employees a fair wage and providing them with good working

conditions an ethical initiative or good motivational management and sound HR practice? Karnani (2010) takes this argument a stage further. He believes that fuel efficient cars and healthier foods were not popular with business until they became profitable and that energy conservation only became an issue when energy costs rose to unacceptable levels.

Business creates conflicts

These conflicts are incompatible with doing business ethically. For example, business is based on the relationship between buyers and sellers, each of whom want the best deal for themselves. In Chapter 11 we identify the dilemma of operations management, whereby firms seek the lowest cost operation, which conflicts with the customer need for quality goods and services at a competitive price.

Weak evidence

We have indicated that it is difficult to prove that concern for ethical business and social responsibility will improve the performance of the company. In supermarkets we are confronted by products claiming 'fair trade' and 'ethical sourcing', yet such claims are difficult to prove. Social damage and business benefits are difficult to quantify and for every study claiming a connection there is another offering a more sceptical perspective.

- Margolis and Walsh (2003) examined over 100 studies carried out between 1972 and 2002 on the relationship between CSR and corporate financial performance. They identified a positive relationship in 50 per cent of studies, a negative relationship in 6 per cent and inconclusive findings in the remaining 44 per cent. This study seems to be cited both by those seeking to prove a positive relationship and by those who are more sceptical. The sceptics are quick to point out the methodological shortcomings of many of the studies.

- Verschoor (1998) did a study of the USA Fortune 500 companies with a management commitment to ethical and socially responsible business, which was backed up by practices. He found a statistical relationship between such practices and the financial performance of the company.

- Van der Merwe et al. (2003) argued from their research finding that whereas those companies whose performance was excellent had strong ethical codes and practices, there were other companies that had such codes where performance was anything but excellent. Having ethical codes was not a guarantee of excellent performance. Many companies possessing such codes and practices did not perform well at all. In our discussion of corporate culture, in Chapter 6, we made a similar comment in suggesting that strong cultures were the products of success rather than the other way around. Firms that are performing well have the luxury and financial capacity to engage in social responsibility programmes.

- Brammer and Millington (2008) identify the difficulties of such studies in terms of the inability to define the determinants of CSR and the problems of establishing clear links with performance. Their study examined the financial performance of 500 large UK firms over 10 years and linked this with philanthropic donations as a measure of CSR. The findings were inconclusive. Certainly those firms that made the largest donations were among the most financially successful. However, this was a position they shared with those firms making the least donation.

However most of the studies look at the relationship between CSR and measures of financial performance. Few examine other impacts such as those on customer satisfaction or employee commitment.

REFLECTION POINT

What measures would you use to establish a link between ethical business and the performance of the firm?

Structural barriers

Many firms operate in highly competitive markets with demanding shareholders. Under such conditions the pressures on managers to cut costs and maximize profit are considerable. However, there is evidence to suggest that cutting costs can lead to problems. In the three cases we have mentioned – Ford Pinto, Union Carbide (Bhopal) and Esso (Exxon Valdes) – the resulting problems were partly the result of attempts to cut costs.

How widespread is the concern?

While awareness and acceptance are widespread among large firms like Daimler-Benz and Shell, there are still many traditional managers who still believe there to be a conflict between ethical business and profitable business. This is particularly true among small businesses. In many firms, changing entrenched attitudes is difficult and takes time.

Ethics as a sham

In some cases, the greening of products has been a marketing ploy, and consumers are deliberately misled into thinking they are buying a 'green' product when this is not the case. Some commentators refer to this as 'greenwash'. In the section on corporate culture in Chapter 6, we illustrate how some firms use values, not as a means of involving employees, but as a way of controlling them. Many companies are fond of stating in their literature that 'employees are our most valuable asset' when employment conditions and work practices would suggest otherwise. The fast-food chain McDonald's has been at the centre of much criticism both for its attitude to the environment and to its employees.

If not a sham, then many companies may be accused of sending out messages that appear to conflict with their business goals. Philip Morris International, one of the world's leading tobacco manufacturers with brands such as Marlboro and Chesterfield, makes the following statements on its website in 2009:

> *We are driven to create the best possible returns for shareholders, while proactively engaging regulators and the public health community to address the complex issues surrounding tobacco use.*
>
> *For us responsibility begins with the product. That is why we are committed to communicating about the health risks of smoking in an open and transparent way and supporting the regulation of tobacco wherever our products are sold.*
>
> *We recognize and acknowledge that we manufacture a product that is addictive and causes serious disease. That is why we openly communicate about the health risks of smoking in an open and transparent way and supporting the regulation of tobacco wherever our products are sold.*
>
> *Cigarette smoking is addictive. It can be very difficult to quit but, if you are a smoker, this shouldn't stop you from trying to do so.*

REFLECTION POINT

What conclusions do you draw from these extracts from the Philip Morris website?

High cost

In some cases, the costs of environmentally friendly business can result in unacceptably high prices. There may also be contradictions. For example, in car manufacture, the switch from solvent-based to water-based paint is better in terms of the environment, yet it increases drying time and, with it, energy consumption that both pushes up the cost and is environmentally unfriendly. In 2009, the UK government backed the continued development of the electric car, yet critics have claimed that the environmental and financial costs involved in the manufacture of the battery and the use of electricity are greater than for those cars using petrol.

What happens when ethical businesses change ownership?

Walsh (2006) believes that relatively small companies with a reputation for ethical business are in danger of being taken over by large multinational concerns. For the multinational this is an opportunity to buy into an ethical agenda. However, Walsh poses the question whether such firms can operate comfortably within a global corporation and cites Body Shop's take-over by L'Oréal, Green and Black becoming part of Cadbury Schweppes, which in turn became part of the Kraft Foods empire, and Ben and Jerry's ice-cream being taken over by Unilever. She notes that in most cases the rating of the ethical credentials of such companies falls dramatically after takeover.

Cultural variations

Different standards, both legal and cultural, apply in different parts of the world. Firms that operate in many markets may have the increased cost of ensuring their products meet the requirements of each country. Products that can be legally sold in one market may be illegal in another, as with hand-guns, legal in the USA but not the UK.

Stakeholder differences

Different stakeholders may have different requirements as we have seen in our section on corporate social responsibility. In the Brent Spar case, the dumping of the oil platform by Shell was acceptable to the UK government, but opposed by some other European countries, such as Germany, and environmental groups, such as Greenpeace.

Such problems as the above create dilemmas for managers in their attempts to pursue an ethical business strategy. Survival of the most ethical of companies depends on achieving financial targets. In 1999, many believed that the Body Shop stood at the crossroads. Its business performance left much to be desired and the company underwent restructure. This involved bringing in fresh blood, but also making people redundant, including the closure of its manufacturing operations. Optimists believed the company's ethical stance would emerge yet stronger and its reliance on a wider group of suppliers would see its value spread to other companies. Pessimists feared that the company would become just another company, undifferentiated from its competitors in its unique ethical stance. As we have seen, the company was subsequently sold to the French multinational cosmetic firm, L'Oréal.

So can business be ethical?

In this section we have explored argument and counter-argument about the relationship between business and ethics and whether or not corporate social responsibility as carried out by many firms is genuine. There is strong evidence that companies are more environmentally aware, especially when it comes to cutting energy costs. Studies linking CSR with financial performance have more mixed results. More positive evidence comes out of the articles of Porter and Kramer

(2006, 2011), which argue that there is profit to be made by focusing corporate strategy on solving society's problems. Blowfield and Murray (2011) offer a more optimistic scenario. They see an increase in the number of companies producing non-financial reports relating primarily to their CSR activities. They see a marked change in attitude of senior managers in companies such as Nike and Wal-Mart, companies that have been heavily criticized in the past for their apparent lack of ethics. They cite the case of successful companies such as Marks and Spencer adopting a holistic approach to CSR that embraces employee health and working conditions, supply chain management, climate change and sustainability. They see lead firms having an influence across their sectors and across their supply chains.

In the next section we examine mechanisms that can be used by organizations to promote and ensure ethical behaviour and social responsibility.

Mechanisms for ethical business and social responsibility

Strategically, in terms of ethical business and social responsibility managers may operate at any point along a continuum, as we can see from Figure 9.1.

There are several mechanisms a firm may use:

- **Ethical audit.** An important foundation to behaving ethically is for management to carry out an audit of all the firm's activities and relationships to assess shortfalls in practice and to establish action plans. Areas for the ethical audit include products and services, processes, terms of employment and conditions for employees and the firm's relationships with its suppliers, local community and the environment. Issues may be raised about the safety of products and processes, how customers are treated before, during and after sales, how employees are treated, and so on.

- **Codes of practice.** These outline the firm's stand on ethical business in terms of a mission. Most codes also contain policy and operational manuals that attempt to establish appropriate decisions and courses of action in specific circumstances as, for example, with the receiving of gifts from potential customers. Such codes of practice exist not only for employees but also for suppliers. For example, Levi Strauss, Reebok and Nike all challenged the practices of some of their suppliers in Asia and refused to do business with those where there was evidence of the use of forced labour and/or child labour. As a result,

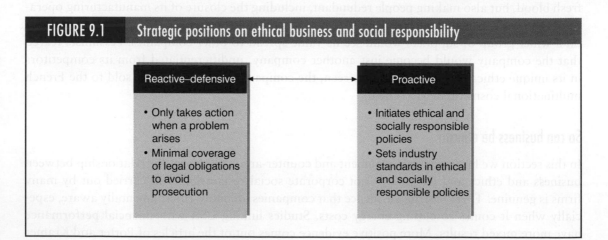

FIGURE 9.1	Strategic positions on ethical business and social responsibility

Reactive–defensive

- Only takes action when a problem arises
- Minimal coverage of legal obligations to avoid prosecution

Proactive

- Initiates ethical and socially responsible policies
- Sets industry standards in ethical and socially responsible policies

Levi Strauss established a code of practice for suppliers on employment practices, pay and health and safety.

- The growth of global business has led to the publication of international codes by such organizations as OECD and ILO, and the UN Commission on Transnational Corporations. Such codes cover a broad range of issues dealing with human rights and work practices. These include statements about the disclosure of financial information, levels of pay, the right of employees to unionize and the length of the working week. Despite publication of such codes by many organizations, little is known about their impact on employee behaviour or the firm's activities. While such codes exist, it is reckoned that knowledge and application of them is far from widespread within individual organizations.

- **Ethics department.** Some organizations have institutionalized ethics and social responsibility within their structure. In 1980, the World Bank established an ethics function and a few years later incorporated it as the ethics office within the HR department. Since 1990 it has operated as a standalone department and has developed an ethical toolkit to assist decision-making in different cultural settings wherever the bank operates. A separate department was established in 1997, the department of institutional integrity, with the task of investigating and advising on fraud and corruption in bank projects (Johnson, 2002). Some companies appoint an ethical officer, whose primary role, in many cases, is to assist the firm to achieve one or more of the international standards identified above.

- **Company reports.** In the 1980s, companies began to include ethical and CSR issues in their company reports and this led to separate reports focusing on such issues. The belief is that such reporting mechanisms will be based on some kind of audit and guide the company in its future actions. However, there is a danger that such reports become a 'glossy sham'.

- **Employee induction and training.** For many firms this is an important mechanism for transmitting values and practices about ethical business and corporate social responsibility. Employees joining a Korean corporation, such as Samsung, Hyundai and LG, will begin their employment with up to three weeks' induction, which focuses on the values of the organization, including their commitment to social responsibility (Needle, 2000).

- **Whistleblowing.** Some firms, such as the World Bank, have set up whistleblowing hotlines. Employees may phone in, without fear of reprisal, to report any practice or incident where members of the company have been behaving unethically. Such mechanisms are not always popular with staff. In Case 5.1, we noted that Wal-Mart employees in Germany were reluctant to use whistleblowing as a mechanism to inform on fellow employees.

- **Non-executive directors.** The theory behind the appointment of non-executive directors is that they have no direct involvement in the management of the enterprise and are able to provide experience from elsewhere and can operate as an impartial voice in influencing strategic direction. As people with an interest outside the organization, they are often considered as an important agent of social responsibility. The Higgs Report in the UK on the role and effectiveness of nonexecutive directors sees their function in terms of:
  - widening diversity of board membership to prevent corrupting practices;
  - providing critical and independent thinking in board level decision-making;
  - providing a vehicle for the greater shareholder access to the board.

  However, the independence of non-executive directors has been questioned. They have to be closely involved in the workings of the company to be able to offer any critical input.

This means they must work closely with management, making it more difficult to maintain distance and retain independence. Moreover, many are appointed because they are well-known to executive directors, thereby compromising their potential for independence still further. The Higgs Report noted that only 4 per cent of non-executive directors were formally interviewed before appointment.

- **Implicit mechanisms.** In addition to the explicit mechanisms identified above, there are more implicit measures to champion ethical practice. These operate through corporate culture, management leadership, performance appraisal and incentive schemes. For example, ethical business and socially responsible practice could be part of employee job descriptions and form an important factor upon which performance is judged.

CASE 9.1   ENRON

Enron was founded in 1985 as the result of a merger between Houston Natural Gas and InterNorth, both relatively small regional companies in the USA. The chairman of the new company was Kenneth Lay, who remained in post until Enron's bankruptcy in 2001. The company grew rapidly and had become by the 1990s, the largest energy trading company in the world and the USA's seventh-largest company. Every year from 1996–2001 the company was ranked by *Fortune* magazine as the 'most innovative company' in the USA. Between 1996 and 2000 sales value increased from US$13.3 billion to US$100.8 billion. The company was praised by Wall Street and the White House alike. Enron's growth generated considerable wealth for both investors and employees, more especially a small number of senior staff, some later accused of fraud.

Enron portrayed itself as a highly competitive, global business, strongly in favour of the free market and deregulation. It also portrayed itself as a socially responsible organization through its concern for the environment (it had won awards in the USA and in other countries and supported the Kyoto summit on greenhouse gas emissions), its involvement in local communities (it donated generously to schools) and its activities in the developing world (it saw itself as contributing to raised living standards). The company was also keen to stress its empowerment of the workforce in that employees at every level were encouraged to put forward ideas that contributed to the growth of the business. Employees were rewarded handsomely for profitable ideas.

In December 2001, the company filed for bankruptcy with debts of US$15 billion. Later reports estimated a much larger debt of US$23 billion. At the time this was the biggest bankruptcy in US history, a distinction taken over by WorldCom some eight months later. The demise of Enron was responsible for the bringing down of Arthur Andersen, one of the world's leading accounting firms.

What did Enron do?

Enron was engaged in a range of activities:

- Enron built pipelines, gas plants and power stations around the world.

- The company diversified into a range of products, including water, petrochemicals, steel, paper, plastics, shipping and weather risk management.

- Although the company was highly diversified on paper, its core business and the source of its greatest revenue came from the energy industry and more especially energy trading. It benefited from the deregulation of the energy and utilities industries (those providing energy and water, among other things, to the public) in many countries. As a result, Enron was able to expand rapidly in the 1980s. The company sold energy to industries and utilities in the USA and elsewhere. More significantly, it sold contracts to deliver natural gas, electricity and other energy products at some date in the future.

- To support the sale of energy in the future, Enron developed and sold financial instruments to its customers, designed to protect them against large shifts in energy prices. These instruments are known as derivatives in that they are derived from an asset or a product. Their purpose is to allow companies to offset financial risk. The two types of derivative in this case were futures and options. A future is a contract which places an obligation to buy or sell at a set price on a given future date. An option is similar to a future except that the contract offers the right, but not the obligation.

- Enron invested in other activities and business, many of them, particularly in the years preceding bankruptcy, unrelated to its core business of energy.

Enron was one of the first companies to take advantage of Internet trading through the creation of Enrononline. Internet business was considerable so that, in the first quarter of 2001 alone, the company was involved in US$27 billion worth of transactions online. Such volume boosted Enron's rising share price and its appeal to investors and the US government.

By 1999, Enron was involved in a quarter of all natural gas and electricity deals in the world and the company had large operations in Brazil, India and the UK. In the UK, Enron had bought Wessex Water, power stations on Teesside and was one of the largest traders on the London Metals Exchange. In all, the company employed over 20 000 people, 5000 in Europe, 4000 of them in the UK.

To many commentators, Enron was not an energy company in the traditional sense. The company had capitalized, not only on the deregulation of the energy industry, but also upon deregulation and product innovation in the financial markets. In particular, it made a large proportion of its income from derivatives. The complexity of many of these financial products and associated deals meant that Enron's finances were difficult to unravel and even senior employees were not aware of the full extent of the dealing.

Important people and organization culture

Kenneth Lay as the founder and chairman (a role he combined with that of chief executive following Skilling's resignation) was the central figure throughout. A friend of George W. Bush from the latter's time as governor of Texas, Lay was involved in advising Bush on his elevation to the White House and Enron was a major contributor to the Bush presidential election campaign.

Jeffrey Skilling was an ex-McKinsey energy consultant. He joined Enron in 1990 and became chief executive in 1996. He helped move Enron aggressively into the energy trading and derivatives markets and championed the move into non-core businesses such as broadband. Skilling resigned in 2001 as the scandal was about to break.

Andrew Fastow was the finance chief. He was a key player in moving assets and debts out of the core business into other companies Enron had created. It is estimated that 3500 such companies were created as part of a 'structured finance' strategy. The financial information, much of which would be damaging to Enron, was effectively hidden and off the Enron balance sheet. This made Enron appear to be in a much better position than it was and kept the share price artificially high. Some of the companies were given interesting names, like Raptor, and one, LJM, was run by Fastow. Fastow was close to decision makers in banks and persuaded them to invest heavily in both Enron and these off-balance sheet companies, including LJM. Fastow was dismissed in 2001 following disclosures by one of his staff to Lay.

Lay and Skilling led a macho culture that pervaded senior staff and traders at Enron. Traders in particular were given plenty of freedom and were encouraged to be creative and take risks. Some of the dealings were highly questionable but traders gained large bonuses for profitable business. The macho culture was present in the performance review system. This was a forced distribution rating system where at least 10 per cent of staff each year had to be given the lowest rating. Those with the lowest rating were dismissed.

Lay and Skilling were instrumental in maintaining excellent PR for the company, even on the brink of bankruptcy. They saw the benefits in a good relationship with government figures (including the president), politicians, bankers, Wall Street analysts, and journalists. As a result, Enron was favoured by government, banks, Wall Street and the press.

What went wrong?

The collapse of Enron happened in a matter of months. In a few weeks, between October and November 2001, the share price fell by 90 per cent

(Continued)

and by the end of November three independent credit rating agencies considered Enron to be worthless. Around that time a rescue attempt was made by a smaller, rival energy company, Dynegy. This ended when Dynegy withdrew, claiming that Enron had misrepresented its financial position and its position was far worse than Dynegy had thought.

The market was alerted when Skilling suddenly resigned as the chief executive of Enron in August 2001. Lay, the chairman, took over the role. From October 2001, a number of factors came together which led to the bankruptcy of Enron. Sherron Watkins, an executive vice-president in Fastow's department, sent a memo to Lay, warning him of irregularities in Fastow's deals. She said in the memo: 'I am incredibly nervous that we will implode in a wave of accounting scandals.' Soon afterwards, Fastow was dismissed.

There have been many accusations of fraudulent behaviour and a number of senior Enron executives were tried over four years. Fastow, his wife and seven other executives were in the first group accused on charges of fraud, insider trading and the falsification of accounting records.

However, throughout, the company maintained that it had always operated legally and had simply taken advantage, as had many other companies, of the complexities of the newly deregulated markets in both energy and finance. Several investigating teams have been brought in since bankruptcy, including PriceWaterhouseCoopers. None of the teams has been able to sort out the complexities of Enron's dealings. The following attempts to give a flavour of Enron's 'wrongdoings':

- In essence, Enron had inflated its earnings through the use of dubious accounting procedures. For example, it included in its accounts derivative contracts at gross rather than net value.

- Enron took advantage of innovations in financial instruments, notably derivatives, to manipulate earnings and avoid regulation. These activities were known to the firm's consultants and auditors, Arthur Andersen, and by Wall Street investment banks.

- Enron's staff exploited the deregulated energy and derivatives markets to the full. They became involved in increasingly complex deals with networks of companies (over 3500 were linked to

Enron in some way) as well as banks. Incentives given to staff to make such deals led to yet more deals, and even some senior managers were not aware of what was happening. The company was unable to control its staff. Fastow's department was central to this process, as were companies such as LJM.

- Enron was borrowing heavily to finance many of its deals. The debts incurred by this borrowing were 'hidden' in companies and did not appear on Enron's balance sheet. This process artificially inflated the value of the company and drove up the share price. This was also a key factor in Enron's demise. The company conceded that it had not fully met accounting requirements and, as a result, was forced to reduce its equity by US$1.2 billion. This led to a fall in share price and a loss of confidence in the company.

- In 2001, the state of California was hit by 38 power blackouts. The whole state was affected for some of the time. The cost to businesses was estimated at around US$30 billion as well as irritating millions of private customers. The blackouts were a product of a poorly constructed deregulation that gave all the power to the energy providers and saw prices rise. In effect, power companies operated as a cartel and charged what they liked. Moreover, there was evidence that the companies were manipulating the supply, causing blackouts and then raising the price. El Paso, a major supplier, was found guilty of such practices. Enron was one of a number of firms, including Dynegy, accused.

- The company made highly speculative and ultimately poor investments, many of them not connected with energy, its core business. Many of these investments were 'buried' in subsidiary companies and not declared on the balance sheet.

- In the weeks around the declaration of bankruptcy, older accusations resurfaced. These included accusations of human rights violations against protesters at the building of a power station in Dabhol, India. Amnesty International became involved in the case of the protesters and the World Bank had publicly criticized the cost of the project. Also in India, Enron had been involved in a political corruption scandal concerned with the privatization of energy supply.

- Just before bankruptcy, 286 senior staff received bonuses totalling US$72 million. The company argued that the bonuses were to ensure that key staff stayed with them during difficult times. A group representing redundant Enron workers and those that had lost their pension took out a lawsuit to recover the money for the pension fund.

The effect of Enron's bankruptcy

Ultimately, the Enron scandal involved both the White House and the UK government. Senior White House staff had talks with Enron during 2001, but the details were not disclosed. Similarly, in the UK, Enron held talks with the Blair government in 1998–2000. The former Conservative energy minister, Lord Wakeham, was a non-executive director of the company and the ex-Europe chairman, Ralph Hodge, was favoured in the UK New Year Honours. It is clear that Enron sought political protection, although the Bush administration has distanced itself from such corporate scandals and introduced revised laws on pensions and disclosure of financial information.

With the collapse of the share price, many investors lost considerable amounts. These investors included many employees, who had been encouraged to back their own company, particularly in view of its remarkable rise. Many of these employees were prevented from selling their shares before the collapse of the company. Some senior employees, however, did sell their shares before the worst of the collapse, attracting accusations of insider trading. For example, Skilling was found by the court to have sold shares worth US$63 million in the 18 months before the collapse of the company. Many of those same employees not only saw their share investments rendered worthless, they lost their jobs and they lost their pensions. Over 20 000 employees are estimated to have lost US$1 billion in a pension fund tied to Enron stock.

Financial institutions lost money and many lost reputation. Credit Lyonnais had US$250 million tied up with Enron. JP Morgan Chase and Citigroup between them agreed to pay US$255 million to settle charges of helping Enron commit fraud. The

money will be paid into the pension fund. Most of the world's big banks were keen to gain from Enron's success. They vied for business and made money from fees and interest payments associated with Enron's acquisitions and loans. The creditors believe these same banks assisted Enron in questionable deals and many are being pursued through the courts.

The case of Arthur Andersen

Arthur Andersen was one of the 'big five' global accounting firms and employed 85 000 people. Andersen was both a consultant to Enron, with a contract worth US$50 million a year, and also acted as Enron's auditors. The whole Enron case highlighted a debate within the accounting profession and governments: that of the independence of auditors. The main argument is that firms which act as both consultants and auditors are likely to be compromised in their auditing duties by their close association with companies, especially where high fees are involved, as with Enron.

The Houston office of Andersen admitted to destroying documents relating to the Enron case. Staff members were disciplined and the partner responsible was dismissed. More significantly, in June 2002, Andersen was found guilty in a Houston court of obstructing justice. The verdict meant that Andersen was not allowed to audit public companies in the USA and it announced that it would cease practice by the end of 2002. The other large accounting firms have been working with Andersen to transfer their clients. Essentially, they are accused of not doing their job by spotting discrepancies in the accounts and alerting investors.

In June 2005, the US Supreme Court unanimously overturned Arthur Andersen's conviction of obstructing justice related to the destruction of Enron documents and the US Justice Department announced that it would drop the criminal case against the company. In 2009 Arthur Andersen paid US$16 million to the Enron Creditor's Recovery Group (see next section) to settle negligence claims relating to its auditing and advisory services. However the damage was irreparable. Thus the Enron affair brought down one of the oldest and largest

(Continued)

CASE 9.1   *(Continued)*

firms of accountants. There are those who believe that Arthur Andersen deserved all that has happened so far and more. Others see the backlash of a USA government wishing to send out a strong message about corporate fraud.

What happened?

In 2001 the company filed for Chapter 11 bankruptcy, which allowed it to continue to operate, on the basis that a going concern was more likely to pay its creditors. For a time, the new Enron chief, Stephen Cooper, saw a future as a scaled-down company. A message on the Enron website in July 2003 stated:

> *Enron is in the midst of restructuring its business with the hope of emerging from bankruptcy as a strong and viable, albeit smaller, company.*

This did not happen. Enron sold off whatever assets it could to pay creditors and effectively became a 'shell' company, with no operations. In 2007, Enron Corp changed its name to Enron Creditor's Recovery Group to reflect its true status and purpose. The Recovery Group filed lawsuits against 11 US and international financial institutions and alleged their involvement in fraud and misrepresentation. By 2011, US$21.74 billion had been redistributed to creditors. Most of the banks and financial institutions agreed to settle out of court. For example, Citigroup paid US$1.66 billion, JPMorgan Chase paid at least US$982 million and Barclays paid US$144 million.

More than 20 000 Enron employees lost their jobs and with that, medical insurance. The average severance pay was US$4500. In addition, they had lost between them $3.2 billion in retirement and pension funds.

Lay was convicted of fraud and perjury but died of a heart attack in 2006 before he was sentenced. He faced up to 45 years in prison. Jeffery Skilling was sentenced to 24 years and four months and ordered to forfeit US$45 million for redistribution to creditors. He was found guilty in May 2006 on 19 counts of conspiracy, fraud and insider trading. In 2013, his sentence was reduced to 14 years, when

he agreed to withdraw his challenges to the conviction and agreed to pay US$42 million to the Recovery Fund. Andrew Fastow was originally sentenced to 10 years, a relatively light sentence on the basis of his testimony against Lay and Skilling. This was reduced to six years upon further review of his cooperation. In addition, he paid back US$24 million. He was released in December 2011.

The last 15 executives to be sentenced received punishment in June 2007 ranging from probation to six years, largely on the basis of pleading guilty and avoiding trial.

The Enron trials and sentencing have given rise to a legal debate in the USA focusing on the issues related to leniency for giving information and for guilty pleas.

A further perspective

In 2003, Frank Partnoy, writing in *The Guardian* newspaper stated:

> *Relative to many of its peers, Enron was a profitable, well-run and law-abiding firm. That does not mean it was a model of corporate behaviour – it obviously was not. Although the media seized on its collapse as the business scandal of the decade, the truth was that Enron was no worse than Bankers Trust, Orange County, Cendant, Long-Term Capital Management, CS First Boston, Merrill Lynch and many others to follow, including Global Crossing and WorldCom, which collapsed soon after Enron.*

Questions

1 What aspects of corporate social responsibility are represented by the Enron case?

2 In your opinion, did Enron behave ethically and if not why not? How do you place your position on this issue alongside that of Frank Partnoy (stated at the end of the case)?

3 Examine the role of Arthur Andersen in the Enron affair. Was the outcome for Andersen fair?

4 What steps can be taken and by whom to ensure that an Enron case never happens again?

In addition to mechanisms employed internally by organizations, there are two external mechanisms that may have an influence on the approach and behaviour of organizations:

- **League tables.** League tables are published that rate companies along some measure of ethical behaviour or CSR. Jensen (2001), while supporting the long-term value to the firm and its stakeholders of a CSR approach questions the relevance and value of such measurements. Do such measurements reflect reality? As we see in Case 9.1, Enron was acclaimed in a number of countries for its attitude to CSR.

- **Ethical investment measures.** We have noted the growth of ethical investment funds such as the Dow Jones Sustainability Index and FTSE4Good. There is an assumption that companies that wish to be included in such listings will change their policies and behaviour and become more ethical. The motivation here may lie in the performance of such listings. There is some evidence that ethical listings have out-performed the standard listings on both the Dow Jones and FTSE indices since they were introduced.

- **Strategic choice.** We have already seen that some like Porter and Kramer (2006, 2011) see business ethics and CSR as an issue of strategic alignment between the economic needs of the company and the needs of society. In this way the choice of strategy, especially in terms of products, markets and supply chain management can enhance both the profitability of the company and solve important social and environmental problems.

SUMMARY

- Business ethics and corporate social responsibility are both about conducting business in an ethical manner and acting responsibly towards stakeholders and looking after the environment.
- Both business ethics and corporate social responsibility are complex ideas and there are numerous issues to be considered in satisfying the needs of stakeholders and in behaving responsibly towards the environment.
- At the heart of business ethics is a debate about the nature of business and whether business is the best agent for social responsibility.
- There are strong business arguments that socially responsible business is successful business, although much of the evidence is weak and contradictory.
- Organizations have a choice of strategies and practices to operate in a socially responsible way.

DISCUSSION QUESTIONS

1   What do you understand by the concepts of business ethics and corporate social responsibility? To what extent can we distinguish between the two concepts?

2   In an organization known to you (company, college, etc.) identify the various stakeholders. What does corporate social responsibility mean in the case of each?

3 What issues emerge when an organization attempts to be socially responsible to different stakeholders?

4 To what extent do you agree with the view that 'the business of business is business' and that social responsibility is best handled by other means?

5 What arguments can you put forward to support the view that socially responsible business is successful business? Support your arguments with evidence and illustrations.

6 How does the strategic case for ethical business differ from the traditional business case?

7 What are the pros and cons of whistleblowing?

8 What specific issues in business ethics emerge as a result of globalization?

9 Examine the Railtrack case study in Chapter 6 and the Executive Pay case in Chapter 7. What aspects of business ethics and corporate social responsibility are involved?

FURTHER READING

Good coverage in general texts can be found in:

Blowfield, M. and Murray, A. (2011) *Corporate Responsibility: A Critical Introduction*, 2nd edn. Oxford University Press: Oxford.

Crane, A., and Matten, D. (2010) *Business Ethics*, 3rd edn. Oxford University Press: Oxford.

Crane, A., Matten, D. and Spence, L.J. (2014) *Corporate Social Responsibility: Readings and Cases in a Global Context*, 2nd edn. Routledge: Abingdon.

A more pragmatic perspective is offered by:

Visions of Ethical Business, Financial Times Management: London.

Porter, M.E. and Kramer, M.R. (2006) 'Strategy and society: the link between competitive advantage and corporate social responsibility', *Harvard Business Review*, Dec., 78–92.

Porter, M.E. and Kramer, M.R. (2011) 'Creating shared value', *Harvard Business Review*, 89, 62–77.

A good source of research is the *Journal of Business Ethics*.

PART THREE
THE ACTIVITIES CONTEXT

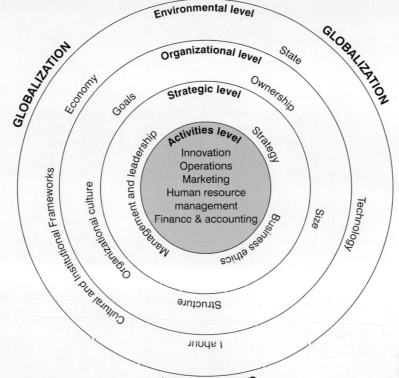

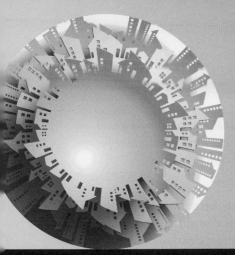

INNOVATION

LEARNING OBJECTIVES At the end of this chapter you should be able to:

- Identify and differentiate between the concepts and activities of invention, innovation, design, entrepreneurship and research and development (R&D).

- Identify different types of innovation and assess their relative significance to organizational success.

- Explain how innovation is the product of the interaction of a number of environmental and organizational variables.

- Explain the relationship between innovation and other functional areas of business such as operations and marketing.

- Assess critically the meaning of entrepreneurship and the role of the entrepreneur and identify the variables influencing entrepreneurial success.

- Critically assess the contribution of innovation to a firm's profitability and nation's economic growth.

- Assess the role of state intervention in innovation.

- Explain and evaluate the concept of national systems of innovation.

- Assess the link between innovation and technology.

- Critically assess the relative influence on innovation of organization size, structure and culture.

- Explain and assess strategic approaches to innovation.

INTRODUCTION

There can be little doubt that those activities which contribute to the efficient introduction and exploitation of new and improved processes and products are extremely important for the competitive performance and long-term growth of any industrial economy.

(Freeman, 1989, p. 199)

Innovation is a core business activity linked to both the growth of national economies and the survival and growth of individual firms. In Chapter 8 we spoke of differentiation and cost leadership as generic strategies for competitive advantage. Innovation clearly lies at the heart of differentiation but also contributes to cost reduction through improved product development and design and through changes in process technology.

The DTI (2006) identified advantages associated with innovation in a survey. For the **individual firm** the advantages lie in:

- A higher and sustainable profit.
- The ability to challenge competition.
- Offering value-added to the customer in the form of improved quality, lower price and greater choice.

For **national economies** the survey echoes Freeman's quote above. The advantages are:

- The growth in terms of economic output.
- Improved productivity.

For **society** the advantages are seen in terms of:

- Improved health care.
- Improved education.
- A better environment.
- Improved transport systems.

We can see that innovation is the key ingredient for survival in a competitive market. In the electronics industry, where product lifecycles have reduced, constant innovation is essential. Seventy per cent of the products of Siemens, the large German electronics company, are less than five years old, and such companies must undertake a constant process of product renewal. In the previous chapter we saw how General Electric's launch of a series of new products under their 'Ecomagination' arm greatly increased their revenues.

Undoubtedly, innovation is a function of business since it is related to entrepreneurship – the driving force behind business growth and development. In this chapter we attempt a broad-based view of innovation. We will start by examining the differences between the related concepts of innovation, invention, research and development, design and entrepreneurship. We then move on to examine the relationship between innovative business activity and the environmental aspects of the model, in particular its impact on economic growth, the role of governments in stimulating innovation and entrepreneurship, and, especially, differences in government policy and attitudes towards innovation in different nation states. Much government policy focuses upon the encouragement of new technologies, yet it is our contention that the development and design of products needs to be accompanied by corresponding developments in marketing and in management and organization. In the latter part of this chapter we extend this view of innovation further by examining how it operates within organizations, and, in particular, the relevance of organizational structure and culture to innovative activity. The chapter ends by focusing on generic innovation strategies.

Our discussion of innovation is not confined to the technological hardware of products and processes. Product and process innovation invariably requires accompanying innovations in marketing, organization structure and management processes. These are sometimes referred to as administrative innovations as opposed to technical innovations of the product and process type. Research has pointed to the need to balance both technical and administrative innovation (Daft, 1982; Damanpour et al., 1989). The benefit of technical change can be lessened without accompanying changes in administration. For example, the adoption of a new client database in a large organization is of little value unless staff are trained to use it. In retailing it is mostly innovations that the customer cannot see, as with the logistics of getting produce to supermarket shelves that have given firms their greatest competitive advantage.

The link between innovation and entrepreneurship is important, since it establishes innovation as a function of all businesses. Many people associate innovation with the process of product design in the manufacturing industry. Yet, examples of innovation can be drawn from every organizational context. In the financial services industry, banking has been transformed by the introduction of automatic cash dispensers and then online banking, giving the general public easier access to cash and account information. In the entertainment industry, multi-screen cinemas offer the public a wider choice and have contributed to increases in attendance and hence revenue. In the travel industry, the booking of airline seats has been revolutionized by computerized booking systems directly accessible by travellers on the web. As we saw in Chapter 4, significant claims are made for the impact of e-commerce. In education, innovations occur through the development of courses or new methods of presenting those courses, such as online learning. In most of the above cases the innovation is viewed as offering the adopter a competitive advantage.

IDENTIFYING THE CONCEPTS

The terms 'invention', 'innovation', 'research and development', 'design' and 'entrepreneurship' are all used in a variety of contexts, often interchangeably. There is a further confusion in that while all are processes, 'research and development' or R&D as it popularly known, is frequently used in an organizational context to identify a department whose primary objective is the creation and development of products and new ways of making them. In this section, we offer some definitions of invention and innovation, R&D, design and entrepreneurship. Finally in this section we explore the link between innovation and knowledge. In the next sections we examine in more detail the types and scope of innovation and look more closely at R&D expenditure and entrepreneurship.

Invention and innovation

These terms are often confused, yet if we take Schumpeter's line there is a very clear distinction between them:

As long as they are not carried into practice, inventions are economically irrelevant.

(Schumpeter, 1961, p. 88)

KEY CONCEPT 10.1   INVENTION VERSUS INNOVATION

Invention is the discovery or creation of a product or process, whereas innovation is the process through which inventions and ideas become a business or operational reality. An innovation can include new products, processes, strategies and organization structures. Innovation is claimed by many as an important source of competitive advantage.

Tidd et al. (2005) remind us that the originators of some of the most famous inventions are not remembered, while those who commercially exploited them are. Thus, few have heard of J. Murray Spengler, the inventor of the vacuum cleaner, yet most know Hoover, initially a leather-goods maker, to whom Spengler sold his idea. On the other hand, most would link the discovery of penicillin with Alexander Fleming, who chose to give his findings to the scientific community. The commercial production of penicillin was patented by a US firm, which reaped the financial benefits.

Invention is the creation of something new, be it computer software, a computer design, a method for painting cars, a form of selling, a university course, or a form of organization structure. An invention becomes an innovation when the idea becomes a reality, when the new software and computer go into manufacture and start selling, when the new technology for painting cars offers a more efficient and effective system, or when the new university course recruits students.

This reinforces the notion that innovation operates in a variety of forms and in a variety of contexts.

Research and development

We can define research and development as the organization of innovation at the level of the firm. It is this activity of an organization that both seeks to satisfy a market need by developing new products and methods, and find uses for scientific and technological inventions. This introduces the concepts of demand–pull innovation (fulfilling a market need) and technology–push innovation (applying existing knowledge). R&D is clearly associated with science and technology, although the R&D function can be performed in all types of industry. We have seen that the process of product development occurs in non-scientific and technical situations. In many organizations there is a group of people whose primary task is the generation of business ideas, as in the case of television companies, which have departments for new programme development.

KEY CONCEPT 10.2   RESEARCH AND DEVELOPMENT

Research and development, or R&D, is the name given to the organizational function that is usually the focus for innovation within a firm. R&D can refer to an activity or the name of a specific department. Expenditure on R&D and the size of an R&D department have been used as measures of levels of innovative activity, although they are probably best used as indicators rather than exact measures owing to the presence of other variables which can and do influence innovation.

In some industries, especially those involved in complex, competitive environments, R&D is vital. Firms such as IBM and Apple in the computer and telecommunications industry, and Bayer and GlaxoSmithKline (GSK) in the pharmaceutical industry, have large teams of staff engaged exclusively in R&D work. The importance of R&D to GlaxoSmithKline is shown in Case 10.1. However, the institutionalization of R&D can bring its own problems, which are raised when we look at organizational aspects later in the chapter.

KEY CONCEPT 10.3 DEMAND–PULL VERSUS TECHNOLOGY–PUSH

Demand–pull and technology–push refer to the sources of innovation. Demand–pull refers to the development of new products and processes as a direct result of market demand. Technology–push is the use of known technologies to develop innovative products and processes. Many innovations, for example the CD player, are developed as a result of both demand–pull and technology–push.

REFLECTION POINT

Identify and consider examples of both demand–pull and technology–push innovation. Which do you think is the most common?

Design

This is usually the final stage in the R&D process, which translates the development into the final product for the consumer. The design stage attempts to fuse certain elements, which are referred to as the design mix. These elements are effective operation, safety, ease of maintenance, value for money and aesthetic considerations. These are all focused on satisfying customer needs.

The design aspect of research and development is an obvious area of overlap with both the production and marketing processes, to the extent that product design is seen as an essential element in both fields. Design and styling assume particular importance in industries such as car manufacture, where products are often sold as much on their appearance as their inherent product qualities. A firm like Bang & Olufsen produces televisions and hi-fi equipment to high technical specifications, yet its distinctiveness owes much more to its visual appeal. Making their products look very different from their competitors is a deliberate Bang & Olufsen strategy.

It is not only in the manufacture of products that design is important. In the retail industry the design of the store layout and how goods are displayed is known to influence the purchasing habits of consumers. In the hotel industry, the French designer Philippe Starck has created innovative designs and furnishings. Hotels that have used his services use his involvement as a brand to attract customers.

Entrepreneurship

Entrepreneurship is the process of creating new products and services, new processes, new methods of management and new markets. Entrepreneurs are therefore central to the process of innovation. Entrepreneurship is often linked to the operation of small businesses. However, true entrepreneurship involves some form of innovation. We explore entrepreneurship in more detail later in the chapter.

Innovation and knowledge

We can identify two types of knowledge, explicit and tacit. **Explicit** knowledge is that derived from an external source such as a book or a published paper. It is therefore available to all and can be copied. Explicit knowledge on its own is rarely a source of competitive advantage. **Tacit** knowledge on the other hand is knowledge that is developed over time by organization members and is unique to a particular firm. Tacit knowledge is therefore an important source of innovation. It can reside in a product or process and can be part of an organization culture. It is difficult to copy and is a source of competitive advantage.

There is a wider link between innovation and knowledge through the higher education system. A DTI survey found that companies active in innovation had twice the number of university graduates as employees than non-innovative companies (DTI, 2006).

KEY CONCEPT 10.4 EXPLICIT AND TACIT KNOWLEDGE

Explicit knowledge is obtained through rational processes of data collection and is often contained in documentation. As such it is relatively easily available to all. Tacit knowledge is the sum total of knowledge acquired by the organization and passed on to subsequent generations of employees. It is rarely documented and is difficult for outsiders to penetrate and copy. Since tacit knowledge is unique to an organization it is an important source of innovation and competitive advantage.

TYPES AND SCOPE OF INNOVATION

Types of innovation

We can identify a number of types of innovation:

- **Product innovation** is the development of a product such as a new model of a mobile phone, a new influenza vaccine, a new form of insurance policy, or a restaurant introducing a vegetarian menu for the first time.
- **Process innovation** is concerned with how the product is made or delivered to the customer. The development of robots in the manufacturing industry is a form of process innovation, as is a restaurant opening a self-service section in addition to waiter service. In cases like the Toyota production system, process innovations can be wide-ranging and offer a firm an enviable competitive advantage.
- **Organization and management innovation** is a broad category covering different types of innovation. Such innovation has been defined by Hamel (2006, p. 75) as:

  ... a marked departure from traditional management principles, processes and practices or a departure from customary organizational forms that significantly alter the way management is performed.

  Hamel identifies a number of management innovations including the establishment by Edison of a research laboratory at General Electric and the development of methods of calculating a return on investment at DuPont. The creation of the divisional structure as we saw in Chapter 6 enabled multinational firms like General Motors to control its international operations more effectively and gain competitive advantage. The Toyota production system, copied throughout the automotive industry and in other manufacturing contexts is much more than just a process innovation; its lean, just-in-time approach is an innovation in the management of the entire operations system and supply chain. We deal with this in more detail in Chapter 11.

We argued in the introduction that increasing attention has been given to management innovation. In a DTI survey of firms in the UK, 30 per cent of institutions claimed product and/or process innovations in 2002–04. In the same period, 61 per cent of institutions claimed broader innovations involving strategy, structure or management practices (DTI, 2006).

REFLECTION POINT

Identify an organization and management innovation that you believe has radically changed how organizations operate.

Marketing innovation This is a broad category and involves innovations in pricing such as 'buy-one-get-one free', and packaging, such as Pringles placing crisps in cardboard tubes, as well as novel ways of promoting products. There is inevitably some cross-over with product innovation. For example, Dell developed a system not only where customers could purchase computers online but also determine the size of memory and a range of computer functions to suit their needs.

Tidd et al. (2005) refer to **position** innovation, which they define as changing the context of a product. They cite the case of Lucozade, whose original target market was those recovering from illness. The drink has been successfully repositioned as an energy drink for sportspeople or for the keep-fit market. The washing powder Surf was experiencing a declining market share as every new product appeared to come with a new formula for washing whiter. The company aimed the product at a segment of the market it had identified as 'anti-gimmick'. To emphasize this point, it offered the product with a changed name, which suggested to consumers that they were getting a better deal than those offered by competitors. The change and repositioning of the product were very successful and sales increased. We deal with aspects of market segmentation and positioning in more detail in Chapter 12.

Mensch (1979) would label Square Deal Surf and similar marketing tactics as **pseudo innovations.** He argued that such innovations were often introduced to revitalize a stagnant market, when, in fact, no real change had taken place. Pseudo-innovations are often the product of marketing campaigns to change the fortunes of a flagging product. The product may be re-launched under a different name, repackaged to suggest product changes or advertised as containing a 'new improved formula' when no significant change has taken place.

However, the case of Square Deal Surf illustrates the complexity of innovation. To Mensch, it represents a pseudo-innovation in terms of product, yet the marketing strategy employed was innovative. Moreover, not all innovations are visible. Where washing powders have radically changed their formula this is not apparent to the consumer and the company relies on its marketing effort to convey this information, reinforcing the importance of an integrated innovation and marketing strategy.

REFLECTION POINT

Identify some examples of marketing innovations. How influential have they been?

The scope of innovation

Innovation can be viewed as a continuum incorporating product modifications at one end and changes in the nature of society at the other. We identify three broad categories; incremental, radical and paradigm shift. Table 10.1 presents some illustrations of incremental and radical innovations.

TABLE 10.1	Examples of radical and incremental innovation	
Innovation type	**Radical**	**Incremental**
Use of raw materials	Using plastic to make bottles instead of glass	Changing the nature of the plastic in plastic bottles to make them tough enough to hold carbonated drinks
Product	Using integrated circuits on microchips to replace transistors	A sandwich shop using new combinations of fillings for its sandwiches
	The hybrid car that runs on both electricity and petrol	Creating different forms of the same shampoo for different kinds of hair
	The contraceptive pill	Changing the dashboard display of a car for easier recognition
Process	The float glass process for making flat glass devised by Pilkington	Grouping jobs on a manufacturing assembly line to be carried out by teams
	Using robots instead of people for welding in the car industry	Introducing YouTube clips to enhance a PowerPoint lecture presentation
	The use of online learning instead of lectures at university	
Marketing	Selling computers online instead of using retailers	The use of cars painted with the company name and logo by an estate agent to drive prospective buyers to view properties
Organization	The creation of divisional structures with profit centres to improve efficiency and control of global operations	Outsourcing the payroll function from the HR department
Management	Toyota's production system	Rotating senior management staff into different roles every three years

- **Incremental** innovations are essentially modifications and improvements on existing products and processes, but their cumulative effect can be significant, as shown by computers and cameras. The majority of innovations in business are such incremental changes, often of a minor nature. This is understandable since radical breakthroughs are rare and there is considerable scope for permutations within an existing framework and knowledge base. This incremental approach to innovation is pursued by many Japanese companies and is the reason why camera producers, such as Nikon and Canon, bring out new models at regular intervals.

- **Radical** innovations, sometimes referred to as **discontinuous** innovations, change the nature of a product or process. This form of innovation can be disruptive and there is a likelihood that firms will go out of business if they are unable to adapt. An example of a radical innovation in camera technology would be the digital camera.

- **Paradigm shift** innovations change the nature of markets and societies. The industrial revolution was one such paradigm shift, followed by the change from craft to mass production. Lean production (explored in Chapter 11) could be considered a paradigm shift in terms of its impact on manufacturing and other industries and upon those who work in them. There is a clear link between radical or discontinuous innovations and a paradigm shift and they are really stages along the same continuum. Sometimes paradigm shift innovations follow changes in the political economy. The liberalization of the Chinese and former Soviet Union economies has given people and businesses the freedom to develop new forms of enterprise and new ways of doing business. The growth of international joint ventures in China represents a paradigm shift. Some argue that deregulation in some sectors has changed the nature of business. Examples of this would be the deregulation of the energy market that allowed firms like Enron to create new forms of doing business (see Case 9.1) and the deregulation of the airline business, which has spawned the entry of low-cost carriers such as easyJet and Air Berlin.

REFLECTION POINT

Think of your own examples to place in the categories identified in Table 10.1.

EXPENDITURE ON RESEARCH AND DEVELOPMENT

The British government, initially through the Department of Trade and Industry (DTI), renamed in 2007 as the Department for Business, Innovation and Skills (BIS), published annual league tables of R&D spending. The UK R&D Scoreboard, as it was known, became a benchmarking device, not just for UK firms but for international firms as well. It listed the top 800 firms in the UK and the top 1250 firms globally in terms of their R&D spending and their R&D intensity. R&D intensity is spending as a proportion of sales turnover (BIS, 2010). Such information is now available for stock-exchange-listed companies as a requirement of SSAP 13 (Statement of Standard Accounting Practice). The Department of Business, Innovation and Skills ceased publication of the R&D Scorecard after 2010 as a cost-cutting exercise. Similar information is still published by the EU (European Commission, 2013 http://epp.eurostat.ec.europa.eu).

Tables 10.2 and 10.3 show expenditure on R&D by companies in the UK and worldwide respectively. Table 10.4 shows the latest data from the European Union. Tables 10.5 and 10.6 show how this spending is concentrated in five countries and the proportion of R&D spending by sector.

TABLE 10.2	Ranking of top 20 companies in the UK by R&D expenditure and as percentage of sales (2009)

Company	Rank	2009 R&D spend (£ million)	Proportion of sales (%)
GlaxoSmithKline	1	3629	12.8
AstraZeneca	2	2746	13.5
BT	3	1029	4.9
Unilever	4	792	2.2
Royal Dutch Shell	5	679	0.4
Royal Bank of Scotland	6	559	1.4
HSBC	7	472	1.0
Rolls Royce	8	471	4.5
Airbus	9	367	14.7
BP	10	363	0.2
Shire	11	347	18.6
Pfizer	12	326	25.5
Land Rover	13	314	6.9
Ford	14	313	4.5
Vodafone	15	303	0.7
Barclays	16	264	0.8
BAE Systems	17	234	1.1
Bentley Motors	18	230	27.7
Roche Products	19	208	20.7
Nokia	20	197	11.4

A number of conclusions may be drawn from this R&D expenditure information.

- R&D spending worldwide is dominated by five countries, which in 2009 accounted for 77 per cent of all expenditure. Not surprisingly, given the size of its economy, the USA dominates within this group although its proportion of spending has fallen. In the 2013 data in Table 10.4, eight US companies are amongst the top 20 R&D spenders. The tables also illustrate the increased spend by Swiss companies, which by 2009 was the same as the total UK spend. It reflects the significance of pharmaceuticals and biotechnology to the Swiss economy. Comparing Tables 10.3 and 10.4, the biggest expenditure increase is by Samsung electronics in South Korea, reflecting its upward market share in highly competitive markets. The EU reports that for 2012–13 that while US companies increased expenditure by 8.2 per cent, the largest percentage increase in R&D expenditure was in China with a 12.2 per cent increase followed by South Korea with 8.9 per cent. By comparison the increase in the EU was 6.3 per cent and in Japan only 0.4 per cent (European Commission 2013 http://epp.eurostat.ec.europa.eu).

- Around 56 per cent of all the expenditure is in three sectors. These are technology hardware (computers, mobile phones, etc.), pharmaceuticals and the motor industry.

- Expenditure varies among sectors in different countries. For example, the majority of expenditure in the UK is in pharmaceuticals, as is also the case with the Swiss. We return to this theme later in the chapter when we examine national differences in innovation.

TABLE 10.3	Ranking of top 20 global companies by R&D expenditure (2009)				
Rank	Company	Sector	Country	R&D spend (£million)	Proportion of sales (%)
1	Toyota Motor	Automobiles and parts	Japan	6014	4.4
2	Roche	Pharmaceuticals and biotechnology	Switzerland	5688	19.4
3	Microsoft	Software and computer services	USA	5396	13.9
4	Volkswagen	Automobiles and parts	Germany	5144	5.7
5	Pfizer	Pharmaceuticals and biotechnology	USA	4802	15.5
6	Novartis	Pharmaceuticals and biotechnology	Switzerland	4581	16.7
7	Nokia	Technology hardware and equipment	Finland	4440	12.2
8	Johnson & Johnson	Pharmaceuticals and biotechnology	USA	4326	11.3
9	Sanofi-Aventis	Pharmaceuticals and biotechnology	France	4060	15.3
10	Samsung Electronics	Electronic and electrical equipment	South Korea	4007	5.4
11	Siemens	Electronic and electrical equipment	Germany	3805	5.6
12	General Motors	Automobiles and parts	USA	3758	5.3
13	Honda Motor	Automobiles and parts	Japan	3746	5.6
14	Daimler	Automobiles and parts	Germany	3700	5.3
15	GlaxoSmith-Kline	Pharmaceuticals and biotechnology	UK	3629	12.8
16	Merck	Pharmaceuticals and biotechnology	USA	3619	21.3
17	Intel	Technology hardware and equipment	USA	3501	16.1
18	Panasonic	Leisure goods	Japan	3445	6.7
19	Sony	Leisure goods	Japan	3308	6.5
20	Cisco Systems	Technology hardware and equipment	USA	3225	14.4

- In 2005 four of the top six companies in terms of expenditure globally were in the automotive industry, which has been far from profitable in recent years. This is a theme we return to when assessing the outcomes of innovation strategy. By 2013 five automobile companies feature in the top 20. The biggest spender in most years seems to come from this sector with Toyota in 2009 and Volkswagen in 2013.

- There are marked variations in the amount of expenditure as a percentage of sales revenue. This is much lower in the car industry than it is in pharmaceuticals, reflecting the higher costs involved in the development and testing of drugs.

TABLE 10.4	The world's top 20 companies by their total R&D investment (€ millions) in the 2013 EU Scoreboard		
	Company	Country	R&D investment
1	Volkswagen	Germany	9 515
2	Samsung Electronics	South Korea	8 344
3	Microsoft	USA	7 890
4	Intel	USA	7 691
5	Toyota Motor	Japan	7 070
6	Roche	Switzerland	7 007
7	Novartis	Switzerland	6 922
8	Merck	USA	5 995
9	Johnson & Johnson	USA	5 809
10	Pfizer	USA	5 740
11	Daimler	Germany	5 639
12	General Motors	USA	5 584
13	Google	USA	4 997
14	Robert Bosch	Germany	4 924
15	Sanofi-Aventis	France	4 909
16	Honda Motor	Japan	4 906
17	Siemens	Germany	4 572
18	Cisco Systems	USA	4 503
19	Panasonic	Japan	4 398
20	GlaxoSmithKline	UK	4 229

TABLE 10.5	Global R&D expenditure 2005 and 2009 as a percentage of the total by country	
Country	R&D spending (%)	
	2005	2009
USA	41	34
Japan	20	22
Germany	10	11
France	6	6
UK	5	4
Others	18	22

- Among the top UK spenders in 2009 are three major banks, with the Royal Bank of Scotland (RBS) and HSBC featuring in the top 10. This illustrates the importance of R&D in the non-science-based industries and the service sector. The EU data for global expenditure in 2013 shows six banks in the top 200 with Banco Santander spending most in 101st position. The other banks listed in order are RBS, Deutsche Bank, ANZAC Bank, HSBC and Barclays.

TABLE 10.6	Global R&D expenditure 2005 and 2009 as a percentage of the total by sector	
Sector	**R&D spending (%)**	
	2005	**2009**
Technology hardware	19.2	17
Pharmaceuticals	18.7	19
Automotive	17.6	16
Electronics	7.4	7
Software	6.6	7
Others	30.5	35

- The EU report notes that the expenditure trends show resilience in the face of economic uncertainty. The findings for 2013 show that major companies are increasing R&D expenditure at a higher rate than sales revenues; an overall 6.2 per cent increase for R&D against a revenue increase of 4.2 per cent (European Commission, 2013).

ENTREPRENEURSHIP

We noted at the beginning of this chapter that the activities of the entrepreneur were crucial to innovation. The entrepreneur creates new products, new markets, and new means through which products are made and markets reached, based around new forms of organization and new means of managing people. Entrepreneurs such as Thomas Edison and Henry Ford have therefore been important in business history. More recently, entrepreneurs such as Bill Gates of Microsoft, Steve Jobs at Apple and Richard Branson at Virgin have become household names.

There has been a tendency to equate entrepreneurship with small firms. However, not every small firm is entrepreneurial, since many merely replicate existing forms of business. Becoming self-employed to run a newsagent's shop has little to do with innovation and entrepreneurship. In fact the majority of sole traders and small businesses are not entrepreneurial. This view of entrepreneurship also detracts from the importance of entrepreneurship in large businesses. In his study of General Motors, Sears, Dupont and Standard Oil, which we referred to in our discussion of structure in Chapter 6, Chandler stressed the importance for managers to be able to see beyond the daily problems of controlling a large corporation and develop new business ideas for the future. However, the qualities that give rise to an entrepreneur are not necessarily those of an 'organization man'. This may make entrepreneurs difficult to manage, an issue we discuss later in the chapter.

KEY CONCEPT 10.5   ENTREPRENEURSHIP

Entrepreneurship is the activity of entrepreneurs, who are responsible for the creation of new products, processes, services and markets. They develop new ways of doing business, create new organization forms and new ways of managing people. Entrepreneurship achieves such changes through the mobilization of physical, financial, human and information resources. These resources are often combined in new ways to create something new or to achieve improved levels of performance. Entrepreneurs are usually willing to lead and to take responsibility for their actions.

What is entrepreneurship?

Various attempts have been made to define the entrepreneur. Schumpeter presented a romantic view of the entrepreneur as someone who possessed:

The dream and the will to found a private kingdom ... the will to conquer ... the joy of creating.

(Schumpeter, 1961, p. 93)

A conference in 1998, sponsored by the UK government, set out the following characteristics of entrepreneurial activity (DTI, 1998):

- A desire to own and be accountable for one's performance.
- A willingness to engage in a rich and broad network of learning situations and to incorporate learning into one's activities.
- A fundamental motivation to be successful and make a contribution for one's self and/or other groups within society as a whole.
- The capability and willingness to move beyond the accepted and orthodox if such methods are failing to achieve sufficient added value.
- An intellectual and skill-based capability to weigh up the riskiness of innovative courses of action and the ability to manage such risk for the benefit of self and others.
- The capacity to focus activity upon the achievement of tangible and recognized outputs.
- A willingness to move ahead and innovate without being constrained overly by currently available resources.

A model of entrepreneurship

Bessant and Tidd (2007) identify three types of entrepreneur:

- **Lifestyle** entrepreneurs. These seek independence through self-employment. Very few of these will be innovative.
- **Growth** entrepreneurs. These seek wealth, influence and reputation and many have created large, aggressive organizations as in the case of Rupert Murdoch and News Corporation.
- **Innovative** entrepreneurs. Their main interest lies in the creation of something new. Growth is a by-product.

The above classification is interesting and is based largely around individual choice and preferences. However, it conflicts with our earlier definition of entrepreneur, which sees entrepreneurship inextricably linked with innovation.

Figure 10.1 presents a model of entrepreneurship, which serves as a summary of research into the characteristics of successful entrepreneurs and the conditions in which such people thrive (further summaries of this research can be found in Bridge et al., 1998; Burns, 2001; Chell, 2001, Bessant and Tidd, 2007). The model distinguishes between types of entrepreneur as well as identifying variables that influence successful entrepreneurial activity. Unlike the previous classification, the three types focus on different types of innovative activity rather than on the motivation for becoming an entrepreneur.

Three types of entrepreneur are identified:

- **Craftsman.** The craftsman focuses on the product, which he or she has invented and/ or developed. He or she possesses a specific skill that originates from a trade, craft or

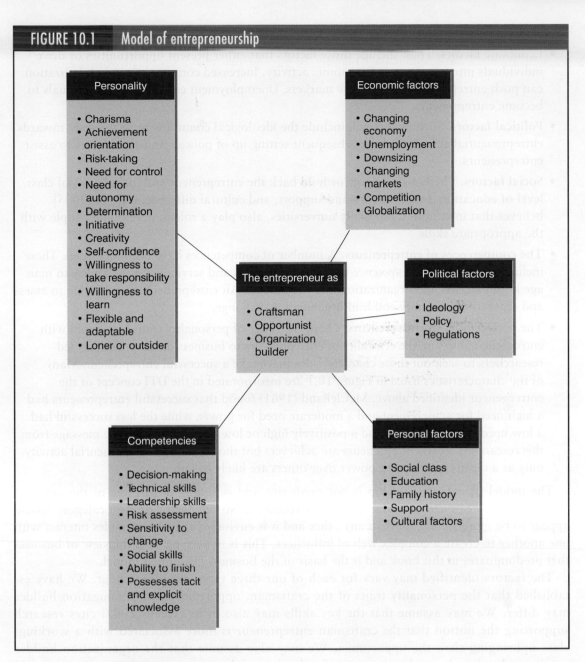

FIGURE 10.1   Model of entrepreneurship

Personality

- Charisma
- Achievement orientation
- Risk-taking
- Need for control
- Need for autonomy
- Determination
- Initiative
- Creativity
- Self-confidence
- Willingness to take responsibility
- Willingness to learn
- Flexible and adaptable
- Loner or outsider

Economic factors

- Changing economy
- Unemployment
- Downsizing
- Changing markets
- Competition
- Globalization

The entrepreneur as

- Craftsman
- Opportunist
- Organization builder

Political factors

- Ideology
- Policy
- Regulations

Competencies

- Decision-making
- Technical skills
- Leadership skills
- Risk assessment
- Sensitivity to change
- Social skills
- Ability to finish
- Possesses tacit and explicit knowledge

Personal factors

- Social class
- Education
- Family history
- Support
- Cultural factors

engineering background. Craftsmen tend to operate as sole traders or at least in small businesses. They are often characterized as loners.

- **Opportunist.** The opportunist focuses on the market and has the ability to seek out and develop opportunities. They are often characterized as confident and outgoing.

- **Organization builder.** The organization builder focuses on making things happen and effecting change within organizations. They are often characterized in terms of their strong vision and inspirational leadership skills.

The variables we identify are:

- **Economic factors.** These include those factors that either present opportunities or drive individuals into new forms of economic activity. Increased competition and globalization can push entrepreneurs to seek new markets. Unemployment can motivate individuals to become entrepreneurs.

- **Political factors.** Such factors will include the ideological commitment of the state towards entrepreneurial activity and the subsequent setting up of policies and regulations to assist entrepreneurs.

- **Social factors.** These may support or hold back the entrepreneur and include: social class, level of education, family history and support, and cultural differences. Koen (2005) believes that institutions, especially universities, also play a role in developing people with the appropriate skills.

- **The competences of entrepreneurs.** A number of competences have been identified. These include the technical competence to develop products and services and the ability to manage both external and organizational environments. An entrepreneur must be able to assess and react to opportunity and lead organizational change.

- **The personalities of entrepreneurs.** There is a range of personality traits associated with entrepreneurship and the centrality of entrepreneurs to business development has led researchers to seek out those characteristics that make a successful entrepreneur. Many of the characteristics listed in Figure 10.1 are incorporated in the DTI concept of the entrepreneur identified above. McClelland (1961) found that successful entrepreneurs had a high need for achievement and a moderate need for power, while the less successful had a low need for achievement and a positively high or low need for power. The message from this research is clear: entrepreneurs are achievers but those seeking entrepreneurial activity only as a means of achieving power over others are likely to fail.

The model of entrepreneurship is not predictive and is simply descriptive of the range of variables which can and do influence the entrepreneur. No one factor or even category would appear to be more significant than any other and it is envisaged that the variables interact with one another to create a complex web of influences. This is in keeping with the view of business that predominates in this book and is the basis of the Business in Context model.

The factors identified may vary for each of our three types of entrepreneur. We have established that the personality traits of the craftsman, opportunist and organization builder may differ. We may assume that the key skills may also differ. Chell (2001) cites research supporting the notion that the craftsman entrepreneur is more associated with a working-class upbringing than the opportunist. We may also assume that the organization builder would tend to be educated to university level, whereas the craftsman and opportunist would be more represented among early school leavers, although some like Koen (2005) question this image of the modern entrepreneur.

However, we may argue that certain characteristics and certain skills could be the prerequisite of all entrepreneurs and that the differences between craftsman, opportunist and organization builder, as illustrated above, are merely stereotypes to be challenged. For example, many successful individual inventors have been both university educated and middle-class. Research in the whole area is far from conclusive, occasionally contradictory and any conclusions should be drawn with caution.

REFLECTION POINT

How would you define an entrepreneur? Are entrepreneurs born or made?

ENVIRONMENTAL ASPECTS OF INNOVATION

Four aspects of our model are significant here. We will look first at the relationship between innovation and the economy, which leads logically to a discussion on the role of the state in encouraging innovation. This, in turn, leads to the differences in the way nations approach innovation, which we examine by looking at cultural influences. There is a clear relationship between technology and innovation, which we acknowledge in our assessment of the contending influences of technological development and the marketplace. We will not discuss the relationship between innovation and the labour market here since we examined the impact of changing technology on jobs at some length in Chapter 4. The relationship between innovation and labour is important, since the skills of the workforce and their attitude towards change, more especially changes in technology, are crucial to the successful implementation of innovation. A core element is the role of the economy, and the belief that innovation stimulates economic growth.

The role of the economy

There have been many attempts to link innovation with economic and financial growth both in terms of national economies and individual firms. In general, innovation is perceived as the means through which economic regeneration occurs. As such it has held a fascination for those who see government investment in R&D as a strategy for tackling the problems of economic decline. More specifically, economists have attempted to prove links between innovation and such factors as per capita growth and export competitiveness. In this section we will examine two assumptions:

- Innovation is the key to national economic growth and lifts national economies out of recession.
- Innovation is a prerequisite for organizational survival and success and is linked to organization growth, financial growth and market share

We will assess these two assumptions in the light of available evidence.

Innovation and long-wave cycles

The relationship between innovation and economic activity owes much to the work of the Russian economist Kondratieff (1935). He put forward the view that economic activity exhibits regular long-wave economic cycles of growth and depression, followed by a further period of growth and so on. The explanation for the operation of these cycles has been taken up by a number of economists. For Schumpeter, the key was innovation. Each phase of economic recovery can be attributed to clusters of innovations, enabling capitalism to evolve and usher in a new period of prosperity (Schumpeter, 1939). He thought that most innovations occurred when the economic climate appeared more favourable, thus acting as a stimulus for entrepreneurial activity. However, some believe that innovations only occur in the depths of depression, when profits are so low that entrepreneurs are stimulated into risk-taking ventures (Mensch, 1979).

The problems are identifying when the cycles begin, how long they last, and what the key innovations are. There is another problem of identifying and dating the innovations and the highly deterministic nature of cyclical activity, leaving some economists to view the theory as convenient rather than meaningful.

R&D expenditure and performance

A government survey of UK firms in 2002–04 found that managers identified the following outcomes of R&D expenditure that contributed to growth and profits (DTI, 2006):

- Improved product range and product quality.
- Access to new markets.
- Improved processes with reduced costs per unit, increased capacity and increased flexibility.

Such data is based on management belief rather than hard economic or financial measures. Other studies have attempted to use harder data. An early study by Solow (1957) concluded that as much as 90 per cent of improvements in productivity and output could be attributed to process innovations.

If we use the data from the 2006 R&D scoreboard, there is a link between R&D expenditure and shareholder value. Those companies shown on the scoreboard with a higher intensity of R&D that are in the FTSE100 index show a higher value growth than the average for the FTSE 100. The 2006 scoreboard also points to the importance of R&D expenditure in a recession. An examination of the technology hardware sector, which includes firms such as Nokia, Hewlett-Packard and Intel, during the 2001–04 recession revealed the significance of R&D expenditure. Of the 19 largest firms that increased R&D expenditure during recession, 18 had increased sales. Of the 17 that had cut R&D expenditure by more than 10 per cent, 13 had lower sales over the period.

Patents and performance

Table 10.7 is concerned with patents. As with published expenditure, patents represent an easily measured output of R&D. The dominant market position of GSK's drugs Zantac and Zovirax is, in part, a function of patent protection, and the expiry of the patent resulted in other manufacturers entering the market (Case 10.1).

KEY CONCEPT 10.6   PATENTS

A patent is a legal device that enables the holder to maintain a monopoly in an invention for a stated period, which in most countries stands at 20 years. The state grants this monopoly in return for a full disclosure of the invention. Such a system exists in all industrialized countries. A patent protects the inventor from would-be copiers and enables him or her to exploit the invention for profit and/or the good of society. It is believed that the benefits of such a system will encourage invention and innovation. A patent holder may issue manufacturing licences to third parties and thus derive financial benefit.

Table 10.7 shows those firms receiving the largest number of US patents over a period of 36 years, represented by data from three years, 1987, 2007 and 2013. The table is dominated by US and Japanese companies, the US accounting for 26 top 20 positions over the three years and the Japanese for 25. A correlation exists between the number of registered patents and export performance. The dominance of Japanese products, particularly electrical goods, cameras, office

TABLE 10.7	Top 20 firms receiving US patents by rank order 1987–2013					
Rank	**1987**		**2007**		**2013**	
1	Canon	847	IBM	3 148	IBM	6 809
2	Hitachi	845	Samsung	2 725	Samsung	4 676
3	Toshiba	823	Canon	1 987	Canon	3 825
4	General Electric.	779	Matsushita Electric	1 941	Sony	3 098
5	US Philips	687	Intel	1 865	Microsoft	2 660
6	Westinghouse	652	Microsoft	1 637	Panasonic	2 601
7	IBM	591	Toshiba	1 549	Toshiba	2 416
8	Siemens	539	Sony	1 481	Hon Hai Precision Industry	2 279
9	Mitsubishi Denki	518	Micron Technology	1 476	QUALCOMM	2 103
10	RCA	504	Hewlett-Packard	1 470	LG Electronics	1 947
11	Fuji Photo	494	Hitachi	1 397	Google	1 851
12	Dow Chemical	469	Fujitsu	1 315	Fujitsu	1 806
13	DuPont	419	Seiko Epson	1 208	Apple Inc	1 775
14	Motorola	414	General Electric	914	General Electric	1 739
15	AT&T	406	Infineon Technologies	856	GM Global Technology	1 626
16	Honda Motor	395	Denso Corp	803	Seiko Epson	1 494
17	NEC	375	Texas Instruments	752	Ricoh	1 470
18	Toyota	375	Ricoh	728	Intel	1 455
19	Bayer	371	Honda	719	Hewlett-Packard	1 360
20	General Motors	370	Siemens	700	BlackBerry	1 334

technology and cars in the US is reflected in the table. In 1987 the top three companies receiving patents in the USA were all Japanese. In fact, eight Japanese companies feature in the top 20 for 1987 and five out of the top eight in 2007. In more recent years, IBM has been the leading company in terms of US patent activity, with Samsung also prominent. This may reflect the continuing impact of the 1990s recession in Japan as well as the increase in investment among US firms, particularly in computer hardware and software and in South Korea in telecommunications and domestic electrical goods. Although there are seven Japanese firms in the top 20 for 2013, the fall in both the number of representatives and their position in the table has almost certainly been affected by a decline in R&D investment in 2012–13 compared to the USA, South Korea and Taiwan (European Commission, 2013).

Problems of linking innovation and performance

Despite attempts to show links between innovation and various measures of performance both at the national and organizational levels, the links between innovation and economic performance remain speculative.

One difficulty is our inability to measure innovation. Indicators that have been used, such as patents and the amount of money a firm has invested in its R&D activities, can at best be considered a rough guide. For example, a patent may be registered and then never used to produce anything of value; improvements in products and processes can originate as much from individual inventors and equipment users as they can from organized R&D departments.

There is also the difficulty of establishing a causal relationship between innovation and economic growth due to the presence of a large number of variables. The export success of 'upper range' German cars such as Mercedes-Benz and BMW may well be attributed to the technical superiority of the product when compared with other cars in the same range and hence justify investment in R&D. There is another explanation. Both firms have run carefully targeted advertising campaigns, which not only stress the technical superiority of their product but also attempt to give the product an image of exclusivity and high status. To what extent are their sales attributable to technical innovation and how much to advertising? This illustration confirms the interrelationship of innovation and marketing identified earlier. It also emphasizes a theme in this book: that business activities are interrelated and there are dangers in viewing one activity, such as innovation, in isolation. This view is backed by NESTA, a body representing science, technology and the arts in the UK. They believe that the UK invests more in innovation than depicted by measures of innovation relying only on R&D expenditure. Their estimate is that R&D represents only 11 per cent of expenditure on innovation by UK firms; the rest is in the form of design and styling, training in new skills, innovations in organization and management and new brand development. NESTA argues that these innovations have a greater impact on productivity growth and can be found across a wide range of business sectors, whereas traditional science-based R&D does not (NESTA, 2009).

In 2005 Ford was the top investor in R&D, spending US$4.6 billion. Third in the list was General Motors, spending US$3.9 billion. Yet in 2006, Ford announced its biggest losses to date of US$12.7 billion and announced proposed global job cuts of 40 000 and the proposed closure of 12 plants. In late 2007, General Motors announced record losses of US$39 billion.

Expenditure in R&D would seem to be no guarantee of short-term financial success. This illustrates again the difficulty of examining R&D in isolation. R&D expenditure by firms like Ford and GM may well have contributed to product and process improvements, but these could have been negated by other factors such as the stagnant US car market or a lack of management strategy to capitalize upon the investment. Furthermore, the time horizon for the investment may be such that the pay-back will be at some time in the future. We may also speculate that without the investment in R&D the losses might have been even greater. Again this demonstrates the difficulty of showing causality.

REFLECTION POINT

What conclusions do you draw from the expenditure of Ford and General Motors on R&D?

Throughout this chapter we have made reference to the interest of the state in innovation based on the assumed link with economic growth. We now examine the role of the state in more detail. We will view the role of governments in general terms and explore how governments operate with respect to the stimulation of innovation, an area referred to as 'national systems of innovation'. There are strong links here to models of capitalism that we discussed in Chapters 3 and 5.

The role of the state

In almost every country, the state is involved in innovation. Three main reasons may be given as motivation for this involvement:

- Using the kind of economic argument presented in the last section, innovation and entrepreneurship appear to be factors in economic expansion and export competitiveness.
- We have noted that investment in innovation is both long-term and high-risk. The mechanism of the free market may be inadequate in generating those innovations upon which economic expansion is based, hence the need for state involvement.
- Intervention is often necessary for political and strategic as well as for social reasons. In Britain and the USA, defence spending forms a major part of all expenditure on innovation. Many countries have seen space exploration as a goal of national importance and prestige. Investment in renewable forms of energy is viewed by governments as a desirable strategy.

The state's financial investments are biased towards technological innovation in the manufacturing and defence industries, but exhortations for innovation and enterprise are usually aimed at all firms in all sectors. In this section, we attempt a classification of the types of intervention specifically concerned with innovation and examine the associated problems.

Types of state intervention in innovation

We examine state intervention under six main headings; procurement, subsidies, education and training, patents and licensing, restrictive and enabling laws and, finally, import controls. Such interventions occur even where the government has expressed its ideological opposition to interference in the workings of the free market.

Procurement The need of the state for certain products has stimulated research in many areas. Defence offers the clearest illustration with implications not only for the armaments industry itself, but also in electronics, computing and aerospace. Businesses in the USA have seen the armed forces as a very large and very stable market. In most countries the needs of health provision have stimulated developments in the pharmaceutical industry and, in most nations, concern for the environment and sustainability has led to government-backed research in many areas.

Subsidies Subsidies to firms occur in the form of investments, grants and tax concessions. Most subsidies aim to support a particular form of R&D. For example, EU funding, particularly through the European Social Fund, is biased towards the use of more innovative business solutions, particularly in IT. Subsidies can conflict with free market ideologies and, in some cases, as with the EU, subsidies to individual firms are not allowed.

Education and training There is an assumption that state investment in education and pure science will increase the level of innovation and thus benefit both the economy and society. The relationship between primary research and the knowledge-based activities of higher education institutions is supposedly one of the features of the modern age. Developments in 'Silicon Valley' in California and, in the UK, the growth of the science parks around major universities, such as Cambridge, show the relationship between industrial research and universities with a reputation for science. The growth of some US high-technology companies such as Hewlett Packard in Palo Alto, California, is clearly associated with this phenomenon. We note in Case 10.1 that Glaxo chose to locate one of its US research laboratories in the midst of universities in North Carolina. Such illustrations support the view that competitive endeavour among firms in close proximity to each other is a spur to economically successful innovations and that there is synergy to be gained both through such competition and through collaboration with the university sector.

In spite of such developments, British institutions of higher education are often subjected to financial stringencies as part of the government's determination to reduce public expenditure. On the positive side this has, in many cases, pushed industry and universities much closer together.

The state sometimes intervenes in skills training. Many ascribe Germany's advantage in product and process innovation to its superior craft training schemes. Clearly a skilled workforce is one that can adapt readily to technical changes.

Patents and licensing A patent is a legal device that enables the holder to maintain a monopoly in an invention for a stated period, usually 20 years. In exchange for granting this monopoly, the owner of the invention must make available its details to the general public. The patent system operates in almost every country. The stated benefits of such a system are:

- It encourages new developments by offering protection to the patent holder against others copying the invention, as illustrated in Case 10.1 with Zantac and Zovirax.
- By revealing the details of the invention, it encourages further inventions and innovative activity along similar lines.
- It prevents the duplication of research.
- It ensures that the benefits of research are passed on to society.
- A real benefit to the patent holder is the opportunity to issue manufacturing licences.

A firm holding a patent on a particular type of manufacturing process may allow another firm in the same business to use that process upon the payment of an agreed fee. In the case of major inventions this can be an important source of revenue for the patent holder and may make the company an attractive prospect for acquisition. Licensing is clearly a vital source of revenue for some companies. In certain cases the law has had to intervene to enforce the issue of licences where it was felt that some companies were operating an unfair monopoly.

Restrictive and enabling laws Most countries possess laws that control manufacturing standards and relate to such aspects as safety and pollution. Not only do these laws ensure that innovations conform to certain standards, but they aim to encourage research into socially desirable end-products, such as electric cars or exhaust systems that restrict air pollution. The ends are not only socially desirable but can have an effect on business performance as well. A firm that meets government standards of product quality enters the marketplace with additional competitive edge.

Such regulations can benefit some firms but handicap others. The determination on the part of the US administration to reduce the health care budget posed a threat to GlaxoSmithKline (Case 10.1), but may lead to the development of cheaper generic drugs. The use of restrictive laws has been greatest in the USA and there is a lobby that sees a danger that excessive regulation may hold back technological innovation and hence the country's economic growth. However, as with the relationship between innovation and economic growth, there is a difficulty in establishing a direct causal link between such laws and innovative activity at the level of the firm.

Import controls The theory here is that restriction on the imports from other countries will have a beneficial effect in stimulating research in the home country or intensifying the search for a substitute product or process. Import controls enforced by Japanese governments have often been cited as the impetus for innovations by Japanese businesses. There is, however, a danger that other countries may well retaliate and impose their own restrictions. The World Trade Organization has been part of the process to bring an end to such import controls (see Chapter 3 for more details).

REFLECTION POINT

Which of the above state interventions do you believe will have the greatest impact on innovation?

Problems with state intervention in innovation

We have seen that the main motive for state intervention to encourage and support innovative activity is the desire to improve economic performance. We have also seen the difficulties of showing a direct relationship between investment in innovation and economic growth, whether measured at national or organizational levels. There are other difficulties with the state's involvement:

- An over-reliance on state funding may have repercussions at times of reductions in government expenditure.
- A difficulty lies in the ability of government employees to make decisions in highly specialized technical and scientific areas, and decisions that are in the best interests of the business community as a whole. Government support may well be important in stimulating innovation but the critical skills and knowledge reside in the firms themselves or the higher education sector.
- There is the general conflict between government intervention and the freedom of firms and individuals, especially in laissez-faire systems.
- Underpinning many of the difficulties outlined above is the view that governments have the power to constrain innovation and entrepreneurial activity by bureaucratic interference and restrictive legislation.
- The direction of state intervention may raise conflicts with interest groups as well as raising ethical issues. Such issues surround R&D spending in the defence industries, in aerospace and in nuclear energy. Issues like these deal with aspects of business ethics and question the purpose, direction and outcomes of innovative activity.

Despite these difficulties many see an important role for the state in innovation activities of individual firms. A considerable literature has developed about national innovation systems. This literature argues that cultural and national differences are a product, not just of the role of the state but a whole series of institutional relationships within a country that result in different patterns of innovation. We explore this in the following section. There are links here with the notion of economic systems and institutional frameworks as sources of diversity that we introduced in Chapters 3 and 5.

National and cultural differences

So convinced have we become of the dependence of the total social, political and economic order on technical development that national output of scientific discoveries and the rate of technological advance have begun to appear as the ultimate criterion of culture and different political and social systems are compared as facilitators of this kind of achievement.

(Burns and Stalker, 1966, p. 19)

Burns and Stalker recognized that innovation was the product of a number of influences operating together. The configuration of these influences often leads to national differences. The term 'national system of innovation' is generally attributed to Lundvall who defined it as

> ... the elements and relationships which interact in the production, diffusion and use of new, and economically useful knowledge ... and are either located within or rooted inside the borders of a nation state.

(Lundvall, 1992, p. 12)

According to Lundvall, two features of the national system of innovation are:

- The relationship between the actors and institutions in the system, including governments, firms, banks and universities. We identify these in more detail in the next section.
- The flows of knowledge in the system. Lundvall believed that the actors and institutions engage in interactive learning that increases the value of knowledge as it flows through the system and as it is used.

A good example of how these relationships produce different approaches to innovation is illustrated by Freeman (1995) in a comparison of Japan and the USSR in the 1970s, as seen in Table 10.8.

The differences between Japan and the USSR reflect the differences in the two political and economic systems at the time. The USSR was a state-controlled economy with a strong internal focus, except in the cold war with the West and the USA in particular. Individual firms received instructions and dealt directly with the government. There was no competition but also no reason to collaborate. Japan typifies a coordinated market economy where the state encourages individual firms to innovate as a means of achieving competitive advantage. The de-militarization of Japan following World War Two has meant that defence R&D has played a very small role indeed.

Elements of the national system of innovation

We can identify a number of elements. The **state's involvement** includes the extent of subsidies to companies especially for basic research; the funding of universities and training and the

TABLE 10.8	An example of contrasting national systems	
Japan	**USSR**
High R&D spending as a % of GNP (2.5%)	Very high R&D spending as a % of GNP (4%)
Less than 2% investment in military and space	Over 70% to military and space
Integration of R&D, production and imported technology	Almost no integration of R&D, production and imported technology
Strong links between firms	Non-existent links between firms
Incentives to innovate at firm level	Mostly disincentives for innovation at firm level
Almost 70% of R&D company financed and operational at enterprise level	Less than 10% operating and financed at enterprise level
Intense international competition	Weak exposure to international competition except in arms race with the USA

protection of home markets. As can be seen in the above example of the communist USSR, the entire political and economic ideology influences the direction and levels of innovative activity. The nature of **economic organization** will determine the degree of sector specialization as in the case of the dominant role played by pharmaceuticals in Switzerland. In the USA and Japan, large firms predominate in terms of innovation, while in Italy a much greater role is played by smaller firms working together. Innovation is also a feature of competition both nationally and internationally. At the **level of the firm**, innovation strategies are important as well as the level of investment in innovative activity. The integration of the **banking system** with business can determine the amount of venture capital flowing into organizations. The significance of **stock market behaviour** can influence levels of investment especially where the system is geared to maintaining share price and paying high rates of dividend, which may operate against longer-term investment in R&D. The facilitation of **knowledge flows** through interaction with other firms and with universities as well as labour mobility can all be contributing factors. We may also identify **cultural influences**. The incrementalism that defines much of innovation by Japanese firms may well be a product of avoiding uncertainty, so encouraging a step-by-step approach involving detailed planning. The lack of innovative activity in many UK firms, with the exception of pharmaceuticals, may reflect educational preferences away from science and engineering.

KEY CONCEPT 10.7	NATIONAL SYSTEMS OF INNOVATION

National systems of innovation comprise a number of actors and institutions that collectively operate to determine the nature of innovation. The different influence of actors and institutions in different countries can lead to very different approaches to innovation. Influences include the state, banks, individual firms and the universities. The national system is influenced by economic and political ideologies as well as underlying approach to education and training. A key element in the system is the flow of knowledge between the participants and the development of knowledge as a product of the education system and through international links.

We do know that the interaction of the various actors and institutions and the nature of knowledge flows produces different approaches to innovation as illustrated in Table 10.9. In Chapter 5 we noted the difference between coordinated market economies (CMEs), typified by Japan and Germany, and liberal market economies (LMEs), typified by the UK and USA. We can see how these different systems impact upon innovation.

Table 10.9 gives examples of differences in two types of market systems. However, there is some evidence that many US firms have adopted a more long-term approach to R&D while, largely as a result of economic problems, firms in Germany and Japan have adopted more short-term approaches.

However, differences remain. Historically in Japan, innovation has always been supported by the state. The government Ministry of International Trade and Industry has, since the 1960s, encouraged innovation through the establishment of research consortia, in which R&D staff from major firms in each sector are seconded to government centres to collaborate on developments that will benefit the sector and ultimately the economy.

In comparison with other major industrial countries, the UK spends less on R&D as a proportion of GDP and employs fewer research scientists as a proportion of its labour force than its main competitors. In some industries, notably pharmaceuticals, the UK has world-class R&D performers in the likes of GlaxoSmithKline and AstraZeneca, but this is not the case in most

TABLE 10.9 Coordinated market and liberal market economic systems and their impact on innovation

CME (Germany/Japan)	LME (UK/USA)
Innovation is based on tacit knowledge accumulation	Innovation is based on demand, risk and time costs
Innovation is seen differently to other investments	Innovation is measured as just another investment
Long-term approach supported by banks	Short-term approach, with banks demanding a return on investment
Power in firms rests with engineers, scientists and practitioners	Power in firms rests with accountants
Rigorous general education and specific vocational training	Less rigorous general education and less attention paid to training and development, especially in the UK
Strengths in science and engineering	
Stable stock market supporting a long-term approach	More volatile stock market leading to a short-term approach
Government support and some intervention	Government adopts a more hands-off approach

other industries and innovation is concentrated in relatively few firms. The reasons can be found in the specific features of the UK national system of innovation:

- The behaviour of the stock market is frequently cited, more especially the payment of high rates of share dividend linked to short-termism.

- The withdrawal of the state from direct support is also given as an explanation. This was particularly apparent under the free market ideologies of successive governments since 1979.

- The lack of R&D activity in UK firms is also a function of the nation's industrial structure. The USA, in particular, has a much higher proportion of high-tech firms engaged in leading-edge research. UK industry is typified by low-tech firms and the GlaxoSmithKlines are the exception rather than the rule.

- There has been an over-emphasis on defence and prestige projects.

- Historically, high interest rates and the difficulties of raising investment capital are also cited.

- A relatively smaller number of university graduates in science and engineering than in many other countries.

While such comparative data and analyses are revealing, it is difficult to show precise links between cultural and national differences, R&D expenditure, innovation and economic growth. Our discussion of cultural and national differences has focused almost exclusively on R&D and technology. We should not forget that other forms of innovation exist. While the behaviour of financial markets is blamed for the lack of investment of UK manufacturing firms in R&D, firms specializing in finance have themselves been highly innovative, developing new products to keep one step ahead in a highly competitive business. As we have seen earlier, R&D investment in the banking sector has been growing.

Globalization versus national systems

The diffusion of knowledge flows and innovation has accelerated as a result of globalization. In particular, the creation of global business networks has facilitated knowledge exchange and similar innovations have been taken up in diverse national and cultural contexts. Does globalization mean that national systems are no longer important? There are two strong areas of evidence supporting the importance of national systems.

First, Porter (1990) argues that national systems are very important and these support the development of local competences, resulting, in some countries, in clusters of successful firms in the same sector. In the USA, there is the development of the automobile industry around Detroit. In Germany, we find clusters representing the chemical and precision engineering industries. In Japan there are clusters representing the automobile, electronic and camera industries. The UK is represented by a strong financial industries sector. It is clear that some countries focus on some types of R&D more than others. Almost 70 per cent of Swiss expenditure on R&D is from the pharmaceutical companies. Pharmaceuticals also dominate in the UK accounting for around 48 per cent of expenditure. In South Korea the electrical and electronic companies account for 60 per cent of all R&D expenditure and in Germany the automobile and parts industry accounts for around 48 per cent of R&D spending. In the USA the spending, while larger in most sectors by comparison with other countries, is spread across a number of different sectors (BIS, 2010).The second argument supporting national systems is based on the concentration of R&D activity in the home country of large multinationals. Examining the data from a number of studies carried out in the 1990s, Tidd et al. (2005) conclude that only 12 per cent of the innovative activities of the world's largest 500 firms they define as technologically active were located outside of their home country. This compares with 25 per cent of their production activities. However, more recent research by Tellis et al. (2008) suggests the position has changed and that multinationals are increasingly seeking to locate R&D in developing economies. Their research of the largest multinationals as defined by the Fortune 500 global listing found the top five locations for their R&D facilities as follows:

USA	502
Germany	153
Japan	152
UK	109
China	98

Moreover, they noted that India was ranked seventh with 63 facilities (Tellis et al., 2008).

REFLECTION POINT

Has globalization made obsolete the role of national systems of innovation?

Innovation and technology

There is an obvious relationship between technology and innovation. Numerous illustrations exist where developments in state-of-the-art technology result in business innovations and the development of new products and processes: the microchip being a good example.

There are some, like Schumpeter, who see technical breakthroughs as the force that changes the whole nature of business, and the ability of firms to respond is crucial to their survival (Schumpeter, 1961). The emphasis on the role of technology is referred to as technology–push. There is another view in which demand plays a leading role in determining the direction, extent and impact of inventions. While some industries undoubtedly have a richer knowledge base than others, notably chemicals and electronics, the profitability of the application of that knowledge was predominantly a question of demand. This process is referred to as demand–pull (Schmookler, 1966). This was referred to earlier in this chapter (see Key concept 10.3).

Attempts have been made to support the primacy of demand–pull over technology–push and vice versa and illustrations can be given on both sides. The development of synthetic fibres is clearly a case of demand–pull, while the growth of the mass market in electronic calculators is clearly a case of the use of developments in integrated circuits and hence technology–push.

In most instances, the distinction between technology–push and demand–pull is too simplistic. The growth of sales of the CD is the product of both the application of laser technology to produce consumer goods (technology–push) and a function of rising discretionary income and market segmentation (demand–pull). The two forces would appear to operate side by side. The development and rapid expansion of International Direct Dialling by British Telecom in the late 1970s was a direct response to a growing market demand among the business community for telephone communication with overseas associates. Having developed the technology, BT found that the resources were being under-used outside peak business periods. The company therefore launched an advertising campaign to increase private and domestic use of the available technology. The initial development was demand-led, while subsequent developments were clearly a case of technology leading the market, and a company anxious to obtain a healthy return on its investment.

We can see from these illustrations that the marketing function is both an important guide and support to the direction of innovation. Marketing activity helps in the selection of R&D projects by providing information on the probability of their commercial success. It then assists in persuading the consumer that change is desirable. We can see then that invention, innovation, research and development, manufacturing and marketing have a complex relationship that is not always fully explored by those seeking to prove a correlation between innovation and economic growth.

As well as being the catalyst for innovation, in some cases an established technology can be difficult to change. Whittington (2000) cites a number of examples, the most famous of which is the development of the QWERTY keyboard on typewriters. It is acknowledged that this particular configuration for keyboards is not the most efficient. Its development was a function of mechanical constraints of early typewriters and the insistence of the Remington Company that a keyboard should have all the letters to type 'typewriter' on one line. The system persists despite the fact that the mechanical constraints no longer exist.

ORGANIZATIONAL ASPECTS OF INNOVATION

Innovation varies significantly between different sectors, and between firms in the same sector suggesting that both structural and organizational factors influence the effect of innovation on performance.

(Tidd et al., 2005, p. xiii)

When we examine innovation at the level of the individual organization, the most significant aspects to emerge are those of size, structure and organization culture. Ownership variables do not appear to be significant and, despite the obvious interest of the state in the innovation process, there is certainly no evidence to suggest that innovation in publicly owned companies is any more significant than that in private firms. Indeed, critics of public ownership may well argue that political involvement can slow down the process of innovation. We shall see that the question of goals is invariably tied up with issues of size, and we deal with these aspects together in our next section.

Organizational size and goals

The impact of organizational size upon innovation presents us with conflicting evidence as to the relative merits of large versus small firms. We will examine some of that evidence and attempt to show the relationship of size with changing goals as well as illustrating the dynamic process of innovation at the level of the firm. However, we must remember the major difficulty in our assessment of innovation, that of measurement. While R&D expenditure is clearly an indication of innovative activity, firms can be highly innovative in their products, marketing and organization without having an organized R&D function.

The argument for large firms includes the following:

- Large firms dominate when developments in technology depend upon expensive research programmes of the kind that can only be found in the large corporation. The complexities of modern technologies and the corresponding development costs set up irrevocable pressures on organizations to grow. This is certainly the case in the pharmaceutical and aerospace industries. Evidence in the 1960s was fairly clear in that large manufacturing firms spent proportionally more on R&D, had a larger share of innovation and were quicker to adopt new techniques of manufacturing (Mansfield, 1963).
- Large firms also feature more prominently where risk is high. They are able to spread risk more easily than small firms and are generally better placed to attract government funding and to obtain bank loans.
- In general, large firms are able to generate more funds internally that can be used for development funding.
- Large firms also dominate where high volume sales are needed in competitive industries. This explains both the dominance and high R&D expenditure of major firms in the automobile industry.
- Large firms can exploit economies of scale and therefore get more for their research expenditure.
- Large firms dominate the R&D Scoreboards (see Tables 10.2, 10.3 and 10.4).

The argument for small firms includes the following.

- Small firms spend more on R&D as a proportion of total sales and employ proportionally more staff in R&D than the larger firms, though this could be a case of economies of scale operating in favour of the larger firm rather than any differences in their innovative capacities.
- Smaller companies do have higher R&D intensities, measured in terms of the relationship between R&D expenditure and sales. However, this may be because they are in the process of establishing themselves and are in the research phase of their development. It may also be a function of their lower sales compared with those of larger firms.

- Those who subscribe to the small-firms lobby would argue that the smaller company is more flexible and adaptable, less bureaucratic, closer to the consumer and, hence, the source of far more significant innovations than the big firm. We deal with such arguments in more detail in the section on small businesses in Chapter 6.

- Some evidence favours the small firm. Pavitt (1983) found that firms of less than 1000 employees accounted for more than 20 per cent of innovations in Britain, far greater than their share of R&D investment but less than their share of employment or net output. However, Bessant and Tidd (2007) argue that much of the research is biased towards specific, notable examples and ignores the fact that the majority of small firms are not innovative at all.

There are three complicating factors: competition, the nature of the industry and time. We deal with each in turn.

Jewkes has championed the cause of the small inventor but found that size is a far less significant factor than the **competitive nature of the market** in which the firm operates (Jewkes et al., 1970). We may conclude from this that highly innovative firms are more likely to be found in very competitive markets, as is the case with cameras, and that this occurs irrespective of the size of the firm.

There are also important variations according to the nature of the **sector in which the firm operates.** Most innovations in the electrical, electronic, food, chemical and vehicle industries occur in large companies. In the case of mechanical engineering, instrumentation, leather and footwear, it is the smaller firm that tends to dominate (Pavitt, 1983). There is a danger with such analyses in that they confine innovation to products and processes. Significant innovations in, for example, retailing and financial services tend to be overlooked.

The relationship between innovation and size of firm can **vary over time.** Henry Ford produced five engines in quick succession, before the Model T, in a relatively small, jobbing-based organization. No product change then took place for 15 years, as the emphasis shifted to the development of mass-production process technologies and incremental product improvements (Abernathy and Utterback, 1978).

Examinations of business histories show that the most fundamental product innovations usually take place at a relatively early stage of a firm's development, when it is relatively small. As the firm develops, more emphasis is placed on process innovations. A stage may well be reached where the growth of mass markets and the need for economies of scale in the production process mean that fundamental change is resisted as being too costly. In other words the goals of the company change over time with changes in size and the nature of the innovations. A longitudinal study of the development of computer aided design (CAD) systems in manufacturing found that from 1969 to 1974 initial innovations took place in small computer software companies. From 1974 to 1980 the main developments were taking place in much larger companies. Either the original firms had expanded or they had been bought out by firms, such as General Electric, wishing to buy into the new technology. In both cases, size was seen as an important factor in the attraction of venture capital. From 1980 onwards, smaller firms once again entered the market, concentrating on the development of highly specialized CAD systems, with a limited field of application (Kaplinsky, 1983).

We may conclude that there is no clear relationship between size and innovation, but we are able to make the following observations:

- The investment required in some types of innovation, and the need for high volume production for a return on that investment, clearly operates in favour of large companies, as in the chemical and pharmaceutical industries.

- An influencing factor would seem to be the sector of operation. Some sectors, like chemicals, tend to be dominated by large companies while in others, especially instrumentation, the small firm still plays a significant role.

- There are cases of breakthroughs being made by small firms in all sectors, but they may have to align themselves with larger companies to obtain the necessary development capital, production capacity, or access to markets.

- Where markets are especially volatile, any firm, irrespective of size, may have to keep innovating to maintain market share. It is in such situations that entrepreneurial activity becomes most important.

- The relationship between size and innovation varies over time as does the link between product and process innovation.

REFLECTION POINT

Does size matter when it comes to innovation?

Innovation and organization structure

When novelty and unfamiliarity in both market situation and technical information become the accepted order of things, a fundamentally different kind of management system becomes appropriate from that which applies to a relatively stable commercial and technical environment.

(Tom Burns, in the preface to *The Management of Innovation*, Burns and Stalker, 1966, p. vii)

The starting point is appropriate, since it was Burns and Stalker's study of the post-war electronics industry and, in particular, the failure of some of the Scottish firms in their study to innovate, that has been so influential, not only in the development of organization theory, but as a practical guide to innovative firms on the development of appropriate structures. In this section we will examine why such a 'fundamentally different kind of management system' is necessary, the problems encountered in setting up such a system, and the attempts that have been made to provide solutions to these problems. We illustrate the arguments by focusing on the R&D department in typically science and technology-based industry. The same arguments apply for any group within an organization with the primary responsibility for initiating innovation. For example, in an advertising agency tensions often arise between staff who manage client accounts, and who have to adopt a business orientation, and those whose primary responsibility is the generation of creative ideas.

Burns and Stalker identified two ideal types of organization, which they called the mechanistic organization and the organic organization. In their view the organic organization was more effective for innovation. The differences between these two types of organization are presented in Table 10.10.

REFLECTION POINT

In what situations would mechanistic structures be more effective than organic structures?

TABLE 10.10	Differences between mechanistic and organic organizations
Mechanistic	**Organic**
Highly specialized tasks. Fragmentation and differentiation	Contribution of individuals to a collective common goal
Tasks follow abstract rules	Tasks related to the needs of real situations
Roles and jobs are defined in a precise way	Roles and jobs are loosely defined and are continuously being redefined
The structure is very hierarchical with location of key knowledge at the top	Responsibility and authority are delegated throughout the organization. Knowledge exists anywhere in the organization
Interaction and communication tends to be vertical	Communication flows in all directions. Teamworking and networking are encouraged
Members of the firm are expected to be loyal and obedient	Members of the firm are expected to be committed to the goals
The focus tends to be on experience and knowledge built up within the organization	The focus is on external experience and knowledge is drawn from a variety of sources
Innovation strategies tend to be based on rational approaches using SWOT analysis	Innovation strategies tend to be incremental, changing and creative

The R&D function and those connected with it have various claims for different treatment from the rest of the organization.

- There is a fundamental belief that the creativity inherent in the function requires its workers to communicate freely both within and outside the organization and to be free of the bureaucratic controls to which other departments are subject.

- The very nature of the work demands that there be flexibility as far as the allocation of priorities, patterns of working and normal management control systems are concerned.

- Specifically there is a demand for the relaxation of hierarchical controls and a need to see investment in R&D as a long-term issue.

Those companies where innovation is a key activity have tended to respond by creating R&D departments. This can create a problem, in that this can set up a clash of cultures between R&D and the other departments. The need for flexibility, as outlined above, challenges bureaucratic controls and with it the existing power base. The old order with its allegiance to the organization and the status quo can be shaken by a group with allegiance to a knowledge base whose source lies outside the organization. In such a situation it is often convenient for top management to isolate the R&D department both politically and sometimes geographically. In this way it presents less of a challenge to the status quo and can be conveniently amputated when costs need to be cut. It is not uncommon, in times of economic recession, for firms to cut back or close down altogether their R&D function. This sets up an interesting paradox between the need to reduce expenditure and the central role ascribed to innovation in economic recovery. However, it is often the R&D staff who support this isolation within the organization. It absolves them of responsibility and gives them the kind of freedom they seek to pursue their own goals.

The result for the organization is invariably a lack of coordination between R&D and production and marketing; which retards the innovative process and is detrimental to the effective operation of the firm as a whole. A great deal of time can be wasted on internal politics and the situation can lead to a proliferation of committees and intermediaries.

In many ways, the R&D department needs to be different because its goals are different, the time horizon on which it is evaluated is different, and it has different needs with regard to the formality of its operations. An R&D department needs an informal structure because of the uncertain nature of its work and its need for a flexible response to both technological and market changes. Specialists may need to be brought in from outside, possibly on a temporary basis, decision-making and responsibility may have to be decentralized, and there will usually be a very loose specification of jobs and work procedures. Integration may be achieved through the management information system, by creating cross-functional teams, or by using some managers in special integrating roles.

There are dangers with this approach. Catering to the special demands of the R&D function can lead to the kind of isolation we have already discussed and attempts at integration can all too often result in paperwork jungles or the creation of supernumerary roles.

Communication and coordination would appear to be key issues. Multinationals that can draw effectively upon a worldwide network are generally more innovative than those who operate as separate national entities. Companies such as GSK and Siemens have established global innovation networks, vital in fast-moving industries such as pharmaceuticals and electronics. In all firms, a close relationship between R&D and marketing is essential to provide information which reduces uncertainty concerning the acceptability of innovative products.

Firms operating globally would seem to have three options. Innovation can be the prerogative of some centralized unit such as a central R&D division, or it can be a decentralized activity or a combination of both systems. A centralized system offers economies of scale and may offer advantages in the development of new technologies. However, where it is important to develop local products for local markets, particularly where supply chains are involved in the development process, a decentralized system may be more effective. Most global firms, such as HP and Ford, have R&D operations in most of their main markets. Tidd et al. (2005) argue that the factors involved in centralization versus decentralization and global versus local are:

- Where basic research is important, as in the pharmaceutical industry, centralization tends to be the norm, as it does where a period of trial and error is needed after a breakthrough.

- Firms following long-term strategies tend to have more centralized R&D than those pursuing more short-term, market-led strategies.

- There is a tendency for most global firms to locate the majority of their innovative activity in the home country. In the case of Germany, Japan and the USA, Tidd et al. (2005) note that as much as 80 per cent of high-spending R&D is located at home. The main use of foreign R&D would appear to be to adapt products for local markets. Of course, in the case of certain complex products, such as passenger aircraft, even this may be unnecessary. Localized R&D would seem to operate best when there is a need to exploit local conditions, as in the case of working with local raw materials or using specialized local knowledge and skills. We also noted that there is a trend to locate R&D in emerging markets, especially China and India (Tellis et al., 2008).

Some believe that effectiveness is achieved through the organization of the firm around its dominant competitive issue. In this way, if innovation were identified as the priority then the firm should locate its centre of power and influence around that activity. Innovative firms not only see innovation as a priority but build an entire organization culture based on innovation. In the next section we reinforce this theme.

Organization changes, which follow technical innovations, can underline the competitive advantage of the innovation. The impact of containerization and advances in telecommunications offered opportunities to shipping companies, but full advantage was only gained following corresponding changes in jobs and organization structure.

The role of organization culture

In the previous section we dwelt at length on the structural issues pertaining to the operation of an R&D function. We have maintained throughout that innovation is not the sole prerogative of science-based manufacturing industry, nor does it depend on the existence of a formally established R&D department. We have established that innovation applies to all forms of business, and many firms are entrepreneurial and innovative largely because it is seen as a responsibility of all staff, irrespective of their function.

A culture of innovation may be built up in a variety of ways. One way may be to recruit innovative and entrepreneurial staff and, by using training programmes, to develop creative thinking. More significantly, the lead normally comes through the activities and energy of senior management, and their creation of an organization to foster innovation. Ekvall (1991) reported on a research programme about creativity and found, not surprisingly, that creative organizations were typified by high trust, freedom, idea support, playfulness and risk-taking.

INNOVATION AND MANAGEMENT STRATEGIES

Throughout this chapter we have seen that both management and representatives of governments have operated on the clear assumption that innovation is linked to increased productivity, market share and profitability, as well as being an indication of the state of a nation's economic health. An innovation strategy would appear to be the key to competitive advantage, based on the belief that firms must innovate to survive, since strategies that depend on imitation and following market trends will ultimately lead to a saturation of the market.

In this section we will examine two types of innovation strategy, 'first to the market' and 'follower strategies'. Following our discussion of organization structure and culture we will revisit the concept of integrated strategies before closing the section with an examination of some constraints to innovation.

Types of strategy

In Chapter 8 we identified a number of approaches to strategy formulation that we called the 'strategic process'. We noted that a popular approach to strategy was the rational approach based on an assessment of the firm's environment and of its strengths and weaknesses. We argued that such an approach was unlikely to produce innovative solutions since much of the knowledge is also available to competitors and therefore strategies are likely to be copied.

Whittington (2000) and Tidd et al. (2005) argue that an innovative strategy is more likely to arise from an incremental process. This allows strategy to develop in a step-by-step approach and is constantly amended as new things are learnt about the environment, the organization and the customers. Such a process goes hand-in-hand with a form of organizational learning, in which the organization members develop knowledge and understanding that is unique to their firm and situation. We have referred to this as tacit knowledge (see Key Concept 10.4). As we noted in Chapter 8, no single approach to strategy is necessarily better than any other. However, in terms of innovation, two generic strategies have been recognized. These are 'first to the market', sometimes referred to as 'first-mover' and 'follower'.

'First-to-the-market' strategy

According to Ansoff and Stewart (1967), organizations pursuing this type of strategy display the following features:

- Research and development is viewed as a central part of their operation.
- There is a strong commitment to basic research, technical leadership and hence a willingness to take risks with comparatively large investments.
- Research tends to be close to the state-of-the-art and the organization employs a high proportion of top-rate research scientists.
- There is considerable coordination between research, production and marketing and planning is usually long-range.

The large pharmaceutical companies, like Pfizer, Roche and GlaxoSmithKline, fit into this category. They use R&D and a 'first-to-the-market' strategy as a deliberate attempt to dominate the market. As we see in Case 10.1, GSK and its predecessors have always employed large numbers of research scientists, have close links with universities in various parts of the world, and developed the anti-ulcer drug Zantac before its rivals, thereby achieving a very large and very profitable market share.

However, a first-to-the-market or a first-mover strategy is not confined to science and technology-based industries. First-mover advantages can be found also in the banking industry (ATM machines, telephone and online banking) and in the tourist industry (being first to develop a resort, or in the case of Club Med, develop a new holiday formula).

First-mover advantages Being first to the market gives a firm distinct advantages, many of which were identified by Lieberman and Montgomery (1988):

- The firm has technical leadership and can do something that no-one else can, thereby creating a steep learning curve for others to follow. The advantage may lie in the uniqueness of the product or process. It may also lie in the complexity, as in the case of large jet aero-engines developed by Rolls-Royce. The advantage may also lie in combining a bundle of attributes that others find difficult to replicate. This was an advantage gained by Japanese cars in the US market in the 1980s. This is very similar to the concept of core competence, discussed in Chapter 8.
- The firm can use the patent system to create a monopoly position and earn income from licensing activities, as with Pilkington and its float glass process or with many products in the pharmaceutical industry, such as GSK's Zantac or Pfizer's Viagra.
- Those first to the market can control limited resources. These include raw materials and labour, but other factors as well. The first development in a beach resort can occupy the prime site and buy land when prices are relatively cheap. Those following, especially if the resort becomes fashionable and popular, are faced with less desirable locations and higher prices. Such locational advantages can also give a competitive edge in retailing.

- Those that are first can set the industry standards that others must follow, as in the case of computer hardware and software. The battle for market share in the UK satellite television industry was fought between Sky and BSB, with the two companies operating different systems. In some respects BSB operated a technically superior system but being first enabled Sky to gain the largest market share. BSB experienced financial difficulties and was eventually taken over by Sky.

- Once a market is established, those coming after incur significant costs in getting buyers to switch from the first mover product. This is especially true if the first mover establishes a strong brand.

Being a first mover and being first to patent the invention may not be sufficient in itself. Sony was not the first company to patent the Walkman but was the first to produce it cheaply and market it effectively. Rank Xerox was first to the market with the photocopying machine and used the patent to create an effective monopoly but failed to compete effectively for several years with Canon and Toshiba when they entered the market as followers. Being a follower can have advantages and it is to this we now turn.

'Follower' strategies

A variety of follower strategies can be identified. Some firms, such as Philips operating in the domestic electrical market, are highly innovative and take state-of-the-art technical knowledge invented elsewhere and use this to develop their own product range. Other firms will follow cautiously behind the state-of-the-art technology, concentrating more on design modifications. Follower companies possess R&D departments and, while not first to the market, are still concerned with innovation. By contrast there are some followers who have no R&D function as such. They exist largely on a strong manufacturing base and have the ability to copy products quickly and effectively. Successful firms of this type operate on low costs, have a comparatively low selling price and the ability to deliver on time. They rely on being highly competitive as opposed to innovative. Firms operating in this way do not tend to be household names.

Follower advantages

- Goods can often be introduced more cheaply as high development costs do not have to be recouped. Followers are able to acquire technology much more cheaply.

- There are fewer risks and the costs associated with them.

- Those coming after can learn from the mistakes of the pioneers. For example, Boeing developed its highly profitable 707 range of aircraft by learning from the metal fatigue problems that dogged the early versions of the British Aircraft Corporation's Comet and, as a result, gained a much larger market share (Bowen et al., 1992). In turn, Airbus, a relative newcomer, learned from Boeing and in certain areas became the market leader.

- Coming second also means that a market with support mechanisms such as knowledgeable retailers, service and maintenance facilities, and complementary products, is established. In the computing arena, later arrivals entered a marketplace where software standards were established and they could develop their products accordingly.

- The consumer is more aware and has developed product knowledge.

Follower strategies have been summed up by Lieberman and Montgomery (1988) as 'free-rider' effects'. Such a strategy can be pursued in specific circumstances by otherwise highly innovative and well-known companies. We have noted that, when Rank Xerox's patent on the photocopier expired, several companies, including Canon, Toshiba and Gestetner, used the available technology to manufacture their own versions. In many cases those coming second not only have the advantages highlighted above but can build upon their reputations in other fields. In the case of Canon and Toshiba they developed photocopiers that were not only cheaper but more reliable. This, in turn, resulted in Rank Xerox rethinking its own strategy and led to a focus on quality and the development of 'total quality management' (TQM) techniques in an attempt to recapture its former market position.

REFLECTION POINT

Identify a range of first-mover and follower firms and their products.

Integration: strategy, structure and culture

Although innovation is a primary source of competitive advantage, it is usually an effective source only if it can be deployed in concert with some other sources of competitive advantage, or if it is at least supported by other strategic weapons.

(Kay, 1992, p. 127)

Our illustrations of the 'first-mover' and 'follower' strategies above suggest that the two are not mutually exclusive and that a firm can pursue different strategies in different product markets. The above quote from Kay (1992) suggests that whatever strategy is pursued it is insufficient in itself without the support of the rest of the organization. This reinforces the theme raised in our discussion of the relationship to innovation of organizational structure and organizational culture. We may conclude from the works of Kay (1992), Tidd et al. (2005), other authors and case histories that the strategic implications for a firm wishing to be innovative are:

- Leadership is important in setting the agenda. Individuals such as Edison and Ford have set examples for others to follow. Without such leadership, firms can lag behind. Tidd et al. (2005) argue that General Motors delayed implementing lean production, following Toyota's lead, on the mistaken belief that the Japanese advantage came from unfair trading practices.

- In general there needs to be a risk-taking ethos that is supported by top management. Such an ethos is an important part of the firm's vision statement, widely accepted by employees. There ought to be a willingness to experiment and therefore a freedom to fail. Employees should be empowered, encouraged and supported. Individual contributions should be recognized and publicized throughout the organization.

- This should be supported by the recruitment of people with creative talents and, where appropriate, with good technical backgrounds in the specific industry sector. This in turn needs to be supported by a creative culture reinforced by flexible structures and styles of leadership

- Recruitment policies need to be reinforced by training and development programmes which place emphasis on innovation and the acquisition of the required technical knowledge. Promotion strategies should include technical know-how and a commitment to innovation as key criteria. Development targets should stretch individuals.

- The exchange of ideas should be encouraged, not just within the firm but, especially for those operating in science-based industries, also by fostering links with universities and other research establishments. Innovators tend to have an external focus.

- Mechanisms that facilitate communication can be set up, such as suggestion schemes and more radical methods of employee participation, but, more generally, innovation may be encouraged if the organization is flexible and decentralized.

- Effective structures tend to be based on small flexible teams, where employees have broadly defined jobs. Employees should be encouraged to interact with people and ideas from outside their own organization. While structures are important they need to be flexible enough to change as circumstances change.

- Innovation is about learning and change, and it is linked to the concept of the learning organization. There should be a focus on tacit learning that is used for competitive advantage.

- Whether a special R&D department is created or not, attention needs to be paid to integrating the function of innovation with the rest of the organization's activities. Kay (1993) goes further and speaks not only of the importance of integration within the firm – between departments, management and labour – but also between the firm and its suppliers and the firm and its customers. The close relationship between many Japanese manufacturing firms and their components suppliers illustrates this. In short, innovation is the responsibility of all people in the organization (and those outside who work with it) and not just members of the R&D department.

Probably the most significant feature to emerge from the points made above is the need to create a particular organization culture or climate that is supportive of innovation. This in turn needs to be supported by an environment where emphasis is placed on developing the skills of the workforce, and where innovation is encouraged by banks and by effective political policies instead of rhetoric. The absence of these features presents the innovative firm with considerable constraints.

Constraints to effective innovation strategy

Despite the central role ascribed to innovation, there are constraints that may limit its effectiveness. We can identify them as failures of management and of structure and problems associated with costs, operations, the behaviour of employees and other difficulties relating to the political and economic environment.

A failure of management

- A UK DTI survey concluded that the main inhibitor to innovation was the lack of vision and leadership of senior managers. Many did not see the market need to innovate (DTI, 2006).

- For any new idea there is a high probability of failure. If we add this to a tendency on the part of many managers to underestimate the costs involved, then it is easy to see why some companies have found innovation a risky strategy. Lockheed and Rolls-Royce in the aerospace industry are good illustrations of this.

- Managers in many industries, faced with the pressure for career development and pressures from shareholders for a generous dividend, may opt for safer short-term investments, which preclude more radical innovative strategies. Undoubtedly the problems associated with short-termism in general highlight the importance of a supportive financial system for effective innovation.

Cost is a major inhibitor as are the difficulties of raising finance. This is reinforced by the issue of the time lags between development and commercial exploitation which can be highly variable, a process taking an estimated 22 years as far as television was concerned.

Structure. Kanter (1997) concluded that the main structural constraints were a dominance of vertical relationships and poor lateral communications.

Behavioural constraints include resistance to change and coping with organization changes that change the power relations within organizations.

In addition to all these problems, economic, social and political conditions may militate against effective innovation. We have already seen the importance of a skills infrastructure and supportive political policies. Objections by trade unions fearing losses in job security, either real or imagined, can set back the introduction of process innovations, as we have seen in the newspaper industry (News International case in Chapter 4).

Difficulties of the kind identified above have led to a preference by some firms to seek other strategies. A common option is the use of the patent and licensing system identified in this chapter. Instead of developing products and processes itself, a firm will manufacture a product or use a process that has been developed elsewhere, on the payment of a licence fee to the patent holder. This is not only a strategy for the avoidance of R&D costs but can save a great deal of time in the development process by eliminating duplication of effort. The high cost of development in the electronics industry was considerably reduced for many firms by using, as their starting point, the original patent for the transistor owned by the Bell Telephone Corporation. Licensing may not be totally passive and may, in fact, be a spur to modifications, resulting in a company developing its own innovations.

In addition to licensing, the costs of innovation may be reduced by undertaking joint development with another company, buying in specific research work as needed from a specialist research consultancy firm or even through acquisition strategy. In this way, a firm can add to its stable of new products, processes and patents by purchasing particularly innovative companies that are operating in their chosen direction of diversification. In some cases a spin-off company can be established to focus on a specific project, as SmithKline Beecham did with Adprotech before its merger with Glaxo Wellcome.

In discussing innovation, students should remember that the strategies are never as discrete as textbook models would like them to be. We have noted that a firm can be first to the marketplace with some of its product range while following other firms in other types of product. A firm may well have a strong R&D department with a record of successful innovation. At the same time it could license developments from its competitors and even pursue an acquisition strategy of buying up certain highly specialized units.

What does appear to be important is an integrated strategy, a theme that appears central to the innovative process. A good idea may be wasted without corresponding policies in operations and marketing, the respective themes of our next two chapters.

CASE 10.1   GLAXOSMITHKLINE (GSK)

In 2000, Glaxo Wellcome and SmithKline Beecham merged to create the largest UK pharmaceutical company. On the Forbes Global 2000 list it is the fifth ranked pharmaceutical company in the world behind the USA firms Merck, Pfizer, Johnson & Johnson and the French company Sanofi-Aventis. The motivation behind the merger was the creation of a research-led company to challenge the best in the world in terms of its ability to invent and deliver new drugs to the market. The merger was estimated to save the two companies £1.89 billion. The company now employees 99 500 employees in 87 manufacturing sites and offices in 115 countries. Its major research sites are now in the UK, USA, Spain, Belgium and China. The corporate headquarters are in London.

This case focuses on developments that occurred in Glaxo Wellcome before the merger and deals with the recent problems that have arisen since the merger.

Glaxo Wellcome was itself formed by a merger in 1995 between Glaxo and Wellcome. At the time, Glaxo Wellcome controlled 35 per cent of the world gastrointestinal drug market, 25 per cent of the antibiotic market, 25 per cent of the respiratory market and 70 per cent of the anti-viral market. The focus of the company remained the prescribed pharmaceuticals market, despite considerable growth in the over-the-counter, non-prescription drugs market. At that time Glaxo Wellcome had a presence in over 50 countries, manufacturing in over 30 of them. Glaxo Wellcome operated in a competitive world market where research played a significant role both in terms of expenditure and in terms of the ever-present need to develop innovative products.

Glaxo had risen to prominence with the development and manufacture of the world's best-selling drug, Zantac, a treatment for ulcers. The drug was launched in 1981 and became the world top-seller by 1986. However, the company had not emerged as a leading-edge researcher until the 1960s when the acquisition of a research-based operation led to the development of Ventolin, a drug for asthma sufferers. The company had developed in the early part of the 20th century as a family business selling powdered milk for babies, with a gradual extension into products related to infant nutrition. The real point of entry into the drugs market came with the Second World War when the company began to produce penicillin. Zantac transformed Glaxo from a moderate UK company into a world leader. Wellcome was founded in the late 19th century as a UK company, Burroughs Wellcome, by two Americans. The company developed the rubella vaccine, but its best-selling item, Zovirax, a treatment for herpes, was launched, like Zantac, in 1981. By 1996, Zantac was the world number one and Zovirax the world number six in terms of drug sales. Overall, the company had six medicines in the top 40 best-selling pharmaceutical products.

Before the merger, both Glaxo and Wellcome were noted for their commitment to R&D. Between 1987 and 1992 more than half of Glaxo's capital spending went on equipping research laboratories. In 1992, Glaxo built a complex at Stevenage to employ 1700 research scientists. In 1992, the Stevenage research laboratories were the largest investment project in the UK after the Channel Tunnel and Sizewell B nuclear reactor. The laboratories became the research base for Glaxo Wellcome. Following the merger, the company was able to rationalize its R&D operations, saving £600 million a year. At the same time, it became the top listed UK company in terms of R&D expenditure, spending £1.14 billion in 1997. By 2013, in world terms, the R&D expenditure of the new company GlaxoSmithKline was the fifteenth largest of all companies and fourth among all pharmaceutical companies, behind Pfizer and Johnson & Johnson of the USA, and Sanofi-Aventis of France. For many years it has been the largest R&D spender in the UK.

Glaxo Wellcome had its research HQ in the UK, and then had research operations in the USA, Japan, Spain, France, Singapore, Switzerland and Italy. Glaxo Wellcome's R&D strategy was an extension of that pursued by Glaxo. The company had a fairly ruthless approach to weeding out the potentially successful from the unsuccessful developments at a relative early stage and the marketing of innovative drugs at relatively high prices. There was a strong belief in different approaches to solving problems and Glaxo Wellcome not only capitalized upon cultural differences in the approach to research but moved its researchers around the various locations. The organization of research was invariably flexible with the emphasis upon small teams feeding into project approval committees. There was a strong support of pure research and links with the university sector were seen as crucial. In 1992, Glaxo supported university chairs and projects and the location of its laboratory in North Carolina was in the 'research triangle' between three of the state's most prestigious universities. The Stevenage research site was deliberately designed to resemble a university campus. Such a commitment to pure research underlined the long-term view of R&D strategy. This is inevitable in an industry where it is not uncommon for the development process to take between 10 and 15 years. An important feature here was the good relationship that the management of the company had fostered with City financial institutions.

The development of Zantac by Glaxo owed much to initial work carried out by a British scientist, James Black, whose findings were published in 1972. Black was working for the US firm SmithKline French, which was the first to the marketplace with an anti-ulcer drug, Tagamet, in 1978. Scientists at Glaxo were convinced that by reworking Black's studies they could develop a superior product. An intensive research programme and product trial resulted in Zantac being launched in 1981. The R&D period for Zantac was highly concentrated, with a subsequent shortening of product lead-time. Effective use was made of patent protection to differentiate the product from its main rival.

The success of Zantac as a product was invariably linked to its acceptance in the USA. Apart from its being the largest market for drugs there were fewer price controls than elsewhere and, hence, greater potential for profits. Zantac was initially marketed in the USA by the Swiss company Hoffman-La Roche, well known through its own products, Librium and Valium – the world's biggest-selling tranquilizers. Zantac was priced higher than Tagamet and it is widely acknowledged that the marketing campaign was aggressive. Not only were the superior claims of Zantac over Tagamet forcibly made but Glaxo emphasized the negative side-effects of the rival drug. Subsequent pressure by the US regulatory body, the Food and Drug Administration, has resulted in Glaxo withdrawing some of the claims made concerning the superiority of Zantac. Nonetheless, Zantac took the US market from Tagamet to become the world's best-selling drug. At its peak, sales of Zantac accounted for some 40 per cent of Glaxo's total sales.

However, by the mid-1990s there were threats to the market dominance of both Zantac and Zovirax

- In 1993 a new administration was elected to power in the USA. A key policy of the new administration was the reduction in health care costs, which were the highest of any nation. There was considerable pressure to reduce the costs for the elderly, who generally have inadequate insurance and must pay the full cost of treatment. There was also pressure to bring down health insurance premiums and to reduce the cost of state-funded health care. The drug companies, who charged premium prices for their products, became an obvious target. The government encouraged the purchase of cheaper generic drugs developed in lower-cost labour markets, such as Puerto Rico. The threat at the time to both Glaxo and Wellcome was significant given their reliance on the sales performance of Zantac and Zovirax in the USA.

- The above threat was magnified by the expiry of the patents on both Zantac and Zovirax in 1997. This meant that others could enter the market, producing generic versions of the drugs at a much lower price. This, in turn, forces the originator to lower their prices to remain competitive, with the risk of a substantial fall in profits. Glaxo Wellcome tried a number of legal manoeuvres to retain their patents to no avail. The company also attempted to gain some ground on the generic drugs manufacturers by negotiating a deal with the manufacturer, Novopharm, to produce Zantac ahead of the patent expiry date. Nonetheless, the expiry of the patent led to a 3 per cent fall in total sales for Glaxo Wellcome in 1997.

Several factors mitigated these threats:

- The merger between Glaxo and Wellcome gave the new company a broader product portfolio.

- As well as saving on R&D costs, the merger resulted in a global reduction of labour costs, with 7500 jobs being lost.

- Opportunities had opened up in emerging markets, which by 1997 accounted for 15 per cent of world sales in pharmaceutical products.

(Continued)

CASE 10.1   (Continued)

- The management considered that its continued investment in R&D enabled it to replace Zantac and Zovirax with other best-selling drugs. Between 1990 and 1997, Glaxo Wellcome launched 24 products, which in 1997 represented 34 per cent of sales. The company has great hopes for drugs to treat migraine and Aids. Other developments included drugs to alleviate the side-effects of chemotherapy and considerable investment in the development of 'gene guns' to deliver vaccines and treat cancers.

Since the second merger in 2000 to create GSK, the company, now with even greater investment in R&D, has strengthened the position of its predecessors as one of the world's leading companies. However, there have also been problems:

- The sheer size of the firm has been questioned in some quarters, particularly as new drugs have not been developed at the speed and volume predicted. To offset this, the company established six specialist drug discovery units. However, within a short time the heads of three of these units had left to join rival companies.

- During 2002, the share price halved. Although the UK stock market fell during this period, the performance of GSK was seen as poor.

- The patent protection of two of its more recent best-selling drugs was under threat from generic manufacturers. The drugs were Paxil, an anti-depressant that outsold Pfizer's Prozac, and Augmentin, an antibiotic.

- The company was criticized for its position on the sale of AIDS drugs to Africa. In common with its predecessor companies, GSK insisted on selling drugs at premium prices. Opponents claimed this put them out of the reach of most African states, where AIDS is a serious problem. The company eventually relented following the intervention of the UN and its then secretary general, Kofi Annan.

- In May 2003, in an unprecedented action, shareholders blocked proposals on the contract of the then chief executive, Jean-Pierre Gamier. Under the terms of the proposed agreement he was to be promised a settlement of over £20 million, to be paid when he decided to leave the company. Shareholders considered this as excessive. The issue arose at the same time as criticism was levelled at the appointment of several non-executive directors. The criticisms were based on the poor records of several of those directors with companies in other sectors.

- In 2012 net income was over 13 per cent down on the previous year. Price controls on drugs were introduced by several governments, including those of Spain, France, Germany, Turkey and South Korea. This affected GSK's revenue by 7 per cent and operating profit by 11 per cent despite a reduction in operating costs of 3 per cent. As a result GSK embarked on a restructure of its European operations to reduce costs further.

- GSK along with many other pharmaceutical companies was put under pressure by the Chinese government to reduce the prices of medication as the nation's medical services were struggling to cope with an ageing population. GSK executives in China were also accused of bribing doctors and hospital staff to gain market share for GSK products.

Despite these problems GSK has done well in emerging markets and their fastest growth has been seen in China, Latin America and India. The growth in emerging markets was 14.7 per cent between 2007 and 2012 compared to 3.4 per cent growth in the largest market, North America In 2012 the contribution of its various markets were as follows.

North America	£221bn	42.8%
Europe	£120bn	23.35%
Emerging markets and Asia Pacific	£112bn	21.7%
Japan	£63bn	12.2%

GSK is one of the few pharmaceutical companies targeting research in medicines and vaccines aimed at the World Health Organization priorities of tuberculosis, malaria and HIV/AIDS. In 2012 the company was ranked first in making medicines available to the poorest countries and its vaccine business remains one of the largest in the world.

CASE 10.1 (Continued)

Questions

1 What advantages are to be gained by the various mergers that resulted in GlaxoSmithKline?

2 What conclusions can you draw from the case about product innovation in the pharmaceutical industry?

3 What does the case tell us about the organization of innovation?

4 What are the major threats facing GlaxoSmithKline?

SUMMARY

- Invention, innovation, research and development, design and entrepreneurship are all related concepts.

- For businesses it is the process of innovation that is the key concept, turning an invention into something profitable. Innovation can relate to products, processes, marketing and organization and management, and can range from fundamental to minor changes.

- Evidence suggests that the more successful innovations are those that are integrated, with product, process and organizational change occurring together. Integration would appear to be an important theme in innovation.

- Entrepreneurship plays a key role in innovation. We can identify different types of entrepreneur and factors that contribute to the development of entrepreneurs, although predicting who will become an entrepreneur is still difficult.

- We view innovation as the key to increased productivity, increased market share and hence profitability and the firm's continued survival. The theme has been translated to the scale of national economies and we have seen how some regard innovation as the source of economic recovery out of a recession. These relationships are difficult to prove but there can be no denying that without innovation there can be no new products or processes.

- The importance of innovation has been recognized by governments, although there are considerable variations in the extent and direction of intervention. Government support for innovation is seen not only for economic, but for political and social reasons too, although there can be ideological and practical difficulties in the state's involvement.

- We are able to identify differences between nations in the nature and type of innovation. This is a product of the national innovation system. It would appear that such differences persist in a global economy.

- There are clear links between innovation and technology, although in practice it is difficult to determine whether an innovation is a result of 'technology–push' or 'demand–pull'.

- Most important innovations in business are the product of a range of factors. An understanding of the marketplace is particularly important, and innovation and marketing are interrelated activities.

- At the level of the individual firm there is no clear evidence linking the size of a company with its propensity and ability to innovate, although very expensive research tends to be concentrated in large companies. The sector in which the firm operates and the volatility of the market all interact with the size of establishment in a complex way.

- What is fairly clear is that firms with an R&D department have special problems in the integration of R&D with other activities and in particular, production and marketing. The most successfully

SUMMARY   (Continued)

innovative companies tend to be those that have paid attention to the creation of a particular organization culture and the encouragement to all staff to be creative.

- Some firms clearly see themselves as technical and market leaders and invest a high proportion of their income in developing new ideas, products and processes. Other firms are more content to sit behind the field and rely upon minor developments or strategies of copying. Strategies can be adopted either singly or together.

DISCUSSION QUESTIONS

1   What do you understand by the concept of organization and management innovation? Are such innovations as important as scientific and technological innovations?

2   What are the relative advantages and disadvantages for a firm pursuing radical/ discontinuous innovations versus incremental innovations?

3   Examine Tables 10.2 to 10.5 relating to expenditure on R&D. What conclusions do you draw?

4   Assess the relationship between innovation and economic growth. Which criteria would you use to show such a relationship?

5   Examine the ways through which the state can subsidize, encourage and protect innovation in private firms. Why should the state get involved, and what difficulties arise with such involvement?

6   What is a national system of innovation and how significant are such systems in determining differences between nations?

7   Examine Table 10.7 relating to patents. What conclusions do you draw?

8   Select a range of consumer domestic products that illustrate the relationship between technology–push and demand–pull. Which of these two is the more significant?

9   What contribution can the size of the firm make to innovative activity?

10   Identify problems associated with the existence of a special function responsible for the initiation of business ideas, such as an R&D department. What structural devices would you employ to reduce these problems?

11   Assess the innovation strategy options for a manufacturer of consumer electrical goods, a major computer firm, a package holiday company, and a university.

12   Assess the relative advantages and disadvantages of being a first mover and those of being a follower.

FURTHER READING

A good general approach to innovation in general can be found in:

Drucker, P.E. (1985) *Innovation and Entrepreneurship*, Heinemann: London.
Tidd, J., Bessant, J. and Pavitt, K. (2005) *Managing Innovation: Integrating Technological, Market and Organizational Change*, 3rd edn, John Wiley: Chichester.

A good coverage of entrepreneurship can be found in:

Bessant, J. and Tidd, J. (2007) *Innovation and Entrepreneurship*, John Wiley: Chichester.

Although it was written over 40 years ago, some of the best insights into organizational and strategic aspects of innovation are found in:

Burns, T. and Stalker, G.M. (1966) *The Management of Innovation*, Tavistock: London.

Two important articles covering national systems of innovation and strategic aspects respectively are:

Freeman, C. (1995) 'The "national system of innovation" in historical perspective', *Cambridge Journal of Economics*, 19: 5–24.
Lieberman, M. and Montgomery, D. (1988) 'First-mover advantages,' *Strategic Management Journal*, 9: 41–58.

Useful websites include:

UK Department for Business, Innovation and Skills: www.berr.gov.uk
The EU information on R&D can be found at: http://iri.jrc.ec.europa.eu/scoreboard13.html

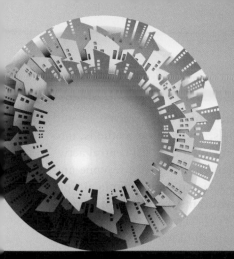

OPERATIONS

11

LEARNING OBJECTIVES At the end of this chapter you should be able to:

- Identify the objectives of operations and their contribution to competitive advantage and explain the conflicting nature of those objectives.
- Explain the difference between the operations function in a manufacturing and service organization.
- Define operations as a system and as a transformational process.
- Identify and explain the main activities of operations management and assess their contribution to organizational effectiveness.
- Articulate the problems and issues involved in planning and control.
- Assess the approaches to quality control.
- Explain supply chain management and just-in-time.
- Explain the link between technology, the design of operations systems and the effect on jobs.
- Explain the impact of operations on the size and structure of the organization.
- Identify and assess operations strategies.

INTRODUCTION

Operations is concerned with the creation of the goods and services offered to consumers and the transformation of inputs, such as information, people, materials, finance and methods, into outputs, such as goods, services, profit, customer and employee satisfaction. It is a central activity in most types of organization. This means that operations activities influence revenue and costs as well as organization structure. Although traditionally associated with manufacturing, the operations function also plays a key role in supermarkets, restaurants, banks, local government, schools and hospitals, in fact in all kinds of organizations.

The growth of the non-manufacturing sector has encouraged a rethinking of the operations concept. We can see clearly that significant operations issues exist in managing an airport as busy as Schiphol in Amsterdam or Heathrow in London. Planes must take off and land safely and on time. For this to occur, operations must be coordinated, including air traffic control, ground crews, baggage-handling, passport control and customs, aircraft cleaning, refuelling and catering. In busy regional hospitals, surgical operations must be carefully timed and scheduled, patients transferred to and from wards, equipment prepared and the various support systems, from nursing to catering, properly briefed.

Competitive advantage is derived from the objectives of the operations system. It is generally acknowledged (for example, Slack et al., 2014) that these are:

- quality
- dependability
- speed
- flexibility
- cost efficiency and effectiveness.

KEY CONCEPT 11.1   OBJECTIVES OF OPERATIONS MANAGEMENT

The main objectives of operations management are acknowledged by many to be quality, dependability, speed, flexibility, cost efficiency and effectiveness. A focus on these issues will result in competitive advantage. It has been suggested that real competitive advantage will come from a primary focus on quality, followed by dependability, speed, flexibility and, finally, cost. The belief is that attention to the other factors will lead to both a reduction in cost and a customer who is willing to pay more for a high-quality, reliable product. In reality, operations strategies vary in the way these items are mixed.

These objectives recur throughout this chapter and a more detailed discussion of their role in operations strategy can be found in the final section. We begin with a more detailed definition of operations and examine differences between manufacturing and non-manufacturing, as well as looking at inherent tensions in the operations process. We then review issues in operations design, operations planning and control with a focus on improvement processes and introduce some aspects of supply chain management. As with all our treatments of business functions we explore some environmental and organizational issues before closing the chapter with an analysis of operations strategies.

IDENTIFYING THE OPERATIONS FUNCTION

We have seen that an operations system exists to provide goods and services, which it does by transforming inputs into different kinds of output. We can view this as a system comprising inputs, process and outputs, as in Figure 11.1.

Figure 11.1 shows that the operations function transforms the various resource inputs into the required goods and services. Three aspects of the model need explanation:

- Not all the outputs of the system are necessarily desired outcomes. Waste, in the form of either substandard products or unused raw materials, can be a costly item in manufacturing, while in the form of polluting chemicals it can constitute an environmental hazard. Customer dissatisfaction can be an unintended output. The consequence of diners at a restaurant receiving bad service may well mean they decide never to return.

- The concept of environmental pollution introduces the notion that outputs of one system are invariably inputs to other systems. The manufactured outputs of a car components

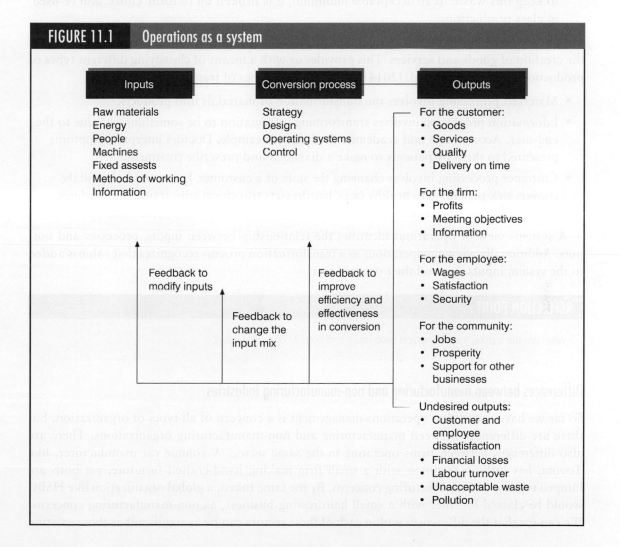

FIGURE 11.1   Operations as a system

Inputs

Raw materials
Energy
People
Machines
Fixed assests
Methods of working
Information

Conversion process

Strategy
Design
Operating systems
Control

Outputs

For the customer:
- Goods
- Services
- Quality
- Delivery on time

For the firm:
- Profits
- Meeting objectives
- Information

For the employee:
- Wages
- Satisfaction
- Security

For the community:
- Jobs
- Prosperity
- Support for other businesses

Undesired outputs:
- Customer and employee dissatisfaction
- Financial losses
- Labour turnover
- Unacceptable waste
- Pollution

Feedback to modify inputs

Feedback to change the input mix

Feedback to improve efficiency and effectiveness in conversion factory are clearly inputs to other firms. The increasing use of systems of global sourcing and global sub-contracting by manufacturers has led to developments in operations strategies and placed emphasis on supply chain management. Wages paid to workers will invariably be passed on to shops and supermarkets and also to banks and other financial institutions, in the form of mortgage payments or savings, which are then used to fund further investments.

- Outputs may also be considered as inputs to the same system. In this way, information gained during the production process can be used to improve the operation of the system, such as changing the supplier to improve the quality of parts and reduce the number of rejects. A large number of dissatisfied customers at a restaurant or a hairdressing salon is an indication that some element of the process needs attention. This is known as feedback. Another type of relationship can be built up between output and input when materials are recycled. In the manufacture of large sheets of glass, the smoothing of edges, the cutting of glass to size, and the generally fragile nature of the product mean that there are always quantities of broken glass. While measures are taken to keep this waste to an acceptable minimum, it is broken up to form 'cullet' and re-used in glass production.

We can see from the systems model that production is a transformation process resulting in the creation of goods and services. This provides us with a means of classifying different types of production system. Slack et al. (2014) identified three types of transformation:

- Materials processing involves the transformation of materials into products.
- Information processing involves transforming information to be something of value to the end-user. Accountants and academics do this, for example. Doctors interpret symptoms presented to them by patients to make a diagnosis and prescribe treatment.
- Customer processing involves changing the state of a customer. For example, hospitals convert sick patients into healthy ones, hairdressers transform appearances and airlines change a person's location.

A systems view of operations identifies the relationship between inputs, processes and outputs. Additionally, viewing operations as a transformation process recognizes that value is added to the system inputs, beyond their original cost.

REFLECTION POINT

What are the inputs, transformation processes and outputs of a university?

Differences between manufacturing and non-manufacturing industries

So far we have stated that operations management is a concern of all types of organization, but there are differences between manufacturing and non-manufacturing organizations. There are also differences between firms operating in the same sector. A volume car manufacturer, like Toyota, has little in common with a small firm making hand-crafted furniture, yet both are lumped together as manufacturing concerns. By the same token, a global organization like HSBC would be classed together with a small hairdressing business, as non-manufacturing concerns. We can see that the differences within each of these sectors can be as significant as those existing between them. At this stage, however, it is worth pointing to the differences between manufacturing and non-manufacturing:

- Manufactured goods tend to be more tangible, storable and transportable.
- In a non-manufacturing concern, the customer is generally more of an active participant in the process. This is especially true in education and hospitals and those organizations offering a personal service, such as hairdressers, solicitors and financial advisors. The interaction of the customer means that the process is often less predictable, and operation systems correspondingly more complex.
- Unpredictability means that operations are more difficult to control in the non-manufacturing sector. The degree of contact with the customer can affect the efficiency of the operation. For example, doctors may not be able to plan their work as effectively as they would like owing to the variability in the consulting needs of patients. Productivity therefore becomes more difficult to measure and quality becomes much more a matter of subjective assessment.
- The quality of a service tends to be assessed on the basis of not only output but also the way it is delivered. Aspects of delivery can be important for perceptions of quality in manufactured goods, but less so than for services.

We examine the implications of these differences when we look at the elements of the operations process later in the chapter.

Conflicting objectives and changing solutions

Any operations system, be it in manufacturing or service, is concerned with the production of a certain number and type of goods and services at a designated level of quality. Completion and delivery must be within certain time limits and within acceptable financial and social costs. The price charged must be acceptable to the consumer and must ensure sufficient quantity of sales to secure an acceptable return for the organization. The entire system should have sufficient flexibility to be able to adjust to changing demands.

KEY CONCEPT 11.2	POTENTIAL CONFLICTS IN AN OPERATIONS SYSTEM

In most operations systems, there is inevitable tension between the needs of management to construct an efficient operation and the needs of customers. The needs of the former tend to focus on costs, while those of the latter focus on design, quality, price and delivery. Many of the techniques in the design, scheduling and control of the operations system aim to resolve such potential conflicts.

Consumers want goods and services to their specific requirements of quantity and quality and perhaps to be tempted by a selection of offerings. The goods and services should be easy to obtain at the time they are needed and should be sold at a price the consumers deem reasonable. If we buy an item of flat-pack furniture from a store like Ikea we can take the item home with us. On the other hand, if we decide to buy handcrafted furniture from an upmarket department store we know that it will cost more than the flat-pack item, and that we may have to wait for delivery. Many consumers are willing to make trade-offs: to pay more for quality, or to wait for made-to-measure items. Many are not willing to do this and managers are left with the task of balancing potentially conflicting objectives to achieve both customer satisfaction and the efficient use of resources. This is illustrated in Figure 11.2.

FIGURE 11.2	The conflicting objectives of operations management

Customer satisfaction	V	Efficient use of resources
Availability of goods and services in the quantity required		Low levels of stock
		Scheduling which meets all demands
Best quality for price		Best price for quality
Good selection of innovative goods and services		Limited range creating long runs and repeat offerings. Low-cost design
		Scheduling to fit resources and constraints. Efficient use of raw material and labour
Fast, reliable delivery		Low-cost location. Restricted hours of working and opening
Flexible delivery on demand and easy access		

Such conflicts exist in all types of operations systems. We may wish to fly from London to Singapore but cannot travel on the day we wish because all the seats are booked. We travel two days later but, when we arrive, we must wait two hours to get into our hotel room, because the room-cleaning schedule means the room is not ready. In both cases solutions might have been found by upgrading our flight to business class or upgrading the standard of the room to an available suite. However, such options may be at an unacceptable price. We could have re-routed our journey via another European city, but this would have added to the length of journey or required us to fly with an airline on which we could not accumulate frequent flyer points. We could have changed hotel but our original choice was made on the basis of a convenient location and good price.

The main reason for conflict goes back to the interrelated nature of the operations system. In an attempt to reduce costs, managers have options. They can cut back on the cost of materials or staff, which may result in lower-quality goods and a generally poorer service. They can expect the workforce to increase productivity for the same reward or they can gear up for higher productivity by ensuring long production runs (in the case of manufacturing) or reducing the time spent with clients (in the case of the service industry). All these options give rise to potential conflicts. Goods of lower quality may not be acceptable to the consumer, unless the price is cut, so negating the original cost-cutting exercise. The workers may resist attempts by management to increase the tempo of work. In manufacturing, the introduction of long production runs has a trade-off in the form of reduced flexibility and lack of choice for the consumer. A doctor faced with a waiting room full of patients may be more efficient by limiting consultation time but with the attendant danger that a potentially serious illness could be overlooked.

The operations manager needs to balance the forces that are the cause of such conflicts. Operations managers emerge as mediators, coping with different demands, both within the operations system itself and between that and other systems. This role is sometimes termed boundary management. We develop these themes in more detail in our discussion of operations strategies at the end of the chapter. In the meantime, we look a little more closely at the relationship between operations and the other activities.

REFLECTION POINT

What conflicts of the type identified above have you experienced as a customer of goods and services?

The relationship between operations and other functional areas

The centrality of the operations function and the boundary role of the operations manager bring into focus the relationship between the operations function and the other functional areas. Examples of such relationships include the following areas.

Innovation

As we saw in the previous chapter, innovation is at the heart of product development, with obvious implications for the operations function. In both manufacturing and service industries, production capabilities and capacities must be important considerations at the design and development stage of any product. An innovative product design is of little value if it cannot be made by the workforce within certain cost parameters. Similarly, a new design for a business management degree course must take into account the skills of the teachers and the capabilities of the students.

Marketing

Information about consumer requirements is essential to those in operations. Operations managers need to know the total demand for their products and services and when they will be required. This forms the basis of planning. Feedback from consumers on the utility of the product or service or its value for money can assist both the R&D and operations functions in the design and creation of future products. Holiday companies frequently ask clients to complete a questionnaire about every aspect of their holiday, not only as a public relations exercise but also to improve the product and the way it is delivered.

Human resource management

HRM will assist in recruitment and selection (employee resourcing); in training and development; in the management of pay and performance; and in ensuring good employment relations including the control of the safety, health and welfare of the workforce. Staff selection and training are crucial to the success of those service industries with high levels of customer contact.

Finance and accounting

The accounting function clearly interfaces with operations in the development of budgets and targets. In return, operations information is essential to such decisions as pricing and wage determination. The accounting function will also play a role in decisions to replace items of capital equipment.

CASE 11.1   ZARA

By Francisco Puig (University of Valencia, Spain) and Miguel González-Loureiro (University of Vigo, Spain)

When managers from the fashion industry are asked to explain the sources of competitive advantage, the majority would identify marketing issues such as brand and the interpretation of social trends. Few would assert that competitive advantage stems from logistics and operations management. This case is about the Spanish fashion group Inditex, owner of the well-known brand Zara. Zara is the group's largest

CASE 11.1 *(Continued)*

brand and for the sake of simplicity we will refer to the company as Zara to represent all the brands developed by Inditex. We shall show how Zara developed a logistics system while expanding internationally and that its operations management is an essential part of its competitive advantage. At the same time, its operations system imposes a barrier of entry for new competitors willing to develop similar business models in this market segment, because of the large investment needed in ICT and the experience gap that Zara has built. Zara's market is sometimes referred to as 'quick fashion'. Zara will reinterpret the latest haute couture fashions, almost overnight and get them in their shops at affordable prices.

Zara is a global, vertically integrated company that in 2012 had more than 6000 stores around the world, more than €15 946 million sales and a net annual profit of more than €2 367 million. It employs 120 000 people. Zara opened on average 463 new stores each year between 2008 and 2012. Its main suppliers are located in India, Bangladesh, Turkey, China, Morocco, Brazil, Portugal and Spain. The company aims to achieve over 50 per cent local supply of Zara's manufactured goods in each of the countries where it has stores. This meant increasing the total number of suppliers to 1 434 by 2012 at the same time that the group expanded internationally. More than 30 000 product items are created by the Group each season. With 6000 stores to stock, a very large number of products must be moved large distances virtually every day.

The value chain in the fashion industry starts with raw material either natural (such as cotton) or artificial (such as nylon) and all the different components that make the final product (e.g. buttons, zips, and the like). Flexibility to make quick changes and utilize small batches of production may be as important as speed. Processes such as fabric spreading, cutting or sewing/assembling can be outsourced. Meanwhile, activities related to design as well as activities at the end of chain are conducted internally. Only the final touches such as ironing, labelling and packaging are carried out at the central warehouse.

The company has a policy of only making goods to order, linked directly to sales or projected sales. This increases the complexity of managing the huge number of relationships across the supply chain as it requires speed and flexibility in its operations on a global scale. The system is based on knowing the exact requirements of each store on a daily basis. In the words of a senior Zara manager, *'We sell tomatoes, and when a tomato is not sold as quickly as possible, then it rots'.* This message not only puts the emphasis on speed and on shortening the time to market, but illustrates the fast moving nature of the business. Items have a very short shelf life and for Zara and its associate brands, a season can mean only 15 days. This in turn creates an urgent need to buy on the part of consumers, particularly as items are produced in a limited number for each store.

Each store around the world is in contact with the Spanish headquarters at the end of each day and sends data on all items sold including information on colour and size. This has two major implications for the supply chain management. First, with those items which do not reach the expected sales at a given store, supply stops in that item to that store and is diverted to stores with higher sales. If this happens for an item across several stores, then the manufacture of that item is stopped immediately. Second, if the central warehouse does not have enough stock of a particular item which is selling well, then an order is automatically generated for immediate manufacture.

Zara's current policy is that an item for sale should be in the store for two days or less. European stores operate on a stock turnover of between 24 and 36 hours, while for those in the rest of the world it is 48 hours. This policy lowers the cost of inventory, even when the number of stores has grown at impressive annual rates. This policy would not be possible without the aid of ICT and a complex, automated system that incorporates suppliers and external transport companies. The hub is the automated warehouse located in Arteixo, which has been replicated in Zaragoza and in Tordera, near Barcelona. The warehouse has an automated aerial handling system that was designed and installed by Toyota, based on the principles of just in time and lean manufacturing. The system can deal with 60 000 items an hour. The aerial rail system itself is around 250 kms long. However, as some operations must be done by hand, the maximum number of goods handled is nearer 30 000 per hour.

The system begins with an order from one of the group's stores. The automated system locates the goods in the warehouse and the number of items required by size and colour are placed in a box for

CASE 11.1   (Continued)

TABLE 11.1	Milestones for Zara's logistics system
Dates	**Milestones**
1963–1988	Zara begins its activity as a manufacturer of clothes and apparel. Several plants are opened over this period, distributing the products among the stores located in the main cities of Spain and some nearby countries such as Portugal (Porto was the first store opened in a foreign country by 1988).
1986–1987	The group's plants run their entire production to the Zara brand and Inditex lays the foundation for a strong logistics system to match the planned growth.
1989–1990	Inditex begins its activity in the USA and France.
1991	Pull & Bear is born and Inditex buy the 65% of Massimo Dutti corporation. The logistics system is shared with both brands.
1992–1994	Stores are opened in Mexico (1992), Greece (1993), Belgium and Sweden (1994). The stores are all in the downtown shopping locations, and all stores are owned by Zara.
1995–1997	Inditex acquires the full equity of the Massimo Dutti brand. Zara moves into Malta, Cyprus, Norway and Israel.
1998	The brand Bershka is born to focus on younger females. Stores are opened in several countries across the world.
1999	Stradivarius is acquired becoming the fifth brand owned by the corporation. Stores are opened in Europe, North and Latin America and in Saudi Arabia and Bahrain
2000	Inditex locates its headquarters in Arteixo (near A Coruña, Spain). The central warehouse is a totally automated computer controlled system with direct extranet connections to each store. It continues opening new stores
2001–2002	Oysho is launched as the lingerie new brand. Inditex begins trading on the public stock market. It opens more stores in current markets (e.g. in Ireland and Italy), and in new markets in Latin America and the Caribbean.
2003	A new brand is born: Zara Home, the group's seventh brand focused on household goods. The logistics centre in Zaragoza is opened.
2004–2006	Inditex opens its store number 2000, and now operates in 56 countries of Europe, America, Asia and Africa. In 2006 a store opens in China.
2007	Zara Home opens the first Inditex's online store. Two new logistics platforms are inaugurated in Spain. Zara opens its store number 1000. Bershka and Pull & Bear both now have over 500 stores each.
2008	A new brand, Uterqüe, is born, specializing in fashion accessories. Inditex opens the store number 4000 in Tokyo and reaches 73 countries.
2009	Inditex signs a deal with Tata Group to open stores in India from 2010 onwards. The other brands enter China. A new logistics platform opens in Barcelona (Spain).
2010–2011	In September, 2010, the online store becomes active across 16 European countries. With openings in Australia, the group now operates in the five continents with more than 5500 stores in 82 countries.
2012	Inditex reaches 6000 stores opened all over the world

(Continued)

CASE 11.1 (Continued)

TABLE 11.2	Breakdown of stores by brand
Brands	**No. of stores**
Zara (+Zara Kids)	1770 (+166)
Pull & Bear	825
Massimo Dutti	634
Bershka	910
Stradivarius	816
Oysho	533
Zara Home	363
Uterqüe	87
Total	6104

TABLE 11.3	Geographical distribution of Zara's suppliers (2012)
Asia	672 suppliers
European Union	444
Non EU Europe	136
Africa	112
Central and South America	68

each store. Once the boxes are completed, they are moved to the corresponding cargo bay. The final process of loading the trucks was initially done by hand. As the automated part of the system was much faster than the manual handling, the result was a bottle-neck. However, the shift was not allowed to end until all the orders were loaded. This led to an industrial dispute that was settled with a net increase of 12 per cent in bonuses and salaries. The settlement also included a reduction in the number of hours for the people in the warehouse. It also meant a small increase in the hiring of temporary labour.

An additional challenge for the Zara group is the management of a global supply chain comprising nearly 1500 suppliers spread far and wide (see Table 11.3). The solution was seen in the creation of clusters based on geographical area. These clusters are audited by Zara or by an auditing firm hired by Zara. Each cluster is coordinated by a board made up of suppliers' representatives in that region. The aim of creating clusters was twofold: first, the number of direct relationships with each supplier would reduce; and second, through the cluster system suppliers would be encouraged to exchange best practice. Country clusters have been formed in each area and the company carries out specific programmes with each cluster group. These include training and technological support for all the players involved in the supply chain. The company operates specific initiatives known as 'Clear to Wear' and 'Safe to Wear', tailored to help suppliers comply with the production standards fixed by the group. Both initiatives relate to health and safety standards of the product itself and those in the supplier's factory. The production standards also relate to standards of housekeeping and conditions of employment, including rates of pay.

Clusters include both direct suppliers and suppliers of auxiliary products as well. The boards running the clusters are given responsibilities by Zara. For example, the Bangladesh cluster was placed in charge of the internal investigation to examine the tragedy, which happened on January 26, 2013, when a fire broke out in the Smart Fashion factory located in Dhaka. It was found that the local supplier in charge of manufacturing the articles had transferred production to this factory without informing Zara beforehand.

The Group carries out more than 3500 annual audits to monitor the supply chain activities and suppliers are expected to comply with the company's requirements. Factories are ranked from A (the best) to D. Improvements on key aspects are expected within each cluster. In addition to the annual audit, suppliers are periodically screened to check whether they are fulfilling the terms of their contract with Zara. During 2012, 474 suppliers had their contracts cancelled while 418 new suppliers were given contracts (see Table 11.4).

The complexity in the supply chain increased when the Group decided to open online stores for all the group's brands. By the end of 2013, online stores for Zara were available in a limited number of European countries (Spain, Portugal, France, Italy, Germany, UK, Austria, Belgium, Holland, Ireland, Luxembourg, Sweden, Norway, Denmark, Monaco, Switzerland and Poland) and in the USA, Canada, Japan, China and Russia.

An additional level of complexity is related to the strategy of regional or even national prices and the possibility of consumers comparing prices between

CASE 11.1   *(Continued)*

TABLE 11.4	Group supply chain in 2012			
Region	Suppliers used in 2011	Suppliers not used in 2012	New suppliers in 2012	Suppliers used in 2012
Africa	127	30	15	112
America	66	22	24	68
Asia	686	271	257	672
Non-EU Europe	134	45	47	136
EuropeanUnion	477	106	75	446
Total	1 490	474	418	1 434

stores in different locations. In addition, the online store is a new channel to be managed along with the whole supply chain.

The company has direct management of its stores, operates a large and complex supply chain and pursues a strategy of rapid design and rapid turnaround of goods. As if this were not enough, the company faces additional challenges. There seems to have been a greater focus on ICT and information systems than on staffing issues. The short-cycle logistics operated by the group have put great pressure on the stores' workers. Up to 2008 there were two deliveries each week and sales staff had to replenish the shelves before opening. A pilot study was conducted in 17 stores across Spain. The study recommended that dedicated shelf fillers could be employed between 2 a.m. and 10 a.m. The existing stores' employees could then concentrate on sales. By July 2014, this recommendation was carried out in Spain and nearby countries but it was still under consideration in the rest of locations. This became an even more relevant issue when the Group moved to more frequent deliveries, placing even more pressure on sales staff. There are also concerns about the carbon footprint of the entire logistics operation. All transportation and distribution operations are carried out by external operators and local firms.

Questions

1 Under the principle of *fast-fashion* and lowering the time to market, analyse what processes of the value chain you would recommend to out-source and why.

2 Assess the impact of the ICT on the global efficiency of Zara's supply chain. Identify positive and negative implications for the logistics-related HR. Which management issues emerged from the large number of relationships with suppliers? How has Zara tried to manage them? What is the role of policies and norms in managing and controlling the supply chain?

3 Why does Zara insist that 50 per cent of manufacturing must be carried out by local suppliers? What implications does this have for their logistics operations?

4 A key issue for logistics in global organizations is the balance between universal HR policies and the need for adaptation to local factors. What factors will affect the mix?

5 Identify non-related businesses where Zara's logistics model could be extrapolated. Would it be necessary to make relevant changes? If so, which one(s)?

THE MAIN ACTIVITIES OF OPERATIONS MANAGEMENT

Table 11.5 offers a classification of the main activities of operations managers. A distinction is drawn between the design of the operations system and the operation of that system.

TABLE 11.5	The activities of operations management
System design	**Systems planning and control**
Product design	Operations planning
Forecasting demand	Scheduling
Capacity planning	Quantity control
Work design	Quality control
Location	Technology control
	Cost control
	Supply chain management

The design of operations systems

This involves the design of the products and services that people require and the design of the processes to supply those products and services efficiently and effectively. As we saw in the last section, this invariably involves operations managers with other functional areas of the organization. We deal in turn with product design, forecasting demand and capacity planning, work design, issues relating to location and, finally, the design of operations networks.

Product design

There are two major decisions in product design:

- The styling and function of the product, sometimes known as the product specification.
- The range of products or degree of standardization to be offered.

Design issues clearly interface with innovation (Chapter 10) and marketing (Chapter 12), and issues relating to these aspects are discussed more fully in those chapters. Decisions about both the product specification and the product range involve the kind of conflicts discussed previously. Customers desire goods and services that conform to their expectations of function, quality, reliability and cost. For the operations manager those same goods and services must be both easy and cost-effective to produce and deliver. For this reason, issues of product design also involve issues of process design.

The product design process invariably involves the development of product concepts. These can originate from a R&D department or a more informal design team within the organization. Important sources of product ideas also lie outside the organization. They can originate from market research information, through discussion with customers about their needs or from examining what the competition is doing. Information about competitors' products is important in the design stage. Many firms buy the products of their rivals to see what they comprise and how they have been put together. Academics involved in teaching an MBA at one university might obtain the course outlines and syllabuses from another university to gain ideas for course development. In the manufacturing industry this can involve the more complex process of reverse engineering, where products are systematically taken apart to see how they were made.

The decision on which product design to follow involves considerations of acceptability, feasibility and viability for both the firm and its customers. Will it be acceptable to the market and will it be reliable enough or safe enough for customers to use? Can it be produced at a price that meets company cost and profit requirements and is attractive to the consumer? In many industries these tensions have been assisted greatly by the development of modularization. A modular system exists where products are built up by the combination of a family of standard items. In the car industry, for example, a great number of different models can be offered, based around combinations of the same chassis, but with variations in engine size, gear box, number of doors, interior finish and so on.

Developments in modular systems can simplify the operations process and represent a form of standardization. A lunchtime sandwich bar may appear to have a very large range of products, when in fact all are based on different combinations of a limited range of ingredients and are made using similar production techniques. This is a case of increased standardization giving the impression of increased variety. Many companies see standardization as an important means of cost reduction. Standardization often means a better use of resources, such as longer production runs and the opportunity to obtain discounts on the purchasing of raw materials and components in bulk. For the consumer, however, it may mean less choice, which may be acceptable if prices are reduced. One of the advantages of the modular system lies in the attempt to maximize both standardization and choice. An important operations decision is the extent of standardization that is both desirable and feasible.

Forecasting demand and capacity planning

These two tasks form the basis of a series of decisions central to operations management, since it is here that the direction for the entire operation is set and resources are acquired and deployed. There is a particular need for market information and accurate predictions of demand. This is obviously much easier where goods are made or services delivered to order, less so when goods are made to stock or services are on demand. In this case historical data is important but even this may prove inadequate in a volatile market of changing demand, high levels of competition and variations in supply. In any case the demand for goods and services changes over time for a number of reasons. These may be seasonal as in the case of an increased demand for certain types of goods at Christmas or for sunscreen products during the summer holiday period.

Even where demand can be forecast with some accuracy, capacity planning may not be straightforward. It can be especially sensitive to product and process innovation, and it will be affected by decisions on the type of technology used, organization size and structure, the extent of sub-contracting and policies concerning the intensity of labour, the size of the labour force and the hours of operation. Organizing the capacity to meet demand in some kind of sequence is known as scheduling, which we deal with under operations planning.

Capacity planning is especially difficult in service industries. In most instances, the product on offer cannot be stored when the capacity is not fully utilized, as with airline seats and hotel rooms. The concern for unused capacity in the hotel industry has led some hoteliers in popular destinations to overbook rooms. This works well if the predicted number of cancellations occurs. If not then it results in customer dissatisfaction and damages reputation.

A number of strategies are used by service industries to reduce the difficulties imposed by capacity planning by attempting to control demand:

- Demand can be channelled or delayed to match available resources. A bus company or an airline will dictate demand and capacity by operating a fixed schedule and, in some cases, insisting that passengers buy tickets beforehand.

- Extra capacity can be laid on in times of known high demand: many department stores hire additional part-time staff during the Christmas period.

- Some services can operate a delayed delivery system to control demand and plan capacity. A garage will attempt to match the cars it accepts for servicing work with available equipment and labour and will delay bookings to times when capacity is available. The system can and does break down, through overbooking, staff absenteeism, and jobs taking longer than planned. In such situations the problem may be solved by overtime work, but this increases cost and any delay can impair the service the customers feel they are getting.

In the case of the bus company and the car service there is a certain flexibility in both equipment and staffing levels. Such flexibility is not available in all situations. A telephone company must establish a capacity to cope with peak demand, which occurs during office hours. At other times the capacity is under-used and represents a net cost to the company. In most countries, telephone companies attempt to smooth out demand through the use of cheaper rates for off-peak usage.

REFLECTION POINT

How are demand and capacity reconciled in your university or in your organization?

Work design

We are concerned here with two types of decision:

- the physical layout of the operations system;
- the design of individual jobs.

The dominant considerations here are economic (meeting demand and keeping within cost constraints), technical (product design and utilizing available equipment), and behavioural (fulfilling the needs of both the consumer and the work force). Variations in these economic, technical and behavioural factors often result in different types of operations system.

The layout of a department store usually involves the grouping of like products to capitalize on staff expertise and meet customer expectations. The layout caters for both demand and buyer behaviour by locating fast-moving goods and frequent purchases on the ground floor. With goods such as furniture, the purchase is planned and deliberate and the store can afford to locate the furniture department on the upper floors. Staffing policies often follow such decisions on layout. Permanent, specialist and more highly-trained staff tend to be located where customers require specialist advice, as in buying furniture and carpets. Where goods have a quick turnover and customers generally know what they want, lower-paid temporary staff are used.

The minimization of cost is a major management consideration and the technique used is known as work study, comprising method study and work measurement. **Method study** seeks to find more efficient and effective ways of doing work and, as such, embraces equipment design and ergonomics as well as more subjective, psychological aspects of the person/job relationship. **Work measurement** is 'the application of techniques designed to establish the time for a qualified worker to carry out a task at a defined level of performance' (British Standard 3138).

Work study is useful in planning and scheduling, cost estimation, the determination of maintenance schedules, human resource planning and employee training. It also forms the basis for most types of output-related incentive schemes. The technique is applied to both manufacturing and non-manufacturing concerns.

Location decisions

The location of the operations system is generally a combination of several factors:

- The availability and the cost of labour are important issues in determining location. The creation of science parks in close proximity to universities enables firms to have easy access to research skills. The decision of many manufacturing firms from Europe, USA and Japan to locate in countries such as China and Vietnam is an attempt to reduce costs by outsourcing to lower wage economies.

- The availability of raw materials and proximity to energy supplies and transport systems are often important for the location of manufacturing plants. This is why many manufacturing plants were historically located on or near ports or rivers.

- The cost of land and property rentals is important for both manufacturing and non-manufacturing organizations alike. This was a factor in the UK government moving many of its services out of London.

- Specific local issues also play a part. These can include the cost of local taxes, the degree of financial assistance available, the ease or difficulty associated with planning procedures and local amenities in general.

Globalization has offered many firms potential competitive advantage through location as we saw in our discussion of off-shoring and outsourcing in Chapter 2.

Location is an important consideration in the service industry, especially where customers are expected to travel to obtain a service. The location of a hospital on the outskirts of a town may solve the land constraint problems of a central site but the new site must be easily accessible by patients and visitors, otherwise it is failing in its service function. Similarly, large supermarkets located on the edge of towns must make the effort of travel worthwhile in terms of a wider range of produce at cheaper prices. There must be ample car-parking space and an incentive can be offered in the form of discounted petrol prices at the supermarket's own petrol stations, with even further discounts tied to the amount of purchases bought in the main store. A professional practice, such as an accounting or law firm, may need to balance the advantages of operating from a city centre site, especially for client consultation and prestige purposes, against the rising costs. A prestigious location, even at considerable cost, can be seen as important for reputation and as a form of marketing.

The above factors link location decisions with the proximity of customers, their ease of access and their expectations, although proximity to customers is not a factor in electronic commerce or with call centres. The proximity to competitors on the other hand may be important. In retailing, proximity to other shops can mean a larger number of potential customers. The same logic also applies to the location of restaurants in major cities, as in London's Chinatown or New York's 'restaurant row'. In most cities, areas have developed that are famous for specific activities such as the legal district, the financial district, the garment district and so on. Close proximity to rivals is seen as an important source of competitive information and while such firms compete they can also collaborate to assist clients. Usually an entire support industry grows up around the firms, including specialist recruitment agencies, specialist book shops and office equipment suppliers.

REFLECTION POINT

Identify those businesses where location is important and those where it is less important. What reasons can you offer for the differences?

Operations planning and control

Operations planning

The aim of operations planning is to ensure that sufficient goods or services are produced to meet demand. The activity determines what the organization can achieve in terms of:

- the quantity of goods and services it produces;
- the quality of those goods and services;
- the timing of their delivery;
- the cost of production;
- the degree of flexibility the organization has at its disposal.

The key influences are the extent to which management can control the supply side and the demand side of the equation. In manufacturing, known customer demand over time and a dedicated just-in-time (JIT) supply system can result in an effective low-cost operation. However, where there are large fluctuations in both demand and supply, inefficiencies are bound to occur with a corresponding increase in the cost of operations. Even where planning is based on accurate information, things can go wrong. A university is able to plan its schedule of lectures for the term, semester or year based on the known numbers of students registered to take certain subjects, the availability of rooms and the constraints of staff and student timetables. However, the sudden illness of a lecturer may mean that the lecture cannot take place, rooms can inadvertently be double-booked or, in the case of open courses, there may be more students than space available.

A basic consideration in manufacturing is whether goods are made to stock or to order. Historically, Ford had a policy that all cars were ordered before manufacture. On the other hand Chrysler, in the USA, made various models which were then sold from stock. The fast-food chain McDonald's produces hamburgers to stock based on carefully prepared demand forecasts. Hamburgers that are not then sold within a certain length of time are discarded. McDonald's claims that this system provides greater operating efficiency, and it still has the flexibility to produce goods to order when stocks are inadequate. Making items to stock can mean that goods are always available when needed, but it can be costly in terms of having stock lying around. Making goods to order is more efficient but can mean that the customer has to wait.

Operations planning overlaps with issues of capacity planning. In the service industry, problems of manufacturing to stock or order reveal themselves in the provision of standardized or customized items. A hairdresser will offer a standardized service to all customers, such as a haircut and wash, and a customized service in the form of styling. Restaurants often attempt to offer the best of both worlds. An 'a la carte' menu offers the consumer flexibility of choice but within a limited range of dishes. In general, more choice presents more problems for the operations planner. The more dishes the chef must make to order the longer the potential delay for the customer and the greater the difficulty in serving a group of customers at the same time. This is the reason that many restaurants will insist that large groups order from a set menu.

The above examples illustrate the problems of loading, sequencing and scheduling.

Loading refers to the amount of work that can be allocated to a particular work centre, be it a department, unit or person. Effective planning usually aims to equalize the load through a process known as load levelling, both over time and across employees and groups. Where demand is known in advance, as in the allocation of lecturing duties in a university, loading should be a relatively straightforward operation, provided there are agreed rules as to what constitutes a fair load. In certain areas, such as the health service, where resources are tight and demand may be high, demand can be controlled by an appointments system. However, such a system must have the capacity to deal with emergencies, often requiring those with scheduled appointments to wait or have their appointments cancelled.

Sequencing relates to the order in which work is done. The basis of this can vary among firms. A simple method of sequencing is on the basis of first come, first served. In certain food shops, where demand can build up periodically, this problem is tackled by having a customer numbering system, which ensures that customers are dealt with in order. In some manufacturing firms it may be more appropriate to batch work irrespective of the order date, since this is a more efficient use of resources. Some firms may prioritize work by customer.

Scheduling attempts to balance the costs of production against demands for goods and services to ensure that demand is met in the most efficient way possible. Many theories and techniques have been developed to deal with such problems including queuing theory, linear programming and the more complex models of operational research.

REFLECTION POINT

What will influence loading, sequencing and scheduling in organizations with which you are familiar?

The problem with all such techniques is that, while they can offer optimal solutions to the problems of production planning and scheduling, they cannot allow for all the constraints operating in a given situation, many of which cannot be measured and many of which are highly subjective. Coping with variations in supply and demand depends upon having some measure of capacity. Manufacturing firms use measures of machine and labour utilization, both hospitals and hotels use beds, universities use staff-student ratios and room size, and so on. Where variations occur between capacity and demand there are three generic coping strategies:

- Variations in demand are simply ignored and activities are constant. This results in stable employment and, in times of high demand, high utilization of resources. When demand falls, however, costs will rise through problems of over-staffing or too much stock being created. In the case of a specialist art or antiques dealer, where margins are high, long periods without customers may be acceptable. In the case of the public sector, where resources are tight, stable levels of staffing mean that customers might have to queue or wait for the service they require.

- Capacity can be adjusted to meet demand. This is done in manufacturing firms by overtime or hiring temporary labour when demand is high and laying off workers when demand is low. The use of overtime and the growth of contract, part-time and temporary employment are prime examples of the use of labour flexibility to adjust to changes in demand. However, overtime can be expensive and hiring extra staff is only possible if spare capacity in the other resources is available, particularly space, machinery and equipment. Reducing the workforce carries social costs as well as financial costs where redundancy is involved. In the service industry, customer contact often makes scheduling difficult owing to the variations in time demanded by each client. Banks have tackled the problem by the introduction of automatic teller machines (ATMs) and have designated staff to deal with standard transactions and another group of staff to deal with more complex enquiries. The gains of adjusting capacity to meet demand are in the form of increased revenue, although where resources are stretched there may be costs associated with reduced quality.

- Demand can be adjusted to fit capacity. It may be increased to make use of spare capacity through price reductions, advertising and promotional campaigns and even the development of new products. Airlines often cut the price of their fares and hotels the price of their rooms to encourage more travellers in low season. A university may use spare capacity during vacations by hiring out rooms and residential accommodation for conferences. Where there is excess demand this too can be controlled. Most doctors' surgeries now operate appointment systems and football clubs ensure that demand does not exceed capacity by making certain games all-ticket affairs. Other strategies here might include persuading the customer to accept a delay in delivery or subcontracting the work to another company.

REFLECTION POINT

Identify a situation where each of the three generic coping strategies would work best.

Scheduling decisions can be highly sensitive and illustrate the relationship between the firm and the environment in which it operates, which is especially true of the public sector. For example, planning and scheduling problems are contentious in the health services. Hospitals must schedule operations according to their available resources; this means that only a specific number of non-emergency operations can be budgeted in any one year, resulting in a build-up of waiting lists.

All these illustrations take production planning and scheduling out of the domain of programmed decisions and simplistic techniques and involve social, political and ethical considerations.

Operations control

There are various types of control used in any production system. As with all forms of control, those managing the system must determine the standards that are to operate. In some types of system such standards may be difficult to measure. For example, there has been considerable debate over definitions of quality in education or social work. In other situations there may be conflict concerning the appropriateness of certain standards, for example between the firm and its customers over service standards, between marketing and production about delivery times, or between management and employees over levels of productivity. We identify the types of control below and then focus on quality control.

- **Quantity control** is sometimes known as production control and sometimes as progress chasing. Quantity control ensures that the throughput of goods and services goes according to the planned schedule.

- **Quality control** ensures that the quality of the finished product or service meets the standards set in the design stage and also meets with the approval of the customer. In manufacturing, quality control involves quality considerations about components and raw materials. It can be especially difficult in services, where standards are both variable and highly subjective. We deal with issues of quality in more detail in the next section.

- **Technology control** refers to the maintenance of plant or equipment. While issues of maintenance are invariably linked with manufacturing industry, the use of computers and other types of office equipment places technology control on the agenda of all organizations. The issue in technology control is the determination of when a piece of equipment is in need of service. Many firms solve this problem by instituting a system of planned preventive maintenance. In some firms technology management is sub-contracted through service agreements with suppliers, as in the case of photocopying machines. In many such cases equipment is leased rather than bought outright and, in the case of problems, repair or replacement is automatic.

- **Labour control** includes issues relating the extent and style of supervision and the nature and use of incentives.
- **Cost control** has strong links with cost accounting and budgeting. Cost control involves the collection and analysis of accounting information about all aspects of the business and the use of comparisons, which are either historical and/or based on benchmarking against another organization.

We can see from the five types of control that there is considerable overlap. Labour control has a close relationship to quantity, quality and cost control; productivity is a function of quantity, technology, labour and cost control.

With all types of control someone must decide upon the appropriate form of action when deviations from the standard occur. Various options are available. For example, in the case of a bottling plant, the decision is straightforward. Empty bottles are washed and then closely inspected before being filled; bottles that are cracked or chipped are broken up, bottles that are still dirty are sent through the washing process again. A clothing manufacturer making garments for a retail chain, such as Zara or H&M, has other options. It may be possible to sell elsewhere items that are not acceptable to the original client. Some manufacturers sell less than perfect goods to their own staff or to the public as 'seconds'. Such decisions get more complex in businesses such as a restaurant, where overall quality may not be judged until the meal has been eaten, and the only redress is in the form of compensation. Assessments, especially of quality, can be highly subjective and a potential source of conflict between producer and customer.

Quality planning, control and assurance

In this section we will attempt to define quality, examine its importance and review both traditional and more modern approaches to it. The latter will take us through benchmarking and total quality management (TQM). The traditional view of a quality product is that it conforms to specification. This is a narrow approach that has been superseded by a view that focuses much more on the perspective of the customer. Slack et al. (2014) view quality in terms of **customer expectations versus customer perception.** Where expectations are met, quality is acceptable. Where expectations are exceeded, quality is deemed to be high, but where expectations are not met quality is seen as poor. This does mean that quality is ultimately subjective. Nonetheless, both manufacturing and service organizations must plan to achieve standards of quality based on their operating experience. Deming (1986) argues that improved quality is a virtuous circle of lower costs, lower prices, increased market share and the provision of more jobs. The importance of quality is thus seen in terms of enhanced reputation, increased sales revenue and a better deal for customers, employees, shareholders and society at large. Some consumers are willing to pay more for goods of higher quality.

The cost of quality failure can be significant. There are the famous examples of Chernobyl and Union Carbide (see Chapter 9 for more details). At a more mundane level, an electrical fault in a dishwasher, a battery that does not work or services that are not delivered when promised are the kind of quality problems experienced by consumers every day. In such cases the costs are those incurred by the company in scrap or replacement. However, other costs may be less easy to define, such as the customer buying another make of dishwasher or battery the next time or changing their service provider. Furthermore, stories of poor quality are passed around and reputations can be damaged.

Methods of quality control, assurance and improvement

In this section we compare more traditional approaches to quality, based on the notion of measurement against a performance standard, with alternative approaches, such as benchmarking and total quality management (TQM). Historically, methods associated with quality have moved from control to assurance to, more recently, a focus on quality improvement.

The traditional approach to quality control involves measurement against a performance standard, which is sometimes referred to as conformance to specification. A number of steps are involved:

- First, the performance standard or quality characteristics must be defined and specific measures applied. These can relate to such factors as dimensions, appearance, reliability, durability, speed of service, behaviour of staff, after-sales service and so on. For hotel rooms the specification will include the number of towels and toiletries to be provided for each bathroom and the frequency with which they are changed. McDonald's uses specifications relating to the customer ordering process. This involves attempts to define specific measures for customer greeting, taking the order, assembling the order, presenting the order, obtaining payment and thanking the customer. Thirty-five separate steps are identified, each with its own associated measure.

- Once a measurable standard has been set, the next step is to assess goods and service against that standard to determine what is acceptable and what is not acceptable. In most processes, this can be done in stages. In the manufacturing industry, it is common to find quality checks on incoming materials and components, regular checks at each stage of production and then a final examination of the finished product. This kind of process can be vital in ensuring that problems are dealt with as soon as they arise and are not passed on to the next stage in the process. The boundary between acceptable and unacceptable can vary depending on the type of product or service. In certain types of precision engineering there may be no allowable deviation from the standard. In the accident and emergency department of a busy hospital a standard may be set that each patient is seen by a nurse within 15 minutes of arrival. At exceptionally busy times or in the event of a major emergency, the standard will have to be revised. In most cases standards will have a tolerance factor built in. A number of methods are used for measuring performance against the standard. The record company in Case 11.2 uses a mixture of visual and audial checks. A decision must be made whether to check every product or service item or operate a sampling method. The next decision involves the corrective action needed to close or reduce the gap between performance and the standard. This can take a variety of forms. In manufacturing, faulty items can be reworked or scrapped. In retailing, faulty or damaged goods can be replaced or a refund made to the customer. Where flights have been delayed by some time, particularly where mechanical problems are concerned, some airlines will offer free flights as compensation. For many service industries, recovering a problem situation to the total satisfaction of the customer can be a useful way of reinforcing customer loyalty.

- Once corrective action is taken, the process should not end. The information obtained in the quality control process should be fed back to other parts of the operating system, so that quality improvements can be made.

REFLECTION POINT

What kinds of quality control would be effective in a university? What measures would you use?

There are two problems associated with more traditional methods involving measuring performance against a standard. First, the approach tends to be inward-looking and emphasizes organizational criteria rather than customer criteria. Second, the approach tends to be historical, in that faults are rectified after they occur. These problems have led managers to seek other approaches. We will examine benchmarking and TQM next.

Benchmarking

Benchmarking is the comparison of performance in one organization or part of an organization against that in another, with a view to finding ways of improving performance. This is a common technique used by car manufacturers. Interest in the success of the Toyota production system led managers from most western car manufacturers to benchmark their company's performance along several dimensions with that of Toyota and make visits to Japan to see such systems first-hand. Comparisons were made of the hours taken to build a car, the amount of work in progress, stock levels and vehicles made per employee. In practice, benchmarking can be done in many ways. Comparisons can be made with other departments in the same organization, or with other organizations in the same business – or even in a different kind of business.

Benchmarking is used extensively outside the manufacturing sector as well. A service has been established for the legal profession in the UK offering inter-firm data on all aspects of operations, including the number of partners, number of staff, client profile, profitability and so on. The UK government offers benchmarking data to educational establishments in the form of performance league tables.

Benchmarking does not replace traditional methods of quality control and can operate alongside them. What benchmarking does offer is a focus on the marketplace and on performance improvement.

KEY CONCEPT 11.3   BENCHMARKING

Benchmarking is the process of improving quality through comparison with another organization or a different part of the same organization. Quality improvement is achieved through learning from the practices and methods of others and adopting them for use in your organization. There can be limitations in the transfer of such practices, especially where different cultures are involved.

Total quality management

Total quality management (TQM) is a strategic approach to quality that permeates the entire organization. It goes beyond control and assurance in that it incorporates a number of techniques and approaches, and is part of a culture change in the organization. While many see TQM as a relatively recent phenomenon, the concept emerged from the work in statistical quality control at the Western Electric Hawthorne plant in the 1930s and was primarily associated with the work of W. Edwards Deming and Joseph Juran, although the concept of total quality management (TQM) is attributed to Armand Feigenbaum. The ideas were introduced to Japan by the Americans as the occupying force in the immediate post-war era and found its greatest expression in the Japanese manufacturing industry. Japanese techniques associated with TQM can be found in the work of Ishikawa and Taguchi. The concepts and ideas in the development of TQM can be found in Feigenbaum (1961), Deming (1986) and Juran (1988).

KEY CONCEPT 11.4   TOTAL QUALITY MANAGEMENT

TQM is a strategic approach to quality that embraces all members of the organization. The aim is to create a corporate culture that focuses on the needs of the customer by building quality into every aspect of the operation. The claimed advantages are a cost saving for the organization and added value for the customer. It is a method of long-term continuous improvement that is linked to national standards and international standards. Common criticisms include its association with the introduction of a cumbersome bureaucracy and the problems of introducing such systems in low-trust cultures.

The essence of TQM incorporates the following:

- It is a top-down management philosophy that focuses on the needs of the customer.
- TQM values are depicted by slogans such as 'customer awareness', 'getting it right first time', and 'continuous improvement'.
- TQM comprises a quality plan, which offers a structured, disciplined approach to quality and incorporates a number of systems, tools and techniques. Emphasis is given to the collection and analysis of information and to employee training.
- TQM covers all parts of the organization and often those organizations in the supply chain. Relationships between departments in the same organization, as well as those between firms in the supply chain, are governed by detailed service level agreements.
- As we can see from the key values, TQM is culturally based. Involvement of all staff is central to its philosophy. TQM statements abound with references to teamwork and creative thinking and often contain slogans about empowerment as a means of adding value.
- TQM focuses on the elimination of costs associated with control and failure. These are seen as signs of poor quality. Instead, the emphasis is on prevention through the involvement of all staff.
- Through its focus on continuous improvement, TQM is essentially a long-term approach.

There are also a number of criticisms of TQM. Despite the culture of involvement and the slogan of empowerment, the focus is often on management control, leading, in some cases, to management by stress:

- TQM systems tend to be bureaucratic, time-consuming and expensive to setup and run. It has been dubbed 'quality management by manual'. The gains from introducing TQM are often less than those anticipated. This can lead to demotivation and lack of interest and the effect of introducing TQM fades over time.
- In many cases TQM is bolted on to existing quality control and assurance systems and is less effective as a result. As with strong corporate cultures, there is a paradox between a top-down system, which inevitably involves control, and the same system, which urges involvement and empowerment.

- TQM requires high levels of trust across the entire organization. It is, therefore, difficult to introduce TQM effectively in low-trust situations. For this reason TQM is often difficult to operate where there is downsizing.

REFLECTION POINT

Can total quality management be effective in all types of organization?

Supply chain management

In Chapter 2 we saw how a globally dispersed supply chain lay at the heart of the new global economy. In Case 11.1 we see how the management of the supply chain is the key factor in giving the Spanish company Zara its competitive advantage.

Supply chain management combines several more traditional activities of purchasing and supply, stock control, distribution and logistics. Purchasing and supply is concerned with the interface with suppliers. Inventory or stock control is involved with the management of stock once it has reached the organization. Distribution is concerned with the interface with customers. Logistics is concerned with the planning and management of materials flows in the organization, particularly at the downstream end of operations, and as an interface with distribution. Supply chain management is an attempt to integrate these various activities and in doing so:

- takes a holistic view of the movement of materials, components and information within an organization and in its relationship with suppliers and customers;
- extends the boundaries of a single organization to incorporate those organizations involved in upstream activities (suppliers) and those involved in downstream activities (distributors, retailers, customers). An effective supply chain usually involves a close relationship with suppliers and with customers;
- takes a strategic view of the supply chain and manages the process to reduce costs for the organization and to create added value for the customer.

KEY CONCEPT 11.5   SUPPLY CHAIN MANAGEMENT

Supply chain management brings together a number of related activities, including purchasing and supply, inventory management, logistics, materials management and distribution. These are combined as part of an integrated strategy which aims to reduce costs for the organization and enhance satisfaction for the customer. Like many approaches in operations management, it aims to resolve the classic dilemma of both satisfying customer needs and ensuring the efficient utilization of resources (articulated in Key Concept 11.2 and Figure 11.2). Such an approach can involve suppliers and distributors in joint ventures with the organization.

In any organization there are likely to be many supply chains, which vary in length. A major decision, which must be made in manufacturing in particular, is the extent to which control of a supply chain extends into ownership through various forms of vertical integration by acquisition or joint venture. The supply chain concept can be applied to non-manufacturing organizations as well. In universities, students are part of a supply chain. Full-time students are 'supplied' by schools and colleges and part-time students by local employers. The students must meet certain quality requirements in the form of qualifications to gain entry. Once they have entered the university they are processed through a number of teaching, learning and assessment stages and emerge with a degree and enhanced career opportunities. While all too few universities take a holistic and strategic view of this process, elements of supply chain management are emerging. Many universities make great efforts to build close relations with certain schools and colleges to ensure a consistent supply of known quality. In the case of the recruitment of students from overseas, universities establish joint ventures with agents in a number of countries to manage the flow more effectively. At the downstream end of the chain, most universities have an established careers service to assist in employment. As students pass through the system there is attention paid to completion rates and the reduction of wastage as a measure of the quality of provision.

The management of the supply chain has a significant impact on costs and profitability.

Given that supply chain management is a subject in its own right, we will focus on a selected number of issues involved in purchasing and just-in-time.

Purchasing issues in supply chain management

The variables of purchasing are source, quantity, quality, time and price. We will examine each of these in turn.

Source Management is faced with decisions concerning the source of the firm's raw materials, components and services. The obvious strategy is one that maximizes the other four variables, obtaining supplies and services in the quantity and quality required, when they are needed, and at an acceptable price. In achieving these aims, managements must decide whether to produce their own materials, components and services or buy them from other manufacturers; and if the latter, whether to opt for a single supplier or buy from several suppliers.

The make-or-buy decision involves consideration of vertical integration. This can be achieved through the acquisition of a material, component or service supplier or by doing it yourself. Either approach will give management greater control over the reliability of supplies, and it may well add a dimension to the firm as a supplier to others. However, the trend in manufacturing is that firms make less of the total product and rely much more on outsourcing (see Chapter 2).

There are advantages to using a limited number of suppliers. A good relationship can be built up over time, which leads to mutual commitment and dependability. Frequent communication enables problems to be solved as they arise and leads to improvements in the quality of supply. A greengrocer supplying a top restaurant will know through discussion and experience that the chef will only accept first-class produce and preselects accordingly. The greengrocer will also be able to advise the chef when certain types of produce are particularly good, which may affect the quantity of the order. Using several suppliers can offer volume flexibility and a range of experience through dealing with different customers. Where suppliers are competing for the same order, the purchaser may be able to reduce costs through price competition.

The relationship between supplier and purchaser is often a question of relative power (see the discussion of Porter's 'Five Forces' model in Chapter 8). The personal relationships between buyers and sellers are therefore an important ingredient in purchasing, although cases exist where personal relationships have resulted in contracts being unfairly secured and even bribery used.

Quantity The decision here is how much to order at any one time. This is a function of cost, storage capacity, and the nature of the operations system. The decision can be difficult. For example, a firm operating complex machinery for a continuous process may need to stock expensive replacement machine parts, even though they may be needed only infrequently. JIT is an attempt to minimize material costs. The greater the purchasing requirements, the greater the possibility of obtaining discounts and some highly diverse organizations operate a central purchasing function to maximize such discounts.

Quality The quality of incoming raw materials, components and services is a vital ingredient in the quality control function. Inspection of incoming materials is a significant part of controlling the process.

Time and price The timing of a purchase is, like order quantity, a function of the needs of the operations system, storage capacity and price. Certain commodities are particularly price sensitive which has led to buyers speculating on price. Some firms, to offset the costs involved in stockholding, engage in hedging, a process of buying materials and stock at the current price for delivery at some future date. This may involve futures and options trading, although the volatile nature of some markets increases the risk in decision-making.

Two trends are noticeable in the manufacturing industry. These are the extension of the manufacturing process down the supply chain and the globalization of the supply industry:

- The nature of the manufacturing industry has changed. A factory that makes the majority of its own components is now a rarity. The large manufacturing plants concentrate on the final assembly of components made elsewhere. Wages are generally lower in the components industry with cost savings accruing to the lead firm.

- In our discussion of globalization, in Chapter 2, we noted that global supply chains were now common, taking advantage of lower wage costs in many cases but also specialist know-how in others.

REFLECTION POINT

Why is supply-chain management such an important issue for contemporary organizations?

Just-in-time (JIT)

The origins of this system are ascribed to the Toyota car plant and are part of the process of 'lean production' and 'lean management' that we examine later as part of the section on operations strategies. The effectiveness of the system meant that it became common practice firstly in Japanese manufacturing industry and then globally. Just-in-time (JIT) aims to obtain the highest volume output at the lowest unit costs. The system is based on the simple principle of producing goods and services only when they are needed. Because of this, JIT is described as a 'pull-through' system, as is shown in Figure 11.3. Exact quantities are produced and specific requirements are placed on materials and parts suppliers, as well as each stage in the production process, to deliver just-in-time for the next stage of operations. Materials intake, work-in-progress and finished stock are therefore kept at minimum levels.

KEY CONCEPT 11.6   JUST-IN-TIME

JIT aims for the highest volume of output at the lowest unit costs, based on producing goods and services only when they are needed. Starting with the customer demand for the product or service, the JIT system works backwards. Goods and services are produced for each stage of the operation only as required. For this reason JIT is sometimes referred to as a pull-through system. JIT eliminates the need for maintaining costly inventory and uses specific techniques such as Kanban.

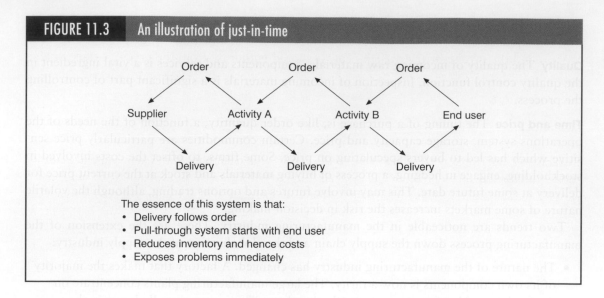

FIGURE 11.3   An illustration of just-in-time

The essence of this system is that:
• Delivery follows order
• Pull-through system starts with end user
• Reduces inventory and hence costs
• Exposes problems immediately

Elements of the JIT system are:

• it is based on customer demand;
• there are implicit notions of quality and continuous improvement;
• it eliminates waste;
• operations become more cost-effective;
• it includes employee involvement and teamwork;
• it is based on close links with suppliers and customers.

In the more traditional approaches, buffer inventories of parts and components are built up at the start of the whole process and between each activity. This means that cash is tied up in stock and fairly large numbers are employed in inventory management. Moreover, a system that relies on buffer stocks will hide inefficiencies in any part of that system. With JIT, problems are immediately brought to light and must be dealt with.

For the system to work effectively the operation must exist as an integrated and interdependent whole. High quality materials and components must be available at every stage. Materials and components must flow quickly through the system. The system must be flexible enough to cope with variations in supply and demand.

Advantages claimed for the system include:

• JIT smooths out the production flow, reduces inventory and hence costs.
• By preventing production delays it enables the firm to meet its delivery deadlines.
• It eliminates time wasted in waiting for components, as well as over-production.
• Through the involvement and interdependence of staff it creates flexibility and improved teamwork throughout the organization.
• JIT encourages a much closer relationship with suppliers and those able to meet the demands of the system are often offered high-volume contracts, sometimes as the sole supplier. To obtain the maximum flexibility from JIT, it is often introduced with new multi-purpose machinery, enabling the firm to manufacture a wider range of product types in shorter runs.

At the Toyota factory, the system is controlled by an information system known as 'Kanban'. This is a system of cards or signals that inform Toyota of the quantity to be produced by each process and the precise quantity each process should withdraw from the previous stage, which may be either another process, a materials store, or even a supplier. In Toyota, the Kanban system is extended to sub-contractors, which must conform to the precise delivery requirements of the parent factory. Kanban is the most commonly used JIT technique and lies at the centre of the entire system. Nothing happens unless the Kanban is received. This technique is now widely used in manufacturing industry.

While JIT can strengthen the ties between the company and supplier, the system can place considerable pressure on sub-contractors. The system can only work given the willingness of suppliers to participate. This situation frustrated some Japanese companies when they started operating in the UK and led to protracted negotiations with British supply companies, some of which found the demands placed upon them too great for the rewards involved. JIT also means that disruptions in supply, for whatever reason, can threaten the entire system. For example, an earthquake in the Kobe region of Japan disrupted road and rail links. Although many manufacturing plants were undamaged, supplies could not reach them and they were unable to operate because they carried insufficient stock.

We return to wider issues of lean operations at the end of the chapter.

OPERATIONS AND THE ENVIRONMENT

The job of operations management is to produce goods and services for the customer through the most efficient use of resources. The achievement of these goals requires predictability in the supply of materials, labour, finance and so on. This may be difficult in a turbulent environment and explains why managers set up buffer systems to protect operations from unexpected changes. In practice, this is achieved by having certain levels of buffer stock and groups of workers who are available when needed. This can be expensive and more effective operations systems are generally those that can respond to environmental change rather than being isolated from it.

Since the mid-1980s, the biggest changes for operations management have come from globalization, new technology and the diffusion of Japanese manufacturing methods such as JIT. The globalization of business has added to the complexity of operations management. We have noted elsewhere that organizations are generally part of a global network. A single manufacturing firm can be involved in global operations in different countries assembling components also from different countries. A Hollywood film can be made in the UK using technical expertise from the UK film industry at the same time that a UK film is made in Ireland with USA financial backing.

All the environmental aspects of our model relate in some way to the operations function. In this section we will explore aspects of that relationship. We deal first with the interaction of operations, the economy and the state, with a focus on the manufacturing industry. The theme of manufacturing also emerges in the examination of operations and technology, where the emphasis is on techniques based on computerization and automation. We end the section with an examination of operating systems in different societies.

Operations, the economy and the state

Given that the operations function is central to any organization, it can be deduced that the value added is central to GDP growth. Until the 1980s, successive UK governments recognized the economic importance of manufacturing through policies to encourage its growth, and through its attempts to regenerate flagging industries and firms. Since then, advocates of continued support of manufacturing industry have lost out to those who favour the operation of the free market. The state is involved in the operations function in that:

- Operations can be affected by laws relating to environmental pollution and health and safety. In some cases the introduction of such laws has led to increased costs for organizations.

- National and international quality standards have been developed such as BS 5750 in the UK and ISO 9000 globally. The UK government has stated its intention by favouring those firms that possess BS 5750 in its award of contracts. There is evidence that some firms will only buy goods and components from firms that have been quality assessed, and it is predicted that such standards will influence the purchasing habits of consumers.

- As part of regional policy, many governments have attempted to influence the location of both the manufacturing and non-manufacturing industry. This has generally focused on measures to encourage firms to locate in areas of high unemployment by giving them generous grants and tax allowances.

Operations and technology

Chapter 4 discussed issues relating to technology and labour. The impact of technological change on operations can be seen in terms of cost, speed, flexibility, quality and dependability. Technological change creates change in operations strategy. We can view these changes in two ways. First, we can identify changes in the shift from craft production, through mass production to lean production. Second, we can identify those changes that affect directly the way products are made and services produced by looking at flexible manufacturing systems.

Flexible manufacturing systems (FMS) bring together elements of advanced manufacturing engineering to solve the problem of offering consumer choice and a quick response to market changes using a minimum of working capital. Potentially, FMS offers manufacturing industry a solution to the dilemmas of operating efficiency and customer choice outlined in Figure 11.2. The system enables different models to be built using the same assembly line and pieces of equipment. The claimed advantages are in terms of speed, flexibility, improved quality and lower costs. Most flexible manufacturing systems comprise linked computer-controlled machines, robots and computerized transport systems. The programmed FMS selects the right tools and components for a particular job and usually has built-in mechanisms for automatic fault finding in the job and the equipment.

In car manufacture, an FMS would enable a range of models to be built on the same production line, with the necessary tool changes being automatic, and the required parts being delivered automatically to work stations in the quantity and at the time they were required.

However, developments in computerized systems have affected all types of organization. In the service industry, developments in customer processing technology and the use of the Internet have changed the way people access information or obtain services, such as the booking of tickets for a rock concert or football match.

Despite this potential for variety, the reality for many companies is that the payback on such substantial investments as FMS is only feasible on long runs. Furthermore, only a limited range of product variety is feasible before costly programming and tooling changes are required. Innovations in operations technology undoubtedly carry the potential for a more effective and efficient operations system but such enthusiasm needs to be tempered by the high cost and recognition of the limitations of the technology.

National and cultural influences and operations

We have already explored this theme in some detail in Chapters 2 and 5, when we examined the extent to which operations systems around the world have converged as a result of the growth of the large transnational corporation and the associated factors involved in globalization. One explanation for the rise of the Japanese economy has been the well-planned and executed methods of operations management, especially in the manufacturing industry. Often cited is the Japanese attention to detail; the importance of lean production and a totally integrated production system using techniques such as JIT and TQM; and acceptance by labour of a system demanding flexibility.

The key issue is the extent to which systems developed in one culture can be transferred to another (for more detail see Chapter 5). Lean production and just-in-time were developed in Japan in response to specific conditions. These included a scarcity of raw materials, uncertainty following the Second World War, rising labour costs in the 1960s, the absence of supply of immigrant labour (unlike Germany), a customer call for product variation and a manufacturing system comprising of large numbers of smaller firms feeding large conglomerates. Just-in-time also fitted the core cultural characteristics of the Japanese. A high level of uncertainty avoidance is met by the JIT requirement for meticulous planning, and JIT builds on values associated with loyalty, dependence, duty and responsibility. Despite these culturally specific features, JIT has been adopted by European and US firms with some measure of success.

ORGANIZATIONAL ASPECTS OF OPERATIONS

The centrality of the operations function to an organization means that, more often than not, the nature of the organization is influenced by the nature of the operations system. In this section we will explore the interaction between the operations function and size and structure, key organizational elements of our model.

Operations and organization size

The size of the firm, expressed in terms of both numbers employed and capital invested, has a close relationship with the operations function. A firm dedicated to mass production is invariably large, in terms of both the number of employees and capital investment. A mass producer of cars, such as Toyota or Ford, will employ many thousands of workers at any one of their assembly plants throughout the world. As with most elements of the Business in Context model, the influence is two-way. The sheer size and complexity of the operating system in a volume producer of automobiles will influence the size of the workforce and the capital employed. By the same token, the size of the firm and its output requirements will determine the precise nature of the operations system and, in particular, the technology employed. For example, only the largest of firms with high outputs are able to invest in highly automated production systems at profit.

The production technology employed in an oil refinery requires only a small work force to that employed in mass production technologies, yet the emphasis on sophisticated process technology means that capital investment is generally much higher. A very large insurance firm will almost certainly use a factory-style flow line for the processing of the very large numbers of policies it has to handle.

The relationship between size and the operations system reveals itself most clearly through the way the operations process is organized and its impact upon organization structure.

Operations and organization structure

In Chapter 6, we introduced the link between production technology, size and organization structure. We argued that the relationship also involved other variables, such as strategy, culture and the behaviour of interest groups. Nevertheless, since the operations function represents the firm's central activity it would be surprising if the structure did not reflect both the technology and the strategies associated with producing the goods and services of the organization. There are clear overlaps with our discussion of structure in Chapter 6 and you are advised to refer to the relevant parts of that chapter.

OPERATIONS STRATEGIES

We have established in this chapter that operations management is the central function in all organizations. We have also noted that there is often a conflict between operating efficiency and achieving customer satisfaction. Throughout, we have emphasized a number of objectives:

- quality
- dependability
- speed
- flexibility
- cost.

We can identify the specific contribution to competitive advantage made by each of the five strategic objectives. A number of these factors come into play in Zara (Case 11.1).

The **quality** of goods and services offers competitive advantage in terms of the dependability and attractiveness to the consumer. From the firm's perspective an emphasis on quality reduces costs and increases value added. This can be achieved via error-free processes to produce error-free goods and services. This reduces the costs associated with waste and making corrections as well as the costs associated through the creation of dissatisfied customers. Goods and services of higher quality can often be offered at a higher price. Given the advantages that can be gained by focusing on quality, many see this as a starting point in the achievement of the other objectives.

Dependability refers to the capability of the firm to deliver its goods or services to the customer's satisfaction, not just to meet consumer expectations of quality, price and durability but more importantly on time. This may be achieved by carrying large stocks, but this can be costly. Inevitably, it involves investment in operating systems such as JIT and TQM. Both applications can reduce time and cost, while at the same time increasing dependability.

Speed of operation involves two aspects. First, there is the speed associated with the time between the product idea and its appearance on the market. Considerable advantage can be gained through the delivery of innovative products ahead of the competition. Second, there is the speed associated with the time it takes between order and delivery to the customer. This minimizes customers' waiting time, reduces inventory and can improve forecasting. The second approach is implicit in JIT and lean production.

The **flexibility** to alter products and meet volume demands with minimum lead-time is often a strategy for survival in highly competitive or, in the case of Orlake Records (Case 11.2), survival in declining markets. Flexibility in terms of product range and volume can offer considerable advantages in terms of the attractiveness of a wide selection of goods and services, the ability to deal effectively with fluctuations in demand, and the ability to deliver on demand at the convenience of the customer. This approach does require a flexible and often multi-skilled labour force, as well as good relations with suppliers. While flexibility can be a distinct advantage, there may be just as great an advantage in going for high-volume production in a single product market. This allows the firm to take advantage of the experience curve, which can result in a virtuous circle of expansion. An increased market share leads to greater experience in operating the production system, resulting in lower costs. When these are passed on in the form of lower prices, the result is even greater market penetration. Such a virtuous circle can be enhanced by investment in production technology to reduce operating costs. This kind of strategy, while potentially successful in an expanding market, has severe limitations when the market is declining.

Cost advantage results from taking costs out of the operations process. These costs are involved in product development, the product itself and in the operating system, and involve those associated with materials, facilities and staffing. In some organizations there can be a trade-off against quality. A restaurant that attempts to reduce costs by buying cheaper raw materials may find that it loses its reputation and trade. A problem faced by managers is that cutting costs is an easy option. However, on its own it may not give competitive advantage unless it is integrated with improved quality, dependability and speed.

REFLECTION POINT

Why is quality considered to be a lead objective?

Managers must decide the most appropriate strategy for their organization. It is possible for firms operating in the same industry to have very different strategies. Texas Instruments traditionally opted for high-volume production, reasonable prices and high market share of calculators and measuring equipment. HP, on the other hand, operating in the same markets, concentrated on low-volume, high-quality, innovative products. Different strategies can even exist within the same organization. Several restaurant businesses have a flagship restaurant that operates at the high end of the market producing highly individual, expensive meals in luxury surroundings. At other restaurants, they offer meals at lower prices and aim at those customers on a lower budget seeking a similar brand experience.

Most airline companies operate a variety of services on the same route, first class, business class, economy, excursion, stand-by and so on. These are all priced according to the quality of service and the dependability and flexibility offered to the customer. Table 11.6 shows the cost of a return fare of a British Airways flight from London to New York in March 2015.

Table 11.6 demonstrates that two passengers travelling on the same plane to the same destination, one with a first-class ticket and one with an advanced purchase economy ticket can pay £10 738 and £483 respectively. From an operations perspective, the first-class ticket offers more flexibility, in that it can be used on any flight and guarantees a full refund if not used, whereas

TABLE 11.6	British Airways return fare structures London Heathrow to New York JFK, March 2015 (based on booking in August 2014)
Service	**Fare, including Taxes (£)**
First class: fully flexible open ticket	10 738
First class: advance purchase non-refundable	6 305
Business class: fully flexible open ticket	6 630
Business class: advance purchase non-refundable	2 572
World Traveller Plus (Premier economy): fully flexible open ticket	2 393
World Traveller Plus (Premier economy) advance purchase non-refundable	949
World Traveller (Economy class): fully flexible open ticket	1 624
World Traveller (Economy class): 3-day advance purchase non-refundable	483

the advanced purchase ticket can be used on specified flights only and is not refundable. The table also demonstrates the price difference between a fully flexible open ticket, which allows travel at any time, and advanced purchase tickets, which restrict travel to nominated flights. The lower price for advanced purchase encourages the consumer to nominate specific flight times and thus assists the airline with capacity planning and scheduling.

The first-class passenger uses much more of the aircraft's resources in terms of space and staffing levels and receives a much higher quality of service including lounge facilities at the airports. Greater speed is offered in the check-in process and with the destination baggage handling. There are other less tangible benefits, such as exclusivity and privacy. These factors increase the cost of the product and this is reflected in the price. There are, however, other factors at work, including a price based partly on what the market will bear and partly on that many first-class and business class seats are usually paid for not by individuals but as part of business travel. Such issues of pricing strategy illustrate the overlap between operations and marketing, which is discussed in the next chapter. The variations in airline ticket prices are compounded by seasonal factors, and the variation in tax that is taken by the UK government on each ticket purchased.

Approaches to operations strategy

There are a number of views on the most effective operations strategy:

- Strategies can be grouped around a theme, using one of quality, dependability, speed, flexibility and cost. In the previous section we made a case for grouping strategies around quality as this would lead to the achievement of other objectives such as dependability and cost. However, it is difficult to view such strategies in isolation. Some approaches to quality improvement could increase costs. There are cases of firms that have pursued cost advantage to the neglect of others with damaging effects on quality, dependability and flexibility.

- For the above reason, it is suggested that operations strategy should not only be internally consistent but also the overall corporate strategy and the strategies of the other functional areas, notably innovation and marketing.

- However, such a focused strategy will need to be flexible to respond to the different needs of customers and, if necessary, to match the competition.

- The reality of operations strategies in many organizations is that compromises have to be made. There may be trade-offs between quality and cost/price, quality and speed, dependability and flexibility, cost and flexibility and so on.

In both manufacturing and service organizations an integrated strategy has developed based on the concept of lean production.

Lean production

Lean production is a totally integrated manufacturing strategy that was developed in Japan by Eiji Toyoda and Taiichi Ohno, senior engineers at Toyota. They developed a mass production system based on flexible technology operated by multi-skilled teams and organized a supply chain based around just-in-time methods (Ohno, 1988, Womack et al., 1990). This was known initially as the Toyota production system and was later known as lean production.

The essence of lean production was the elimination of all waste in the production process from the time the order is taken to the time that cash is received for the product. In so doing it will speed up the production process, maintain a flow of work, reduce costs and result in high value added. The work at Toyota and similar methods used by firms in the Toyota supply chain, as well as elsewhere in Japan, were elevated to celebrity status through the work of the International Motor Vehicle Program at MIT in the USA. This was a detailed study, 1986–90, of Japanese techniques focused on the decline of such US producers as GM relative to their Japanese competitors. In the best-selling book that emerged from the study, *The Machine that Changed the World*, Womack et al. (1990) claimed that the productivity in Japanese car plants was twice that of their US counterparts and set the standard for the rest of the world. Their view was that lean production, while owing its origins to mass production, was a discretely different and superior system, and if adopted would result in the US automobile industry closing the gap on Japan.

KEY CONCEPT 11.7   PRODUCTION

Lean production is a totally integrated strategy for manufacturing that came out of the Toyota factory in Japan and quickly found favour among managers in the manufacturing industry across the globe. It integrates a number of features. These include value engineering in design, flexible manufacturing systems, an integrated supply chain with a close relationship with suppliers and distributors (Key concept 11.5), just-in-time (Key concept 11.6) and total quality management (Key concept 11.4). Lean production also represents a cultural shift for all employees, with an emphasis on flexibility and teamwork. Massive improvements in operating efficiency are associated with lean production, but these are questioned by some writers who feel they may be limited to specific contexts. Nonetheless, the impact of lean production methods in all types of manufacturing has been significant, together with its application in non-manufacturing contexts.

Lean production represents a holistic approach to manufacture and integrates a range of methods and philosophies, including JIT and TQM. Many stress that lean production is less of a technique and more of a philosophy. Indeed some refer to it as 'lean thinking'. Certainly the approach has spread beyond manufacturing to many types of service industry. The following represent the features of lean production:

- Supported by JIT, close contact and joint activities with a limited number of dedicated suppliers, including design and costing, leading to a mutual understanding of expectations.

For example, Toyota made only 15 per cent of its parts in-house. Focus on costs at all stages of the process, including the use of value engineering in design;

- Problem-solving at the source of the problem with time out to consider improvements. This is part of the process of continuous improvement, which the Japanese call *kaizen*;

- State-of-the art flexible technology enabling fast set-up and changeover times and supported by preventive maintenance methods;

- Small batch manufacture with the ability to offer considerable variety. This is supported by flexible manufacturing systems technology;

- Employees are flexible and multi-skilled and work in teams to perform a range of jobs that often involve housekeeping, maintenance and quality control;

- A delayering of management and a sharp increase in delegation throughout the organization.

Womack et al. (1990) argued that the integration of the above represented a fundamental change in manufacturing strategy and covered product design, the organization of operations and relationships across the entire supply chain:

> *(Lean production) … uses less of everything compared to mass production – half the human effort in the factory, half the manufacturing space, half the investment in tools, half the engineering hours to develop a new product in half the time.*
>
> (Womack et al., 1990, p. 13)

Womack et al. argue that these advantages were found in plants with similar investment in automation and that the least automated plants in Japan were more efficient than automated plants in the USA. They further argue that the products that emerged from such systems carried half the average defects and used one-tenth of the inventory and one-fifth of the number of suppliers. Given such evidence, it is hardly surprising that *The Machine that Changed the World* became a best-selling business book and findings, such as those of the research team at MIT, led to the senior managers of the top US car firms making study tours of Japanese car plants. Undoubtedly, the interest generated led to a change in the way leading western firms such as GM and Ford attempted to change their operations processes and accelerated the take-up rate of JIT among western manufacturers.

However, lean production is not without its critics. The claims made by the MIT research team and in Womack et al. have been challenged by Williams et al. (1992). They argue that, Toyota apart, the margin of superiority of Japanese car manufacturers is small and, in some cases, bettered by European and US car manufacturers. They argue also that the downside of labour savings is the intensification of work for employees. Further they claim that the gains in labour efficiency achieved in Japan cannot be compared with those of western firms because of the greater reliance in Japan on the sub-contracting system. The headcount is in effect pushed down the supply chain, giving the impression of the 'lean organization'. In a similar vein there is the difficulty of separating the relative effects of lean production from gains derived from plant modernizations.

Reichhart and Holweg (2007) argue that lean production has focused on the relationship between the manufacturer and the supplier and that, by comparison, distribution has been neglected. While lean production creates smooth production flows, it still has difficulty meeting variable market demands. As a result, lean techniques still struggle to solve the dilemma of meeting both operating efficiency and customer needs. Through their studies, however, they are optimistic that systems of lean distribution can be developed that deliver the right product to the end customer at the right time and location.

Lean services

While the initial focus on lean production and lean thinking was in the automobile industry, its application has been widespread not just across all forms of manufacturing but also in retail and the service industry. The application has been used to reduce waiting times for customers, to eliminate errors in transaction, to avoid duplication of activities and to focus on customer care to achieve repeat custom. The following examples offer a flavour of such applications.

Tesco used lean thinking to redesign its supply chain. In the past, individual stores dealt directly with individual suppliers. As a result each supplier could make a number of journeys to several stores, adding to the cost of goods. Moreover, stores varied in their ability to control stocks. Tesco introduced a system of central warehouses. Suppliers were able to make central deliveries. Tesco then supplied individual stores from this central depot on a continuous basis as determined by a computer-controlled stock control and replacement system, based on the sales patterns in each store. Such a system is replicated by most big supermarket chains around the world. Attention has also been paid to the lay-out of stores and the organization and location of check-outs to speed the flow of customers through the store. In some supermarkets this is further enhanced by introducing self-check-out systems.

British Airways in conjunction with BAA, the company owning the main airports in the UK, used lean approaches in its design of Terminal 5 at Heathrow to simplify processes, eliminate unnecessary processes and to ensure a smooth flow of passengers through the terminal with no build-ups. Unfortunately, the opening of the terminal coincided with a failure of the baggage handling system to maintain a smooth flow. Subsequently, however, the systems have been seen as a success.

Lean production and lean thinking has also been used by some hospitals to create an efficient and effective flow of patients through the various treatments and processes and to reduce waiting times in A&E and ER units. One application has been to reduce the movement of patients, as between outpatient services and the X-Ray department by rethinking layouts and the availability of equipment, and by performing simultaneous treatments on patients in the same location.

Lean operations: endpiece

The adoption of lean production methods in whole or part, by many manufacturing and service organizations, is some indication that the investment is seen as worthwhile. There is no disputing its global impact on major organizations and on operations processes and outcomes. Nissan in the UK claims that lean production, as a transplanted operations system from Japan, has contributed to its status as the leading producer of cars in Europe as measured in terms of number of cars built per employee per year. However, an aggressive lean production system can threaten the security of many employees and it is understandable that the system has been examined closely by trade unions in many countries, including Japan itself.

While much has been made of its application in service organizations, such applications could be interpreted in other ways. They have perhaps less in common with the Toyota production system than more traditional approaches to work study that seek to improve the effectiveness of operations. In the early 1960s, as a result of studies carried out in hospital wards in the UK, the drugs trolley was introduced. This replaced a system in which drugs administered to patients on the ward had to be fetched for each patient in turn from a locked drugs cabinet located in the nurses' office. This was time-consuming and involved nursing staff in repeat journeys from the ward to the central drugs cabinet for each patient. A secure, mobile drugs trolley was introduced, which contained all the drugs required for all the patients on the ward, and which was wheeled from patient to patient. Was this the application of lean production before its time or simply a good idea to reduce unnecessary work?

REFLECTION POINT

Find examples of lean production in non-manufacturing contexts.

CASE 11.2   ORLAKE RECORDS

Orlake Records made vinyl gramophone records on an old industrial estate in Dagenham, East London, and for a time was a classic case of survival in a declining market. The company was bought by the First Sound and Vision Group (FSV) in 1999. Orlake continued to make vinyl discs, but the new company focused on its North London operation selling CDs and cassettes. FSV placed its faith in the development of self-adhesive pads to protect CDs and invested heavily in the project, diverting income from across the group. The new product failed and FSV along with it.

FSV was placed in administration on 6 November, 2000. The North London operation was closed but the production of vinyl records was allowed to continue at Dagenham. The company was bought in November 2001 by private owners and the company traded under the old name of Orlake Records. Around this time, one of its competitors, EMI, closed its record manufacturing plant in Hayes, West London. The plant and machinery had been bought by Orlake's new owners and, after a period of cold storage, the vinyl plant in Hayes was reopened, trading as Portal Space. While the EMI plant was not ready, Orlake in Dagenham took up much of the capacity of the former EMI plant. EMI's share of the vinyl market declined and it shifted its production overseas. Orlake and Portal Space became two of the largest players in the UK vinyl market.

Work at Orlake and Portal Space settled into a pattern reflecting their traditional customer bases. Orlake was essentially a jobbing factory that took excess production capacity from major producers. Its production runs tended to be small and it dealt with a mixed selection of clients. However, around the time that Portal Space re-opened the EMI plant, Orlake had developed a major client, Universal, who came to account for almost half of Orlake's output. Portal Space had a different client base and traded on EMI's name in the business. Portal Space acquired a portfolio of larger clients at the high end of the market and was able to charge a price that was over 8 per cent more than Orlake. Portal Space invested more in R&D, but the two companies collaborated on technical developments.

Market history

From 1979 to 1986, the annual trade delivery of vinyl singles in the UK fell from 89.1 million to 67.4 million, and LPs from 74.5 million to 52.3 million. Over the same period the sales of cassettes increased threefold to reach 69.6 million in 1986. In the 1990s the sales of vinyl declined again and CDs eclipsed both vinyl and cassettes in the marketplace. By the end of 1998, this trend had continued apace, as Table 11.7 illustrates. Competition in manufacture had become intense, not just in this country but internationally as well. At the end of the 1990s only six manufacturers of vinyl discs remained in the UK and Orlake had the capacity to meet UK market needs in its entirety. In spite of this dramatic decline in the market, Orlake not only managed to maintain its output levels but has seen a dramatic increase in market share. In 1999 Orlake received a substantial order from the major record company, Polygram. Orlake had produced vinyl records for Polygram for a number of years, achieving high levels of satisfaction by fulfilling small orders to quality specifications, flexibly and on time.

The vinyl market itself had changed. A mixed market of 7-inch singles, 12-inch LPs, and variations in the form of shape discs, picture discs and colour discs had shifted to a focus on the production of 12-inch singles for the dance market. Much of this growth was accounted for by independent

CASE 11.2   *(Continued)*

TABLE 11.7	Recorded music sales by type as a percentage of the total in terms of volume and value									
	1996		**1997**		**1998**		**1999**		**2000**	
	Volume	*Value*	*Volume*	*Value*	*Volume*	*Value*	*Volume*	*Value*	*Volume*	*Value*
Singles										
7 in	0.8	0.2	0.7	0.2	0.5	0.1	0.2	0.07	0.18	0.04
12 in	2.8	1.4	2.5	1.3	2.2	1.2	2.5	1.3	3.0	1.5
Cassette	7.1	1.9	6.9	1.7	7.1	1.9	7.0	1.7	4.8	1.2
CD	15.9	7.5	19.1	8.6	19.2	9.4	18.9	9.1	15.4	7.6
Total	26.6	11.0	29.2	11.9	29.0	12.6	28.9	12.2	23.4	10.4
Albums										
LPs	1.0	1.0	0.8	0.9	0.8	0.8	0.8	0.6	1.12	0.7
Cassette	17.8	16.1	14.2	13.2	12.2	10.8	6.6	6.2	4.0	3.5
CD	54.6	71.9	55.7	74.1	57.9	75.9	63.6	80.7	71.4	85.2
Total	73.4	89.0	70.8	88.2	71.9	87.5	71.0	87.5	76.6	89.4

record producers and record brokers. The latter represented a one-stop shop for cutting, sleeve and label design. In this respect the BPI figures presented in Table 11.7 under-represented the sales of 12-inch singles by about half. Official statistics focus on selected shops, while the 12-inch market also includes sales from small specialist shops, in clubs and pubs, as well as exports. These do not feature in the UK statistics. Nonetheless, the table still reveals the overwhelming dominance of the CD market. However, in a period of CD dominance, the 12-inch singles market had both held its own and increased in value and the real decline of the period was in cassette sales.

It is estimated that the vinyl market in 2009 has declined by around 20 per cent from the height of dance music in 2001. The boost to vinyl sales from the dance music phenomenon fell as interest in the music fell after 2005. However, many young people were exposed to vinyl as a product.

The production system at Orlake

Orlake was able to turn around orders in seven days for new releases and five days for repeat orders.

Such turnaround times were considered essential in small-batch jobbing manufacture.

The actual manufacture was the following stage from the recording studio. There, the final tape was converted to a series of vibrations, which cut grooves into a master disc, known as the lacquer master. Orlake had a plating shop, which took this master and, through an electro-forming process, made its own moulds to form the basis of record production. Several moulds were required depending on the number of presses to be used, the length of the run and the uncertain working life of each mould. The actual record was made in the production department by compression moulding which pressed extruded plastic on to the mould on a specially designed machine. This took around 25 seconds for the average disc. Operations at Orlake were based in two buildings. The smaller building housed the plating shop, the library of production moulds, and acted as storage for labels and sleeves. The larger building housed the production presses and the offices and offered some storage space for the finished product. However, there was not a great requirement for storage, given the fast-moving nature of the business.

(Continued)

CASE 11.2 (Continued)

Record companies tended to use several manufacturers, particularly on high-selling items. Orlake manufactured for a range of companies and as a competitive strategy attempted to meet customer requirements of high quality, low cost products in as short a time as possible.

The variety of the work meant that there were no standard production runs. Very large production runs associated with a vibrant 7-inch singles market were a thing of the past. The market comprised of 85 per cent 12-inch singles. The largest run in 1998 was 8000 units, but production runs of 500 became not uncommon with an average run of 1250 units. The firm used two types of presses, fully automatic and manually operated. Orlake had 14 automatic presses: two of them for 7-inch singles. In addition the company had five manual presses, more than any other producer, offering Orlake additional flexibility. The presses gave Orlake a capacity of around 4.5 million units a year operating with two five-hour shifts.

Certain products such as 'picture' discs and 'shape' discs could only be produced using manual machines. However, the demand for both products declined as they were associated largely with the 'heavy metal' boom of the late 1980s. Since 2001 there was an increase in the production of picture discs with the revival of such bands as Metallica and Iron Maiden. Management saw it as important to retain the capacity to produce special discs on manual machines, and Orlake was the only company offering such a variety of products. It was felt that it offered Orlake both a competitive edge and a means of gaining access to higher-volume business with some companies.

Production planning and scheduling was carried out continuously at the point of order and was the responsibility of the sales order clerk and the production controller. Schedules were drawn up on the basis of 'first come, first served'.

Quality control was the responsibility of the supervisor in the plating shop – the area where master moulds were made that determine the quality of the entire operation. Quality control throughout the company relied on visual checks. At the pressing stage, one finished record in every 20 was checked visually. Ninety per cent of all faults were spotted visually by a trained operator. In addition, a particular pressing was checked audibly every hour. Before storage, a further one record in 40 was checked visually, a process that was repeated after nine hours had elapsed to allow the plastic to cool down. Faults found with the moulds were sometimes rectified manually. At the pressing stage, if repetitive faults were found in a particular run, the batch was destroyed. Management moved to a system whereby quality was the responsibility of all employees and was reflected in the bonus scheme.

Orlake operated with a core staff of 50 employees. About 30 of these were full-time staff working a 40-hour week. The rest were part-timers, each operating a five-hour shift. Two such shifts were run each day. Overtime was used extensively to meet fluctuations in demand. Many of the staff had been with Orlake for several years and the company had a pool of experienced, skilled staff in the local community that they could draw upon as necessary. The employees were extremely loyal to the company and had a considerable commitment to and interest in the product.

A benefit of the move to a two-shift day system was the improved levels of quality with increased levels of management supervision. No job descriptions were used and all staff were expected to work flexibly across a range of tasks. Operators became packers and vice versa, and both supervisors and management helped out in the production and packing process. As with other industries operating in areas of declining demand, some skills were difficult to find, more especially those in compression moulding.

Orlake did well in a declining market and survived the collapse of its parent company, FSV. Its strengths could be summed up as follows:

- Management used quality and service to gain competitive advantage. There was a desire to improve service levels further.

- Orlake had never chased volume through price discounts and maintained a niche market with several customers. Price discussions were held with customers once a year, discussions about quality were held for every order.

- Emphasis was placed on cost efficiency. In the 1990s much of this was achieved through staffing cuts, the elimination of the night shift, improvements in quality, continued staff flexibility and in increased use of automation coupled with a production focus on the 12-inch

CASE 11.2   (Continued)

disc. From 2000, cost reduction focused on expanded capacity on the automatic presses without increasing staffing. As a result, gross margins continued to rise despite increased materials costs.

- Speed of response and dependability of delivery times was seen as vital in a business where the life span of the product might be relatively short. The firm had a strategy of fulfilling customer orders for any type of gramophone record in as short a time as possible and a reputation had been built up for low lead-times and prompt delivery.

- While special items such as shape discs, hologram discs and picture discs became much less significant in terms of volume, the company retained the flexibility to produce such items as and when required. Such flexibility enhanced the company's reputation in the marketplace.

The closure of Orlake

Despite the best efforts of the management and staff to stay profitable, the owners of Orlake Records decided to close the business and focus on operations at Portal Space in Hayes, West London. Orlake ceased to trade in late summer 2007. The reasons for closure were several. The market for vinyl had declined. Competition had increased, especially from producers in Eastern Europe, where vinyl was less of a niche product. Orlake lost its big client, Universal, which decided to put its business to tender. Much of the work went to Eastern Europe, the Czech Republic in particular. Orlake considered a revised strategy based on low price, but this could not be justified by the volume. The lease on the land and

buildings of Orlake's Dagenham site was due for renewal. Finally, its traditional labour pool of temporary contract workers in the local area was disappearing, some through retirement and others who had moved away following the closure of a manufacturing plant by the area's largest employer, Ford.

Vinyl Factory Manufacturing

Portal Space changed its name to Vinyl Factory Manufacturing and in 2009 was the only major producer of vinyl records in the UK. Its main production item remains current releases from popular groups. Some labels, such as Domino with artists such as the Arctic Monkeys, are keen to exploit their releases on vinyl. More recently, the company has moved into the production of high-price specialist limited edition sets containing several discs, high quality artwork and the artists' signature. Such sets have been produced for the Pet Shop Boys, Radiohead and Oasis, the last with a planned run of 20 000 copies.

Questions

1 Assess the market factors that have contributed to the success and failure of Orlake in a music industry dominated by the CD.

2 How would you summarize and define Orlake's operating system?

3 Assess the operations strategy of Orlake in terms of quality, speed, flexibility, dependability and cost.

4 What does the future hold for Vinyl Factory Manufacturing and upon what does its continued survival depend?

SUMMARY

- The operations function is a transformation process that takes inputs such as materials and labour and turns them into goods and services.

- The function operates in a variety of industries and settings and is not limited to manufacturing.

- The main activities of operations management involve the design of a system to process inputs and setting up control devices to ensure effective operation.

- It is acknowledged that the operating system has expanded to incorporate all the elements of the supply chain from components to customers.

- The objectives of any operations system are quality, dependability, speed, flexibility and cost.

SUMMARY (Continued)

- A central problem in operations management is the reconciliation of customer satisfaction with the efficient use of resources.
- Traditionally, techniques of operations management have emphasized efficiency. However, there is a growing awareness of other elements, such as the flexibility to respond to changing market demand and a need to focus on quality.
- Globalization has affected operations through the geographical extension of the supply chain and the growth of global, interactive operating systems.
- The centrality of the function means that it exerts considerable influence on organization structure.
- Changes in technology have particular relevance for operations systems, in terms of both product and process innovation. In manufacturing and the service sector alike there have been changes in the way goods and services are both produced and accessed by the customer.
- Japanese methods, especially in manufacturing industry, have been very influential and include JIT, TQM and in particular lean production.
- Operations strategies are a core element of a firm's overall corporate strategy. The most successful strategies would appear to integrate all elements of the operations system, display a clear focus and are consistent with the strategies of the other functional areas.

DISCUSSION QUESTIONS

1 Examine the similarities and differences to be found in the operations systems of manufacturing and non-manufacturing organizations. How do the operations priorities differ in a firm producing television sets for a mass market compared with those of a large regional hospital?

2 Design a systems model for a manufacturing firm, a retail organization and a hospital. Show both the types of transformations that are taking place and the other systems with which the firm interacts. What are the main activities and relationships?

3 Define the objectives of a firm manufacturing television sets, a hospital and a fast-food restaurant in terms of quality, dependability, speed, flexibility and cost.

4 What strategies can be employed to solve the conflicting objectives of operating efficiency and customer satisfaction?

5 What types of impact can product design have on the operations process? How does it affect the objectives of quality, dependability, speed, flexibility and cost?

6 Assess the effect of globalization on operations management.

7 Identify the operational aspects that influence scheduling in a restaurant, at an airport, and for a national daily newspaper. What strategies and techniques would you employ to solve scheduling problems in these three situations?

8 Why is supply chain management an important aspect of manufacturing industry? To what extent have techniques imported from Japan assisted this process?

9 To what extent can the techniques associated with lean production be applied to a department store, a hospital and a university or college?

10 Examine the links between TQM and corporate culture.

FURTHER READING

Probably the most comprehensive text, in terms of coverage and examples, available is:

Slack, N., Brandon-Jones, A. and Johnston, B. (2014) *Operations Management*, 7th edn, FT Prentice Hall: Harlow.

Some good cases from both manufacturing and the service sector can be found in the companion volume to Slack et al.'s main text:

Johnston, R., Chambers, N., Harland, C., Harrison, A. and Slack, N. (2003) *Cases in Operations Management*, 3rd edn, FT Prentice Hall: Harlow.

An emphasis on and integrated approach to strategy is the theme of;

Slack, N. And Lewis, M (2011) *Operations Strategy*, 3rd edn, FT Prentice Hall: Harlow.

Detailed coverage of operations in the service industry with some good illustrative cases can be found in:

Johnston, R. and Clark, G. (2012), *Service Operations Management: Improving Service Delivery*, 4th edn, FT Prentice Hall: Harlow.

A good introduction to lean production and lean thinking as well as a good summary of the historical development of manufacturing systems can be found in:

Womack, J., Jones, D.T. and Roos, D. (1990) *The Machine that Changed the World: The Story of Lean Production*, Rawson Associates: New York.

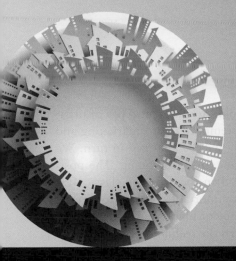

MARKETING

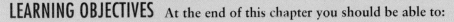

LEARNING OBJECTIVES At the end of this chapter you should be able to:

- Define marketing and trace its development as an activity.
- Identify the differences between business to consumer and business to business marketing.
- Identify the elements of marketing.
- Explain how these elements form the basis of the marketing mix and articulate how this operates.
- Assess the various approaches to buyer behaviour.
- Critically assess the significance of branding, targeting, positioning, market segmentation and the value of the product life cycle.
- Explain the role of marketing in relation to the economy and the state.
- Assess the impact of technological and social change on marketing through the development of digital and social media marketing.
- Assess the factors influencing the operation of marketing in different organizational contexts.
- Evaluate different marketing strategies.

INTRODUCTION

In this chapter we will examine the nature of marketing as it applies to different types of organization and to different types of product and services. We will attempt to define marketing and chart the development of the concept. The elements of marketing will be analysed in turn. We start with market research and link this to segmentation, targeting and positioning. The positioning of products leads us into consideration of branding. We then focus on the classic 4Ps, product, price, promotion and place. All these elements make an important contribution to the marketing mix and to marketing strategy. We look at the interface of marketing and the environmental context of our model. A key development here has been the technological and social changes that have led to the growth of digital and social media marketing. We examine how marketing is carried out in organizations and its links, particularly to innovation and operations management. We close the chapter by reviewing the elements of marketing in a strategic context.

Decisions in marketing generally focus on the nature of the markets and on the products and services to serve those markets. In terms of products and services, marketing is concerned with design, prices, promotion, the means through which they are distributed and the interface with the customer. In most advanced industrial societies, individuals are faced with a vast choice of such products and services, which can be acquired in a variety of ways, often at a range of prices. Advertising is a pervasive feature of modern life, its scope and reach having been expanded through the developments in digital media technologies.

Marketing, probably more than any other business activity, attracts strong feelings. Many members of the public, as well as many business and management students, associate careers in marketing with the glamour and fictional lifestyles of the people portrayed in advertisements. Such a view is misleading, for marketing is much more than advertising and the tasks can involve the much less glamorous work of collecting detailed market information or the packaging and delivery of industrial components.

It is the high-profile nature of marketing that attracts critics. Marketing is accused of creating an excessively materialistic society, planned product obsolescence, the high-pressure selling of poor-quality products and the excessive political power of the multinational. Marketing specialists would counter this, listing their credits as the development and supply of products and services demanded by consumers, the provision of essential information for the shopper, and the use of marketing to create public awareness for such socially acceptable goals as improving a nation's health. They would point also to the growing involvement of the consumer in the spread of marketing information via social media websites. Given the increasing use of marketing in political elections, it might also claim to be an important part of the democratic process.

DEFINITIONS AND ORIENTATIONS

The process by which companies create value for customers and build strong customer relationships in order to capture value for customers in return.

(Armstrong and Kotler, 2007, p. 6)

Marketing consists of individual and organizational activities that facilitate and expedite satisfying exchange relationships in a dynamic environment through the creation, distribution, promotion and pricing of goods, services and ideas.

(Dibb et al., 2006, p. 1)

The achievement of corporate goals through meeting and exceeding customer needs better than competition.

(Jobber, 2001, p. 5)

Marketing is not a specialized activity at all. It encompasses the whole business. It is the whole business seen from the point of view of its final result, that is from the customer's point of view. Concern and responsibility for marketing must therefore permeate all areas of the enterprise.

(Drucker, 1968, p. 54)

The above definitions introduce a number of aspects. Marketing is seen as:

- an interactive process;
- being aimed at satisfying (or exceeding) customer needs;
- operating in a competitive and dynamic environment;
- concerning goods, services and ideas (and therefore existing in all types of organization);
- involving activities of design, pricing, promotion and distribution;
- the responsibility of all members of the organization.

KEY CONCEPT 12.1   MARKETING

Marketing is an interactive process aimed at satisfying or even exceeding customer needs. It is concerned with the design, pricing, promotion and accessibility to the customer of goods, services and ideas. It exists in all types of organization and is the responsibility of all members of the organization.

The following approaches to marketing present a generalized view of the historical development of marketing ideas:

- The **product** orientation assumes that goods and services will sell themselves. There are usually two reasons for this. First, demand is greater than supply and goods and services are relatively easy to sell. This was the case with the expanding populations of Europe and the USA at the end of the 19th century. The second reason is linked to the inherent quality and performance characteristics of products and services and therefore sales promotion is largely unnecessary. This approach also assumes that consumers are generally well informed.

- The **selling** orientation assumes that consumers will not buy sufficient goods and services unless they are persuaded to do so by advertising, sales promotion and incentives to the sales force. This approach is often necessary when supply outstrips demand, or in the case of what Kotler (1983) defines as 'unsought' goods, such as encyclopaedias, or with the promotion of political candidates. The concept emerged with the development of the techniques of mass production and its origin is particularly associated with the depression of the 1920s and 1930s, more especially in the USA.

- The true **marketing** orientation shifts the attention to the consumer, whereas the production and selling orientations concern themselves with the needs of the organization. The true marketing approach involves the determination of consumer needs and values and the design and supply of goods and services to satisfy them. The assumption here is that the consumer is sovereign and the survival of any organization depends upon the satisfaction of its customers. In this context, customers can include organizations as purchasers of components for manufacture or office equipment; individuals when they buy a car, go to the supermarket or eat in a restaurant; visitors to a holiday resort; supporters of a particular political party; and even students of a university. Such an approach underpins most modern definitions of marketing. The development of the marketing orientation is linked to increased competition, the deregulation of markets and advances in information technology. It is also linked to rational approaches to management that are based on investigation and analysis as the basis of strategy. This, in turn, is linked to the emergence of market research as an important activity. Piercy (2009), while rejecting the effective contribution of much market research and traditional marketing theory, strengthens the case of the marketing orientation. He argues most vociferously that there can be no other legitimate approach to 'going to market' (a phrase he uses rather than marketing) than by satisfying customer needs.

• **Relationship marketing** takes the marketing orientation a stage further. It is focused on the creation of a strong bond between the organization and its customers as well as its suppliers, distributors and retailers. Relationship marketing is based on two premises. First, good relations with customers create customer loyalty and result in repeat purchases. Second, it is more expensive to seek new customers than it is to retain existing ones.

• **Societal** marketing takes the previous orientation a stage further. With societal marketing the attention is still focused on the consumer's needs, but the assumption here is that those needs are satisfied in such a way as to enhance the well-being of the consumer and society as a whole; goods and services should be socially acceptable, non-harmful and non-polluting. This approach arises from the enhanced consumer awareness of environmental issues. In many major supermarkets, shelves are dedicated to the presentation of organic foods and new product lines, such as toilet rolls and kitchen towels made from recycled paper, or coffee filters using unbleached paper. Washing powder and certain foodstuffs are packaged in refillable containers and recycling bins have sprung up at supermarkets, colleges, parks and car parks. Supermarkets such as Tesco and Sainsbury have made considerable investment in the design of stores to present attractive buildings constructed using environmentally-friendly materials. In many organizations, distribution logistics, which has always been concerned with fuel efficiency, now has traffic reduction as a goal.

• **Social media marketing.** Many believe that marketing has been transformed by developments in social media technologies and the increase in the usage of social media websites such as Facebook and YouTube. The marketing concept is extended not just by focusing on the consumer but by involving the consumer in the marketing process itself. Consumers use social media to comment upon and review products and services, reaching large audiences and having a significant impact on brand awareness and sales.

While the above approaches to marketing do approximate to the historical development of marketing, we can see them working side by side today. Precision engineering tools tend to sell on the reputation of the product and because they are engineered to meet the exact requirements of the customer; while certain double-glazing and kitchen installation firms use aggressive promotion and selling techniques.

REFLECTION POINT

What examples can you give that illustrate the product, selling, marketing, relationship marketing and societal marketing approaches?

The view of marketing that focuses on consumers and the determination and satisfaction of their needs is not without its sception. Galbraith (1972) challenges the consumer-oriented marketing concept, which he calls the 'accepted sequence'. He believed that the growth of big business, the complexity of modern technologies and the correspondingly massive investments in product development have disenfranchised the consumer. 'The revised sequence' has taken over, in which complex products, beyond the understanding of the average consumer, are developed at great cost. The emphasis shifts from the satisfaction to the creation of consumer demand through investment in promotion to safeguard investments in product development.

Galbraith's view may be challenged in two ways. First, a discussion that focuses on individual consumers and manufactured products presents a restricted view of marketing. In the next section we examine the extent to which the marketing is applied in other contexts. Second, we shall see later in the chapter, the process of marketing has been revolutionized by digital and social media technologies, the latter in particular stressing the participation of the consumer.

Marketing in different contexts

Marketing as an activity is carried out in a variety of contexts, the most obvious being, of course, the sale of goods and services to individual consumers as end-users. This is commonly referred to as business-to-consumer marketing (B2C). Marketing also occurs when a firm manufacturing petrol tanks sells them to vehicle and lawnmower manufacturers and others who use petrol tanks in their products; this is sometimes referred to as industrial or organizational marketing, or, more commonly, business-to-business marketing (B2B). Equally, it is not only manufactured products that may be marketed, but also services, such as banking and management consultancy. Holiday resorts, such as Disneyland Paris (Case 12.4), have always marketed themselves to attract tourists. In 1965, Singapore needed inward investment to offset the loss of British bases. The government established the Economic Development Board (EDB) and set up marketing offices in the USA and other countries. The EDB represented a one-stop shop for would-be investors, offering a fast response and eliminating the need for investors to negotiate with a range of government agencies (see Case 3.1 for more details). In addition to the marketing of products and services, some firms promote themselves by presenting a corporate image to the public. Marketing is far from being the sole prerogative of profit-making organizations, as governments, political parties and charities have discovered. We will deal with each of these aspects in turn.

Business-to-business marketing

Business-to-business marketing embraces any marketing exchange between two or more organizations. It involves both products and services. There is a clear overlap with purchasing and procurement, but business-to-business marketing is much more than a buyer–seller relationship and differs from business-to-consumer marketing for the following reasons:

- Business-to-business marketing in the manufacture of products, particularly with the development of global factories and global supply chains (see Chapter 2), involves networks of components suppliers. In this case the component is not the end product but is being used to manufacture the end product. More importantly, this process involves discussion and negotiation over the design, price, delivery times and after-sales service to a degree not found in business-to-consumer exchanges. The elements of the marketing mix involved in the component supply are worked out between the businesses involved. This is true of any product manufactured in this way, be it airliners, cars, or computers.

- There has been a significant growth in the business-to-business marketing of services especially in the provision of accounting and consultancy services.

- Whereas consumers buy goods and services for a variety of reasons, which may include less tangible considerations of status, organizational buyers tend to be more concerned with the utility of the product or service as well as its contribution to their costs.

- Organizational buying is institutionalized and is often carried out by professionals using formalized procedures involving quotations and contracts and often as part of a close, continuing relationship between buyer and seller (see relationship marketing). A feature of most car manufacturers is the process of joint design and the exacting demands they place on their components suppliers. For their part the components suppliers have to compete on the basis of quality, price and delivery schedules.

REFLECTION POINT

How does business-to-business marketing differ from the procurement and purchasing function in organizations? What examples can you give to illustrate the difference?

The marketing of services

It is in relatively recent times that many service organizations have fully acknowledged the need to consider marketing in a serious way. The historical reluctance of the service industry to engage in marketing may be due to the relatively small size of the many service operations, the intangible nature of some of the products and, in the case of the professions, constraints imposed by their own professional bodies. The specific characteristics of services presents a number of marketing problems. The following characteristics are taken from Cowell (1984):

- Intangibility. Most services have no physical product and therefore cannot be seen or touched before purchase. This is often seen as the key difference between services and goods.

- Inseparability. In most cases acquisition and consumption of services occurs at the same time and there is often some personal contact between buyers and sellers. As a consequence, 'relationship marketing' is important.

- Heterogeneity. Many services are customized and the nature of the personal relationship between seller and buyer can vary significantly. As a result consistency is a problem and control is difficult.

- Perishability. Most services cannot be stored for future use as in the case of theatre tickets or purchasing seats on an airline.

- Ownership. In the case of services such as a table at a restaurant or a seat in the cinema, the buyer does not own it but purchases the right to use it for a limited period.

However in reality there are few pure services or even pure goods. A restaurant sells not only a service and a dining experience but plates of food as well. A university provides its students with lectures and seminars, but increasing attention is paid to the less tangible aspects of student life such as personal feedback on performance and the climate of staff–student relations. A car showroom sells cars but also after sales service and ongoing advice.

Significant changes have taken place. The service industry has grown and become fiercely competitive, as is the case with banking and financial services. Companies in this sector have invested heavily in advertising and other kinds of sales promotion. Many consumers are now deluged by direct mail from credit card organizations. A student opening a bank account for the first time is wooed by offers such as free overdrafts and gifts. Airlines have decided to package their products in a much more tangible way; business travellers are now invited to buy BA's 'Club Class' or Singapore Airline's 'Raffles Class' and enjoy a number of distinctive product advantages. Some of these are tangible such as larger seats, faster check-in and access to dedicated lounges at airports. Other benefits are less tangible incorporating feelings of exclusivity and status. The lifting of advertising restrictions on the legal profession in the UK has led, in some cases, to vigorous promotion of price differentials on services such as conveyancing and of services to assist clients in accident compensation claims.

The marketing of images

Companies such as McDonald's and Shell have spent heavily to convey a specific image, which may well stress efficiency, experience, breadth of operations, company size, social responsibility or all of these characteristics. Theatrical agents have always existed to promote their clients, but the concept of marketing people has been extended to present any celebrity figure who may be 'packaged' to enhance his or her earning capacity through paid public appearances. The marketing of ideas has also grown in popularity. Many governments have launched campaigns to inform the population about AIDS, the perils of smoking or potentially dangerous epidemics such as SARS or swine flu.

Political elections in most countries are now fought by parties that invest heavily in marketing an image as well as an ideology. The UK Labour Party, conscious of a need to widen its appeal after three successive election defeats, targeted the young, professional middle classes and repackaged itself as 'New Labour'. The repackaging and subsequent promotional campaign, particularly the use of high-quality image advertising, was seen as vital to their election victory of 1997. The marketing of political parties presents an interesting combination of organizational image, ideas and people.

The use of marketing by governments raises ethical issues: it invariably supports the particular ideology of the party in power, and may be abused by some individuals to promote their own political careers.

REFLECTION POINT

Identify some images and ideas that you have seen being marketed.

International and global marketing

This is often considered as a separate marketing context requiring adaptations of the product, its price and the way it is promoted to account for differences in cultural expectations or constraints imposed by the economy or by governments. Such differences have led many firms to appoint local agents to market their products or else engage in a joint venture with a local firm. International and global marketing can be seen as part of a continuum from selling goods and services overseas, from a home base, through various forms of equity joint venture, to wholly owned subsidiaries in different countries.

We can also identify stages in the evolution of global marketing in much the same way as we looked at the transition of the international to the transnational company in Chapter 2.

Bartlett and Ghoshal (1995) identified a number of stages in the development of global and transnational organizations. Each of these stages is associated with a different approach to marketing. The international company is typified by the export of goods manufactured in the home base. The multi-domestic company establishes operations in several countries to develop goods and services aimed at specific local markets. The global company is focused on linked regional strategies with a standardization of products, services and promotion within a specific region and the creation of global brands. The transnational company has global brands and regional standardization, but also produces local products and services for local markets.

THE ELEMENTS OF MARKETING

We have already seen that the marketing concept focuses on the consumer and his or her needs. Marketing strategy is enshrined in the concept of the marketing mix, popularly referred to as the 4Ps – product, price, promotion and place. The concept of the 7Ps has been developed for service marketing and adds people, process and physical evidence. We will deal with all these concepts in this section. While many consider them to be the key elements of marketing they are also the basis of the marketing planning process and marketing strategy. In this section we identify the elements as market research, segmentation, targeting, positioning, branding, the 7Ps and buyer behaviour, and we deal with each in turn.

The elements will be treated separately, although in practice there is considerable overlap between them. The price of a product, especially when higher than comparable offerings, can be used as a product feature, part of the brand and even a method of promotion, stressing the exclusivity of the offering. This also involves the company positioning the product in a target market and the consumer perceiving and acknowledging a relationship between price and quality.

KEY CONCEPT 12.2   THE MARKETING MIX

The marketing mix generally refers to an overall marketing strategy which involves the manipulation of four elements. These are decisions concerning the nature of the product and its design, price, sales promotion, advertising and customer awareness, and distribution. These four factors are popularly referred to as the 4Ps: product, price, promotion and place, a classification ascribed to McCarthy (1960). Two important aspects of this are not made explicit: market research and buyer behaviour. Decisions about the marketing mix cannot be made without researching the market in all its aspects and that includes a thorough understanding of buyer behaviour. Some refer to the 7Ps, which add elements stressing customer service. These elements are people, physical evidence and process.

MARKET RESEARCH, SEGMENTATION, TARGETING AND POSITIONING

Market research

Market research deals with the collection and analysis of information to assist the marketing planning process. Four types of market research can be distinguished, although there is considerable overlap between them, and most firms engage in all types.

- Management needs to possess accurate information about its current marketing activities. This includes the number and value of sales of its range of products and services, and its market share compared with competitors. Such information can provide useful feedback on sales variations by region or by salesperson, and may well provide the basis for implementing changes.

- Management needs to be aware of developments that are occurring in the market place, which may have a direct or indirect bearing upon the business. Such information may be about products brought out by competitors, the relative prices of goods in shops, how competitors are promoting their products, or whether changes are taking place in the way consumers buy goods. This activity is sometimes referred to as market intelligence for it enables management to build up a picture of the market in which they operate and chart the changes and trends so that strategies may be initiated and altered as appropriate.

- Market research involves feasibility testing: to assess the market potential of a new product or service; to assess the consumer reaction to pricing policies or price changes; to assess the reaction of consumers to a particular advertisement, and so on. When a company such as Nestlé launches a chocolate bar, the product has invariably been tested on a wide range of people, and their reactions to appearance, taste, price, value for money, and, sometimes, the method of promotion, are carefully assessed. An essential element of feasibility research is an analysis of the market itself, especially its size and composition in terms of age, sex and occupation. The film industry tests new movies on target audiences and as a result of audience feedback changes can be made. A similar practice is used in the theatre, where plays and shows are tested in the provinces before being brought to a major venue such as New York or London. Customer reactions to products are often tested using in-depth interviews with individual consumers or using focus groups. A focus group is a means of discovering more about a particular product through engaging a small group of consumers or potential consumers in a group discussion led by a trained facilitator. Such groups are used in business-to-business marketing as well as in the marketing of consumer goods and are used widely by such firms as Hewlett-Packard and British Oxygen.

- The fourth type of research is a mixture of the previous three in that it collects information to evaluate a product and the way it is priced, promoted, acquired, perceived and experienced by the consumer after the launch. Continuous data of this type can be collected by consumer panels. These are groups of consumers, who may be representative of the population as a whole or some specific segment of the market. Panels are then asked to monitor their purchasing and eating habits, their television viewing, and so on. However, information of this type has proliferated as consumers comment on products and services via social media websites or contribute to websites such as Tripadvisor posting comments on hotels and restaurants. In some cases such comments elicit replies from the organization that is being reviewed. More recently some organizations have used techniques developed in neuroscience such as MRI scans and other such measurements of brain activity and sensors to measure heart rate. Such techniques attempt to assess a consumer's cognitive and affective response to products and to marketing images in advertising. The application of neuroscience to marketing is based on the assumption that many purchases are made at a sub-conscious level. However such techniques are expensive, are difficult to apply to large numbers and have questionable validity.

Individual organizations, especially if they are large, can do their own market research. However, research has developed as a specialist activity and numerous agencies, such as Mintel and Taylor Nelson Sofres have arisen, offering a variety of services. Many such firms operate globally and, among their many services offered to clients, provide regular television viewing figures, so enabling firms to target and evaluate television advertising campaigns. Such firms provide their clients with regular market intelligence on market share and trends, tasks often beyond the resources of an individual company. Some market research agencies specialize by product or the type of service offered and some have built up reputations for consumer interviewing.

KEY CONCEPT 12.3   MARKET RESEARCH

Market research involves the collection and analysis of information to gain feedback on current marketing activities, including those concerned with product launches and testing the market response to product proposals. It is concerned with collecting and reviewing information about competitors' products, pricing, promotions and distribution policies. Effective market research enables managers to make more objective marketing decisions.

REFLECTION POINT

A college department is planning to revise and re-launch its degree in business and management. What types of market research would you carry out to support this plan?

Segmentation, targeting and positioning

These are three related elements of marketing. **Segmentation** occurs when the market is broken down along a number of dimensions. Kotler (1983, p. 40) defines a market segment as: '... consumers who respond in a similar way to a given set of marketing stimuli.' Some form of segmentation is central to the efficient use of marketing resources in that it focuses on those groups most likely to buy the product or the service.

Commonly used segments include geographical location, age groups, gender groups, income groups, occupation groups, social classes and so on. Segmentation can also be based on psychographic aspects such as differentiating groups by lifestyle or personality traits. An increasing feature of cosmopolitan urban areas is segmentation based on ethnic groups. For example in Case 2.2 we saw how Sleek aimed its hair and cosmetic products at the younger, female Afro-Caribbean community. Segmentation can also be based on consumer behaviour targeting those who make frequent or repeat purchases. This is linked to the concept of customer loyalty.

Targeting involves identifying those market segments the organization wishes to pursue and target marketing is about developing products and a marketing mix which meets the needs of that segment. **Positioning** involves placing the product in the market so that it meets customer's expectations and perceptions in comparison with other products in terms of price, quality, and so on. In positioning it is important that the customer has a clear image of the product.

Market segmentation, targeting and positioning, and product differentiation go hand in hand, in that products and services are designed, developed, promoted, and even priced and distributed with a particular market segment and position in that market in mind. True segmentation occurs when genuinely different products are made for the different market segments. However, segmentation is not just a consideration in product design, it also encompasses all aspects of the marketing mix, including promotion. In 1971, Coca-Cola offered a global product using a global promotion campaign, emphasizing a unified world with the slogan: 'I'd like to teach the world to sing in perfect harmony' Here was a case of an undifferentiated product promoted in an undifferentiated way. In 1993, Coca-Cola, in the face of increasing competition, especially from own brands, changed its approach. The company launched a promotional campaign, which varied its approach and techniques to appeal to different segments, differentiated by age, culture, social class and lifestyle. From 1993–97, world sales of Coca-Cola rose by 21 per cent (*Financial Times,* 5 May, 1997).

In 2009, Thomson offered 35 different holiday brochures revealing significant product differentiation and targeting different markets segmented by age, income, lifestyle, couples with children, couples without children and so on. While few holiday companies aim to match Thomson for product differentiation, others do target specific markets. Saga has always designed its holidays and cruises for the older age groups and marketed them accordingly. While its products are aimed at a growing market, the company recognized that an increasing proportion of that market were fitter and more active than the previous generation and did not wish to be associated with 'an older generation'. The company therefore attempted to change its image and broaden its market position by offering products to over-50s, emphasizing attractive lifestyle holidays.

Not all such product differentiation is motivated solely by the desire to cater for consumer needs. The growth of the winter holiday market in the UK is undoubtedly related to affluence and changing lifestyles. It is also related to the hotel owner and tour operator's desire to use capacity all the year round. In some cases, winter holidays are aggressively promoted and attractively priced to push up market demand. In this case some segments, such as the retired population, are singled out.

So far, we have focused upon consumer goods and services, but segmentation is a feature of business-to-business marketing as well. Many components manufacturers such as the Japanese firm Denso, and computer and electronics firms such as Hewlett-Packard, have successfully targeted specific customer groups and tailored their products accordingly.

An important strategic decision in marketing is the determination of the most appropriate segments for the marketing effort. There would appear to be three options:

- a single or a small range of products or services is offered for a single segment or limited range of segments;
- many products and services are offered to many market segments;
- a single product or service is offered to an undifferentiated mass market.

The choice will depend on factors such as: whether the segment can be accurately identified; if it is large enough to be profitable; whether it can be served within certain cost constraints; and, of course, management goals.

REFLECTION POINT

Identify products that fit each of the three segment categories listed above.

A truly undifferentiated product is a rarity. A fairly ordinary product, such as a can of baked beans, is offered in a number of variations, with various added ingredients, such as sausages or with less salt and sugar (a variation aimed at health-conscious consumers). As we saw in the case of Coca-Cola, an undifferentiated product can still be offered in different ways to different market segments. In addition, the same product can be offered at different prices to different segments in different places. A bottle of Scotch whisky can be bought at one price in a local supermarket, yet the same bottle can cost four times as much when bought via room service in an upmarket hotel. The premium charged is a function of the added service element but it is also based on the knowledge that the type of client at such a hotel will probably perceive price as a less important factor than convenience. All these examples show how aspects of the marketing mix can be manipulated for different segments of the market.

Aiming for a limited market segment can be a highly successful strategy but it can be restricting once a certain market size and share have been reached. Then the company may need new products and markets to continue growing. A deliberate attempt to change its market segment by repositioning was adopted as a survival strategy by the British motorcycle industry in the mid-1970s. Faced with overwhelming competition from Japanese bikes, the British industry continually retreated upmarket, ultimately to be defeated in that segment as well by the Japanese. The British manufacturers went for an inappropriate segmentation strategy and might have been more successful had they invested in the process technology to manufacture reliable, low-cost, mass-produced bikes. This interrelationship of marketing, product development and process technology recurs in our discussion of the product life cycle and marketing strategy.

A differentiated product range serving different markets has long since been the strategy followed by car producers and both product development and acquisition strategies are informed by a desire to extend their range and reach new segments. The financial services industry offers investment plans to suit the needs of different groups, often at different stages in their lives and careers.

Positioning refers not only to choosing the correct market segment for your product but also to finding the appropriate niche in that market, to differentiate it from its competitors on such matters as price and quality. Repositioning occurs when the same product is offered to a different group, either to combat falling sales or as a general growth strategy. This was done by Guinness, which aimed its promotion at a younger drinker with very successful results. Manikin, the cigar manufacturer attempted the same ploy but was less than successful. The new target market found the cigar too strong for their taste, while the original market disliked the new style of promotion. For positioning to work, the features, benefits and price of the product must meet the needs of its market segment and they must be both comparable to similarly positioned products yet be distinctive from the competition. Lucozade repositioned its product and found a new market. Traditionally the drink was associated with ill-health and was bought as an aid to recovery. The product was repositioned as an energy drink for people who saw keeping fit as an important part of their lifestyle.

Excessive segmentation can pose problems and it has been referred to as 'marketing mania' (Levitt, 1975). The development, production, promotion and administrative costs associated with product differentiation can render excessive segmentation an expensive strategy, particularly where minor product changes result in major process adjustments. Differentiation may be a strategy for survival in a declining market, as shown by Orlake Records in Case 11.2, but the strategy may not always work. The willingness of the UK textile and steel industries to take on any order, whatever its size, led to dramatic cost increases and merely hastened the decline of those industries, when product concentration might have been a more appropriate strategy.

Overall, segmentation, targeting and positioning would appear to offer more benefits than costs. The following can be listed as the advantages:

- It can assist in market penetration by catering more precisely to the needs of a particular group than competitors.

- Knowledge of the most appropriate segments for targeting products and services can lead to competitive gains.
- Knowledge gained of a particular sector of the market can assist a company in the development of products for that sector.
- Products developed for one segment can be adapted to be attractive to other groups.
- Targeting can make more efficient use of a firm's resources.
- Appropriate positioning and repositioning can add value to the product and appeal to a new market segment and thus broaden its appeal.

The issue of resources in segmentation is taken up by Piercy (1997). He believes that a successful segmentation strategy is linked to structure and culture. He argues that effective segmentation depends partly on the ability of the firm to organize itself so that different segments are 'owned' by different groups. He argues further that segments need to be compatible with the values of members of the organization, and that the movement into new market segments can threaten the status quo and existing power relations within the organization.

KEY CONCEPT 12.4   SEGMENTATION, TARGETING AND POSITIONING

Segmentation is the process through which the total market is broken down to create distinctive consumer groups. The criteria used to form such groups varies and may include geographical location, social class, occupation, sex, lifestyle, and so on. Once market segments have been identified, products can be developed that focus upon a particular group in an attempt to maximize both the marketing effort and the needs of consumers. **Targeting** involves the evaluation of segments to determine the most appropriate segment for the product and **positioning** involves placing the product in the market so that it meets customer's expectations and perceptions in comparison with other products.

REFLECTION POINT

Select a company that offers a number of different products. What conclusions do you draw about the segmentation policy of that company? On what are the market segments based?

BRANDING

Branding is the process through which the product is given a name, logo or symbol to distinguish it from other products on offer. Branding has become more important as competition increases and products have become easier to copy. Brands are used extensively in the fashion industry, where they are used to differentiate similar products but also to signify a position in the market appealing to a particular market segment. In this way brands such as Armani and Versace have targeted the high income market while the Spanish company Zara has positioned itself in the fashion conscious but lower income market. Branding has become important in the entertainment industry. The globally popular boy band, 'One Direction' has become the brand and is registered as a trademark. The brand is used not only to sell concerts but also DVDs, CDs, downloads and a whole range of souvenirs such as fashion dolls and key rings. The One Direction brand is also used to sell perfume, cosmetics, hair dryers, clothing, bedding and furniture. Michael Jackson achieved similar brand status in the popular music world and his brand continues to be used by business interests after his death. There are many examples of brands outliving the company that created them, Gillette being a good example of a long-lived brand, although the company has been sold many times over, and is now part of the Procter and Gamble Group. Calvin Klein is no longer an independent company but is owned by Philips Van Heusen (PVH), which also owns such brands as Tommy Hilfiger, Speedo and Izod. Such brands are recognizable not just by their name but in many cases by a distinctive logo. Some manufacturers feel it is important to create a brand style so that any one of their products from a given range is recognizable. Alfred Sloan insisted to his design teams that all GM cars in the USA possessed a definitive 'GM look' (Sloan, 1986). Alfa Romeo cars are also differentiated from rival brands by the use of distinctive styling.

KEY CONCEPT 12.5	BRANDING

Branding involves giving the product a name, logo or symbol to distinguish it from products offered by competitors or even by the same organization. Branding is an important source of product differentiation in a competitive and dynamic environment and can apply to a single product, a range of products or an entire organization. It is used to create awareness and build up customer loyalty to ensure repeat purchases. A well-known brand is seen as a financial asset that can provide firms with considerable competitive advantage.

Types of brand

A brand can represent a number of aspects, each of which offers meaning to the consumer. The following typology has used Aaker (1996) as its starting point. Brands can be one or any combination of these aspects.

- The brand can represent a **product** as in the case of Cadbury's chocolate, Kellogg's cornflakes and Michelin tyres. Brand names can be given to a single product or a range of products. Using the same high profile brand across a range of products has clearly benefited Apple's sales of cellphones, tablets and laptops. Such use of brands across a range is known as brand extension. In other cases it may be important to differentiate individual products, even though they originate from the same stable. For example, the washing powder market is dominated by two producers, Lever and Proctor & Gamble, yet each markets a range of washing powders under different brand names. In this way the brands assume an identity of their own, so much so that many people believe them to be from different companies.

- The brand can represent the **organization**. In this case the company has as much if not more meaning to the consumer than the product. There are certain types of consumers who favour certain high profile retailers, such as Harrods in the UK or Bloomingdales in the USA and use them to purchase a range of different products. Universities such as Harvard, Oxford and Cambridge are arguably more attractive to students than the course they wish to study (i.e. the product). The brand as organization is especially important in Japan, to the extent where employment with a big corporation, such as Sony, is an important source of social status. This is an important source of competitive advantage for such as the Disney Corporation (Case 12.4).

- Some organizations extend the concept of the organization brand through the development of a 'generic' or 'own' brand. These can be found especially in supermarkets and retail chains such as Sainsbury, Tesco, John Lewis, Maceys and Bloomingdales. A 'generic' is a product that is sold under the brand name of the retailer and applies to all kinds of products. It may, in fact, be identical to a nationally known brand on the same shelf, but is generally sold at a cheaper price to appeal more to the price-conscious shopper. In some cases generics have acquired a brand image that goes beyond price and value for money to indicate product quality. Historically, Marks & Spencer promoted this image through a single generic brand, St Michael. In more recent years the company has launched a range of brands such as 'Per Una' (in association with Next), 'Blue Harbour', 'Classic Collection' and 'Collezione', each targeting a different market segment.

- Piercy (2009) argues that, in some firms, a **person** becomes the brand, usually in the form of the founder or leading character. To a greater or lesser extent this can be seen with the likes of Richard Branson at Virgin or Bill Gates at Microsoft. In sport and entertainment there are many examples of people as brands. We have already mentioned One Direction and Michael Jackson and, in football, players such as Ronaldo and Beckham have negotiated, as part of their contract, rights to a proportion of the income derived by the club from selling merchandise bearing their name.

- The brand can acquire a **personality** that is nurtured by advertising and promotional campaigns. Thus the Marlboro cowboy associates cigarette smoking with the rugged outdoor life and Bacardi reinforces the association between the drink and a carefree lifestyle on a tropical island. Aaker (1997) has identified five personality traits that are associated with brands. These are: competence, excitement, ruggedness, sincerity and sophistication. There is however little evidence as to how such associations affect the purchase decision. The brand can be a **symbol** that can represent exclusivity and quality at a high price, as in the case of Harrods, Rolls-Royce and Rolex. It can also represent good value for money, as in the case of Boots or Wal-Mart, or even acceptable cheap goods, as in the case of Superdrug and Primark.

- In some cases **the country of origin** becomes a brand. Many German products have acquired a reputation for excellent manufacturing quality, as with Mercedes Benz. The image may not be consistent across a range of goods, so that German supermarkets such as Aldi and Lidl trade on low-end, value-for-money pricing. The country of origin image can change. Japan, once known for cheap imitative products, became a byword for quality and innovative products, especially in the car and domestic electrical goods market. China's leading companies, such as Haier in refrigeration, are moving its position as a producer of cheap goods to one of a brand representing quality at an affordable price. Studies such as Vida and Reardon (2008) examine why some consumers wish to buy own country products. There would appear to be a range of complex reasons including the belief in the superiority of such goods and the belief that it saves jobs and is good for the national economy. However, as we saw in our discussion of globalization in Chapter 2 products are now made in many different countries, which only adds to the complexity.

Co-branding

Co-branding refers to two (or more) brands being presented in association with the aim of increasing exposure, customer awareness and market share of one or more of the brands. Intel initially co-branded with IBM and Compaq/HP computers. As the relationship proved to be successful Intel processors became industry standard and the company now co-brands with most computer manufacturers. While Intel clearly benefitted by association with early market leaders, in recent years Intel is sought as a co-brand by a wide range of manufacturers as a mechanism to increase their market share. In the same way, hotel chains, holiday and car rental companies hope to gain by being co-branded as preferred partners with major airlines as with Hertz and British Airways. In some cases co-branding enables some brands to move into market segments where they have previously had limited exposure. Concha-Y-Toro, Chile's largest wine producer and one of the largest wine companies in the world, has co-branded a range of wines with Manchester United Football team attempting to widen their appeal in hitherto traditionally non-wine drinking market segments and to promote themselves to markets outside Chile. Nike and Apple have formed a co-branding relationship clearly aimed at increasing the market share of both brands. The 'Nike+' app on both the iphone and the ipod is linked to a sensor that fits into a pocket in the Nike running shoe. The sensor tracks distance, pace, time and calories used and transmits the information to the Apple devices. Both Apple and Nike view themselves as partners in emerging technologies aimed at athletes.

The reasons for branding

- Brands are a means of differentiation and attraction. The speed of technology transfer has meant that less time is available to capitalize on competitive advantage through technological change. The brand takes over from technology as the source of differentiation. The development of a brand could mean increased market share and even appeal to more or different segments of the market.

- The markets for most consumer goods in Europe, the USA and Japan have become stagnant. Brands are an attempt to give a product more prominence in the marketplace and on the shelves of retailers. Brands also help customers search for goods. Some shops, particularly in clothing and cosmetics, organize their department around brands.

- The creation of a popular brand can also mean market leadership, which means increased revenue through volume sales and/or price leadership. However, the market leadership and, in particular, the price leadership of several brands has been challenged by the growth of own-brand goods.

- Through the development of brand loyalty, organizations can ensure repeat purchases of the product, calls on the service, or visits to a particular shop. However, through the development of a strong brand it is hoped to break the loyalty between a customer and a rival brand and encourage brand switching.

- A brand image can be a great attribute to a company when launching products and entering new product markets. The new products acquire the favourable attributes of other products belonging to the same brand. Ralph Lauren has used the presence of a strong brand in clothing to extend the product range into bed linen, home furnishings and furniture. Such brands are sometimes referred to as 'banner' brands. The presence of a strong brand enabled Virgin and Sainsbury to enter the competitive financial services sector. In this way, some companies use a single brand for a range of products.

- Branding can be valuable for all products, new or otherwise, in that it can add value to the product. It is for this reason that many firms protect their brand names by registering them as trademarks. The registration of a trademark enables its owner to use the law to prevent competitors from using the same or similar brand name or mark for the same type of product or service. This also protects the consumer from being deceived and confused about the origin of the goods. The added value provided by a brand and the use of the brand as a primary source of competitive advantage is referred to as brand equity.

> *Brand equity is a set of assets (or liabilities) linked to a brand's name and symbol that adds to (or subtracts from) the value provided by the product or service to a firm and/or that firm's customers.*

(Aaker, 1996, p. 7)

- Attempts have been made to measure brand equity both in financial terms and in terms of the strength of attraction to customers. Apart from being subjective, the methods are usually complex. It is also debatable whether a brand in isolation can maintain its value if separated from the organization. Nonetheless, the acquisition of Rowntree by Nestlé is often cited as an example of the power of brand equity. In 1988, Nestlé bought Rowntree for £2.5 billion when the tangible assets were valued at around £1 billion (although the actual sums vary depending on the source). The difference between purchase price and asset value is the value to Nestlé of brands such as Kit Kat, Polo mints and After Eight mints. Table 12.1 lists the top 25 valuable brands, an annual survey that attempts to combine brand perception by members of the public and estimate the added value to the company of the brand. Such estimates of value are, to a certain extent, speculative.
- Branding can be a means of structuring the organization around brands to create healthy internal competition, as in the case of Proctor & Gamble.

Global brands

Much attention has been given to the growth of global brands such as Apple, Coca-Cola, IBM, Disney, Microsoft and McDonald's. The world's leading brands have been identified by a number of groups. There are now a large number of such brand listings. Not all are based on rigorous research and some are even funded by the brands themselves. BrandZ is a listing of leading brands produced by research carried out by Millward Brown, a research agency that is part of the WPP group. Their methodology identifies the world's most valuable brands based on a formula that comprises consumer views, sales and company financial data. Their list of the world's top 25 brands is presented in Table 12.1.

Most global brands share common features. They are a strong brand in their home market and often carry with them into the global market specific country of origin values. They address similar customer needs and are positioned the same in all countries. The rationale for global brands is the same as for all brands with some additional factors. A global brand with global sales offers economies of scale in terms of product manufacture and promotion, with related cost reductions. A strong global brand gives a company increased market control.

REFLECTION POINT

What do you think are the most popular brands in your country? Test your list out against the companies listed in Table 12.1. Will US companies continue to dominate? What conclusions can you draw from the inclusion of four Chinese companies?

TABLE 12.1	Most valuable global brands 2014. (Firms are USA origin unless stated)
1	Google
2	Apple
3	IBM
4	Microsoft
5	McDonald's
6	Coca-Cola
7	Visa
8	AT&T
9	Marlboro
10	Amazon
11	Verizon
12	GE (General Electric)
13	Wells Fargo
14	Tencent – *China*
15	China Mobile – *China*
16	UPS
17	ICBC (Industrial and Commercial Bank of China) - *China*
18	Mastercard
19	SAP – *Germany*
20	Vodafone – *UK*
21	Facebook
22	Wal-Mart
23	Disney
24	American Express
25	Baidu – *China*

However, the economies of scale argument for global brands can be misleading. Many global brands like McDonald's differentiates its offering in different markets (see Case 12.2). A product can mean different things to different cultural groups and may have to be positioned differently and/or targeted at different groups.

The critics of branding

Critics claim that brands mislead consumers by drawing false distinctions between products and directing investment away from product development and into packaging and promotion to maintain the myth of product differentiation. As a result, certain brands can charge higher prices than other goods of similar function and quality.

Branding is also attacked for its encouragement of status consciousness and the elevation of style and popularity over utility. For many young people a simple pair of training shoes or jeans will not suffice; they must be the brand favoured by their peer group at that particular time. It is not just the young person market that is pursued by firms promoting a particular brand image. In recent years 'top brand' league tables have been augmented by the top **'Cool Brands'**. A 2013 survey in the UK identified the top five 'Cool Brands' as Apple, Aston Martin, Rolex, Nike and

Glastonbury, the music festival (http:www.rankingthebrands.com). Such brands are supposedly chosen on the basis that they are stylish, innovative and desirable.

While we may criticize branding for many of the reasons above, markets have become highly differentiated and branding can assist in the process of market segmentation as discussed earlier in this chapter.

REFLECTION POINT

What do you believe is the purpose of branding? Who does it help the most – the producer, the retailer or the customer? What do 'Cool Brands' represent?

PRODUCT, PRICE, PROMOTION AND PLACE (THE 4PS)

Product, price, promotion and place are key elements in marketing, form the basis of marketing strategy and together may be manipulated to form the marketing mix (see Key Concept 12.2). Collectively, they are known as the 4Ps and we will examine each in turn. An interesting interpretation of the 4Ps is offered by Armstrong and Kotler (2007) in which they equate each of the 4Ps with 4Cs (Table 12.2). A similar attempt has been made by Ettenson, Conrado and Knowles (2013) substituting 'SAVE' for the 4P's. At the end of the section we will examine briefly the 7Ps, an extension of the 4P concept, which place emphasis on service to the customer and the 'SAVE' model which the authors claim is more appropriate for business-to-business marketing.

TABLE 12.2   The 4Cs

Customer solution: equated with the product

Customer cost: equated with price

Convenience: equated with place

Communication: equated with promotion

CASE 12.1   ABERCROMBIE & FITCH

Case prepared and co-written by Grace Merkin

Abercrombie & Fitch, the fashionable clothing store of today has little in common with its predecessors other than the name and a tradition of branding based on exclusivity. The original store was founded by David T. Abercrombie in 1892. He was a man who loved the outdoor life and, after working as a prospector, miner, trapper, and railroad surveyor, settled in New York and opened a small shop and factory producing camping equipment. Ezra H. Fitch, an attorney by profession, was a regular customer. He joined Abercrombie as a partner in 1900 and the company, now a retail store selling sporting and outdoor goods, was renamed as Abercrombie & Fitch in 1904. Abercrombie & Fitch did not share the same

(Continued)

CASE 12.1   (Continued)

vision for the company and became incompatible partners. In 1907, Abercrombie resigned and Fitch proceeded to expand the business, extending its clothing range and, in 1910, became the first retailer to sell men's and women's clothing in the same store. In 1917, the company moved into its 12-storey flagship store on Madison Avenue in New York and eventually proclaimed itself 'The Greatest Sporting Goods Store in the World'. As well as sporting goods, other types of outdoor clothing and footwear accounted for a substantial proportion of its sales volume.

Although sales fell in the depression of the late 1920s, its reputation as an elite supplier of sporting goods to high society had already been well established. At some point in their lives, every US president from Roosevelt through Ford was a customer of Abercrombie & Fitch. The company outfitted the famous aviators Charles Lindbergh and Amelia Earhart. Its other prominent customers included the Duke of Windsor, Clark Gable, Ernest Hemingway, Kathryn Hepburn and polar explorers Roald Amundsen and Richard Byrd. The company had a clear policy of supplying high-priced goods to up-market customers through most of the 20th century. The company ignored the growing social diversification of those buying sporting goods. It failed to appeal to the hikers and backpackers and growing leisure market of the 1970s. It stuck to its tradition of supplying the gentleman sportsmen of yesteryear. As a consequence, Abercrombie & Fitch went bankrupt in 1977.

The company name was bought by Oshman´s Sporting Goods of Texas. Under new ownership, Abercrombie & Fitch maintained its focus as a sporting goods store, but expanded its leisure clothing range and added a broader range of casual clothing. The new Abercrombie & Fitch was never very successful and did not last very long. In 1987 the company was acquired by the clothing store, 'The Limited' (now known as 'L Brands'), who moved the company HQ to Ohio. Some shares were made public in 1996 and in 1998 Abercrombie & Fitch was launched as an independent company with shares initially offered to existing shareholders of 'The Limited'.

A key change had occurred in 1992, when Michael Jeffries was appointed as the new head of the company. Between 1992 and 2008,

Abercrombie & Fitch enjoyed unprecedented growth under the guidance of Jeffries, both in terms of sales and the opening of new stores both in the USA and globally. Between 1995 and 2008, the company increased the volume of sales by a factor of 23 and net income by a factor of almost 58. It was during this time that the brand image we see today was developed. By 2014 the company had 842 stores in the USA and 157 across several other countries. As well as the flagship brand Abercrombie & Fitch, the company launched 'Hollister' stores selling less expensive apparel, 'Gilly Hicks', specializing in underwear and sleepwear and 'abercrombie kids'.

The brand image was driven by Jeffries who enlisted the help of photographer Bruce Weber, who had previously designed and shot the Bloomingdales catalogue and had worked for Versace, Pirelli and Ralph Lauren, among others. For Abercrombie & Fitch he produced iconic black and white photographs of models. These 'models' were mainly Abercrombie & Fitch employees, selected by Weber because they embodied the A&F image. Store employees who deal with customers are not called 'sales assistants' but are referred to as 'models'. A key criterion in their hiring is that they possess the A&F 'look'. Men must be lean and muscular and women must possess what was once described as the 'cheerleader look'. Both men and women must also be youthful, attractive, energetic, and look good when smiling. The more attractive men, who can show off their muscular 'six packs', are selected to be topless store greeters. This image was maintained by racy advertising and enhanced by very darkly lit interiors, except for well-lit displays of merchandise, loud music creating a high-energy night club atmosphere and the use of a powerful fragrance throughout. Pricing is pitched towards the high end of the market and the brand has variously been described as 'aspirational', 'youthful', and 'cool'. For many years the company refused to hold special offer promotions. CEO Jeffries thought the company 'too cool' to have a sale and saw promotions as short-term solutions with damaging long-term consequences.

There has been much criticism of the company's overt policies of elitism and the requirement of certain looks and appearance of its staff. The policies were vigorously defended by Jeffries in an interview with Salon.com, the US arts, culture and style online magazine in 2006. He said. 'We aim at the all-American kid with a great attitude and a lot of friends. A lot of people don't belong in our clothes and they can't belong. Are we exclusionary? Absolutely. Those companies that are in trouble are trying to target everybody … you don't alienate anybody but you don't excite anybody either.' Defending the company image he said. 'We hire good-looking people in our stores, because good-looking people attract other good-looking people and we want to market to cool, good-looking people. We don't market to anyone other than that.'

Few objections to the CEOs stance were raised internally while the going was good and while his business model worked. Externally it was somewhat different. Over the last 20 years, A&F has had its share of legal problems and bad publicity. It had to pay out US$50 million to settle three class-action race discrimination lawsuits. The lawsuits alleged discrimination against African American, Latino and Asian American applicants and also some of those hired, who claimed they were only offered less visible backroom jobs in the storeroom. A similar case went to tribunal in the UK when a female employee with a prosthetic arm claimed discrimination in that she was only allowed to work in areas not seen by customers. While the tribunal did not uphold the claim of discrimination, damages were awarded for harassment. An ex-pilot of the company's private jet accused the company of age discrimination, when he was replaced and attempted to ridicule the company's dress and appearance manual for aircraft staff, which specified, among other things, how the CEO, his guests and dogs had to be treated and that cabin crew and pilots had to wear Abercrombie & Fitch underwear. The various legal cases attracted a considerable coverage in both national and international media, many of whom were keen to either repeat quotes from CEO Jeffries, similar to the ones given to Salon.com and to publish the more bizarre requirements of the behaviour and dress code requirements for the private jet. The company has been regularly attacked by feminist groups objecting to its suggestive promotional photography, inappropriate female T-shirt slogans ('Who needs a brain when you have these') and its children's range which included push up bikini bras for children. The company also attracted publicity when it offered to pay a star of the popular US TV reality show *Jersey Shore* to **not** wear A&F clothes, because they disliked his foul-mouthed and sexist behaviour and felt this was an inappropriate brand image.

Michael Jeffries himself came under fire for setting up his own private company to look after 'the personal interests of Abercrombie & Fitch's CEO' and headed by his partner, Matthew Smith. Jeffries' compensation package of US $48.1 million in 2012 was also widely publicized, especially as it exceeded the average A&F store worker's pay by a multiple of 1640. The company also refused to confirm the age of the CEO, even though this was a matter of public record.

Despite the bad publicity the company and its CEO have received over the past few years, opinion is divided on the impact on Abercrombie & Fitch's performance. Some even go so far to claim that it has helped market the company by giving it so much prominence. However the company did respond to accusations of discrimination by carrying out a review of its recruitment and selection policies and by appointing a diversity and inclusion officer. There has been a fall in demand for luxury goods and clothing in particular following the financial crisis of 2008 and the rise in unemployment, especially among teenagers, Abercrombie & Fitch's main target group. The company's sales revenue and profit figures for the last four years are presented in Table 12.3.

These figures do not show that in June 2014 sales showed a decline for the 7th quarter running and in the 2nd quarter of 2014, sales fell by 13 per cent in Abercrombie & Fitch and 16 per cent in Hollister.

TABLE 12.3	Abercrombie & Fitch revenue and profit 2010–14	
	Sales revenue US $ billions	**Gross profit US $ billions**
Feb 2010–11	3.5	2.2
Feb 2011–12	4.2	2.6
Feb 2012–13	4.5	2.8
Feb 2013–14	4.1	2.6

(Continued)

CASE 12.1   (Continued)

Moreover, revenue per share also shows a fall. Many feel that the company is losing its appeal to its target markets that seem to favour mobile phones and tablets over 'aspirational' clothing. The cost of maintaining stores in prestigious high street locations in major cities is costly when faced with declining sales. Mistakes have been made in expansion strategies. The company has been criticized for over-expansion, especially in foreign markets. In addition, Jeffries launched an even more up-market brand, Ruehl, selling even higher priced clothing, which failed and was closed down in 2009.

In response to its declining market position the company made a number of policy changes. It has clearly played down its sexually explicit image, certainly in its online presentation of its product lines. It has introduced price promotions on most products, some discounted by as much as 60 per cent. In 2014 the company changed its policy on sizing. Previously, selling larger sized clothing, especially to women was not seen the right image for Abercrombie & Fitch, but larger sizes for both men's and women's clothing have been introduced. There have also been some changes management announced in 2014. While Jeffries remains as CEO, his role as chairman has been taken by a non-executive director with experience at a senior level with Macys. In June 2014 the company announced the appointment of Christos Angelides as brand president. Up to then he had spent his entire career with the UK company, Next, rising from graduate trainee to become its successful fashion head. His role in Abercrombie & Fitch will include responsibility for all product ranges and the financial performance of the brands.

In 2013 in face of continuing adverse publicity, CEO Jeffries released the following corporate statement on Facebook:

I want to address some of my comments that have been circulating from a 2006 interview. While I believe this … quote has been taken out of context, I sincerely regret that my choice of words was interpreted in a manner likely to cause offence. Abercrombie & Fitch is an aspirational brand that, like most speciality apparel brands, targets its marketing at a particular segment of customers. However, we care about the broader communities in which we operate and we are strongly committed to diversity and inclusion. We hire good people who share these values. We are completely opposed to any discrimination, bullying, derogatory characterizations or any other anti-social behaviour based on race, gender, body type or other individual characteristics.

Questions

1 Has the Abercrombie & Fitch of the early part of the 20th century anything in common with the modern company?

2 How would you define the brand image of Abercrombie & Fitch today. Why do you think this brand has been successful?

3 To what extent are criticisms of the brand justified?

4 Compare the quotations given by CEO Jeffries to Salon.com in 2006 and via Facebook in 2013. What conclusions do you draw?

REFLECTION POINT

Why do Armstrong and Kotler stress the 4Cs as well as the 4Ps?

The product

In our discussion of the contexts of marketing, we saw how the term 'product' has a wide connotation and may include manufactured goods, services, people, organizations, places and ideas. A product comprises several elements. These include functions and benefits, the main features, quality level, styling, brand name, packaging, after-sales service, delivery, installation, after-sales service and warranty. Marketing needs to consider all these aspects of the product. Free delivery or extended guarantees may be seen as essential product characteristics by some consumers. After-sales service and the provision of replacement parts are important sources of income for car dealers. In this section we look at aspects of the product and explore the concept of the product life cycle.

A **product line** is the total number of variations of the same basic product, differentiated by quality, cost or extra features. A sandwich shop will make several versions of the same basic model with variations in the type of bread and different combinations of filling. An airline offers product differentiation both before and during its flights through different levels of service in each class. In response to price competition from companies such as easyJet, some airlines have launched their own subsidiaries offering low-cost, 'no-frills' flights. The breadth of a product line is closely related to the degree of market segmentation.

A **product mix** is the total number of products offered by the firm, sometimes referred to as the product portfolio. The size of a firm's product mix can affect its profitability, in that the effect of poor performers may be lessened by income from better-selling items. However, too broad a product mix can cause problems of control.

Marketing considerations are an important input in the process of developing new products. We saw in Chapter 10 that product development was not only potentially expensive but that the risk of failure was high. Extensive market research is needed concerning such aspects as the utility and acceptability of a design, the target market and likely acceptable price of a new product. An estimate may be made about likely future sales which, when set alongside likely development costs, is essential in assessing the business viability of a new project.

The product life cycle

The product life cycle assumes that all products have limited lives during which they pass through stages, all of which have implications for sales and profitability. The classic life cycle is depicted by four phases (Figure 12.1). The concept can apply equally as well to services as manufactured goods. Shaving was once a popular service offered by barber shops. With the introduction of safety razors and easy-to-apply shaving cream the need for the service declined.

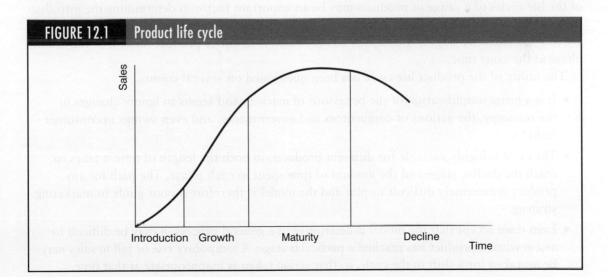

FIGURE 12.1   Product life cycle

The growth of the unisex hairdresser salon led to a further decline in the number of traditional barbers. However, by the mid 1990s male grooming had become a highly profitable business and there emerged a small number of male-only hairdressing salons, offering shaving as one of the services. In this way the product life cycle is revived through the repositioning of the product.

- During the **introduction phase** sales are slow as both consumers and distributors become aware of the product and decide whether to adopt it. The costs of development and promotion are high and firms may suffer initial losses.

- During the **growth phase** there is a rapid acceptance of the product and a dramatic increase in sales. This is generally sustained by improved distribution, product improvements and even price reductions. There are normally high profits for pioneering firms but a growing market attracts competitors, leading to brand differentiation. While the production learning curve may lead to a reduction in costs, the need to satisfy an expanding market can involve costly investment in new production processes. The end of this phase is marked by a high level of competition, recognized by Wasson (1978) as a separate phase, which he termed 'competitive turbulence'.

- As it becomes saturated the market reaches a **mature phase.** Sales and profits are still high but there tends to be considerable investment in maintaining sales. This is achieved through product changes, increased promotional activity and price cutting. Products are sometimes re-launched at this stage, usually with new features, different packaging and often an attempt to create a different image. Firms seek to maintain brand loyalty at the same time as attempting to broaden the market by repositioning. At this stage, the less competitive firms drop from the product market.

- The **decline phase** is marked by a falling off in sales and, while some firms do well as others leave the market, survival is often dependent upon successful product diversification.

The product life cycle can be useful as a framework for planning a marketing campaign and as an indication that marketing strategies need to be adjusted to match changes in the cycle. This may include changing the price or increasing the promotion activity to boost sales. There is an implicit assumption that the cycle may be manipulated by the marketing mix. An understanding of the life cycles of a range of products may be an important factor in determining the introduction of new products and ensuring that the product mix is well represented at the introductory, growth and maturity stages. A company has problems if its entire product range is in the decline phase at the same time.

The utility of the product life cycle has been questioned on several counts:

- It is a gross simplification of the behaviour of markets and seems to ignore changes in the economy, the actions of competitors and governments, and even swings in consumer fashion.

- The cycle is highly variable for different products, in both the length of time it takes to reach the decline stage and the amount of time spent in each phase. The path for any product is extremely difficult to plot and the model is therefore a poor guide to marketing strategy.

- Even if we accept that the model is descriptive of a general process, it may be difficult to assess when a product has reached a particular stage. A temporary rise or fall in sales may be mistaken for a shift in the cycle, so that action taken is inappropriate at that time.

Each stage of the product life cycle has implications for the design of the product, the volume and variety of production, and the nature of the process of manufacture or delivery of the service to the customer. In manufacturing, the product life cycle is closely related to a process life cycle. The introductory stage of the product life cycle is marked by a highly flexible production process. As markets reach their maximum potential the capacity can only be met by relatively inflexible mass production systems. The cost of such systems necessitates a high market demand and long production runs. There is a similarity here with the 'revised sequence' (Galbraith, 1972), discussed earlier in this chapter. In this situation, marketing becomes led by production rather than demand. However, in the case of manufactured goods, the relationship between the product and process life cycles has been complicated by the introduction of flexible manufacturing systems (see Chapter 11).

REFLECTION POINT

Think of the product life cycle for a range of products. How useful is the concept?

Price

If marketing strategy were based entirely on the analysis of the neoclassical economists then price would be the most significant feature of that strategy and would be based on the concept of the price elasticity of demand. A product is price elastic if changes in price influence changes in demand. All things being equal, an increase in price will lead to a fall in demand and consequently a fall in revenue and vice versa. All things are rarely equal, and consumers can behave in an unpredictable manner. Many factors influence price and pricing strategy and operate at the environmental, organizational and strategic levels of our model and involve factors such as branding, discussed in the previous section. We deal with some of those factors under the following headings.

Cost

A business wishing to make a profit must use the cost of making a product or providing a service as an important base point in setting its prices. However, the sensitivity of most pricing decisions lies less in the cost of raw materials, labour and the like, than the understanding of those factors that may determine the extent of mark-up on the basic cost price. These include most of the factors identified below. Moreover, costs can be distorted by accounting methods, particularly those associated with apportioning overheads. For example, should overheads be calculated for individual cost centres or averaged for the whole organization? Cost and price are linked through economies of scale and the belief that volume production will lead to price reduction. While this may be true for some products, there are many exceptions which challenge both the notion of economies of scale and the necessity of tying price to volume production. We revisit this approach in our discussion of marketing strategy.

Consumer behaviour

The price of a product may well be related to what a consumer can afford and to what he or she is prepared to pay. This, in turn, is related to income levels, the consumer's perceptions of quality and value for money, and the consumer's budget. In purchasing a camera for a special holiday or a word processor for the office of a small business, the consumer's own target price based on what he or she wants to pay may be the primary factor. The range of products considered will then be limited to those priced within a range around or below the target price. A firm aiming at a particular target market may be best advised to discover the budgeting behaviour of its potential consumers before setting the price. Some firms use target pricing to influence product design. For example, where costs are likely to exceed target price, value-engineering methods will be used to reduce costs. Consumer perceptions can, of course, be influenced by promotional activity. Many brands are marketed as highly priced products in the knowledge that certain market segments will pay for specific brands. This strategy is successfully pursued in the fashion industry to establish products in a highly competitive market. Such strategies depend on brand image, trends and social influences. Case 12.1 examines the retail store Abercrombie & Fitch and explores the significance of the brand on price.

Economic factors

Price is related to the economy in a number of ways, all of which have a potential impact on an organization's pricing policy:

- The affluence of consumers will have an obvious influence on their level of budgeting and regional variations may produce differential demand, especially for luxury items.
- The role of the state in managing the economy may affect both demand and prices.
- The control of interest rates will influence the extent of consumer credit and hence the size of an individual's budget, as will levels of taxation.
- During periods of high inflation the government may well introduce measures to control prices.
- One influence on price in the global economy is the currency exchange rate, which fluctuates according to the state of the economy. Fluctuations between UK sterling and the US dollar have had a major impact on trade between the two countries. In 2008–09 the UK currency fell sharply against the euro. Many UK residents who had chosen to retire in countries such as Spain and France found that they were no longer able to afford to live in those countries on a UK pension. In addition, the housing market had collapsed, which meant they were unable to sell properties they had bought. As a changing exchange rate brings prices of products more into line with competition from domestic suppliers or other country's imports, criteria other than price become more important.

Competition

Many firms price their products by reference to an existing market, basing their price around that offered by competitors for products of similar features and quality. The growth of the low-cost airline business has affected national carriers, who in response have lowered prices or even cut routes to stay in business. In such industries price is used prominently in promotion. In the airline business some companies have been accused of misleading the customer by promoting an initial low price but then charging for extras such as baggage handling, food and drink and even a booking fee.

Management goals

The price of goods is often related to the extent to which managements wish to optimize profit. Management goals rarely conform to simple economic models and are complicated by considerations of power, politics and personal preference. The desire of a group of managers for a larger market share for their products may result in a low-price strategy to build up demand. In some firms price may be used as a promotion strategy to create an image of product quality in the eyes of the consumer.

Organizational size

The size of an organization may give it market power and the ability to manipulate market prices. This is especially true of oligopolies such as oil companies. We saw in Chapter 10 how GlaxoSmithKline's market dominance with Zantac and Ventolin enabled it to charge high prices. A major supermarket chain, such as Wal-Mart or Tesco, is able, because of its purchasing power and stock turnover, to insist on large price discounts from its suppliers. It is then able to price some of its goods lower than the competition to attract customers. We noted in our discussion of business ethics in Chapter 9 that Wal-Mart's pricing policy enabled it to gain advantage over the competition, so much so that rival supermarket chains were put out of business. Fishman (2006) referred to this as the 'Wal-Mart effect'.

We began our discussion of price by challenging the all-important view attributed to the price element in marketing by neo-classical economists. The role of price in marketing strategy is, as we have seen, highly complex. Nonetheless it is the only element of marketing strategy that generates income, all other items incurring cost. Pricing policy is therefore a vital strand of strategy which, because of the complexities involved, is often difficult for management to judge.

REFLECTION POINT

Which factor has the most influence on price?

Promotion

We can identify five traditional types of promotion: advertising, sales promotion, direct marketing, personal selling and publicity. The expansion of promotion as a marketing activity is a function of the growth, complexity and competitiveness of markets and the developments of appropriate technology, as in the newspaper and television industries. Advertising is a vital source of revenue for commercial television stations, for newspapers and magazines and for websites. In the last few years, promotional activity has changed radically with the increased use of digital and social media marketing. We examine these changes in a separate section later in the chapter.

All types of promotional activity use psychological theory and communication models of human behaviour, but the nature of the promotion used will depend on a number of factors, including the strategy of the organization, the available budget and the type of market. While television advertising may be an appropriate medium for the promotion of consumer goods and services, such as cars and home contents insurance, a specialist magazine may be preferred for expensive camera equipment, and personal selling may be the best way to market industrial goods to other organizations. Some forms of promotion, such as television advertising, are obvious, while others, such as shop design, are less so. The Burton Group, on taking over Debenhams, invested heavily in redesigning the department store interiors to project a new image and attract different market segments.

Promotion, like distribution, often involves management working together with representatives of other organizations. Advertising, for example, may involve the marketing manager working closely with an agency as well as representatives of the media. We will return to these aspects when we discuss the organizational aspects of marketing, and turn our attention, for the time being, to the types of promotion.

Advertising

The management of advertising involves four considerations: the design of the message, the selection of the media, the cost of both production and exposure, and the evaluation of its effectiveness.

- The design of the message reflects the three functions of advertising:
  - First, it operates to inform the consumer and may be useful in creating initial demand for a product or informing consumers about price changes or the addition of new product functions or services.
  - Second, it operates to persuade the consumer to buy the advertiser's product rather than that of a rival. This form of promotion tends to focus on features which distinguish a product from its competitors, and by building up a brand image.
  - The third function serves to remind the consumer of the product and encourage repeat purchases. Such promotion is not aimed solely at consumers, but also at wholesalers and retailers to give products shelf space. In general, the nature of the message will vary in all these cases. For example, an advertisement that aims to change the buying habits of consumers will often use images with which the potential consumer identifies.
- Advertisers have a wide choice of media, including national and local newspapers, magazines, cinema, television, radio, posters and the Internet. The selection of appropriate media involves considerations of the target market and timing. A campaign may be staggered using a variety of media for maximum effect. The choice has broadened. Newspapers as well as offering space in the main paper, offer advertising opportunities in a range of magazine supplements, in online versions of the paper and through the newspaper apps on mobile phones and tablets.
- The cost of promotion will vary with the media selected. Advertising costs in newspapers vary widely and are dependent on circulation, the day of the week, the space and position on the page and whether the paper is national or local. Special deals may be struck between the buyers and sellers of advertising space. The problem with such expenditure is the degree of waste, since much advertising can be ignored by large sections of the population, and the real impact is often difficult to evaluate. We will deal with the evaluation of advertising in our discussion of marketing strategy.

Sales promotion

This incorporates a variety of techniques, including free samples, money-back coupons, special offers on loyalty points and competitions. Manufacturers promoting goods through the trade often provide attractive point-of-sale displays or product expertise in the form of a specialist salesperson. Fashion, furniture and cosmetic manufacturers train and pay their own staff to work in department stores. Exhibitions and trade fairs are popular ways of promoting goods both to the trade and industry as a whole. Such forms of sales promotion apply to services as well as manufactured goods. New restaurants often invite a specially targeted clientele to a launch evening. Railway companies have introduced several types of fare structure to attract off peak users, in the same way that many restaurants offer reduced-price meals to attract customers outside the hours of peak demand. These examples illustrate the interaction between sales promotion and pricing strategies.

Sales promotion is sometimes referred to as 'below-the-line' advertising and is often under-estimated in considerations of promotion. It is estimated that sales promotion comprises over 70 per cent of all expenditure on promotion activity and has achieved a particularly rapid growth since the 1960s. The consumer has become better informed and more aware of special offers, while managements have apparently grown sceptical of the effectiveness of advertising and believe there to be a much clearer and direct relationship between expenditure on sales promotion and sales.

REFLECTION POINT

Identify the various types of promotion used by a store with which you are familiar.

Case 12.2 illustrates a promotional campaign by McDonald's in Singapore that used cultural stereotypes and proved to be an outstanding financial success for the company.

Direct marketing

This is both a form of promotion and a channel of distribution. In direct marketing, organizations deal directly with the customer without using intermediaries such as shops. There are many forms, which include direct mail shots, inserts in magazines, mail order catalogues, telephone sales, coupon response forms, door-to-door leaflets and the use of websites, social media and emails.

Most businesses now have websites and will deal directly with customers (we discuss this further in our discussion of the impact of technology on marketing and in the section on digital and social media marketing). Theatres and restaurants use emails and leaflets to promote special offers or simply to make potential customers aware of their product. The websites of many restaurants contain menu details. Direct marketing is used to sell to organizations as well as to individual consumers. Most firms obtain their most frequently purchased office supplies online or from mail order catalogues or a combination of both.

The advantage claimed for direct marketing over other forms of promotion is that it can be targeted at specific groups. Unlike television or other forms of advertising, the target audience is reached with minimum wastage. Critics of direct marketing attribute to it the growth of 'junk mail' and 'junk email'. Despite its critics, direct marketing has grown in popularity and some firms, such as Dell, have used it to increase their market share. The popularity of direct marketing is associated with increasing market segmentation and developments in information technology and telecommunications. A key factor has been the growth of name and address lists of all types, which form the basis of databases used by firms in direct marketing.

CASE 12.2   McDONALD'S KIASU BURGER AND THE FOURTH FLAVOUR

The global fast-food restaurant chain McDonald's has built its reputation on a range of products that it offers around the world. The similarity in its global product range is matched by a similarity in its approach to marketing. The restaurants are easily recognizable by a common approach to design and layout. In almost every location the restaurant can be spotted underneath the sign of the 'golden arch', representing the 'M' in McDonald's. Promotional campaigns everywhere tend to emphasize family values, low cost, good-value nourishing meals and use a 'Ronald McDonald' character to appeal to children.

In reality there have always been variations in the taste and appearance owing to variations in local suppliers around the world, but the core product range remained sacrosanct. In the 1990s the product policy was relaxed to allow the introduction of local products appealing to local tastes, usually accompanied by a fierce promotional campaign. Since 1993 such a policy has operated in Singapore. The first of such products was the Kiasu Burger. Kiasu is a local Chinese dialect word in Singapore which roughly translates as a 'fear of losing out'. The positive connotation of this word is generally associated with healthy competition and the need to be first. The negative attributes are associated with aversion to risk and even selfishness and cowardice. Kiasu-ism is a well-known concept in Singapore and, since 1990, has been popularized through a comic strip character, Mr Kiasu. The character was developed by four young Singaporeans and his adventures usually depict the worst elements of Kiasuism, such as gluttony and pushing to the front of queues. The comic strip developed cult status, but soon gained wider appeal and became a local craze. The comic strip character was augmented by a range of Mr Kiasu merchandise, such as T-shirts.

A decision was made to launch a product in May 1993 using the concept of Mr Kiasu. The company developed a local product, the Kiasu Burger, described as 'an extra large chicken patty seasoned with extra spices, marinated in extra sauce, topped with fresh lettuce, all sandwiched in an extra-large sesame seed bun'. The product was sold at S$2.90 and was cheaper than the rest of the McDonald's hamburger range. The product was also introduced as part of a range of value-for-money meal combinations and purchasers of the Kiasu Burger were entitled to buy a Mr Kiasu figurine for 90 cents. Four figurines were offered, each bearing a typical Mr Kiasu slogan, such as 'Everything also I want!' and 'Everything also must grab!' Such slogans poked fun, not only at Singaporean attitudes, but also at 'Singlish', a local dialect version of English. The campaign was supported by television advertising, featuring Mr Kiasu as a cartoon character for the first time.

Within two months of the launch, a million were sold and the Kiasu Burger itself had become a craze. Demand for the figurines was also high. At the end of July 1993, McDonald's launched a further promotion celebrating the success and congratulating Singaporean customers for being able to laugh at themselves. For a limited period the company offered its Kiasu Burgers and figurines at half price.

The Kiasu Burger was developed as part of a series of promotions under the banner of the 'fourth flavour'. The aim of the promotion was to increase turnover by catering specifically to local taste and the use of novelty items. Any specific 'fourth flavour' was never destined to become a permanent feature of the McDonald's product range. Instead, it was planned that interest would be maintained by the introduction of a new product at regular intervals, with the subsequent phasing out of the previous 'fourth flavour'. A year after the launch of the Kiasu Burger, McDonald's Singapore introduced the chicken-based Kampung Burger. This too was based on a popular cartoon character, Kampung Boy, and the cartoon characters were seen in animation for the first time as the product was launched by a television commercial. McDonald's saw the product as representing traditional community values associated with village life. The promotion was accompanied by a caption contest.

In 1995, McDonald's introduced another chicken product in the form of the Love Burger. It linked the product with the importance of love within the family and ran a competition to find Singapore's longest-married couple – the prize being an anniversary party at McDonald's. Another competition was launched for newly-weds and prizes of McDonald's wedding receptions were offered for the most creative love messages between couples. The Love Burger was followed the following year by the McPepper Burger, a beef hamburger in a thick spicy black pepper sauce.

CASE 12.2 (Continued)

This was the most successful promotional item to date and the company sold over half a million in the first two weeks of the launch.

Promotional items also included desserts such as McDonaldland, an ice-cream exclusively for the Singapore market. The ice-cream container was designed as the head of one of four McDonald's characters, 'Ronald McDonald', 'Hamburglar', 'Birdie' and 'Grimace'. Earlier desserts to appeal to local taste had included mango and durian milkshakes.

While the promotions varied in their popularity, the cumulative effect was an increase in turnover for McDonald's, with a knock-on effect to its main product range. During the period of these launches from 1993–97, McDonald's presence in Singapore grew from 50 to over 80 outlets on a small island of then under four million people.

Questions

1 What risks was McDonald's taking with its launch of the Kiasu Burger?

2 What other forms of promotion does the company use?

3 How could a similar campaign be launched in the UK or in another European country?

KEY CONCEPT 12.6 DIRECT MARKETING

Direct marketing involves setting up a direct channel between the organization and its customers. It is thus a channel for both promotion and distribution, targeting specific groups and enabling them to respond without the use of an intermediary. There are many methods ranging from mail shots to the use of the Internet.

Personal selling

This is a specialized form of direct marketing favoured in business-to-business marketing, recognizing the importance of building good personal relations between seller and buyer. However, the cost of employing a sales force to maintain regular contact with customers can be expensive In recent years a much cheaper form of personal selling has developed in business-to-consumer marketing, especially among the manufacturers of double-glazing and fitted kitchens, by employing part-time workers to contact potential consumers by telephone. Such unsolicited selling has attracted much criticism from irritated consumers.

Publicity

This can be an important form of promotion in that the credibility of products or services may be enhanced by linking them with news stories. Many newspapers now have specialist business features or even supplements and such stories can be an effective way of keeping a firm and its products in the public eye. Some of the larger firms institutionalize this function by employing a specialist public relations department.

An examination of promotion raises many important issues. Advertising, in particular, has been challenged for developing an overly materialistic society, and the ethics of advertising goods such as cigarettes and alcohol has been questioned by a number of interest groups. The high cost of promotion campaigns using television advertising sets up considerable barriers to the entry of new firms and may operate in favour of big business. This is another reason for the growth of direct marketing.

Place

Place refers to the processes by which products and services reach the consumer and involves consideration of marketing channels and physical distribution. A marketing channel represents the flow of goods and services and may comprise several stages, involving intermediaries, such as transporters, agents, wholesalers and retailers.

Intermediaries play a number of roles. They are usually able to distribute goods to customers in a more cost-effective way than the manufacturer, particularly where goods are mass-produced and items are fast moving. The most popular daily newspapers in the UK sell millions of papers between them. This would be impossible without a complex and well-organized network of transport, wholesalers and retailers to ensure that newspapers are available for readers each morning. In this case, the intermediaries break down the number of newspapers into more easily managed batches and are geographically dispersed to ensure an effective delivery. Such wholesalers and retailers handle a range of daily newspapers and so facilitate the buying process by offering consumers choice. Manufacturers and consumers are therefore linked in a cost-effective network. The cost of a single newspaper establishing its own network would push up prices to many times their current value. In recent years such networks have been transformed through technological developments which have made possible the printing of newspapers almost at the point of sale. This has reduced the number of distribution channels and meant that UK holidaymakers in popular resorts around the world can obtain a daily paper on the same day it is published.

An intermediary is also an important source of market research and sales promotion since it stands in closer proximity to customers than the manufacturer. For the same reason intermediaries are often better placed to offer a comprehensive after-sales service. Some intermediaries may offer limited processing facilities, such as cutting glass or mixing paint to order. For the manufacturer, the intermediary shares some of the risk by buying goods in bulk to sell on (some of which may not sell) and, in so doing, helps finance the manufacturer's operations. The case of Sleek in Chapter 2 demonstrates how a business has grown as an intermediary.

Those manufacturers seeking greater control over the distribution process have tried to integrate vertically the marketing channel network. Perhaps the clearest example of this is franchising. However, we have already noted in this chapter the power that can be wielded by big supermarket chains over some manufacturers; a case of the marketing channel controlling the supplier.

In charting the growth of direct marketing, we noted that not all marketing channels involve intermediaries. In the case of business-to-business transactions it is more common for the manufacturer to deal directly with the purchaser, often by building up a relationship between the sales and purchasing departments in the respective organizations. As we saw in the discussion of supply chain management in Chapter 11, there is a tendency for very close relationships to be built up between components suppliers and manufacturers, particularly with the introduction of JIT production methods.

In all cases it is important that the marketing channel makes the goods and services accessible to those who seek them. The importance of accessibility varies with the nature of the product on offer and the needs and wants of consumers. It is important for a fast-food restaurant to be located near centres of population and to be sited so as to encourage casual callers. Accessibility becomes less important for the prestigious restaurant rated by food guides, since customers will often be willing to travel several miles. Hospitals, especially those offering casualty services, also need to be located close to and be easily reached by the populations they serve. The increase in the sale of flowers worldwide is a direct result of the widened access that telephone sales and, more recently, the use of the Internet have produced (see Case 12.3).

The concept of the marketing channel has been revolutionized by the growth of e-commerce and online marketing. This was featured in Chapter 3 and will be raised later in this chapter in our discussion of the relationship between technology and marketing. It is also a central feature of Case 12.4.

REFLECTION POINT

Is location becoming less important for customers? Is this true for all types of business?

Customer service and the 7Ps

The concept of the 4Ps has been extended to 7Ps to emphasize aspects of customer service. The additional aspects are:

- **People.** This focuses on all staff in the organization and recognizes that they play an important part in creating customer satisfaction and customer loyalty. The emphasis is on how staff treat customers to give them added value. There is a recognition that all staff need to be trained in customer care, especially those that deal directly with customers. Many organizations use call centres to interface with customers and their effectiveness in delivering customer satisfaction has been questioned on the basis that call centre staff are not employed directly by the organization providing the service.

- **Process.** Effective service requires effective processes for the identification of customer needs, for the effective handling of orders and for dealing effectively with complaints.

- **Physical evidence.** An attractive environment as perceived by the customer is an important element of the service provided. This is a key feature in the design of airport terminals, department stores, supermarkets, hairdressing salons and restaurants and bars. It has also become an important consideration in the design of medical centres and local authority offices dealing with customer services. As well as attractiveness being important, customers must find the organization easy to use. A department store and an airport terminal should have layouts that are easy for customers to negotiate and waiting rooms in hospitals and local authority services should be both comfortable and provide key information on such things as waiting time.

Many have argued that the 4Ps is a somewhat dated model (see Armstrong and Kotler's 4Cs earlier in this section). Ettenson, Conrado and Knowles (2013) have argued that the 4Ps model is inappropriate for business-to-business marketing and they offer an alternative based on their work with Motorola. They propose the SAVE model, comprising:

- **Solution** (which they prefer to 'product'). This focuses on meeting the needs of the customer rather than emphasizing the features and functions of the product.

- **Access** (which they prefer to 'place'). This de-emphasizes specific locations and channels and focuses instead on accessibility and preferred channels for the customer.

- **Value** (which they prefer to 'price'). This emphasizes the value of the offering relative to the price instead of its relationship to production costs or the price offered by competitors.
- **Education** (which they prefer to 'promotion'). This emphasizes the information relevant to the customers need, and recognizing this may change over time, instead of blanket advertising and personal selling.

BUYER BEHAVIOUR

An understanding of the needs, wants and behaviour of consumers is vital in designing a marketing strategy. Buyer behaviour involves considerations of why people buy and how they arrive at the decision to buy. Several writers have attempted to formulate theories of consumer behaviour to predict the outcomes of various strategies. As yet, the predictive validity of such theories and models leaves much to be desired. The weakness of such theories lies in the complexity of buyer behaviour. We have seen how changes in an economy can affect consumer perceptions of their own purchasing power. In addition we can identify psychological and sociological influences, including: perception, attitudes, patterns of learning, motivation, personality, social class, peer groups and culture. Knowledge of such factors is an important contribution to marketing strategy and may be used in the development of the marketing mix. Advertisers use these influences by, for example, linking products to certain social groups with whom the consumer identifies and by using 'experts' to extol the virtues of particular brands in an attempt to influence the perceptions and attitudes of the consumer.

Predicting buyer behaviour becomes particularly important with innovations and is an important ingredient in decisions concerning new product development. Rogers (1962) attempted to differentiate people according to their response to innovative products and identified five types:

- innovators
- early adopters
- the early majority
- the late majority
- laggards.

The innovators and early majority comprise an estimated 15 per cent of the population and are important as opinion leaders in the diffusion of innovations. The implication for the marketing specialist is to establish the characteristics of these groups and focus the marketing communication accordingly. The diffusion of new products is seen as a chain reaction of influence between pioneering consumers and the mass market. While Rogers found that early adopters tended to be younger, more affluent and more cosmopolitan than later adopters, such generalizations, like so many models, have foundered at the sheer complexity of buyer behaviour. For example, a consumer may be an early adopter of the latest in camera technology but particularly conservative where furniture, clothes or holidays are concerned. In this case we would need to identify the opinion leaders for each product group.

Whatever the product or the target market, considerable attention is paid by many managers to the attainment of customer loyalty, based on the assumption that the costs of retaining customers are less than those associated with gaining new customers and that loyal customers not only make repeat purchases but also recommend the company and its products to other potential buyers. In the late 1990s, the related concepts of customer care and relationship marketing became fashionable. West, Ford and Ibrahim (2010) feel that the emphasis on relationship marketing has been recognized in business-to-business marketing for many years, it was applied relatively late to business-to-consumer marketing. While for many consumers there is rather more rhetoric than reality, in many organizations customer care has become the focus of training and culture-change programmes. For many organizations retaining a close relationship with all customers is difficult, which is why there tends to be a focus on identifying and building up relationships with those customers who represent most value to the company.

In the UK and other countries, supermarkets and retail chains have attempted to increase customer loyalty through the introduction of 'loyalty cards', in which purchases attract points which can then be converted into cash refunds, exchanged for goods or, in some cases, converted to air miles. In most cases the cash benefit of such loyalty cards is worth a 1 per cent discount off the cost of the shopping and most analyses conclude that exchanging loyalty points for goods is simply not cost-effective, because, in most shops, customers would need to spend several thousand pounds to earn enough points to buy even simple household goods. It is questionable whether such schemes increase loyalty since many customers are members of several such loyalty schemes. Piercy (2009) challenges the notion of loyalty cards as an effective strategy in that they are easy for competitors to copy and sees them as a gimmick that does little to create real customer value. Perhaps the greatest benefit to the organization is that such schemes enable them to collect information about shopping habits; the loyalty card has become an important source of market information.

Piercy (2009) questions several of the assumptions that underpin traditional approaches to customer loyalty. In particular, he challenges the assumption that there is an automatic link between customer satisfaction and loyalty, as illustrated in Figure 12.2.

The classic model of customer loyalty is illustrated by the 'happy stayer'. However, there are customers who gain satisfaction yet enjoy switching brands. These Piercy describes as 'happy wanderers'. 'Hostages' are customers who have no choice either because they are tied in by contract or they are dealing with a monopoly supplier who can exploit market power by charging a high price. 'Dealers' are customers who forever seek the best deal irrespective of brand or supplier.

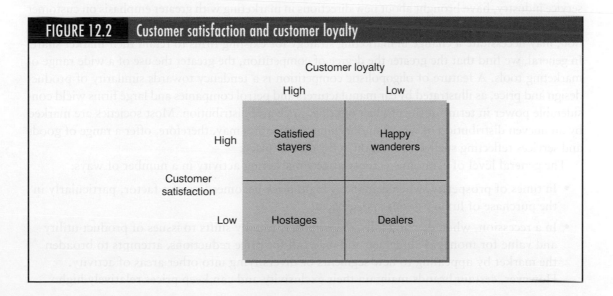

FIGURE 12.2   Customer satisfaction and customer loyalty

Because the link between loyalty and satisfaction is complex, Piercy questions the value of loyalty programmes.

The complexities of buyer behaviour have led some to conclude that consumer marketing is inherently more complex than is the case with business-to-business marketing. Such a perspective ignores the complexities in B2B marketing, which may be different from those in consumer marketing but are just as real. These complexities include the nature of management values and organizational politics, and those involved in the relationship between the buyers and sellers of industrial and organizational goods and services.

REFLECTION POINT

What do you believe to be the most important determinants of buyer behaviour?

ENVIRONMENTAL ASPECTS OF MARKETING

Marketing activities are not only influenced by environmental factors, the management manipulation of the 4Ps represents a deliberate attempt to shape consumer behaviour and hence the market environment within which the firm operates. Marketing strategy is, therefore, vital to the corporate strategy of any organization. We will view the relationship of marketing with the environment of the firm by looking in turn at the economy, the role of the state and consumer interest groups, technology and, finally, cultural and social factors.

Marketing and the economy

The subject of marketing has always been associated with applied economics, and economic theory is used as the basis for the development of marketing strategies. Marketing activity is influenced by economic factors in a number of ways. Major economic shifts, as in the case of manufacturing to service industry, have brought about new directions in marketing with greater emphasis on customer service. The entry of new firms into the market place, especially in the form of overseas competition, may necessitate a change in marketing strategy for existing firms to retain their market share. In general, we find that the greater the degree of competition, the greater the use of a wide range of marketing tools. A feature of oligopolistic competition is a tendency towards similarity of product design and price, as illustrated by car manufacturers and petrol companies and large firms wield considerable power in terms of the product offering, price and distribution. Most societies are marked by an uneven distribution of wealth and income. Companies may, therefore, offer a range of goods and services reflecting such segmentation in the market place.

The general level of economic activity affects marketing activity in a number of ways:

- In times of prosperity, when demand is high, price becomes less of a factor, particularly in the purchase of luxury goods and services.
- In a recession, when demand falls, the emphasis usually shifts to issues of product utility and value for money. Falling demand may call for price reductions, attempts to broaden the market by appealing to new segments or diversifying into other areas of activity. However, certain brands maintain their exclusivity and can keep prices relatively high.

- In economically depressed areas, attempts by the unemployed to set up small businesses in retailing and food and drink outlets are often doomed to failure owing to the low levels of demand in that area. Where demand is so low, little in the way of marketing strategy can change the basic position.

- Changing rates of inflation and changes in interest rates will affect savings and the availability of credit. Where price inflation rises at a faster rate than wage inflation the demand for certain luxury goods may fall. Some firms combat this by offering favourable credit terms to customers in an attempt to boost sales.

- Expenditure on advertising is often seen as an indicator of the economic health of a nation. A recession in the UK during 2001 and 2002 affected advertising revenues. Overall expenditure on advertising fell by 11 per cent in 2001, with television most affected. Most television companies reduced their slot prices by 13 per cent. The situation became even worse in 2002 with the advertising industry taking its worst cuts for 50 years.

These illustrations show how marketing strategy has often reacted to changes in the economy. However, many firms will attempt to manipulate the economy through its marketing activities. In Chapter 10 we examined the link between levels of investment in product development and economic growth at both the level of the firm and nationally. We have seen that one of the functions of promotional activities is to persuade consumers and hence attempt to manipulate demand. We have noted several times in this book how very large companies, especially those operating globally, are able to manipulate markets to their advantage through product development, pricing and promotional strategies in such a way as to affect national economies.

While the relationship between marketing and the economy is significant, we saw in our discussion of price elasticity that economic theory has its limitations in our understanding of marketing behaviour, ignoring as it does a range of important cultural, social and psychological influences. Political and pressure group influences also play a part and it is to these we now turn.

Marketing and the role of the state

The state represents a powerful presence in the market place as a dominant employer, supplier and purchaser. Since the 1980s both privatization and deregulation in the UK have changed the marketing environment. The state is involved in marketing in a number of ways:

- The state markets its services and provides information on government policy.

- Advertising is often used to direct the behaviour of individuals, as in the case of health information and education, and to encourage the unemployed to take advantage of training schemes.

- The pricing and promotional policies of state-controlled industries can be used to direct public expenditure and consumption, as was the case with energy. With the privatization of the energy industry across Europe, the emphasis has shifted to the establishment of price controls for private organizations.

- The state attempts to regulate the marketing activity of private firms. Most of these measures are aimed at regulating free competition and protecting individual consumers and the environment.

- In terms of product, most governments have devised technical standards to which products should comply to ensure minimum standards of quality, and to protect both the consumer and the environment against potentially dangerous products.

- We have seen in Chapter 10 that the granting of patents gives inventors a monopoly to market their products in return for making their invention public. The aim of such legislation is both to reward and stimulate innovation.

- Through its law relating to monopolies and mergers, the state tries to define and prevent unfair competition. In the UK this is controlled by the Competition Commission (formerly the Monopolies and Mergers Commission). In the USA it comes under the legal framework of the Sherman Anti-Trust Laws.

- Many governments have tackled the problems of deception in advertising and sales promotion through legislation, which also sets out the contractual rights of consumers on such issues as the return of goods and warranty.

- Many governments attempt to limit the advertising of certain types of products such as cigarettes and alcohol.

- Within the jurisdiction of the EU, organizations are subject to a range of regulations affecting companies and consumers alike, as with the pricing of agricultural produce or the description of products when promoting them for the European market.

- The state has become a powerful consumer and a very large market in its own right. The state can use this power for social and political ends, by awarding contracts to firms in economically depressed areas or by withdrawing contracts from firms that do not adhere to government policy in such areas as environmental protection or employment rights.

- In the UK the deregulation and privatization of the 1980s and 1990s meant that many local authority services were outsourced, involving processes of competitive tendering from would-be suppliers. Many authorities used a principle known as 'best value', in which organizations marketing their goods and services to them must conform to stringent criteria.

Government intervention in the marketing activity of private firms is a complex issue, no better illustrated than in the case of cigarette advertising. In 1997, the UK government attempted to ban all cigarette advertising. The proposals were met with intense lobbying by interested parties. For a number of years there has been a ban on the television advertising of tobacco products. This had led to the tobacco companies seeking other forms of promotion, notably the use of billboard advertising and sports sponsorship. Firms controlling advertising sites and billboards naturally objected to a complete ban. The biggest opposition came from sports bodies, especially those with an interest in Formula One motor racing. This is a very expensive sport that historically has derived considerable revenue from cigarette companies, with brands such as Marlboro sponsoring teams. Legal restrictions banning cigarette advertising in many countries resulted in conflict between the Grand Prix organizers and various governments. The threat to cancel the Grand Prix in Canada in 2004 was averted only by a deal at the last minute. Lobbying earned the ban a reprieve in the UK but Formula One has readily embraced new venues such as Malaysia and Bahrain. Here, state-of-the art facilities have been provided with government backing as well as a more liberal approach to cigarette advertising to attract the Grand Prix circus.

REFLECTION POINT

Why do governments want to control marketing? Over which elements do they have greatest control?

Consumerism

The concept of consumerism has developed in the past 50 years. The importance of consumerism was highlighted in the US Congress in an address by President Kennedy in 1962 in which he identified consumers as ' the only important group ... whose views are often ... not heard'. (cited in www.consumersinternational.org). In that address Kennedy identified four basic rights:

- The right to be informed, by being given the facts to make informed choices.
- The right to safety, to be protected against harmful products, processes and services.
- The right to be heard, especially by governments in making policy.
- The right to choose from a range of good quality products at affordable prices.

Since Kennedy's address, the rights have been built upon by Consumers International (formerly the International Organization of Consumers Unions) to comprise also:

- The right to satisfaction of basic needs, comprising access to essential goods and services.
- The right to redress including compensation for unacceptable goods and services and also for misrepresentation.
- The right to consumer education to acquire knowledge and skills to make choices.
- The right to a healthy environment. (www.consumersinternational.org)

In recent years there has been an additional focus on the right to privacy, based on concerns about the uses of personal information of customers held by organizations.

If we accept that marketing is nothing more than the effective satisfaction of consumer needs and wants, then consumerism would, in fact, be synonymous with marketing and the presence of organized consumer groups would be no more than a source of information and market research. The consumer movement has, however, developed as a political interest group to represent the rights of consumers, largely because those rights are seen to be threatened by the activity of many firms.

The crusades against dangerous products, by people such as Ralph Nader in the USA, the growth and success in the UK of organizations such as The Consumers' Association, and, more recently radical magazines such as 'Adbusters' have raised the public awareness of consumer issues. At the same time, magazines and programmes on television and radio have fed the public need for information. Consumer information exists to satisfy a need but, like marketing promotion itself, it has created an even greater need. The number of consumer magazines has proliferated. National newspapers in many countries now give editorial space to consumer matters and concern themselves with consumer issues, from testing new cars and bottles of wine, to offering advice on financial matters, to highlighting illegal and dubious practices in the business world.

KEY CONCEPT 12.7   CONSUMERISM

Consumerism has developed as a social movement to inform and assist consumer choice and to act as a pressure group to represent the interests of consumers. These interests are represented to organizations in an attempt to influence product design, price and distribution. Consumer interest groups also act as watchdogs to guard against unsafe products and dishonest producers. That consumers are now more aware and better informed is due largely to the activities of consumer groups and the publicity given to consumer matters.

As well as feeding off its own publicity and success, the growth of consumerism is often related to factors such as:

- The public needs protection against the effects of dangerous products. Articles in the US trade press and newspapers during the 1970s focused the public's attention on the large number of fatal accidents involving Ford Pinto cars: all a direct result of the location of the petrol tank. The pressure was such that Ford withdrew the model.

- The public needs protection against the dishonest behaviour of some producers. For example, there have been cases of finance companies, particularly those dealing with short-term 'pay-day' loans, misleading the public about the true cost of loans or credit.

- The growth of pressure groups, such as the Campaign for Real Ale (CAMRA) in the UK, is a reaction to the monopoly power wielded by the main producers in a particular industry. CAMRA became so successful that it changed the product policies of major brewers as well as encouraging the growth of independent breweries. PETA (People for the Ethical Treatment of Animals), provides information on the cruelty to animals in food production, cosmetics, clothing, in zoos and in 'seaworld' shows involving dolphins and orcas. PETA has enlisted the help of Hollywood celebrities to communicate their message. Consumers themselves are better educated, more affluent and, largely because of the growth of the consumer press, more informed. The result has been increased expectations and demand for products of a higher quality. While this is probably true for all consumers, the growth of consumerism is undoubtedly a middle-class phenomenon closely related to the degree of affluence of particular consumer groups.

In some cases consumer pressure has been very successful. Environmental groups in Europe such as Greenpeace enlisted considerable public support to oppose Shell's dumping of its dis-used oil platform, Brent Spar, in deep water in the North Sea. The lobby caused Shell to rethink its actions. In more general terms, the consumer movement has been influential in broadening public awareness of consumer matters and bringing about a range of protective legislation. In many cases this has led to improved goods and services and more effective marketing. There are still those who feel that the consumer lobby needs to go much further to protect the rights of consumers, while others, particularly in business, may resent the influence of consumer groups on governments, fearing that excessive regulation may stifle innovation.

Marketing and technology

Marketing and technology interact in a number of ways:

- We have seen in Chapter 9 the process of product design and development and its protection through the patent system. We also noted that marketing was an essential vehicle for the information and promotion of new products and processes.

- In our discussion of the product life cycle we identified the relationship between process technology and levels of demand. It is no good management using product development, pricing and promotional strategies to increase demand if that demand cannot be met by the production system. For example, the development of computerized stock systems has provided greater information and access for both buyer and seller.

- Developments in technology have changed the marketing process itself. Among the most obvious aids to marketing have been developments in retailing to simplify the process of purchase.

These include massive changes through the use of the Internet (a fuller discussion of e-commerce can be found in Chapter 4 and an illustration of its use in Case 12.4). The most significant impact on marketing has been in the areas of digital and social media marketing. Both these activities have emerged out of developments in communications technology, the lowering of cost and widespread availability of such technology and changes in social behaviour. We discuss this more fully in the next section.

- Developments in transport have not only improved distribution systems but enabled consumers to access a wider range of goods. The transnational or even transcontinental shopping trip is commonplace.

E-marketing, digital marketing and social media marketing

In Chapter 4 we discussed e-business and e-commerce. **E-marketing** is an essential component of the wider activities of e-business and e-commerce. Certain types of business have been transformed. Instead of buying CDs at a music store, most people choose to buy them online through websites such as Amazon.com. Even this market is changing. Instead of buying CDs as physical entities, many buy the right to download them. Both developments have transformed this particular market with the result that many retail outlets have closed, including formerly large stores such as HMV.

Digital and social media use similar technologies and their usage overlaps. The development of both owes much to the availability of cheaper technology enabling access to and use of new forms of communication. Social media in particular has been facilitated by high speed Internet access and a social as well as technological change in the way people communicate with each other.

Digital marketing is any marketing activity that uses digital technologies such as the Web, email, apps, digital TV and digital data about products, markets and customers. It makes use of smart phones, tablets, and computers. While digital marketing can be aimed at broad groups, its main value lies in the ability to target specific segments. It has changed the marketing strategies of organizations, so much so, that by 2011 online advertising had exceeded the amount spent on TV advertising in the UK (Baines and Fill, 2014). There are a number of reasons for this change; online advertising is much cheaper than that on TV; it is more flexible, enabling rapid changes to be made and has the capability of creating personalized messages for target groups; it can also be activated in any location, unlike TV (Baines and Fill, 2014). It is however viewed by some consumers as an annoying intrusion.

Digital marketing uses a number of specific techniques. These include:

- **Email marketing.** Email messages are sent regularly to existing or potential customers whose email addresses have been captured on the organization's database. A similar process can be operated using text messages.
- **Display advertisements.** These are most commonly found on Internet sites and take the form of pop-up advertisements or banner messages that appear on screen. Increasingly, many such messages make use of multimedia presentations, replicating TV and cinema advertising.
- **Search engine marketing.** This is a process that is aimed at increasing the visibility of an organization, its products and services on search engines such as Google or Yahoo. Visibility can be increased by the manipulation of the organization's own website and key words

can be selected to enhance the profile of a company on a particular search engine. This has spawned a new group of consultants who advise companies on ways to increase their visibility. On some search engines a high position on the listings can be purchased. Search engine manipulation can also involve the use of contextual advertisements. This enables an organization to link an advertisement to whatever topic the Internet user is accessing online. An Internet user checking a holiday destination will find pop-up advertisements offering deals on specific hotels at that destination. The whole issue of search engine marketing was raised in a 2014 court case in which the UK cosmetics company 'Lush' used trademark law to prevent Amazon, the global online store from using the word 'lush' to direct search engine users to the Amazon cosmetics site. Amazon does not sell 'Lush' company products. The UK court found in favour of 'Lush'. Amazon were ordered to stop using the word 'lush' to direct search engine users to its site and also instructed them to cease using 'lush' in their advertising. At the time of writing this finding was subject to appeal by Amazon. The case does however illustrate how search engines can be manipulated.

Social media marketing uses such vehicles as Facebook, Twitter and YouTube. As the use of social media has grown, so has its use in marketing. The dramatic increase in usage can be seen with Facebook. It was launched in 2004 largely among student groups in the USA. By 2006 there were 12 million users and by early 2014 there were 1.23 billion users worldwide and its use had expanded to many different groups, including older users (www.theguardian.com/technology/2014/feb04/facebook/). Initially social media marketing involved consumers interacting with one another. However, its growth as a social phenomenon has attracted the interest of companies such as Coca-Cola, Starbucks and Ford, who use social media channels to market their products. Ford, for example, posts information on both Facebook and Twitter about their products. Generally, their posts have a lighter touch than their advertisements in other media.

The key difference that marks out social media marketing from other forms of digital marketing is that the emphasis has shifted from the organization to the customer. Social media websites enable consumers to generate marketing information on products and services themselves. Berthon et al. (2012) identify a number of ways in which this takes place:

- Social media users set up informal discussions on products, services and their experience with organizations;
- Customers submit reviews and evaluations on their experiences;
- Customers suggest changes in the design of products and services;
- Through their comments they can promote or destroy a brand. As Weber (2010) states,

  These days, one witty Tweet, one clever blog post, one devastating video, forwarded to hundreds of friends at the click of a mouse can snowball and kill a product or damage a company's share price.

Weber (2010) cites the example of Dave Carroll, a Canadian folk singer who was refused compensation by United Airlines after baggage handlers had damaged his guitar, valued at US$3500. He posted a music video about his experiences on YouTube. Within a month it had been watched by five million people and within six months by over nine million. This is an example of **viral marketing**, albeit with negative connotations for the company. There is strong evidence that advertisements and marketing messages are passed on via social media, especially if they are seen as funny, odd or provocative. There is however no clear evidence as to who is most likely to send on such messages so that they can be targeted.

It is clear that social media has become a powerful tool in marketing. There are, however, some constraints. The technology needed for some social media websites, such as the large bandwidth needed for YouTube is not available everywhere. In some countries such as China there are government controls on social media, and currently in China, Facebook is not available. From a company's perspective the choice of social media may be important as some forms are more popular in some countries than in others. For example, Facebook is not widely used in Japan. Since much of the information on social media is generated by customers, organizations have no control over the content. There has been considerable publicity, not least on social media sites themselves, about fake or 'promotional' reviews of products or services. Review sites such as Tripadvisor have come under scrutiny, for example, for hotel owners posting positive reviews for their own property and negative reviews for hotels in competition with them.

CASE 12.3   THE GROWTH OF TELEMARKETING IN FLOWER SALES

At first glance the market for cut flowers would seem to be the province of a large number of small outlets. The reality is a highly competitive market, dominated by a small number of organizations such as Interflora in the UK and 1-800-Flowers in the USA. The business of selling and distributing cut flowers has been one of high growth and profitability. A major reason for that growth lies in the choice they offer the customer in terms of marketing channel and the widening of that choice through the use of telephone sales and the Internet.

The four main customer requirements would appear to be easy access, the ability of the business to meet target prices, fast delivery and the availability of expert advice. These requirements are met by three main channels. The flower shop provides expert advice and offers the customer the opportunity to choose a particular arrangement first hand. This channel is important when customers are concerned to pick the flowers themselves or when they wish to take the flowers as a gift, as in the case of hospital visits or as a token when invited to someone's home. The flower shop may be preferred when buying flowers for oneself. Telesales, either through a call centre or a shop, still offer the opportunity to obtain expert advice, but this method may simply be more convenient, as when sending flowers as a thank you gift or to commemorate someone's birthday or anniversary. Such a method, while saving a visit to a flower shop, does carry a handling and delivery charge. A more recent development has been the opportunity to buy and organize the delivery of flowers online. The advantage of this channel lies in its speed, easy accessibility of product and price information, and convenience. Websites are used by some organizations, such as Interflora, as a means of making more sales. Such organizations offer an email service to remind people of dates such as birthdays and anniversaries. The service is usually free and inevitably accompanied by an easy means of ordering flowers for immediate delivery.

In the UK, the largest operator is Interflora. This is an international organization trading as FTD in the USA, Canada and Japan and as Fleurop in parts of Europe. Interflora is a non-profit trade association owned by its members. These comprise over 58 000 florist shops across 146 countries. The members elect the company board from among their constituents and the board members serve for a fixed period before they are replaced. Interflora trades not only in flowers, but also chocolates and other similar gifts. The company aims to provide a seamless service to customers and prides itself on its responsiveness and innovation. The company has grown largely on the basis of telephone sales made by customers to individual shops. In the case of a delivery outside the area the florist will check the nearest Interflora member to the delivery address and pass on the order. This process used to be carried out exclusively by telephone, but the company introduced a computerized system linking member shops. There has been a recent growth in online business but the telephone is still by far the main source of orders.

Teleflorist is the second-largest UK organization behind Interflora and operates in much the same way.

(Continued)

CASE 12.3 (Continued)

However, Flowers Direct, another growing firm in the UK market, operates in a different way. This is a privately-owned company that uses few intermediaries. Flowers Direct claims an advantage over Interflora through the operation of a 24-hour call centre. It sells and delivers not through shops but via a central warehouse and the use of couriers to deliver the flowers. Like Interflora and Teleflorist, it offers an international delivery service.

1-800-Flowers is a USA company and, at a consistent annual growth rate of 25 per cent maintained over the past few years, is claimed by many as one of the fastest-growing companies in any market. Initially a private company specializing in flowers, 1-800-Flowers made a private equity placement in May 1999 and began share trading on Nasdaq in August, 1999. Its product range has widened to include garden products, including furniture, home decor items, specialized foods and, most recently, gourmet foods. The company has its own headquarters and central staff, some of which specialize in market research to develop new product ranges and also to monitor quality and service standards. The company operates call centres and has its own shops branded as Bloomnet. Despite having its own shops, the majority of trading is carried out through partner florists, which number over 1500. The company started with telephone sales and direct sales through its own outlets. Internet sales, while only 15 per cent of the total for 1998–89, increased 85 per cent on the previous year and are viewed by the company as its focus for the future. The company launched its website in 1995, which is not only used to promote and sell its products, but is also used to announce job vacancies and invite applications.

Questions

1 What advantages do telephone sales and online sales offer in the flowers and associated products market?

2 What are the disadvantages of telephone and Internet sales in this market?

3 Why are telephone sales more popular than Internet sales? Is this likely to change in the future and what would be the advantages and obstacles for both the sellers and buyers?

KEY CONCEPT 12.8 DIGITAL MARKETING

Digital marketing makes use of the Internet and email technology accessed via computers, tablets and smartphones to change the way in which organizations create marketing communications. Advertisements and even personalized messages are sent through emails and via display, pop-up and banner ads on a range of different websites. The organization can also increase its visibility on search engines such as Google and use this as a marketing tool.

KEY CONCEPT 12.9 SOCIAL MEDIA MARKETING

The use of social media such as Facebook, Twitter and YouTube has emerged as a powerful marketing tool. The marketing focus has shifted from the organization to the consumer who can share their opinions about products and services with other social media users. While this can be and occasionally is damaging to the reputation of an organization, many companies use social media themselves to post company and product information and to place paid advertisements.

The role of national, social, cultural and institutional influences in marketing

In our discussion of segmentation we suggested that markets were increasingly segmented and the marketing effort was correspondingly targeted at specific groups. Invariably the basis for such segmentation is national, social and cultural. Differences between societies and between culturally distinctive groups have resulted in different patterns of product adoption. The way a product or service is promoted varies widely in different parts of the world as a result of cultural differences and differences in legal requirements and government codes governing advertising. The popularity of a product among one cultural or social group is no guarantee that it will appeal to any other group. Despite the expansion of international travel, the food preferences of cultural groups can vary widely. For example, the durian is one of the most popular fruits in South-East Asia, yet its taste and smell are unpleasant to many westerners. However, marketing does not simply react to social and cultural differences, it is actively used to promote products. As with other aspects of our model, the influences are invariably two-way with marketing acting as both a product and a cause of social change. Several national, social and cultural factors illustrate our point.

Social influences

Values and attitudes are important influences on the marketing process. Core cultural values, such as family life and concern for children, are constantly used in advertising, and marketing specialists take care not to transgress such social mores. An interesting variation to this is shown in Case 12.2. McDonald's in Singapore launched the Kiasu Burger. Both the naming of the product and the accompanying promotion poked fun at a particular cultural characteristic of Singaporeans. However, the ensuing success of the product would indicate that this was taken in good part by the local population.

Changing demographic patterns relating to age, sex, location and, naturally, incomes may have a profound effect upon marketing. An ageing population in many western industrial societies has opened up marketing opportunities in such industries as tourism and in general focused the attention of marketers towards a sector they had previously seldom considered. Geographical shifts in population can alter consumer demand and property prices. Rising property prices in London and the south-east of England have had a knock-on effect on property market in surrounding areas. This has manifested itself in changes in the types of property being built, house prices and the way that property is promoted by estate agents. Such changes also affect the marketing of public transport systems.

Reference groups, such as experts, peers, social classes, and those groups portraying a desired lifestyle, are frequently used in marketing communication as mechanisms of attitude change. This would seem to operate across all cultures. In many countries in South-East Asia a highly visible rich elite, who often favour western and Japanese goods, are used as trendsetters for the aspiring middle-classes and play their part in cultural change.

Cultural and institutional influences

Globalization has inevitably led to a degree of convergence in marketing. The creation of a single television advertising campaign across several countries makes it cheaper for producers. The growth of global media and satellite television have increased the amount of media space available and also brought down costs. There are some similarities in advertising in different countries in the use of humour and stereotyping, especially gender and nationality. For example, Ford in the USA sold the German-built Lincoln-Mercury Scorpio as 'imported from Germany for select dealers' building on the widely-held belief that the Germans develop superior technical products. Such cultural stereotyping has benefited the Germans considerably as exporters of manufactured goods, and they have been especially successful with more technical products such as machine tools. Japan, on the other hand, had to overcome a damaging stereotype, which saw its exported goods in the 1920s and 1930s as cheap, imitative products. However, as with all stereotyping we should always remember that the differences within a country are often greater than those between countries. We also have evidence of variations in marketing as a result of cultural and institutional differences. Several of the following examples are taken from Usunier and Lee (2009). Many of the illustrations relate to marketing communications in sales promotion and advertising.

- Advertising spending by companies varies considerably between countries. The highest spenders are in the USA and Japan, with Germany and the UK some way behind. The Americans are noted for their emphasis on promotional activities while in Japan, it seems to be driven by an emphasis on market growth and incremental product development. Additionally, in Japanese consumer markets, competition is rarely based on price but on product differentiation and service. These qualities need to be communicated to customers.

- There are cultural differences on the emphasis placed on elements in the marketing mix. The Germans are noted for their emphasis on product development and careful targeting in many segments while their supermarkets such as Aldi and Lidl focus on value and price. As we have noted, the emphasis in the USA is on selling, advertising and promotional activities. In the USA, the population would seem to have a high tolerance and even expectation of a large number of TV advertisements. The French, on the other hand tend to be less tolerant and more sceptical.

- Language is an important tool in most aspects of marketing communications. This tends to be culturally specific because of the frequent use in marketing communications of colloquial and slang expressions. However, in Asia, English is often used in TV advertising in the belief that this adds weight to the advert.

- Colour, metaphors and symbols have different meaning in different countries. For example, use of the colour white in many European countries symbolizes cleanliness and purity, whereas in many Asian countries it signifies death. De Mooij (2005) cites the example of an advertisement by the Korean company LG in the US *Newsweek* magazine. The advert contained a large illustration of a fish, which in Asian countries is a symbol of prosperity, but the symbol was lost on many western readers of *Newsweek*.

- Advertising is controlled by laws in most countries and these laws vary. For example, there is variation between countries on the advertising of alcohol and tobacco products. In France, there are strict restrictions on the use of children in advertisements. In some countries there are stricter taboos, so that in Saudi Arabia there must be no portrayal of gambling, alcohol or of scenes depicting cheating or adultery.

- The type of advertisement varies between countries. Comparative advertising, where a product is directly compared with its main rival is commonplace in the USA but not allowed in France, Germany and Italy. How products are portrayed also varies. Lasserre and Schutte (1999) cite the case of Club Med's attempts to sell holidays to the Japanese. The company had traditionally sold its holidays on the image of easy-going resorts and the emphasis on simple pleasure seeking. They found little interest in the Japanese market until they stressed the opportunity for holidaymakers to learn and participate in organized sporting activities. This is a classic example of the same product with a different promotional message suited to a particular market segment, in this case identified by nationality. Case 12.4 examines cultural difference and the associated problems in the early days of Disneyland Paris.

- De Mooij (2005) makes extensive use of Hofstede's work and sees linkages between advertising and Hofstede's cultural dimensions. In countries with large power distance advertising stresses status symbols and the wisdom of experts. In individualistic cultures advertisements are more direct and tend to be more verbal, whereas in collectivistic societies they stress group activities, tend to be more visual and make greater use of metaphors. In countries with high uncertainty avoidance there tends to be a strong need for scientific evidence and the competence of the producer is emphasized. In masculine societies advertisements emphasize winning and being the best and depict gender role differentiation. In those countries with short term orientation, instant gratification is a common theme.

With all such examples there is a danger of cultural stereotyping. In addition, situations can, and do, change. In Japan, the recession of the 1990s has led to increased price competition and in many cities there has been the growth of discount stores. The younger buyer in Japan is more attracted to western products that reflect individualism than the more traditional older population and is more likely to buy on credit.

REFLECTION POINT

Identify a number of products that reflect cultural differences.

ORGANIZATIONAL ASPECTS OF MARKETING

We have already dealt with several organizational issues elsewhere in this chapter. In examining the different orientations to marketing we saw how marketing goals have developed over time and how much they vary between organizations. Several references have been made to the impact of organizational size on marketing. We have noted that increasing size has led to increasing specialization within the marketing function and how the costs associated with marketing activities have acted as barriers to entry, favouring big business in the achievement of market dominance.

An important element of strong corporate cultures is a close identification with the needs of the customer.

In this section we will focus on structural issues pertaining to marketing, dealing first with the way the function is organized and second with the relationships between the marketing and other functional areas.

The organization of marketing

Marketing was initially viewed as being synonymous with sales. With the growth of the firm and the development of its markets came the problems of organizing the sales force, often achieved by creating sales territories operating under a hierarchy of district and regional managers. The need for improved market research and sales promotion created research and advertising units as sub-divisions of the sales department.

The growth of increasingly complex markets, the emergence of large organizations and changing attitudes by management towards consumers all called for corresponding developments in the functional organization of business activities. Marketing emerged as a function in its own right, with the previously dominant sales department as a subsidiary activity. The marketing effort now spawned specialisms in advertising, sales promotion and market research, and some marketing departments also assumed responsibility for new product development. In the larger organizations, marketing management became the coordination of a range of specialist marketing activities.

This functional organization of marketing mirrored functional developments occurring elsewhere in the firm, but some companies were experimenting with other forms of organizational structure. As we saw in Chapter 6, in our discussion of structure, divisionalization occurred because some firms such as GM found it most appropriate to organize around products or markets. The marketing efforts in many organizations went down the same route. Piercy and Morgan (1993) take up this theme of structure following strategy and see product market segmentation as the basis of organization structure that, if it is in harmony with the needs of the market, is a source of competitive advantage.

Forms of structural arrangement in marketing

Product management

In the 1920s, Proctor & Gamble developed the concept of product management. Under this arrangement, the firm is organized around its products and each brand or group of brands has its own manager. Such a structural arrangement may be necessary where product knowledge is highly technical, or where the firm is dealing in totally different product markets. The benefits that may be gained by management from such an arrangement include an increased knowledge of the product market and an ability to respond quickly to changing market demands. A healthy internal competition can be built up, leading to increased sales. Furthermore, product management has often been a good training ground for aspiring senior managers, as it interfaces with most aspects of the firm's operation. The customer gains by dealing with people who have real product knowledge. Product and brand management can be costly ways of organizing the marketing effort. Specialist activities, such as advertising, may be unnecessarily duplicated, or product managers may lack expertise in the more specialized areas of marketing. In firms where every brand has its own manager there may be over-staffing of management at the lower and middle levels, with the ensuing problems of career progression.

Organize around markets

An alternative structural arrangement would be to specialize around markets. The markets may be differentiated geographically, by industry, or even by customer. In consumer marketing some form of geographical specialization is a traditional approach. Sales forces have tended towards regional organization for ease of administration and control, and television advertising is invariably regional. The US firm Colgate-Palmolive derives the larger part of its sales revenue and profits from overseas activities and traditionally has based its organization on individual country operations linked through a regional structure. Staff mobility within this structure has been viewed as an essential part of career development within the company.

Industry or customer focus

It is in the marketing to organizations, with the prospect of high-volume, high-value orders, that specialization by industry or by customer is regarded as a factor in increasing sales. The Xerox Information Systems Group switched from selling by product to selling by industry, and organized its marketing efforts accordingly. The advantages of this approach lie in building up a close relationship with individual customers and gaining insights into their operations. Some firms operating in the computer market, such as IBM and HP, offer a consulting service to potential customers. This has led to improvements in the customer's own operating systems and potentially more sales for the computer company. Gaining experience of the customers' operating problems and their marketing environment is often invaluable to the process of developing products. Such a structure would seem most appropriate where the market is becoming more competitive and there are long-term advantages to be gained from building up such close relationships with customers. This emphasizes the importance of relationship marketing.

Outsourcing to agencies

The past 40 years have seen the growth of advertising agencies. Some, like Saatchi & Saatchi, have achieved a very high public profile. Specialist agencies also operate in market research and sales promotion. The advantages of outsourcing to an agency lie in its ability to stand back and offer an independent assessment of the firm's marketing activities, to offer specialist expertise, which the company may not possess, and to act as a source of ideas.

Dealing with outside agencies can be a costly exercise and may be a potential source of conflict. In fact, any structural differentiation within the marketing function itself may set up internal conflicts. Brand differentiation and management may create competition but that same competition has the potential for conflict. Tensions can exist between marketing management who direct operations and the sales force who must carry them out. Much wider tensions can exist in the relationship between marketing and the other functional areas as we see in the next section.

As seen in Chapter 6, organization structures rarely conform to ideal models. Many firms have marketing departments that display elements of all the structural variations identified above. A system of brand management can be backed up by a centralized research or advertising function. The marketing effort can be organized according to industrial markets but may be further differentiated according to product. The system is further complicated in that marketing departments frequently use agencies external to the firm.

Marketing and other functions

The stereotypical view of the relationship between marketing and operations is one of conflict. Operations staff view marketing staff as people who make their life difficult through promises to customers that are difficult to meet. For its part, the marketing department sees operations staff as inflexible and more concerned with the efficiency of their own systems rather than satisfying customer needs. Such myths have some basis in fact. Historically, the two functions have been evaluated according to different criteria. Marketing personnel have tended to be rewarded for achieving a high sales turnover and a high market share, while the primary orientation of operations has been towards the achievement of minimum cost and a smooth operation flow. The marketing staff have been encouraged to create change by developing opportunities, while the operations staff have tended to resist any change that increases costs. Moreover, the cultures of the two groups have traditionally differed. Marketing specialists tend to deal with vague concepts like image and customer preference and have their focus outside the organization, while operations staff tend to be internally focused and more comfortable dealing with the quantifiable.

Such conflict is not necessarily dysfunctional. Persuading customers to adopt standardized goods and services may enable the firm to offer a better service as well as reducing costs. Where conflict is disruptive it may be tackled in several ways. Management might consider different reward criteria. Marketing staff could be rewarded for accurate forecasts rather than meeting some artificially contrived quota and operations staff rewarded for meeting delivery times. Conflict may also be avoided by encouraging more interaction through joint project teams and mixed career paths.

Similar tensions may occur between other functions, as with R&D over product design or with accounting over methods of payment. Nor are such conflicts the sole property of the marketing department. We have already identified the type of conflict that can emerge between the R&D and operations functions and in the next chapter we see the traditional antagonisms that occur between the HR department and line management. Such conflicts are the inevitable consequence of organizational size and managerial specialization. They may, however, be minimized by strategies focusing on coordination.

THE STRATEGIC ASPECTS OF MARKETING

Competitive marketing strategy is a market-oriented approach that establishes a profitable competitive position for the firm against all forces that determine industry competition by continuously creating and developing a sustainable competitive advantage from the potential sources in the firm's value chain.

(West, Ford and Ibrahim, 2010, p. 5).

The process of developing a marketing strategy bears a striking resemblance to the process of developing a firm's corporate and business strategies, underlining the centrality of marketing to the firm's planning process. Opportunities are analysed, target markets are defined, market share objectives are set, segmentation strategy determined and the particular marketing mix is developed. The marketing mix, including issues of positioning, branding and competitive differentiation, is central to the whole process since it identifies and guides the strategic options. Strategic considerations in marketing therefore embrace all of the factors we have discussed in this chapter and can be viewed as a hierarchy of intentions. First, objectives must be decided upon about such factors as desired market share and market growth and the emphasis to be placed on such issues as new product developments and customer loyalty. Second, management must decide on its product range and which markets it will target with these products. Third come the decisions about competitive tactics, including targeting, positioning, pricing and promotion. We will use all the elements discussed in this chapter to examine the various aspects of marketing strategy. Finally, we see how these elements may be combined and stress the integrated nature of marketing and the other functional strategies.

Segmentation, targeting, and positioning strategy

There are a number of key issues to be addressed:

- Management must decide which segments are to be targeted and what the cost of this is in terms of product variety.
- Management should assess the effectiveness of their targeting strategy. According to Kotler (1983) targets should be measurable (by size, income level, etc.), accessible, substantial (large enough to generate profit), differentiable (truly distinct) and actionable (a distinct marketing approach can be identified).

- West, Ford and Ibrahim (2010) believe the key to successful positioning is to find out what the consumer believes and how the consumer acts. They advise against tinkering too much with the image of a product as this can confuse the market.

Branding strategy

Brands can be important in achieving both differentiation and cost leadership. A clear brand image is an important part of marking out a company's products from those of its competitors. Cost reduction can be achieved through **brand leveraging**. Where a brand is already well-known, the costs of building consumer awareness of a new product are therefore lower. Two companies that have achieved this with considerable success are Sony and Apple. Co-branding, discussed earlier in this chapter, works in a similar way.

Product strategy

The historic fate of one growth industry after another has been its suicidal product provincialism.

(Levitt, 1960, p. 34)

References have been made to product strategy in our discussion of innovation and operations in the previous two chapters, as well as earlier in this chapter. Levitt's quote from his influential article 'Marketing myopia' is a plea to management for a marketing-led product development strategy. Most industries, he feels, restrict themselves by defining their businesses too narrowly, largely because they are product-oriented rather than customer-oriented. He cites the case of the decline of the US railway business, which identified itself too rigidly with railways rather than the transport needs of its customers and lost ground to the airlines and car industries.

Following the market in this way may be desirable but depends upon the firm possessing the appropriate financial resources and skills. A firm's competitive edge may lie in the production of highly specialized goods and skills, and resources may not be easily transferred. In such cases survival may depend upon acquisition or merger.

In general terms, a product strategy needs to consider the type and range of products on offer, the size of the product line and product mix, the style and quality of those products, the use of brand names and packaging, the nature of the services that are offered with the product, such as warranty and after-sales care and the capability of the organization to develop new products. As we discussed in our chapter on innovation, a successful product innovation is important not only for differentiation but also for cost reduction.

Pricing strategy

We have already discussed the various constituents that determine the price of goods and services, and, singly or together, these form the basis of pricing strategy. **Cost-plus pricing** consists of a standard mark-up after all costs have been taken into consideration. **Target-profit pricing** involves establishing the price in accordance with projected demand using some form of break-even analysis. In this way, a book, for example, can be priced according to two criteria: the minimum sales required to cover production costs and the required profit margins based on estimated sales figures.

Both the cost-plus and target-profit methods are based on the assumption that prices are related solely to cost and demand. As we saw earlier, this is too simplistic a view. The pricing strategy needs to take account of factors external to the firm, in particular prices charged by competitors and the perceived value of the product by the consumer. In the former case there is a tendency for firms operating in the same product market to adopt a going rate, although, as we shall see later, more aggressive tactics can be pursued by firms breaking into new markets. By contrast to the going rate, pricing goods according to their perceived value can lead to considerable variation. Such a strategy is based on the customers' assumption that 'they are getting what they pay for' and they relate price to quality and hence to the cost of producing the goods or services.

However, a high price can be used to denote exclusivity and so attract a particular market segment. New Zealand wine has for a long time been more expensive than many Australian wines of the same grape variety. This was a deliberate strategy on the part of New Zealand growers to maintain high quality, and the mass market is shunned. New Zealanders, in their own country, have traditionally purchased Australian wine for everyday drinking and New Zealand wine for the special occasion. However, this strategy has shifted in recent years as New Zealand producers have tried to increase market share. This has been very successful in the UK with wines made from the Sauvignon Blanc grape. Even with high rates of government taxation in the UK contributing to the price, a bottle of Sauvignon Blanc wine can be purchased at a lower price in the UK than in New Zealand. This has created high demand for this wine in the UK and in other countries such as the USA. This in turn has had a knock-on effect on vine planting with Sauvignon Blanc grapes dominating in several wine growing areas, changing the nature of New Zealand wine production.

Brands can be used by the producer to protect price and premium prices are often demanded for fashionable brands. Some UK supermarkets such as Tesco have attempted to break free from such price control in the sale of branded denim jeans such as Levi 501 by offering them at almost half the price of the usual retail outlets. Such a strategy was seen as damaging to Levi's exclusive advertising campaign and to its relationship with its existing retailers. As a result, Levi refused to supply Tesco. Undeterred, the supermarket chain obtained the jeans direct from factories in Mexico. The demand was so high that Tesco had to set up a helpline to direct customers to stores with availability.

All these factors come together in the pricing strategies relating to new products. The simplest method may well be to price goods by comparison with the nearest equivalents, roughly in accordance with the going-rate method. Traditionally, two general strategies have been used, skimming and penetration, although skimming has become somewhat dated as a pricing strategy.

- **A skimming strategy** operates when the initial price is high. The product must appeal to a market segment where price is not an important consideration. The target market is generally a high-income group of market leaders but it may comprise, for products such as cameras and hi-fi equipment, the lower-income 'enthusiast'. The price will offset the high development cost for this type of product. Once a reputation and a market have been established there may be a reduction in price to broaden the market, using the original purchasers as opinion leaders. Price reductions may also be necessary to maintain a market share as competitors arrive on the scene. Both the VCR and the CD player entered the market at high prices, with considerable price reductions as the market expanded and the competition increased.

- **A penetration strategy** involves setting a low price to attract a mass market at the outset. Such a strategy is used where demand is sensitive to price and where economies of scale can be gained by mass production. Penetration is usually associated with competitive markets.

However, the strategy can be used to discourage competition by raising the barriers of entry, since those entering the market must be certain of high sales to offset development costs. In the early days of personal computers Amstrad attempted to dominate the business market for personal computers by selling at half the price of its rival, Apricot.

We can see that the pricing decision needs to take account of a range of interconnected factors. Additional complexities can and do exist:

- The same product may be differentially priced for a number of reasons. It may be discounted for bulk purchase or to specific groups such as senior citizens and students. The same cinema seat may be differentially priced for different performances to even out demand and particularly to attract customers to less popular showings in the week.
- The price may be a function of the number and type of distribution channels. Imported goods may be more expensive because they pass through more intermediaries, and products are generally more expensive in a prestigious store.
- Pricing strategy generally changes over the life of a product as a function of demand, market share, and changes in the economy. Price cuts may be introduced to regenerate a product nearing the end of its life cycle or to beat off competition, and price rises may be needed to keep pace with inflation.
- Price can be used as a promotion strategy on market entry.
- There is also a strong link between price and place/distribution. For example, premium priced watches will not be found at discount outlets. Estate agents in London are careful to locate themselves in areas where property prices match their brand image.

Such variations can be confusing and lead to customer complaints, as some airlines have found. The price of the same seat on the same flight may vary considerably depending upon when and where the ticket has been bought.

Promotion strategy

Earlier we identified the three main functions of a promotion strategy: to inform, persuade and remind. We also suggested that an effective strategy was dependent upon selecting the most appropriate message and media for the product and target market. Earlier in this chapter, in our discussion of digital and social media marketing, we have noted a perceived shift from traditional forms of advertising towards providing images and information that can be gained on search engines and through social media. For all types of promotion, two important decisions are key: how much to spend and how to gauge whether a campaign has been effective or not. Both are important as any form of promotion adds cost in the short term.

It is clear to management that a promotion strategy must be affordable, yet setting an appropriate budget is far from easy. Three common methods are:

- **The percentage-of-sales method** sets the budget according to the previous year's sales figures or is based on sales forecasts. The inherent flaw in such a strategy is that promotion is a function of sales rather than vice versa. Nevertheless, such a method is simple and may appeal to the cautious decision-maker.
- **The competitive-parity method** pegs promotional expenditure to that of the major competitors in proportion to the market share.

- **The objective-and-task method** has probably the most rational appeal in that specific targets are set and the budget apportioned accordingly. Such a method enables the results of the expenditure to be assessed against the objectives.

Promotion may be evaluated on three levels:

- The first consideration is that the particular advertisement or sales promotion has been seen and by how many and what type of people.
- The second consideration is that the public and, in particular, the target market are aware of the product and its attributes.
- The final and most important consideration is that the promotion results in the desired action on the part of the target market. In the case of consumer products, the ultimate test lies in the number of sales; whereas a government campaign to reduce drinking and driving will have to be measured by the number of convictions.

The evaluation of a promotion campaign is especially difficult for two reasons:

- First, a decision has to be made about the time scale for such an evaluation. Is the impact of an advertisement to be measured over a week, a month, several months or longer?
- Second, it may not be possible to isolate the effect of a promotional campaign from the influence of other variables such as changes in the economy, the behaviour of competitors and changes in social behaviour. Accurate evaluation may require extensive econometric models or a level of experimentation not feasible in most organizations. Few firms have followed DuPont and tested advertising expenditure in their paint market by varying the amounts in parts of the same territory to assess the impact on sales. It discovered that the effect of the heaviest expenditure was weakest in areas where it had a high market share. Perhaps this is a pointer to the diminishing returns of advertising expenditure.

In 2002, Honda sales in the UK were falling. Its agency developed a TV advert which followed the passage of a cog across various car parts before displaying the finished Accord. The campaign coincided with a reduction in media spending by Honda and promotional outlay by dealers, an increase in the price of cars and a reduction in the number of dealerships. The campaign was not run in France, Germany, Italy and Spain. As a consequence, Honda was able to measure the effectiveness of the campaign and claim an increase in revenue of £352 million directly attributable to the campaign against a campaign cost of £47 million. In addition, the TV advert became a focus of attention. There were news features and a documentary was made about how the advert was made. The company received numerous requests for a DVD of the advert and distributed a DVD with a national newspaper in some areas (*Media Guardian*, 16 March 2009, p. 6).

Distribution strategy

We have already noted how this is linked to price. Distribution strategy is concerned with such issues as the type and number of channels, the location of those channels and how they might be controlled. Many channels are available, including a traditional sales force, using a part-ner firm to handle distribution aspects of the business, distributors, wholesalers and retailers, telemarketing and the Internet. The choice of channel depends on the nature of the product or service. Traditionally, many organizations used sales representatives. However, the maintenance of a full-time sales force is expensive and may only be justified where transactions are complex, require face-to-face interaction, involve an element of customer training, and where there is clear value added by using this form of distribution. Many organizations no longer need this kind of service. Costs can be reduced through the use of telephone sales, call centres and the Internet. Such forms of telemarketing and websites often have the advantage of operating 24 hours a day all week. The use of a single channel may limit access to customers and a mix of channels may be required, or the use of different channels for different products.

Traditionally in the manufacturing industry, distribution strategy has focused around stock policy. Incentives in the form of discounts were often given to persuade intermediaries such as warehouses to hold stock. Such strategies became less important with the increased use of JIT strategies. Distribution has become the key to success for many organizations. The emergence of Dell from a small firm to a leader in the PC market in less than five years is attributed both to its customer care approach and to its use of direct marketing. Dell was the first computer company to focus on telesales and the Internet and its methods have been copied by competitors such as NEC. First Direct has emerged as a success in banking largely through its round-the-clock accessibility to customers by telephone and a call centre is a much cheaper way of operating a bank than a high street branch. Case 11.4 examines the growth of flower sales through telemarketing and the Internet and demonstrates how an industry has widened its customer base by focusing on specific distribution channels.

The advantages of using technology-based distribution strategies lie in lower costs, access to an expanding market and being able to focus investment and staff where they can be most effective, as in after-sales service or customer training (Friedman and Furey, 1999).

An integrated marketing strategy

Integration can occur in a number of ways: within each component of the mix; between the various elements of the mix; between marketing and the other functional strategies; and integration of the whole company around marketing strategies focusing on enhanced customer loyalty and satisfaction. We will deal with each in turn:

- Activities and strategies associated with each component of the mix should work together. For example, effective promotion is generally achieved through a campaign in which press and television advertising and sales promotion are coordinated to achieve the maximum impact upon the consumer.

- The elements of the mix should work together. Price reductions are often accompanied by a promotion campaign and both need the reinforcement of sufficient stocks and effective distribution in anticipation of increased demand. Improvements in product quality necessitating increases in price need to be sensitively handled in promotion.

- Effective integration of marketing with the other functional strategies, especially those of innovation and production, is considered essential to the firm acquiring a competitive advantage. An effective product portfolio should be built around the skills and other resources of the organization. A business school that attempts to offer courses in international business but lacks staff with the necessary expertise may attract a poor reputation and see support for all its courses suffer as a result. Some see this integration of functional strategies as an iterative process, requiring the constant monitoring of markets, products, processes and technology, and the firm working these elements around its chosen field of distinctive competence.

- As far as marketing itself is concerned, many suggest that the strategic focus should be towards customer satisfaction and customer loyalty. To be effective, this should permeate across the entire organization and therefore is in itself an integrative strategy. Integrated strategies aim to enhance the reputation of the company and secure repeat purchases, but also act as an opportunity to sell additional products. Mercedes-Benz at its Sindelfingen plant and headquarters on the outskirts of Stuttgart has established a visitor centre. This is linked to visits around the plant and embraces a cafeteria and luxury restaurant, a shop selling both souvenirs and more expensive extras for the cars, model displays, a film theatre and a financial services department. Buyers of a new Mercedes have the option of collecting it themselves from the factory. Those who exercise this option are met by a personal courier and given a personalized tour, at the end of which they pick up their car. Not only does this generate enhanced customer satisfaction, it is often treated as a family outing, which includes a meal at the restaurant, the inevitable purchase of souvenirs and, perhaps, signing up for a special Mercedes credit card at the financial services desk.

Many supermarkets try to enhance the customer experience by introducing extra services. These include ample car parking, petrol stations and car-wash facilities, cash points, cafeterias, loyalty cards and staff employed solely to give customer information. There are dangers with such multifaceted approaches to marketing in that dissatisfaction with a peripheral element of the service can cause the customer to go elsewhere and the main sale is lost.

CASE 12.4   DISNEYLAND PARIS

Disneyland Paris opened for business as Euro Disney in April 1992. It was the fourth Disney theme park and followed the successes of Disneyland in Los Angeles (opened in 1955), Disney World in Orlando, Florida, (1971) and Disneyland Tokyo (1983).

The idea of opening a theme park in Europe had been around for some time. Disney had noted that while only 5 per cent of the visitors to its US parks came from Europe, that figure represented two million visitors a year. The company felt there was a large potential European market waiting to be tapped and it had been encouraged by the success of its Tokyo operation. This was a faithful copy of Disneyland in California and convinced Disney executives that if the Disney experience could work in Japan, the concept could be transplanted to a European location with ease.

Proposals for the development began in the early 1980s. Several countries were interested, among them France, Italy, Germany, Spain and, for a short time, the UK. Although Spain was a strong candidate (mainly for its weather), the eventual location was the area around Mame-la Vallee, some 30km outside Paris. The choice of location was due to a number of factors:

- France had a stable economy and low rates of inflation.

- The location was within easy reach of a large proportion of the French population and near a main road route from Germany. Around 17 million people were two hours away by road or rail and over 300 million people were less than two hours away by air. The park was easily accessible from the Paris airports of Orly and Charles de Gaulle. Market surveys had shown that tourism in Europe was predicted to expand.

- Paris was already a popular holiday destination and the proximity of the park meant a large number of visitors would have an extra attraction.

- The French government was very supportive. Finance was made available for extending road and rail links to the park. Low interest loans with delayed repayment terms were made available to Disney and tax concessions were granted through the reduction of VAT on goods sold in the park. The enthusiasm of the French politicians was, in part, a product of rising unemployment in the 1980s and the promise that the park would create at least 15 000 jobs.

- Market research was carried out among the French and the general feedback was that the park would be welcomed.

Euro Disney was launched by a share issue in 1989, at a share price of £7.07. The Walt Disney Corporation took a 49 per cent share and 51 per cent was offered, in the first instance, to European investors. The flotation was popular and at the time of opening the shares were worth £16.

All the theme parks are based around Disney characters. These have universal appeal and are reinforced in the public's imagination by the regular re-release of films such as *Snow White*, *Pinocchio* and *Fantasia,* and the more recent policy of releasing some of the films on DVD including both earlier Disney classics and more modern films such as the *Toy Story* and *Pirates of the Caribbean* series. In Disneyland Paris a feature of the experience and creation of fantasy is the interaction between staff dressed up as characters and the customers. While the Disney characters create the main theme, each of the parks is divided into imaginary worlds, each stressing a theme. In Disneyland Paris, the imaginary worlds comprise Main St USA, Frontierland, Adventureland, Fantasyland and Discoveryland. An element of all these 'worlds' is a number of experiences and rides with an emphasis on creativity and state-of-the-art technology. The Disney Corporation has a policy of continuous technological updating. Another goal is quality of service, which extends beyond the theme park to hotels, catering and souvenir shops. To that end, staff are carefully selected and trained. Stringent criteria embrace appearance codes, including rules on dress, hairstyle, size, weight and so on. Disney has created a distinctive corporate culture for its theme park employees. For example, employees are known as 'cast members' and their uniforms as 'costumes' to reinforce the concept of fantasy. In support of this, all events are meticulously planned. At any time there may be several employees dressed up as the same character, but only one may be seen at any one time in the park. The characters emerge from underground tunnels responding to a centralized control using two-way radio. The fantasy is everything and two Mickey Mouses in the park at the same time would never do.

When it opened, Euro Disney had 29 rides, six hotels, a campsite, golf course and assorted restaurants, food outlets and souvenir shops. At the outset, an additional 3000 acres were acquired for expansion. By 1996 it was expected that the theme park itself would be much bigger and be joined by a conference centre to capture offseason trade. Disney was proud of its new European park and claimed it as technologically superior to any that had gone before it.

Despite the overwhelming support of the government, Disney met problems in dealing with the local bureaucracy and planning regulations. In the first few weeks of opening, the company encountered demonstrations by local villagers objecting that the park would damage the quality of their lives. However, many locals gained substantially from the sale of land and used the money to build motels, shops and restaurants in the area.

Initial reactions of the paying public were mixed. There were many complaints of high prices, long queues, poor service and teething problems with many of the rides. The French were critical of the apparent lack of intellectual content in the park's attractions and the quote by arts commentator, Ariane Mnouchkine, that Euro Disney was a 'cultural Chernobyl' was widely reported in the world's press. The initial problems caused another commentator to refer to it as 'corporate America's Vietnam' (*The Observer,* 14 November, 1993). The target attendance of 11 million for the first year was almost reached but, thereafter, attendance figures fell to 9.8 million in the second year and 8.9 million in the third, but rose to 10.7 million in 1995. Despite criticism from the world's press, in its first year of operation Euro Disney was easily France's top attraction, with several million visitors more than the Pompidou Centre, the Eiffel Tower and the Louvre.

Perspectives on the success or otherwise of the attraction were mixed. The then Disney chief Michael Reisner was quick to point out that attendance patterns at other Disney theme parks were similar in the early years. The financial failings of the European operation were, however, inescapable. In the first two years of operation the park had lost US$1.7 billion and, from its buoyant position at opening, the share price fell from £16 to £3.55. In 1994, trading was suspended on the French stock exchange when the share price fell to less than £2. In 1993, over 10 per cent of staff were made redundant. The park was becoming a drain on the highly profitable Disney Corporation and to protect USA shareholders, executives put pressure

(Continued)

CASE 12.4   (Continued)

on French banks and the French government to support the financial restructuring of Euro Disney. The eventual restructuring of 1994 included a relaxation of loan repayments, the leasing of some attractions and a rights issue, with a Saudi Arabian prince accumulating a large number of new shares. Despite the problems in France, the Disney empire was extended in 1995 through the purchase of ABC Television in the USA to make Disney the world's largest entertainment network.

The relative failure of Euro Disney in its early years has been attributed to economic/financial and cultural causes. In the early 1990s, the French currency was stronger than some other European currencies, notably those of the UK, Italy and Spain. French interest rates had risen, placing an additional burden on loan repayments. The effective devaluation of sterling meant a fall in UK visitors to the park of about half. It was only marginally more expensive for a UK family of four to visit Disney World in Florida, given the relatively cheap rate of the US dollar. Even for those who did visit, spending was down on accommodation, food and souvenirs. Most commentators agreed that both entrance and hotel prices were too high. Price cuts were made during the first year of operation but this meant that, for the hotels, occupancy rates had to rise to levels beyond the most optimistic estimates. While park attendance targets were almost reached, levels of operating profit were well down on targets. Market research discovered that families who stayed overnight preferred cheaper accommodation in Paris where a visit to the park could be combined with other attractions. A vicious circle was created whereby a lack of revenue meant that expansion plans for a second phase were shelved. The park needed more attractions so that people would need to stay overnight and push up occupancy rates. As it was, the park's attractions could all be visited in a day. The postponement of the second phase also delayed the construction of a conference centre, which was planned to take up hotel space in off-season periods. Not only were the hotels contributing some 30 per cent to the overall deficit, but their lack of success meant that the company was thwarted in its plans to sell them off at a profit after the first few years of operation.

Many critics claim that the early disappointments were rooted in cultural differences. The Disney

experience is very American and alien to elements of the French market. The French claimed that the attractions were lacking in intellectual content and failed to build in any way upon French cultural heritage. While US theme parks favour fast food and ban the sale of alcohol and cigarettes, French visitors preferred table service and alcohol with their meals. The Japanese park made little concession to Japanese culture and had proven a great success. Disney executives believed that if the concept could work in Japan it could work anywhere. However, the Japanese were attracted to the family orientation, uniforms and regimentation and the opportunity to buy souvenirs at every turn, all of which fitted Japanese culture. The French were less enthusiastic and early concessions were made, including: the sale of cigarettes, the availability of alcohol at table-service restaurants, the choice of non-US-style food, the incorporation of European themes into the attractions and the widespread use of the French language. This became even more important as the recession in Europe made the park even more dependent on the French paying public.

Language was a big issue. The attractions at Disney are based largely on US cultural themes and the predominant language used is English. However, the location of the park was so that it could attract visitors from many countries, who spoke different languages. Disneyland Paris tried to deal with this by making most of its attractions non-dependent on language as its main form of interaction. This restricted the introduction of new attractions. A popular addition to Florida's Disney Park in 2005, following the success of *Finding Nemo*, was a talking turtle, located in a real aquarium. The turtle interacted with children by asking and receiving questions. The language barriers meant that the attraction could not transfer to Paris.

There were early problems with some of the cast members who had difficulty embracing their roles with the dedication required by Disney and labour turnover rates were around 25 per cent in the first two years. Staff morale was further undermined by redundancies. Disney was also criticized for its lack of cultural awareness in its promotional activity. The same style of promotion was used across Europe and no account was taken of cultural differences.

The financial problems of Euro Disney resulted in the company rethinking other aspects of the

CASE 12.4   (Continued)

park's operation. In 1995, the name was changed to Disneyland Paris to give the park a stronger sense of geographical identity and associate it with the image of Paris. At the same time, the name change was an attempt to disassociate the park from its earlier failures and from the link some commentators had made with other failed 'Euro' projects. Further price cuts were made of up to 20 per cent from entrance fees, hotels, food and souvenirs. The company ran its own promotional packages, including special winter deals and free entry and hotel accommodation for up to two children under 12-years-old when accompanied by two paying adults. Strict codes covering working practices and dress were relaxed in an attempt to reduce labour turnover and improve morale. New attractions were added, including a convention centre and the Space Mountain – heralded as the most technically advanced ride in the world. Further attractions were continually planned and in 2005 a development budget of €240 million was set.

In the late 1990s the company moved into operating profit and there was a steady growth of revenue each year. Guest spending in the park had also risen, and hotel occupancy rates exceeded 80 per cent. Recovery was aided by a weaker French franc in the latter part of the 1990s. Gilles Pelisson, the chief executive of Euro Disney SA (controlling company of Disneyland, Paris) stated in his 1998 report:

> In a tourism environment largely affected by the Football World Cup, Disneyland Paris has confirmed its position as the leading European leisure destination. Nineteen ninety-eight was characterized by a strong improvement in operating performance and the start of important developments aimed at diversifying our product offering. All these elements strengthen our confidence in the future of the Company and we look forward to the major event of 1999, the opening of our new attraction 'Honey, I Shrunk the Audience!'.

The attraction, whose name would have matched ideally the attendance trends of the early years, represented a growing confidence in the future of the park. In 2002, it expanded with an investment of £370 million in a new theme based on Hollywood films. However, another crisis hit in the summer of 2003. Debts had mounted to £1.5 billion. Despite the Disney Corporation waiving its management and royalty fees, there was insufficient revenue from tourists to service the debt. Once again, the company faced bankruptcy. The problem was a shortfall in tourists to France and, in particular, the sharp fall in US tourists, due in part to the French lack of support for the USA in the Iraq war and a subsequent US boycott of French goods.

On the 15th anniversary of the park in 2007 and after two financial restructurings, the company continued to make a loss but there was optimism. In 2007, losses were halved from the previous year, attendance was up from 12.8 to 14.5 million and revenue had increased by 14 per cent over the previous year.

By 2012 Disneyland Paris was the most visited tourist destination in the whole of Europe and boasted 58 attractions across two theme parks, the Disneyland Park and the Walt Disney Studios Park. The resort employed 15 000 people and offered seven themed hotels with 5800 rooms. Tables 12.4–12.6 show attendance patterns, hotel occupancy and spending by visitors from 2010–2013.

TABLE 12.4	Disneyland Paris attendance and average spend 2010–13	
	Attendance (millions of visits)	**Theme park average spend (euros)**
2010	15.0	45.21
2011	15.6	46.16
2012	16.0	46.44
2013	14.9	48.14

(Continued)

CASE 12.4   (Continued)

TABLE 12.5	Disneyland Paris hotel occupancy and average hotel spend 2010–13	
	Occupancy rate (%)	Average spend per room (euros)
2010	85.4	208.92
2011	87.1	218.80
2012	84.0	231.33
2013	79.3	235.01

TABLE 12.6	Disneyland Paris breakdown of attendance by country of origin 2012
	%
France	51
UK	14
Spain	8
Belgium and Luxembourg	6
Netherlands	6
Italy	3
Germany	3
Rest of World	9

While the number of visits increased by almost 7 per cent over the three-year period, the average spend increased by only 2.7 per cent over the same period. While hotel occupancy rate actually declined by 1.4 per cent, spending per room rose by 10.7 per cent. The country of origin of visitors is overwhelmingly France. This is not surprising given the location of the park but, given the earlier objections by French people to the park, many seem to have been won over. The attraction may lie in the increased use of the French language in the park and the greater emphasis on French culture. This also may partly explain the relatively low number of visitors from Germany especially given the ease of access by road for many Germans.

While visitors continue to rise, the financial performance of the company continues to be less than satisfactory. The share price fell from €8.56 in April 2011 to €4.70 in July 2012 and the company continued to record losses, rising from a loss of €45 million in 2010 to €100 million in 2012 and €78.2 million in 2013 (http://corporate.disneylandparis.com/investor-relations/financial-indicators/)

In part the losses can be explained by heavy borrowing to cover losses from previous years, heavy discounting on both entry tickets and hotel rooms to boost visitor numbers, higher staff wages and the expensive upgrading of existing attractions. However, no new attraction has been added since 2006. Although wage costs have risen there has been significant unrest among employees including a strike in 2009. The main concerns of staff have been job cuts, the increasing accident rate, which exceeds that in the building industry, and the lack of opportunity for career development. As a result the company sanctioned a social audit aimed at improving working conditions and employee satisfaction.

Questions

1 What are the marketing issues displayed by this case?

2 What were the reasons for Disney opening in the Paris area? Were these reasons justified?

3 What initial problems faced Disneyland Paris and how were they tackled?

4 What marketing strategies could the company use to move out of its ongoing financial problems? Are there any non-marketing strategies that would help?

5 What reasons can you give for the company continuing to make losses after operating for over 30 years?

SUMMARY

- Marketing involves the understanding of customer needs and behaviour and the researching of markets for the effective development, pricing, promotion and distribution of goods and services. These activities operate in a number of consumer and organizational contexts and can incorporate the marketing of people, places, company image and ideas as well as goods and services.

- The product, price, promotion and distribution elements of marketing are known as the marketing mix and are elements of marketing strategy. There is a trend for firms to segment the markets in which they operate, calling for variations in the marketing mix for each target market. Another important element of the mix is the branding of products and services and their positioning in the market.

- Marketing operates at the interface between the organization and its environment, and changes in the economy, state regulation, technology and social trends all call for changes in marketing strategy. Marketing managers use their knowledge of the environment, especially of those social and cultural influences that shape behaviour, in an attempt to manipulate demand for their product. In recent years marketing activities have been affected by globalization, consumerism and technology-based developments such as telemarketing and online marketing.

- The development of an effective marketing strategy depends upon an understanding of the workings of the market place, of customer needs and the appropriate mix for the market segment and prevailing environmental conditions. The implementation of that strategy depends upon the integration of marketing with the other functional specialisms, with a focus on the customer.

- In the last few years a key development has been the use of both digital and social media channels for marketing, the latter reinforcing the central role of the consumer.

DISCUSSION QUESTIONS

1 Assess Drucker's claim that marketing is not a specialized activity since it encompasses all the activities of the firm.

2 How far and in what industries do the orientations to marketing operate today?

3 For what reasons do governments engage in marketing? Does this raise any ethical problems?

4 What type of market research information would you need in the following situations: a holiday company offering a new resort location; a manufacturer developing a new vacuum cleaner; a restaurant owner planning a more expensive menu?

5 What factors would you consider to determine the price of the following: a new high-performance sports car; a new breakfast cereal; an MBA at an internationally known business school?

6 Why does market segmentation occur and what are its advantages and disadvantages for management and the consumer?

7   Assess the contributions of branding to the marketing process and to the success of the business.

8   Assess the contribution of the selection of appropriate distribution channels to effective marketing strategy.

9   To what extent can marketing activities change the environment in which the firm operates?

10   What are the essential ingredients of an effective marketing strategy for fast-moving consumer goods (e.g. toothpaste), a luxury yacht and a firm of professional accountants?

11   Assess the problems and opportunities presented by developments in digital and social media marketing.

12   What is the difference between targeting and positioning?

FURTHER READING

There are a number of good general texts on marketing. The following can be recommended.

Baines, P. and Fill, C. (2014) *Marketing*, 3rd edn, Oxford University Press: Oxford.
Kotler, P., Armstrong, G., Harris, R. and Piercy, N.F. (2013) *Principles of Marketing*, 6th European edn, FT Prentice Hall: Harlow.

The following book takes a predominantly strategic perspective.

West, D., Ford, J. and Ibrahim, E. (2010) *Strategic Marketing: Creating Competitive Advantage*, 2nd edn, Oxford University Press: Oxford.

An interesting perspective on marketing can be found in:

Piercy, N.F. (2009) *Market-led Strategic Change: Transforming the Process of Going to Market*, 4th edn, Butterworth-Heinemann: Oxford.

Some good international examples can be found in:

Ghauri, P. and Cateora, G. (2014), *International Marketing*, 4th edn, McGraw Hill: Maidenhead.
Usunier, J.-C. and Lee, J.A.(2009) *Marketing Across Cultures*, 5th edn, FT Prentice Hall: Harlow.

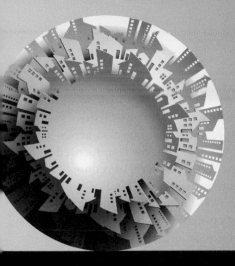

HUMAN RESOURCE MANAGEMENT

13

LEARNING OBJECTIVES At the end of this chapter you should be able to:

- Define and identify the main activities of HRM and explain how the role is performed.
- Identify the components of employee resourcing and the issues in recruitment and selection.
- Explain the role of training, development and employee branding in the processes of employee development.
- Identify the factors determining pay, explain different kinds of reward system and assess the contribution of performance management.
- Identify the process associated with employment relations and distinguish between these and industrial relations.
- Identify and explain variations in HR practice due to economic, political, social, legal and cultural differences.
- Explain variations in HRM with the size of the organization and critically evaluate the relationship between HR specialists and other managers.
- Identify and assess a range of HRM strategies and critically assess the effectiveness of HRM in achieving organizational goals.

INTRODUCTION

Throughout this chapter we will refer to human resource management as HRM. We will attempt to define HRM and examine how the function has developed. More than most business activities, HRM is shaped by the environmental context with which it operates. The role is influenced by the national framework within which it works. For example, changes in the level of economic activity or changing technology have implications for employment levels and the kind of skills needed. HRM is affected by regulatory and institutional frameworks, including employment laws and institutions for the development of skills. These vary between countries and different models and approaches to HRM have developed in different countries. Alongside this we have the growth of global business and the need for effective international models of HRM. We explore all these issues. In the past 20 or so years HRM has developed a much stronger strategic focus and we will explore different approaches to HRM strategy. The effectiveness of such strategies often depends on the relationship at organizational level between HRM specialists and other managers, another theme explored in this chapter.

We look first at definitions of HRM before examining the key activities and how they are performed in organizations. We then explore the relationship of HRM to environmental and organizational variables before examining HR strategies and their contribution to organizational effectiveness.

Since 1980 a large UK database has been accumulated by regular large scale surveys into workplace employment relations. This database charts the development of the HRM function and its activities. The research is sponsored by the government and is generally referred to as WERS (Workplace Employment Relations Survey). The latest findings relate to the 2011 survey, published both as a book, *Employment Relations in the Shadow of Recession* (van Wanrooy et al., 2013) and as a summary report (van Wanrooy et al., 2014). This chapter refers to this research, but wherever possible, findings from other countries are introduced and international comparisons are drawn.

DEFINING HRM

HRM used to be called personnel management. In the UK the function developed out of welfare roles performed by paternalistic employers such as Cadbury and Rowntree. With the increasing size of organizations and, especially in the UK, the growth of trade union membership, the role of personnel management expanded. By the 1960s the role incorporated among other activities, recruitment, selection, training and pay. However, in the UK in large organizations there was a focus on industrial relations and personnel specialists spent a great deal of their time negotiating and generally dealing with trade unions.

In 1963, the Institute of Personnel Management (IPM), now the Chartered Institute of Personnel and Development (CIPD), defined personnel work as follows:

Personnel management is a responsibility of all those who manage people as well as being a description of the work of those who are employed as specialists. It is that part of management which is concerned with people at work and with their relationships within an enterprise. It applies not only to industry and commerce, but to all fields of employment. Personnel management aims to achieve both efficiency and justice, neither of which can be pursued successfully without the other. It seems to bring together and develop into an effective organization the men and women who make up the enterprise, enabling each to make his own best contribution to its success, both as an individual and as a member of a working group. It seeks to provide fair terms and conditions of employment and satisfying work for those employed.

The definition is interesting because of its idealistic stance, the absence of precisely defined tasks and duties and its reference to the dual goals of serving the needs of employees and the organization. It also serves the useful purpose of distinguishing between a business function and a departmental presence within an organization. The definition also introduces some of the potential conflicts in the role. HRM is a specialist function but it also involves a set of activities practised by all managers. The definition also refers to the needs of the organization as well as those of the employees. We return to these themes throughout the chapter.

The term 'human resource management' can be traced to a course of that name at the Harvard Business School in the USA. The course reflected a more strategic focus for personnel management. One of the texts that emerged from Harvard at the time defined HRM thus:

Human resource management (HRM) involves all management decisions and actions that affect the nature of the relationship between the organization and its employees – its human resources.

(Beer et al., 1984, p. 1)

The approach focused on commitment as a route to improving organizational performance and was apparent in large US companies such as Hewlett-Packard and IBM. The approach was also found in some UK firms. In the UK, the emergence of HRM coincided with the weakening of the trade unions, extensive privatization and the notions of 'best practice', a view that there was one best way of managing human resources. Early adopters of HRM included British Airways and Marks & Spencer. In Case 13.1 we see how British Airways invested heavily in a widespread training programme to change the culture of its organization towards a greater emphasis on customer care.

The approach to HRM that had developed in both the USA and UK at the end of the 1980s can be summed up as follows:

- Treating employees as individuals but, at the same time, developing teams.
- The careful selection, training and development of core staff.
- Reward systems that stress individual performance and commitment and which are linked to employee appraisal and development.
- Communication networks and the involvement of all employees.
- Emphasizing a culture that stresses commitment to organizational goals, quality and flexibility.
- The development of HR strategies as part of overall business strategy and the integration of HR strategies themselves.
- Business values as an over-riding consideration.

Many of these characteristics are incorporated in Figure 13.1.

There was a distinct shift in the activities of human resource management away from industrial relations. This change spawned a vast literature examining both the language and ideology of HRM as well as questioning whether much had changed apart from re-launching personnel

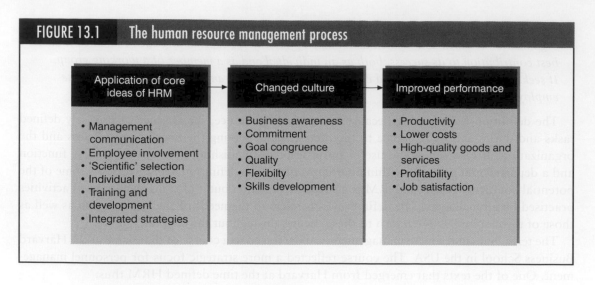

FIGURE 13.1 **The human resource management process**

Application of core ideas of HRM

- Management communication
- Employee involvement
- 'Scientific' selection
- Individual rewards
- Training and development
- Integrated strategies

Changed culture

- Business awareness
- Commitment
- Goal congruence
- Quality
- Flexibilty
- Skills development

Improved performance

- Productivity
- Lower costs
- High-quality goods and services
- Profitability
- Job satisfaction

management as HRM. It is now generally acknowledged that HRM takes a more strategic view of the role and is more aligned with the objectives of the organization. Studies have revealed that, in the UK at least, the personnel function has been renamed HRM and its practitioners are known as HR managers. Hoque and Noon (2001) note that, with this change, practitioners were more likely to be professionally qualified and more likely to be involved in the development of strategy.

The term HRM is now commonplace, as shown in Table 13.1. The table relates to a survey of job advertisements in the UK profession's journal from March 1993 to April 2009. Three types of job advertisement were identified:

- Those specifying a human resource manager or similar incorporating human resources in the job title.
- Those specifying personnel manager or similar in the job title.
- Those seeking a specialist role, such as in training, reward or equal opportunities.

In March 1993, the title human resource manager tended to be reserved for the higher-status and more highly paid positions. By 2003, human resources featured in the large majority of jobs, even those of a fairly junior nature. The number of positions titled personnel manager had

TABLE 13.1 **Job titles advertised in IPM/CIPD professional journal March 1993 to April 2009 as per cent of total jobs**

Job title	Positions advertised (%)			
	March 1993	*May 1999*	*May 2003*	*April 2009*
Human resource manager or similar	26	44	61	66
Personnel manager or similar	36	20	11	2
Specialist job title	38	36	28	32

declined markedly and were found mostly in the public sector. By 2009, the job title of personnel manager had all but disappeared.

REFLECTION POINT

Is there something distinctive about HRM that differentiates it from personnel management?

What are the activities of HRM?

In this text we take a broad definition of HRM as expressed by Boxall and Purcell (2003, p. l):

All those activities associated with the management of the employment relationship of the firm.

We group these activities under four headings:

- **Employee resourcing.** This includes planning, recruitment and selection, and issues relating to equality and diversity and work–life balance.
- **Employee development.** This involves training and development and a more recent focus on employee branding.
- **Pay and performance.** This involves methods and types of remuneration and how performance is managed.
- **Employment relations.** This includes various approaches to communication and participation, the relationship between management and unions and in general issues relating to the employment relationship.

We deal with each of these in turn later in this chapter. This focus is supported by the findings of a survey by the CIPD (2007). It revealed that the responsibilities and activities carried out most by HR professionals were recruiting and retaining staff, developing employees, improving the management of performance and the involvement and engagement of staff. The survey also noted a shift in focus in how the role was carried out and how time was spent as perceived by practitioners. This is shown in Table 13.2.

The findings in Table 13.2 reinforce the view that HRM has become more strategic in focus and that strategy is linked to overall business strategy. It is also a reflection of how practitioners view themselves. The shift from personnel management to HRM has been associated with the specialists themselves seeking more status within the organizations in which they work.

TABLE 13.2 Percentage of time spent on HR activities as perceived by practitioners			
	Three years ago (%)	**Now (%)**	**Three years from now (%)**
Administrative functions, e.g. maintaining records	50	36	24
Operational activities, e.g. recruitment	39	41	41
Strategic inputs	12	26	35

KEY CONCEPT 13.1   HUMAN RESOURCE MANAGEMENT

In many organizations, human resource management or, as it is often referred to, HRM or HR, performs the roles and duties formerly ascribed to personnel management. Many would argue that there is more than a name change and that the function has undergone an ideological shift. Traditional personnel management was concerned with recruitment, selection, training, pay, welfare and industrial relations. HRM deals with all of these, but integrates them within the overall strategy of the enterprise and sees business values as an over-riding consideration. An important element of HRM is the development of a culture that stresses commitment to organizational goals, quality and flexibility.

An influential model in this respect and one used as a framework by the CIPD in their survey (CIPD, 2007) is that of Ulrich (1997). The emphasis is not so much on the basic activities themselves but on what they can deliver to the organization. Ulrich identifies HR activities as comprising 'three legs of a stool':

- HR as the centralized provision of administrative services for the whole organization. This would involve the keeping of staff records or acting as a service centre giving information and advice as needed.

- HR as a centre of expertise. In this respect HR would provide 'expert' operational skills in areas such as recruitment and selection or remuneration schemes.

- HR as a business partner. In this role HR would have an input in the development of strategy for the organization and through that identify HR priorities.

It is in this final role that the CIPD and practitioners see the greatest change. This is reflected in some job titles. Referring to Table 13.1, six of the job advertisements for HR specialists in April 2009 had 'HR business partner' as the job title. Ulrich's model is in part a statement of how the role is performed, which we examine in the next section.

How HRM is performed

The HRM function may be performed in a number of ways:

- HR managers can be generalists, performing all activities or specialists in one or more of the functions.

- The role may be performed by a specialist HR manager or a general manager with responsibility for HR matters, or by individual managers themselves acting alone. WERS 2011 found that a general manager with responsibility for HR spent an average of 26 per cent of their time on HR matters and that 22 per cent of workplaces had a specialist HR manager (van Wanrooy et al., 2104).

- In some cases, HR specialists operate only in an advisory capacity to other managers. Members of the HR department will advise on the setting up of HR systems, which will be operated by other managers. Examples of this could include the establishment of an equal opportunities policy or developing criteria for promotion.

- In many cases, HR specialists work with other managers as, for example, in interviewing candidates for a vacancy, or designing and implementing a training programme for a sales department.

- In all kinds of organizations there is increasing use made of HR consultants, particularly in the fields of recruitment and training.
- An increasing trend is the use of outsourcing. We have referred to such offshore outsourcing more generally in Chapter 2 and examine HR outsourcing briefly below.

In smaller firms the activities tend to be carried out by all managers and no specialist is employed. In larger firms, with formalized procedures, a mixture of all methods occurs. The use of consultants and outsourcing is appropriate for small firms where specialist HR inputs are an intermittent requirement. In larger firms, consultants are seen as a more cost-effective method of delivering certain HR services than bearing the cost of maintaining a large internal department. This is particularly the case in training and some recruitment and payroll activities.

We have noted the trend towards **outsourcing.** For many years firms have outsourced aspects of HR work, notably recruitment, training and the administration of the payroll. However, the practice would appear to be growing in all countries, but particularly in the USA and UK. Even if the activity is not outsourced there is evidence of increasing use of consultants, especially lawyers, accountants and government agencies. The increasing use both in the UK and elsewhere is partly linked to changes in employment law (van Wanrooy et al., 2014). The growth of both outsourcing and the use of external experts is motivated by a number of factors:

- As with all forms of outsourcing, cost is a prime consideration. For example, it is not cost-effective to employ specialists in aspects of technical training whose services are only required intermittently.
- In some cases expert knowledge and skills may be needed as with the administration of psychometric tests or in an increasingly complex legal environment, particularly where the firm operates in a number of countries.
- Some tasks like payroll administration can be dealt with more easily and more effectively through an outsourced operation.
- Firms are increasingly engaged in activities in several countries. Local HR managers may not possess the knowledge and experience to deal with certain aspects of operations in other countries.
- Outsourcing HR can also be a response to downsizing and cost cutting.

We can identify three types of outsourcing:

- Specialists in specific areas. The most commonly outsourced HR activities are payroll, recruitment, training and pensions.
- Large providers offering a wide range of services. In some cases a large proportion of the HR function can be outsourced. This is a growing trend and firms such as PricewaterhouseCoopers, KPMG, IBM, and Accenture have diversified into offering wide-ranging HR services.
- Specialist providers of HR software and support.

We now examine the major HR roles and responsibilities; resourcing, development, pay and performance and employment relations.

REFLECTION POINT

Why has outsourcing become a growing trend in HRM?

EMPLOYEE RESOURCING

The HR manager will attempt to meet the organization's demand for labour. This will be achieved mainly through recruitment, selection and training, often within the framework of a staffing plan.

In some cases the labour market will act as a constraint to the extent that severe labour shortages in a given area may cause management to rethink its plans. In other cases the labour market operates as a partial constraint, and attempts will be made to entice workers away from existing jobs by offering them attractive pay packages and opportunities for career development. This can cause high levels of mobility among certain groups with scarce skills in an otherwise depressed labour market. A good example of this in the late 1990s can be found in the IT consulting industry, where scarce skills and an abundance of work resulted in high levels of mobility and higher salaries. In other cases the firm attempts to change the composition of the labour market, meeting shortages by training substitute labour or by attracting certain groups back to work, such as married women with children, by providing working conditions compatible with school hours. The introduction of 'family-friendly' employment policies is an example of such an approach. The increased use of flexible employment practices has been one of the reasons for the increase in the proportion of women in the work force. As we can see, employee resourcing overlaps with other activities of HR management such as training and development, pay and performance and employment relations.

In this section we examine recruitment and selection and the issues it raises in global firms and issues relating to equality and diversity including the more contemporary debate relating to the work–life balance.

KEY CONCEPT 13.2   EMPLOYEE RESOURCING

Employee resourcing involves a set of processes that fulfill the organization's demand for labour. The primary processes are recruitment and selection. Recruitment involves attracting candidates to apply for jobs in the organization. Selection involves choosing the most appropriate applicant from the pool of attracted candidates. Important considerations in recruitment and selection are the reliability and validity of the methods used and ensuring that the processes used conform to legal requirements and to cultural norms. An important consideration is one of equal opportunities.

Recruitment and selection

These are related processes. Recruitment involves attracting candidates to apply for jobs in the organization. Selection involves choosing the most appropriate applicant from the pool of attracted candidates. Both are important processes for a number of reasons:

- They are a means of achieving strategic goals, including culture change within the organization. For example, the recruitment and selection of a new chief executive is often accompanied by the bringing in of a new senior management team.

- Recruitment and selection can contribute towards a core competence and create a competitive advantage. For example, firms attempt to recruit leading performers from other firms to enhance their competitive position.

- Recruitment and selection can be expensive. This is not just the cost of advertising or the cost of the selection process itself, but also the costs of getting it wrong. Making poor appointments can result in poor performance, damage relations with clients, lead to increased training costs and in general, increase the costs associated with hiring and firing.

The traditional approach to recruitment and selection has been to focus on costs and to establish a one-sided process focused on the needs of management and the needs of a specific job at a specific time. Recent thinking has questioned these approaches.

- Recruitment and selection is an opportunity in which both parties can influence outcomes. The concept of employer branding has emerged. Employers wish to brand themselves as attractive organizations to influence candidates to join them. It is no longer just the responsibility of candidates to create a favourable impression to be selected. Brewster et al. (2005) identify strong employer branding as a features of firms such as Diageo, Shell and Rolls-Royce primarily to attract and retain talented workers but also to create strong corporate values to assist them in managing a more distributed global work force.

- Recruitment and selection is an opportunity to change the composition of the work force to change the culture as identified above, but also, perhaps, to target underrepresented groups as part of a policy of diversity management.

- Traditional approaches that focus on specific jobs at a specific time may be inappropriate in a rapidly changing global environment. This is partly the rationale for employer branding identified above.

Recruitment

The first stage in any recruitment process is to establish the need to recruit. Given the costs associated with hiring full-time staff on permanent contracts, many firms use other approaches to deal with increases in workload or to fill vacancies when someone leaves. These include reorganizing the work between existing staff, using overtime, employing part-time or temporary workers, outsourcing and, in some cases, changing the technology to reduce the need for staff.

Once a decision to recruit is made then the traditional approaches are usually based around a job description and a person specification. The former identifies the tasks and responsibilities of the job, while the latter identifies the knowledge, skills and attitudes required of candidates. Traditional approaches to both job descriptions and person specifications are becoming less relevant due to the increasing need for flexibility, multi-skilling, frequent restructuring and coping with operations in a changing global environment. Other approaches include a focus on competences, which emphasize behaviours rather than ticking off qualifications and skills. Key behaviours are seen as evidence of flexibility, excellent performance and the ability to operate in different and changing environments.

Various methods are available to attract candidates. Recruiting from inside the organization, **internal recruiting,** is the cheapest option and has the advantage that candidates are known to the organization. It is a source of motivation for employees but can be limiting in both the range of candidates and the ideas they bring to the organization. Methods of **external recruiting** include:

- Some firms rely heavily on referrals from specialist recruitment agencies, from existing staff and from people who write in or simply walk in to the organization seeking a job.

- The preferred method of recruitment is advertising, a requirement in some organizations as part of equal opportunities policy. Both local and national press are used, as are specialist journals and the media used will depend largely on the nature of the job and the level within the organization.

- There has been a significant growth in the use of online recruitment, either through the organization's website, which can identify current vacancies, or specialized recruitment websites.

A problem with some methods of recruitment, especially advertising, is that they result in a large field of candidates. While this can be an advantage it can be costly in terms of administrative time. The effectiveness of a particular method of recruitment can be evaluated in terms of the quantity and quality of candidates, offer and acceptance rates and the tenure and performance of those hired.

REFLECTION POINT

When would you use internal recruiting and when would you use external recruiting?

Selection

Most view selection in terms of a matching process between the candidate and the job description. The decision to employ or reject a candidate is ultimately the prerogative of line managers, but the administration of the process tends to be carried out by HR specialists.

Problems with selection methods include reliability and validity. Reliability refers to the extent to which a measure of consistency can be achieved, as, for example, in getting interviewers to behave in a similar fashion and ask candidates similar questions. Validity refers to the extent to which a selection method actually discriminates between suitable and unsuitable candidates and the extent to which it can predict future job performance. The conclusion drawn from many studies of selection techniques is that they are highly variable in terms of reliability and validity and managers use intuitive and subjective criteria and make selection decisions that are far from scientific.

REFLECTION POINT

How would you explain reliability and validity in the selection process?

A number of selection methods are used:

- **Application form** information is used to pre-select or to shortlist candidates for interview.
- **Interviews** are the most popular form of selection. Much research has been conducted into the reliability and predictive validity of the interview (a good summary of much of the significant early research is offered by Arvey and Campion, 1982). Research suggests that interviewers are biased, that unfavourable information is given greater weight than favourable, that decisions tend to be made on first impressions and that interviewers tend to have poor recall of candidates. Despite this, interviews are popular with both interviewers and candidates and can be useful in determining verbal fluency and motivation. Interview reliability and validity can be enhanced by interviewer training, the use of structured interviews for all candidates and the use of situational questions. Interviews tend to be liked by managers because they allow them to exercise judgement in the selection process. Interviews are also an important method of employer branding (explained in more detail in the next section), in which the candidate is 'sold' the values of the organization.

- **Tests** are used to measure personality traits, cognitive ability and other skills. They can be useful for collecting information from large numbers of candidates, they subject all candidates to the same experience, and they can be relatively easy to administer and score. The validity of personality tests has been questioned by many researchers and a common argument used is that the same job can be done effectively by people with different personality traits. The use of tests in general has been challenged by those who claim that they tend to be culturally biased and therefore discriminate unfairly. Many managers prefer tests that are a sample of the kind of work to be carried out by the successful candidate, e.g. keyboard skills, because they feel this will have a higher predictive validity. There is evidence of an increased use of tests which replicate or approximate to performance at work and these are now widely used in 46 per cent of UK organizations (Kersley et al., 2006).

- **Assessment centres** usually involve a group of candidates and a range of selection methods, including discussion groups, tests, problem-solving exercises and interviews. The assessment centre attempts to replicate real work behaviour in various job simulation exercises. The exercises test job skills, interactive skills, leadership skills and the ability to work under pressure. The centre requires a large number of trained assessors, tends to be expensive and is used primarily in graduate recruitment or for more senior jobs. Assessment centres can also be used for promotions and for the early identification of management talent. Some evidence suggests the predictive validity of assessment centres is higher than in many other forms of selection (Thornton and Rupp, 2006), although evidence is mixed. A particular difficulty is knowing what weight to give to each of the different elements involved in the selection.

Recruitment and selection in global firms

The usual pattern here is where a multinational firm recruits and selects staff for an assignment in one or more of a number of countries in which it operates. In many multinationals, such as Ford, cross-national mobility was a feature of many management positions. UK managers could be posted to Germany, Belgium, Spain or the US headquarters in Michigan. In companies such as Colgate-Palmolive, international posting was a key ingredient of management development and an expected part of moving up the management hierarchy. Such expectations have been modified by a number of factors:

- There is the growing use of locals from host countries to fill positions in that country.

- Finding suitable candidates who can operate cross-nationally and cross-culturally has been difficult for many organizations.

- There is an increased reluctance on the part of some managers to move (Dowling and Welch, 2004). For example, Colgate-Palmolive found an increasing number of managers who were unwilling to move due to their partner being unwilling to disrupt their own career (Bartlett and Ghoshal, 1995, pp. 622–37).

In addition to these trends, recruiting and selecting to work in other countries adds complications to the process:

- There are cultural issues to consider. As we saw in Case 2.1, Chrysler found that sending young managers to work at their joint venture in China did not meet with the approval of their Chinese partners, who equated age with knowledge and experience. However, there are many false assumptions that can be made, particularly the view that international appointments are the sole prerogative of white males.

- There may be legal and institutional differences that need to be reflected in policies.
- In some countries, appointments need to be approved by politicians.
- There may be any number of issues that are specific to the location and the nature of the job.
- There is also a choice of selection strategy. For example, historically, many firms have pursued an ethnocentric approach by giving important positions only to people from the home base of the multinational. A polycentric approach tends to appoint locals to positions in the host country, while reserving HQ jobs for home country employees. There is a notable trend towards a geocentric approach in the appointment of the best person for the job irrespective of nationality, an approach taken by both Nissan and Sony in the selection of chief executives.

We can see that the recruitment and selection of international staff is complex and, as one might expect from such a complex situation, there would seem to be no acknowledged best practice.

Equal opportunities and diversity

Attempts have been made to differentiate between equal opportunities and diversity management. Equal opportunities is usually related to establishing operational procedures to ensure that the organization complies with the laws covering discrimination against specific groups of people such as women, ethnic minorities and those with disabilities. Diversity management tends to be more strategic, focuses more on individuals and is founded on the assumption that the organization will be more effective if all people feel more valued. In practice, there is significant overlap between the two concepts.

There is evidence that job and promotion opportunities are limited by gender, race, age, disability, sexual orientation and so on (a good summary can be found in Kirton and Greene, 2005). In many countries there is legislation covering discrimination and many organizations have developed equal opportunities policies. WERS 2011 found that a growing number of employees in all kinds of workplace were aged 50 or older, had some form of disability and came from a minority ethnic group. In addition half the UK labour force was female (van Wanrooy et al., 2014).

Three reasons have been offered for treating people equitably and there is considerable similarity with the rationale offered for ethical business (see Chapter 9). First, there is a moral imperative that all people should be treated equally and that societies have a moral duty to provide opportunities for all. Second, there is a legal and financial case in that illegal or unfair discrimination leads to court and tribunal cases and the potential of damaging fines and perhaps even more damaging publicity. Finally, there is a business case for diversity, which incorporates a number of points:

- It enables firms to select from a wider pool of labour.
- It makes better use of existing resources.
- It exposes firms to a wider range of ideas that can lead to more effective decisions.
- Customers themselves are generally diverse. The employment of a diverse staff will match the profile of customers and sends a message to them as well as offering more knowledge of potential markets. As a result market share can be increased.
- Effective diversity policies can motivate employees and can lead to a reduction in absenteeism and turnover.

Dickens (2005), writing about the UK, notes that many organizations have policies on equal opportunities and diversity and she acknowledges also that there has been an increase in the employment of women and ethnic minorities. Despite this, she argues that discrimination is still a feature of employment and, in particular, women and ethnic minorities are underrepresented in senior positions. This is backed up by WERS 2011, which found that 76 per cent of organizations had equal opportunities policies but less than 23 per cent of them carried out monitoring or reviewed their policies with regard to recruitment and selection, and less than 10 per cent with regards to pay or promotion (van Wanrooy et al., 2014).

A number of approaches can be taken to manage diversity. These include:

- Monitoring employment statistics as a basis of questioning policies and practices on the hiring and promotion of those likely to suffer discrimination. As we see above, this is only carried out in a minority of workplaces.

- Taking affirmative action to ensure that the organization employs and promotes people from specific groups.

- Attempting to change the culture of the organization through training, by challenging assumptions of existing staff and using mentors and role models.

KEY CONCEPT 13.3   EQUAL OPPORTUNITIES AND DIVERSITY MANAGEMENT

Action on equal opportunities usually comprises a set of procedures that comply with laws that prevent discrimination against certain groups. The early focus was on women and ethnic minorities but the legal provision had broadened to include, for example, disabilities, religious allegiance, age and sexual orientation. Policies related to equal opportunities have been criticized as being reactive. Diversity management takes both a more proactive strategic approach and focuses more on individuals rather than groups to ensure that the organization benefits from the contribution of all employees.

Work–life balance

An important contemporary issue in equal opportunities and diversity management is that of providing opportunities for employees who have responsibility for children or caring for others in general. Such responsibilities often clash with the organization's need for people to work long hours as required by the needs of the business. Work–life balance refers to two main issues:

- The number and pattern of hours worked.

- Providing arrangements for child-care and those with responsibility for caring for the elderly or for people with disabilities.

The debate about the work–life balance is related to the rising employment of women with children, the growth of one-parent families, the increased focus on 'family-friendly' policies, the need for employer flexibility and the issue over long hours worked or expected in some managerial and professional jobs. Walsh (2013) sees, in the UK at least, positive signs in the promotion of work–life balance employment practices, supported by legislation on such issues as parental leave and the employees' right to request flexible work time arrangements. She also recognizes problems. In many jobs there is still a 'long hours culture' and that the flexibility created by forms of teleworking at home can actually heighten the work–life conflict.

Policies that may be used can involve changing the hours, allowing for more flexible patterns of work and providing sponsored child-care facilities. In some organizations there are constraints on such flexibility due to the nature of the operations and because of cost. Work–life balance was subject to EU legislation in the Working Time Directive, which places a limit of 48 hours a week on the time employers can ask employees to work. However, in some organizations there is a culture of working long hours as a demonstration of commitment to the organization. In this respect the issue of work–life balance and legislation to set limits on the working week has the objective of protecting the health, family life and leisure time of employees. However, WERS 2011 found that an increased number of UK managers believed it was the individual's responsibility to manage the balance between work and other responsibilities and saw obstacles in terms of the nature of the work, the operating hours required and the cost (van Wanrooy et al., 2014).

EMPLOYEE DEVELOPMENT

Employee development or, as it is sometimes known, human resource development, involves all activities related to the training and development of staff. In this section we examine some changes, identify the processes and look specifically and briefly at management training and development and employee branding. As we shall see, there are many overlaps with employee resourcing. Employee development is essentially a learning activity, when employees acquire knowledge, skills, attitudes and qualifications and in so doing learn to work with others to contribute towards organizational performance. The activity is important in terms of competitive advantage both at the level of the firm and in terms of national economies. Employee development is also an important contribution to succession planning as an alternative to external recruitment. For example, Ford traditionally operated a policy of identifying and training suitable candidates for promotion to first line supervisor, but only placing them in post when a vacancy was created.

We can identify three developments:

- There is an increasing link between training and development and employee resourcing. The need for flexibility and multiskilling means that it is probably more important to select people who can be trained rather than employing people with specific skills. This approach is also central to employee branding (see later in this section), where employees are selected on the basis of their acceptance of the values and culture of the organization.

- The focus of training and development has shifted from manual skills to 'soft' skills involved in the performance of effective interpersonal behaviour. This reflects a global shift from manufacturing to service industries.

- Although training varies considerably between sectors, occupations and even firms in the same sector, there is a clear focus on management training and development and on leadership (see Chapter 7). In the UK, WERS 2011 found that training had extended to more employees but that the duration of training had shortened. There is evidence of training cuts in recession, but firms are more likely to impose pay freezes and delay recruitment as forms of cost cutting (van Wanrooy et al., 2014).

KEY CONCEPT 13.4   EMPLOYEE DEVELOPMENT

Employee development is concerned with all activities related to the training and development of staff. It is an important activity that contributes to the economic health of a nation, the competitive advantage of firms and to employee motivation. There are strong overlaps with employee resourcing.

The training and development process

We can view training and development as a process:

- **Analysis of training and development needs.** Traditionally, this has been based on identifying the gap between the requirements of the job description and the skills of the individual carrying out the job. A simple model involves an assessment of the likelihood of failure without training, together with the cost of failure without training. This enables managers to focus training budgets where they are most needed. Increasingly, there is emphasis on the need for greater flexibility and the requirement for employees to develop a range of skills. Some organizations base training and development not just on the needs of the organization but also upon the wishes of employees. Asking employees to identify their own training needs is a common feature of most appraisal schemes.

- **Training methods.** The traditional classification is between on-the-job training and off-the-job training. On-the-job-training involves learning by doing and can involve a trainer or a mentor. Japanese firms tend to prefer on-the-job-training for the acquisition of job skills, which involves job rotation within a department with each employee supported by a mentor. Off-the-job training invariably involves the use of a training course which can be carried out either internally or externally. In contrast to their typical approach to training, Japanese firms often use off-the-job-training for induction programmes focusing on the transmission of corporate values.

- **Who does the training?** Training and development can be carried out by agencies. It has long been a specialist activity within HR and firms with regular training needs may well use their own specialists. In many cases on-the-job-training is carried out by line managers within individual departments. In many firms training is outsourced to specialists. Outsourcing occurs even in large firms, particularly where the training is specialized or of a highly technical nature. There is a distinction to be drawn between those who are responsible for training and those who carry it out. In the case of outsourcing it is inevitably the HR specialist within the firm, who in consultation with line managers, draws up the training specification and seeks out the most appropriate provider. As training budgets are increasingly devolved to line managers, problems have been noted in that line managers do not necessarily see training as a priority and often view it as a cost rather than an investment.

- **The evaluation of training and development.** Evaluation is traditionally based around cost-benefit analysis in which the total costs of training, including the opportunity costs of people being trained, are compared against the value of the outcome of training, for example, increased output. While it is relatively easy to assess the total cost it is much more difficult to quantify the benefits, which may not reveal themselves until some time after the training event or may be affected by other variables, such as a planned reduction in output. While such measurement of outcomes is difficult for all jobs, it is even more difficult in the case of management development or professional training, where time horizons may be several years. As a result of these difficulties attempts have been made to establish other approaches to evaluation, usually involving subjective feedback from trainers, trainees and even clients.

REFLECTION POINT

How would you evaluate the effectiveness of the course for which you are using this text?

Management development

It is generally accepted that there are three components of management development. These are:

- Education including MBA programmes, undergraduate business and management programmes and some specialist masters and professional programmes.

- Training, including the acquisition of specific skills such as time management, decision-making and presentation skills.

- Development as an ongoing process within the firm including mentoring and coaching. Management development is seen as important in the attraction and retention of managerial talent and as an important contribution to organizational performance. More recently, as we have seen in Chapter 7, there has been an emphasis on leadership skills. Given that these are, arguably, difficult to train, there has been a focus on methods of management recruitment and selection to identify leadership potential among recruits.

Despite the high profile of management development in the literature there is little evidence concerning its effect on performance. Given the difficulties of establishing measurable criteria and the time frame of management development, it is difficult to show a return on investment. Two other factors complicate evaluation. First, managers, particularly in the USA and UK tend to be highly mobile and have moved to another firm before any sensible evaluation is possible. Second, in many organizations there has been delayering of management levels (see the section on structure in Chapter 6), which again acts as an obstacle to the evaluation of training and development processes.

Employee branding

Employee branding is the process of 'ensuring that employees act in accordance with the organization's brand values' (Edwards, 2005, p. 266). Employee branding is a means through which an organization's core values are communicated and embedded in its staff. As such we can see links with corporate culture (see Chapter 6). In terms of HR activities, it has specific implications for recruitment, selection, induction and training.

Employee branding extends the concept of brand as used in marketing. Through such branding, employees become the representatives and even the embodiment of the corporate brand. In our discussion of corporate social responsibility in Chapter 9 we noted how some organizations develop themselves as a brand that is attractive to prospective employees and also to prospective investors and customers.

Organizations using both employer and employee branding, such as easyJet, clearly see branding as a means of attracting and developing high quality employees and enhancing the performance of the organization. However, Edwards (2005) concludes that there is little evidence of its impact on performance.

KEY CONCEPT 13.5   EMPLOYER AND EMPLOYEE BRANDING

Employer branding occurs when employers wish to brand themselves as attractive organizations to influence candidates to join them and also to create strong corporate values to assist them in managing a more distributed global work force. Employee branding is a means through which an organization's core values are communicated and embedded in its staff so that they behave in accordance with those values.

In the public as well as the private sector we can identify increased attention being paid to performance management. This is a result of increased competition in the latter and increased pressures from both governments and clients in the former. Issues of low pay and equal pay have been debated by governments. Pay represents a major cost and large organizations in both the private and public sectors have responded to local and global economic problems by shedding employees to reduce these costs. Multinationals operating in the global economy have attacked labour costs as a means of increasing profits by moving jobs out of high-cost countries to those areas where pay is lower. The global banking crisis of 2008–09 was blamed partly on the generous pay and bonuses of senior managers and the lack of any meaningful link between pay and performance.

In this section we will examine the relationship between pay and performance and look at trends in performance management.

Pay and reward systems

Reward systems form part of the employment contract and are also used to gain increased effort and output from employees. There is therefore a link between reward and theories of motivation. Reward systems can be classified as:

- **Intrinsic rewards.** These include job satisfaction, esteem and self-fulfilment. There is an assumption that with the shift towards knowledge working, intrinsic rewards will become more important.
- **Extrinsic rewards.** These include basic rates of pay, overtime payments and performance-related pay such as bonuses. Such rewards also include non-pay factors such as company car, health insurance and pension scheme.

In this section we look at factors determining pay, payment schemes and some recent trends.

Factors determining pay

Many factors have an influence on the rate and type of pay. The importance of these will vary dependent on the situation:

- The concept of equity features in any discussion of reward systems. It is a consideration in setting basic rates of pay, e.g. do they constitute a fair return for effort? It is also a consideration in determining the relative rates of pay between each type of job. Such considerations of equity have become more complex in a globally networked economy as the same type of work in the same organization can attract very different rates of pay in different countries.
- There may be variations in the supply and demand for labour and in what other firms are willing to pay.
- Economic changes affect rates of pay. In a recession some firms ask their employees to take pay cuts. In 2009, British Airways announced a scheme to ask all employees to forgo a month's salary to assist the organization's weak financial position. In many cases the rate of pay is determined by what the firm can afford.
- The rate and type of pay is clearly influenced by the nature of the job. In many organizations the relative rate of pay between jobs is determined by some form of job evaluation.

- Recently there has been a closer link between the goals of the organization and its rates and systems of pay. In this way pay has been used to achieve certain strategic ends. In more general terms pay may be a form of employer branding as in the case of a firm wishing to be a 'pay leader' in the sector to attract talented recruits.
- The type of technology has an effect, as in the shift from craft to mass production. Qualified craftsmen with a legitimate claim for higher rates of pay were replaced by lower-paid, semi-skilled production workers. As a result, organizations could produce more at a lower cost.
- Pay is also determined by regulatory systems as in the case of collective bargaining involving trade unions or government policies, which affect the public sector in particular.

Many of the above factors work together in combination although different factors have been influential at different times. Traditionally in the UK and in other countries, trade unions have influenced pay rates through collective bargaining procedures. However union influence over pay has been in significant decline. WERS 2011 found that only 6 per cent of workplaces in the UK engaged in collective pay bargaining, involving only 16 per cent of employees. The decline has also affected the public sector (van Wanrooy et al., 2014). In most organizations pay is unilaterally set by management.

Devising pay and reward systems

Decisions to be taken when devising a system for pay and reward include:

- What is to be the basic rate for the job? This can be expressed either as an hourly rate or as a monthly or annual salary.
- Whether there should be some kind of pay scale. If so, how large should it be and how will individuals move along the scale?
- Whether there should be some form of incentive scheme.
- What offerings are to be made apart from pay, e.g. company car, pension scheme and so on? These are sometimes referred to as fringe benefits.

We can see that a combination of some or all of the above factors offers a very wide choice of pay and reward system.

In most organizations the **basic rate** is determined by some kind of job evaluation scheme, which attempts to compare jobs in the same organization according to agreed criteria and then allocate a relative value to that job. As we have seen, there are several factors which can influence pay and many organizations are influenced by the market rate. This can be built into the equation with job evaluation but there may be cases where the market rate distorts relative rates of pay determined internally. Most basic rates are linked to hours worked and can also include overtime payments for additional hours and increments along a pay scale, usually based on age and length of service. The assumption behind such scales is that employees will develop over time and their contribution will be greater. Such a system was the cornerstone of the employment contract in Japan for many years. The advantage of basic rate schemes lies in their simplicity, transparency, ease of administration and they offer managers greater control over labour costs. Apart from an incremental system that may encourage retention, such schemes offer little in the way of incentive.

Many organizations prefer to link pay with performance through some kind of **incentive scheme.** WERS 2011 found in the UK some form of incentive scheme in 54 per cent of organizations. Incentive schemes were most prevalent in the private sector but WERS found they were found also in 22 per cent of public sector organizations. The use of incentives varied widely across sectors with 68 per cent of employees in financial services receiving some form of incentive compared to only 4 per cent in education. (van Wanrooy et al., 2014).

The main decisions about incentive schemes are:

- Whether the scheme is based on individual, group or organization performance.
- Whether it is based on some form of measurable output or whether it is based on input factors such as skills and effort.
- Whether pay is directly linked to some output measure, e.g. a fixed amount is paid for each unit of production above a certain level or whether a bonus is paid based on some qualitative assessment of contribution. Such qualitative assessments are usually subjective and come under the heading of merit pay.

The simplest form of incentive scheme is piecework. This links the incentive directly to each piece produced or to a fixed element of a job. Such incentives are commonly found in the clothing industry, where payment is based on each garment or piece of garment produced; in sales, where it is directly linked to items sold; and in some professions, such as dentistry, where the dentist is paid according to the nature of the procedure carried out. There are some types of job where piecework is the only means of payment and there is no basic rate. Some selling jobs operate on this principle and such systems are often linked to the type of 'sweat shop' arrangements in the clothing industry.

Incentive schemes based on the unit of production work best where there is a short job cycle (the worker can see an immediate return for effort), where jobs are repetitive and where there are few fluctuations in output due to external factors, such as parts delivery. More complex jobs require incentive schemes that involve a greater degree of judgement by managers and such schemes are invariably linked to appraisal and the wider issue of performance management. It is here that merit pay predominates.

Studies of the link between pay and performance and hence the effectiveness of incentive schemes have yielded mixed results. The problem of establishing a clear link is the presence of so many variables, as with many HR interventions and management decisions in general. In Chapter 7 we noted problems with executive pay. The experience with some firms such as leading banks was that executive bonuses were paid even though profits and share price had fallen.

Trends in pay

We can identify the following trends:

- With the move of jobs away from manufacturing and to the service sector there has been a corresponding shift in the way people are paid, particularly with regard to performance-related pay. Incentives in manufacturing relied heavily on measured outputs. In the service industry, the focus is more on rewarding appropriate behaviour with customers and clients. Some supermarkets use 'mystery shoppers', whose real role is to assess the behaviour, effectiveness and service quality of employees. Sears Roebuck carries out customer surveys with the prime intention of rating employees on their service provision (Deery, 2005).
- There has been a shift in emphasis from reward based on historical information such as output and past performance to reward based on an individual's value and potential to the organization. This gives a key role to the HR department since it links pay strategy with organization strategy. The 'total reward approach' focuses on offering employees a bundle

of pay and non-pay benefits. Some firms, such as AstraZeneca, operate this as a 'cafeteria system', whereby employees can choose those benefits that most suit their needs. Some firms have used this as part of 'family-friendly' policies and include such options as flexible working hours, child-care provision and paid paternity leave. The most popular fringe benefits are company cars and private health insurance. Final salary pensions, in which the pension obtained on retirement was a fixed percentage of the final salary, were considered important in attracting and retaining employees. Nearly all pension funds are invested in stock markets and the fluctuations in share values together with people living longer has, in some cases, created large pension fund deficits. As a result many firms have withdrawn such schemes.

Performance management

Traditionally, performance management, if it happened at all, comprised an annual appraisal of an employee by a line manager. In recent years there has been a growth in the use of formal appraisals and an increased emphasis on performance management. This is linked strongly to developments in the HR function since performance management is the means through which individual effort and contribution become part of the process of achieving organizational goals.

> *Advocates of performance management claim that its value resides in the cycle of integrated activities, which ensure a systematic link is established between the contribution of each employee and the overall performance of the organization.*
>
> (Bach, 2013, p. 223)

The increased attention on performance management is a function of:

- Increased competition.
- The increased use of targets not just in the private sector but as a means of adding value to public sector services.
- The greater focus in many organizations on culture change.
- The need to carry out restructuring which will inevitably include downsizing and delayering.

The purpose of performance management

A number of reasons have been given. These range from the visionary to the more mundane operational and include:

- The communication of organizational goals and the creation of a shared vision.
- Setting individual goals and giving clear expectations of performance and contribution.
- Developing mechanisms whereby employees can monitor and improve performance both of themselves and others.
- Motivating and gaining commitment.
- Improving communication.
- Identifying individual development needs and managing careers.
- Mentoring and counselling to improve performance.
- Identifying future talent.
- Using it as a management control device.
- Assisting in pay, promotion and even in disciplinary matters.

We may conclude that some of the above may be difficult to achieve in combination. For example, the use of performance management to motivate and achieve greater commitment may be at odds with its use as a management control device and as part of a disciplinary procedure.

KEY CONCEPT 13.6   PERFORMANCE MANAGEMENT

Performance management involves procedures and techniques, such as appraisal, to assess the performance of individual employees and to ensure that a link is forged between their contribution and the overall performance of the organization.

Trends in performance management

First, we can observe its broadening use to all employees. Performance appraisals were traditionally only for managers and even then the most senior managers were rarely appraised. Now, appraisal schemes have embraced all levels within an organization. Armstrong and Baron (2005) found in a UK survey that 87 per cent of organizations surveyed operated a formal appraisal scheme with fairly wide coverage, which was a 30 per cent increase compared with their survey some seven years earlier. Similar findings were made by WERS 2011 where the percentage of workplaces formally appraising non-managerial staff rose from 43 per cent in 2004 to 69 per cent in 2011 (van Wanrooy et al., 2014).

Second, there has been a broadening of approach and the development of new techniques. These include variations on the traditional appraisal, such as 360-degree appraisal to those approaches that use a broad range of measures, such as the balanced scorecard. The idea of **360-degree appraisal** has developed as organizational structures have become more flexible and individuals no longer report to just one line manager. Under this scheme, individuals are appraised by a number of stakeholders, including, in some organizations, clients and customers. The **balanced scorecard,** developed by Kaplan and Norton (1996) as an alternative to traditional accounting perspectives on organizational performance, can be used as a basis of individual performance management. This has much in common with the 'best value' approach developed in the public sector. A balanced scorecard approach attempts to judge performance along a range of criteria, which usually include: financial measures of outputs; the value of outputs as seen by the customer; co-workers and other stakeholders; individual productivity and associated costs; and measurements of learning and growth. Armstrong and Baron (2005) note that such multi-faceted approaches are commonly used by large organizations such as Shell and AstraZeneca.

Third, there has been a renewed belief that the greater involvement of employees in performance management processes will increase the likelihood that organizational goals will be achieved. This inevitably has led to an increased focus on employee development needs. In contrast there is also some evidence of ranking as a means of removing the lowest-ranked performers from the organization. This technique was a feature of Enron, as mentioned in Case 9.1, but is also found in organizations such as Microsoft and General Electric.

Problems with performance management

A considerable critique has been built up around the uses of appraisal schemes. Many of the issues raised about appraisal apply equally to performance management in general:

- If we review the above list identifying the purposes of performance management and the subsequent comments it is apparent that there are many and conflicting objectives. The appraiser is being asked to play different roles including those of evaluator and developer.

- In some jobs it is difficult to set targets that can be measured or targets that are totally under the control of the employee.

- The appraisal of individual performance is confronted with similar problems experienced in the selection interview; problems of subjectivity, bias and stereotyping. In some firms there are gender and cultural issues, where the stereotype of an effective performer is that of a white male employee.

- Some managers find the process time-consuming and consequently do not take performance management seriously.

- Some managers find it difficult to make assessments about staff performance.

- Reviews can be unduly influenced by recent events and fail to take a balanced view of performance over a period of time.

- Studies have shown that criticism has an overwhelmingly negative impact on employees.

- Some like Townley (1989) have argued that the dominant purpose of appraisal is as a form of management control.

Many issues in pay and performance management have been central to employment relations.

EMPLOYMENT RELATIONS

Employment relations was known as industrial relations. For many HR departments, particularly in large scale manufacturing organizations, industrial relations was a primary role, especially in the UK. For a company such as Ford, a large number of HR specialists were employed to solve minor disputes as they occurred and so prevent major disputes and ensure smooth production flows. An element of this role involved negotiations with trade union representatives. As a result, the image of industrial relations was one of conflict and of adversarial relations between management and unions.

In the 1980s, a number of changes occurred around the same time. Trade union membership fell and in countries like the UK unions were weakened by new laws (we introduced such issues in Chapter 4). There was a shift to employee representation outside trade unions, through such bodies as works councils. As we have seen already in this chapter, the HR role itself had changed to reflect the increased competition of the new global economy. New approaches were brought in by global firms from different countries and HR practices were modified accordingly. For example, the Japanese brought practices aimed at employee consultation, fostering commitment and focusing on team approaches to quality. American HR focused on culture change, employee commitment and improved performance. The EU was influenced by continental-style systems of employee involvement through works councils as developed in Germany and Scandinavia. As a result, the term 'employment relations', with an emphasis on cooperation, commitment and involvement of the entire work force replaced industrial relations.

The HR role itself changed. It now involves:

- Working with trade unions where membership is still a feature of employment. In these organizations wages and conditions are still negotiated through collective bargaining. As we have noted, in the UK this is becoming less common, even in the public sector.

- In many organizations the emphasis has shifted from adversarial bargaining to partnership between management and unions. This has been greatly influenced by European social models.

A partnership approach stresses joint working between management and unions, long pay deals, agreements on job security, information sharing and joint problem solving. The effectiveness of such practices depends on high levels of trust between owners, managers and employees.

- Establishing and operating procedures for discipline and grievance. In the UK, WERS 2011 found that 88 per cent of organizations had a formal grievance procedure and 89 per cent a formal discipline procedure (van Wanrooy et al., 2014). There is some overlap here with performance management as many organizations have formal procedures to deal with poor performance. However, many organizations employ informal processes, through which problems are resolved before formal procedures are employed. In many countries and especially in the UK the incidence of individual disputes has risen and the incidence of collective disputes, especially strikes has fallen.

- Establishing and operating procedures for communication, consultation, participation and involvement.

- Increasingly, we have seen the development of procedures to deal with employment relations issues arising from and in non-standard forms of employment such as part-time working, contract working and outsourcing.

KEY CONCEPT 13.7   EMPLOYMENT RELATIONS

Employment relations involves all matters in the relationship between the individual and their employing organization. It involves consideration of contractual issues related to terms and conditions and formal procedures for grievances, discipline and poor performance. It is also concerned with those non-legal processes that form part of the psychological contract between the individual and their employer, including measures for employee involvement and participation. Where trade unions operate, employment relations will involve negotiation, consultation and bargaining. However, the processes have shifted away from groups to individual employees.

Employee involvement

This has strong links to the development of HRM in the 1980s and the strengthening of the link between employee contribution and the goals of the organization. It is based on the assumption that the involvement of employees in making decisions improves performance. We can identify three approaches to involvement: representative, direct and task-based. Forms of direct involvement would appear to be the most popular.

Representative employee involvement includes trade unions and work councils. The European Works Council Directive was adopted by the EU in 1994, but took until 2005 to be adopted by the UK. The directive applies to all organizations with more than 1000 employees in member states and any organization employing 150 in two or more member states. The focus is on the involvement of employees across transnational organizations but covers organizations operating in a single state. The works council must meet at least once a year and can comprise up to 30 elected representatives. The general focus of such councils was intended to be on structure, performance and future developments.

Direct employee involvement tends to be favoured by management since it offers them greater control and focuses on all employees as individuals. Bryson (2000) reported in the UK that between 1994 and 1998 forms of representative involvement halved, with a corresponding quadrupling in forms of direct involvement. Similar trends have been found elsewhere in Europe and in the USA. Direct involvement can take many forms. Downwards direct involvement includes newsletters, emails and briefing groups. Upwards direct involvement includes suggestion schemes and quality circles. WERS 2011 noted an increase in all types of communication to provide employees with information. The main methods used were meetings involving all staff and team briefings (van Wanrooy et al., 2014).

Task-based employee involvement occurs where involvement is an inherent part of the job. In some cases this is designed in as with job enrichment schemes to improve the motivational content of the work. It is clearly a feature where work is carried out by autonomous work groups, who have been given responsibility for parts of the operation.

In general, the evidence on employee involvement and the performance of individuals and of organizations is mixed. Some studies report increases in productivity, others that it has little effect on either employee motivation or absenteeism. There are reports of both management and employee scepticism. As with many interventions, there is a difficulty of demonstrating a causal link between involvement and performance due to the influence of so many other variables that cannot be controlled.

ENVIRONMENTAL ASPECTS OF HRM

Changes in the competitive environment of most companies have placed greater emphasis on the need to innovate, improve the quality of their goods and services and, above all, be more cost-effective in their use of labour. This, in turn, has resulted in many of those companies re-examining the way they select, train, use, motivate and reward employees. An aspect of this new competition has been its global nature and organizations have often looked to global competitors for other models.

The development of HR as a specialist management function in organizations owes much to the influence of external events:

- The growth of markets and the creation of the joint stock company led to increases in the size of the firm with a corresponding demand for recruitment, training and some centralized payment administration system.
- The growth of trade unions, especially in Britain, created the need for industrial relations specialists among management.
- The impact of two world wars created problems for the labour supply and a corresponding attention being paid to training methods and employee consultation.
- Full employment in the 1960s once again focused the attention on labour shortages and methods used to tackle them, such as the retraining of staff and recruitment from other companies.
- In the 1980s, the growth of the global economy and the expansion of multinational firms created challenges for the HR specialist.

HR and globalization

The relationship between HR and globalization involves issues relating to the economy, the role of the state, cultural and institutional differences as well as the kind of HR strategies organizations wish to pursue. Here we look at the changes as a result of globalization that affect HRM and examine their effect. A fuller discussion of globalization can be found in Chapter 2.

Changes resulting from globalization

- The growth of global business through multinationals and networks of cooperation.
- An increase in competition.
- Organizations now operate in a variety of economic, political, cultural and institutional settings.
- Many organizations must now deal with a distributed, diverse work force in a number of countries.
- With the changing nature of global operations and with the growth of mergers, acquisitions and joint ventures there have been frequent shifts in power and control.
- Accompanying all the above have been job mobility, structural change, downsizing and delayering.

The effect on HRM

- The need to develop policies to manage staff in cross-border situations. Historically, the focus of HR has been on the management of expatriate workers, but this is now just one of many considerations.
- The importance of developing international managers.
- The need to develop policies and practices that operate effectively in different locations to reflect cultural, institutional and legal differences. Variations including trade union membership, local versus expat rates of pay and policies on recruitment and selection will need to be managed.
- The need to understand comparative issues, particularly the why and the how practices may vary between international locations.
- The need to deliver business strategies in a cost-effective way. This may mean transferring jobs to low wage economies. It can also mean investing in employee development to deliver enhanced performance.
- In the case of offshore and outsourced operations HR may be involved in ensuring that employment practices in both subsidiaries and contracted firms conform to certain standards with regard to health and safety, pay and conditions.

Approaches to global HRM

We can identify three generic approaches:

- The **universalist approach** is linked to convergence and notions of best practice. The assumption is that there is a model of HRM that can be applied in all countries. Such approaches tend to be found in those multinationals with a strong, centralized corporate culture, as with HP and IBM. The reality is that even in such firms there tends to be a modification of policy and practice to meet local legal and cultural requirements. In such situations it is likely that senior managers come from the lead organization in the home country.
- The **contextualist approach** deems that the most effective HR policies and practices are those that work best in specific situations. This is a culture-specific approach and echoes the work of Geert Hofstede, described in Chapter 5. He believed that HR practices needed to vary as core values differed between cultures. His main study was IBM, thereby refuting the universalist perspective. An example he gave was that of individual

performance-related pay. He argued that this worked best in Anglo-Saxon cultures displaying individualism, risk taking and masculine characteristics (Hofstede, 1980b). Firms employing the contextualist approach tend to use more local managers in senior positions.

- The **globalist approach** argues for a mix of global and local practices, and that the universalist and contextualist approaches can be mixed to good effect. For example, there can exist a global policy about rewarding staff or about employee welfare. However, the application of such a policy will vary depending on local laws and customs. Brewster et al. (2002) found that the most global activities in common were communication, recruitment and selection, benefits, training and development and performance management, while the most localized ones were employment law, equality and diversity and industrial relations. Brewster et al. (2005) in a study of 64 multinationals conclude that the value of the HR function lies in achieving a balance between centralized, coordinated systems and sensitivity to local needs.

REFLECTION POINT

What have been the main effects on HRM of globalization?

HR and the economy

Edwards and Rees (2006) argue that a strongly performing economy is likely to attract the attention of others to its HR methods. They cite as evidence the post-war dominance of the USA and the diffusion of its HR policies and practices. In the 1980s, the focus turned to Germany and Japan and an interest in commitment and involvement. We see a re-emergence of interest in US methods in the late 1990s as US practices are viewed as more flexible than the embedded systems of Germany and Japan.

There is some evidence to link the fortunes of HR specialists with economic growth. During a period of growth there is an emphasis on recruitment, selection, training and reward policies. In the UK, economic growth in the 1960s led to the growth of trade union activities and a corresponding expansion of the roles of HR specialists. However, there is some evidence for the durability of HR specialists during economic decline as well. Here, there is a focus on HR inputs to restructuring plans and in an emphasis on performance management in the face of increased competition.

The role of the state

The state, operating through government policies and the legal system, has had considerable influence on the HR function through legislation, employment policies concerned with such issues as the supply of labour and education and training, and third-party intervention.

Employment legislation is concerned with the rights and obligations of employers and employees and the conduct of employment relations. The growth in employment law in the 1960–70s, the industrial relations legislation of the 1980s and various EU laws and directives have changed the work of the HR specialist in the UK. Employment legislation has similarly increased in other countries. Much of this legislation affected the day-to-day work of HR managers and some commentators see the expansion of employment law as a vehicle for the increased status of the HR function. Managers, faced with a complex array of new legal provisions, seek expert advice and often turn to the HR specialist as their source. A trend in many countries has been the greater willingness on the part of individuals to use the legislative process to protect their own rights and often to pursue claims against employers.

Most governments try to achieve a stable balance between supply and demand in the labour market through employment policies. This has involved the funding of university courses and training initiatives. Governments have been willing to use **third party intervention** in those industrial disputes they see as damaging to the nation's economy. The UK government currently funds ACAS, set up in 1974, and it was given statutory rights under the Employment Protection Act 1975. ACAS is a state mechanism which attempts to influence the conduct of industrial relations without either party having recourse to the use of law. As we will see later in the chapter, the extent of state intervention in HR matters varies between liberal market economies such as the UK and USA and coordinated market economies, especially Germany.

Technology

In Chapter 4 we examined how technology and, in particular, technical change, affected jobs. Such changes have implications for the HR function including training and retraining, recruitment, selection, payment systems and managing change in general. Historically, technical change has been an issue in industrial relations, as we saw in the News International case study in Chapter 4.

Technical change invariably results in a mismatch between the needs of the firm and the skills of the workforce. Some firms tackle this mismatch by the use of outside contractors, but longer-term cost-effectiveness will probably lie in developing training programmes. Such training focuses not only on the development of skills but upon general workforce orientation towards using technology. In many firms the creation of a more flexible workforce has been identified as a training priority.

The traditional view is that technical change creates problems, largely because trade unions resist change. This resistance is inevitably linked to fears over job losses, deskilling and increased management control. However, certain factors may temper this perspective. Not all technical change is viewed unfavourably and it can come with investment and optimism, and a route to better jobs and higher wages.

The nature of the technology offers some groups of workers more bargaining power than others because they operate and control vital technologies. This has an effect on policies concerning access to retraining and inevitably on payment systems.

Cultural and institutional influences

In this section we will observe differences between the operation of HRM in various countries linked to differences in the cultural and in the economic and political contexts of those countries. In Chapters 3 and 5 we introduced broad differences in economic systems that we identified as Anglo-Saxon, social market and Asian. In Chapter 5 we also looked in some detail at accounts of cultural differences and their impact on business policies and practices. We use the ideas introduced then as a basis for our analysis of HR policies and practices in different countries.

More than most business functions and activities, HR policies and practices are embedded in the social, political, economic, legal and cultural contexts in which they operate. In Case 5.1 we saw how many of Wal-Mart's difficulties operating in Germany were caused by its insistence on employing US practices in a very different cultural and institutional context. Two studies support this position.

REFLECTION POINT

Review the Wal-Mart case study in Chapter 5. What HR issues can you find in this study?

Aycan (2005) linked HR practices with cultural differences drawn from well-known theoretical perspectives. For example, he argued that recruitment and selection criteria varied according to cultural differences. In performance-oriented and universalistic (rule-based) cultures, criteria were based on job knowledge, qualifications and competences. In status-oriented, particularistic (relationship-based) cultures, criteria were more likely to focus on inter-personal skills, social class and age. He also suggested that internal recruitment would more likely be found in high uncertainty avoidance, particularistic cultures. However, his research is based on propositions derived from cultural theory rather than a systematic study of HR practices. It is therefore a starting point for research rather than a plausible explanation in its own right.

Pudelko (2006) carried out an extensive literature survey of theories of culture and of social, economic and political contexts together with an examination of HR in organizations in the USA, Japan and Germany. He concluded that, in general, HR practices conformed to a 'best fit' model with their respective economic and cultural contexts. He found that firms in the USA and Japan displayed very different approaches to HR with Germany somewhere between the two. That is supported by our knowledge of different economic and political systems.

HR in different economic and political systems

In Anglo-Saxon systems, such as in the USA and the UK, there is an emphasis on the free market, job mobility, managerial autonomy and the weakening of trade unions. As a consequence, managements are generally given a greater freedom to respond to a dynamic competitive environment and there is less emphasis on job security. Rates of pay, particularly top management pay, can be higher than in other systems but labour tends to be used as a flexible resource. For example, redundancies are a common way to control costs.

There are differences between the UK and USA. In the UK there has been a greater focus on industrial relations, although with the decline of trade unions this has changed. HR in the UK is also influenced by EU regulations and directives such as those relating to working time and to works councils, although such practices are less embedded in the UK than, for example, in Germany and Sweden. There are, of course, wide variations in practice ranging from fairly sophisticated HR approaches in some multinational companies to an apparent lack of concern for HR issues in other companies.

In social market systems there is typically greater concern for employee welfare and representation, codified in law. In Germany, there is a highly legalized approach to employee and employer rights and duties. Collective bargaining is highly centralized at an industrial level and industrial relations is not a concern for the HR manager. Specialist management functions such as HR play a much smaller role in Germany than elsewhere, a correspondingly higher status being accorded to line management. In Scandinavia, management autonomy is challenged by the presence of strong trade unions and employee rights reflect their disposition towards social equality.

In Asian systems there is an emphasis on welfare provision in the form of housing and sports facilities and upon other mechanisms to cement commitment between the employee and the firm as with the emphasis placed on corporate values and lengthy induction processes in many Japanese and Korean firms. However, there are differences both between and within countries.

In big companies in Japan, HR policies bestow considerable advantages on core employees, including lifetime employment, seniority payments and welfare provisions that are not available to temporary or non-contract workers.

HR as a standardized practice

Despite the differences between these three models, there is some evidence of practices converging. Much of this convergence is attributed to multinationals. In some cases there is standardization based on size and the need for greater centralization and formalization. We return to this theme in our discussion of 'best practice' strategies at the end of this chapter.

Pudelko (2006) found evidence of what he called cross-cultural learning. He found evidence of both Japanese and German firms adopting US-style HR practices. Warner (2002) found evidence of Chinese firms differentiating themselves by adopting western practices and Nguyen (2003) noted similar developments in a study of Vietnamese firms. Such cross-cultural learning was also associated with the interest in Japanese management methods by western companies in the 1980s. For example, many US and UK firms introduced Japanese-style quality circles as a form of employee involvement.

A common European HRM model was investigated as part of a study of practices across Europe (Brewster and Bournois, 1991). The study found considerable variation, particularly between the UK and the rest of Europe, despite a growth of regional policies and legislation in the EU. It would appear that the influence of underlying cultural and institutional systems persists. We may conclude by restating our earlier position, that HR practices more than most activities in the organization tend to be embedded in their social, political, economic and cultural context.

In addition to these contexts, variations in HR can also be found with respect to organizational and strategic influences, to which we now turn.

ORGANIZATIONAL ASPECTS OF HRM

In this section we will view the relationship between organization size and HR activities and focus on the relationship between HRM and other management activities in the organization structure. A theme to emerge in the dealings with management from other functional areas is that of goal conflict. Attempts to resolve such conflict are currently focused upon organizational culture and strategic HRM. We will deal with strategies in more detail in the final section of this chapter.

Organization size

The development of personnel management departments in UK and USA firms during the early part of the 20th century can be attributed to the increasing size of the organization. A control mechanism was needed, particularly for recruitment and payment, giving rise to specialist positions of 'wages officer' and 'labour officer'. Such positions concerned themselves with recruitment, discipline, timekeeping and general administration of the payment system, including the control of bonus payments. Furthermore, the increasing size of the firm has led to increasing specialization within HR itself, although current practice may be reversing that trend.

We have also noted a relationship between the size of the firm and attempts to standardize HR practices in multinational companies.

Organization structure and goals

In terms of the operation and organization of the HR function within organizations, several trends can be seen:

- There is a shift towards strategic inputs and away from operational issues by HR specialists.

- As a consequence, there has been a devolution of some HR responsibilities and practices to line management. This may be linked to an increase in outsourcing as line managers are sometime reluctant to perform HR practices.

At the heart of these issues is the status of the HR function within the organization and its relationship with top management, with line management and with other functional areas. There are ambiguities and potential problems which give rise to goal conflict within the organization:

- HR is a specialist function but its activities such as selection and performance management are carried out by all managers. This is a source of potential conflict between HR and other functional managers particularly those in operations (these are sometimes referred to generically as line managers).

- This conflict is not helped by the difficulties encountered by HR managers in proving their worth to the organization either because of the suspicion of line management towards new techniques or because of the way HR managers organize their work.

- HR specialists generally operate in an advisory capacity, so advice can be rejected or ignored.

- A central feature of many HR activities is the well-being of employees. Yet HR must also make difficult decisions as in making people redundant during a restructuring exercise.

In general, research has focused on case studies where problems have been identified in the relationship between HR and other departments. A classic case was presented by Karen Legge (1978). Her study deals with the conflicts and ambiguities identified above related to what she called 'personnel management'. Legge saw the relationship between HR and line management as one of potential conflict in that the latter had a hazy perception of the personnel department's activities and 'tended to consider them "out of touch" with the kind of problems and constraints line managers face' (Legge, 1978, p. 52). In particular, other managers felt that HR did not identify as closely as they might with the profit goals of the organization. This was a central theme in the development of HRM in the 1980s.

Legge saw a vicious circle operating, as in Figure 13.2. HR was not involved in planning and decision-making, resulting in human resource problems that were left for HR to sort out. Pressure of time and lack of resources led to crisis management resulting in line management having a poor perception of the HR function and hence its non-involvement in decision-making. The circle was reinforced by the failure on the part of some line managers to recognize the need for a specialist role for HR since many HR activities are carried out by all managers. Attempts were made to break free of the circle by HR specialists by adopting specialized techniques based on the behaviourial sciences. These were often rebuffed by a suspicious line management. As a result, Legge saw that many personnel managers 'opt for an easy life' and they concentrated on a more acceptable welfare role.

A theme that runs through the discussion above and the literature of HRM in general is that of HR managers having difficulty in demonstrating their effectiveness and being viewed as acting strategically. We examine this in more detail in the next section.

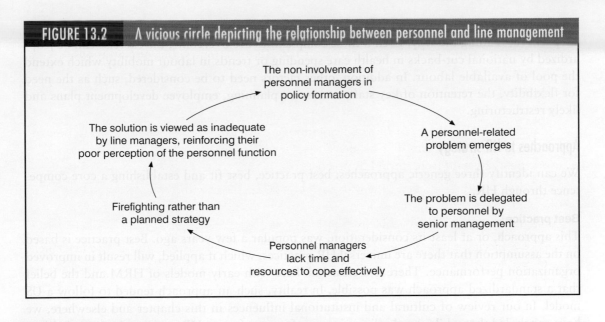

FIGURE 13.2   A vicious circle depicting the relationship between personnel and line management

The non-involvement of
personnel managers in
policy formation

The solution is viewed as inadequate
by line managers, reinforcing their
poor perception of the personnel function

A personnel-related
problem emerges

Firefighting rather than
a planned strategy

The problem is delegated
to personnel by
senior management

Personnel managers
lack time and
resources to cope effectively

HR STRATEGIES

The emergence of HRM in the 1980s emphasized a strategic approach to human resource issues. In this section we examine human resource planning as the basis of strategy, we look at approaches to HR strategy and finally make an attempt to assess the contribution of HR strategy to organizational performance.

Human resource planning

This is a fundamental technique used in most HR departments. The process is concerned with matching future staffing requirements with future staffing availability and involves consideration of both the quantity and the quality of the labour force, including the analysis of such factors as the age profile of the staff. Several techniques have been used, from simple demand–supply models to sophisticated statistical models. The output of a planning exercise should set the guidelines for HR strategies in recruitment, selection, training, retirement and so on. The resulting strategies will vary depending on the relationship of the predicted future demand to predicted future supply.

For example, a firm whose demand for labour exceeds the predicted supply may have to consider changes in its remuneration strategies with a view to attracting more recruits, or investigate the possibilities of introducing technology to replace labour. Where the labour supply exceeds the predicted future demands, plans may have to be formulated for early retirement, redundancy or perhaps looking to marketing strategies to increase the demand for the firm's goods and services. Even where demand and supply are evenly matched, a human resource planning exercise may give management useful insights into the nature of labour utilization and suggest where improvements can be made.

The reality, of course, is much more complex. Such complexities are often the result of long lead-times and other variables over which management has little control. The planning of the supply of future doctors is an exercise that must incorporate projected birth and death rates, take account of the age profile of the nation and examine trends in disease and illness.

Given that the training time for a doctor is at least seven years, allowance must be made for drop-out rates along the way. Even if these complexities are overcome, the exercise can be jeopardized by national cut-backs in health care spending or trends in labour mobility which extend the pool of available labour. In addition, other factors need to be considered, such as the need for flexibility, the retention of key staff, succession planning, employee development plans and likely restructuring.

Approaches to HR strategy

We can identify three generic approaches: best practice, best fit and establishing a core competence through HR.

Best practice

This approach, or at least its consideration, was popular a few years ago. Best practice is based on the assumption that there are universal HR practices, which if applied, will result in improved organization performance. There is a clear link here with early models of HRM and the belief that a standardized approach was possible. In reality, such an approach tended to follow a US model. In our review of cultural and institutional influences in this chapter and elsewhere, we have concluded that while standardization was a feature of some HR practices in some multinationals, in general the most effective HR policies and practices are those that fit the contingencies within which they operate; in other words some kind of 'best fit'.

Best fit

We have already examined the notion of best fit of HR strategy with regard to economic, political, social, legal and cultural factors. This would imply the need for a best fit with external contingencies. There is also a need for a fit with contingencies that are internal to the organization. We can define these in terms of:

- An internal consistency between HR policies and practices themselves. For example, payment policy needs to reflect recruitment and training policies.
- A consistency between HR policies and those of other functions. For example, a change in operations will have an impact on the demand for and utilization of labour.
- A linkage between HR strategy and that of the overall strategy of the organization. This was a key issue in the development of HRM itself.

There are obvious examples where a change in business strategy leads to a corresponding change in the HR strategy. Survival in a recession may depend on either cutting back on operations or developing new areas of operation. In a recession, policies may need to emerge on redundancy, or more flexible ways of working are introduced to cut costs. The development of new products and markets calls for new skills, which may necessitate recruiting staff or retraining employees.

Purcell (1989) argues that different product markets call for variations in HR strategy. A simple way of illustrating this is to use the BCG matrix from Chapter 7. When firms have a cash cow, the emphasis is upon stable, low-cost production to 'milk' the profits. HR policies associated with cash cows are those that ensure stability and continuity and may focus on the need to keep costs to a minimum and use flexible forms of labour force. However, as Purcell points out, the very profitability of cash cows may lead to complacency, such as over-staffing. Where stars and question marks are concerned, the emphasis shifts to operating a more flexible approach. HR priorities become the selection and development of innovative staff and the creation of teams across functional specialisms. The long-term uncertainty associated with both stars and question marks places emphasis upon the management of change. For dogs, the focus turns to cutting losses. This may mean redundancy programmes and it could involve retraining, transfer and even relocation.

REFLECTION POINT

What is the difference between best practice and best fit as far as HR strategies are concerned?

Differentiation through HRM

A problem with best fit with the prevailing business strategy is that HR strategies can only be reactive. Another approach is to use HR strategy to achieve leadership, differentiation and, ultimately, competitive advantage. This has much in common with the strategic model based on the resource-based view of the firm (RBV) and core competence that we introduced in Chapter 8. It could be argued that the key elements that make Southwest Airlines so successful (see Case 8.1) can be copied by competitors. However, what makes them work is the uniqueness of the employment relations and corporate culture.

In the literature considerable attention has been given to high performance work systems (HPWS). Wood sees HPWS as a concept that comes out of high commitment management and high involvement management and offers an alternative to the employment relationship from systems based on control. There is some measure of agreement (Huselid, 1995, Pfeffer, 1998, and Becker and Huselid, 1998) that HPWS comprise:

- Security of employment.
- Rigorous recruitment and selection procedures.
- Self-managed teams and the decentralization of decision-making.
- Relatively high rates of pay tied to performance.
- Extensive development and training based on the needs of the organization.
- Reduced status differences in organizations.
- A specific commitment to employee involvement.
- Widespread sharing of financial and performance information.

The key point that links this to the resource-based view and differentiates it from best practice is that the bundling of these practices into a coherent and effective system is not easy and therefore difficult to imitate. In a survey of 968 firms Huselid (1995) found that the application of HPWS practices resulted in lower labour turnover, higher sales per employee, larger cash flow per employee and a higher stock market value of the organization. He did however claim that the effectiveness was dependent upon employees having the necessary skills, motivation and opportunity to use their skills and abilities (since referred to as the SMO approach). In other words there is some overlap with the best fit approach in that the HPWS needs to be integrated with organizational contingencies such as leadership style, and organization structure.

Effectiveness of HR strategies

In assessing the effectiveness of HR strategies we must first determine what we mean by effectiveness. The majority of approaches to effectiveness take an organizational perspective.

Effectiveness is seen in terms of profit, sales, productivity, share price, employee retention and labour turnover, and so on. There may be an alternative approach which places greater emphasis on the needs of employees in terms of job satisfaction, involvement and in terms of skills and personal development. The stakeholder approach would see effectiveness in terms of meeting the needs of a range of people or groups, including employers, shareholders, employees, unions and customers. However, as we have seen earlier in this book, meeting the conflicting needs of all stakeholders at the same time is very difficult.

It is therefore no surprise that studies of HR effectiveness have focused on variables such as profit and productivity and share value, partly because these are measurable but partly because they address the age-old concern of HR managers being able to prove their worth. Studies of effectiveness seem to have become the dominant HRM debate, more especially studies linked to the effectiveness of high performance work systems (HPWS). In this area there have been several meta-studies (summaries and conclusions about a range of research findings in a given area). More notable meta-studies have been offered by Boselie et al. (2005), Combs et al. (2006) and Jiang et al. (2012).

The majority of studies point to a strong relationship between HR practices and measures of financial and operational performance as well as with employee retention and reduced turnover. There are also strong links established between HPWS and performance. Guest (2011) argues that the majority of studies show evidence of association between HR practices and performance but not causation. Several writers have spoken about a 'black box' that represents a set of assumptions we make about the relationship between HR and performance without knowing exactly what the mechanisms are that make it work.

Numerous authors ... call for a better understanding of the black box between HR practices and performance.

(Wright and McMahan, 2011, p. 293)

As with many management practices, establishing a link with performance is difficult due to the presence of so many variables which may affect the outcomes. Guest et al. (2000) identified a further problem. They interviewed 462 chief executives and 610 HR managers in UK companies. Their conclusions were as follows:

- Most chief executives recognized the link between HR practices and performance but still failed to prioritize HR issues.
- There was disagreement between the chief executives and HR people as to which practices were the most significant.
- Both chief executives and HR managers rated the performance of the typical HR department as low.
- The research identified effective practices from other studies. Most organizations failed to make use of these practices. In some ways these results are similar to the findings of Legge (1978) about the role and status of HR managers some 30 years earlier.

The mixed findings of the various studies raise doubts about our current ability to measure the contribution of HR and hence show links between HR strategy and organization performance and most of the articles we have cited identify the need for more research.

CASE 13.1   BRITISH AIRWAYS

The beginnings

British Airways was formed in 1972 through a merger between BEA and BOAC. It possessed an extensive route network, an exceptionally good safety record, and, in Heathrow, an enviable operating base within easy reach of London. The company had high levels of union membership across all types of employee.

The first decade of operation was typified by problems and in 1982 the company reported losses of £100 million. The problems were over-staffing, a lack of operating efficiency compared with its competitors, industrial disputes and a poor image with the travelling public. Part of the problem was attributed to a bureaucratic organizational structure and decision-making, typical of many nationalized industries. In BA's case, the problem was compounded by a hierarchical structure that reflected the armed forces rather than a business operating in a fast-changing environment. By the 1980s, the airline business was more competitive than ever and new entrants such as Virgin had quickly developed favourable reputations based upon competitive pricing and quality service.

Privatization and culture change

In 1983, the government had announced its intentions to de-nationalize the airline and the recently appointed chairman and chief executive were given a clear message that the company had to be made commercially viable. Privatization eventually took place in 1987.

The workforce was cut by some 20 000 and certain routes were withdrawn. Greater attention was paid to marketing and organizational changes, including a reduction in hierarchical levels and a reduced emphasis of status differences and job titles. In 1983, the company launched a culture change initiative, which used as its focus customer care. This was based on research into effective behaviour in the caring professions and the experience of SAS (Scandinavian Airlines) in implementing a similar programme. British Airways enlisted the help of the same consultants as those involved in the SAS project.

Two training initiatives were launched. The 'Putting People First' campaign was aimed, initially, at employees in direct contact with the general public, such as check-in staff and cabin crew, although it was extended to other groups as well. A 'Managing People First' campaign was aimed at middle and senior management. Both campaigns were based on customer perceptions that portrayed BA as bureaucratic and saw its staff, while competent, as aloof and uncaring. The campaigns were launched on the assumptions that people performed best when given the maximum support by their peers and, most importantly, by their supervisors, and also when given maximum involvement and discretion in solving problems. Human resources staff were given training in organization change by the consultants and much of the responsibility for HR issues was passed to line management.

Putting People First training confronted staff in groups with the negative image of BA held by its customers and encouraged employees to suggest ways of changing it. Role play was also used through which staff were encouraged to use their initiative to resolve customer problems, such as flight delays and lost luggage. Presentations were given of what various people and groups in the organization did each day in an attempt to break down barriers and build a greater sense of identity. An important part of the process was the involvement of the chief executive, Colin Marshall, who was present for at least part of the training sessions.

Managing People First was a five-day residential programme for managers. It comprised three elements: the encouragement of managers to adopt a more visible, open and dynamic style and an attempt to get managers to link their department's goals with the company's objectives. At the same time, a management appraisal scheme was launched and tied in to an individual reward system with both performance-related pay and share options.

In 1988, the year following privatization, profits of £320 million were reported by BA. Customer feedback was good and the airline won awards for its customer service in the business press. The feedback from employees was equally encouraging. Measured in terms of profitability and customer and employee satisfaction, the change programme was successful.

(Continued)

CASE 13.1 (Continued)

Into the 1990s

At the start of the 1990s the airline industry was hit by both a recession and the impact of the first Gulf War. BA experienced further financial problems by the mid-1990s and embarked on cost-cutting exercises in the light of falling demand, especially for business-class seats. The Boeing 777 was introduced on long-haul flights instead of the more expensive 747. In response to the threat offered by low-cost airlines BA introduced 'Go' – its own low-cost service as a wholly-owned subsidiary. The initiative was a failure and short-lived.

The late 1990s saw a sharp fall in the share price and a worsening of relations with both cabin crew and pilots. In 1999, the company decided to strengthen its message of earlier years in an attempt to win the hearts and minds, not only of its employees, but of its customers as well. The new initiative was called, not surprisingly, 'Putting People First Again'.

Into the new millennium

Problems continued to hamper the company. There was increased competition in an industry that had too many carriers. Short-haul routes were under attack from budget carriers such as easyJet, Ryanair and Air Berlin. All airlines had suffered as a result of the terrorist attacks on New York on 11 September 2001 and the war with Iraq in 2003.

In 2005, BA appointed Willie Walsh as chief executive. He previously ran the Irish carrier Aer Lingus, where he had acquired a reputation for cost control. The company continued to shed labour in response to rising costs and falling profits. This became urgent in 2006 when the company announced a deficit on its final salary pension scheme of over £2 billion. This was higher than the market value of the company. In the face of this pensions crisis, BA announced proposals to end the final salary pension scheme for new recruits and to increase the retirement age for pilots and all staff to 60 and eventually to 65. These proposals became a source of further unrest and strike threats. Pilots had hitherto enjoyed generous pensions at a compulsory retirement age of 55. Around the same period, there were short strikes or threatened strikes over pay, pensions, sick leave policy and proposals to launch a subsidiary airline with pilots recruited from elsewhere and paid lower salaries than BA pilots. Even a strike that was

threatened but did not take place affected ticket sales and it was estimated that industrial disputes had cost the company £200 million since 2000.

However, in 2008, the company announced a £922 million profit, 45 per cent up on the previous year. Much of the increase was due to cuts in routes and services, a reduction in staffing costs and an increase in transatlantic business travel. Even as the profits were announced BA was preparing for a year of austerity based on predicted increases in fuel prices.

Fears for the financial performance of the company in 2008–09 were well-founded. BA announced annual losses of £401 million, the highest since privatization. The causes were identified as high fuel prices, the collapse of business travel as a result of the credit crunch and the banking crisis, and a weak pound against other currencies, notably the US dollar and the euro. More cuts were planned along with a freeze on pay rises and on management bonuses.

The 2010 cabin crew strike and the aftermath

In March 2010 cabin crew began a 3-day strike over issues that were first announced by BA management late in 2009. A planned strike over the Christmas period was halted by a High Court injunction. The key issues were a planned reduction of cabin crew staff of 1700, initially by voluntary redundancy; a reduction of the cabin crew on each flight on some routes; pay to be frozen for two years; and new recruits to cabin crew jobs would be hired on less favourable terms and conditions than existing staff. The changes were proposed by management in light of the recession following the 2008 banking crisis, a loss of £342 million in the last 9 months of 2009 and a potential pension fund deficit of £3.7 billion. Cabin crew operating out of London Gatwick were already on lower rates of pay than those at Heathrow and BA were aware that their Heathrow staff were on much higher rates of pay than in some rival airlines and enjoyed a basic pay that was almost twice that paid by Virgin Atlantic.

The strike continued as a series of 3- and then 5-day strikes over a period of almost 16 months and a total of 22 days of strike action. This was the first major dispute involving BA cabin crew for over 10 years and each strike ballot was strongly supported by union members with around 80 per cent in

CASE 13.1   (Continued)

favour. The strike was typified by hostile bargaining stances and bad feeling between management and unions. This was especially true between CEO Willie Walsh and the joint general secretaries of UNITE, Tony Woodley and Derek Simpson. In addition the courts were involved, starting with the prevention of the 2009 action on account of voting irregularities.

CEO Walsh saw the union as a continuous obstacle to BA achieving its operational and financial performance targets. The unions were accused of leaking information to the press that resulted in passenger cancellations and a fall in the share price. Union activists were accused of over-aggressive tactics and of disrupting meetings. As a reaction to the first strike action, management withdrew staff travel privileges with immediate effect for those on strike. Such travel privileges are seen as a key perk of the job and staff can obtain a 90 per cent discount on all flights for themselves and nominated family and friends. For some staff from France and Spain it was not just a perk but a means by which they got to work. In addition, management had organized 21-day training courses for ground staff and a 4-day course for pilots, so they could replace cabin crew on strike. Management also took the first steps to create a separate cabin crew fleet based on lower wages and less favourable terms and conditions.

For its part, the union leadership had a lack of trust in BA management and accused them of failing to negotiate and using bullying tactics. The union saw the withdrawal of staff travel privileges and organizing fast-track training courses for replacement cabin crew as tantamount to 'declaring war'. During the early part of the dispute, UNITE sent a letter to the airline's major shareholders claiming that they 'have been thwarted by a management that is ... putting ego and machismo ahead of your interests as investors...and playing fast and loose with the airline's future'.

The dispute ended in June 2011. The union agreed to accept staff cuts and BA restored staff travel privileges and granted a pay award of 7.5 per cent over 2 years. There was also agreement that those staff that had been dismissed or disciplined during the dispute could have their cases dealt with by ACAS. The agreement followed a change in leadership in both BA and the union. Willie Walsh had moved to head BA's parent company International Airlines Group (IAG) and was replaced by Keith Williams. Len McCluskey replaced Woodley and Simpson at UNITE. An official statement was made by BA.

The skills and professionalism of British Airways cabin crew are second to none, and we are delighted this dispute is behind us.
CEO Williams stated.

One of the things we need to do is rebuild the brand image, which inevitably suffers during a protracted dispute.

At the end of 2010 BA reported record losses of £531 million and that the strike was responsible for a fall in revenue of £1 billion. However in the two years following the strike, the airline moved into profit. During the dispute BA merged with Iberia, the Spanish Airline, to form International Airlines Group (IAG), although BA was much the stronger partner financially. In 2012 IAG acquired BMI from Lufthansa and the Spanish low-cost carrier Vueling. While Vueling was kept as a separate brand, BMI was integrated into the BA fleet.

During the strike BA had pushed ahead with the recruitment of an entirely new group of cabin crew. There was a clear policy of hiring younger people and the interview process included questions on attitudes to trade union membership. An initial fleet of 1250 were hired (approximately 10 per cent of all BA cabin crew). Their initial basic wage was around 50 per cent of that paid to existing Heathrow-based cabin crew and the terms and conditions included less stop-over time on international flights and less generous expense allowances. The new crew were, however, offered discounted staff travel privileges. The new recruits always flew on separate planes to the 'old' cabin crew and were generally allocated to routes that had traditionally been associated with the most generous stop-over times and expense allowances.

In June 2014 there was a threat of strike action by the new cabin crew fleet, who had initially rejected a pay offer based on the inflation rate and were seeking a reduction in the pay gap between themselves and the 'old guard' cabin crew. They further claimed that they were earning less than rates paid to staff on Ryanair and easyJet and that some employees were claiming tax credits (state benefits paid to workers on low income).

(Continued)

CASE 13.1   (*Continued*)

Questions

1 What aspects of HR are exhibited in this case?

2 What were the factors which led BA to introduce 'Putting People First' and related programmes?

3 How do we know that such initiatives were successful? What other factors might we need to consider?

4 To what do you attribute the causes of the problems experienced by BA since 1990?

5 What HR strategies could the company consider to tackle these problems?

6 Compare and contrast the culture change initiatives of the early 1980s with the cabin crew dispute of 2010–11 and subsequent company strategies.

SUMMARY

- Human resource management emerged as a concept in the 1980s, initially in the USA as a more strategic approach to what was formerly known as personnel management.

- The role is performed in a number of ways and is particularly influenced by the size of the organization. In large organizations there are specialist departments, but the role is performed to some extent by all managers, which is a source of potential conflict. In recent years, there has been a large growth of outsourcing in HRM.

- We can identify four overlapping activities: employee resourcing, employee development, pay and performance issues, and employment relations.

- Employee resourcing involves processes of recruitment and development using reliable and valid methods that provide equal opportunities. Equal opportunities and diversity management are aspects of all HR activities.

- Employee development involves processes concerned with the training and development of all employees although a recent focus has been on management and leadership.

- Several factors determine pay and people's pay and reward can be made up of many elements, including performance related pay and fringe benefits. Performance management has become a consideration in many organizations with links to employee development and the organizations' strategic objectives.

- More than most activities, HRM is shaped by the environment in which it operates. In particular, policies and practices are influenced by the economic, political, legal, social and cultural context in which they operate.

- An issue in the operation of HR practices is the relationship with other managers and the status of HRM in the organizations. These issues are frequently a source of tension.

- HR strategies are influenced by the same contexts and by the strategic objectives of the organization, although there are difficulties in demonstrating the contribution of HR strategies to organization success criteria.

DISCUSSION QUESTIONS

1 What is HRM and what is its contribution to the organization? What does Ulrich mean by 'HR as a business partner'?

2 Is there a case for the elimination of HR specialists, so that the function can be performed by all managers?

3 Why should managers be concerned with issues of equality and diversity?

4 How would you set about developing a training programme for: (a) a newly appointed operations manager; (b) a legal secretary in a busy law practice; and (c) a university lecturer?

5 What factors determine pay and which, if any, are more significant than others?

6 What are the main difficulties with effective performance management?

7 How are HR policies and practices influenced by cultural differences?

8 What are the factors in an HR strategy for: (a) a small, expanding computer software developer; (b) a medium-sized manufacturer of electrical components for the car industry; and (c) a new university? What issues emerge in each case?

9 What are high performance work systems (HPWS) and in what ways can they enhance the performance of organizations?

10 What are the problems involved in demonstrating the effectiveness of HRM strategies?

FURTHER READING

An excellent source of current thinking and research in HRM can be found in:

Bach, S. and Edwards, M.R. (eds) (2013) *Managing Human Resources: Human Resource Management in Transition*, 5th edn, Blackwell: Oxford.

Current textbooks with an excellent coverage are:

Bratton, J. and Gold, J. (2012), *Human Resource Management: Theory and Practice*, 5th edn, Palgrave Macmillan: Basingstoke.
Claydon, T. and Beardwell, J. (2010) *Human Resource Management: A Contemporary Approach*, 6th edn, FT Prentice Hall: Harlow.
McKenna, E. and Beech, N. (2013) *Human Resource Management: A Concise Analysis*, 3rd edn, FT Prentice Hall: Harlow.

A good coverage of international issues can be found in:

Edwards, T. and Rees, C. (2010) *International Human Resource Management: Globalization, National Systems and Multinational Companies*, 2nd edn, FT Prentice Hall: Harlow.

A still useful account of role conflict involving HR specialists is available in:

Legge, K. (1978) *Power, Innovation and Problem-solving in Personnel Management*, McGraw-Hill: London.

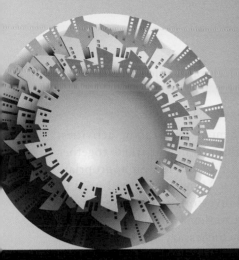

FINANCE AND ACCOUNTING

14

LEARNING OBJECTIVES At the end of this chapter you should be able to:

- Outline the contribution of finance and accounting to business decisions.
- Distinguish between the types of funding for business activities and assess their relevance.
- Identify and explain the contribution of management accounting to business decisions.
- Identify the types of financial report and explain their value to business decisions and stakeholders.
- Identify the growth of interest in corporate governance and the role of accounting in this process.
- Identify differences in accounting practice around the world and offer a limited explanation.
- Assess the effect of organization size and structure on accounting practices.
- Describe the limitations of accounting information in its contribution to strategy.

INTRODUCTION

In this chapter we examine the role played by the finance and accounting function in the operation of a business. We identify the following functions:

- The raising of funds or **financial management**.

- The contribution of accounting to management control and decision-making, often referred to as **management accounting**.
- The function of **financial reporting** sometimes known as financial accounting.

We show these three elements in Figure 14.1, and portray them as overlapping activities. For example, a business that decides on a strategy of expansion into new markets together with investment in new process technologies will need to base the decision on appropriate forecasts and investment calculations (management accounting). Management will need to present accounting information to a bank or another potential investor (financial reporting) to persuade them to back not only the plans for expansion but to demonstrate the financial health of the business. If all is well the company will obtain the necessary capital (financial management).

Accounting procedures and processes are very much a product of the organization and wider environments in the way that they operate. In most countries, accounting information plays a vital role in corporate governance. We will examine the economic, legal and social influences on the finance and accounting function, and examine variations resulting from the size of the organization, ownership patterns and organization structure. We shall also examine the accounting practices of large multi-divisional companies by examining procedures for cost allocation and transfer pricing. We end the chapter by giving an overview on the contribution of finance and accounting strategies to overall management strategy.

Throughout this chapter it is the intention to present accounting not as a series of technical calculations but as a management function that is influenced by those who prepare and use accounting information. For example, the determination and disclosure of profit levels will be guided by regulations governing accounting practice. It may also be influenced by the wish to minimize liability for tax and the relationship with stakeholders, including employees and shareholders. Budgets are determined by management to guide activities in accordance with plans. The process of budget setting and resource allocation is, in many organizations, a product of organizational politics, power and influence.

It is not our intention to give an introduction to book-keeping and accounting techniques. Introductory books that students may consult are recommended at the end of this chapter. We shall begin our examination by looking at the activities depicted in Figure 14.1.

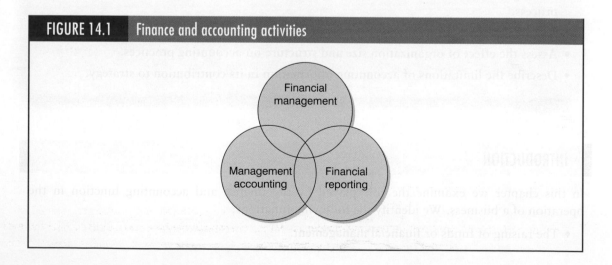

FIGURE 14.1   Finance and accounting activities

FINANCIAL MANAGEMENT

Financial management is concerned with raising capital to finance an organization's operations and with ensuring that a company can generate sufficient revenue to cover the cost of raising this finance. That cost may be in the form of interest rates payable to banks or dividend paid out to shareholders. There is a clear overlap with management accounting in that the funds must be managed by putting them to the most effective use. For example, investments must be carefully appraised. We may identify four sources of finance: share capital, loan capital, internal funding and the state.

Many factors influence the source of finance. The attitude of management to risk may be an important factor. A cautious manager may wish to limit the extent of bank borrowing at all costs. The extent to which internal funds can be made available depends on the ability of management to satisfy its shareholders through paying dividends. There are also differences in the funding of activities between large and small firms, a point we shall return to later.

KEY CONCEPT 14.1   FINANCIAL MANAGEMENT

Financial management is a part of the finance and accounting function that is concerned with the financing of an organization's activities. Finance is normally raised through share capital, loan capital, state finance or through internally generated funds.

Share capital

The issue of shares is a means whereby capital can be raised by devolving ownership of a company to shareholders. In return for their investment, shareholders become part-owners of the company and are entitled to a payment each year in proportion to the number of shares held, and, usually, in proportion to the firm's profit levels. Such payments are known as dividend. As noted in Chapter 6, this process, resulting from legal changes in most industrial countries in the 19th century, enabled firms to get much bigger. The creation of the limited liability company not only raised finance in this way but reduced the risk for individuals, who could not be held personally responsible for financial losses incurred by the firm.

KEY CONCEPT 14.2   SHARE CAPITAL

Share capital is funding raised through the issue of shares offering shareholders part ownership in the firm and an annual payment in the form of dividend. Dividend is usually paid in direct proportion to the amount of profit after tax. Shares are mostly a source of finance for the firm only at the time of the initial share issue. Thereafter, shares may be bought and sold on the stock market with no capital accruing to the organization. The two main types of share are preference shares and ordinary shares.

Three types of share capital are:

- **Preference shares** attract a fixed rate of dividend, usually payable twice a year. Such agreed dividend must be paid irrespective of the financial performance of the company but, in times of hardship, payment may be deferred until such time as it can be afforded by the company. In this case, the shares are known as cumulative preference shares, since the dividend accumulates until it is paid. Preference shareholders have a preference over other shareholders when assets are sold in cases of liquidation.

- **Ordinary shares** form the majority of all share capital. Owners of ordinary shares do not receive a guaranteed dividend, but they are normally entitled to a share of the profits after deductions for tax and payment to preference shareholders. There are two types of ordinary share, those with voting rights and those without. However, non-voting shares are becoming rare and several companies have changed the status of their non-voting shares to give the owners voting rights. Ordinary shareholders can vote to elect the directors of the company.

- **Golden shares** are retained by governments in the case of privatization issues. The retention is to protect the interests of the public and to prevent a hostile takeover. Such shares have accompanied privatization in the UK and in other countries, including the transitional economies of Eastern Europe. To achieve a measure of continued government control, limits may be placed on the number of shares any private investor may hold. For example, when it was privatized no one shareholder was allowed to own more than 15 per cent of the BAA, the company formed from the government-owned British Airports Authority. Such restrictions and even the government ownership of shares last only for a limited number of years. Golden shares in BAA were eventually sold and in 2006 BAA was bought by a consortium led by the Spanish construction company Ferrovial. This led to BAA's delisting from the London Stock Exchange.

The main source of finance from shares comes in the form of new share issues. However, relatively little finance comes from share capital in most countries. There are exceptions. For example, venture capital is important in financing small firms. Overall, however, shares play a minor role in the raising of funds and evidence suggests that where new share issues do play a part, the money is spent not on investing in current activities, but to fund acquisitions and, in recent years, in attempts to save banks from collapse. In the case of the Royal Bank of Scotland, the issue of new shares to shore up an ailing balance sheet simply caused the share price of the company to fall sharply.

Stock markets were created to encourage potential investors to finance businesses over which they had no direct control, yet for the majority it is simply a secondary market in which shares are bought and sold by investors, with no funding activity involved. A great deal of stock market activity revolves around the dealings of financial intermediaries. We have discussed their role alongside more general issues relating to the separation of ownership and control in Chapter 6. While funding and share trading are separate activities, those holding large numbers of shares can influence management decision-making in that, if sufficient numbers of shares are traded, the company itself is traded. Managements tend to be aware that new owners may have different agendas from those of their predecessors.

REFLECTION POINT

How important is share capital in the financing of organizations?

Loan capital

This is a riskier form of financing than share capital. With share capital, dividend payment can be deferred and the capital itself does not have to be paid back except when the company is liquidated. With nearly all forms of loan capital, interest must be paid on due dates and some interest charges can be high. The usefulness of loan capital depends on the rate of interest, the time required for repayment and the security that needs to be offered. There are many types of loan financing and we examine a selection below.

Debentures are negotiable instruments that can be bought and sold on the stock market. They are issued in return for loans secured on the fixed assets of a company. The advantage of debentures over shares is that interest paid can be offset against tax, whereas this is not the case for share dividend.

Bank borrowing is more common than raising finance through share issues, but its use varies between countries. On the whole, UK banks are less willing to lend and less willing to take a role in the management of business activities than their counterparts in other countries. Banks play a much greater and more integrated role in coordinated market economies such as France, Japan and Germany. In Germany, lending terms have traditionally been favourable to industrial borrowers as far as both interest rates and the length of the pay-back period are concerned. In liberal market systems such as those of the UK and USA, banks are institutional investors and are likely to sell their shares when things go wrong. Inadvertently, through their activities on the stock market, banks may weaken the financial position of a company, which, in turn, can encourage a takeover bid.

In the UK, banks have become conscious of their poor image as far as investment is concerned and all the high street banks engaged in costly advertising and publicity campaigns to attract the business borrower. Managers, especially in the UK, have been suspicious of high interest rates and control ceded to banks when borrowing large amounts. The banking crisis of 2008–09 changed the picture for bank borrowing, not just in the UK but elsewhere. Interest rates had fallen but banks became reluctant to lend.

Overdrafts are used by many businesses as a source of loan capital and many firms have permanent or semi-permanent overdraft arrangements with a bank. Many firms are only able to operate through a permanent overdraft.

Leasing is a form of loan capital in that the firm will acquire assets it has not bought, but leased from another firm. Company cars, security systems and photocopiers are often acquired in this way. Leasing agreements usually provide other benefits such as service agreements or replacement after so many years or in the case of a breakdown. Leasing has become popular for many items, although the tax advantages vary in different countries and in the UK tax advantages have been reduced.

Factoring is a means of raising capital. A factoring company will buy debts owing to a firm at some 70–80 per cent of the invoice value. While money is lost on the value of the invoice, this can be a useful way of improving cash flow quickly.

Trade credit is a form of loan capital in that payment is delayed for an agreed period, thus assisting cash flow.

KEY CONCEPT 14.3   LOAN CAPITAL

Loan capital is raised by borrowing money from a third party and can take many forms. Forms of loan capital include loans from banks or other financial institutions, debentures, overdrafts, factoring, leasing and trade credit. Loan capital carries more risks than other forms of financing in that interest must be paid and, with most types of loan credit, the capital must be paid back within a stated period of time.

Other forms of financing

Internal funding is used by most private companies in developed industrial nations. For existing firms, as much as 90 per cent of funding is generated internally in the USA and UK, with around 70 per cent in Germany and Japan (Corbett and Jenkinson, 1997). The position has not changed. Internal finance comes mainly from the redistribution of profits, although funding can be raised through the sale of assets. Management often prefers to finance their businesses internally. The main factor is the fear that the involvement of banks and shareholders will weaken their control of the company. This is certainly the case as far as bank borrowing is concerned, but less so for shareholders. However, as we saw in Chapter 6, institutional investors can influence management decisions. The shareholding route may be especially resisted by small business owners fearing a diminution of their control over the business.

State funding plays a relatively minor role in the funding of business in most countries. China is a major exception with its state controlled economy, but even here there has been a significant growth of private equity firms and equity joint ventures with foreign companies (see Chapter 3 for more detail on changes in the Chinese economy). The liberalization of many economies has led to a shift away from state funding. The privatization of many state enterprises in the UK in the 1980s and 1990s saw almost a complete withdrawal of state funding. In EU countries, governments are restricted in funding companies because this is considered a form of unfair competition. (See Chapters 3 and 10 for a further discussion of such issues). Although many governments have reduced or even stopped the direct funding of business, indirect funding still plays a role. Japanese firms, such as Nissan, have benefited from government assistance in their establishment of UK bases. In Singapore, the government has pursued a policy of providing infrastructure and offering tax advantages to attract leading high-tech companies.

REFLECTION POINT

What are the respective advantages of loan capital and internal funding as methods of financing an organization?

MANAGEMENT ACCOUNTING

Management accounting is the application of accounting techniques to provide management with the information to assist in planning and control. There is an overlap with financial management in that management accounting is concerned with the use of funds, and with financial reporting in that management accounting uses the data collected as a basis for its calculations.

KEY CONCEPT 14.4   MANAGEMENT ACCOUNTING

Management accounting is concerned with the planning, coordination and control of funds. It involves such activities as budgeting, costing, investment appraisal and the management of cash flows. Through such activities, management is provided with necessary information to assist in making decisions.

In terms of planning, management accounting helps formulate plans for other functional areas. For example, an assessment of future labour costs will assist human resource planning. Predictions of the future cost of raw materials will help in devising appropriate purchasing strategies and, where predicted costs are high, may even stimulate the development of products using other materials. An important contribution to the planning process is the assistance offered by management accounting techniques of investment appraisal in selecting the most appropriate course of action from a range of options. Such techniques are more valuable as environments become increasingly complex.

Management accounting plays a vital role in the wider process of management control. It enables clear parameters to be set in the form of budgets and represents a method by which many problems can be sensed and measured. It is especially useful as a control tool for three reasons. First, the data produced offer management one of the few methods of quantifying the effect of their decisions and of the organization's operations. Second, management accounting integrates the information from all the activities of the business and enables management to view operations as a whole. Third, it deals with the control of funds that are essential to an organization's survival.

We deal with five aspects of management accounting. These are budgeting, cost accounting, investment appraisal, the management of cash flows, and the contribution of the management accountant to management decisions. There is considerable overlap between these categories. For example, the control of assets would inevitably involve budgetary control, and the contribution to general management decisions would include all the other categories. Management accounting is central to strategic planning and many of the issues reappear when we discuss strategy at the end of this chapter. For the moment we examine each of the categories in turn.

Budgeting and budgetary control

A budget is a quantitative statement of expectations concerning the allocation of resources and performance. The two aspects of budgeting are the establishment of standards and the setting up of mechanisms to measure and control performance. As a result, budgeting has a central position in the design of most management and accounting information systems.

KEY CONCEPT 14.5 BUDGETING

Budgets are devices for planning and control. They establish standards to be attained, including those for income and expenditure and mechanisms through which activities can be measured against the standards. Budgeting is a means of allocating funds and resources, of delegating authority and of motivating employees and is, above all, a vital control of all activities.

Budgets are used in many ways: to allocate funds and supplies, as a means of delegating management authority, as targets to motivate employees, and as a means of control of both spending and performance. For example, a university allocates funds to each department designated as a cost centre. The allocation varies according to the size of the department and the nature of its work. Medical schools by the nature of their work and the size of external funding will attract a large slice of any university budget. Science and engineering departments may get a large capital expenditure budget to purchase equipment. Budgets are allocated under headings such as staffing, research, equipment, office supplies, library purchases and the funding of conferences for staff. Such a mechanism serves two main purposes. First, it attempts to ensure that expenditure keeps within defined limits. Second, it spreads the complex task of managing this expenditure by delegating to department heads.

Budgets are normally based on historic information, usually last year's budget. In a highly bureaucratic organization, resistant to change, this can cause difficulties when the needs of organization members change, or in dynamic environments. In such cases, changes may not be represented in budget allocation, which is based on out-of-date information.

In all organizations there are often difficulties in changing budget allocations. This is because budgeting is a bargaining process dealing with the allocation of scarce resources. Those with most to lose have a vested interest in maintaining the status quo. It is for this reason that attention has focused on the behavioural aspects of budgeting. The bargaining process can be useful in that it can force management to confront long-held assumptions and face up to underlying tensions that affect decision-making. However, there is a danger that conflict will be dysfunctional. This is especially true where budgeting in the form of targets is used as a control device, and more so where it forms the basis of the organization's reward system. In this case, and also where scarce resources are at stake, there may be a temptation for managers to distort information to place both them and their departments in the most favourable light.

Budgeting is therefore inseparable from the process of organizational politics and the way the organization is structured. In many cases this process has been acknowledged and attempts have been made to introduce some form of participation or, at the very least, consultation in the budget planning process.

REFLECTION POINT

What are the advantages and disadvantages of participatory budgeting?

Cost accounting

Cost accounting involves the analysis and allocation of costs. In large organizations this can be a complex process involving paper transactions between different units, especially in firms with many divisions. We return to this aspect when we discuss the influence of organization structure on accounting procedures. The nature of costs varies considerably, but most can be classified as fixed or variable and direct or indirect.

KEY CONCEPT 14.6   COSTING

Costing is the means by which the costs of producing goods and services are calculated. It is therefore an important ingredient of pricing. Some costs, such as those associated with bought-in raw materials and components, are relatively easy to ascribe to particular goods and services. Others, such as rent, labour or the costs of providing a prestigious head office, are more difficult to relate to specific items. As a result, costs are defined as fixed, variable, direct and indirect. Several costing techniques, such as absorption costing and activity-based costing, have been developed to apportion such indirect costs.

- **Fixed costs** are costs, such as rents, that are unaffected by the level of activity.
- **Variable costs** change in direct proportion to the level of activity. For example, the amount of raw materials used by a manufacturer will vary with the intensity of production. The amount of paint used by a decorator will vary with the size of the rooms to be painted.

- **Direct costs** are those that can be linked directly to a specific product or activity. Variable costs are generally direct costs.
- **Indirect costs** are those that cannot be linked directly to a specific product or activity and are generally therefore fixed costs. These are sometimes referred to as overhead costs and usually relate to more general overheads such as labour, heating, lighting and so on and are difficult to allot to a particular product or activity.

There are, of course, costs that are semi-variable. The cost of labour is generally fixed but can vary with the level of activity, as when additional work is required to complete a job. Similarly, ventilation, heating and lighting, while considered overheads, can and do vary with the level of activity. Some costs, such as wages, are highly detailed, while others, such as expenditure on hospitality, can be relatively vague.

Absorption costing is the traditional method for sharing out fixed and indirect costs across the organization. Here, costs are allocated to cost centres in the organization on the basis of some formula, such as the size of the cost centre. In this way, larger departments will pay more towards overheads than small departments.

Activity-based costing has replaced absorption costing in many organizations. This form of costing method focuses on those activities that drive the costs in a particular product or activity. It is reckoned to be a more realistic method for apportioning costs, especially in more advanced technological systems where indirect costs are much more significant than direct costs.

Activity-based costing is a technique that challenges traditional cost accounting methods. In many manufacturing organizations, technological and competitive changes are taking place, which are challenging the basis of historical costs, and management needs to devise new methods. These changes include the introduction of manufacturing technology to reduce the cost of production, and a renewed emphasis is placed upon improving quality, increasing operating efficiency and reducing the uncertainty of materials and components supply.

REFLECTION POINT

What elements would you consider in identifying the cost of a university course?

Investment appraisal

Capital investment involves the commitment of funds now with the expectation of acceptable earnings in the future. Such decisions are made about the purchase or renting of new or additional premises, investment in equipment, the development of a new product, or even the acquisition of another business. A careful appraisal of such investments is necessary owing to the large sums involved and the effect such investments may have on the future viability of the company. Investment appraisal methods include pay-back, rate of return, net present value (NPV) and yield.

KEY CONCEPT 14.7   INVESTMENT APPRAISAL

Investment appraisal is the process of calculating whether an investment is cost-effective in the short, medium or long term. Such appraisals can relate to the acquisition of another firm, the development of a new product or the purchase of equipment. A commonly used technique is net present value (NPV).

NPV is a popular method because it estimates future returns on investment, but assesses them on current values. Management is therefore able to make a more informed judgement. Despite the popularity and frequency of their use, NPV calculations are not without problems. They are difficult to use for long-term investments without management making some big assumptions about the future behaviour of markets and the future costs of raw materials. The more assumptions that have to be made, the less accurate the forecasts are likely to be. A problem associated with this is that strong management commitment to a particular investment project may result in a self-fulfilling NPV calculation. The figures are simply made to work to justify the decision.

The management of cash flow

Cash flow is concerned with the movement of cash into and out of the organization. This is an important activity since the firm needs to ensure that it has sufficient cash to cover current expenditure. Many small firms find the most severe problems occur in managing cash flows. A business start-up has a considerable cash outflow to begin with and it may be some time before sufficient revenue is established to cover these initial costs. Several businesses have ceased trading with seemingly healthy order books, simply because they have insufficient incoming cash to pay bank interest charges and so are unable to stay in business and capitalize on their orders.

KEY CONCEPT 14.8	CASH FLOWS

> Cash which flows in and out of a firm is vital to its survival. Without adequate cash flows a firm may have insufficient funds to pay its bills and may cease to trade, even though it may possess a high-quality product and a healthy order book.

Cash-flow management can be particularly difficult in times of high inflation, when there is a danger that profits become absorbed by escalating costs. Some firms also experience difficulties in expanding economies. In such situations there is a temptation to turn profit not into cash but into new investments, by budgeting against future profits. For example, a firm could invest in equipment on the basis of forecasts that predict market growth. Competitor behaviour and/or changes in market conditions can leave the firm with a massive expenditure but no increase in business. Firms that over-reach themselves in this way are often faced with liquidation.

In times of recession, a big concern of cash-flow management is the management of stocks. Many manufacturing firms attempt to reduce their outgoings through a better control of inventory. Strategies employed include the development of close links with a limited number of suppliers and operating such production control methods as JIT (Chapter 11 has a fuller discussion of such strategies).

Contribution to management decision-making

Any discussion of the elements of management activity can give the misleading impression that such activities are discrete. In reality, the work of the management accountant does not focus on any one of these activities but uses them all in conjunction to assist in the general process of management decision-making. The accountant would be expected to contribute to most types of management decision, and certainly would have an input in decisions such as the closure of part of the business and in decisions to make the product or deliver the service versus buying it in or outsourcing.

FINANCIAL REPORTING

Financial reporting involves the collection and presentation of data for use in financial management and management accounting. In most countries there are legal requirements governing the kind of statement that must be produced. In the UK, the requirement is for a profit and loss account, a balance sheet, a director's report and an auditor's report. For those firms listed on the stock exchange there is an additional requirement of an interim, usually half-yearly, report. Within the legal requirements, some variation is allowed. For example, some companies, such as British Airways, now report in euros. In recent years, the Internet has become significant as a reporting channel, and it is a requirement in the USA for some companies to post results on websites. Most large companies and many small ones publish their annual report and accounts online. Financial reporting differs from financial management and management accounting in that it has an important role in the governance of the organization. As we shall see, financial reports are used by a variety of stakeholders and are an important mechanism for establishing the probity of an organization.

KEY CONCEPT 14.9 FINANCIAL REPORTING

Financial reporting is the presentation of financial information in a form that is useful to interested parties. In most countries the form of such information is prescribed by law. Such information is useful in management decision-making, for potential investors and for a firm's competitors. Since the financial information is available to such a wide audience, management must decide on the extent of disclosure beyond the minimum required by law.

Three forms of financial statement for companies are the balance sheet, the profit and loss account, and the cash flow statement. The form and content of such statements in the UK are determined partly by law and partly by the requirements of professional bodies and other interested parties, such as the government and the Bank of England. The legislation and regulations set out by governments and professional bodies combine to form generally accepted accounting practice (GAAP). There is a UK GAAP and a USA GAAP, which are sets of practically-based accounting rules. There are, of course, differences between the UK and the USA regulations, although some companies, such as Shell and BT, report under both systems. There is a divergence of accounting practices across the world. For example, whereas the UK and USA operate to more practically-based rules, Germany and France are more strictly controlled by legislation. Such divergence has led to the creation of a supranational body, the International Accounting Standards Committee, which has a goal of harmonization.

KEY CONCEPT 14.10 TYPES OF FINANCIAL REPORTING

There are two main types of financial report. The balance sheet is a statement of assets and liabilities at the close of business on the last day of the accounting year. The profit and loss account is a statement of profit and loss In a defined accounting period. The report presents a summary of revenues and shows the expenses incurred in earning the revenues. The difference between the two is the profit or loss. In addition to these two reports, some firms prepare a statement of cash flows, which is a measure of the solvency of an enterprise.

The balance sheet

The balance sheet represents the summary of an organization's financial position at a point in time and is a measure of the solvency of the organization. The balance sheet is a statement of a firm's assets, liabilities and capital at the end of the last day of the accounting period. Assets are resources owned at a particular time. A balance sheet will differentiate between fixed assets, such as land, buildings and machinery, and current assets, such as cash and stock. Assets can also include such intangible aspects such as goodwill. Liabilities are resources owed by the organization at a particular point in time. Capital is the cumulative amount invested by owners at a particular point in time. Figure 14.2 shows the layout of a typical balance sheet.

Adjustments are often made in accounts for depreciation, stock and inventory value, costs and bad debts.

The profit and loss account

The profit and loss account provides detail of a firm's income and expenditure throughout a stated period of time, known as the accounting period. The profit and loss account must include the figures from two accounting periods. In almost all cases this involves presenting a comparison of the current figures with those from the previous year. Income represents the value of resources delivered to customers over a period of time. Expenditure represents the value of resources used in producing items or services to the customer over a period of time. The profit and loss account also provides details of distributions, which involve the transfer of the surplus of income over expenditure for the accounting period. A typical distribution for a public limited company will be the payment of share dividend. Figure 14.3 shows the layout of a typical profit and loss account.

Cash flow statements

A third form of statement is produced by some companies. This is the cash flow statement. It details the movement of cash during an accounting period and is very useful for planning and control purposes and as a general indication of the financial health of the business.

FIGURE 14.2	Components of a typical balance sheet

Balance sheet of Company X at a certain date

Fixed assets		xxx
Current assets	xxx	
Less current liabilities	xxx	
Net current assets		xxx
Total assets		xxx
Less long-tem liabilities		xxx
Net assets		xxx
Capital and reserves		xxx

FIGURE 14.3   Components of a typical profit and loss account

Annual profit and loss account for Company X for the period ended 31 Dec 2014

	2014	2013
Sales	xxx	xxx
Less: cost of sales (direct costs in relation to sales)	xxx	xxx
Gross profit	xxx	xxx
Less: other costs (administration, distribution)	xxx	xxx
Operating profit	xxx	xxx
Add: income from other investments	xxx	xxx
Profit before interest and tax	xxx	xxx
Less: net interest	xxx	xxx
Profit before tax	xxx	xxx
Less: tax	xxx	xxx
Net profit	xxx	xxx
Less: dividends	xxx	xxx
Retained profits	xxx	xxx

REFLECTION POINT

What are the purposes of the balance sheet, the profit and loss account and the cash flow statement?

Ratio analysis

Methods have been developed to analyse published accounts and collectively they are known as ratio analysis. Such analyses are important in providing comparisons with performance in previous years and as a comparison with other companies and industry standards. We can identify several methods.

Profitability ratios examine the extent of profit or loss and its derivation. Three profitability ratios are normally used. **Gross margin** is an expression of sales revenue over direct costs. **Net profit** is a ratio that examines net profit relative to sales revenue after expenses apart from distribution of dividend have been accounted for. **Return on capital employed** (ROCE) is a ratio of net profit to capital employed to generate that profit. This is a useful aid to decision-making in that the capital employed may be put to more profitable use.

Activity ratios assess the efficiency of the company in the use of its resources. Several measures are used. **Inventory turnover** examines the number of times the average inventory is turned over during the year. In manufacturing, this refers to the speed with which parts and components are used. The higher turnover, the cost of financing the purchase and the cost of storage come down, as does the risk of deterioration. **Debtors collection period** is a measure of the time taken to obtain cash from debtors. This has clear implications for a healthy cash flow. **Sales to capital employed** is similar to ROCE and is a measure of the efficiency in the use of capital employed to generate sales.

Liquidity ratios examine the company's cash and liquidity position. Such ratios compare assets and liabilities to ensure that the organization has sufficient assets to cover liabilities.

Gearing ratios examine how the firm is financed and are a measure of risk in borrowing. The **debt to equity** ratio is a measure of the relationship between the value of the company and the amount it owes. A high ratio is a good indication of the vulnerability of the company.

Market ratios are measures of the performance of the company on the stock market. Such ratios are only applicable to listed companies. **Dividend yield** is a measure of the amount of dividend paid relative to the market value of the company and is a reflection of the return on investment. **Earnings per share** is a measure of how much each share has earned over the accounting period.

Ratios provide useful assessments of the financial health of a business, identify problems and guide decision-making. They are criticized for placing total emphasis on financial information. An approach put forward by Kaplan and Norton (1992, 1996) was 'the balanced scorecard'. Its aim was to complement traditional financial reporting and include consideration of longer-term developments. Norton and Kaplan's balanced scorecard contained four elements or in their terminology, perspectives:

- The financial perspective includes ratio analyses and measures of profit and cash flow.

- The customer perspective includes assessment of delivery effectiveness and customers' perception of quality and satisfaction.

- The internal business perspective includes measures of cost, productivity and relationship with suppliers.

- The innovation and learning perspective covers investment in R&D, in training and assesses the HR profile of the organization in terms of age, gender and so on.

There are a number of models of the balanced scorecard, which are variations on the above. It is used by large companies such as Wal-Mart and General Electric, but a criticism is that many of the measures are based on subjective scoring by managers.

KEY CONCEPT 14.11   RATIO ANALYSIS

Ratios are used to interpret and analyse data presented in financial reports such as the balance sheet and profit and loss account. Ratios dealing with profitability, operating efficiency, liquidity and borrowing assist the users of accounts in examining trends in a single organization over time and in comparing that organization with others.

REFLECTION POINT

Which ratio analysis would you find most useful in assessing the financial health of a business and why?

Users of published accounts

Financial reports are particularly useful to management in the planning, organizing and controlling of resources. It is not only managers who are interested in the financial information of individual businesses; the following also have need of such information:

- **The state** requires public companies to be accountable and present their accounting information in a standardized form according to various laws and regulations. In the

UK, all public companies must present to Companies House a balance sheet, a profit and loss account, a directors' report, an auditor's report and notes on the accounts where necessary. There is some relaxation of these requirements for smaller businesses but only relating to the extent of information provided. However, small firms must still produce detailed information for the tax authorities and usually banks. As well as stipulating the accounts to be presented, the law also determines what must be disclosed and the state requires financial information to levy appropriate taxes on businesses. The nature of the tax laws certainly affects how firms report, and most use reporting conventions that minimize their liability for tax.

- **Investors** need the information to make informed judgements about future investments, as well as needing to protect their investments. The accountability of public companies to their investors encouraged the development of rules governing disclosure.

- **Employees** may need the information, especially if they are involved in a profit-sharing or share ownership scheme. There is evidence of the increasing use of profit sharing. Published accounts are, of course, particularly useful to trade unions in planning wage negotiations as part of collective bargaining, although the extent of this has declined, especially in the UK and USA. In more general terms, a company concerned with involving its employees in the running of the enterprise may see the disclosure of financial information as an important element of the participation process.

- **Creditors** such as banks and suppliers are naturally concerned with the firm's liquidity and need to assess the risk involved in offering credit and, of course, to safeguard against fraud.

- **Competitors** use financial information as a yardstick against which their own performance may be measured, and may derive insights into what other firms are doing.

- **Customers** use the information to ascertain the risk of placing expensive or long-term contracts and perhaps to assess the fairness of a company's pricing policy. This is particularly important in business-to-business deals.

An issue in financial reporting is the extent of disclosure. The wide availability of the accounts of public companies influences their content and the way information is presented. Managements have a fair amount of discretion since much of the content of accounts is subject to interpretation, such as allowances for depreciation and the valuation of assets. As a result, firms are often accused of manipulating their financial information to minimize tax liability or to present a strong position to shareholders. In addition, firms are also conscious that financial information will be available to competitors and may wish to hide certain facts from them. We have seen, in our discussion of management accounting, that financial information can be presented in such a way as to legitimize certain courses of action in preference to others.

All this reinforces the notion that accounting is a behavioural and political rather than a technical exercise. Clarke et al. (1999) go further in an Australian study of the collapse of certain Australian firms, such as the Bond Corporation, the Adelaide Steamship Company and the Parry Corporation. They show how accounts for such companies were not only produced under existing regulations, but were subject to the legal requirements of external audit. Despite this, the firms concerned managed to keep hidden their real financial positions and eventually collapsed. Similar cases can be found in the UK, notably Polly Peck, BCCI and Maxwell Communications. Cases like these have focused attention of both the professions and academics on both the content and format of financial reports and the role of the auditor. A classic case is that of Enron, presented in Chapter 9. In this case there were issues of hidden accounts that should have been picked up by the auditors and communicated to shareholders and other stakeholders. The involvement of the auditors, Arthur Andersen, in the proceedings brought down one of the world's largest firm of accountants.

Accounting and corporate governance

The collapse of Enron and the banking crisis of 2008 has brought attention to the concept of corporate governance and the role the finance and accounting can play, more especially financial reporting. Corporate governance has been defined as:

> The system of checks and balances, both internal and external to companies, which ensure that companies discharge their accountability to all their stakeholders and act in a socially responsible way in all areas of their business activity.

(Solomon, 2007, p. 14)

The essences of this and similar definitions are that:

- Corporate governance is more than how an organization is managed and controlled.
- It concerns the overall direction of the organization but also seeks to ensure that decisions made are accountable and acceptable to both internal and external stakeholders.
- It is concerned that all stakeholders are satisfied and that policies and practices are socially responsible.

There are links here with business ethics and corporate social responsibility, which we discussed in Chapter 9 as well as discussing the difficulties of satisfying the needs of all stakeholders. The provision of accounting information in financial reports clearly plays a vital role in providing the checks and balances to which Solomon refers. There would appear to be two stages in the process. First, in many countries the financial reports must be audited by independent experts as a legal requirement to ensure they give a true and fair representation of an organization's financial position. Second, the accessibility of published accounts to a large number of stakeholders offers an opportunity for public scrutiny.

Whilst the theory is sound, the process has been questioned. First, financial reports can be presented in such a way as to hide information. Second, the auditing process may not be completely independent. As we saw in the Enron case (Chapter 9), the auditor, Arthur Andersen was also a consultant acting on the company's behalf. As a result some have called for auditing to be a central government function and not, as at present, to be carried out by private accounting firms.

Yet good governance appears to have a number of positive benefits as follows:

- There is an assumption that effective governance contributes to effective performance and financial and economic growth.
- It enhances confidence among investors and other stakeholders. For example, it can play a part in employer branding and employee commitment.

We know that examples of 'bad' governance create bad publicity and may, in some cases, lead to insolvency and/or legal action, fines and imprisonment. However effective governance is not straightforward. Many business activities are complex and hidden and difficult to regulate. As we have seen with executive pay, the actions of senior managers are sometimes difficult to control. Guidelines for effective governance have been laid down by the OECD and the Financial Reporting Council (FRC) of the UK. The FRC have focused on the selection and training of board members; the role of non-executive directors; the need for clear and understandable financial reports; transparent auditing procedures; executive pay; and dialogue with shareholders.

ENVIRONMENTAL ASPECTS OF FINANCE AND ACCOUNTING

In the last section we saw that financial reporting was greatly influenced by state regulations concerning the disclosure of information for public accountability and for reasons of collecting taxes. In this section we focus on two other environmental influences on the accounting and finance function: the economy and differences in culture and national systems.

In keeping with our Business in Context model, influences are two-way. The finance and accounting practices of firms affect the environment in which they operate. Economic resources in society are often allocated on the basis of accounting information. We have noted elsewhere the growing tendency for firms to engage in the buying and selling of other companies. Financial information is vital to this activity.

The role of the economy

In general, accounting practices will vary according to the nature of the economy in which they operate. For example, in many developing countries there is little need for sophisticated accounting techniques and systems of basic cash accounting predominate. The raising of finance discussed in the previous section is a function of the market and the way this influences profit levels, share prices and bank interest rates. Two economic features have held particular interest for accountants: inflation and currency exchange.

A problem in times of high inflation is that profits can be overstated by basing costs on historic data made largely irrelevant by inflation. In such situations, systems of adjusting balance sheets to account for fluctuating prices were developed. While these have less relevance today, inflation accounting techniques have been widely used in such countries as Brazil. Like inflation, fluctuations in currency exchange rates make historic cost accounting difficult. The effect is significant for those firms reliant on export markets, as with Swiss firms Nestlé and Ciba Geigy with 90 per cent of their business outside Switzerland.

Differences in culture and national systems

Two main issues are discussed here, differences in ownership and the financing of business, and variations in financial reporting.

Differences in ownership and financing a business

There are differences in both ownership patterns and in the way firms are financed. Much of the work in this area has focused on comparisons between the UK and USA, as liberal market economies on one hand and Germany and Japan as coordinated market economies on the other (see Chapter 5 for more detail). We look first at patterns of ownership and then at the way firms are funded.

In the UK, around three-quarters of all shares are owned by institutional shareholders, who tend to hold diversified share portfolios and have little if any connection with the firm. The stock market in the UK is volatile with a much higher proportion of shares being traded than in any other country. As a result of such share trading activity, the UK experiences a higher proportion of takeovers, many of them hostile. Banks own shares in UK companies but tend to operate like other institutional shareholders. Under such a system, the primary objective of institutional investors is to make money for their own shareholders. They, therefore, have a preference for selling shares when events are not going to their liking, rather than attempting to influence policy. In response, managers tend to be very aware of the need to maintain share price and to keep such investors happy with high rates of dividend. Indeed, the dividend paid by UK companies is higher than in Japan and Germany and even marginally higher than in the USA.

In Germany, ownership patterns are much more stable. There are fewer firms quoted on stock markets. Those with shareholders tend to be dominated by one or two shareholders owning around a quarter of the company and having a seat on the supervisory board. Takeovers are controlled by law and hostile takeovers are rare. Banks tend to have a much closer relationship with firms and bank representatives regularly take a place on the board. Employees in Germany also play a role as board members, enshrined in the laws relating to co-determination.

In Japan, as in the UK, three-quarters of shares are owned by institutions. However, unlike the UK, trading of such shares occurs infrequently. Most of the trading is among those householders owning shares. This is a reversal of the situation in the UK. The institutional shareholders have a close relationship with the firms and takeovers are rare. Banks play a major role and, in some cases, are members of large corporate groupings or have a substantial ownership interest in companies. In manufacturing, suppliers are often part-owned by the firms they supply. The Japanese system is one where there is a very close relationship between firms, banks and suppliers.

Such differences as those existing between the UK, Germany and Japan have led many to hold the UK financial system as being responsible for the spread of short-termism, lack of investment and long-term strategy and, hence, the comparative industrial decline of the UK. While Owen (1996) agrees in part with such an analysis, he raises questions. He argues that in the period 1950–80 the UK was indeed outperformed by Germany, but it was also outperformed by France and Italy. All three countries possessed different financial systems, thereby making links between industrial performance and specific financial systems difficult. He further argues that if long-termism was such an advantage to Germany then it would show up most in those industries where long-term investment would be an advantage. He examines pharmaceuticals and electronics. In the former, both the UK and Germany have performed well, whereas in the latter, both lag some way behind the Japanese. He suggests that there are other factors at work in these cases.

Corbett and Jenkinson (1997) examined sources of finance for firms in the UK, USA, Germany and Japan between 1979–94. Their findings are summarized in Table 14.1.

TABLE 14.1	Percentage sources of finance 1970–94			
	Germany	**Japan**	**UK**	**USA**
Internal	78.9	69.9	93.3	96.1
Bank finance	11.9	26.7	14.6	11.1
New equity	0.1	3.5	−4.6	−7.6

The data in Table 14.1 is extracted from a longer list that includes bonds, trade credit, capital transfers and makes certain statistical adjustments. The key points to emerge are the relatively low contribution made by new equity (i.e. new share issues) to the funding of firms in all countries and the differences shown. Internal funding makes a much greater contribution in the UK and USA and banks play a proportionately larger role in the funding of firms in Germany and particularly Japan. This reinforces the differences between these two sets of countries highlighted in Chapter 5.

Differences in financial reporting

Many differences can be observed in national accounting practices. These reflect factors such as the nature of the legal system, the pattern of ownership and control, the system of taxation, the strength of the accountancy profession, and the social climate. Such variations were noted in the section on financial reporting.

The discussion of the Beijing Jeep venture in Chapter 2 noted that AMC/Chrysler found it difficult working with the Chinese system of accounting. This was different to the one used in the USA and was based on a Russian system and designed for state-controlled enterprises. It offered little information on costs, for example.

In France and Germany, financial reporting systems are highly prescribed by law, yet there tends to be less emphasis on financial reporting in France largely because of the dominance of family ownership and, hence, the private nature of many companies. In the UK and USA reporting requirements are less prescriptive but the information needs of shareholders are much greater, especially in the USA where share ownership is more diffuse. Patterns of ownership are themselves related to the influence of the accounting profession. Public ownership requires accountability and hence accountants have to audit company accounts. Much less auditing is required in France, which may account for its relatively low numbers of accountants. In general, a social climate that encourages openness, social responsibility and consumerism, as in the USA, results in different patterns in the disclosure of financial information than is found in a more closed society such as Switzerland.

There has been pressure to standardize accounting practices across countries. This is partly a function of increased international business via globalization and joint ventures. Harmonization is one of the tasks of the International Accounting Standards Committee. Some harmonization has taken place within the EU. The pressure for standardization comes from a variety of quarters. Financial reports prepared in one country are used by financial analysts and investors in another, as part of the growing internationalization of capital. In manufacturing, global operations and sourcing of components have hastened the need for internationally usable financial information. Standardization would assist multinational companies in consolidating their accounts, assessing potential acquisitions and even enabling them to transfer accounting staff from one country to another more easily. This is just part of the vast changes that have accompanied the globalization of the economy. It should not be forgotten that many accounting firms operate multinationally too and harmonization would greatly assist their operations.

REFLECTION POINT

Why do we find differences in the funding of business and in financial reporting between organizations in different countries?

ORGANIZATIONAL ASPECTS OF FINANCE AND ACCOUNTING

The nature of any organization impinges upon accounting procedures. This is inevitably shown when changes occur in ownership or in the goals of the enterprise, bringing about changes in the organizational culture. For example, the takeover of one firm by another may well result in the consolidation of accounts and perhaps a change in accounting practices. The privatization of companies in Britain since the 1980s has changed the nature of many of those organizations from a service centre to a profit centre with a corresponding effect on accounting practices. The liberalization of economies around the world has resulted in changes in accounting practices as with firms in many Eastern European countries.

This section focuses on two organizational issues: the accounting implications of the size of the firm, and the influence of structure on accounting procedures. The two issues are linked, as we shall see when we examine the problems of cost allocation and transfer pricing in large multi-divisional firms.

Accounting requirements of large and small firms

Differences in the size of businesses affect their ability to raise capital, the complexity of their accounting procedures and controls, and the extent of their financial reporting. Differences are therefore to be found in all the three aspects of finance and accounting. Larger firms, not surprisingly, have much more complex procedures and employ professional accountants in a specialized department. In smaller firms, the accounting function is often external to the firm with a subsequent reliance on the advice of outsiders, who may not have the detailed knowledge of an internal management accountant. Larger firms may have the problems of satisfying large numbers of shareholders, but their very size often gives them an advantage in raising funds from external sources. In any event, large and complex organizations can often finance themselves internally by switching funds from one unit to another. Small firms have much more problem raising finance and tend to be more concerned with the management of cash flows.

Organization structure, cost allocation and transfer pricing

We have already seen how organization structure and accounting procedures tend to reinforce one another, in that a large organization may delegate responsibility and control costs through the creation of individual budget centres. In very large organizations, the structure generally matches the finance and accounting responsibilities of the firm. A centralized headquarters will act as an investment centre determining new initiatives, as well as allocating profit targets for each division. In turn, the divisions will determine targets for each operating unit and designate each one as a cost centre in control of a budget. There are occasions when mismatches can occur, as in the case of a department manager who has no effective budget and, hence, limited powers of operation.

The operation of budgetary control can produce a more efficient and effective management control system. It also carries the potential problem of encouraging functional insularity to the detriment of the firm as a whole. Units can become so preoccupied with their own targets and keeping within their own budgets that they may refuse calls for assistance from other units through the fear that this will erode their own performance. In some manufacturing firms, this has resulted in a total lack of continuity between departments and between production shifts.

Such problems increase with the size of the firm and with the necessity for funds to flow across many units of the same organization. The problems come to a head in firms with many divisions where each unit operates as a profit centre and is accountable for the achievement of predetermined profit targets. We examine two aspects of this problem: cost allocation and transfer pricing.

Cost allocation

The problems of cost allocation occur when central services, such as headquarters administration, research and development, and perhaps maintenance, must be paid for by those units in the organization with responsibility for generating income and profit. A decision needs to be made on the basis of the apportionment of such costs (see the reference to absorption costing in the section on management accounting). Some firms vary cost allocation according to the size of the profit centre, as a proportion of their costs, or the extent to which use is made of the central services. The final criteria is often difficult to measure accurately, but any method is open to challenge by those managers who see their profits eroded by costs that lie outside their control. Some managers are resentful that their efforts are diluted by sections of the firm that do not generate income but merely incur costs. In some cases this has resulted in the marginalization of service departments such as HRM and R&D. Once again accounting becomes the focus for political debate at the level of the firm. While accounting is itself a largely advisory function, the importance to decision-making of financial information, which is largely controlled by accountants, often enables the accountant in the organization to wield power and influence.

Transfer pricing

Transfer pricing is the process through which goods and services produced in one section of the organization are sold internally for use by another. The need for transfer pricing mechanisms is a function of the development of the multi-divisional firm and associated profit centres. An effective transfer pricing mechanism can contribute to the optimum allocation of a firm's resources and to the motivation of division managers towards efficient operation and hence to the overall prosperity of the organization.

Such mechanisms occur wherever there is a need in one unit of the organization for the services of another. A form of transfer pricing occurs in higher education, as the following illustration reveals. Universities and other colleges tend to be organized around specialist subject departments. A department that offers a business management course may have the need for specialist law inputs which reside outside that department. In many colleges a transfer pricing system has been devised whereby those departments servicing another are allocated points based on the number of hours and students they service. These points, with those generated from their own departments, form the basis for staffing allocations. A problem with such a mechanism is that it may encourage departments only to service those areas where they can ensure high rates of return.

A source of potential conflict exists when individual units within an organization must operate as a profit centre and are encouraged to seek external clients as sources of revenue. Management may be faced with the dilemma of having to meet internal demand for goods and services when higher returns may be obtained through meeting the requirements of customers external to the firm.

The issue of transfer pricing is particularly pertinent to the operation of global firms.

Transfer pricing and the global firm

A great deal of transfer pricing activity occurs between member organizations of multinational corporations. Such activity has increased with developments in the global economy. While this can cause the kind of organizational political problems outlined above, there are three main reasons for the extensiveness of such activity. These relate to issues of taxation, competition and issues relating to the need of the multinational to protect itself against social, economic and political changes occurring in the host country. These issues should be viewed in conjunction with the discussion on globalization and multinationals in Chapter 2.

Tax reasons Through its activities worldwide, a multinational company can move profits from high to low-tax areas using the transfer pricing mechanism. Firms operating in high-tax regimes are charged inflated prices for goods and services produced in low-tax areas. While this represents only a paper exchange of funds within the same organization it can result in some firms showing a much greater profit than others. In normal circumstances pressure is brought to bear on poorly performing profit centres. Such problems may be avoided by the use of dual reporting systems, one for external consumption and the other for internal use.

Competition reasons Some multinationals subsidize member firms through the transfer price mechanism. So that a new company may develop itself in an established market, other firms belonging to the multinational could supply goods and services at low prices, buying back the finished products at a high price.

Protection against change A multinational will wish to protect itself against economic and political changes that threaten its prosperity and ultimate existence. Problems caused by high inflation, currency exchange and devaluation in a particular country can be tackled by charging high prices for goods supplied to the subsidiary in that country, and buying goods back at low prices. By operating in this way the multinational keeps finance in the family and prevents money being siphoned off by individual nation states.

News Corporation, a global company controlled by Rupert Murdoch, makes very good use of its global presence by accessing the advantages accorded by the tax laws and accounting regulations in the many countries in which it operates. Indeed the attractiveness of some of those countries is their status as a tax haven. News Corporation has a highly complex financial structure with a large number of subsidiary companies, many registered in the British Virgin Islands where corporation tax is 1 per cent per annum and in the Cayman Islands under a similar tax regime. As a general rule, the company will pay loans in countries with high levels of corporation tax and collect profits in countries where tax levels are low. News Corporation also makes large capital investments and is renowned for setting up new businesses. This it does with maximum tax benefit, particularly where it can obtain tax relief in high-tax countries. All this has been achieved within the laws and accounting regulations of the various countries within which News Corporation operates.

In 2012, the UK government held an investigation into several major companies, including Amazon, Google and Starbucks, that were accused of diverting their UK profits to tax havens. For example, Amazon reported all European sales to Luxembourg with 12 per cent corporation tax and Google reported in Ireland with 12.5 per cent tax, less than half the rate in the UK (Syal, 2012).

REFLECTION POINT

Why is cost allocation and transfer pricing more of an issue in global firms?

STRATEGIC ASPECTS OF FINANCE AND ACCOUNTING

The three aspects of finance and accounting represent strategies of financing and controlling operations, of distributing resources and power through budget allocation, and of information disclosure. Additionally, financial tools and information are invariably used in making strategic decisions in other functional areas, such as the decision to invest in products or equipment, or to take on staff. Financial analyses form the basis of most acquisition attempts.

We can therefore see that the finance and accounting function assists management decision-making on issues that are central to the viability of the firm. These issues include the sources of funds, investment decisions, acceptable levels of debt, the minimization of tax liability and the extent of the pay-out to shareholders.

As with all the functional areas discussed in this book there is a growing recognition that the strategies associated with the different activities are linked in a synergistic way. In the manufacturing industry, evidence is emerging that cost and quality are not necessarily trade-offs but essential ingredients of the same strategy. Focusing greater attention on improving quality can also lower costs. This can become a virtuous circle in that extra funds are released for investment in quality improvement.

Throughout this chapter we have been careful to point out the inexact nature of accounting methods. We can summarize the limitations on the use of accounting information in strategy formulation:

- Because of problems in measuring many aspects of business activities, accounting information can be subjective.

- Financial statements are summaries. Information is therefore selected and interpreted according to the needs of the compiler and user of financial statements.

- As a result of the above, financial information is often used to achieve political ends, such as the justification of an investment decision or a pay offer.

- There is an added danger in all this in that many assume the data to be scientific and objective, and use it accordingly.

- Because of the bias to what can be measured effectively, management may place undue emphasis on short-term results and neglect the longer-term implications of strategic decisions, or base too many decisions on historic data which is made redundant by changing circumstances.

CASE 14.1   FOOTBALL FINANCES: OUT OF CONTROL?

Football is the UK's most popular spectator sport. Attendances at games were larger in 2008 than every other European country except Germany. Average capacity utilization of Premier League stadiums was 92 per cent in 2007–08 with half of clubs enjoying a level of over 96 per cent. The game has a huge following on television, not just in the UK, but globally as matches from the English league are shown live around the world. In the UK, around 18.6 million follow the game and 7 million play including 3.9 million children and 1.1 million girls. The game in England is organized in four divisions. There is the elite Premier League of 20 clubs, the Championship and Divisions 1 and 2, each with 24 clubs. There is movement between the leagues as a result of promotion and relegation and the most successful

(Continued)

CASE 14.1   (Continued)

clubs in the Premier League are rewarded by being selected to play in European competitions in addition to their normal league programme.

Each year, the accountants Deloitte publish a report on the finances of the English game. In its 2009 report, it noted that while the UK economy grew at an average annual rate of 5.4 per cent between 1992 and 2008, the revenue of the Premiership clubs in England grew 16 per cent and the other leagues were not far behind. The Premier League has the highest revenue by some distance of any league in Europe, as shown in Table 14.2.

Despite the growth of revenue in the English league, problems exist. Only 11 of the 20 premiership clubs made an operating profit in 2007–08 and in the other divisions the position is much worse. Clubs in the second-tier league, the Championship, made a collective operating loss of £102 million. The extent of the problem can be seen in Table 14.3.

Given the credit crunch and the global recession that is expected to continue for several years, the position may get worse and problems are predicted for lower league clubs, where there is much less chance of obtaining revenue from broadcasting, sponsorship and commercial activity. For many of these clubs there is a danger of bankruptcy and entering administration. Premier League clubs have already taken measures to keep customers, with seven clubs cutting seat prices, seven clubs freezing prices and most offering cut-price deals for children and pensioners for the 2009–10 season. Only one club, Manchester United, has announced a price increase.

Fears that the game's finances are out of control are not new. The rising wages and player transfer costs were the major cause of financial problems in the 2001–02 season, Then, Arsenal, one of the biggest clubs, lost £22 million, eclipsed only by Fulham with losses of £40 million and Leeds with £34 million. The problem was not confined to England. In the same season, teams in Italy's Series A, the top division, had a collective loss of over £500 million. Several English clubs, having formed public limited companies saw share prices fall and in 2002 the sector suffered the biggest drop of any sector outside technology. For example, the share price at Leeds went from a high of £0.24 to a low of £0.04. The club gambled on heavy investments, including £100 million on players to achieve domestic and European success. As a result, debts rose to £77 million (an increase in three years of 838 per cent). Salaries had increased by 290 per cent over three years from 1999 and the numbers employed on the non-playing side rose during the same period from

TABLE 14.3   Revenue and profit of English league clubs 2007–08 in (£m)

	Revenue	Operating profit/ (loss)
Premiership	1932	185
Championship	336	(102)
League 1	125	(24)
League 2	65	(8)

TABLE 14.2   Revenue growth of major European football leagues 1996–2008 (€m)

	1996–07	2001–02	2006–07	2007–08
England	685	1747	2273	2441
Germany	444	1043	1379	1438
Spain	524	776	1326	1438
Italy	551	1017	1064	1421
France		643	972	989

91 to 246. At the end of the season in 2007, Leeds was relegated to Division 1, the third tier of English football, where they stayed for three years before gaining promotion to the Championship (Tier 2).

The financial position of football clubs in England will be examined in terms of revenue, expenditure and overall financial position.

Revenue

On the revenue side, the picture is healthy. For English clubs in 2007–08 there was an increase in revenue of 21 per cent over the previous year. The large majority of this was accounted for by the Premier League. Even here there are big differences between clubs, as Table 14.4 shows.

The key component of revenue for clubs in the Premier League is not ticket sales but earnings from broadcasting. Revenue here rose from £464 million in 2006–07 to £767 million the following year. The total package for the premiership for the sale of its media rights until the end of the 2010 season was negotiated at £2.7 billion. The position is similar in other European countries and the relative contribution of various income streams for the major European Leagues is seen in Table 14.5.

Revenue from broadcasting does not apply equally to all clubs and those clubs who make most appearances gain the most income. Invariably there is greater coverage of the big clubs. There are potential threats. The subscriber television channel Setanta ceased to trade in 2009, but the impact will

TABLE 14.4	Turnover of selected premier league clubs 2007–08 (£m)
Manchester United	256.2
Arsenal	222.5
Chelsea	213.6
Liverpool	159.0
Tottenham Hotspur	114.7
West Ham	57.0
Blackburn Rovers	56.4
Fulham	53.7
Middlesbrough	48.0
Wigan	43.0

The above represents the top five and bottom five in terms of turnover for clubs in the Premier League 2008–09 and is taken from published accounts.

be greatest on smaller clubs outside the Premier League. There is increasing use of online and mobile phone technology to access highlights of games and this is seen as a threat to TV broadcasting.

Expenditure

The most significant contribution to expenditure is wages, followed by transfer fees for players. Premier League total wage costs for 2007–08 were

TABLE 14.5	Sources of revenue for the major leagues 2007–08 as a per cent of revenue		
	Match day	*Broadcasting*	*Sponsorship and other commercial*
England	29	48	23
Germany	24	33	43
Spain	28	40	32
Italy	13	61	26
France	14	56	30

(Continued)

CASE 14.1 (Continued)

£1.2 billion, an increase of 23 per cent on the previous year and over twice those in the respective league in Germany, some 31 per cent higher than Spain and 29 per cent higher than Italy. There were large variations by club and by league as shown in Tables 14.6 and 14.7. The inflation in the cost of wages represents a threat to finances. Furthermore, such costs are difficult to control due to the global nature of the sport. For example, if a wages cap were employed, as in some sports in the USA, players could move to other leagues where caps were not in operation. Any harmonization of wage regulation would need to be at least Europe-wide.

The gap has widened between the Premiership and other leagues, although in the Championship wages from 2006–08 increased three times more than revenue. In the Premiership, the top four wage payers have been consistently the top performing clubs over the past few years and overall in this league there is a correlation between wage costs and performance. This is not the case for the other leagues.

TABLE 14.7	Estimated player wage bills in the English leagues 1992–2008 (£m)			
	1992–03	**1997–08**	**2002–03**	**2007–08**
Premier League	54	135	548	787
Championship	29	80	149	179
League 1	14	33	48	57
League 2	8	17	26	27

Spending on player transfers also increased in 2007–08 by 35 per cent on the previous year. Of the £779 million spent by English clubs, £664 million was spent by the Premier League clubs. About 45 per cent of transfer expenditure was on players from overseas clubs.

Financing

At the end of the 2007–08 season, Premiership clubs carried a total debt of £3.1 billion, mainly in overdrafts and loans. Around £2 billion of this debt is attributable to the top four clubs, although a large proportion represents investment in stadiums and other facilities and in players. There are, however, important differences. In the case of Manchester United and Liverpool, the clubs were bought by US owners with borrowed money. In both cases, the loans were transferred to the clubs, loading them with heavy interest payments. In the case of Arsenal, the debt is related largely to the cost of building a stadium at £260 million and the renovation of the old stadium for housing at a cost of £130 million. The new stadium led to a doubling of income from ticket sales. The housing development was hit by falling property prices and the credit crunch of 2008. In Chelsea's case, their debt is from interest-free loans over five years of £700 million from the owner, Roman Abramovich.

Like Chelsea, other clubs in the Premier League have benefited from such soft loans or from takeovers

TABLE 14.6	Rank order total wage costs of Premier league clubs 2007–08	
	Wage bill (£m)	**% increase on 2006–07**
Chelsea	172	30
Manchester United	121	31
Arsenal	101	13
Liverpool	90	17
Newcastle	75	31
Portsmouth	55	48
Manchester City	54	49
Tottenham Hotspur	53	21
Aston Villa	50	17
Everton	44	16

CASE 14.1   (Continued)

by rich owners. Randy Lerner, another investor from the USA, bought Aston Villa after selling the credit card company MBNA, and Fulham is subsidized by the Harrods owner, Al Fayed. At the end of 2008, Manchester City was bought by a consortium from Abu Dhabi headed by Sheikh Mansour. The club immediately broke the UK transfer record, paying £35.5 million for a player and their subsequent transfer bids and wage offers have raised the stakes in an attempt to buy success.

In other divisions there are few such saviours. In the Championship the net debt at the end of 2008 was £325 million and for many clubs in the other leagues there is a threat of insolvency.

Questions

1 What are the opportunities and threats to English football that arise from its reliance on income from broadcasting contracts?

2 Examine Tables 14.6 and 14.7. What potential problems can be identified from the data and trends presented? How can the problem be tackled?

3 Are the high levels of debt carried by English clubs sustainable? What problems are likely to arise?

4 Why does football seem to operate in a different way from other types of business?

SUMMARY

- The finance and accounting function in business comprises financial management, management accounting and financial reporting.

- Financial management is concerned with the funding of the business and ensuring such funds can be met by the organization. Sources of finance include share capital, loan capital, state finance and internally generated funds, usually through the reinvestment of profit. It is this last source that would appear to be most significant for firms in Britain.

- Management accounting is concerned with assisting management in planning and control. It involves the preparation and control of budgets, the analysis and allocation of costs, the appraisal of capital investments, the management of cash flows and general contribution to strategic decision-making.

- Financial reporting involves the preparation of financial statements such as the balance sheet, profit and loss account and cash-flow statements. Financial reporting must conform to a legal and regulatory framework and take account of the needs of the groups that use this information. Issues are whether the accounts represent a true and fair picture and the extent of disclosure.

- The finance and accounting function is influenced by the environment in which it operates. Financial reporting is subject to state controls and accounting practices have developed to cope with economic changes such as inflation and fluctuations in the value of currency. Despite pressures to harmonize accounting practices there are considerable differences between countries, reflecting cultural influences.

- Accounting practices vary also with the size of the organization, with large and small companies having their own special problems. As organizations increase in size and develop appropriate structures, decisions have to be made on the allocation of costs and transfer pricing. The latter becomes a particularly useful mechanism in the hands of the multinational corporation.

- Accounting information forms the basis for most strategic decisions within the organization. Its value should be placed alongside a number of limitations, not least of which are the subjective nature of accounts and the role played by accounting information to justify organizational political decisions.

DISCUSSION QUESTIONS

1 What is the value of the professional accountant to business?

2 Why is the internal funding of business so popular in the UK and USA?

3 What would be the most appropriate methods the following organizations could use to raise revenue to fund new activities: a very small firm just making a mark in the office supplies market; a university; a multinational car manufacturer?

4 What specific contributions can the management accountant make to strategic decision-making? What limitations can be placed on the value of this contribution?

5 Identify the different needs of the users of accounting information. To what extent can current methods of financial reporting hope to satisfy them all?

6 What are the specific finance and accounting problems and priorities for small as opposed to large companies?

7 What are the advantages and disadvantages to various interested parties associated with cost allocation and transfer pricing activities in global firms?

8 Identify the behavioural and political nature of management accounting. What problems does this cause and how might they be minimized?

9 What is the relationship between financial reporting and corporate governance?

FURTHER READING

This text covers the fundamentals of finance and accounting and offers a discussion on the organizational and environmental influences:

Berry, A. and Jarvis, R. (2011) *Accounting in a Business Context*, 5th edn, Cengage Learning: Andover.

A good basic text is:

Atrill, P., McLaney, E. and Black, G. (2013) *Accounting and Finance for Non specialists*, 8th edn, FT Prentice Hall: Harlow.

A good source of information on management accounting is:

Drury, C. (2013) *Management Accounting for Business*, 5th edn, Cengage Learning: Andover.

An excellent guide to financial reporting and the interpretation of company reports and accounts is:

Holmes, G., Sugden, A. and Gee, P. (2008) *Interpreting Company Reports and Accounts*, 10th edn, FT Prentice Hall: Harlow.

REFERENCES

Aaker, D.A. (1996) *Building Strong Brands*, Free Press: New York.

Aaker, D.A. (1997) 'Dimensions of brand personality', *Journal of Marketing Research*, 34, 347–356.

Abernathy, W.J. and Utterback, J.M. (1978) 'Patterns of industrial innovation', in R.R. Rothberg (ed.), *Corporate Strategy and Product Innovation*, 2nd edn, Free Press: New York.

Abrahamsson, M. and Rehme, J. (2010) 'The role of logistics in retailers' corporate strategy – a driver for growth and customer value', *Supply Chain Forum: An International Journal*, 11, 4, 14–23.

Aiello, P. (1991) 'Building a joint venture in China: the case of Chrysler and the Beijing Jeep Corporation', *Journal of General Management*, 17, 2, 47–64.

Amable, B. (2003) *The Diversity of Modern Capitalism*, Oxford University Press: Oxford.

Anderlini, J. (2010) 'Foreign Companies Losing Out in China', *Financial Times*, 2 September.

Andrews, K. (1971) *The Concept of Corporate Strategy*, Irwin: Homewood, IL.

Ansoff, H.I. (1968) *Corporate Strategy*, Penguin: Harmondsworth.

Ansoff, H.I. and Stewart, J.M. (1967) 'Strategies for a technology-based business', *Harvard Business Review*, 45, Nov–Dec, 71–83.

Armstrong, G. and Kotler, P. (2007) *Marketing: An Introduction*, 8th edn, Pearson Education: Upper Saddle River, NJ.

Armstrong, P. and Baron, A. (2005) *Managing Performance: Performance Management in Action*, CIPD: London.

Arvey, R.D. and Campion, J.E. (1982) 'The employment interviews: a summary and review of recent research', *Personnel Psychology*, 35, 281–322.

Atkinson, J. (1984) 'Manpower strategies for flexible organizations', *Personnel Management*, August, 28–31.

Aycan, Z. (2005) 'The interplay between cultural and institutional/structural contingencies in human resource management practices', *International journal of Human Resource Management*, 16, 7, 1083–1119.

Bach, S. (2013) 'Performance Management', in S. Bach and M. R. Edwards, *Managing Human Resources: Human Resource Management in Transition*, 5th edn, John Wiley & Sons: Chichester.

Bach, S. and Edwards, M.R. (2013) *Managing Human Resources: Human Resource Management in Transition*, 5th edn, John Wiley & Sons: Chichester.

Baines, P. and Fill, C. (2014) *Marketing*, 3rd edn, Oxford University Press: Oxford.

Barclays Bank (2002) *Barclays Bank Survey on Family Business*, www.smallbusiness.barclays.co.uk.

Barkema, H.G. and Schijven, M. (2008) 'How do firms learn to make acquisitions? A review of past research and an agenda for the future', *Journal of Management*, 34, 594–634.

Barney, J. (1991) 'Firm resources and sustained competitive advantage', *Journal of Management*, 17, 1, 99–120.

Barney, J.B. and Hesterly, W.S. (2012) *Strategic Management and Competitive Advantage: Concepts*, 4th edn, Pearson: Saddle River, NJ.

Bart, C.K. and Baetz, M.C. (1999) 'The relationship between mission statements and firm performance: an exploratory study', *Journal of Management Studies*, 35, 6, 823–853.

Bartels, F.L., Buckley, P. and Mariano, G. (2009) *Multinational Enterprises' Foreign Direct Investment Location Decisions within the Global Factor*, Research and Statistics Branch Working Paper 04, UNIDO: Washington, DC.

Bartlett, C.A. and Beamish, P.W. (2011) *Transnational Management; Text, Cases and Readings in Cross-border Management*, 6th edn, Irwin: Chicago, IL.

Bartlett, C.A. and Ghoshal, S. (1995) *Transnational Management; Text, Cases and Readings in Cross-border Management*, 2nd edn, Irwin: Chicago, IL.

Bass, B.M. (1985) *Leadership and Performance Beyond Expectations*, Free Press: New York.

Bass, B.M. (1990) 'From transactional to transformational leadership: learning to share the vision', *Organizational Dynamics*, 18, 3, 19–31.

Batt, R., Doellgast, V. and Kwon, H. (2006) 'A Comparison of Service Management and Employment Systems in US and Indian Call Centers', in S. Collins and L. Brainard (eds), *Offshoring White Collar Work – the Issues and Implications*, Brookings Institute: Washington, DC.

Becker, B.E. and Huselid, M.A. (1998) 'High Performance Work Systems and Firm Performance: A Synthesis of Research and Managerial Implications', in G. Ferris (ed.), *Research in Personnel and Human Resource Management*, Vol. 16, JAI Press: Stamford, CT.

Beer, M., Spector, B., Lawrence, P., Quinn Mills, D. and Walton, R.E. (1984) *Managing Human Assets*, Free Press: New York.

Berggren, C. and Nomura, M. (1997) *The Resilience of Corporate Japan: New Competitive Strategies and Personnel Policies*, Paul Chapman Publishing: London.

Berle, A.A. and Means, G.C. (1932) *The Modern Corporation and Private Property*, Macmillan: New York.

Berthon, P.R., Pitt, L.F., Plangger, K. and Shapiro, D. (2012) 'Marketing meets Web 2.0, social media, and creative customers: Implications for international marketing strategy', *Business Horizons*, 55, 261–271.

Bessant, J. and Tidd, J. (2007) *Innovation and Entrepreneurship*, John Wiley and Sons: Chichester.

Bhaskar, K. (1980) *The Future of the World Motor Industry*, Kogan Page: London.

Bird, D., Beatson, M. and Butcher, S. (1993) 'Membership of Trade Unions', *Employment Gazette*, May, 189–196.

Birkenshaw, J. and Mol, M. (2006) 'How management innovation happens', *Sloan Management Review*, 47, 4, 81–88.

BIS (2010) *R&D Scoreboard*, UK Department for Business, Innovation and Skills: London.

Blake, R.R. and Mouton, J.S. (1964) *The Managerial Grid*, Gulf: Houston, TX.

Blowfield, M. and Murray, A. (2008) *Corporate Responsibility: A Critical Introduction*, Oxford University Press: Oxford.

Blowfield, M. and Murray, A. (2011) *Corporate Responsibility: A Critical Introduction*, 2nd edn, Oxford University Press: Oxford.

Boddy, D. (2002) *Management: An Introduction*, Financial Times/Prentice Hall: Harlow.

Bolton, J. (1971) *Small Firms: the Report of the Committee of Inquiry on Small Firms*, HMSO, Cmd. 4811, London.

Bonnin, A.R. (2002) 'The fashion industry in Galicia: Understanding the "Zara" phenomenon', *European Planning Studies*, 10, 4, 519–527.

Boselie, P., Dietz, G. and Boon, C. (2005) 'Commonalities and contradictions in HRM and performance research', *Human Resources Management Journal*, 15, 67–94.

Bowen, A., Buxton, T. and Ricketts, M. (1992) 'The Economics of Innovation: Setting the Scene', in A. Bowen and M. Ricketts (eds), *Stimulating Innovation in Industry: The Challenge for the United Kingdom*, Kogan Page/NEDO: London.

Bowles, P. (2012) 'Rebalancing China's growth', *Canadian Journal of Development Studies*, 33, 1, 1–13.

Bowman, C. and Faulkner, D. (1996) *Competitive and Corporate Strategy*, Irwin: Chicago, IL.

Boxall, P. and Purcell, J. (2003) *Strategy and Human Resource Management*, Palgrave Macmillan: Basingstoke.

Brammer, S. and Millington, A. (2008) 'Does it pay to be different? An analysis of the relationship between corporate social and financial performance', *Strategic Management Journal*, 29, 1325–1343.

Bratton, J., and Gold, J. (2012) *Human Resource Management: Theory and Practice*, 5th edn, Palgrave Macmillan: Basingstoke.

Braverman, H. (1974) *Labour and Monopoly Capital*, Monthly Review Press: New York.

Brewster, C. and Bournois, F. (1991) 'Human resource management: a European perspective', *Personnel Review*, 20, 6, 4–13.

Brewster, C., Sparrow, P. and Harris, H. (2002) *Globalizing HR*, CIPD: London.

Brewster, C., Sparrow, P. and Harris, H. (2005) 'Towards a new model of globalizing HRM', *International Journal of Human Resource Management*, 16, 6, 949–970.

Bridge, S., O'Neill, K. and Cromie, S. (1998) *Understanding Enterprise, Entrepreneurship and Small Business*, Macmillan: London.

Brossard, M. and Maurice, M. (1976) 'Is there a universal model of organizational structure?', *International Studies of Management and Organization*, 6, 11–45.

Brouthers, K.D., Brouthers, L.E. and Harris, P.C. (1997) 'The five stages of the co-operative venture strategy process', *Journal of General Management*, 23,1, 39–52.

Brown, A. (1998) *Organizational Culture*, 2nd edn, Financial Times Pitman: London.

Bruce, M. (1987) 'Managing people first – bringing the service concept into British Airways', *Independent and Commercial Training*, March–April.

Bruce, A., Buck, T. and Main, B.G.M. (2005) 'Top executive remuneration: a view from Europe', *Journal of Management Studies*, 42, 7, 1493–1506.

Bryce, R. (2002) *Pipe Dreams: Greed, Ego and the Death of Enron*, Public Affairs: London.

Bryman, A. (1992) *Charisma and Leadership in Organizations*, Harper & Row: New York.

Bryson, A. (2000) *Have British workers lost their voice or have they gained a new one?*, PSI Discussion Paper 2, Policy Studies Institute: London.

Buchan, J. (1993) 'Withdrawal symptoms', *Independent on Sunday Review*, 23 April, 2–5.

Buiter, W. and Rahbari, E. (2011) *Global Growth Generators: Moving Beyond Emerging Markets and BRIC*, http://blog.citigroup.com/2011/03/global-growth-generators-moving-beyond-emerging-markets-and-bric.shtml.

Burns, J.M. (1978) *Leadership*, Harper Row: New York.

Burns, P. (2001) *Entrepreneurship and Small Business*, Palgrave: London.

Burns, T. and Stalker, G.M. (1966) *The Management of Innovation*, Tavistock: London.

Cantwell, J., Dunning, J.H. and Lundan, S.M. (2010) 'An evolutionary approach to understanding international business activity: the co-evolution of MNEs and the institutional environment, *Journal of International Business Studies*, 41, 567–586.

Carlson, S. (1951) *Executive Behaviour: A Study of the Workload and Behaviour of Managing Directors*, Strombergs: Stockholm.

Carr, A.Z. (1968) 'Is business bluffing ethical?', *Harvard Business Review*, 46, Jan–Feb, 143–153.

Carroll, A. (1991) 'The pyramid of corporate social responsibility', *Business Horizons*, July–Aug, 39–48.

Carroll, D.T. (1983) 'A disappointing search for excellence', *Harvard Business Review*, 63, Nov–Dec, 78–88.

Castells, M. (1996) *The Rise of the Network Society*, Blackwell Publishers: Oxford.

Caulkin, S. (2005) 'A heap big pile of chiefs', *Observer*, 22 May, p. 10.

Chaffin, J. and Fidler, S. (2002) 'Enron's alchemy turns to lead for bankers', *Financial Times*, 28 Feb.

Chandler, A.D. (1962) *Strategy and Structure: Chapters in the History of American Capitalism*, MIT Press: Cambridge, MA.

Chandler, A.D. and Mazlish, B. (2005) *Leviathans: Multinational Corporations and the New Global History*, Cambridge University Press: Cambridge.

Channon, D.F. (1973) *The Strategy and Structure of British Enterprise*, Macmillan: London.

Chell, E. (2001) *Entrepreneurship: Globalization, Innovation and Development*, Thomson Learning: London.

Chen J. and Yao, S. (eds) (2006) *Globalization and Growth in China*. Routledge: Abingdon.

Child, J. (1969) *The Business Enterprise in Modern Industrial Society*, Collier-Macmillan: London.

Child, J. (2005) *Organization: Contemporary Principles and Practice*, Blackwell: Oxford.

Chong Li Choy (1990) 'Business in the development of Singapore', in Chong Li Choy et al. (eds), *Business, Society and Development in Singapore*, Times Academic Press, Singapore.

CIPD (2007) *The Changing HR Function*, CIPD: London.

Clark, A. (2006) 'White collar criminals find quality of mercy increasingly strained', *The Guardian*, 24 October.

Clarke, F.L., Dean, G.W. and Oliver, K.G. (1999) *Corporate Collapse: Regulatory Accounting and Ethical Failure*, Cambridge University Press: Cambridge.

Claydon, T. and Beardwell, J. (2010) *Human Resource Management: A Contemporary Approach*, 6th edn, FT Prentice Hall: Harlow.

Combs, J., Liu, Y., Hall, A. and Kitchen, D. (2006) 'How much do high performance work practices matter? A meta-analysis of their effects on organisational performance', *Personnel Psychology*, 59, 501–528.

Conger, J. (1990) 'The dark side of leadership', *Organizational Dynamics*, 19, 2, 44–55.

Conn, D. (2008) 'What the credit crunch means for the Premier League', *The Guardian*, Inside Sport, 6–7, 22 October.

Conn, D. (2009) 'Inside sport special report: Premier League finances', *The Guardian*, Inside Sport, 3 June.

Connon, H. (1992) 'Glaxo invests £1bn. Hot-house to foster discovery', *Independent*, 9 June.

Corbett, J. and Jenkinson, T. (1997) 'How is investment financed? A study of Germany, Japan, the United Kingdom and the United States', *The Manchester School Supplement*, 69–93.

Council for Excellence in Management and Leadership (2002) *Managers and Leaders: Raising Our Game*, Council for Excellence in Management and Leadership: London.

Cowell, D.W. (1984) Sales promotions and the marketing of local government and leisure services, *European Journal of Marketing*, 18, 2, 114–120.

Crane, A. and Matten, D. (2010) *Business Ethics*, 3rd edn, Oxford University Press: Oxford.

Crane, A., Matten, D. and Spence, L.J. (2014) *Corporate Social Responsibility: Readings and Cases in a Global Context*, 2nd edn, Routledge: Abingdon.

Cyert, R.M. and March, J.G (1963) *A Behavioural Theory of the Firm*, Prentice Hall: Englewood Cliffs, NJ.

Daft, R.L. (1982) 'Bureaucratic v non-bureaucratic structures and the process of innovation and change', in S.B. Bachovach (ed.), *Research in the Sociology of Organizations*, JAI Press: Greenwich.

Damanpour, F., Szabat, K.A. and Evan, W.M. (1989) 'The relationship between types of innovation and organization performance', *Journal of Management Studies*, 26, 587–601.

Daniel, E. and Wilson, H. (2002) 'Adoption intention and benefits realized: a study of e-commerce in UK SMEs', *Journal of Small Business Enterprise Development*, 9, 4, 331–348.

Datta, D.K. (1988) International joint ventures: a framework for analysis, *Journal of General Management*, 14, 2, 78–91.

Davis, S.M. and Lawrence, P.R. (eds) (1977) *Matrix*, Addison-Wesley: Reading, MA.

Dawson, S. (1986) *Analysing Organizations*, Macmillan: London.

Dawson, S. (1996) *Analysing Organizations*, 3rd edn, Macmillan: London.

De Cuyper, N., De Jong, J. and De Witte, H (2008) 'Literature review of theory and research on the psychological impact of temporary employment: towards a conceptual model', *International Journal of Management Reviews*, 10, 25–51.

De Mooij, M. (2005) *Global Marketing and Advertising: Understanding Cultural Paradoxes*, 2nd edn, Sage: London.

De Wit, B. and Meyer, R. (2010) *Strategy: Process, Content, Context: An International Perspective*, 4th edn, Cengage Learning: Andover.

Deal, T.E. and Kennedy, A.A. (1982) *Corporate Cultures*, Penguin: Harmondsworth.

Deery, S. (2005) 'Customer service work, emotional labour and performance', in S. Bach (ed.), *Managing Human Resources: Personnel Management in Transition*, 4th edn, Blackwell: Oxford.

Deming, W.E. (1986) *Out of Crisis: Quality, Productivity and Competitive Position*, Cambridge University Press: Cambridge.

Department for Transport (2011) *Realising the Potential of GB Rail; Final Independent Report of the Rail Value for Money Study*, Department for Transport: London.

Dibb, S., Simkin, L., Pride, W.M. and Ferrell, O.C. (2006) *Marketing Concepts and Strategies*, 5th European Edition, Houghton Mifflin: Boston, MA.

Dicken, P. (2011) *Global Shift: Mapping the Changing Contours of the World Economy*, 6th edn, Sage: London.

Dickens, L. (2005) 'Walking the talk? Equality and diversity in employment', in S. Bach (ed.), *Managing Human Resources: Personnel Management in Transition*, 4th edn, Blackwell: Oxford.

Dix, G., Forth, J. and Sisson, K. (2008) *Conflict at Work: The Pattern of Disputes in Britain since 1980*. London: ACAS.

Dore, R. (1973) *British Factory – Japanese Factory*, University of California Press: Berkeley, CA.

Dore, R. (1997) 'Good jobs, no jobs and bad jobs', *Industrial Relations Journal*, 28, 4, 262–268.

Dore, R. (2000) *Stock Market Capitalism: Welfare Capitalism: Japan and Germany Versus the Anglo-Saxons*, Oxford University Press: Oxford.

Dowling, P. and Welch, D. (2004) *International Human Resource Management: Managing People in a Multinational Context*, Thomson: London.

Driffield, N. and Du, J. (2007) 'Privatization, state ownership and productivity: evidence from China', *International Journal of Economics of Business*, 14, 2, 215–229.

Drucker, P.E. (1964) *Managing for Results*, Harper & Row: New York.

Drucker, P.E. (1968) *The Practice of Management*, Pan Books: London.

DTI (1998) *Entrepreneurial Activity and Entrepreneurship within Higher Education*, Durham University Business School, DTI Conference, DTI: London.

DTI (2005) *Inspired Leadership: Insights into People who Inspire Exceptional Performance*, DTI: London.

DTI (2006) *Innovation in the UK: Indicators and Insights*, DTI Occasional Paper No 6, DTI: London.

Dunning, J.H. (1993) *Multinational Enterprise and the Global Economy*, Addison-Wesley: Harrow .

Edwards, M. (2005) 'Employer and employee branding: HR or PR?', in S. Bach (ed.), *Managing Human Resources: Personnel Management in Transition*, 4th edn, Blackwell: Oxford.

Edwards, T. and Rees, C. (2006) 'The transfer of human resource management practices in multinational companies', in T. Edwards and C. Rees (eds), *International Human Resource Management: Globalization, National Systems and Multinational Companies*, FT Prentice Hall: Harlow.

Edwards, T. and Rees, C. (2010) *International Human Resource Management: Globalization, National Systems and Multinational Companies*, 2nd edn, FT Prentice Hall: Harlow.

Eisingerich, A.B. and Kretschmer, T. (2008) 'In E-commerce, more is more', *Harvard Business Review*, 86, 20–21.

Ekvall, G. (1991) 'The organizational culture of idea-management: a creative climate for the management of ideas', in J. Henry and D. Walker (eds), *Managing Innovation*, Sage/OU: London.

Elliot, L. (2014) 'Mint condition: countries tipped as the next economic powerhouses', *The Guardian*, 9 January.

El-Namiki, M. (1993) *Contemporary Dynamics of Entrepreneurship*, Netherlands International Institute for Management: Netherlands.

Ettenson, R., Conrado, E. and Knowles, J. (2013) Rethinking the 4P's, *Harvard Business Review*, Jan–Feb.

European Commission (2006) *Europeans and Mobility: First Results of an EU-wide Survey*, European Commission: Brussels.

European Commission (2013) *R&D Scoreboard*, European Union: Luxembourg. (http://epp.eurostat.ec.europa.eu).

Fagan, M. (1991) 'Is it right that the scientists should take the decisions?', *Independent*, 10 June.

Farrell, D. (2005) 'Offshoring: value creation through economic change', *Journal of Management Studies*, 42, 3, 675–683.

Fayol, H. (1949) *General and Industrial Management*, Pitman: London.

Feigenbaum, A.V. (1961) *Total Quality Control*, McGraw Hill: London.

Fiedler, F.E. (1967) *A Theory of Leadership Effectiveness*, McGraw Hill: New York.

Fishman, C. (2006) 'The Wal-Mart effect and a decent society. Who knew shopping was so important?', *Academy of Management Perspectives*, August, 6–25.

Freeman, C. (1989) 'R&D, technical change and investment in the UK', in F. Green (ed.), *Restructuring the UK Economy*, Harvester Wheatsheaf: London.

Freeman, C. (1995) 'The 'National System of innovation' in historical perspective, *Cambridge Journal of Economics*, 19, 5–24.

French, R. (2010) *Cross-cultural Management in Work Organizations*, 2nd edn, CIPD: London.

Friedman, L.G. and Furey, T.R. (1999) *The Channel Advantage*, Butterworth-Heinemann: Oxford.

Friedman, M. (1970) 'The social responsibility of business is to increase profits', *New York Times Magazine*, Sept 13th, New York.

Friedman, T.L. (2006) *The World is Flat: A Brief History of the World in the 21st Century*, Penguin: Harmondsworth.

Galbraith, J.K. (1972) *The New Industrial State*, 2nd edn, Penguin: Harmondsworth.

Galbraith, J.R. (1971) 'Matrix organization designs', *Business Horizons*, 14, 29–40.

Galbraith, J.R. and Nathanson, D.A. (1978) *Strategy Implementation: The Role of Structure and Process*, West Publishing Co.: St. Paul, MN.

Gallie, D. (1991) 'Patterns of skill change: upskilling, deskilling or the polarization of skills?', *Work, Employment and Society*, 5, 3, 319–351.

Gao, X. (2010) State-owned enterprises in China. How big are they? World Bank, Gao Xu's Blog, 2 March.

Gereffi, G. (1999) 'International trade and industrial upgrading in the apparel commodity chain', *Journal of International Economics*, 48, 37–70.

Gereffi, G., Humphrey, J. and Sturgeon, T. (2005) 'The governance of global value chains', *Review of International Political Economy*, 12, 1, 78–104.

Gill, C., Krieger, H. and Froelich, D. (1992) 'The employment impact of new technology: recent European evidence', *Journal of General Management*, 18, 2, 1–13.

Gladwell, M. (2009) *Outliers: The Story of Success*, Penguin Books: London.

Goleman, D. (1995) *Emotional Intelligence: Why It Can Matter More Than IQ*, Bantam Books: New York.

Gomes, E., Angwin, D.N., Weber, Y. And Tarba, S.Y. (2013) 'Critical success factors through the merger and acquisitions process: revealing pre- and post-M&A connections for improved performance', *Thunderbird International Business Review*, 55, 1, 13–34.

González-Loureiro, M., Dabic, M. and Puig, F. (2014) 'Global organizations and supply chain: new research avenues in the international human resource management', *International Journal of Physical Distribution & Logistics Management*, 44, 7, forthcoming.

Goos, A. and Manning, A. (2007) 'Lousy jobs and lovely jobs: the rising polarization of work in Britain', *Review of Economics and Statistics*, 89, 1, 118–133.

Gordan, G.G. and Ditomaso, N. (1992) 'Predicting corporate performance from organizational culture', *Journal of Management Studies*, 29, 6, 783–98.

Grainger, H. and Crowther, M. (2006) *Trade Union Membership*, DTI: London.

Granovetter, M. (1985) 'Economic action and social structure', *American Journal of Sociology*, 91, 481–510.

Guest, D., Michie, J., Sheehan, M., Conway, N. and Metochi, M. (2000) *Effective People Management*, CIPD: London.

Guest, D.E. (2011) 'Human resource management and performance: still searching for some answers', *Human Resource Management Journal*, 21, 1, 3–13.

Haleblian, J., Devers, C.E., McNamara, G., Carpenter, M.A. and Davison, R.B. (2009) 'Taking stock of what we know about mergers and acquisitions: a review and research agenda', *Journal of Management Online First*, February, doi 10.1177/0149206308330554.

Hales, C.P. (1986) 'What do managers do? A critical review of the evidence', *Journal of Management Stores*, 23, 88–115.

Hall, E.T. (1959) *The Silent Language*, Doubleday: New York.

Hall, E.T. (1976) *Beyond Culture*, Doubleday: New York.

Hall, E.T. (1990) *Understanding Cultural Differences*, Intercultural Press: Yarmouth, ME.

Hall, P.A. and Soskice, D. (eds) (2001) *Varieties of Capitalism: The Institutional Foundations of Comparative Advantage*, Oxford University Press: Oxford.

Hamel, G. (2006) 'The why, what and how of management innovation', *Harvard Business Review*, 84, 2, 72–84.

Hamel, G. and Prahalad, C.K. (1990) 'The core competence of the corporation', *Harvard Business Review*, 68, 3, 79–91.

Hamel, G. and Prahalad, C.K. (1994) *Competing for the Future*, Harvard Business School Press: Boston, MA.

Handy, C. (1993) *Understanding Organizations*, 4th edn, Penguin: Harmondsworth.

Harbison, F. and Myers, C.A. (1959) *Management in the Industrial World: An International Analysis*, McGraw Hill: New York.

Harrison, C.R. (1972) 'Understanding your organization's character', *Harvard Business Review*, 50, 3, 119–128.

Hawkins, K. (1978) *The Management of Industrial Relations*, Penguin: Harmondsworth.

Held, D., McGrew, A., Goldblatt, D. and Perraton, J. (1999) *Global Transformations: Politics, Economics and Culture*, Polity Press: Cambridge.

Hickson, D.J., Pugh, D.S. and Pheysey, D. (1969) 'Operation technology and organization structure: an empirical appraisal', *Administrative Science Quarterly*, 14, 378–397.

Hill, C.W.L. (2007) *International Business: Competing in the Global Marketplace*, McGraw Hill-Irwin: New York.

Hirst, P. and Thompson, G. (1999) *Globalization in Question*, 2nd edn, Polity Press: Cambridge.

Hitt, M. and Ireland, D. (1987) 'Peters and Waterman revisited: the unending quest for excellence', *Academy of Management Executive*, 1, 2, 91–98.

Hofer, C.W. and Schendel, D. (1978) *Strategy Formulation: Analytical Concepts*, West Publishing: St. Paul, MN.

Hofstede, G.H. (1980a) *Culture's Consequences: International Differences in Work-related Values*, Sage: London.

Hofstede, G.H. (1980b) 'Motivation, leadership and organization: do American theories apply abroad?', *Organizational Dynamics*, Summer, 42–63.

Hofstede, G.H. (1994) *Cultures and Organizations: Intercultural Cooperation and its Importance for Survival*, McGraw Hill International: London.

Hofstede, G.H. (1999) 'Problems remain, but theories will change: the universal and the specific in 21st century global management', *Organizational Dynamics*, 28, 1, 34–44.

Hofstede, G.H. and Bond, M.H. (1988) 'The Confucius connection; from cultural roots to economic growth', *Organizational Dynamics*, 16, 4, 4–21.

Hofstede, G.H., Hofstede, G.J. and Minkov, M. (2010) *Cultures and Organizations: Software of the Mind – Intercultural Cooperation and its Importance for Survival*, 3rd edn, McGraw Hill: New York.

Holden, N.J. (2002) *Cross-cultural Management: A Knowledge Management Perspective*, FT/Prentice Hall: Harlow.

Hoque, K. and Noon, M. (2001) 'Counting angels: a comparison of personnel and HR specialists', *Human Resource Management Journal*, 11, 3, 5–22.

Horne, M. and Stedman-Jones, D. (2001) *Leadership: the Challenge for All?*, The Institute of Management: London.

House, R.J. and Mitchell, T.R. (1974) 'Path-goal theory of leadership', *Journal of Contemporary Business*, Autumn, 81–97.

House, R.J., Hanges, P.J, Javidan, M., Dorfman, P. and Gupta, V. (2004) *Culture, Leadership and Organizations: The GLOBE Study of 62 Societies*, Sage: Thousand Oaks, CA.

House, R.J., Javidan, M. and Dorfman, P.W. (2001) The GLOBE project, *Applied Psychology: an International Review*, 50, 4, 489–505.

Hu, Y.S. (1996) 'Globalization and corporate nationality', in M. Warner (ed.), *International Encyclopaedia of Business and Management*, pp. 1664–1672, Routledge: London.

Huselid, M.A. (1995) 'The impact of human resource management practices on turnover, productivity, and corporate financial performance', *Academy of Management Journal*, 38, 635–672.

Hutton, W. (2012) 'Globalisation can work but only with a unified international plan', *The Observer*, 29 January.

ILO (2003) *Labour Market Trends and Globalization's Impact on Them*, International Labour Office: Geneva.

ILO (2007) *Key Indicators of the Labour Market*, 5th edn, International Labour Office: Geneva.

ILO (2013) *Key Indicators of the Labour Market*, 7th edn, International Labour Office: Geneva.

IMF (2003) *The Impact of Globalization on Workers and their Trade Unions*, www.imf.org.

Institute of Personnel Management (1963) 'Statement on personnel management and personnel policies', *Personnel Management*, March.

Javidan, M. and House, R.J. (2001) 'Cultural acumen for the global manager: lessons from project GLOBE', *Organizational Dynamics*, 29, 4, 289–305.

Javidan, M. and House, R.J. (2011) 'Cultural acumen for the global manager: lessons from project GLOBE', *Organizational Dynamics*, 29, 4, 289–305.

Javidan, M., House, R.J., Dorfman, P.W., Hanges, P.J. and de Luque, M.S. (2006) 'Conceptualizing and measuring cultures and their consequences: a comparative review of GLOBE's and Hofstede's approaches', *Journal of International Business Studies*, 37, 897–914.

Jensen, M.C. (2001) 'Value maximization, stakeholder theory and the corporate objective', *Journal of Applied Corporate Finance*, 14, 3, 8–21.

Jensen, M.C. and Meckling, W.H. (1976) 'Theory of the firm: managerial behaviour, agency costs and ownership structure', *Journal of Financial Economics*, 3, October, 305–360.

Jewkes, J., Sawers, D. and Stillerman, R. (1970) *The Sources of Innovation*, W.W. Norton: New York.

Jiang, K., Lepak, D.P., Hu, J. and Baer, J.C. (2012) 'How does human resource management influence organizational outcomes? A meta-analytical investigation of mediating mechanisms', *Academy of Management Journal*, 55, 1264–1294.

Jobber, D. (2001) *Principles and Practice of Marketing*, 3rd edn, McGraw Hill: Maidenhead.

Johanson, J. and Vahlne, J-E. (1977) 'The internation-alization process of the firm: a model of knowledge development and market commitment,' *Journal of International Business Studies*, 1, 1, 83–101.

Johnson, G., Whittington, R. and Scholes, K. (2012) *Fundamentals of Strategy*, 2nd edn, FT Prentice Hall: Harlow.

Johnson, G., Whittington, R., Scholes, K., Angwin, D. and Regnér, P. (2013) *Exploring Strategy: Text and Cases*, 10th edn, FT Prentice Hall: Harlow.

Johnson, P. (2007) *The Economics of Small Firms: An Introduction*, Routledge: London.

Johnson, R. (2002) 'Trust funding', *People Management*, 26 Sept., 36–39.

Johnson, S. (2011) 'Takeovers enhance share value – study shows', *Financial Times*, 1 May.

Johnston, R. and Clark, G. (2012) *Service Operations Management: Improving Service Delivery*, 4th edn, FT Prentice Hall: Harlow.

Jones, G. (1996) *The Evolution of International Business: An Introduction*, Routledge: London.

Jones, G. (2005) *Multinationals and Global Capitalism: From the Nineteenth to the Twenty-first Century*, Oxford University Press: Oxford.

Judge, T.A., Bono, J.E., Ilies, R. and Gerhardt, M.W. (2002) 'Personality and leadership: a qualitative and quantitative review', *Journal of Applied Psychology*, 87, 4, 765–780.

Juran, J.M. (1988) *Quality Control Handbook*, McGraw Hill: New York.

Kanter, R.M. (ed.) (1997) *Innovation: Breakthrough Thinking at 3M, DuPont, GE, Pfizer and Rubbermaid*, Harper Business: New York.

Kanter, R.M. and Corn, R.I. (1994) 'Do cultural differences make a business difference? Contextual factors affecting cross-cultural relationship success', *Journal of Management Development*, 13, 2, 5–23.

Kaplan, R.S. and Norton, D.P. (1992) 'The balanced scorecard; measures that drive performance', *Harvard Business Review*, 70, 1, 71–79.

Kaplan, R.S. and Norton, D.P. (1996) *The Balanced Scorecard*, Harvard Business School Press: Boston, MA.

Kaplinsky, R. (1983) 'Firm size and technical change in a dynamic context', *The Journal of Industrial Economics*, 32, 1, 39–59.

Kaplinsky, R. (2000) *Spreading the Gains from Globalisation: What Can Be Learned from Value Chain Analysis*, IDS Working Paper 110, Institute of Development Studies: Brighton.

Karnani, A. (2010) 'The case against corporate social responsibility', *Wall Street Journal*, August 23.

Katz, D. and Kahn, R.L. (1978) *The Social Psychology of Organizations*, John Wiley: New York.

Kay, J. (1992) 'Innovations in corporate strategy', in A. Bowen and M. Ricketts (eds), *Stimulating Innovation in Industry: The Challenge for the United Kingdom*, Kogan Page/NEDO: London.

Kay, J. (1993) *Foundations of Corporate Success: How Business Strategies Add Value*, Oxford University Press: Oxford.

Kennedy, C. (1988) 'Global strategies for 3M', *Long Range Planning*, 21, 1, 9–17.

Kerr, C., Dunlop, J.T., Harbison, F. and Myers, C.A. (1973) *Industrialism and Industrial Man*, Penguin: Harmondsworth.

Kersley, B., Carmen, A., Forth, J., Bryson, A., Bewley, H., Dix, G. and Oxenbridge, S. (2006) *Inside the Workplace: Findings from the 2004 Employment Relations Survey*, Routledge: London.

Kirkbride, P., Pinnington, P. and Ward, K. (2001) 'The state of globalization today', in P. Kirkbride (ed.), *Globalization: the External Pressures*, John Wiley and Sons Ltd.: Chichester.

Kirkpatrick, S.A. and Locke, E.A. (1991) 'Leadership: do traits matter?', *Academy of Management Executive*, May, 48–60.

Kirton, G. and Greene, A.M. (2005) *The Dynamics of Managing Diversity: a Critical Approach*, 2nd edn, Elsevier Butterworth-Heinemann: London.

Knorr, A. and Arndt, A. (2003) 'Why did Wal-Mart fail in Germany', Band 24, pp. 1–30, Institute for World Economics and International Management, University of Bremen.

Koen, C.I. (2005) *Comparative International Management*, McGraw-Hill: London.

Koh, H.C. and Boo, E.H.Y. (2001) 'The link between organizational ethics and job satisfaction: a study of managers in Singapore', *Journal of Business Ethics*, 29, 4, 309–324.

Kondratieff, N.D. (1935) 'The long waves in economic life', *Review of Economic Statistics*, 17, 105–115.

Konzelmann, S., Fovargue-Davies, M. and Schnyder, G. (2012) 'The faces of liberal capitalism: Anglo-Saxon banking systems in crisis?', *Cambridge Journal of Economics*, 36, 495–524.

Kotler, P. (1983) *Principles of Marketing*, 2nd edn, Prentice Hall: Englewood Cliffs, NJ.

Kotler, P., Armstrong, G., Harris, R. and Piercy, N.F. (2013) *Principles of Marketing*, 6th European edn, FT Prentice Hall: Harlow.

Kotter, J.P. (1990) 'What leaders really do', *Harvard Business Review*, May–June, 103–111.

Lasserre, P. and Schutte, H. (1999) *Strategy and Management in Asia Pacific*, McGraw Hill: London.

Lawrence, P.R. and Lorsch, J. (1967) *Organization and Environment*, Harvard University Press: Cambridge, MA.

Legge, K. (1978) *Power, Innovation and Problem-solving in Personnel Management*, McGraw Hill: London.

Legge, K. (1998) 'Flexibility: the gift wrapping of employment degradation?', in P.R. Sparrow and M. Marchington, *Human Resource Management: The New Agenda*, Financial Times/Pitman Publishing: London.

Legrain, P. (2002) *Open World: The Truth about Globalization*, Abacus: London.

Lei, D. (1989) 'Strategies for global competition', *Long Range Planning*, 22, 1, 102–109.

Levitt, T. (1958) 'The dangers of social responsibility', *Harvard Business Review*, 36, Sept–Oct, 41–50.

Levitt, T (1960) 'Marketing myopia', *Harvard Business Review*, 38, July–Aug., 24–47.

Levitt, T. (1975) 'Marketing myopia: retrospective commentary', *Harvard Business Review*, 53, Sept–Oct., 177–181.

Levitt, T. (1983) 'The globalization of markets', *Harvard Business Review*, 61, May–June, 92–102.

Levy, D. (2005) 'Offshoring in the new global political economy', *Journal of Management Studies*, 42, 3, 685–693.

Lieberman, M. and Montgomery, D. (1988) 'First-mover advantages', *Strategic Management Journal*, 9, 41–58.

Likert, R. (1961) *New Patterns in Management*, McGraw Hill: New York.

Lindblom, C.E. (1959) 'The science of muddling through', *Public Administration Review*, 19, 2, 79–88.

Littler, C.R., Wiesner, R. and Dunford, R. (2003) 'The dynamics of delayering: changing management structures in three countries', *Journal of Management Studies*, 40, 2, 225–256.

Lundvall, B.A. (ed.) (1992) *National Systems of Innovation: Towards a Theory of Innovation and Interactive Learning*, Pinter: London.

Luthans, F. (1988) 'Successful v. effective real managers', *Academy of Management Executive*, 2, 2, 127–132.

Lyons, M.P. (1991) 'Joint ventures as strategic choice – a literature review', *Long Range Planning*, 24, 4, 130–144.

Manning, A. (2004) *We Can Work It Out: The Impact of Technological Change on the Demand for Low-Skill Workers: CEP Discussion Paper No 640*, CEP: London.

Mansfield, E. (1963) Size of firm, market structure and innovation, *Journal of Political Economy*, 71, 6, 556–576.

Margolis, J.D. and Walsh, J.P. (2003) 'Misery loves companies: rethinking social initiatives by companies', *Administrative Science Quarterly*, 48, 2, 268–305.

Marjoribanks, T. (2000) *News Corporation, Technology and the Workplace: Global Strategies, Local Change*, Cambridge University Press: Cambridge.

Marris, R.L. (1964) *The Economic Theory of Managerial Capitalism*, Macmillan: London.

Martin, J. (2001) *Organizational Behaviour*, 2nd edn, Thomson Learning: London.

McCarthy, E.J. (1960) *Basic Marketing: a Managerial Approach*, Irwin: Homewood, IL.

McClelland, D. (1961) *The Achieving Society*, Van Nostrand: Princeton, NJ.

McIntosh, M. (1998) *Introduction, in Financial Times Management, Visions of Ethical Business*, Financial Times Management: London.

McKenna, E. and Beech, N. (2013) *Human Resource Management: A Concise Analysis*, 3rd edn, FT Prentice Hall: Harlow.

McLean, B. and Elkind, P. (2004) *The Smartest Guys in the Room: The Amazing Rise and Scandalous Fall of Enron*, Portfolio: New York.

McSweeney, B. (2002) 'Hofstede's model of national cultural differences and their consequences: a triumph of faith – a failure of analysis', *Human Relations*, 55, 1, 89–118.

McWilliams, A. and Siegel, D. (2000) 'Corporate social responsibility and financial performance: correlation or misspecification?', *Strategic Management journal*, 21, 5, 603–609.

McWilliams, A., Siegel, D.S. and Wright, P.M. (2006) 'Corporate social responsibility: strategic implications', *Journal of Management Studies*, 43, 1, 1–18.

Mead, M. (ed.) (1951) *Cultural Patterns and Technology*, UNESCO: Paris.

Medcof, J.W. (1997) 'Why too many alliances end in divorce', *Long Range Planning*, 30, 5, 718–732.

Megginson, W.L. and Netter, J.M. (2001) 'From state to market: a survey of empirical studies on privatization', *Journal of Economic Literature*, 39, 2, 321–389.

Mensch, G. (1979) *Stalemate in Technology*, Ballinger: Cambridge, MA.

Miller, A. and Dess, G.G. (1996) *Strategic Management*, 2nd edn, McGraw Hill: New York.

Mills, R., Dimech Debeno, J. and Dimech Debeno, V. (1994) 'Euro Disney: a Mickey Mouse project?', *The European Management Journal*, 12, 3, 306–314.

Minkov, M. (2012) *Cross-cultural Analysis: The Art and Science of Comparing the World's Societies and their Cultures*, Sage: London.

Mintel (1994) *The Green Consumer*, Vols. 1 and 2, Mintel: London.

Mintzberg, H. (1973a) *The Nature of Managerial Work*, Harper Row: New York.

Mintzberg, H. (1973b) 'Strategy making in 3 modes', *California Management Review*, 16, Winter, 44–53.

Mintzberg, H. (1990) 'The Design School: reconsidering the basic premises of strategic management', *Strategic Management Journal*, 11, 176–195.

Mintzberg, H. and Quinn, J.B. (1991) *The Strategy Process*, 2nd edn, Prentice Hall: London.

Mintzberg, H., Lampel, J.B., Quinn, J.B. and Ghoshal, S. (2003) The *Strategy Process: Concepts, Contexts and Cases*, 4th edn, Prentice Hall: London.

Murton, A. (2000) 'Labour markets and flexibility: current debates and the European dimension', in J. Barry *et al.* (eds), *Organization and Management: A Critical Text*, International Thomson Business Press: London.

Needle, D. (2000) 'Culture at the level of the firm: organizational and corporate perspectives', in J. Barry *et al.* (eds), *Organization and Management: A Critical Text*, International Thomson Business Press: London.

NESTA (2009) *The Innovation Index: Measuring the UK's Investment in Innovation and its Effects*, National Endowment for Science, Technology and the Arts: London.

Nguyen, T.V. (2003) 'Managing change in Vietnamese state-owned enterprises. What's the best strategy?', *Human Resource Management Review*, 13, 423–439.

Nicholls, T. (1969) *Ownership, Control and Ideology*, Routledge: London.

Noon, M. and Blyton, P. (2007) *The Realities of Work*, 3rd edn, Palgrave: London.

O'Neill, J. and Stupnytska, A. (2009) *The Long-term Outlook for the BRICs and N-11 Post Crisis*, Global Economics Paper No 192, Goldman Sachs: London.

Ohno, T. (1988) *Toyota Production System: Beyond Large Scale Production*, Productivity Press: Cambridge, MA.

Owen, G. (1996) 'The impact of financial systems on British and German industrial performance', presented at *PERC Conference on Stakeholder Capitalism*, March 29th.

Owen, G. (2010) *The Rise and Fall of Great Companies: Courtaulds and the Reshaping of the Man-Made Fibres Industry*, OUP: Oxford.

Packard, D. (1995) *The HP Way: How Bill Hewlett and I Built our Company*, Harper Business: New York.

Panitch, L. and Gindin, S. (2013) 'The integration of China into global capitalism', *International Critical Thought*, 3, 2, 146–158.

Partnoy, F. (2003) 'When greed is fact and control is fiction', *The Guardian*, 14 Feb.

Pascale, R. and Rohlen, T.P. (1983) 'The Mazda turnaround', *Journal of Japanese Studies*, 9, 2, 219–263.

Pavitt, K. (1983) 'Characteristics of innovative activity in British industry', *OMEGA*, 11, 2, 113–130.

Pearce, C.L. (2004) 'The future of leadership: combining vertical and shared leadership to transform knowledge work', *Academy of Management Executive*, 18, 1, 47–59.

Peters, T.J. and Waterman, R.H. (1982) *In Search of Excellence: Lessons from America's Best Run Companies*, Harper & Row: London.

Pettigrew, A.M. (1973) *The Politics of Organizational Decision-making*, Tavistock: London.

Pfeffer, J. (1998) *The Human Equation: Building Profits by Putting People First*, Harvard Business School Press: Harvard, MA.

Piccolo, R.F. and Colquitt, J.A. (2006) 'Transformational leadership and job behaviors: the mediating role of core job characteristics', *Academy of Management Journal*, 49, 2, 327–340.

Piercy, N.F. (1997) *Market-led Strategic Change: Transforming the Process of Going To Market*, 2nd edn, Butterworth Heinemann: Oxford.

Piercy, N.F. (2009) *Market-led Strategic Change: Transforming the Process of Going to Market*, 4th edn, Butterworth-Heinemann: Oxford.

Piercy, N.F. and Morgan, N.A. (1993) 'Strategic and operational market segmentation: a management analysis', *Journal of Strategic Marketing*, 1, 123–140.

Pollert, A. (1987) 'The flexible firm: a model in search of reality (or a policy in search of a practice)?', *Warwick Papers in Industrial Relations*, No. 19.

Porter, M.E. (1980) *Competitive Strategy: Techniques for Analyzing Industries and Competitors*, Free Press: New York.

Porter, M.E. (1985) *Competitive Advantage: Creating and Sustaining Superior Performance*, Free Press: New York.

Porter, M.E. (1990) *The Competitive Advantage of Nations*, Macmillan: London.

Porter, M.E. (1996) 'What is strategy?', *Harvard Business Review*, Nov–Dec, 61–77.

Porter, M.E. (2008) 'The five competitive forces that shape strategy', *Harvard Business Review*, January, 79–93.

Porter, M.E. and Kramer, M.R. (2006) 'Strategy and society: the link between competitive advantage and corporate social responsibility', *Harvard Business Review*, December, 78–92.

Porter, M.E. and Kramer, M.R. (2011) 'Creating shared value', *Harvard Business Review*, 89, 62–77.

Porter, M.E., Takeuchi, H. and Sakakibara, M. (2000) *Can Japan Compete?*, Macmillan: London.

PricewaterhouseCoopers (2011) *The World in 2050: The Accelerating Shift of Global Economic Power: Challenges and Opportunities*, PwC: London.

Pudelko, M. (2006) 'A comparison of HRM systems in the USA, Japan and Germany in their socio-economic context', *Human Resource Management Journal*, 16, 2, 123–153.

Pugh, D.S. (1969) 'The context of organization structures', *Administrative Science Quarterly*, 14, 570–581.

Puig, F. and Marques, H. (2010) *Territory, Specialization and Globalization in European Manufacturing*, Routledge: Abingdon.

Purcell, J. (1989) 'The impact of corporate strategy on human resource management', in J. Storey (ed.), *New Perspectives in Human Resource Management*, Routledge: London.

Quayle, M. (2002) 'E-commerce: the challenge for UK SMEs in the twenty-first century', *International Journal of Operations and Production Management*, 22, 10, 1148–1161.

Ranjan, R.G. and Wulf, J. (2006) 'The flattening firm: evidence from panel data on the changing nature of corporate hierarchies', *Review of Economics and Statistics*, 88, 759–773.

Rasiah, R., Zhang, M. and Kong, X. (2013) 'Can China's Miraculous Economic Growth Continue?', *Journal of Contemporary Asia*, 43, 2, 295–313.

Ray, C.A. (1986) 'Corporate culture: the last frontier of control', *Journal of Management Studies*, 23, 3, 287–297.

Reichhart, A. and Holweg, M. (2007) 'Lean distribution: concepts, contributions, conflicts', *International Journal of Production Research*, 45, 16, 3699–3722.

Rifkin, J. (1995) 'The end of work', *New Statesman and Society*, 9 June, 18–25.

Roach, S. (2004) *The Challenge of China and India*, Financial Times.

Rogers, E.M. (1962) *Diffusion of Innovations*, Free Press: New York.

Rondinelli, D.A. and Black, S.S. (2000) 'Multinational strategic alliances and acquisitions in Central and Eastern Europe: partnerships in privatization', *The Academy of Management Executive*, 14, 4, 85–98.

Saner, E. (2012) 'For beautiful people only', *The Guardian*, 28 April.

Schein, E.H. (1996) *Strategic Pragmatism: The Culture of Singapore's Economic Development Board*, Toppan: Singapore.

Schein, E.H. (1990) 'Organizational culture', *American Psychologist*, 45, 2, 109–119.

Schein, E.H. (1992) *Organizational Culture and Leadership*, 2nd edn, Jossey Bass: San Francisco, CA.

Schmookler, J. (1966) *Invention and Economic Growth*, Harvard University Press: Cambridge, MA.

Scholte, J.A. (2005) *Globalization: a Critical Introduction*, 2nd edn, Macmillan: Basingstoke.

Scholz, C. (1987) 'Corporate culture', *Long Range Planning*, 20, 4, 78–87.

Schultz, E.J. (2014) 'Mars seeks 120 day payment terms from vendors', *Advertising Age*, May 23.

Schumpeter, J.A. (1939) *Business Cycles*, McGraw-Hill: London.

Schumpeter, J.A. (1961) *The Theory of Economic Development*, Oxford University Press: Oxford.

Scott, J.P. (1979) *Corporations, Classes and Capitalism*, Hutchinson: London.

Selznick, P. (1949) *TVA and the Grass Roots*, University of California Press: Berkley, CA.

Shirouza, N. (2013) 'Daimler's Mercedes Benz Sees Double-digit Growth in China', Reuters: Chengdu.

Siegle, L. (2013) 'Never again?', *The Observer Magazine*, October 6.

Silver, J. (1987) 'The ideology of excellence: management and neo-conservatism', *Studies in Political Economy*, 24, 5–29.

Slack, N. and Lewis, M. (2011) *Operations Strategy*, 3rd edn, FT Prentice Hall: Harlow.

Slack, N., Brandon-Jones, A. and Johnston, B. (2014) *Operations Management*, 7th edn, FT Prentice Hall: Harlow.

Sloan, A.P. (1986) *My Years with General Motors*, Harmondsworth: Penguin.

Solomon, J. (2007) *Corporate Governance and Accountability*, 2nd edn, John Wiley & Sons: Chichester.

Solow, R.W. (1957) 'Technical change and the aggregate production function', *Review of Economics and Statistics*, 1, 3, 312–320.

Stewart, H. (2004) 'Japan bounces back at last', *The Observer*, 12 December, Business Focus, 3.

Stewart, R. (1967) *Managers and Their Jobs*, McGraw Hill: Maidenhead.

Stogdill, R.M. and Coons, A.E. (1957) 'Leader Behaviour: its Description and Measurement', Research Monograph no. 88, Ohio State University: Columbus, OH.

Stopford, J.M. and Wells, L.T. (1972) *Strategy and Structure of the Multinational Enterprise*, Basic Books: New York.

Straw, W. and Glennie, A. (2012) *The Third Wave of Globalisation*, Institute for Public Policy Research: London.

Streeck, W. (2001) 'Explorations into the origins of non-liberal capitalism in Germany and Japan' in W. Streeck and K. Yamamura (eds), *The Origins of Non-liberal Capitalism: Germany and Japan in Comparison*, Cornell University Press: Ithaca, NY.

Syal, R. (2012) 'MPs accuse Amazon, Google and Starbucks of diverting UK profits', *The Guardian*, 13 November, 10.

Tannenbaum, R. and Schmidt, W.H. (1973) 'How to choose a leadership pattern', *Harvard Business Review*, May–June, 178–180.

Taylor, F.W. (1947) *Scientific Management*, Harper & Row: New York.

Taylor, P. (2010) 'The globalisation of service work: analysing the transnational call centre value chain, in P. Thompson and C. Smith (eds), *Working Life: Renewing Labour Process Analysis*, Palgrave Macmillan: Basingstoke.

Taylor, P., D'Cruz, P., Noronha, E. and Scholarios, D. (2013) 'The experience of work in India's domestic call centre industry', *The International Journal of Human Resource Management*, 24, 2, 436–452.

Teece, D.J., Pisano, G. and Shuen, A. (1997) 'Dynamic capabilities and strategic management', *Strategic Management Journal*, 18, 7, 509–534.

Tellis, G.J., Eisingrich, A.B., Chandy, R.K. and Prabhu, J.C. (2008) 'Competing for the future: patterns in the global location of R&D centers by the world's largest firms', *ISBM Report 06*, Pennsylvania State University, PA.

Tengblad, S. (2006) 'Is there a "new managerial work"? A comparison with Henry Mintzberg's classic study 30 year's later', *Journal of Management Studies*, 43, 7, 1437–1461.

The Economist (2011) 'China's murky ownership rules: who owns what?', 7 July.

Thomas, A.B. (2003) *Controversies in Management: Issues, Debates, Answers*, 2nd edn, Routledge: London.

Thomas, T. and Eyres, B. (1998) 'Why an ethical business is not an altruistic business', in *Visions* of *Ethical Business*, Financial Times Management: London.

Thompson, P. and McHugh, D. (2003) *Work Organizations: A Critical Perspective*, 3rd edn, Palgrave Macmillan: London.

Thornton, G.C. and Rupp, D.R. (2006) *Assessment Centers in Human Resource Management: Strategies for Prediction, Diagnosis and Development*, Lawrence Erlbaum: Mahwah, NJ.

Tidd, J., Bessant, J. and Pavitt, K. (2005) *Managing Innovation: Integrating Technological, Market and Organizational Change*, 3rd edn, John Wiley & Sons: Chichester.

Times Higher Education (2013) *World University Rankings*. http:www.timeshighereducation.co.uk/world-university-rankings/2013–14.

Towers Watson (2014) 'Insurers' shares outperform industry average post-acquisition', http://www.towerswatson.com/en-US/Press/2014/02/insurers-shares-outperform-industry-average-post-acquisition.

Townley, B. (1989) 'Selection and appraisal: re- constructing social relations', in J. Storey, *New Perspectives on Human Resource Management*, Routledge: London.

Transparency International (2013) *Global Corruption Report: Education*, Routledge: Abingdon.

Trompenaars, F. (1993) *Riding the Waves of Culture: Understanding Cultural Diversity in Business*, Economist Books: London.

Trompenaars, F. and Hampden-Turner, C. (2004) *Managing People Across Cultures*, Capstone: Oxford.

Ulrich, D. (1997) *Human Resource Champions*, Havard Business School Press: Boston, MA.

US Bureau of Labor Statistics (2008) *International Comparisons of Annual Labor Force Statistics: 10 countries 1960–2007*, US Bureau of Labor Statistics: Washington, DC.

Usunier, J-C. and Lee, J.A. (2009) *Marketing Across Cultures*, 5th edn, FT Prentice Hall: Harlow.

Van der Merwe, R., Pitt, L. and Berthon, P. (2003) 'Are excellent companies ethical? Evidence from an industrial setting', *Corporate Reputation Review*, 5, 4, 343–355.

van Wanrooy, B., Bewley, H., Bryson, A., Forth, J., Freeth, S., Stokes, L. and Wood, S. (2013) *Employment Relations in the Shadow of Recession: Findings from the 2011 Workplace Relations Study*, Palgrave Macmillan: London.

van Wanrooy, B., Bewley, H., Bryson, A., Forth, J., Freeth, S., Stokes, L. and Wood, S. (2014) *The 2011 Workplace Relations Study: First Findings*, 4th edn, BIS: London.

Verschoor, C.C. (1998) 'A study of the link between a corporation's financial performance and its commitment to ethics', *Journal of Business Ethics*, 17, 13, 1509–1516.

Vida, I. and Reardon, J. (2008) Domestic consumption: rational, affective or normative choice? *Journal of Consumer Marketing*, 25, 1, 34–44.

Walsh, F. (2006) 'When big business bites', *The Guardian*, 8 June, 25.

Walsh, J. (2013) 'Work-life balance: the end of the overwork culture', in S. Bach and M.R. Edwards (eds), *Managing Human Resources: Human Resource Management in Transition*, 5th edn, Blackwell: Oxford.

Walsh, N.P. (2005) 'A special report on Putin's Russia', *The Guardian*, 6 July, G2, 2–7.

Warner, M. (2002) 'Globalization, labour markets and human resources in Asia-Pacific economies: an overview', *International Journal of Human Resource Management*, 13, 384–398.

Wasson, C.R. (1978) *Dynamic Competitive Strategy and Product Life Cycles*, Austin Press: Austin, TX.

Waters, M. (1995) *Globalization*, Routledge: London.

Watson, T.J. (1986) *Management, Organization and Employment Strategy*, Routledge: London.

Watson, T.J. (1994) *In Search of Management: Culture, Chaos and Control in Management Work*, Routledge: London.

Wayne, L. (2012) 'Battling corporate bribery', *New York Times*, March 18.

Weber, M. (1947) *The Theory of Social and Economic Organizations*, Free Press: New York.

Weber, T. (2010) Why companies watch your every Facebook, YouTube, Twitter move, http://www.bbc.co.uk/business-11450923.

West, D., Ford, J. and Ibrahim, E. (2010) *Strategic Marketing: Creating Competitive Advantage*, 2nd edn, Oxford University Press: Oxford.

Whipp, R., Rosenfeld, R. and Pettigrew, A. (1989) 'Culture and competitiveness: evidence from two mature UK industries', *Journal of Management Studies*, 26, 6, 561–585.

Whitley, R. (2000) *Divergent Capitalisms: The Social Structuring and Change of Business Systems*, Oxford University Press: Oxford.

Whittington, R. (2000) *What Is Strategy – And Does It Matter?*, Cengage Learning: Andover.

Williams, A., Dobson, P. and Walters, M. (1989) *Changing Culture: New Organizational Approaches*, Institute of Personnel Management: London.

Williams, K., Haslam, C., Williams, J., Cutler, T., Adcroft, A. and Johal, S. (1992) 'Against lean production', *Economy and Society*, 21, 3, 321–354.

Williamson, O.E. (1975) *Markets and Hierarchies*, Free Press: New York.

Williamson, O.E. (1991) 'Strategizing, economizing and economic organization', *Strategic Management Journal*, 12, 75–94.

Willmott, H. (1993) 'Strength is ignorance; slavery is freedom: managing culture in modern organizations', *Journal of Management Studies*, 30, 4, 515–552.

Wilson, A. (1997) 'Business and its social responsibility', in P.W.F. Davies (ed.), *Current Issues in Business Ethics*, Routledge: London.

Wilson, D. and Purushothaman, R. (2003), *Dreaming With BRICs: the Path to 2050*, Global Economics Paper No: 99, Goldman Sachs: London.

Wolf, M. (2004) *Why Globalization Works*, Yale University Press: Yale.

Womack, J., Jones, D.T. and Roos, D. (1990) *The Machine That Changed the World: The Story of Lean Production*, Rawson Associates: New York.

Woodward, J. (1965) *Industrial Organization: Theory and Practice*, Oxford University Press: Oxford.

World Bank (1997) *The State in a Changing World*, *World Development Report*, Oxford University Press: Oxford.

World Bank (2000) *Poverty in an Age of Globalization*, http://www.1.worldbank.org/economic policy/globalization/documents/poverty globalization.

World Bank (2013a) Data.worldbank.org/indicator/NY/GDP/MKTP/CD.

World Bank (2013b) Data.worldbank.org/indicator/NY/GDP/MKTP/KD.

World Commission on Environment and Development (1987) *Our Common Future*, Oxford University Press: Oxford.

Wright, P.M. and McMahan, G.C. (2011) 'Exploring human capital: putting the human back into strategic human resource management, *Human Resource Management Journal*, 21, 2, 93–104.

Yip, G. (1995) *Total Global Strategy: Managing for Worldwide Competitive Advantage*, Prentice-Hall: Englewood Cliffs, NJ.

Yip, G. (2003) *Total Global Strategy II*, 2nd edn, FT/Prentice Hall: Harlow.

Yukl, G. (2013) *Leadership in Organizations*, 8th edn, Pearson Education: Harlow.

Zaleznik, A. (1977) 'Managers and leaders: are they different?', *Harvard Business Review*, 55, 5, 67–78.

Zhang, P. and Van Deusen, C. (2010) 'French Danone and Chinese Wahaha: yet another example of an unsuccessful international joint venture', *International Business: Research, Teaching and Practice*, 4, 1, 82–100.

GLOSSARY

4 Ps Product, price, promotion and place; these make up the marketing mix.

7 Ps An extension of the 4 Ps to focus on customer service. The additional Ps are people process and physical evidence, and focus on how customers are treated and the service environment.

Absorption costing A traditional method of allocating overhead or indirect costs in which, usually, the total cost is divided according to the volume of activity in each cost centre.

ACAS (Arbitration, Conciliation and Advisory Service) This comprises members representing employers, trade unions and the academic community and is funded by the UK government. Its purpose is to influence the conduct of industrial relations and assist employers and employees in achieving speedy, mutually satisfying agreements and resolutions of conflict. See *Third-party intervention*.

Accepted sequence A consumer-oriented view of marketing in which new products follow consumer demand. Linked to Galbraith (1972). See *Revised sequence*.

Accumulation A key aspect of a capitalist system in which profit is built up by more efficient production methods or through new products and markets. Accumulation is generally linked to expansion. See *Commodification*.

Acquisitions See *Mergers and acquisitions*.

Activity-based costing A system of allocating costs that focuses on the activity that drives the cost rather than simply apportioning overhead costs on a pro-rata basis.

Advertising A form of promotion that involves four major considerations: the design of the message, the selection of the media, the cost of both production and exposure and the evaluation of its effectiveness.

Agency problem With the separation of ownership and control, managers have become the agents of the shareholders. The relationship carries with it a potential problem in that managers, acting in their own best interest, may not act in the best interest of the shareholders.

Anglo-Saxon capitalism A belief in the workings of the free market, individualism and private property. A system in which shareholders play a major role. Found in the USA, UK, Australia, New Zealand and Canada.

Appraisal A formal system of employee evaluation to assess the contribution of individuals to the organization.

Asian capitalism Free market capitalism but with strong state intervention. Based around Asian values of hard work, duty, the role of the family and the importance of savings. A bureaucratic state but weak social welfare provision. Found across Asia, especially in Japan.

Asian tigers A group of countries with rapidly developing economies since the 1970s. The initial tigers were Hong Kong, Singapore, Taiwan and South Korea. They have been joined by a second wave of tigers including Malaysia, China and Vietnam. A 'tiger' economy is now a name given to any rapidly growing economy.

Assessment centres A selection device involving a group of candidates and a range of different selection methods, including discussion groups, tests, problem-solving exercises and interviews. The assessment centre attempts to replicate real work behaviour by testing group working skills and working under pressure.

AUEW Amalgamated Union of Engineering Workers.

Backward integration Obtaining control over the source of raw materials or the supply of components to the firm either by acquisition or establishing close ties with suppliers. See *Forward integration* and *Vertical integration*.

Balance of payments The difference over a given time between the income and expenditure of the economy in its dealings with other nations, involving exports, imports and other transactions.

Balance sheet The summary of a firm's financial position at a fixed point in time. The balance sheet is a statement of a firm's assets and liabilities at the end of the last day of the accounting period.

Balanced scorecard A method of judging the performance of a firm or an individual against a range of criteria, which usually include: financial measures of outputs, the value of outputs as seen by the customer, co-workers and other stakeholders, individual productivity and associated costs and measurements of learning and growth.

Barrier to entry This prevents firms from entering a particular market. In most cases, cost and experience are the main factors, although in some countries, notably China there are legal and political barriers to entry.

BCG matrix A method of portfolio analysis developed by the Boston Consulting Group. Products and/or markets are classified as cash cows, stars, question marks or dogs. See *Portfolio analysis*.

Below-the-line See *Sales promotion*.

Benchmarking The comparison of performance in one organization or part of an organization against that in another with a view to finding ways of improving performance.

Best fit The idea that strategies, policies and practices should be in harmony with the prevailing economic, political, social and cultural context. See *Contingency theory*.

Best practice This is based on the assumption that there are universal practices that, if applied, will result in improved organization performance. The concept is used widely in HRM.

Bolton Report The influential report of the UK Committee of Inquiry on Small Firms, published in 1971, that noted both the decline and economic importance of the small firms sector.

Bounded rationality A concept developed by Cyert and March (1963) linked to decision-making. Information and the choice of strategic direction are taken from a limited range of options due to both complexity and time.

Brand See *Branding*.

Brand equity The value of the brand, which may add substantially to a firm's assets and acts as a major consideration in the price of acquisitions.

Brand loyalty The desired aim of branding, occurring when consumers make repeat purchases of the same branded product.

Branding The process through which the product is given a name, logo or symbol to distinguish it from the range of other products on offer. It is used to create awareness and build up customer loyalty to ensure repeat purchases.

Bretton Woods A conference held in the USA in 1944 by the Second World War Allied Nations, which agreed to set international exchange rates to achieve a measure of regulation and stability. The agreement also established the International Monetary Fund (IMF) and the World Bank. See *International Monetary Fund* and *World Bank*.

BRICS An acronym originally devised by Goldman Sachs to identify countries whose economic growth rates were predicted to challenge the existing economic order. The original BRICs were Brazil, China, India and Russia. South Africa has more recently been added to the group. The five BRICS have now formed an economic and political interest group.

'Bubble' economy The term given to an economy built on speculation as was the case in Japan in the 1980s.

Budgeting The setting of standards for income and expenditure and establishing mechanisms through which activities can be measured against these standards. Budgeting is a means of allocating funds and resources, of delegating authority and of motivating employees and is, above all, a vital control of activities.

Bureaucracy A system of organization for large, complex organizations that operates through hierarchies of control and detailed rules for all activities.

Business ethics The concern for moral standards and individual choices of right and wrong in the conduct of business affairs. It is a function of individual values, corporate culture, prevailing social norms and the laws of the land. See *Corporate social responsibility*.

Business process re-engineering (BPR) A radical approach to adding value for the customer at each stage of the value chain. The aim is for dramatic improvements, which inevitably involves a rethinking of the organization and its operations.

Business strategy This deals with decisions that are linked to specific products and markets that can be differentiated from other products and markets in the same organization. Such strategies apply to strategic business units (SBUs). See *Corporate strategy*.

Business-to-business marketing (B2B) Marketing activities and exchanges between two or more organizations. This has increased with the growth of the global factory, but also includes a growth in B2B services such as accounting and consulting.

Buyer-driven supply chains These are typically found in the clothing and footwear industry and involve the outsourcing of manufacture to low cost producers, usually on a global scale. The lead firm and owner of the brand will normally focus on design, development, marketing and retail. The products that are manufactured elsewhere are branded to represent the lead firm.

Call centre A centralized facility for dealing with customers by phone or email to handle purchases and/or enquiries. In a global economy the call centre may be located to take advantage of low-cost labour or accommodation and calls are re-routed accordingly.

Capacity planning A process to determine the capacity required to fulfil market demand. The capacity could be measured in terms of space, people, machinery and so on.

Cash flow The movement of cash into and out of an organization. A healthy cash flow is essential for survival.

Cash-flow statement A requirement of UK financial reporting that details the movement of cash during an accounting period and is very useful for planning and control purposes.

CBI (Confederation of British Industry) An employers' group that addresses a range of economic and general business and labour issues.

Centrally planned (state controlled) economy State control of the supply and demand of goods and services and targets given to individual enterprises. Control of prices, wages and levels of employment. See *Transitional economy*.

Chapter 11 bankruptcy A USA form in which a firm, although bankrupt, can retain its assets if it can develop a payment plan to satisfy creditors. It is a means of offsetting debts against future cash flows.

Classical organization theory This is associated with the work of Weber and Fayol and offers a rational (and some would say prescriptive) approach to management and organizations. See *Bureaucracy*.

Closed shop A situation where all employees must belong to a trade union as a condition of employment. A compulsory closed shop is not allowed under current UK employment law.

Co-branding Two or more brands are presented together to increase the awareness and sales of each of the brands.

Collective bargaining A process in which the representatives of employers and the representatives of employees (usually trade unions) negotiate wages, conditions and other related aspects.

Command economy See *Centrally planned (state controlled) economy*.

Commodification The development of new goods and services to broaden the nature of consumption and to accumulate profit in a capitalist system. See *Accumulation*.

Common agricultural policy (CAP) An economic policy of the EU that exists mainly to protect the interests of farmers in member states.

Company limited by guarantee A type of UK company, owned by a group of members, whose liability is limited to their financial contribution. Such a company is often found in the voluntary sector.

Company unions Trade unions operated by the company, as is the case with unions in Japan.

Competitor–push The pressure to produce goods and services similar to those offered by competitors.

Confucian dynamism A term coined by Hofstede and Bond (1988) to define core Asian values, which include future orientation, perseverance and an importance attached to savings. It is sometimes referred to as long-term orientation.

Consumerism A social movement to inform and assist consumer choice and to act as a pressure group to represent the interests of consumers. These interests are presented to organizations in an attempt to influence product design, price and distribution. Significant concerns are unsafe products and dishonest producers.

Contingency approach An approach to organization theory that sees organization behaviour and practices as a function of a number of influencing variables. In particular, the contingency approach sees successful organizations operating in harmony with their environment.

Convergence A process in which countries become more like one another. Causal factors include technology transfer and the use of similar productive technologies and the expansion of global products, global markets and multinational firms. See *Globalization* and *Culture free*.

Coordinated market economies Free market economies where there is coordination between competing firms and between firms and the state. Businesses tend to be more regulated than under liberal market economies. Found in Germany and Japan. See *Liberal market economies*.

Core competences Those activities of an organization that give it an advantage over its competitors. Such advantages could derive from factors such as an effective R&D department, an efficient operating system, good internal and external communications, the presence of key individuals or reputation and a loyal customer base.

Corporate accountability Where firms are accountable for their actions to the general public. Firms that transgress socially acceptable standards can expect to be punished, usually by the imposition of fines. In some cases, board members can be held responsible and prosecuted as individuals.

Corporate culture Sometimes referred to as organization culture, although we see corporate culture as the product of management as part of a change and control strategy. See *Organization culture*.

Corporate governance A system of checks and balances to ensure that the organization discharges its responsibilities to its various stakeholders and to ensure that organizations operate in a socially responsible way. Key roles are played by accounting information, company directors, executive management leadership and non-executive directors.

Corporate social responsibility (CSR) The application of business ethics. CSR is concerned predominantly with the firm and its relationship to its various stakeholders, such as shareholders, customers, employees, suppliers and the community, and its relationship to the environment. The assumption is that in all these relationships business decisions are influenced by moral and ethical considerations. See *Business ethics* and *Stakeholder theory*.

Corporate strategy The overall strategy of a firm operating in a number of different businesses. See *Business strategy*.

Cost accounting The analysis and allocation of costs. See *Direct costs* and *Indirect costs*.

Cost control The collection and analysis of accounting information about all aspects of the business and the use of comparisons, which are either historical and/or based on benchmarking against another organization.

Cost leadership The aim of being the lowest cost producer.

Cost-plus pricing A standard mark-up after all costs have been taken into consideration.

Creditors Those to whom the firm owes money.

Culture All human activity that is socially rather than genetically transmitted. It comprises values, norms and beliefs that are displayed in business behaviour and can result in different approaches and business practices in different parts of the world.

Culture specific Each culture is differentiated by its own core values and business ideas. Practices can only be successfully transferred between nations with similar core values.

Culture-free A situation in which culture is less significant than other factors, such as technology or organization size. In a culture free situation, business ideas and practices can be transferred between nations. See *Convergence*.

Current assets Assets that are short term and transitory, such as cash and stock.

Cyclical markets Such markets display periods of varying demand. Many product markets, e.g. automobiles, in mature industrialized economies are cyclical.

Debentures Negotiable instruments that can be bought and sold on the stock market. They are issued in return for loans secured on the fixed assets of a company.

Debtors Those who owe money to the firm.

De-industrialization The decline of the manufacturing sector of the economy.

Delayering The flattening of the organization by removing levels of supervision and management. It is usually accompanied by restructuring and redundancies among the management groups. See *Restructuring*.

Demand–pull The development of new products and processes as a direct result of market demand. See *Technology–push*.

Deregulation The lifting of government restrictions and controls usually aimed at increasing levels of competition.

Derivatives Financial instruments that are derived from an asset or a product. Their purpose is to allow companies to offset financial risk. The two main types of derivative are futures and options. A future is a contract that places an obligation to buy or sell at a set price on a given future date. An option is similar to a future except that the contract offers the right but not the obligation.

Design The final stage in the R&D process that translates the development into the final product for the consumer. See *Design mix* and *Product design*.

Design mix Part of the design process incorporating elements such as effective operation, safety, easy maintenance, value for money and aesthetic considerations. These are all focused on satisfying customer needs.

Deskilling The process of reducing the skill content of work, usually through the introduction of new forms of technology.

Development Takes research a stage further by translating the outcome of research into something more tangible. At this stage in the design of a new product, a prototype or a sample would be produced.

Differentiation A strategy that aims to produce goods and services with certain unique features that make them attractive to customers.

Digital marketing Any marketing activity that uses digital technologies such as the Web, apps, and digital data making use of smart phones, tablets and computers. Through these technologies and methods company and product information and promotion can be sent to specific target groups or segments.

Direct and indirect costs Costs that can be directly ascribed to a specific product. See *Indirect costs*.

Direct marketing Dealing directly with the customer, without using intermediaries such as retail outlets, as with mail shots, mail-order catalogues, telephone sales and electronic commerce. See *Personal selling*.

Distributed leadership See *Shared leadership*.

Distribution The process through which goods and services reach the customer. It involves the use of distribution channels and networks.

Diversification Adding new products or markets to the existing portfolio. Diversification can be *related* or *unrelated* to the existing business.

Diversity management More strategic than equal opportunities and focused more on individuals. Founded on the assumption that the organization will be more effective if all people feel more valued. See *Equal opportunities*.

Dividend The payment made to shareholders of a proportion of profit after tax. See *Ordinary shares* and *Preference shares*.

Divisionalization A form of organization structure that breaks the organization down according to product groups or market territory to form a series of profit centres. A form of organization often found in large complex multinational companies. See *Multidivisional company, Profit centre*.

Dominant coalition The interest group(s) that have the most power and influence in an organization.

Down-sizing Reducing the number of people employed in an organization.

Eclectic paradigm A theory to explain the growth of multinational firms (MNEs) developed by Dunning (1993) by combining a number of existing theories. The key elements are what the MNE owns and controls (patents, technology, brands); the advantages of location (access to raw materials, labour); and the advantages derived from having internal control over operations.

Economies of scale The achievement of cost reduction through the volume of operation. In manufacturing, the higher the volume produced of a single product then generally the lower the costs of producing that item. The concept is sometimes linked to that of *Experience curve*.

Economies of scope A form of horizontal integration when the product range is extended to incorporate similar items. The economies of scope include shared central functions such as finance, marketing and R&D. See *Horizontal integration*.

EETPU The Electrical, Electronic, Telecommunications and Plumbing Union.

Electronic business (e-business) Similar to *e-commerce* below, e-business involves a much broader range of activities, incorporating all business activities. It enables the various elements of global firms to work more closely together and can form the basis of much business to business activity.

Electronic commerce (e-commerce) This involves the connection of suppliers and buyers directly through computer-based systems. E-commerce generally relates to trading activity involving information, goods and services. The initial point of contact is electronic although, in the case of goods and services, delivery is made using more conventional systems. The growth of e-commerce and e-business is directly associated with the development of the Internet and company-wide intranet systems.

Electronic marketing (e-marketing) Linked to *e-business* and *e-commerce* through the provision of information, promotion and sales of products and services online.

Emerging markets These are markets where it is believed that there is considerable potential for growth. Such markets can include newly industrialized nations, such as Malaysia, less developed nations with large populations, such as China and India, and those nations changing from a centrally controlled economy, as in East Europe.

Emotional intelligence A set of interpersonal skills that contribute towards effective leadership. It involves self-awareness, sensitivity to the kind of behaviour that will be effective in a given situation and the social skills to influence and meet the needs of others.

Employee branding A means through which an organization's core values are communicated and embedded in its staff. See *Employer branding*.

Employee development The training and development of staff alongside a more recent focus on employee branding.

Employee relations See *Employment relations*.

Employee resourcing This involves the planning, recruitment and selection of staff and issues relating to equality, diversity and work–life balance.

Employer branding This occurs when employers wish to brand themselves as attractive organizations to influence candidates to join them and also to create strong corporate values to assist them in managing a more distributed global work force. See *Employee branding*.

Employment relations All matters relating to the relationship between employees and management including various approaches to communication and participation, the relationship between management and unions and in general issues relating to the employment relationship. There has been a move away from dealing with employees as groups or as part of a trade union to dealing with them as individuals. See *Industrial relations*.

Enterprise culture A movement that developed in the UK in the 1980s that emphasized individualism, entrepreneurship, innovation and self-help through self-employment. It was associated with the politics of the Thatcher era. See *Thatcherism*.

Entrepreneurship The activity of entrepreneurs, who are responsible for the creation of new products, processes, services and markets. They develop new ways of doing business and managing people and create new forms of organization.

Environmental scanning A process of strategic analysis involving the search for opportunities and threats. See *SWOT analysis*.

Equal opportunities A set of operational procedures to ensure that the organization complies with the laws covering discrimination against specific groups of people such as women, ethnic minorities and those with disabilities. See *Diversity management*.

Ethical audit An audit of all the firm's activities and relationships, including products and services, processes, terms of employment and conditions for employees, and the firm's relationships with its suppliers, local community and environment. The audit checks that ethical practices are being pursued and establishes action plans where they are not.

Ethical investors Investors who seek out companies in which to invest that pursue demonstrably ethical strategies and practices.

Ethics A branch of moral philosophy; the study of morals and principles governing the rights and wrongs of human conduct. See *Business ethics*.

EU The European Union, currently made up of 28 nation states, many operating with a single currency: the euro.

European Exchange Rate Mechanism (ERM) An agreement among member states of the EU to keep exchange rates within fixed limits as a precursor to monetary union.

European Monetary Union (EMU) The creation of a single European currency, now the major currency used in 18 of the 28 EU member states.

Excellent company A term derived from the work of Peters and Waterman (1982). They define 'excellent companies' in terms of eight characteristics including: closeness to the customer; hands on; value driven; autonomy and entrepreneurship, and simple form, lean staff. Such companies usually have strong, well defined corporate cultures. See *Corporate culture*.

Experience curve An advantage gained over time from producing goods or services or operating in particular markets. Cost advantages associated with economies of scale can often be attributed to the experience curve. See *Economies of scale*.

Explicit knowledge Knowledge available within a firm that is usually obtained through rational processes of data collection and is often contained in documentation. Such knowledge is often available to all and, as a consequence, is rarely a source of competitive advantage. See *Implicit knowledge*.

Extrinsic rewards These include basic rates of pay, overtime payments and various forms of performance-related pay such as bonuses. Such rewards also include non-pay factors such as company cars, health insurance and pension schemes. See *Intrinsic rewards*.

Factoring A means of raising capital by selling debts owed at some 70–80 per cent of their real invoice value. While money is lost on the value of the invoice, this can be a useful way of improving cash flow.

Family firm A firm owned and managed by family members. Although there are examples of large family firms, most tend to be very small businesses.

Financial accounting See *Financial reporting*.

Financial management Part of the finance and accounting function that is concerned with the financing of an organization's activities.

Financial reporting The collection and presentation of data for use in financial management and management accounting. In most countries there are minimum legal requirements governing the kind of statement that must be produced. Sometimes known as financial accounting.

Financial Reporting Council (FRC) A UK independent regulator that oversees the professional accounting and actuarial bodies. It produces guiding principles for effective financial reporting, auditing and corporate governance.

Financial services A sector of the economy that includes banking, insurance, pensions and investment activities.

Five Forces model Developed by Porter (1980) to assess the bargaining power of suppliers and buyers, the threat of entry from competitors, substitute products and, ultimately, the competitive rivalry of the firm.

Fixed assets Assets that remain on the books for a significant period of time, such as land, buildings and machinery.

Flexible firm A response to the demands of globalization, competition and cost reduction. Flexibility within organizations occurs in a number of different ways including the employment of part-time and contract workers, outsourcing, multiskilling and introducing variations in pay and times of attendance.

Flexible manufacturing system (FMS) An integrated system comprising the elements of advanced manufacturing engineering to solve the problem of offering consumer choice and a quick response to market changes using a minimum of working capital. An FMS enables a range of models to be built using the same assembly line and pieces of equipment.

Foreign direct investment (FDI) The full or partial ownership and control of a firm located in one country by investors in another country. See *Multinational corporation*.

Forward integration This occurs when producers diversify to control the onward processes of delivering their goods to the consumer, as in the case of a manufacturer setting up a transport or retail operation. See *Backward integration* and *Vertical integration*.

Franchising This allows a firm to produce and market a branded product or service for an initial fee and (usually) a supply contract, e.g. McDonald's.

Free market A market in which firms compete on the same basis with little or no government interference. In reality such a system tends to favour large firms and leads to the creation of monopolies or oligopolies. See *Monopoly* and *Oligopoly*.

Functional strategy A strategy that applies to a functional area of business such as operations, marketing and HRM. See *Business strategy* and *Corporate strategy*.

Futures See *Derivatives*.

G7 (Group of Seven) An economic alliance of the world's major economic nations: Canada, France, Germany, Italy, Japan, the UK and USA.

GAAP (Generally Accepted Accounting Practice) An amalgamation of legislation and regulations to form sets of practically based accounting rules. There is a UK GAAP and a USA GAAP.

Gap analysis A strategic assessment of the difference between what managers want to achieve and what they can achieve with the resources available.

Gastarbeiter A name given, originally in Germany, to foreign migrant workers. The meaning is literally 'guest worker'.

GATT The General Agreement on Tariffs and Trade set up by the Bretton Woods Agreement to facilitate global trade as a means to peace and prosperity. See *Bretton Woods* and *WTO*.

GDP (gross domestic product) The sum total of the net outputs of each sector of the economy, including those of foreign firms but excluding earnings from overseas. GDP is often expressed *per capita* (per head of population).

Global factory The coordination of activities in various locations across the world to design, develop, produce, brand, market and distribute goods or services. Most manufactured goods are now assembled from parts made in different areas of the world to achieve maximum cost effectiveness.

Global market The sale of a product or service in most countries in the world. Coca-Cola and McDonald's can be said to have a global market.

Global value chains The build-up of value along a supply chain comprising a number of international partners. Different revenues are derived from different parts of the chain. Most value is usually derived from design, development, branding and marketing and the least value from manufacture. The former tends to be carried out by the lead form in its own country while the latter is outsourced to firms in countries where wages are lower. See *Buyer driven chains, Global factory, Producer driven chains*.

Globalization A process of economic, political and cultural convergence in which national borders become less significant. The process has been accelerated by developments in information and communications technology.

Globally organized production The coordination of activities in various locations across the world to produce goods or services. Most manufactured goods are now assembled from parts made in different areas of the world to achieve maximum cost effectiveness. See *Global commodity chains*.

GLOBE An acronym for the 'global leadership and organizational behaviour effectiveness programme'. The project sets out to study the impact of culture on leadership, on organizational processes, and on the effectiveness of those processes.

GNP (gross national product) The sum total of the net outputs of each sector of the economy together with the earnings by its residents from overseas investments. Like GDP, GNP is often expressed *per capita*.

Goals Organization goals give direction to the activities of organization members both as broad statements of intent and detailed objectives. Goal formulation can be a highly political process and a source of conflict.

Golden shares Shares retained by governments after privatization issue, usually to prevent a hostile takeover.

Greenfield site This relates to the establishment of a business operation in a completely new location. It usually implies a new building with modern facilities and a new infrastructure.

Hawthorne Studies A series of highly influential studies carried out in the 1920s at the Hawthorne plant in Chicago of the Western Electric Co. The studies are associated with human relations and Elton Mayo, although he was not one of the primary researchers. The studies focused on communications, group behaviour and participation. See *Human relations management*.

Hierarchy of needs A theory of motivation attributed to Abraham Maslow. The theory states that we are motivated by unsatisfied needs and that these are arranged in a hierarchy. We must first satisfy our basic physical needs, but our ultimate goal is self-actualization.

High performance work systems (HPWS) An alternative to management based on control. HPWS involve a number of so-called sophisticated interventions including; rigorous recruitment and selection procedures; extensive employee development, employee involvement and high rates of pay linked to performance. The aim is the creation of highly committed and effective work teams.

Holding company An organization whose main purpose is the ownership and overall control of a group of semi-autonomous companies.

Horizontal integration This occurs most commonly when a firm adds to its portfolio of products by acquisition of companies operating in similar markets. See *Economies of scope*.

Hostile takeover An acquisition of one firm by another, when the firm that is being acquired does not welcome it. See *Mergers and acquisitions*.

Human relations management A set of theories and approaches originating from the early part of the 20th century and, in particular, the work of Elton Mayo. The theory emphasizes group approaches to work, employee involvement, democratic leadership and effective communication. The approach developed throughout the 20th century and is still influential in some forms of management training.

Human resource management (HRM, HR) Management decisions and actions that affect the nature of the relationship between the organization and its employees. A strategic approach to ensuring that people in the organization achieve its goals. It involves recruitment, selection, training, reward systems, performance management, employee relations and employee involvement as an integrated strategy. Also known as HRM and HR. See *Personnel management* and *Hard and soft HRM*.

Human resource planning The analysis of a company's manpower needs in light of its current staffing resources and the nature of the labour market.

Implicit knowledge The sum total of knowledge acquired by organization members throughout the lifetime of the organization and passed on to subsequent generations of employees. It is rarely documented and is difficult for outsiders to penetrate. It is often a source of competitive advantage. See *Explicit knowledge*.

Indirect costs Costs that relate to general overheads such as labour, heating, lighting and so on. See *Direct costs*.

Individualism-collectivism An accepted measure of cultural difference used in studies by Hofstede and Trompenaars. Individualistic societies focus on self and the immediate family, while collectivistic societies are more group oriented and focus on the extended family. Industrialization and globalization are usually accompanied by a shift towards greater individualism.

Industrial relations The relations between employers and employees and their respective representatives with a focus on pay, conditions, job security and participation. They involve negotiation and bargaining. Also known as employee relations. The emphasis has shifted from groups to individuals.

Inflation An increase in the general level of prices usually accompanied by rises in wages.

Information and communication technology The use of developments in computers and telecommunications to enhance the quantity, quality and speed of information transfer.

Innovation The discovery or creation of something new, such as a product, process, strategy or structure, and turning it into economic reality. An innovation is an invention that is economically relevant. See *R&D*.

Institutional framework A model of diversity that recognizes the importance of institutions and regulations as causes of differences between countries. The focus is on institutions such as the stock market, the legal system and the education system.

Interaction-influence model This sees all business activities as a complex series of interactions that are mutually influential, hence business activities influence the national economy, which in turn influences business activities. The *Business in Context* model is an example of an interaction-influence model.

Interest group A grouping within an organization of people with similar goals. Management, the marketing department, a trade union and a work group are all examples of interest groups. Interest groups can combine to form coalitions.

International Monetary Fund (IMF) Part of the United Nations established by Bretton Woods to control the international financial system. The IMF can intervene when changes in a nation's economy threaten to destabilize the economies of other countries. See *Bretton Woods*.

Intrinsic rewards These include job satisfaction, esteem and self-fulfilment. There is an assumption that with the shift towards knowledge working, intrinsic rewards will become more important. See *Extrinsic rewards*.

Invention See *Innovation*.

Investment appraisal A process of calculating whether an investment is cost effective in the short, medium or long term. See *NPV*.

Japanese management A set of practices and techniques associated with businesses in Japan, such as just-in-time, quality circles, single-status firms and company unions. Such practices have been associated with the success of Japanese firms and therefore copied in other countries.

Japanese transplants Japanese manufacturing or service organizations operating in an overseas location and using predominantly Japanese business methods.

Japanization This involves both the process of Japanese foreign direct investment and the adoption or adaptation of Japanese business practices by non-Japanese firms.

Job enrichment The application of the motivation theories of Herzberg to create more challenging and meaningful work.

Joint ventures Two or more firms working together to achieve mutually beneficial objectives. These can include sharing resources, establishing a joint R&D project or setting up a third company with shared ownership. A joint venture is similar to a *strategic alliance,* except that in a joint venture there is an element of shared ownership.

Just-in-time (JIT) A method of manufacture developed initially in Japan as part of *lean production.* Starting with customer demand, goods and services are produced at each stage of the operation only as required. It is a pull-through system that eliminates the need for large stocks but requires close cooperation with suppliers. See *Kanban.*

Kaizen A Japanese system of continuous quality improvement.

Kanban An integral part of a just-in-time system. A *Kanban* is a card or signal which informs how much is to be produced by each process and the precise quantity each process should withdraw from the previous stage, which may be either another process, a materials store, or even a supplier. See *Just-in-time*

Keiretsu A business group around large firms in Japan and typified by a number of cross-holdings.

Keynesian policy An economic policy involving state investment in the economy to create employment.

Labour markets These provide labour for organizations and vary in terms of size, mobility and prevailing skills.

Laissez-faire A model of capitalism emphasizing the free market. See *Anglo-Saxon capitalism.*

Late development effect The advantage enjoyed by newly industrialized countries, whereby they can learn from the mistakes of others, benefit from greenfield sites and catch up economically. See *Newly industrialized countries (NICs)* and *Greenfield site.*

Leadership Influencing the direction of the organization through a focus on change and inspiring the group to improve performance.

Lean production (or manufacture) A totally integrated system of manufacture developed initially by Toyota in Japan. The emphasis is on the integration of state-of-the-art techniques to eliminate waste, a flexible approach and teamwork. Advocates claim dramatic improvements in efficiency and effectiveness.

Lean services The application of lean production principles to the service industry and found especially in retailing and in hospitals.

Leasing A process through which a firm can acquire assets that it has not bought, but rented from another firm. Many company cars, security systems and photocopiers are acquired in this way.

Liberal market economies Free market economies that operate systems of competitive capitalism with minimum state intervention. Found in the USA and UK. See *Coordinated market economies*.

Liberal pluralism A belief in the free market and the recognition that society is made up of different interest groups. The state helps to smooth out difficulties in the operation of a free market and regulates the cooperation and exchange between interest groups.

Liberalization The process of shifting from some form of state control of the economy towards a free market. The most obvious examples are China and the former USSR and its allied states, although there is evidence that capitalist systems have become more liberal. See *Transitional economy*.

Licensing A process whereby the owner of a patent on a product allows another firm to produce that product upon payment of an agreed royalty fee.

Lifetime employment A system under which individuals commit their working life to one firm and whereby the firm guarantees them a job for life. Although associated with Japan, lifetime employment is common in other countries, notably Germany. It is threatened by economic recession and a shift to more liberal economic systems.

Limited company See *Public limited company (plc)* and *Private company (Ltd)*.

Loading A technique in operations management to determine the amount of work that can be allocated to a particular work centre, be it a department, unit or person.

Loan capital finance raised by borrowing money from a third party such as a bank or other financial institution.

Long-term versus short-term orientation A dimension of culture developed by Hofstede. See *Confucian dynamism*.

Long-wave economic cycles Cycles of economic growth and decline spanning over 40 years. Upswings are related to the development of particular industries over time and downswings are the result of saturated and contested markets.

Management The shaping of activities, strategy and organization, coping with the external environment and organizing people to ensure the long-term survival of the firm.

Management accounting The application of accounting techniques to provide management with the information to assist in the processes of planning and control. It involves budgeting, costing, investment appraisal and the management of cash flows.

Management by objectives (MBO) A system of management whereby individual managers are set targets and their performance is judged against target achievement.

Managerial grid An approach to leadership developed by Blake and Mouton, which enables managers to plot their leadership style in terms of their concern for people and for completing the task.

Market research The collection and analysis of information about present and future products, markets, competitor strategies and tactics, and consumer preferences.

Market segmentation See *Segmentation*.

Marketing The design, pricing, promotion and delivery of goods and services to meet or exceed customer needs.

Marketing channel A flow of goods and services, which may comprise several stages, involving intermediaries such as transporters, agents, wholesalers and retailers.

Marketing mix The development of a marketing strategy on the basis of product, price, promotion and place (distribution). These are sometimes referred to as the *4 Ps*.

Markets and hierarchies Markets are sets of relationships where firms or individuals do business with each other on the basis of some form of contract. Hierarchies are sets of relationships within the same organization and tend to be based on some form of ownership as in the case of multinational enterprises.

Marque A brand name usually applied to cars.

Masculinity-femininity A measure of cultural difference used by Hofstede. Masculine societies tend to be assertive and have clearly defined gender roles. Feminine societies have less well-defined gender roles and are more concerned for the welfare of people.

Matrix organization A structural device to manage two or more elements of the organization, be they size, products, markets or customers. In a typical matrix an employee is a member of a functional group and of a product or market grouping. The system works best when two or more elements need to be emphasized but it can cause confusion and dissatisfaction.

Mechanistic organization An organization best suited to stable conditions and similar to classic bureaucracies. High degrees of specialization and operations governed by rules. Clear hierarchies of authority and emphasis on vertical communication. See *Bureaucracy*.

Mergers and acquisitions These occur when two or more firms come together to form a single firm. A merger implies a joining of equals while an acquisition implies a dominant partner.

Merit pay A form of performance-related pay that is usually based on the manager's subjective assessment of an employee's contribution to organizational performance.

Method study A set of techniques which focus on improving how the job is carried out and include not just the methods involved in the tasks themselves, but also equipment design.

Mission A statement of core values which define the purpose of the organization.

MITI The Ministry of International Trade and Industry, an influential branch of the Japanese civil service.

Modes of entry This usually refers to the way in which firms enter international markets. There are a number of possibilities, each with variations in cost, commitment, risk and ease of entry.

MOF The Ministry of Finance in Japan, which controls the Bank of Japan and investment strategy.

Monetarism The control of the economy by the control of the amount of money within it.

Monetary Union See *European Monetary Union.*

Monopoly The control or dominance of a market by a single producer or provider.

Multidivisional company A structural form developed by multinationals in the 1930s to cope with increasing growth and complexity. The organization is divided into separate profit-centres based on product groups and/or geographical area. See *Divisionalization* and *Profit-centre.*

Multidomestic company A company that sets up operations in one or more overseas countries and both produces and sells products for local markets.

Multinational corporation (MNC) One that operates and is managed from bases in a number of different countries. While small firms can and do operate multinationally, most multinationals are large corporations with diverse interests coordinated by a centrally planned global strategy. The growth of the *global factory*, *global supply chain*, *off-shoring* and *outsourcing* has meant that the MNC is defined less in terms of its ownership of foreign assets and more in terms of the value creating activities it controls.

Multinational enterprise (MNE) Same as the *Multinational corporation (MNC).*

National systems of innovation Systems which comprise a number of actors and institutions that determine the nature of innovation in a particular country and lead to variation between nations. Key influences include the state, banks, individual firms and universities.

New technology The use of computers and electronic circuits to process information for greater control, speed, flexibility and quality in work operations.

Newly industrialized countries (NICs) Countries like the Asian tigers that have developed industrial economies later than the advanced nations of the USA, Europe and Japan. They are able to learn from the advanced nations. See *Late development effect.*

NGA The National Graphical Association, a trade union representing print workers.

Non-executive directors Directors with no direct involvement in the management of the enterprise who are able to provide experience from elsewhere and can operate as an impartial voice in influencing strategic direction. Such non-executive directors are seen as an important check and balance and an integral part of corporate governance.

No-strike deal An agreement by a group of employees, usually as members of a trade union, not to withdraw their labour at any time for the duration of an agreed contract period.

NPV (net present value) A popular method of investment appraisal since it estimates future returns on investment, but assesses them on current values.

OECD The Organization for Economic Cooperation and Development, a grouping of 34 nations (at the beginning of 2014) with the aim of improving economic well-being in countries of the world. In 2014 the OECD is in talks with several countries, including the Russian Federation to increase membership.

Off-shoring This involves moving a process to another country. In many multinationals, the process is performed by a unit within the same firm that is located overseas and therefore is not a form of outsourcing. However, where a firm not only locates an activity in another country but also contracts this activity to another firm, it is referred to as offshore outsourcing. See *Global factory, Global value chain, Multinational corporation* and *Outsourcing.*

Oil shocks These refer to two periods in the 1970s (1973 and 1979) when the oil-producing nations made major price increases with a significant impact on the costs of most businesses around the world.

Oligopoly The control or dominance of the market by a small number of firms. Several global markets, such as those for automobiles, oil and pharmaceuticals, can be called oligopolies.

Open systems A view of the organization using the systems approach in which the inputs and the outputs interact with the environment in which the organization operates. See *Systems approach.*

Operations A central role in most organizations, transforming materials, finance, and information into goods and services wanted by customers.

Operations planning A process to ensure that sufficient goods or services are produced to meet demand in terms of quantity, quality, timing and the degree of flexibility.

Operations research (OR) The application of mathematical models to solve complex organizational problems.

Options See *Derivatives.*

Ordinary shares These represent the majority of all share capital. Dividend is not guaranteed but holders are normally entitled to a share of the profits after deductions for tax and payment to preference shareholders. See *Preference shares* and *Dividend.*

Organic organization An organization suited to dynamic changing conditions. Emphasis on flexibility and a loose definition of roles and responsibilities. Typified by delegated authority and free flows of communication both horizontal and vertical.

Organization culture Sometimes referred to as corporate culture, although we see *organization* culture as the product of a number of variables, including history, the economy, technology, product market, strategy, management style and the nature of employees. See *Corporate culture*.

Organization structure The grouping of activities and people to achieve the goals of the organization.

Organizational development (OD) A change strategy popular in the 1970s that used an external or internal consultant to achieve planned change through the development of individuals and groups.

Outsourcing An increasing trend involving the use of another organization to provide essential goods and services. Many manufacturers outsource a proportion of their operations, usually to lower cost operators. Firms often outsource functions such as catering, cleaning and even payroll to other firms. See *Off-shoring*.

Over-capacity Having more factory or office space, machines and people than required to satisfy market demand for goods and services. Over-capacity is expensive in that resources are wasted.

Over-supply When the supply of goods and services is greater than the demand. Over-supply usually results in price falls that can be dramatic, as in the case of microchips in the 1990s.

Partnership A legal form of ownership found especially in the professions. Partners have unlimited personal liability, which may be reduced by forming a *limited liability partnership*.

Patent A form of intellectual property granted for an innovative product which ensures the inventor a monopoly of production over a stated period (usually around 20 years). See *Licensing*.

Payment by results Payment tied to increased output subject to quality, wastage and machine utilization.

Performance management The means through which individual effort and contribution become part of the process of achieving organizational goals. An appraisal usually forms an integral part. See *Appraisal*.

Performance related pay Pay related to the performance of an individual or group based on criteria such as the number of items produced, clients seen, sales made and so on. Pay can also be based on broader criteria involving the assessment of an employee's overall contribution. See *Merit rating*.

Personal selling A specialized form of direct marketing favoured by the sellers of industrial goods, recognizing the importance of building good personal relations between seller and buyer. See *Direct marketing*.

Personnel management A traditional approach to the management of human resources which focuses on selection, training, payment and industrial relations. It has been largely superseded by a more strategically focused HRM. See *Human resource management*.

PEST Analysis comprising a review of four types of environmental influence: political, economic, social and technological. It is a simple model used to identify influences operating on an organization or industrial sector.

PESTLE A variation of PEST that examines in addition the legal and ethical environments and is sometimes known as PESTEL.

Picketing An act of protest and persuasion during times of strike, where (usually) trade union members gather at the entrances to workplaces to persuade others to join them. The activity in the UK is regulated by law.

Pluralist frame of reference See *Unitarist and Pluralist frames of reference*.

Portfolio analysis This is used in firms operating within a number of different businesses and markets or in the same market with a number of different products. The technique enables management to assess the relative attractiveness of their businesses and products in their current markets and assist decisions on the direction of future investment. See *BCG Matrix*.

Positioning Placing the product in the market so that it meets customers' expectations and perceptions in comparison with other products in terms of price, quality, image and so on. See *Targeting* and *Segmentation*.

Power distance An accepted measure of cultural difference used by Hofstede. High-power-distance societies accept that status differences exist and build upon them. Low-power-distance societies introduce measures to reduce such differences.

Preference shares Shares which attract a fixed rate of dividend irrespective of the financial performance of the company.

Private company Different from a public limited company in that shares are not openly available and the company does not have a stock market listing. Shares are owned by the founders, family members or management. Denoted by *Ltd* after the company name. The equivalent type of company in Germany is a *Gesellschaft mit beshrinkter Haftung* (GmbH). See *Public limited company*.

Privatization The selling of state-owned businesses.

Process innovation The development of a new way of making products or delivering them to the customer.

Procurement The activities engaged in the acquisition of the various resource inputs to the primary activities of the organization.

Producer driven supply chains The coordination of production across several organizations, usually in different countries. In most cases, a lead firm develops and controls key technologies and outsources manufacture to firms in lower cost labour markets. See *Global factory*, *Global value chain*, *Multinational corporation* and *Outsourcing*.

Product design This involves consideration of styling and function, the range of products and the degree of standardization. See *Design* and *Design mix*.

Product differentiation A means of gaining a competitive advantage through the development of a product that differs from those of competitors.

Product innovation The development of an original product such as a new model of car or a new form of insurance policy.

Product life cycle This assumes that all products have a limited lifespan during which they pass through a series of stages, usually identified as introduction, growth, maturity and decline, all of which have implications for sales and profitability.

Product line Variations of the same basic product, differentiated by quality, cost or extra features.

Product management The organization of the firm around its products; each brand or group of brands has its own manager.

Product mix The total number of products offered by the firm, sometimes referred to as the product portfolio.

Profit and loss account This provides detail of a firm's income and expenditure over a stated period of time, known as the accounting period.

Profit centre A sub-set of an organization that operates as an independent business with profit targets. These are common in multidivisional companies. See *Divisionalization* and *Multidivisional Company*.

Pseudo-innovation No real change in the product or process has occurred but claims are made to revitalize a stagnant market. Pseudo-innovations are often the product of marketing campaigns to change the fortunes of a flagging product.

Psychic distance The perceived difference between two countries in terms of such factors as language, culture, institutions and business practices. Some believe it explains patterns of multinational expansion in that firms and their managers will move first to countries where they feel most comfortable, i.e. where there is perceived low psychic distance.

Public limited company (plc) A UK company that is a legal entity separate from the owners in which liability is restricted. Unlike a private (limited) company, shares are traded and the company is listed on the stock market. An *Aktiengesellschaft* (AG) is the German equivalent of the UK plc.

Public sector A broad area that includes central and local government, hospitals, universities, schools and nationalized industries.

Purchasing power parity (PPP) A measure of the purchasing power in different countries, a good method of judging the relative cost of living in those different countries.

Quality control A process that ensures that the quality of the finished product or service matches the standards set in the design stage and also meets with the approval of the customer.

Quantity control A process that ensures that the throughput of goods and services goes according to the planned schedule. This is sometimes known as production control or progress chasing.

R&D See *Research and development*.

R&D intensity Expenditure on research and development as a proportion of sales revenue.

Ratio analysis A set of methods for assessing the financial health of a company. They include profitability ratios, activity ratios, liquidity ratios and gearing ratios as well as ratios measuring the performance of shares.

Rational knowledge Knowledge that is derived from scientific and objective methods.

Recession A period of time when the economy stops growing and goes into reverse. A prolonged recession turns into a depression.

Relationship marketing The creation of a strong bond between the organization and its customers as well as its suppliers, distributors and retailers to create customer loyalty and encourage repeat purchases.

Research and development (R&D) The organization function that is the focus for innovation within a firm. R&D refers both to the activity and to the name of a department.

Resource-based view (RBV) An approach to strategy in which a unique strategic position creating competitive advantage can be achieved through the way in which managers use and combine physical, human, organizational and financial resources.

Restructuring This refers to a number of measures generally associated with cost-cutting. Such measures include plant or office closure and reducing the number of employees.

Reverse engineering A process whereby products, usually those of competitor firms, are systematically taken apart to see how they were made.

Revised sequence A system of innovation and marketing in which product development is led by technology and associated costs rather than consumer preferences. Linked to Galbraith (1972). See *Accepted sequence*.

Sales promotion This incorporates a variety of techniques, including free samples, money-back coupons, special offers on loyalty points, contests and so on. Sales promotion is sometimes referred to as *below-the-line* advertising.

Scenario planning A flexible approach to strategy formulation which looks at a number of possible changes in the environment and asks the question 'what if?'.

Scheduling The balancing of the costs of production against demand for goods and services; ensures that demand is met in the most efficient way possible.

Scientific management A highly influential approach to management associated with the work of F.W. Taylor at the beginning of the 20th century. Scientific management is sometimes called *Taylorism*. The key elements are the separation of planning and doing, the scientific analysis and design of work, the application of work study and work measurement and the scientific selection of staff.

Search engine marketing A process to increase the visibility of an organization, its products and services on search engines such as Google.

Segmentation The process by which the total market is broken down to create distinctive consumer groups. The criteria used to form such groups varies and may include geographical location, social class, occupation, gender, lifestyle and so on. Products can be developed which focus upon the needs of a particular group. See *Targeting* and *Positioning*.

Share capital Funding raised through the issue of shares offering shareholders part ownership in the firm and an annual payment in the form of dividend.

Shared leadership Leadership that is distributed across a group rather than being focused on a single individual. It is often found in complex organizations operating in rapidly changing product markets. In such situations leadership moves around as the knowledge and skill base of the organization changes. It is sometimes called *distributed leadership*.

Skimming A pricing strategy involving setting a high initial price. It is used with products that appeal to a market segment in which price is not an important consideration.

SME (Small and medium-size enterprise) The EU classifies SMEs as any enterprise employing fewer than 250 people. SMEs play a key role in the development of the business enterprise and in their contribution to the economy.

Social ethics The belief that ethical standards will vary between societies, reflecting their different histories and influences.

Social market capitalism Free market operation carefully regulated by the state. A mix of public and private ownership with emphasis on social welfare and employee involvement with legal regulation. Found in Germany, Scandinavia and in most countries in continental Europe.

Social media marketing The use of social media websites such as Facebook, Twitter and YouTube to promote products and services. Initially used as a forum for consumers such websites are now used by firms for market research, to provide information, and to promote products and services.

Societal marketing The satisfaction of consumer needs through the provision of goods and services that are socially acceptable, non-harmful and non-polluting.

Society of Graphical and Allied Trades (SOGAT) A trade union representing workers in the print industry.

SOE State owned enterprise.

Sole trader An individual running a company with unlimited personal liability. A common form of business ownership and typical of many small firms.

Stakeholder theory The recognition that the organization is responsible to various groups in society. These may include shareholders, employers, suppliers, banks, government, the local community. See *Corporate social responsibility*.

State The state comprises a number of institutions including government, parliament, judiciary, the civil service, police and armed forces.

Strategic alliance See *Joint ventures*.

Strategic fit A consideration in the choice of strategy or in the choice of a partner. Does the strategy fit with the prevailing organizational and environmental context of the firm? Do prospective partners in a strategic alliance or joint venture offer complementary rather than conflicting or duplicating products and markets? See *Contingency approach* and *Joint ventures*.

Strategy A set of objectives and methods of achieving them, usually formulated by senior management through a combination of analysis and negotiation.

Strategy clock A set of generic strategies to identify a number of strategic options based on the relationship between the perceived value of a product to the customer and the price.

Sub-contracting A system in which the whole or part of the job is done by another firm.

Supply chain This is comprised of suppliers, producers and distributors. In modern business there has been increased emphasis on the management of the supply chain as a route to more cost-effective business and improved customer service.

Supply chain management An integrated set of activities including purchasing and supply, material handling, stock control and distribution.

Supranational organization Political or trade organizations that comprise nation states as their members and therefore cross national boundaries. Examples include the *European Union (EU)*, North American Free Trade Association (NAFTA) and the World Trade Association (WTO).

Sustainability The extent to which an organization's strategy is difficult to copy and is therefore the source of competitive advantage over time.

SWOT analysis An acronym for strengths, weaknesses, opportunities and threats. A simple method of strategic analysis.

Synergy The collective influence of the various activities of the company producing an overall effect that is greater than the sum of the parts.

Systems approach A view of the organization as a set of interrelated parts. Also, a view of organizational activities as a series of inputs, processes and outputs. See *Open systems*.

Tacit knowledge See *Implicit knowledge*.

Tactical ethics The assumption that people pursue ethical standards only because it suits them to do so in particular situations.

Targeting Involves identifying those market segments the organization wishes to pursue and developing products and a marketing mix which meet the needs of each segment. See *Positioning* and *Segmentation*.

Target-profit pricing Establishing the price in accordance with projected demand using some form of break-even analysis. Price is a function of both the minimum sales required to cover production costs and the required profit margins based on estimated sales figures.

Taylorism See *Scientific management*.

Technology A broad concept referring to the application of available knowledge and skills to create and use materials, processes and products.

Technology control The maintenance of plant or equipment.

Technology transfer The process of obtaining technology from another firm or country.

Technology–push The use of technologies to develop innovative products and processes. Many innovations, for example the CD player, are developed as a result of both demand–pull and technology–push. See *Demand–pull*.

Telemarketing The offering and selling of products and services over the phone or via the Internet.

Telesales See *Telemarketing*.

Thatcherism A political and economic philosophy that emerged under UK Prime Minister Margaret Thatcher (1979–91). It espoused the free market, privatization, individualism, self-help and entrepreneurialism. A series of laws were passed to curb the power of trade unions.

Third-party intervention A phrase usually applied to the intervention of the government in disputes between management and labour.

Total quality management (TQM) A strategic approach to quality that permeates the entire organization. It goes beyond control and assurance in that it incorporates a number of different techniques and approaches. TQM is linked to culture change in the organization that focuses on the needs of the customer by building quality into every aspect of the operation.

Trade barriers These are mechanisms erected by national governments to prevent or restrict imports or to place a high tax on imports to protect home producers.

Trade union An association that represents members to goals of job protection, improvements in pay and conditions and achieving greater involvement in decision-making.

Trade union density A measure of trade union membership that identifies members as a percentage of the total employed.

Trademark A name or symbol used to differentiate the goods and services of a particular producer.

Transactional leadership An approach to managing people based on a theory of exchange. Employees must complete tasks in return for which they are rewarded for successful completion.

Transcendental ethics The belief that there are absolute concepts of right and wrong.

Transfer pricing The process through which goods and services produced in one section of the organization are sold internally for use by another.

Transformational leadership A form of leadership in which leaders raise the performance of employees as both individuals and groups to a higher level. Leaders are usually charismatic with a vision that inspires followers.

Transitional economy An economy that is moving from central control by the state towards a free-market model.

Transnational corporation A firm which integrates global resources to achieve economies of scale while still having the capability of responding to local markets. Flexibility, responsiveness and innovation replace control and cost as primary strategic objectives. Such firms generally have weakened ties with their country of origin.

TUC The Trades Union Congress, a UK organization representing all affiliated trade unions.

Uncertainty avoidance An accepted measure of cultural difference used by Hofstede. Uncertainty avoidance measures the extent to which individuals feel threatened by and avoid ambiguous situations.

UNISON A large trade union representing public sector workers in the UK.

Unitarist and pluralist frames of reference The unitarist perspective emphasizes shared goals among all members of the organization and managers find it difficult to acknowledge that trade unions have a legitimate role in their organization. A pluralist frame of reference acknowledges that different groups within the organization may have different goals. Within such a perspective, trade unions are seen as legitimate representatives of the wishes of employees.

Universalism versus particularism A measure of cultural difference. A universalistic culture favours rules over relationships. A particularistic culture favours relationships over rules.

Unlisted securities market Part of the UK stock exchange through which small firms can raise investment capital.

Value added The difference between the value of sales and the cost of the inputs to achieve those sales.

Value chain This offers a view of the organization as a cumulative build-up of added value for the customer through the interaction between key operations activities. The end result is greater than the sum of its parts and, for profit-seeking organizations, means increased margins.

Value engineering The rigorous analysis of the product to investigate where cost savings can be made in the design or manufacture or perhaps where the element can be substituted by one of lower cost.

Vertical integration An integrated system of backward and forward integration. See *Backward integration* and *Forward integration*.

WERS Work employment relations survey. This is a major survey sponsored by the UK government and carried out every few years using a large sample of diverse workplaces.

Whistleblowing A process whereby employees report any practice or incident where members of the company have been behaving unethically.

Work measurement The formulation of standard times needed for an average worker to complete the various tasks involved in a single job and thus a vital component in planning.

Work study An analysis of work. See *Method study* and *Work measurement*.

Work–life balance Concern that employees have a balance between work and home life. It involves issues relating to the number of hours worked and providing arrangements for employees with responsibility for caring for children, the elderly or people with disabilities.

Works council A forum for employee representation in organizations that often exist independently from trade unions. A works council represents all employees and can be involved in strategic discussions.

World Bank An organization set up by the 1944 Bretton Woods conference to initiate and fund development projects around the world. See *Bretton Woods*.

World values survey A series of major surveys carried out every five years or so to identify changing values and how they affect political, economic and social life. An important element is the nature of cultural change and its impact on beliefs and behaviours.

WTO (World Trade Organization) An organization set up by the *General Agreement on Tariffs and Trade (GATT)* in the 1980s to promote free trade, establish rules for international trade and persuade member countries to remove trade barriers.

CREDITS

The following Table has been reproduced with permission of the copyright holders and the credit-lines are listed below:

Table 5.1 p. 153 Source: Hofstede, G., Hofstede, G.J. and Minkov, M. (2010) *Cultures and Organizations, Software of the Mind, 3*rd ed., McGrawHill, ISBN 0-07-166418-1. © Geert Hofstede B.V. quoted with permission.

Referencing citations for the following Figures, Tables, Case Studies are listed below:

Chapter 2

Table 2.1 Source: Adapted from Friedman (2006).
Table 2.3 Sources: IMF (2012); CNN Money (2012).
Figure 2.3 Source: Adapted from Torben Pedersen, Copenhagen Business School.
Case 2.1 Sources: Aiello (1991); *Wards AutoWorld* (October, 1999); http://fpeng.peopledaily.com.cn; Automotive Intelligence (September, 2001), http://www. autointell-new.com; *People's Daily* (26 February 2001); *China Daily* (12 January 2004), Shirouza (2013), Bloomberg.com (various) (2013); various Daimler Benz company websites.
Case 2.2 Sources: www.sleek.co.uk; www.sleekmakeup. com; discussions with founders.

Chapter 3

Table 3.1 Source: International Monetary Fund. Adapted from M.E. Porter (1990).
Table 3.2 Source: Ministry of International Trade and Industry, Japan.
Table 3.3 Source: Adapted from Goldman Sachs Global Economics Paper 9: Wilson and Purushothaman (2003).
Table 3.4 Source: Adapted from Goldman Sachs Global Economics Paper 9: Wilson and Purushothaman (2003).
Table 3.5 Sources: Goldman Sachs Global Economics Paper 9: Wilson and Purushothaman (2003); World Bank (2012).
Table 3.6 Source: Straw and Glennie (2012).
Table 3.7 Source: Chinese Industrial Enterprises Database (2007).
Table 3.8 Source: World Bank (2013a).
Table 3.9 Source: World Bank (2013b).

Table 3.10 Source: Rasiah, Zhang and Kong (2013).
Table 3.11 Source: Rasiah, Zhang and Kong (2013).
Table 3.12 Source: World Bank, world development indicators (2011).
Table 3.13 Source: World Bank, world development indicators (2011).
Table 3.14 Source: US Department of Commerce (2010).
Table 3.15 Source: OICA (2010).
Table 3.16 Source: The Coal Association.
Table 3.18 Source: World Bank.
Case 3.1 Sources: Hofstede and Bond (1988); World Bank Report (1993); Naisbitt (1996); Rohwer (1995); Hampden-Turner and Trompenaars (1997); Henderson (1998); Jomo (1998); *Financial Times* and *The Guardian* (1997–99).
Table 3.19 Source: Hampden-Turner and Trompenaars (1997).
Case 3.2 Sources: The Singapore Yearbook (various years); Chong Li Choy (1990); Wong Kwei Chong (1991); Schein (1996); *Asian Wall Street Journal* (July, 2001, July, 2002).
Case 3.3 Sources: *South China Morning Post* (12–16 November 2001); *Asian Wall Street Journal* (12–16 November 2001); Bloomberg News (2012–13).

Chapter 4

Case 4.1 Sources: *Guardian* Online Business News (18 September 1999–10 November 2008); *New York Times* (15 July 2008); http://www.bbc.co.uk/news; *Financial Times* (2008–2013).
Table 4.1 Sources: International Data Base, US Census Bureau (2011); International Telecommunications Union (2000–2011).
Table 4.2 Source: United Nations Statistics Division, Millennium Development Goals Indicators (2012).
Table 4.3 Source: Adapted from Manning (2004).
Table 4.4 Source: US Bureau of Labor Statistics (October, 2008).
Table 4.5 Source: US Bureau of Labor Statistics (October, 2008).
Table 4.6 Source: US Bureau of Labor Statistics (October, 2008).
Table 4.7 Source: ILO (2007).
Table 4.8 Sources: US Bureau of Labor Statistics (October, 2008); sourced from CIA World Factbook (2012) estimates.
Table 4.9 Source: US Bureau of Labor Statistics (2011).
Table 4.10 Source: http://ec.europa.eu/eurostat (2008).

Table 4.11 Source: www.oecd.org (2011).
Table 4.12 Sources: Grainger and Crowther (2006); BIS (2011).

Chapter 5

Table 5.3 Source: www.walmartstores.com (October, 2007).
Case 5.1 Sources: Knorr, A. and Arndt, A. (2003) 'Why did Wal-Mart fail in Germany', Band 24, pp. 1–30, Institute for World Economics and International Management, University of Bremen; www.walmart stores.com; www.business-week.com/magazine/content/05-15/b3928086-mz054.htm; dw-world.de/dw/article-0,2144,2112746.00.html; http:// dw-world.de/dw/article-0,2144,318142.00.html; http:// dw-world.de/dw/article-0,2144,1519102.00.html; http:// business-guardian.co.uk/story/0,, 1832673,00.html; http:// business.timesonline.co,uk/tol/business/industry-sectors/article694345.ece.

Chapter 6

Case 6.1 Sources: Personnel Management Plus (July, 1993); *Management Today* (July, 1993); *Marketing* (April, 1994); *Financial Times* (1995–98 and 7 February 2002); *The Times* (27 March 2002); *Design Week* (13 June 2002); http://www.zsl.org/.
Figure 6.3 Source: Hyundai group annual report (2000).
Case 6.2 Sources: Galbraith and Nathanson (1978); *Economist* (August 1988), pp. 61–62; *Financial Times* (1998–99); http://www.dowcorning.com; http://www.glassdoor.co.uk/Reviews/Dow-Corning-Company-Reviews-E2771_P2.htm.
Table 6.2 Source: Adapted from Megginson and Netter (2001).
Case 6.3 Sources: *The Guardian* and *Financial Times* (8–11 October 2001); *The Guardian* (April, 2004–December, 2011); www. networkrail.co.uk ; Department for Transport (2011).
Table 6.3 Sources: CNN Money (2011) and UNCTAD World Investment Report (2012)
Case 6.4 Sources: Peters and Waterman (1982); Packard (1995); *Financial Times* and *The Guardian* (September, 2001–2009); http://www.bloomberg.com/news/2013; Hewlett Packard Annual Report (2012).

Chapter 7

Case 7.1 Sources: Horne and Stedman-Jones (2001); DTI (2005).
Case 7.2 Sources: *The Guardian* report on executive pay, www.guardian.com/business/executive-pay-bonuses; articles from *The Observer* and *Sunday Times* (August, 2007–July, 2014).

Chapter 8

Case 8.1 Sources: Porter (1996); Barney and Hesterly (2012); *Financial Times* (June, 2012–July, 2014);

www.Southwest.com; http://Southwest.investorroom.com/company-reports.
Figure 8.4 Source: After Porter (1985).
Figure 8.5 Source: Hofer and Schendel (1978).
Figure 8.5 Source: Kennedy (1988).
Figure 8.7 Source: After Ansoff (1968).
Case 8.2 Sources: SAB and SABMiller annual reports (2000–2013); 'It's Miller time for South African Breweries', *The Guardian* (30 May 2002); 'Miller "is bad deal" for SAB', *The Guardian* (31 May 2002); 'SAB does well everywhere but the US', *The Guardian* (30 September 2003); 'The battle of big beer', *Economist* (13 May 2004).

Chapter 9

Case 9.1 Sources: www.guardian.co.uk/enron; www.enron.com; http://money.cnn.com; http://bloomberg.com; Bryce (2002); *People Management* (21 February 2002); Chaffin and Fidler (2002); Partnoy (2003); McLean and Elkind (2004); Clark (2006).

Chapter 10

Table 10.2 Source: BIS (2010).
Table 10.3 Source: BIS (2010).
Table 10.4 Source: European Commission (2013).
Table 10.5 Source: DTI (2006).
Table 10.6 Sources: DTI (2006); BIS (2010).
Table 10.7 Sources: 1987 – Intellectual Property Owners Inc. (March 1988); 2007 – IFI Claims Patent Services; 2013 – IFI Claims Patent Services.
Table 10.8 Source: Adapted from Freeman (1995).
Table 10.9 Source: Partly based on and adapted from Tidd et al. (2005).
Case 10.1 Sources: Fagan (1991); Connon (1992); Kay (1992); Buchan (1993); *Economist* (25 January 1995); company reports (1998–2013), *Medical Marketing and Media* (May, 1999); *The Guardian* (24 July 2002); *The Observer* (25 May 2003); BIS (2010); European Commission (2013); http://www.forbes.com.

Chapter 11

Table 11.1 Source: Data collected from and Annual Reports and the Corporation's website http://www.inditex.es/en/who_we_are/timeline [accessed on September 2013].
Table 11.2 Source: Website of Inditex http://www.inditex.es/en/who_we_are/stores/ [accessed on September 2013], data updated to 31/07/2013.
Table 11.3 Source: Inditex – 2012 Annual Report.
Table 11.4 Source: Inditex – 2012 Annual Report.
Case 11.1 Sources: Inditex Annual Report (2012); Abrahamsson and Rehme (2010); Bonnin (2002); González-Loureiro, Dabic and Puig (2014); Puig and Marques (2011).
Table 11.5 Source: British Airways (August, 2014).

Table 11.6 Source: BPI Yearbook (2001).

Case 11.2 Sources: Orlake Records, Dagenham, Essex; Vinyl Factory Manufacturing, Hayes.

Chapter 12

Table 12.1 Source: www.millwardbrown/brandz/ top_100_global_brands.

Table 12.2 Source: *Wall Street Journal* (13 June 2014).

Case 12.1 Sources: http://retailindustry.about. com/b/2009/09/07/ceo-mike-jeffries-overvalues-his-own-brand-and-loses-his-cool-after-teen-shoppers-and-investors-dont-aspire-to-abercrombie-any-more. htm; http://www.fundinguniverse.com/company-histories/abercrombie-fitch-co-history/; http://www. bloomberg.com/news/ (various 2010–14); http:// www.businessweek.com/news/2012-11-21/abercrombie-settles-pilot-s-lawsuit-after-ceo-ordered-to-testify; Emine Saner (2012) For beautiful people only, *The Guardian*, 28 April.

Table 12.3 Source: Based on Armstrong and Kotler (2007).

Case 12.2 Sources: McDonald's press releases (1996–1998); *Straits Times* (1999–2000).

Case 12.3 Sources: Company information from Interflora and 1-800-Flowers; Friedman and Furey (1999).

Table 12.4 Source: http://annualreview.disneylandparis. com/2013/#/8.

Table 12.5 Source: http://annualreview.disneylandparis. com/2013/#/8.

Table 12.6 Source: http://annualreview.disneylandparis. com/2013/#/8.

Case 12.4 Sources: *Financial Times* (February–July, 1992, November, 1993, March, June 1994); *The Guardian* and *The Observer* (1993–2009); Euro Disney SA, annual reports (1995–98); Mills et al (1994); http:// corporate.disneylandparis.com/investor-relations/ financial-indicators/2014; http://www.bbc.co.uk/ news/business-17981798; http://www.guardian.co.uk/ world/2012/apr/11/disneyland-paris-20th-birthday-debt; http://www.independent.co.uk/news/world/ europe/the-dark-side-of-disneyland-paris-1964505. html.

Chapter 13

Table 13.2 Source: Adapted from CIPD (2007).

Case 13.1 Sources: Bruce (1987); *Financial Times* (1998–2014); *The Guardian* (2004–2014); *Daily Telegraph* (2010–2012).

Chapter 14

Table 14.1 Source: Adapted from Corbett and Jenkinson (2007), p. 74.

Table 14.2 Source: Deloitte (June, 2009).

Table 14.3 Source: Deloitte (June, 2009).

Table 14.4 Source: Conn (2009).

Table 14.5 Source: Deloitte (June, 2009).

Table 14.6 Source: Deloitte (June, 2009).

Table 14.7 Source: Deloitte (June, 2009).

Case 14.1 Sources: Jones (2009); Conn (2008, 2009); Deloitte and Touche (2003); *The Guardian* and *The Observer* (July and August, 2003, July, 2009).

SUBJECT INDEX

AUTHOR INDEX